History of Central Africa

Volume two

History of Central Africa

VOLUME TWO

edited by
David Birmingham and Phyllis M. Martin

Longman
London and New York

Longman Group Limited
Longman House
Burnt Mill, Harlow, Essex, UK

*Published in the United States of America
by Longman Inc., New York*

© Longman Group Limited 1983

First published 1983

British Library Cataloguing in Publication Data

History of Central Africa
  Vol. 2
  1. Africa, Central—History
  I. Birmingham, David   II. Martin, Phyllis M.
  967   DT352.5

  ISBN 0–582–64675–8
  ISBN 0–582–64676–6 Pbk

Library of Congress Cataloging in Publication Data
Main entry under title:

History of Central Africa.

  Bibliography: v. 2, p.
  Includes index.
  1. Africa, Central—History.   I. Birmingham, David.
II. Martin, Phyllis.
DT352.5.H58 1983   967   83–745
ISBN 0–582–64675–8 (v. 2)
ISBN 0–582–64676–6 (pbk. : v. 2)

Printed in Singapore by
Kyodo Shing Loong Printing Industries Pte Ltd.

*Cover photograph of diamond mining in Angola supplied by Alan
Hutchinson.*

Contents

List of maps

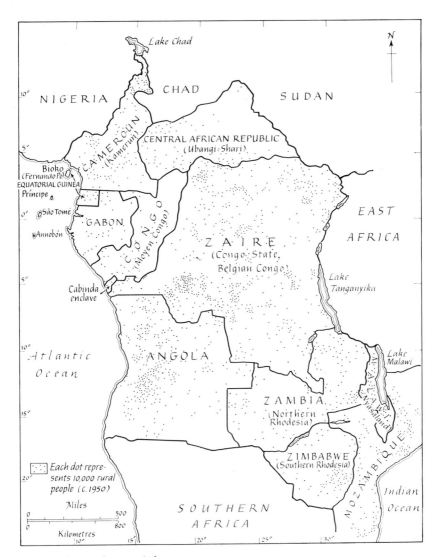

Central Africa in the twentieth century

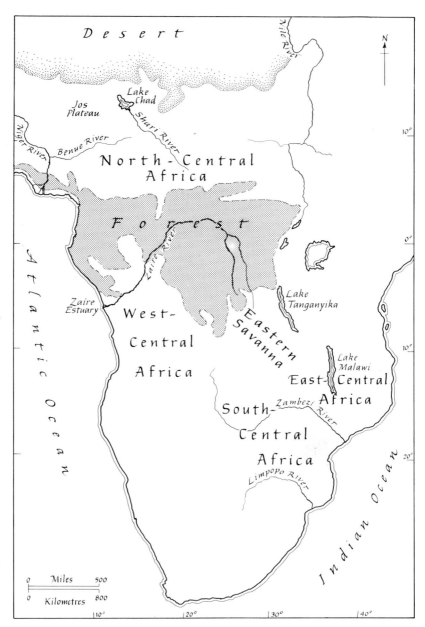

The regions of Central Africa

CHAPTER 1

The violence of empire

PHYLLIS M. MARTIN

By the late nineteenth century Central Africa was in the throes of a grave social and political disruption which involved the whole region from Lake Chad to the Limpopo and from the Atlantic to the Great Lakes. In the northern savanna a widening spiral of violence affected most societies. Everywhere in the forest peoples were facing radical social transformation. In the Atlantic zone, societies faced economic disaster and ecological deterioration, while in the eastern savanna there was the prospect of long-term chaos. In the Indian Ocean zone societies were thrust into general disarray. Only on the Zimbabwe plateau was the intensity of change more muted, but even there the seeds of disruption were evident in the 'distant rumble of economic thunder from the south'.[1]

These dramatic conditions were brought about by the gradual integration of Central Africa into the world system. The demands of expanding Muslim economies in North Africa, in West Africa and in the Nile basin had pushed the slave and ivory frontiers into the savannas between Cameroun and the Uele valley. A second commercial system, fuelled by the international ivory demand and by east-coast slave-labour requirements, infiltrated East-Central Africa between the Great Lakes and the Zambezi. In South-Central Africa the white miners and settlers crossed the Limpopo frontier, and black workers began to trek south to the mines, farms and plantations of South Africa. In addition to the growing interaction between Central Africa and neighbouring regions of the north, east and south, a new trading system was growing. This was based on Western Europe and the United States, and ultimately affected the whole region. The understanding of European expansion requires a closer look at the relations between Europe and Africa in the era following the end of the slave-trade.

1 D. N. Beach, 'The Zimbabwe plateau and its peoples', *History of Central Africa*, volume one, p. 273. The language of this opening statement may seem rather extreme, but all these phrases are taken from the discussion of the nineteenth century in volume one.

The slave-trade was slower to subside on the coasts of Central Africa than in West Africa. By the 1860s, however, it had almost died out. Only in southern Angola did the export of humans persist as São Tomé cocoa planters forcibly recruited their island labour. From Douala to Benguela, old slaving interests were replaced by new shipping and commercial companies which exported raw material such as palm-oil, cotton, rubber and ivory. These included the German firm of Woermann, the British John Holt Company, the Dutch New African Trading Company and the French firms of Régis and Dumas. The industrial giant and pace-maker in the first two-thirds of the nineteenth century was Britain. By about 1850, however, Britain saw a marked decline in agricultural self-sufficiency, a rise in population and a need to increase food imports. Rising costs had to be

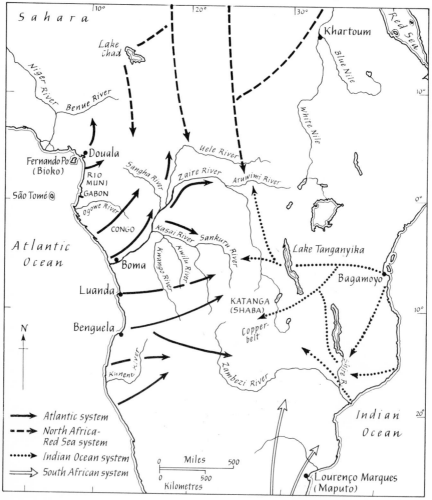

1:1 Central Africa and international trading systems, 1870

balanced by the sale of competitive manufactured goods which Britain supplied to world markets through the new technology and an urban labour force.[2]

In the mid-nineteenth century, the incentives for African traders and brokers to extend their search for commodities further into the interior were heightened as the terms of international trade turned temporarily in their favour. The price of imported goods became lower, whereas the price of the principal African exports was rising or steady until the 1870s.[3] Higher profits and better credit financed the extension of trade routes into the far interior. In the forest zone the trading frontier reached up the Zaire river to the lower Aruwimi and Sankuru by the 1880s. African and Euro-African traders from the Angolan ports crossed the Kasai and Kunene to meet east-coast traders in the Zambezi basin.

Changes both in the type of goods exported and in the scale of commercial activity brought innovation in production and trade organisation. The entrepreneurs and élites who had controlled slave-trading systems could not always adapt to commodity production and transport. Those who had not previously been integrated into the Atlantic system, or who had been marginal participants, were now able to profit. Along the coast, volatile trading conditions were reflected in prolonged negotiations, in skirmishes, in frauds, in the taking of hostages and in reprisals, as established merchant families struggled to maintain their supremacy in the highly competitive business environment. A similar story occurred inland. The new entrepreneurs were mobile bands of hunters and gatherers who trapped elephants, foraged wild rubber and processed gathered wax; villagers who collected palm-oil in the Cameroun, Gabon and Congo forests; firms which marshalled canoe flotillas on the Zaire river; farmers who increased food production to supply specialised workers with their surplus; and small landowners of the Luanda hinterland who established cotton and coffee plantations.

Political and social disruption was common. The most serious losses of human life were in North-Central Africa, in the eastern savanna and in the Indian Ocean zone, where foreigners expanded the slave-trade even as it was declining in West-Central Africa. In the northern savanna, the mercenary and slave armies of newly formed predatory states raided their neighbours. Victims were forced to ally themselves with the invaders or to flee to defensible positions in forests and rock fortresses. Those who fought for survival in centralised polities emulated the tactics of their enemy. In the eastern savanna, coastal merchants infiltrated the area by establishing patron–client relationships with local rulers. They later established their

2 P. J. Cain and A. G. Hopkins, 'The political economy of British expansion overseas, 1750–1914', *Economic History Review*, second series, xxxiii, 4, 1980, 474–6.
3 J. Forbes Munro, *Africa and the International Economy, 1800–1960*, London, 1976, pp. 40–56.

own domains with imported fire-arms, which they also used in order to acquire slaves and ivory for export.

Alien influences affected societies and individuals at different levels. As competition for fixed resources grew, the mobilisation of manpower, womanpower and childpower became more urgent. Family structures were inadequate in the drive to maximise profits, and 'big men' expanded their domestic slave-holdings.[4] Male slaves were employed as porters, manual labourers, boatmen, hunters, gatherers and soldiers. The Chokwe of the Atlantic zone invested heavily in slave-wives who increased human resources, farmed and, with their children, collected rubber and wax.[5] The Bobangi of the middle Zaire even came to value slave children over their own offspring.[6]

Mass-produced European goods became more widely dispersed among ordinary people in the late nineteenth century than ever before. Cattle and traditional measures of value continued to feature prominently in major negotiations such as bridewealth, but imported goods increased in significance as they had previously done among coastal families. Fire-arms were imported on all four trading frontiers for defence, conquest, slave-raiding and elephant-hunting. A Shona worker who bought a gun with wages earned in a South African mine could kill an elephant whose sale would not only recoup the cost of the weapon but also pay for a bride.[7] African involvement in international trading systems did sow the seeds of disaster. At the time, however, the advantages were overwhelming and a refusal to participate was unthinkable. People therefore embraced the new opportunities energetically in spite of the long-term costs, which they could hardly have foreseen.

An underlying continuity characterises Central African history from the mid-nineteenth century to the colonial period. An economic system based on the importation of manufactured goods and the extraction of raw materials affected wide segments of the population by the 1870s. The first 'partition' of Africa among European, American and South African companies was already well advanced, although the process was not completed until about 1930.[8] The formal imposition of colonial rule was a less decisive watershed for Central Africans than once appeared to be the case. Certainly, colonialism did bring major changes in the form of new boundaries, languages, political systems and ideologies; but the integration of Central Africans into the world economy was only made more complete

4 See Cordell and Vansina in volume one.
5 See Miller in volume one.
6 See Vansina in volume one; Robert W. Harms, *River of Wealth, River of Sorrow: the Central Zaire Basin in the era of the Slave Trade, 1500–1891*, New Haven, Connecticut, 1981, pp. 180–5.
7 See Beach in volume one.
8 A. G. Hopkins, 'Imperial business in Africa: interpretations', *Journal of African History (JAH)*, xvii, 2, 1976, 274.

by imperial rule, it was not a new phenomenon. Similarly, the attendant disruption of daily life was intensified, but its roots went back into the earlier period.

THE MOMENTUM FOR EMPIRE

The imperial pulse quickened in the last two decades of the nineteenth century. It took thirty years more to enforce occupation, and even longer to implement fully the systems of administration. By the beginning of the twentieth century, however, the colonial frontiers had been drawn and the patterns of colonial rule under six European powers had been set. The expansion of Europe into the Pacific, the Far East, the Indian Ocean and Africa was unprecedented in its scale. It was made possible in part by new

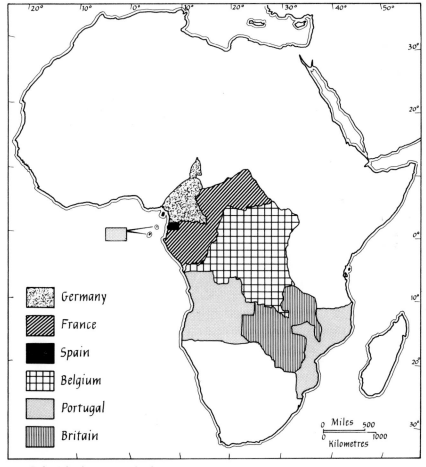

1:2 Colonial rule in Central Africa

technology and owed much to the increasing amount of information supplied by explorers, adventurers, missionaries and traders.

The map of Central Africa produced by the German geographer August Petermann, in 1876, showed a quite accurate knowledge of the savanna regions.[9] Compiled from contemporary scholarship, it included the observations of travellers such as Livingstone, Cameron and Magyar in the central savanna; Bastian and Güssfeldt on the coasts north and south of the Zaire estuary; and Du Chaillu, Compiègne and Marche in the Gabon regions. The band of territory between Angola and Mozambique was also quite well known to the Portuguese. For centuries they had dreamed of joining up their Central African territories of Angola and Mozambique to link the Atlantic with the Indian Ocean. Two Angolan trading agents, Baptista and José, completed a trans-African journey in 1805–1811, and retainers of Silva Porto crossed Central Africa from Benguela to Mozambique in 1852–1854.[10] In the northern savanna, Schweinfurth travelled south from the Nile to the Uele in 1868–1871, and three other Germans – Barth, Nachtigal and Rohlfs – explored the Chad basin. The major blank on European maps was the forest region. Ignorance diminished slowly year by year. As the Geographical Conference sponsored by Leopold II met in Brussels in 1876, Stanley was in the midst of a journey across Central Africa from Bagamoyo to the Atlantic, and Savorgnan de Brazza was travelling on the Ogowe route from Gabon to the Zaire basin.

The growing cartographical knowledge of Central Africa was matched by a new technology. Oceanic cables provided telegraphic links between European concerns and overseas representatives. The telegraph reached Lourenço Marques in 1879 and Luanda in 1886.[11] Coal-burning ships replaced sailing vessels on the long routes by the 1870s. These steamships not only cut the time of journeys but also increased cargo capacities. Small steamers became especially important along navigable inland waterways in the forest zone. Advances in medical research also increased chances of European survival in the tropics. Explorers such as Livingstone, Cameron and Stanley used quinine to control malaria. The European conquest of Africa involved an overwhelming superiority in fire-arms, that resulted from substantive advances in military technology. By the 1860s, muzzle-loading guns were replaced by breech-loaders which could be quickly reloaded in a prone position. Two decades later, this development was superseded by repeating mechanisms used in automatic rifles and

9 Jacques Denis, 'L' Afrique Centrale en 1876: état des connaissances géographiques et cartographiques', in *La Conférence de Géographie de 1876*, Académie Royale des Sciences d'Outre-Mer, Brussels, 1976, pp. 44–56.
10 Ian Cunnison, 'Kazembe and the Portuguese, 1798–1832', *JAH*, ii, 1961, 61–76.
11 Richard J. Hammond, 'Uneconomic imperialism: Portugal in Africa before 1910', in Peter Duignan and L. H. Gann (eds), *Colonialism in Africa, 1870–1960*, Cambridge, 1969, vol. I, p. 359.

rudimentary machine guns.[12] These 'tools of expansion' may not have actually stimulated the European expansion, but they dramatically altered the balance of power and were firmly monopolised in imperial hands.'

In the major European cities, geographical societies which brought together intellectual, military, humanitarian and economic interests funded several expeditions to Central Africa. Many of the early travellers were also prolific writers, and the increasingly literate public was enthused by tales of wealth, both real and imaginary. Public lectures fuelled a concern to end the slave-trade. Scientific curiosity was linked to evangelical Christianity in odd but powerful European notions of 'civilisation'. Thus did churches and colonial societies foster large-scale popular interest in African trade, evangelisation, emigration and colonisation.

The rapid colonial partition of Africa has raised many questions for historians concerning the timing, the speed and the causes of expansion.[13] The search for a single explanation for such a varied and complex set of events has generally been abandoned. However, the general climate created by the unstable political economy in Europe in the late nineteenth century deserves attention. In these conditions governments were receptive to pressure groups with diverse reasons for favouring the annexation of colonies.

Two related trends contributed to a period of economic depression and instability in Europe between about 1873 and 1896. One was the decline of British industrial dominance in the face of competition from France, Germany and the United States. The other was a rise in volume and fall in price of manufactured goods, as the new industrial powers increased their output. The process was advanced by technological innovations in manufacturing and by the growth of finance capitalism. Intense competition caused a more aggressive search for markets and the protection of existing ones. France in 1881, Germany in 1879, and Portugal in 1880, all introduced protective tariffs, while Britain adopted a defensive posture.[14] Some colonial policy-makers were also influenced by a new perception of African resources and by the need to secure privileged access to them. The option of extending colonial empires to protect markets and sources of raw materials by political and military means thus became attractive.[15] When economic interest coincided with other objectives, annexation became probable.

12 Daniel R. Headrick, 'The tools of imperialism: technology and expansion of European colonial empires in the nineteenth century', *Journal of Modern History*, li, 2, June 1979, 231–63; see also, Headrick, *The Tools of Empire*, New York, 1981.
13 There are several anthologies that review the many ways in which historians have answered these questions; see bibliographical essay below.
14 Forbes Munro, *Africa and the International Economy*, pp. 65–71.
15 Hopkins, 'Imperial connections'; and C.C. Wrigley, 'Neo-mercantile policies and the new imperialism', in *The Imperial Impact: Studies in the Economic History of Africa and India*, Clive Dewey and A.G. Hopkins (eds), London, 1978, pp. 9–10, 20–34.

In 1884–1885, Bismarck, the German chancellor, convened a conference of fourteen nations at Berlin. The object was to take the heat out of the escalating crisis over the Zaire basin, and to resolve some of the broader issues of competition for African territories. Informal guidelines were established to minimise the possibility of conflicting claims leading to war among European powers. Imperial claims could be validated through 'treaties of protection' with African rulers, through administrative control of an area and through economic exploitation. The years immediately following the conference were ones of reluctant empire-building, however, for the acquisition of colonies as a means of securing vital interests was a potentially expensive option.

In the 1890s, the speed and temper of expansion changed. As construction of costly transportation systems and mobilisation of African labour became the key to profitable development, business interests sought government intervention to protect their investments and pre-empt the advance of rivals. At the same time, smaller pressure groups such as missionary and colonial societies became more vocal in government lobbies. The movement to incorporate areas into European empires generated its own momentum in capital cities, and was itself inflamed by the international neuroses of the times. Central Africa was an integral part of the heady vision of empire from Germany's *Mittelafrika* policy of joining Cameroun to East Africa to France's trans-Saharan empire from Algeria to the Chad basin, and from Portugal's *à contra costa* aspirations to Britain's 'Cape-to-Cairo' dream.

THE RULE OF THE FEEBLE

This phrase was first applied to colonialism in northern Mozambique,[16] but it can well be used to characterise European rule in the rest of Central Africa, at least before 1920. A striking feature of imperialist expansion in Central Africa was that it did not figure high in the African priorities of the colonial super-powers, Britain and France. Instead the weaker nations, Portugal and Spain, and the opportunists, Leopold of Belgium and Bismarck of Germany, were able to claim large chunks of uncontested territory. Where Britain and France were involved, they granted most of their Central African territories to the private interests of concessionary companies. Company rule continued long after it had become anachronistic elsewhere. This pattern of government profoundly affected the nature of colonial rule and Central African experience of it.

In the 1880s British companies were active at coastal factories from Cameroun to Angola. In 1807, British trade with the Zaire estuary and the adjacent coasts had been negligible, but by 1885 it had risen to about £2

16 Leroy Vail, 'Mozambique's chartered companies: the rule of the feeble', *JAH*, xvii, 3, 1976, 389–416.

million and dominated all other foreign trade.[17] British capital was also invested in Dutch and French shipping and trading. In 1874, the explorer V. L. Cameron had concluded treaties with African rulers in the Zaire basin in order to declare a British protectorate, but his government repudiated the claim. Indeed, the idea of Britain occupying the Zaire region was never seriously discussed by a British government. Reluctance to annex regions formally that were not vital to economic or strategic interests persisted. The Niger basin merited British annexation, but the Zaire basin did not. After 1882, when French treaty-making activities in Gabon and Congo sounded the alarm for British merchants, the British government recognised the claims of Portugal, a friendly power. The powerful Manchester business lobby preferred, however, to support Leopold II, whose avowed commitment to free trade seemed better to protect British economic interests in the Zaire basin. Their opinions triumphed when Britain shifted its support to the Belgian ruler and, with the other powers, recognised the flag of the Congo State at the Berlin Conference.[18]

The British government was also a reluctant participant in the colonial affairs of the south. It had little to do with the white settlers and miners who moved north of the Limpopo into the area that became 'British' Central Africa. This northward surge was financed and organised by South African capital, as Cecil Rhodes, who had been thwarted on the Transvaal gold-fields, sought a 'Second Rand' on the Zimbabwe plateau.[19] The London government was little more than a bystander. No established trade or proven mineral resources needed protection, and the area between the Limpopo and Katanga was not seen as essential to British imperial interests. The arrangement of chartered rule by the British South Africa Company was convenient to both business and government. Rhodes could use the authority of the British government to stake his claim and exclude rivals from north of the Limpopo. The British tax-payer acquired a free colony. A problem arose over the northern extent of British influence. The Company directors appealed to Lord Salisbury to claim Katanga with its possible mineral resources for Britain, but the government refused. Distracted by negotiations over strategic interests in the Nile and East Africa, it was not prepared to alienate Leopold II. Instead Britain adopted a conciliatory policy which allowed Congo State expeditions to claim the area.[20] British Central Africa was thus abandoned to the British South Africa Company. In practice, however, much power was held by local

17 Roger Anstey, *Britain and the Congo in the Nineteenth Century*, Oxford, 1962, pp. 19–20, 30–31.
18 *Ibid.*, pp. 54–6, 60–4, 100–5.
19 I. R. Phimister, 'Rhodes, Rhodesia and the Rand', *Journal of Southern African Studies (JSAS)*, i, 1, 1974, 74–90; also see Smith and Beach in volume one, and chapters by Vail and Phimister, below.
20 S. E. Katzenellenbogen, *Railways and the Copper Mines of Katanga*, Oxford, 1973, pp. 9–18; also see chapter by Vellut, below.

9

settlers and mining interests. Only in the small territory of Nyasaland did missionary interests prevail on a reluctant imperial government to declare a protectorate. Even this area, however, was overwhelmed by the needs of the white economy in South and South-Central Africa.[21]

The French were most active in West-Central Africa. The treaty made by de Brazza with the Tio paramount ruler north of Malebo (Stanley) Pool in 1880, and its ratification by the French parliament in 1882, has achieved notoriety in the annals of the partition of Africa. The French action in the Ogowe and northern Zaire basins is said to have goaded rival European powers such as Britain and Leopold II into claiming other African territories.[22] However, despite the excitement of 1880 to 1882, equatorial Africa remained at the bottom of France's African priorities. De Brazza's expeditions to the Ogowe and Zaire basins in the 1870s had not had the blessing of the French government. On the contrary, policy-makers had been on the point of evacuating Gabon, where Libreville was a mediocre base and trade was dominated by German and British firms.[23] On de Brazza's return to his adopted country in 1881, therefore, the government was reluctant to take action on the fruits of his unauthorised and unwanted diplomacy.

The empire in North and West Africa remained the prime focus of French colonial efforts. Only because equatorial Africa was a back door to Lake Chad and the Nile was the Congo treaty ratified by the French parliament.[24] Large military expeditions were dispatched with fanfare to West Africa in the 1880s, but only a small civilian expedition, mostly financed by the Ministries of Public Instruction and Foreign Affairs, was sent to the Congo. On the eve of his departure to set up administrative posts there, de Brazza was reminded by the French Foreign Office that 'the question of the Congo is not the only important one; we must concentrate our efforts in other areas; ... these impose wise limits that you must not exceed in a country where until now our interests have been relatively weak'.[25] The expedition nevertheless established seven principal stations and nineteen administrative posts, which became the major colonial centres of Gabon and Moyen Congo.[26]

These inauspicious French colonial ventures in Central Africa had barely got off the ground by the end of the century. De Brazza, Commissioner-

21 See chapters by Vail and Phimister, below.
22 Henri Brunschwig, *L'Avènement de l'Afrique Noire*, Paris, 1963, pp. 141–9; Jean Stengers, 'King Leopold and Anglo-French rivalry, 1882–1884', in *France and Britain in Africa*, P. Gifford and W. R. Louis (eds), New Haven, Conn., 1971, pp. 139–40.
23 Henri Brunschwig, *L'Avènement*, pp. 100–1, 111–14, 140–63; K. David Patterson, *The Northern Gabon Coast to 1875*, Oxford, 1975, pp. 121, 136–42.
24 C. W. Newbury and A. S. Kanya-Forstner, 'French policy and the origins of the scramble for West Africa', *JAH*, x, 2, 1969, 263–70; C. Coquery-Vidrovitch, *Le Congo au temps des grandes compagnies concessionnaires, 1898–1930*, Paris, 1972, p. 47.
25 Coquery-Vidrovitch, *Le Congo*, p. 31.
26 C. Coquery-Vidrovitch, *Brazza et la prise de possession du Congo, 1883–1885*, Paris, 1969.

General in Equatorial Africa, 1883–1898, was unable to attract much private capital. In 1887 the government stopped its annual subsidy to Gabon, and warned that 'we cannot stay indefinitely in a period of costly exploration'.[27] The small budget of Moyen-Congo was eaten up by expeditions which used the Sangha and Ubangi routes north to the Chad–Nile region in the 1890s.[28] Unable and unwilling to support an empire in Central Africa, the French government decided to renounce its financial and administrative obligations. In 1898–1899, it adopted the 'solution' of Leopold in the Congo State and divided equatorial Africa into forty enormous territorial concessions. Each was leased to a state-authorised company to exploit and administer.[29] The action acknowledged the impotence of colonial government in the region.

The unwillingness of Britain to protect its merchants in the lower Zaire or to support the ambitions of Rhodes in Katanga allowed Leopold II to step into a huge vacuum and seize the Zaire basin. Britain and France consented in order to keep each other out. The protocols of the Berlin conference 'guaranteed' a free-trade zone and therefore access to traders from both nations. Leopold II was one of the few statesmen to hold the unflinching belief that overseas enterprise could be more profitable than investment at home. In the Zaire basin he hoped to fulfil his ambition for an economic empire. Only pressures from France on the north bank of the Zaire river persuaded him that a political empire was also necessary.[30] Under Leopold, Central Africa became a haven for the gambler and the opportunist. The price of the region's primary exports, ivory and rubber, was rising in the last quarter of the century, whereas manufactured goods were becoming cheaper.[31] In spite of a potentially buoyant economy, however, enormous obstacles had to be overcome before profits could be assured. High transportation costs along routes strung out from Boma, the colonial capital, to the Nile and the Great Lakes, to the Zambezi and the Kasai were an enormous problem. Communications through the forest zone were particularly uncertain. Arab and Swahili merchants who traded with North and East Africa had to be expelled by military action from the northern and eastern Zaire basin.

By the 1890s the costs of exploiting the Zaire region and establishing a colonial infrastructure were more than the Belgian ruler and his administration could bear. In a series of decrees, Leopold converted much

27 Freycinet to de Brazza, 12 April 1886, quoted in R. E. Robinson and J. Gallagher, 'The partition of Africa', in *The New Cambridge Modern History*, vol. xi, Cambridge, 1962, p. 607.
28 Coquery-Vidrovitch, *Le Congo*, pp. 25–46, 75; on French expeditions in North-Central Africa, see Cordell in volume one, and chapter by Austen and Headrick, below.
29 Coquery-Vidrovitch, *Le Congo*; see chapter by Austen and Headrick, below.
30 Jean Stengers, 'King Leopold's imperialism', in *Studies in the Theory of Imperialism*, Roger Owen and Bob Sutcliffe (eds), London, 1972, pp. 248–76; also Stengers, 'King Leopold and Anglo-French rivalry, 1882–1884'.
31 Forbes Munro, *Africa and the International Economy*, pp. 73–6.

Phyllis M. Martin

of the area into a private domain in which uncultivated land was reserved for the state. Thousands of hectares were also leased to companies to administer and exploit in return for tax payments and an allocation of shares. The atrocities carried out in the name of the state and of these companies gradually attracted so much unfavourable international attention that the Congo State was confiscated by Belgium in 1908.[32]

The other opportunist in the colonial partition of Central Africa was Bismarck of Germany. In the same year that the German agent, Nachtigal, signed treaties of protection with Cameroun chiefs at Douala, Germany also annexed Togo, South-West Africa and German East Africa. These actions have been interpreted as an integrated colonial policy devised by Bismarck for reasons of international diplomacy and domestic politics.[33] Although this may have been the case, the economics of trade were also a force behind German action. The Hamburg companies trading in Cameroun benefited by colonial annexations, and one of their directors, Adolph Woermann, was an influential figure in German government circles.[34] In Cameroun, as in the Niger region, fluctuating palm-oil prices

TABLE 1:1

COMMODITY PRICES IN BRITISH MARKETS, 1870–1900

	Palm-oil (shillings per cwt.)	Palm nuts and kernels (£ per ton)	Ivory (£ per cwt.)	Rubber (£ per cwt.)
1870–74	34·8	13·3	34·6	10·7
1875–79	33·8	14·9	46·1	9·8
1880–84	31·5	14·0	45·8	12·9
1885–89	21·6	11·5	47·0	11·2
1890–94	22·9	12·3	47·1	11·5
1895–1900	21·1	11·2	41·5	11·9

Source: J. Forbes Munro, *Africa and the International Economy, 1800–1960* (London, 1976), p. 69.

had created tension among African producers and traders. World prices for palm products dropped sharply from 1873 to 1896 because increased production, improved transportation and favourable prices earlier in the century had led to an oversupply on world markets. The terms of trade turned against African producers and traders as palm-oil prices declined. Conflict developed between producers seeking to hold on to markets, and

32 Robert Harms, 'The end of red rubber: a reassessment', *JAH*, xvi, 1, 1975, 73–88; see chapter by Jewsiewicki, below.
33 See, for example, D. K. Fieldhouse, *Economics and Empire, 1830–1914*, London, 1973, pp. 329–32; Woodruff D. Smith, *The German Colonial Empire*, Chapel Hill, N.C., 1978, pp. 20, 33.
34 Harry R. Rudin, *Germans in the Cameroons, 1884–1914*, New Haven, Conn., 1938, pp. 34–9; Smith, *The German Colonial Empire*, p. 8.

12

French, British and German buyers.[35] In these conditions German traders called on their government to extend political rule to the area so that the situation might be stabilised in their favour.

If Bismarck had been tempted by the colonial lobby in 1884, the attraction did not last long. He would have preferred to limit Germany's African possessions to footholds, and was opposed to costly expeditions and garrisons.[36] As it became evident that the hinterland of Cameroun would have to be occupied to attract trade away from the Niger and Zaire basins, he invited merchants to assume responsibility through a chartered company. The Hamburg merchants, however, declined a burden which would have eroded their profits. Instead, a complete administrative structure was installed in the 1890s, but its limited resources led to great brutalities. On the coast and round Mount Cameroun fertile tracts of land were granted to plantation owners. In the north-west and in southern Cameroun, two private companies were granted large concessions in 1898.[37]

Spain and Portugal, two of the weakest states of Western Europe, shared in the colonial division of Central Africa. In 1900 France ceded Spain the enclave of Rio Muni, which Spanish cocoa-planters on the island of Bioko (Fernando Po) exploited as a labour reservoir before formal Spanish occupation began in 1926.[38] In Portugal, threatened industrialists put pressure on their government to secure colonies which protected markets when falling world prices aggravated competition in the 1870s. For the richer countries of Europe colonial trade was only a small percentage of foreign trade, but for Portugal it was crucial. Although thwarted by the British ultimatum of 1890 from realising its dream of a transcontinental empire, Portugal could nevertheless be well pleased with the large blocks of territory that it came to hold in Angola and Mozambique. High prices for ivory and rubber supported the economy of Angola until the early twentieth century, but much of Mozambique was quickly given over to three concessionary companies dominated by British and South African capital.[39]

The weakness of colonial governments and the power of concessionary companies, white settlers and miners in Central Africa was not merely the result of European preference. It was also a function of local conditions,

35 Forbes Munro, *Africa and the International Economy*, pp. 65–66; A.G. Hopkins, *An Economic History of West Africa*, London, 1973, pp. 133–35, 154; Hans–Peter Jaeck, 'Die Deutsche annexion', in *Kamerun Unter Deutscher Kolonialherrschaft*, Helmuth Stoecker (ed.), Berlin, 1960, I, pp. 29–77.
36 Rudin, *Germans in the Cameroons*, p. 39.
37 *Ibid.*, pp. 92–4, 120–21; Smith, *The German Colonial Empire*, pp. 82–4; see chapter by Austen and Headrick, below.
38 Suzanne Cronjé, *Equatorial Guinea*, London, 1976, pp. 8–9.
39 W. G. Clarence-Smith, 'The myth of uneconomic imperialism; the Portuguese in Angola, 1836–1926', *JSAS*, 1979, v, 2, 171–6; also see chapters by Clarence-Smith and Vail, below.

distribution of resources and the historical development of Central African societies.

Throughout the northern two-thirds of the region there were few large-scale social structures through which Europeans could develop peasant production on the West African cash-crop model.[40] The states of North- and East-Central Africa had emerged through their interaction with Mediterranean, Red Sea, and Indian Ocean slave and ivory markets. The spread of European capital and of colonial rule from the coast of West-Central Africa demanded the overthrow of these states and the reorientation of production networks to serve European ends. Areas which already exported palm-oil, ivory, wax and rubber through European companies were relatively new because of the late suppression of the West-Central African slave-trade. Even palm-oil exports were based on foraging and small-scale units of production. Cash-crop industries comparable to the African palm-oil estates in Dahomey and to indigenous ground-nut enterprises in Senegal and Gambia were virtually unknown. Where an expansion of legitimate trade had been achieved, it had been at the cost of a social and political disruption which fragmented any response to the European advance.

The late-nineteenth-century export trade of equatorial Africa was not nearly as developed as that of West Africa. In 1897 the value of French Equatorial Africa's external trade was only 10 per cent of that of French West Africa; the value of external trade from the Congo State was 25 per

TABLE 1:2

FOREIGN TRADE OF CENTRAL AFRICA AS A PERCENTAGE OF TOTAL SUB-SAHARAN AFRICAN TRADE, SELECTED YEARS (BY VALUE)

	1897	1913	1929	1945	1960
Cameroun[a]	0·7	1·4	0·8	1·1[b]	1·7
AEF[c]	0·5	1·2	0·9	1·2	2·2
Belgian Congo	2·1	2·6	5·4	6·1	7·5
Angola	3·1	1·4	1·5	1·9	2·3
Mozambique	6·5[d]	2·1	2·1	2·0	1·8
Nyasaland	—	0·2	0·3	0·5 ⎫	
N. Rhodesia	—	0·2	1·2	3·1 ⎬	9·7
S. Rhodesia	—	3·2	3·7	5·0 ⎭	
Central Africa	12·9	12·3	15·9	20·9	25·2
Sub-Saharan Africa	100·0	100·0	100·0	100·0	100·0

a After 1919, French mandate area only.
b Includes the trade of Togo.
c Includes the trade of Chad.
d Includes transit trade.

Source: J. Forbes Munro, Africa and the International Economy, 1800–1960, p. 223.

40 For example, see Samir Amin, 'Underdevelopment and dependence in Black Africa: origins and contemporary forms', Journal of Modern African Studies, x, 4, 1972, 521.

cent of that of British West Africa.[41] The total value of Central African foreign trade constituted less than 13 per cent of sub-Saharan trade, and half of this was due to the transit trade of Mozambique (see Table 1:2). The growth of trade was hampered by the high costs of establishing a colonial infrastructure, by the length of supply lines strung from the Atlantic ports to the interior and by the sparse population in the dense tropical forest.

In the southern part of the region, African foreign trade had been oriented to the Muslim powers around the Indian Ocean until a late date. The social structures of the area had also been weakened by the effects of the South African *mfecane*. The nature of colonial rule was primarily affected, however, by the mineral wealth of the area, by the healthy uplands of Zimbabwe, by the fertile lowlands of Mozambique and, above all, by the spread of white South African capital and its demands for labour.

THE VIOLENCE OF COLONIALISM

At times the colonial history of Central Africa becomes a catalogue of violence, both structural and personal. Colonialism involves the subjugation of one group by another, but in some other parts of Africa domination was sometimes a less disruptive influence on daily life. A survey of East African history in the later stages of colonial rule concluded that 'government did not impinge very much on the lives of the people'.[42] This was not at all the case in Central Africa. The very feebleness of colonialism in the early period initiated a time of arbitrary violence, as weak governments and private interest groups scrambled to assert themselves. This era was superseded by a period of more systematic, but none the less violent, rule by government decree. Clearly colonial government could not be omnipresent and its authority varied in time and place. The flexibility and choice of adaptation which Africans retained varied according to local resources. Their freedom of initiative depended on the extent of their integration into the colonial and capitalist world. Often, however, colonialism was an authoritarian, unpredictable and brutal system, whose demands deeply affected the quality of life itself. This is a constant refrain in the following chapters.

The structural violence of colonialism provided the framework within which government auxiliaries and private agencies operated. Coercion within the new boundaries denied participation in decision-making processes. Local African administrators working for colonial government became the tools of foreign occupation, and lost legitimacy in the eyes of their people. In the predatory states of North-Central Africa, the upper Zaire basin and Mozambique, colonial governments merely substituted

41 Forbes Munro, *Africa and the International Economy*, p. 102.
42 Christopher Wrigley, 'Changes in East African Society', in *History of East Africa*, D. A. Low and Alison Smith (eds), Oxford, 1976, vol. III, p. 509.

one dictatorial régime for another.[43] In areas which the colonisers claimed to 'pacify' by ending existing conflicts, ordinary people merely exchanged the uncertainties of local politics for the certainty of colonial coercion. The denial of human rights, detention without trial and corporal punishment became commonplace.[44] Denial of mobility was enforced, and people were confined to specific reserves, towns or villages. Movement was widely controlled through registration and pass systems in settler areas such as Southern Rhodesia and in the Belgian Congo.[45]

The greatest problem of African daily life was the constant colonial demand for labour and for land. Construction, transportation, mining, the collection of wild rubber, crop-growing for new towns, mining centres and export markets, all created a desperate search for labour often in regions which were sparsely populated. In 1899 a new labour code for the Portuguese colonies freely admitted the necessity for forced labour. Africans were legally and morally obliged 'to obtain through work the means that they lack to subsist and to better their social conditions'. Such fine language hardly masked the reality that forced labour could now be legally requisitioned by the state and by private individuals. Those who refused could be treated as criminals. Harsh labour policies continued in Angola and Mozambique into the 1950s.[46] Demands in other colonies were less overt but had the same effect. Taxation and restricted access to land were the main techniques of labour mobilisation. Where peasant production prospered, absorbed labour and competed with foreign enterprises, it was discouraged with seizure of land and cattle and with high taxation until workers were driven into the colonial economy.[47] Loss of land did not always mean banishment to marginal reserves but the best accessible lands were often taken and villagers resettled in strange places dispensable to the colonial economy. Where farmers were permitted to remain on their land, new problems emerged. The enforced absence of male labour, the compulsory production of cash crops and the undermining of the rural economy meant that African land became a sea of poverty around islands of economic growth.[48]

In many parts of Central Africa, family life was a casualty of the colonial system. Enduring marriage relationships became difficult when prolonged absence of men from the villages was required. Some were forced to move

43 See chapters by Austen and Headrick, and by Vail, below.
44 For example, Basil Davidson, *In the Eye of the Storm*, New York, 1973, pp. 157–61; Charles van Onselen, *Chibaro: African Mine Labour in Southern Rhodesia, 1900–1933*, London, 1976, pp. 142–57; see also the powerful novel by the Angolan writer José Luandino Vieira, *The Real Life of Domingos Xavier*, London, 1978; see also chapter by Vail, below.
45 See chapters by Jewsiewicki and Phimister, below.
46 James Duffy, *A Question of Slavery*, Oxford, 1967, p. 140. See chapters by Clarence-Smith and Vail, below.
47 Van Onselen, *Chibaro*, p. 74; see chapters by Vail and Phimister, below.
48 See the discussion in Robin Palmer and Neil Parsons (eds), *The Roots of Rural Poverty in Central and Southern Africa*, London, 1977, pp. 2–4.

16

temporarily to find work; others became permanent town-dwellers; yet others became semi-permanent migrants who participated spasmodically in rural production.[49] The absence of men from rural households for months or even years became common.

Colonies differed in their labour policies. In the Belgian Congo after 1930, the concept of 'stabilised' labour gave the worker a permit to bring his family to the town or the mine compound. Generally men went to urban centres, found work first and only later brought their wives and children to join them. In British Central Africa migrant labourers found it difficult to bring their families out of the rural areas at all, even as late as the 1950s. Employers justified low wages on the grounds that the rural economy was deemed to support the worker's family. The British policy also aimed to discourage the growth of a permanent working class in the towns. The enormous distances in Central Africa precluded frequent visits home. Workers from the Kwilu–Kwango region of the Belgian Congo walked 700 kilometres to Léopoldville or to the Copperbelt towns.[50] A Northern Rhodesian could take two months to walk home from the Copperbelt or could use up the equivalent of two months' wages by taking motorised transport.[51]

In the villages women were left in a vulnerable position. They could be rounded up with their children and held hostage for men who were unable to pay taxes. They were commonly forced to provide virtually unpaid labour for the colonial state to build and maintain roads.[52] They had both to provide adequate food for their families and to participate in cash-crop production. When men were absent at peak agricultural seasons, women had to carry the full burden of providing for both children and old people. When deprived of adequate help for the heavy work of clearing the bush, women had to cut down on the amount of land under cultivation. Protein intake declined when cattle were confiscated, hunting and fishing abandoned, and palm trees neglected.

Village life was also affected by the undermining of its institutions. Social disruption and the spread of disease led to an increase in accusations of witchcraft. Old people with few entrées to the cash economy found their position in society eroded. An imbalance in the age ratio of village populations began to occur, and can be deduced from urban statistics. In the early 1950s, the percentage of people over forty-five was 7·5 in Livingstone, 9·0 in Brazzaville, 10·6 in Stanleyville and a mere 3·5 in the Copperbelt towns.[53] Old people in the villages defended the few privileges

49 Valdo Pons, *Stanleyville: an African Urban Community under Belgian Administration*, London, 1969, p. 59.
50 Jacques Denis, *Le Phénomène urbain en Afrique Centrale*, Brussels, 1958, pp. 174–80.
51 L. P. Mair, 'African marriage and social change', in *Survey of African Marriage and Family Life*, Arthur Phillips (ed.), London, 1953, pp. 105–6.
52 See chapters by Austen and Headrick, Clarence-Smith and Vail, below.
53 Pons, *Stanleyville*, pp. 43–5.

they had left, such as control of women. Bridewealth became less a contractual guarantee of marital stability and more a monetary transaction transferring revenues from young wage-earners to old villagers. In some matrilineal societies, maternal uncles forbade women from leaving the village to follow husbands to town.[54] Young men, on the other hand, had a new economic freedom to seek brides elsewhere if negotiations became too protracted.

Life in the new urban centres of Central Africa was not easy on personal relationships. When the Belgians 'stabilised' town-dwellers, the residence permit required employment and a monogamous marriage. Polygynous men were refused residence even though accompanied by one wife. Only immediate dependants were permitted, and divorced women or widows of less than ten years' residence had to return to the village.[55] In Northern Rhodesia, single women sometimes had to obtain the District Commissioner's permit to enter an urban area. Officials from the Lozi area went periodically to Livingstone to remove 'unauthorised' women back to the villages by force.[56]

The situation of women in towns was full of ambiguities. Most women went to urban areas as dependants. From the Belgian Congo to Southern Rhodesia, in a region where town life was subject to strict controls, administrative restrictions made it difficult for women to find work. They thus lost the economic roles they had had in the villages. In 1952 2 per cent of Stanleyville women over sixteen were wage-earners compared to 90 per cent of the men.[57] Even in Cameroun and French Equatorial Africa where the situation was more flexible, there were few great market women to match those of West Africa. Central African towns-women were therefore forced to turn to the few economic opportunities which were available: petty trading, beer-selling and prostitution. Their future was not bright since education was given to boys in preference to girls.[58]

Central Africa, unlike West Africa, had no great urban tradition or established town population before the colonial period. Since men preceded women to the new towns for employment, they greatly outnumbered them. The numerical imbalance of the sexes was a major cause of social instability, and this, together with poverty, shift-working and a lack of economic opportunities for women, put great pressure on marital relationships. It was not surprising that a high percentage of

54 Jacques Denis, *Le Phénomène urbain*, pp. 357–8.
55 Pons, *Stanleyville*, pp. 36–7, 214, 217; J. S. La Fontaine, *City Politics: a Study of Léopoldville, 1962–63*, Cambridge, 1970, pp. 28–9.
56 Ilsa M. G. Schuster, *New Women of Lusaka*, Palo Alto, California, 1979, p. 20; M. McCulloch, *A Study of the African Population of Livingstone*, Lusaka, The Rhodes-Livingstone Institute, 1956, p. 19.
57 Pons, *Stanleyville*, p. 52.
58 Aidan Southall (ed.), *Social Change in Modern Africa*, London, 1961, pp. 50–1, 56–9.

marriages failed to endure.[59] Although some women were able to achieve an independent status and a wealth beyond that found in village life, material success did not often compensate for the pressures of town life.[60] In the squalid, insecure, deprived conditions of Southern Rhodesia's mining compounds, women and girls suffered appalling personal violence.[61]

TABLE 1:3

RATIO OF WOMEN TO MEN IN SELECTED CITIES
(AFRICAN ADULT POPULATION, EARLY 1950s)

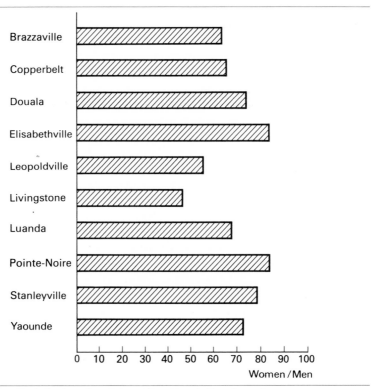

Source: Jacques Denis, *Le phenomène urbain en Afrique Centrale,* Brussels, 1958, p. 202.

The spread of disease was a serious consequence of colonialism. This was in part the result of greater mobility as men moved out of their home environments in search of work. The spread of sleeping sickness in the early decades of the century and the pandemic of Spanish influenza which

59 Pons, *Stanleyville,* pp. 214, 241–2; Schuster, *New Women,* pp. 14–21.
60 For example, see Suzanne Comhaire-Sylvain, *Femmes de Kinshasa, hier et aujourd'hui,* Paris, 1968, pp. 21, 23.
61 Van Onselen, *Chibaro,* pp. 174–9.

swept through Africa in 1918 are mentioned in every chapter in this book.[62] Population movement and marital instability also increased venereal disease. In northern Central Africa, the major tragedy in the lives of many young women was their inability to bear children and the death of their infants.[63] It was not until the 1930s that improved health services began to reduce these human disasters.

The number of Europeans in Central Africa, even in the settler zones, was small, and the weakness of colonial states made the use of African allies imperative. Violence is not power but an instrument of power, and 'power always stands in need of numbers'.[64] The literature on this subject often refers to 'collaborators', but the pejorative connotations[65] are not always appropriate. Often, African leaders believed that incoming European forces widened their policy options and could be used against historic enemies. A European alliance could help pay off old debts, ensure the means of survival and provide opportunity in the new world that colonialism made.[66]

A common European practice was to bring in foreign Africans who had no cultural bonds with local societies. These employees could be recruited individually or contracted from an African government. Stanley, the American explorer, *en route* from Europe to the Zaire estuary, went by way of Zanzibar to contract with the Sultan for 620 porters. Such an arrangement had the double advantage that foreign Africans were less likely to collude with local peoples and had more difficulty in deserting since the territory was unknown.[67] The use of foreign recruits in colonial armies was particularly common: the Germans used Dahomeans, Liberians and Hausa in Cameroun; the soldiers of the *Force Publique* in the Congo State included Hausa, Sierra Leoneans, Liberians, Zanzibaris and Dahomeans; and the Portuguese transported Angolans to fight their colonial wars in Mozambique.[68] In Southern Rhodesia, mine managers

62 The most complete account of health problems and health care is contained in the chapter by Austen and Headrick, below.

63 See Austen and Headrick, below; also see the biographies in Anne Laurentin, 'Nzakara women', in *Women of Tropical Africa*, Denise Paulme (ed.), Berkeley and Los Angeles, 1963, pp. 121–78.

64 Hannah Arendt, *On Violence*, New York, 1970, p. 41.

65 In the European literature, the concept of collaboration is inextricably associated with the alliance of the Vichy régime in France and the Quisling government in Norway with Nazi occupation forces during the Second World War.

66 For a useful attempt at a typology of collaboration, see Allen F. Isaacman, *The Tradition of Resistance in Mozambique*, Los Angeles and Berkeley, 1976, pp. 189–90; also, Allen Isaacman and Barbara Isaacman, 'Resistance and collaboration in southern and central Africa', *International Journal of African Historical Studies*, x, 1, 1977, 31–62.

67 Iain R. Smith, *The Emin Pasha Relief Expedition, 1886–1890*, Oxford, 1972, pp. 69–70, 108.

68 Rudin, *Germans in the Cameroons*, pp. 193–4; L. H. Gann and Peter Duignan, *The Rulers of Belgian Africa, 1884–1914*, Princeton, N.J., 1979, pp. 73, 225 fn.16; Isaacman, *The Tradition of Resistance*, p. 65.

trained foreign Africans as police and guards – for example, Zulu and Xhosa from South Africa, and Yao and Ngoni from Northern Rhodesia and Nyasaland.[69]

The social disruption of Central Africa in the late nineteenth century made it easier for Europeans to follow a policy of 'divide and rule'. Established rivals used European allies against each other – as in Zimbabwe, in the Zambezi valley and on the middle Zaire.[70] Weaker societies, which had suffered at the hands of slave-raiding states, in North- and East-Central Africa, welcomed European colonisers for the protection they provided.[71] Established élites made alliances to preserve their status within society, but anyone could be tempted by incentives to work for Europeans, to increase economic status and to exercise power over fellow men and women. Education was the key to entering the acculturated class of colonial society. Central Africans sought training as clerks, as teachers, as medical assistants, as interpreters and as bureaucrats. To work as a policeman, a tax-collector or a labour-recruiter meant freedom from manual labour and higher wages with better clothing and food for the individual and for his dependents. Privilege could be further increased by abusing power, by demanding gifts and by dominating women. All were common by-products of a violent system.[72]

RESISTANCE, RESILIENCE AND REVOLUTION

African resistance was an important influence in patterns of foreign occupation and domination. If some élites chose to ally themselves to the invaders and profit from their presence, others mobilised their subjects to ward off the threat to political autonomy and economic interest. Violent military confrontation varied in its duration and intensity. In British Central Africa and Mozambique 'primary' resistance[73] had more or less been crushed by 1900; in French Equatorial Africa, in Cameroun and in the

69 Van Onselen, *Chibaro*, pp. 139–40. Also by the same author, 'The role of collaborators in the Rhodesian mining industry, 1900–1935', *African Affairs*, lxxii, 289, 1973, 401–18; also see chapter by Clarence-Smith, below.
70 D. N. Beach, 'Ndebele raiders and Shona power', *JAH*, xv, 4, 1974, 642–8; Isaacman, *The Tradition of Resistance*, pp. 22–37; Jan Vansina, *The Tio Kingdom of the Middle Congo, 1880–1892*, Oxford, 1973, pp. 403–28.
71 Arlette Thuriaux-Hennebert, 'Les Grands Chefs Bandia et Zande de la région Uele-Bomu, 1860–1895', *Études d'Histoire Africaine*, iii, 1972, 167–207; P. Ceulemans, *La Question arabe et le Congo, 1883–1892*, Brussels, 1958.
72 Van Onselen, 'The role of collaborators', pp. 408, 416; Henri Brunschwig, 'French expansion and local reactions in Black Africa in the time of imperialism, 1880–1914', in *Expansion and Reaction*, H. L. Wesseling (ed.), Leiden, 1978, pp. 124–40; Isaacman, *The Tradition of Resistance*, pp. 65, 82–3.
73 A phrase popularised by Terence Ranger to describe early ethnically-based resistance to colonial occupation; see T. O. Ranger, 'Connexions between "primary resistance" movements and modern mass nationalism in East and Central Africa', *JAH*, ix, 3 and 4, 1968, 437–53, 631–41.

Belgian Congo fighting went on as late as 1910; in Angola, Portugal's 'nightmare colony', resisters held out in the eastern region until the 1920s.[74] African ability to challenge European advance has generally been underestimated. In Angola, for example, resisters engaged the Portuguese army in 150 campaigns between 1879 and 1926; between 1902 and 1920 the colonial army spent 83 per cent of its time actively suppressing insurgency.[75]

People also responded as private individuals to European demands. To avoid direct confrontation and resist integration into the colonial world by withdrawal or flight was one option. These tactics were especially common in the early years as colonial expeditions advanced into the interior. On the Ogowe route from Gabon to Brazzaville villagers along river banks and caravan trails abandoned their homes, hid their canoes and fled into the forest to avoid European demands for food, porters, paddlers, guides and river-craft.[76] Elsewhere people moved to inaccessible mountains, swamps and forests to escape labour recruiters and tax collectors. In some areas it was possible to flee across territorial boundaries in the hope of finding a more tolerable brand of colonialism.[77] Sporadic, day-to-day resistance was offered by thousands of subjects through agricultural sabotage, desertion, work slowdowns and strikes. Some rebels hid in remote areas in order to operate as social bandits against those who remained within the colonial system.[78]

The growth of resistance was a cumulative process that passed through various phases. The leaders of early, ethnically-based movements were often successful participants in the international commercial systems, and their actions were based on élite interests, which they mobilised subjects to defend. Another strand of resistance was present in the earliest protest movements, however. As the violence of colonialism was felt in the deteriorating quality of life, people demonstrated their own sense of grievance. Individual and corporate actions were an incremental consciousness-raising process. They could lead to participation in broad-based movements such as multi-ethnic coalitions, industrial action and religiously-oriented groups. By the 1930s, peasant and worker conscious-ness began to cut across ethnic and regional loyalties in the Belgian Congo and on the Rhodesian mines.[79] This 'tradition of resistance' became the

74 Réne Pélissier, *Les Guerres grises: resistances et révoltes en Angola, 1845–1941*, Orgeval, 1977, pp. 306–10.
75 *Ibid.*, pp. 611–12.
76 Coquery-Vidrovitch, *Brazza*, pp. 58–60, 63, 73–85.
77 See chapters by Austen and Headrick, Clarence-Smith, and Vail, below.
78 See chapters by Vellut and Jewsiewicki, below; also see Isaacman, *The Tradition of Resistance*, p. 79, and the comment by Clarence-Smith below.
79 Isaacman, *The Tradition of Resistance*, pp. xxii, 53, 58, 67, 151, 161–6, for the situation in the Zambezi valley. Also chapters by Jewsiewicki, Vellut and Phimister, below.

force behind post-1945 nationalist movements, although leadership came from an educated élite.[80]

The new problems that went with life under colonial rule demanded new solutions. Although an increase in witchcraft accusations was a traditional reaction to misfortune, antidotes were found in religion as well. New cults and shrines arose to counter the tensions and ambiguities which colonialism created, and to satisfy the desire for personal security and success. Religious leaders not only met spiritual and emotional needs; they also played a role in legitimising and coordinating resistance movements.[81] Villagers and townspeople alike turned to new religious forms when neither traditional belief systems nor Christianity answered their needs. Prophets and healers founded syncretic churches which blended strands of religious experience. They foretold an imminent millennium free of Europeans; they preached strict obedience to the church and withdrawal from the colonial system. The new churches were hardly revolutionary in their beliefs or actions, but they drew mass followings and came to be feared by government as a dynamic focus of anti-colonial sentiment. Their leaders were therefore imprisoned and exiled, and their members were persecuted.[82]

Urban centres were the scene of many innovations. A new culture flourished outside the coloniser's orbit. It included popular music, dances, bars and sporting events.[83] Successful, independent women were often pace-makers in setting standards of urban stylishness. They were less commonly subordinated to Europeans at work, and lacked the educational opportunity of men by which to achieve the acculturated status of *evolué* or *assimilado*. It was, therefore, within a largely African frame of reference that they forged a new urban culture more indigenous than European in its inspiration.[84]

In the towns and mining centres, new ideologies and social structures developed to compensate for the loss of village support systems. Immigrants from the rural areas sought out people from the same part of the country. A stronger and wider sense of ethnicity emerged, as these groups occupied specific sectors of towns, spoke a vernacular language standardised by missionaries, promoted their regional culture and continued to prefer marriage within the group. They developed several

80 T. O. Ranger, 'The people in African resistance', *JSAS*, iii, 1977, 125–47, especially 146–7.
81 Isaacman, *The Tradition of Resistance*, pp. 128–9; T. O. Ranger, *Revolt in Southern Rhodesia*, London, 1967, pp. 127–310; also the comment on Ranger's thesis by Julian Cobbing, 'The absent priesthood: another look at the Rhodesian risings of 1896–1897', *JAH*, xviii, 1, 1977, 61–84; and D. N. Beach, 'Chimurenga: the Shona rising of 1896–1897', *JAH*, xx, 3, 1979, 395–420.
82 See chapters by Austen and Headrick, Jewsiewicki, Vellut, Clarence-Smith, Vail and Phimister, below.
83 See chapter by Vellut, below.
84 Pons, *Stanleyville*, p. 215.

kinds of friendly association for help in times of trouble and social institutions with which to celebrate good times. It is a great paradox that by the time African nations came to seek independence, ethnic consciousness was stronger than ever before. It therefore became an obvious power base for political leaders who led the struggle towards independence.[85]

After the Second World War, the demand for an end to colonialism reached a new intensity. Within nineteen years all Central African countries achieved independence except for Spanish Equatorial Guinea, Portuguese Angola and Mozambique, and settler-controlled Southern Rhodesia. The rapid move to independence was partly determined by the history of individual countries. In general, however, the movement for colonial freedom was a continent-wide phenomenon as sudden as the African loss of independence had been at the end of the nineteenth century. Global political, economic and ideological trends all strongly affected both the opening and the closing phases of the colonial relationship between Africa and Europe. In the post-1945 era events as geographically dispersed as Indian independence, the Indo-China wars, United Nations deliberations in New York and the 1945 Pan-African Congress in Manchester, all influenced the struggle for independence in Central Africa. The Second World War had contributed to the shrinking influence of the old imperial super-powers, Britain and France. It had also raised to international pre-eminence the United States and the Soviet Union which had no African colonies and could, therefore, lend their weight to the anti-colonial movement. In Europe the growing influence of social-democratic parties also helped the cause of African nationalism.

World trade and investment entered a settled phase in the period from 1945 to 1960. In the global perspective of the industrial powers of Western Europe, connections with Central Africa seemed relatively unimportant, although existing economic bonds were intensified through investment, management contracts, trade and white immigration. The severing of formal colonial ties was unlikely to affect these imperial economic interests. The economic situation thus made it opportune for the French, British and Belgian governments to concede to the demands for independence by their African subjects. This situation was in direct contrast to the situation at the end of the nineteenth century, when an unstable political economy had helped to propel Europe into Africa.[86]

Despite the violence which colonialism had generated, the move to independence in the northern two-thirds of Central Africa was remarkably peaceful. Only in Cameroun did one nationalist faction take up arms against French imperialism.[87] The popular outcry against France had been stronger in West Africa, and the hard decisions about decolonisation had

---

85 See chapters by Austen and Headrick, Vellut, and Young, below.
86 Forbes Munro, *Africa and the International Economy*, pp. 176–206.
87 See chapters by Austen and Headrick, and Young, below.

been taken before the people of equatorial Africa seriously sought to gain their freedom. Throughout francophone Central Africa, the imperial powers were unwilling to contemplate the level of violence which would ultimately have been necessary to retain control of their colonies in the 1960s. The potential costs of maintaining a colonial presence ultimately outweighed the benefits once continued economic dependence was assured. Problems were already emerging in French Equatorial Africa, where the divergent interests of the four colonies made continued unity problematical without heavy French pressure.[88] The fragility of the colonial presence was most strikingly seen in the Belgian Congo where as late as 1957 the colonial power had no intention of leaving, yet withdrawal came only three years later. Rural unrest and large urban demonstrations had shown that only a large military presence could contain an explosive situation.[89] The cost of such an operation was unthinkable both in moral and financial terms. In the British sphere, the collapse of the Central African Federation was quickly followed by the independence of Zambia and Malawi, thus bringing these countries into line with the British colonies in West and East Africa.[90]

The level of violence necessary to contain the growing tide of African nationalism was only tolerable for Spain, Portugal and the white settlers of Rhodesia. By 1968, however, Spain had given up its effort to protect cocoa plantations through white vigilante forces, and African leaders were given control of the small colony of Equatorial Guinea.[91] The resistance of Portugal was much tougher. Unlike the industrial countries of Western Europe, Portugal lacked the strength to forge informal economic links with its African territories in the event of independence. It feared that the industrial super-powers would quickly take its place in the neo-colonial partnership. Politically and intellectually, the authoritarian régime of António Salazar was out of step with the democratic philosophies in other countries. Nationalists found little support among left-wing dissidents in the metropole. A tough, even brutal, secret police was sent to the African colonies in the 1950s to root out nationalists. For two decades Portugal committed tens of thousands of troops to holding back the liberation forces. At the same time the white settlers of Southern Rhodesia chose to defy world opinion, to ban African nationalist parties and to engage in armed warfare against liberation movements.[92]

Faced with the intransigence of colonial rulers in Angola, Mozambique and Rhodesia, the Central African liberation movements reluctantly espoused the revolutionary philosophy of Frantz Fanon, who had claimed

88 See chapter by Austen and Headrick, below.
89 See chapters by Jewsiewicki, Vellut and Young, below.
90 See chapter by Birmingham and Ranger, below.
91 Cronjé, *Equatorial Guinea*, pp. 11–12.
92 See chapters by Clarence-Smith, and Birmingham and Ranger, below.

that 'only violence pays'.[93] The costs of the violent struggle finally wore down the white governments. Portugal's failure in its African campaigns helped to topple the dictatorship in 1974. The independence of Angola and Mozambique came in the following year. By 1980, economic sanctions, country-wide guerrilla activity and the lack of a viable political alternative caused settlers in Rhodesia to negotiate the independence of Zimbabwe. Liberation enabled Central Africans to begin the long-delayed search for peace and prosperity.

93 Frantz Fanon, *The Wretched of the Earth*, New York, 1968, p. 61; see also H. Arendt, *On Violence*, pp. 53–6.

CHAPTER 2

Equatorial Africa under colonial rule

RALPH A. AUSTEN AND RITA HEADRICK

The goal of all colonial powers is to make their colonies useful to the
metropole by providing raw materials, privileged markets and enhanced
international status. The degree to which they do this is dependent upon the
material and historical endowments of the colony and the level of resources
and energy invested by the metropole. In French Equatorial Africa (AEF)
and Cameroun, this dialectic between the existing African situation and the
strategies of the imperialist powers produced results ranging from the
mediocre to the disastrous. In economic terms, the colonies were marginal;
in political terms, they provided more scandal than prestige.

French and German colonial hopes, when unaccompanied by sustained
interest or sufficient investment, were bound to remain illusions. Even the
few colonial heroes of equatorial Africa were intimately associated with
failure. The founding father of AEF, Savorgnan de Brazza, died on a
mission to investigate the crimes committed by the concessionary
companies through which he once hoped to develop the territory.
Commandant J. B. Marchand's expedition into the interior of AEF ended
in the humiliation of Fashoda, when France lost access to the Nile. The
long-term German governor, Jesco von Puttkammer, was recalled from
Cameroun in personal and political disgrace. Dr Eugène Jamot, who
organised a massive campaign against sleeping sickness, was arrested when
one of his subordinates gave toxic doses of the treatment.

If these territories remained a problem for colonial administrators, the
administrators proved even more of a problem for the African populations.
Whereas the metropoles wanted to transform the region into an effective
counterpart of the Western economy, the goal of Africans was to minimise
the disruption to their own lives and maximise their own wealth and status
within this new European framework. Yet here, too, the interplay between
indigenous resources and alien intervention was such that Africans were
burdened by demands which threatened their livelihood, their health and
sometimes their lives. As for opportunities for upward mobility, they were

significantly less than in colonies with more thriving economies, more respect for traditional social forms and a better educational apparatus.

Of course, there were variations in time and place. The early years in AEF (which consisted of Gabon, Moyen-Congo, Ubangi-Shari and Chad) were particularly marked by under-investment and attempts to extract the expenses of administration from an impoverished population. As René Maran, a colonial administrator, wrote in a novel which won the Prix Goncourt:

> This region was very rich in rubber and very populous. Plantations of all sorts covered its expanses. It abounded in chickens and goats. Seven years were enough to ruin it completely.
>
> The villages were decimated, the plantations disappeared, chickens and goats were annihilated. As for the natives, weakened by unceasing, excessive, and unremunerated work, it was made impossible for them even to devote the necessary time to their sowing. They saw illness settle down among them, famine invade them and their number diminish.[1]

New colonial strategies which began in the thirties, however, involved greater investments to redirect the economy and improve African welfare. Cameroun all along suffered from fewer political and economic disabilities than AEF. It had better soil and was more densely populated. Its immediate pre-colonial history was less traumatic than that of the savannas of AEF, where massive slave-raiding occurred until the turn of the century. Equally important were the political factors. Cameroun was one of few German colonies and, after the First World War a League of Nations mandate, subject to a certain amount of international scrutiny. AEF, on the other hand, was low among France's colonial priorities and had to compete for attention with French West Africa, Indo-China and Algeria.

THE PARAMETERS AND PERIMETERS OF COLONIAL RULE

To understand the colonial period it is necessary to consider natural resources, how Africans had located and organised themselves, and where Europeans had drawn their empires. It was unfortunate for both strategists in colonial ministries and for indigenous populations that the territories were most characterised by what they lacked. There was no Rand or Copperbelt, few easily co-optable states or trade networks, few regions of dense, flourishing population. The area was vast and underpopulated; the continuing quest was for a means to integrate it within the borders imposed by international politics. Even the physical integration of the area was difficult. Though the colonial names of the territories came from bodies of water, the natural transport system was inadequate. Lake Chad offered no

1 René Maran, *Batouala: a True Black Novel* (translated by Barbara Beck and Alexandre Mboukou), Greenwich, Conn., 1972, p. 20. The book originally appeared in 1921.

significant navigation routes, the Congo, Ubangi and Shari rivers were usable only for limited inland stretches and the Gabon and Cameroun coastal rivers penetrated the interior for even shorter distances.

The coastal areas of Cameroun and most of Gabon and Moyen-Congo are rain-forests which contain natural products of immediate interest to the European market: wild rubber, tropical timber and oil-palms. African cultivators, however, were concentrated in western Cameroun, where the volcanic highlands contain some of the most fertile soil in Africa, in Ubangi-Shari and in southern Chad. North of these areas, as far as the Sahara, are dryer savannas, with a mixed agricultural–pastoral economy.

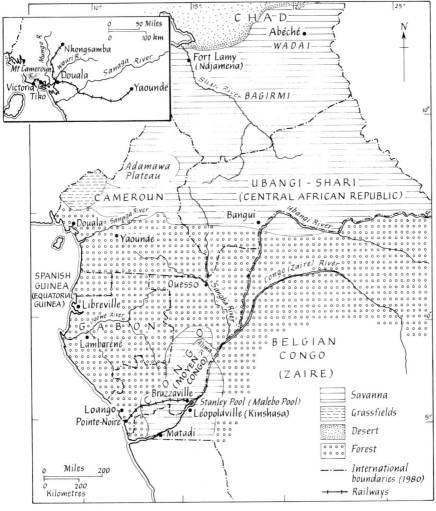

2:1 Equatorial Africa, c. 1920

The sub-soil is not rich in minerals; only Gabon, and then at a late date, provided the world with strategic raw materials. Nor could these colonies be used as a labour reserve for mining centres in nearby countries. They were not to become satellites of wealthier neighbours; financially and commercially they were tied directly to the metropole. The economic systems which evolved were contained within the recently drawn frontiers.

These new borders help to explain the difficulties of creating productive, stable régimes. The most serious problem was that the borders bisected the two great pre-colonial trading zones of the region, those of the Niger and Zaire rivers, thus disrupting African trade patterns. The formal basis for the German and French presence was a series of treaties signed with African rulers such as those of the Duala[2] in Cameroun, the Mpongwe in Gabon and the Tio at Malebo Pool. But the hinterlands of two of these entrepôts were not enclosed by the new political configurations. Douala was on the fringes of the Niger basin commerce; Malebo Pool had been part of a broad network which included not just the Zaire river but the savannas to the south, now under Belgian and Portuguese control. The third city, the Mpongwe port of Libreville, lay before a dense, underpopulated forest zone. In fact neither Douala nor Libreville had ever been a first-rank port, and Loango, the Atlantic outlet of the Moyen-Congo, had declined long before the colonial era.

Although Douala and Malebo Pool were separated from their natural trading hinterlands, they were now attached to vast, inland territories of savanna and desert, the leftovers of more choice colonial claims. Marchand and his troops had hoped to create a band of French territory from the Atlantic to the Indian Ocean. English protests, however, led to French withdrawal from the Nilotic Sudan and left Ubangi as a cul-de-sac. Perhaps as a consolation prize, the English soon afterwards agreed to French occupation of Chad.[3] Within the inland savanna, as in the forest, there were few units which could be incorporated into the new order with their structure intact. Bagirmi and Wadai, once powerful states, were now ruined shells, incapable of restoration despite European attempts. The Adamawa lamidates were cut off by the new border from the rest of the Sokoto Caliphate. Only a few other bureaucratically undeveloped conquest states remained.

A final contribution to the instability of the region was a continuing series of border changes, both international and internal, none of which resulted in a more rational division of territory. The very presence of Germany guaranteed that twentieth-century European power struggles would be played out on African land. Firstly, AEF was truncated by a German salient from Cameroun to the Zaire river, won in the settlement

2 Following standard conventions, the French spelling 'Douala' is used to designate the city, and the English and German spelling 'Duala' to designate the people.
3 Marc Michel, *La Mission Marchand 1895–1899*, Paris, 1972, especially p. 251.

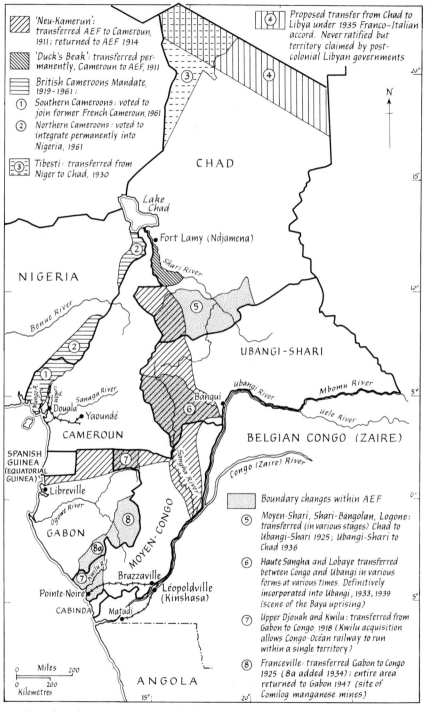

'Neu-Kamerun': transferred AEF to Cameroun, 1911; returned to AEF 1914

'Duck's Beak': transferred permanently, Cameroun to AEF, 1911

British Cameroons Mandate, 1919-1961:

① Southern Cameroons: voted to join former French Cameroun, 1961

② Northern Cameroons: voted to integrate permanently into Nigeria, 1961

③ Tibesti: transferred from Niger to Chad, 1930

④ Proposed transfer from Chad to Libya under 1935 Franco-Italian accord. Never ratified but territory claimed by postcolonial Libyan governments

Boundary changes within AEF

⑤ Moyen-Shari, Shari-Bangolan, Logone: transferred (in various stages) Chad to Ubangi-Shari 1925; Ubangi-Shari to Chad 1936

⑥ Haute Sangha and Lobaye transferred between Congo and Ubangi in various forms at various times. Definitively incorporated into Ubangi, 1933, 1939 (scene of the Baya uprising)

⑦ Upper Djouah and Kwilu: transferred from Gabon to Congo, 1918 (Kwilu acquisition allows Congo-Ocean railway to run within a single territory)

⑧ Franceville: transferred Gabon to Congo 1925 (8a added 1934); entire area returned to Gabon 1947 (site of Comilog manganese mines)

2:2 Transfers of territory in equatorial Africa, 1911–1961

31

surrounding the Moroccan crisis of 1911; then in 1918, Cameroun was divided between Britain and France as a war spoil. The incessant changes within AEF were in pursuit of one of two mirages: less costly government or more effective control. Yet the juggling did little to relieve the incongruities of administering a poor territory strung out from Libya to the Zaire and from the Atlantic to the headwaters of the Nile.

Of all the factors which made this territory seem so burdensome to Paris, none was more critical than low population density. When natural endowments are scanty and metropolitan subsidies meagre, the costs of colonialism must be borne by the colonised. A great deal of administrative energy was invested in 'man-hunts', a phrase which appears and reappears in the local reports. For Africans it meant that, until the mid-1930s, an overwhelming proportion of their income and labour was extracted to support the minimal apparatus needed to control the area.

The population issue dominated the thought of those concerned with the colonies. At a meeting of the Union Coloniale Française a speaker noted, 'the native population is numerically insufficient to assure the economic development of the country'.[4] A handbook written for African mothers explained: 'If the Whites give us advice on raising our children it is because they want them not to die so they can pay taxes when they grow up.'[5]

The scarcity of population was due to low fertility, ecological constraints and the recent slave-trade. To these were added both the unforeseen epidemiological consequences of colonialism and the predictable disasters resulting from the 'économie de pillage' of the early years. Though the rate of infant mortality was high, it seems to have been no more severe than elsewhere on the continent.

The low fertility of the population in the Zaire and Ogowe basins pre-dates the European occupation; however, in many regions fertility fell even lower during the colonial period. For the Belgian Congo the percentage of sterile women rose slightly with each five-year cohort born between 1900 and Second World War. In the districts most affected 40 per cent of adult women bore no living child.[6] Figures for the late 1950s suggest the comparative place of Central Africa in a fertility spectrum. The number of children ages 0–4 per 1 000 women of child-bearing age was 151 in Ghana, 136 in Nigeria, 99 in Cameroun, 75 in Gabon, and 39 among the Nzakara of south-central Ubangi, a particularly infertile group.[7]

Venereal diseases were responsible for most of the sterility and much of the infant morality. These diseases became more widespread with

4 You, 'Observations', *Le Problème de la population*, Union Coloniale Française, Paris, 1920, p.18.
5 Dr Spire, *Conseils d'hygiène aux indigènes*, Paris, 1922, p. 39.
6 Anatole Romaniuk, *La Fécondité des populations congolaises*, Paris, 1967, p. 63.
7 Anne Retel-Laurentin, *Infécondité et maladies chez les Nzakara, République Centrafricaine*, Paris, 1975, p. 8.

European occupation, but it is difficult to account completely for their differential incidence and virulence. Infertility is much greater where marital instability is common, although childlessness can be a cause as well as a result of frequent divorce. Fertility correlates more closely with ethnicity than with particular geographic or environmental zones; there is,

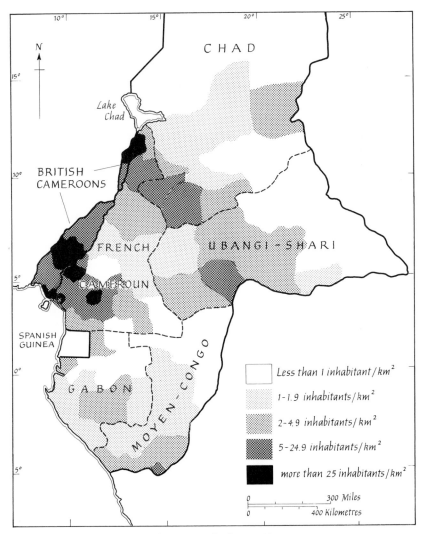

2:3 Population densities, French Equatorial Africa, mid-1930s

Major sources: Services Sanitaires, AEF, *Rapport annuel 1936*; Cameroun, *Rapport annuel 1936*, pp. 100–1; R. R. Kuczynski, *Cameroons and Togoland, a demographic study*, London, 1939, p. 252.

nevertheless, a clear tendency for forest groups to have lower birth-rates than savanna peoples.[8]

Low fertility, though, provides only one explanation for the thinness of population found throughout the forest. Contrary to popular beliefs, the rain-forest is not teeming with edibles, and therefore it cannot support dense populations of hunters and gatherers. Yet agriculture in the forest presents problems beyond the rapid exhaustion of the soil. When farmers clear the land for cultivation, they incur increased health risks. Mosquitoes come down from the tree-tops and settle closer to man, bringing malaria, the single largest cause of infant mortality. Sleeping sickness also increases, for tsetse flies can only live where there is sufficient light.[9] Thus if the population was too low to clear portions of the forests definitively, it could be caught in a health trap.

Whether rain-forests are inherently less healthy than savannas is uncertain. Most colonial doctors and administrators believed them to be so, but this opinion was based on observing the medical problems incurred by workers from savanna regions transplanted to the forest. Gilles Sautter, a geographer who carried out regional studies in Gabon and Moyen-Congo, disagreed; 'For the time being, nothing would allow us to explain the lower average density [of population in] forest areas by their unhealthiness.'[10] Only yaws, a skin disease which is rarely fatal, was clearly more prevalent in the forest. Malaria and sleeping sickness, however, were major killers in both environments.

Undue emphasis should not, however, be placed on tropical diseases. Sickness and death were usually not the result of exotic disease but rather of poverty and poor sanitation. Respiratory and digestive ailments (pneumonia, bronchitis, dysentery, intestinal parasites) which affect any populations without adequate food, clean water and warm shelter, were the major causes of death in equatorial Africa.

Whatever the health status of the population on the eve of colonialism, it declined immediately afterwards. Whereas in East and East-Central Africa a series of cattle and human epidemics paved the way for colonialism, in equatorial Africa the demographic crisis followed partition. Misery is difficult to quantify, but the first three decades of European rule did bring continuing upheaval. Before Europeans penetrated inland there had been disease, epidemics, famines, small-scale warfare and large-scale slave-raiding. Yet the disparity between the means of coercion and the mechanisms of defence, even on the Islamic frontier, was not nearly as great as it became after the imposition of colonial rule; and to the famines

8 Anne Retel-Laurentin, *Infécondité en Afrique noire: maladies et conséquences sociales*, Paris, 1974, pp. 47–58, 98–103; Romaniuk, *La Fécondité*, pp. 108–10.
9 Paul W. Richards, 'The Tropical Rain Forest', *Scientific American*, Dec. 1973, 58–67.
10 Gilles Sautter, *De l'Atlantique au fleuve Congo: une géographie du sous-peuplement*, Paris, 1966, p. 976.

produced by drought were added famines produced by man, as non-existent 'surpluses' were exacted to provision the administration. At the same time, labour was recruited during sowing or harvesting seasons. Finally, there were devastating changes in the disease ecology as new micro-organisms were introduced into previously unafflicted regions. The germs travelled even faster than the régime, and villages which had not yet seen the white man died of diseases like sleeping sickness, the diffusion of which was accelerated by colonial activity.

The burdens of empire fell unevenly. They especially hit those who lived on territory granted to concession companies or to planters, those who were recruited as porters and those forced to work on railway construction. In the rubber regions of Ubangi, in the years before 1914, villagers unable to flee were tied together, and brought naked to the forests to tap rubber vines. They lived in the open and ate what they could find. A French missionary who witnessed the scene wrote: 'The population was reduced to the darkest misery ... never had they lived through such times, not even in the worst days of the Arab [slaving] invasions.'[11]

Regions of Gabon suffered so extensively from famine and incompetent military administration that the colonial office sent an inspection team after the First World War. The government reported that 'the lack of food is particularly found in places where the native has had to suffer the most from contact with us'.[12] Labour and food exactions along with the influenza epidemic of 1918 to 1919 took a severe toll, and in 1920 the governor could only plead that the country needed a rest:

If we continue to see the native as tax payer and worker for Europeans, he will continue to disappear. Or we can ask him to work for himself, increase his crops, make his villages healthier, raise animals and lessen his fatigue.[13]

The sum total of these short-sighted policies and the unforeseen epidemiological consequences of colonialism was a decline in the already small population and its living standards. There are no precise statistics on the population decline because the base-line numbers do not exist. The most reliable estimates of population movement suggest that the population of AEF fell until at least 1923, and the Gabonese population continued to fall, though slightly, until 1955.[14] In Cameroun population

11 R. P. Daigre, *Oubangui-Chari, souvenirs et témoignages 1890–1940*, Paris, 1950, pp. 139–43.
12 Gabon, *Rapport annuel 1921*, Archives Nationales, Dépôt d'Outre-Mer, Aix-en-Provence (hereafter ANDOM) 4 (1) D 19, p. 8; see also Sautter, *De l'Atlantique*, pp. 859–65. The inspection team reports are in ANDOM 3 (D) 4.
13 Gabon, *Rapport annuel 1920*, ANDOM 4 (1) D 17–19.
14 Catherine Coquery-Vidrovitch, 'Population et démographie en Afrique Equatoriale Française dans le premier tiers du XXᵉsiècle', *African Historical Demography*, Centre of African Studies, University of Edinburgh, 1977, 331–51; Sautter, *De l'Atlantique*, pp. 983–6.

decline was more restricted than in AEF, despite the war. Cameroun was located not just geographically, but also demographically, between AEF and Nigeria.

The long-term trends of population concerned the strategists of economic development, but an even more important consideration was the location of the population. In the most general sense the people were concentrated in the savanna. The most densely inhabited region in AEF was from south-western Chad to western Ubangi. Here densities reached eleven per square kilometre in 1936 – low, but still five times the average for Ubangi and non-Sahara Chad.[15] This was the one population concentration in all AEF, and it was located so far from the coast that transporting produce from there incurred enormous costs. In fact, one parliamentarian suggested that Chad be detached from the other colonies since it was faster to travel from Fort-Lamy to Paris by crossing the Sahara than by going through Brazzaville.[16]

At the other end of the population spectrum was Gabon. Blessed by an excellent harbour and a valuable resource, *okoumé* wood, Gabon lacked only one thing, people. The population density of Gabon was less than two per square kilometre. The *okoumé* was scattered in the forest, and its exploitation used up what little manpower was available. None was left to build roads for large-scale development of export crops, and revenue from the *okoumé* was siphoned off to support the government-general in Brazzaville. The labour problem was illustrated by the situation in 1926, when the timber companies requested authorisation to recruit 19 000 labourers, the government allowed 9 000, and, in the end, only 4 800 men could be found.[17]

A series of epidemiological, economic and cultural factors kept the Gabonese population low. Venereal disease was rampant and accounted for a high percentage of medical consultations. Syphilis was probably introduced by European crews in the estuary and was later disseminated with gonorrhea by loggers moving from camp to camp. Gonorrhea led to the extraordinarily high rates of sterility found throughout Gabon. The monetisation of the economy, and the increasing value of women as producers of cash crops, led to sharp rises in bridewealth, particularly among the Fang. It became more difficult for young men to afford wives when young girls were being profitably married to wealthier, usually older, men. Divorce and speculation in wives increased. Thus despite, or

15 Calculations based on population figures in Inspection Générale des Services Sanitaires et Médicaux (hereafter Services Sanitaires) AEF, *Rapport annuel 1936*, Archives of the Colonial Health Services, Pharo, Marseilles (hereafter Pharo).
16 R. Susset, *La Vérité sur le Cameroun et l'Afrique Equatoriale Française*, Nouvelle Revue Critique, Paris, 1934, p. 212.
17 Gabon, *Rapport annuel 1928*, Archives Nationales Section Outre-Mer (hereafter ANSOM), Paris, Fond Guernut B-36; Guy Lasserre, *Libreville, la ville et sa région*, Cahiers de la Fondation nationale des sciences politiques no. 98, Paris, 1958, p. 136.

perhaps because of, the comparative wealth of Gabon, the birth-rate and population continued to fall.[18]

The labour problem in Cameroun was less severe, and average density was five-and-a-half per square kilometre even before the First World War. In the post-war partition, the British skimmed off thickly inhabited regions, while the French were left with three zones of population concentration. The first, north of the Adamawa plateau, was part of the same densely inhabited belt delineated in Chad and Ubangi. More important from an economic standpoint were the two southern areas. The region around Yaoundé had thirty-one people per square kilometre; most populated of all were the western Grassfields, homeland of the Bamileke and Bamoun, where densities reached eighty-three per square kilometre.[19] Thus regions of high density were available to the coast, near the plantations, near where products for export grow wild, near the railways. Roughly three-fifths of Camerounians lived within 300 kilometres of the coast, the zone of economic activity, whereas only one-third of AEF's inhabitants were in Moyen-Congo and Gabon.

The populations, particularly in AEF, were not just 'maldistributed' for efficient exploitation, they were also too fluid for easy control. The colonial occupation had interrupted some large-scale migrations, and administrators also had to contend with the constant shifting of villages as land was used up. In addition, because fields were often located several kilometres from villages, it was difficult to catch people when the government wanted them. African strategies for making themselves scarce led individuals and groups deep into the forest or to inaccessible regions of the savanna. Though it was difficult to grow crops, malnourishment and exposure seemed preferable to labour brigades. People near the borders crossed into neighbouring territories if tax and labour requirements were lower. The cities became a haven.

The administration, of course, wanted people fixed in place so that they could be counted, taxed, recruited and cured at convenience. They tried to relocate and group villages along accessible routes and empty the cities of their 'floating' population. The annual report of Gabon of 1928 listed among the major administrative goals to 'settle the villages, prevent vagabondage'. Local administrative reports contain maps showing scattered villages, a straight road going through the territory, and arrows from each village to the point on the road where the village was to be

18 Georges Balandier, *The Sociology of Black Africa: Social Dynamics in Central Africa*, Douglas Garman trans., New York, 1970, pp. 151–3, 164–87; Camille Jeannel, *La Stérilité en République Gabonaise*, Geneva, 1960; K. David Patterson, 'The vanishing Mpongwe: European contact and demographic change in the Gabon river', *Journal of African History (JAH)*, xvi, 2, 1975, 217–38.
19 Robert R. Kuczynski, *The Cameroons and Togoland, a Demographic Study*, London, 1939, pp. 25–6; *Rapport annuel au Conseil de la Société des Nations sur l'administration sous mandat du territoire du Cameroun* (hereafter Cameroun, *Rapport annuel*) *1936*, 100–1.

relocated. Other reports spoke of moving villages to the automobile route to Brazzaville or flushing out people hiding in the forest and installing them near posts. In Ubangi, the administration worried about pockets of 'dissidents' escaping French control:

> Several training marches of half a company of *tirailleurs*, carried out from time to time in these unpenetrated regions would easily take care of the problem. The air squadron at Bangui would permit us to spot the villages.... About 1 500 natives have been returned to our jurisdiction following the operations of 1932 in the Pana mountains.[20]

Tax exemptions were offered to villages which would settle along the Congo-Ocean railway line. Sometimes these relocations worked, but often, after the official left, the villagers returned to their old settlement.

'Our principal instrument for development [is] the population', wrote one administrator in 1919.[21] This was recognised by everybody working on political, economic and social policies for the colonies. It was also recognised by the people themselves as they tried to extricate themselves from the plans of others. The lack of population, its inconvenient distribution, its 'fragility' (a colonial euphemism for saying that it diminished when maltreated or abruptly moved), were the primary facts which had to be taken into account in any colonial scheme. In the early years, when the costs of development and administration were paid by the population, the demographic consequences were severe. After the 1920s increasing financial contributions by the metropole allowed the population to recover; social and economic opportunities were presented to enlarged segments of society. Yet throughout the colonial period, population size and location often remained the major determinants of economic potential.

THE COLONIAL STATE: AN UNSTEADY EMERGENCE

The first task for both Germany and France was to establish firm territorial control. Their aim was to create an administrative base at minimal cost and then get on with more significant economic undertakings. It was even hoped, in the early years, that the European private sector, both commercial firms and missionary societies, would take much of the responsibility for administration and development.

Contrary to such expectations, Europeans found that the colonies were both expensive and a source of political difficulty. The inadequacy of private investment had to be compensated for by the state, and African resistance was far more drawn out than anyone had anticipated.

20 Boulmer Inspection Mission, 'Situation financière de l'Oubangui-Chari, Deuxième Partie, Recettes budgetaires et capacitè fiscale des indigènes', no. 71, 1932, ANSOM A.P. 3131, p. 8.
21 Lt-Gov., Gabon, to Gov-Gen., AEF, Libreville, 13 May 1919, ANDOM 4 (1) D 17–19.

Meanwhile, sporadic publicity about unfair or inhumane treatment of Africans led to serious criticism of the colonial system from influential voices in the metropole. It was not until the Second World War that an effective system of administration was established throughout the region.

The failure to manage equatorial Africa through the private sector was a major disappointment. Bismarck had hoped to rule Cameroun by organising local merchants into a chartered company such as ruled the Rhodesias, Northern Nigeria and German East Africa. The merchants refused, however, and instead successfully pressured the metropole first to police the rivers, and then to establish a complete administration paid for out of government funds. By the later 1890s, however, large portions of AEF and Cameroun were granted to entrepreneurs who had monopolistic access to their territories:

> Across this vast region, the company has enjoyed an absolute commercial, industrial and agricultural monopoly, almost the right to administer high and low justice, since we have ceded to it our administrative posts, since our administrators defer to it, since it has its own armed men and it polices the region itself.[22]

This system of concessionary companies proved to be an economic failure and also raised the political cost of local rule by provoking African resistance. The inhabitants were coerced into delivering goods by agents who massacred the recalcitrant and burned uncooperative villages. The achievement of territorial control thus required extensive repression.

Because no pre-colonial African states had effectively ruled major portions of equatorial Africa, military conquest was less a matter of concentrated confrontation between large forces than a prolonged campaign involving many expeditions. In Cameroun this process was essentially complete by the end of the German régime. In AEF, however, warfare remained a major government preoccupation up to 1930, when the last major African uprising, the Baya revolt, was finally suppressed. The explanation for this high level of violence lay only partly in the extended resistance put up by slave-raiding states. The defeat of Rabih, the most formidable foe of the French, took three columns of soldiers from Algeria, French Sudan and Ubangi, but it was accomplished by 1900. The continuation of campaigns for another three decades must be blamed on the labour demands of both concessionary companies and government officials. Resistance went beyond attacks on company officials and property. The French found themselves facing rifles and ammunition which a few years earlier they had distributed as gifts or traded for produce. A former administrator in Ubangi described the campaign:

22 Lt-Gov., Gabon, to Gov-Gen., AEF, 13 May 1919.

All the interior of the country had to be conquered, valley by valley, village by village ... the military operations which took place frequently from the end of 1907 were very difficult. Governor-General Merlin presented them in his reports as simple police operations. But throughout, the resistance of Ubangians to this "active occupation" was stubborn and unexpected.[23]

Ironically the First World War led to less unrest in Cameroun, where there was fighting, than in AEF, where the thinning out of the administration gave concessionary companies a freer hand. This, plus the removal of some French forces and intensified wartime labour recruitment, caused uprisings in districts which had been 'pacified' before 1914.

The need for conquest and reconquest meant that the colonial states required a major contingent of military police. The fact that European army officers remained as administrators can partially be explained on financial grounds: their salaries were carried on the metropolitan rather than colonial budgets. Yet even after most areas were placed under civilian rule, the daily administrative tasks were often performed by African militiamen. Their corrupt and uncontrolled behaviour led to a litany of complaints; a weary administrator wrote that there was such a tradition of wrong-doing that it was considered normal.[24] To minimise abuse, officials tried wherever possible to install a locally acceptable chief. One governor could still insist on the militiaman's modernising role: 'more a foreman in charge of educating the natives than a soldier expected to make them do this work by force'.[25] The true impact of such 'education' upon the people is indicated by their own term for the militia: the *tourouko* or *tourgou* ('Turks') were seen as successors to the freebooting forces formerly employed by Muslim slave-raiders[26]

Eventually both Cameroun and AEF were brought under the control of civilian administrators and achieved political stability. In Cameroun by 1914 all districts except the three Fulani 'Residencies' were supervised by district commissioners whose training, morale and standard of pay compared with that in British or Belgian colonies. After France took over, the territory continued to attract exceptionally well-qualified administrators and, uniquely among French possessions, retained them for multiple tours of duty.[27]

23 Pierre Kalck, *Histoire centrafricaine des origines à nos jours*, Ph.D. thesis, University of Lille III, 1973, vol. III, p. 206.
24 Gabon, *Rapport annuel 1933*, ANDOM 4 (1) D 39.
25 Boulmer Inspection Mission, 'Situation financière de l'Oubangui-Chari, Troisième Partie, Dépense locale et économie réalisable,' no. 72, ANSOM A.P. 3031.
26 Kalck, *Histoire centrafricaine*, vol. III, p. 253.
27 Lewis H. Gann and Peter Duignan, *The Rulers of German Africa 1884–1914*, Stanford, Ca., 1977, pp. 67–72, 87–103; William B. Cohen, *Rulers of Empire: the French Colonial Service in Africa,* Stanford, California, 1971, pp. 123–6, 217.

AEF was another story. Military administration and concessionary enterprises survived in some areas to the 1930s. At the same time, there were not enough administrators to fill posts in civilian-ruled districts. Occasionally half the positions in the colony were empty. The turnover of personnel was too great to permit either continuous planning or detailed knowledge of local conditions. The average tenure in one district in Moyen-Congo was sixteen months, and tours of duty were punctuated by extended home leaves.[28] Rarely did a man stay long enough to leave his imprint on a territory. Auguste Henri Lamblin, governor of Ubangi-Shari from 1917 to 1929, was unusual. With few resources other than the force of his own personality and his long incumbency, he had an extensive road network built.

Among the graduates of France's Ecole Coloniale, AEF was the last choice as an assignment, so that administrators posted there, whatever their real qualifications, felt demoted. This sense of marginality was reinforced by the large number of junior officials occupying what should have been senior service posts, and the prevalence of administrators from outlying portions of the French Republic, particularly the West Indies.[29] The status of administrator was further diluted by the practice of maintaining two cadres: a senior service, in theory products of a professional education at the Ecole Coloniale, and junior men with secondary-school education or less, who filled clerical positions. In comparison with British African territories, such a practice increased the proportion of European administrators to African populations, even putting the former in posts which might otherwise be filled by educated Africans. The absence of 'native authority' structures, as fostered under British indirect rule, also decreased opportunities for African clerks and deprived European administrators of an independent local budget.[30]

The lack of local budgets was only one example of the insufficient means given to an administrator. Officials were expected to tour their districts continually, but only rarely did they have a car or motor boat. There were no agricultural or veterinary experts to advise on expanding food or export production; no engineers or machinery to help with road-building. What they did have were crude instruments of coercion. The militia rounded up people to construct roads and administrative buildings, and were less than

28 Kalck, *Histoire centrafricaine*, vol. III, p. 335; Jean Suret-Canale, *French Colonialism in Tropical Africa 1900–1945*, Till Gottheimer (trans.), New York, 1971, p. 313; 'Personnel de sous-préfecture d'Ouesso depuis 1898 [until 1939]', local archives in Ouesso, Congo.
29 Cohen, *Rulers*, p. 46; Brian Weinstein, *Eboué*, New York, 1972, pp. 22–27, 35, 60–1. Precise statistics are available only on West Indians throughout the colonial service, but Weinstein notes that a great number of them preceded and accompanied Eboué in his AEF career.
30 Ralph A. Austen, 'Varieties of Trusteeship: African Territories under British and French Mandate, 1919–1939', in Prosser Gifford and William Roger Louis, (eds), *France and Britain in Africa: Imperial Rivalry and Colonial Rule*, New Haven, Conn., 1971, pp. 515–41.

fastidious in ensuring that people worked only the time legally required of them by the corvée. Chiefs were expected to provide labour and taxes, often on the basis of incorrect censuses. Where legitimate chiefs were non-existent or uncooperative, militiamen were installed in their place. *Capitas* armed with a whip headed the road gangs; *boys-cotons* saw to it that each person planted his assigned amount of cotton. Some chiefs were allowed armed irregulars to enforce compliance with various requisitions. All of these auxiliaries used violent means to ensure that the administration got its quota and that they got a little for themselves on the side. Meanwhile the administrators walked, or were carried in chairs, from village to village, checking on crops and taxes, exhorting people to build pit latrines and clear the bush around the villages, and ensuring the supply of porters or railway builders. The system had to be built on force because without significant metropolitan subsidies there was little money to pay for labour or to provide tangible benefits like schools and clinics which might have justified the taxes in the eyes of the population.

The extent of the territory and the low population densities required tremendous efforts in building and maintaining roads, though they were of less use to Africans than to Europeans. The need for workers was so great that women were continually employed. The demographic results were dire, but directives exempting women were persistently ignored. A Cameroun novelist vividly described the scene, through the words of a French missionary priest: 'They will drive them from their houses, tie them together like beasts and drag them to the site. Then they will work from morning to night, bent under the hot sun.' Later, in a conversation with the local administrator, the priest adds: 'If you build a road ... isn't it under pressure from certain European merchants, cronies of yours? But all the same it's the natives who have to build it. Do you know a single native who owns a transport company?'[31]

The new judicial apparatus was seen by Africans as little more than an additional means of control and a way of providing prison labour for the administration. Under the *indigénat* (native justice code) violations of colonial regulations could be punished summarily by the 'commandant', the military title used by Africans addressing white civilian officials. Crimes ranged from the specific, such as adulterating rubber or failing to appear for obligatory medical treatment, to the less precise, such as insulting France or its representatives. Africans who disobeyed administrators, concession-aires or militiamen were subject to fines or imprisonment. The governor of Chad complained that 'there has been distributed in Chad, under the *indigénat*, in the ten years from 1911 to 1920, 2015 years of prison for a population which is less than a million-and-a-half inhabitants'.[32]

31 Mongo Beti, *The Poor Christ of Bomba*, Gerald Moore (trans.), London, 1971, pp. 41, 152.
32 Jean Cabot, *Le Bassin du Moyen Logone*, Paris, 1965, p. 166.

The inadequacies of the humble, even sordid, instruments of local administration in equatorial Africa help to explain why this area became the subject of sporadic intervention from Europe. In Cameroun, conflict between the Duala and the German colonial government over urban issues escalated into a major political affair when the Duala, unable to get redress from Governor Jesco von Puttkammer (1895–1907), petitioned the Reichstag. Missionary societies led attacks on the government for taking land from Africans in order to create European plantations. These two issues, combined with an official charge that Puttkammer had forged a passport for his mistress, brought about the governor's recall. Both socialist and Catholic Reichstag deputies objected to the amount of money going to the colonies and exposed instances of brutality and immorality by colonial officials and their troops. During the Mandate period, France was criticised for forced labour and taxation policies and was threatened by a German concern to recover Cameroun. Despite severe French punishment for pro-German Africans, no serious political crisis broke before the Second World War.[33]

AEF attracted more attention. Reports of widespread abuses by both government agents and concessionaires hit the Paris newspapers in 1904, in the wake of international humanitarian and left-wing attacks against King Leopold's Congo régime. There were accusations of atrocities, such as the death of women and children taken as hostages to ensure that men would serve as porters, and stories which exposed a general pattern of terror aimed at procuring labour. After a commission headed by Brazza confirmed these reports, the government restricted the authority of the concessionaires.[34] Nevertheless, similar scandals arose again in the 1920s and 1930s, along with appalling accounts of workers' conditions on the Congo–Ocean railway. The effect of this negative publicity was not radical, but at least by the late 1930s local administrations had achieved control over enterprises affecting African welfare and an improved transportation system had lessened the need for porters.

For the indigenous population of equatorial Africa the colonial state was thus a highly authoritarian, often brutal institution. For metropolitan Europeans, however, it was seen as a minimal instrument for controlling rather than developing marginal territories. Yet even France, relatively uninterested in colonies, could not easily abandon its dreams for this region.

33 Ralph A. Austen, 'Duala vs. Germans in Cameroon', *Revue française d'Histoire d'outre-mer*, lxiv, 4, 1977, 477–97; Jonathan Derrick, 'The "Germanophile" élite of Douala under the French Mandate', *JAH*, xxi, 2, 1980, 255–67; Woodruff D. Smith, *The German Colonial Empire*, Chapel Hill, N.C., 1978, pp. 119–64.
34 Félicien Challaye, *Le Congo français: la question internationale du Congo*, Paris, 1909; Catherine Coquery-Vidrovitch, *Le Congo au temps des grands compagnies concessionnaires 1898–1930*, Paris, 1972, pp. 89–224, 231, 263–79; Suret-Canale, *French Colonialism*, pp. 34–6.

Ralph A. Austen and *Rita Headrick*

THE COLONIAL ECONOMY UP TO THE SECOND WORLD WAR

In the pre-colonial period equatorial Africa had produced no commodities of critical value to Western economies, and none of lasting significance was discovered or developed in the first half-century of European rule. As a market the region could offer only the most limited outlet for industrial goods because its population was low and difficult to reach. Capital flowed into the region mainly for expenditure on transport, but the returns on such ventures were too limited to attract much private investment.

The imperial powers switched their economic strategies as each new policy proved disappointing. First they experimented with concessionary companies, but this abdication by the state in favour of private firms was

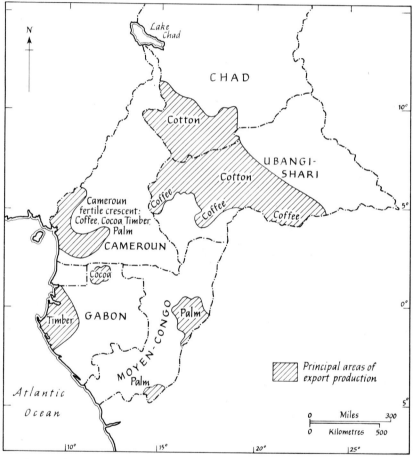

2:4 Principal zones of export production, French Equatorial Africa, inter-war years
   Major sources: Richard A. Joseph, *Radical Nationalism in Cameroun; social origins of the U.P.C. rebellion*, Oxford, 1977, p. 105; Eugène Guernier (ed.), *Afrique Equatoriale Française, Encyclopèdie Coloniale et Maritime*, Paris, 1950, pp. 278–9.

not profitable and led to unacceptable levels of violence. As the concessionary companies were curbed, the government enlarged its own activities by providing an infrastructure and encouraging the export economy. In the course of the depression of the 1930s, however, French strategy shifted towards more serious efforts at incorporating equatorial Africa into the economy of the metropole.

Before the Second World War, investment in this region was modest even by tropical African standards. The approximate amount of public and private capital invested up to 1940 was a little over one thousand million gold francs, of which almost one-quarter went from Germany to Cameroun before 1914. Of the neighbouring territories, Nigeria, with a much larger population but a basically peasant economy, received one and one-half times as much investment; the Belgian Congo, thinly populated but with a major mining sector, attracted three times as much capital. For France, the capital in equatorial Africa represented about 5 per cent of its colonial investment and little over 2 per cent of its total overseas portfolio.[35]

Important changes were brought about in the equatorial economies, despite the low level of capitalisation. Europeans expanded from coastal trading positions to participate directly in inland export markets; they installed new transport systems; and they introduced new forms of export production under both their own control and that of African cultivators. Still, this development was unbalanced. Gabon and the 'fertile crescent' of Cameroun became relatively prosperous. The rest of the territory remained poor and in some cases suffered a major decline in welfare. The economy provided the key arena in which imperial strategy and equatorial African society confronted each other.

FROM PRE-COLONIAL ECONOMY TO CONCESSIONARY SYSTEM

Pre-colonial commercial patterns suggested two possible modes of organising a colonial economy for equatorial Africa. One was to assume that the region represented the margin of several more promising surrounding zones and thus divide it between Nigeria and the Belgian Congo. The second was to regard it as sufficiently large and rich to be integrated on its own through new infrastructures. As it turned out, the European régimes vacillated between these choices and a third, dysfunctional, strategy of competition between Cameroun and AEF. In an

---

35 S. Herbert Frankel, *Capital Investment in Africa*, Oxford, 1938, pp. 158–9, 170; Institut de Science Economique Appliquée, Cahiers, Series A. *Les Plans monetaires internationaux* 8, Paris, 1951, pp. 110–12; Jacques Marseilles, 'L'Investissement français dans l'Empire colonial: l'enquête du gouvernement de Vichy (1943)', *Revue historique*, cclii, 2, 1974, 409–20; Jean-Jacques Poquin, *Les Relations économiques extérieures des pays d'Afrique noire de l'Union française 1925–1955*, Paris, 1957, p. 188.

area more favourably endowed such a pattern would have imposed high costs of development; in equatorial Africa it provided elements of tragic disaster.

Neither Germany nor France had dynamic plans for local economic development when they annexed their respective territories. It was hoped by both régimes that European merchants already established at Libreville and Douala would take advantage of the general security offered by European sovereignty to expand their commercial ventures. Such expansion did take place, but at a considerable cost in political conflict with Africans, and without any matching growth in profits. In west Cameroun an impressive plantation economy was initiated, but elsewhere commerce remained a petty affair, with elaborate networks of African middlemen intervening between the European firms and scattered primary producers. Given the low level of metropolitan interest in the economy, such a stagnant situation might have been tolerable. However, the competitive political postures which had triggered the original scramble now took an economic form when German and French officials became aware that products from their hinterland were being diverted to concessionary companies in the Congo State. On the other side of Cameroun, the Germans were anxious about the exploitation of Adamawa through the British Royal Niger Company and the political and economic consequences of French military expeditions near Lake Chad.

The solution to these problems was to emulate the Congo State and establish French and German concessionary companies. This strategy could at once mobilise new capital, including Belgian, British and Dutch funds, and also make sure that the interiors of AEF and Cameroun were tapped through their own ports. For AEF, the history of concessionary companies is identified with an entire phase of the economic history of Gabon, Moyen-Congo and Ubangi-Shari. In 1899 almost 80 per cent of these territories was assigned to forty private firms. After the first French Congo scandals the concessions were greatly cut down but the companies continued to be the major economic force until about 1930. In German Cameroun two firms, the Gesellschaft Süd-Kamerun and the Gesellschaft Nordwest-Kamerun, were conceded about 50 per cent of the territory; the grants excluded the northernmost savanna and the zones adjacent to the coast where merchant firms and plantations were already established.[36]

The conditions under which the concessions were granted remained ambiguous. The receiving firms generally held neither freehold over their ceded zones nor the right to exclude other merchants, but exercised a

36 Jolanda Ballhaus, 'Die Landkonzessionsgesellschaften', in *Kamerun unter Deutscher Kolonialherrschaft* Helmuth Stoecker (ed.), vol. II, East Berlin, 1968, pp. 99–179; Coquery-Vidrovitch, *Le Congo*; Harry Rudin, *Germans in the Cameroons 1884–1914: a Case Study in Modern Imperialism*, New Haven, Connecticut, 1938, pp. 290–6.

monopoly over local 'exploitation'. Because this came to be defined as any direct relationship between African producers and European buyers, other merchants were, in effect, kept out and a series of monopolies was established. The protests of excluded 'free traders' played an important part in publicising the abuses of the concessionaires. Although Leopold's Congo State served as a model for AEF and Cameroun, there were differences between the two sets of territories.[37] In AEF and Cameroun the companies received state support for security and labour recruiting, but essentially operated as private enterprises required to contribute tax revenues and infrastructural investments for the total development of the colony. Under Leopold the Congo State, itself a kind of private enterprise, participated directly in the activities of the concessionary companies.

Total private investment in the Congo State was greater in 1900 before major mining efforts began, than it was a decade later in AEF and Cameroun combined. Most of this capital, as well as the non-concessionaire investment in French and German equatorial Africa, was devoted to ordinary commerce, transportation, mining and plantations. For concessionary companies engaged in collecting export goods the ratio of investment to territory varied over a limited range. The French and German companies were generally better capitalised than their Belgian counterparts. Generally, however, investment by all concessionaires was very low. Indeed the basic motive for taking up concessions was often stock-market speculation in Europe rather than entrepreneurship in Africa. For those concessionaires who actually took up their territories, the principal goal was not long-term investment but the realisation of quick profits from ivory, palm-oil, palm kernels and rubber. Ivory supplies soon diminished, however, and the more plentiful but less valuable palm products could not be profitably gathered by the terror usually applied to villagers.

The concessionaires who did succeed depended almost entirely on wild rubber, a commodity which dominated exports until the First World War. The advantage of rubber was that it could be gathered easily from trees and vines which abounded in the forest zones of all three territories. In the Congo State, however, crude gathering methods rapidly depleted the *Landolphia* vines and production began to fall off after the turn of the century.[38] AEF and Cameroun, on the other hand, depended on more durable trees and could thus maintain their more limited output until 1913. Then the bottom fell out of the African wild-rubber market due to competition from Brazilian-type quality rubber produced on South-East

37 Coquery-Vidrovitch, *Le Congo*, pp. 47–9; Robert Harms, 'The end of red rubber: a reassessment', *JAH*, xvi, 1, 1975, 73–88; Heinrich Waltz, *Das Konzessionswesen im Belgischen Kongo*, 2 volumes, Jena, 1917.
38 Harms, 'Red rubber', pp. 81–3, 87–8.

TABLE 2:1

MAJOR EXPORTS, EQUATORIAL AFRICA (UNITS OF 1000 METRIC TONNES)

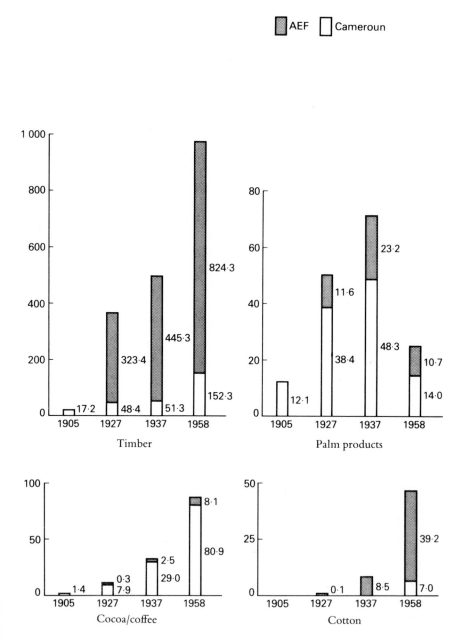

TABLE 2:2

DISTRIBUTION AS A PROPORTION OF VALUE (CURRENT AND CONSTANT FRANCS)

AEF 1905

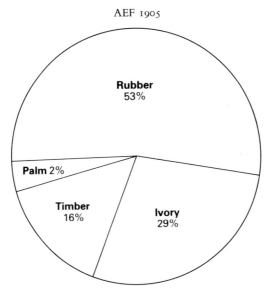

Total value: 13 933 000 francs (current and constant)

Cameroun 1905

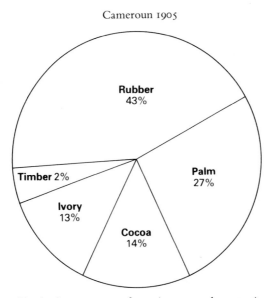

Total value: 13 303 000 francs (current and constant)

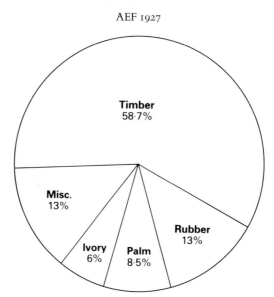

AEF 1927

Timber
58·7%

Misc.
13%

Ivory
6%

Palm
8·5%

Rubber
13%

Total value: 136 747 844 francs (current)
23 247 132 francs (constant)

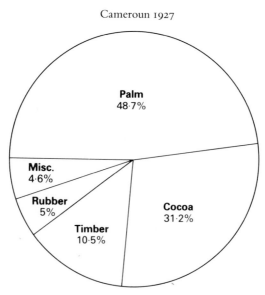

Cameroun 1927

Palm
48·7%

Misc.
4·6%

Rubber
5%

Timber
10·5%

Cocoa
31·2%

Total value: 160 252 203 francs (current)
27 242 874 francs (constant)

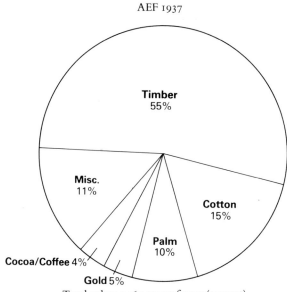

AEF 1937

Timber
55%

Misc.
11%

Cotton
15%

Palm
10%

Cocoa/Coffee 4%

Gold 5%

Total value: 256 353 000 francs (current)
45 117 776 francs (constant)

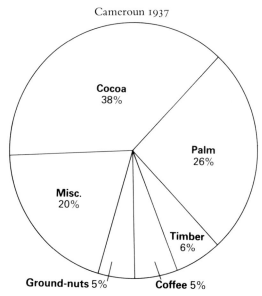

Cameroun 1937

Cocoa
38%

Palm
26%

Misc.
20%

Timber
6%

Ground-nuts 5%

Coffee 5%

Total value: 263 307 000 francs (current)
46 343 032 francs (constant)

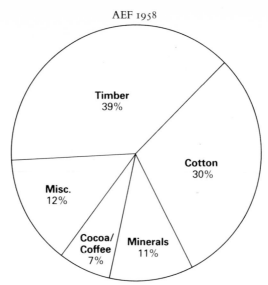

AEF 1958

Timber
39%

Cotton
30%

Misc.
12%

Cocoa/
Coffee
7%

Minerals
11%

Total value: 19 887 000 000 francs (current)
206 824 800 francs (constant)

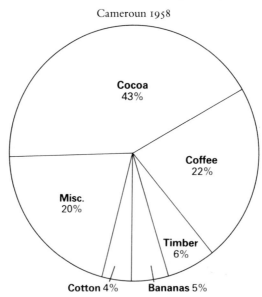

Cameroun 1958

Cocoa
43%

Coffee
22%

Misc.
20%

Timber
6%

Cotton 4%

Bananas 5%

Total value: 22 291 000 000 francs (current)
245 201 000 francs (constant)

Sources:
AEF, *Statistiques coloniales, 1905*, pp. 405, 461–5, 477; *Renseignements généraux sur le commerce des colonies françaises, Paris, 1927*, pp. 42, 274–5, 278–9, 282–3, 296–7, 312–13, 318–19; *Annuaire statistique*, pp. 264–5, 283–5; FIDES, vi, viii, xii; Coquery-Vidrovitch, *Le Congo*, 421–79, and *passim*; Georges Bruel, *La France équatoriale africaine, Paris, 1935*, p. 351. Cameroun: *Deutsches Kolonialblatt*, 17, 1906, p. 528; *Rapport annuel, 1927*, pp. 67–9; *ibid.*, 1937, p. 35; France, Ministère des Finances et des Affaires Economiques, Institut National de la Statistique et des Etudes Economiques, *Bulletin Mensuel de Statistique d'Outre-Mer*, xvi, 4, Oct.–Dec. 1960, 69; currency conversion: *La Grande Encyclopédie Larousse, Paris, 1973*, vol. 8, p. 5057.

Asian plantations. It is indicative of the weakness of the inter-war AEF economy that it still depended heavily on wild rubber and on ivory after their respective prices had fallen to marginal levels. Moreover, the export which finally replaced them was *okoumé* timber from Gabon, which was also gathered in a wild state.

The best way to understand the concessionary companies is to see them as enlarged and distorted versions of pre-colonial states. The methods of gathering and processing goods did not incorporate any new technology beyond hand presses for extracting palm-oil. The concessionaires built no roads and brought in few vehicles. Their major achievement was immediate control over territory through the use of government and private militias. This allowed goods to be extracted at lower prices than would have been possible in a free market, but left Africans with too little

TABLE 2:3

CONCESSIONARY COMPANIES AND OTHER PRIVATE INVESTMENT BEFORE THE FIRST WORLD WAR, EQUATORIAL AFRICA

		Total invested (francs)	Investment per square km.
AEF[1]	All private capital	69 900 000	
(in 1914)	All non-concessionaires	28 900 000	
	All concessionaires	41 000 000	
	Compagnie Forestière		
	Sangha-Oubangui	12 000 000	70·6
	Compagnie des Sultanats	2 251 000	
		or	16 *or*
	du Haut Oubangui	3 600 000	25·7
Cameroun[2]	All private capital	119 375 000	
(in 1913)	All non-concessionaires	110 000 000	
	All concessionaires	9 375 000	
	Gesellschaft Süd-Kamerun	3 750 000	46·3
	Gesellschaft NW-Kamerun	5 625 000	70·3
Congo State[3]	All private capital	245 000 000	
(in 1900)	All concessionaires	n.a.	
	Anglo-Belgian Indian Rubber and		
	Exploration Company (Abir)	232 000	2·9
	Société Anversoise du Commerce		
	au Congo	1 700 000	24·3

[1] C. Coquery-Vidrovitch, *Le Congo au temps des grandes compagnies concessionnaires, 1898–1930*, Paris, 1972, pp. 25, 49–53, 342–50, 368, 371–2, 411; the imprecise nature of the figures for actually invested, as opposed to nominal, capital is indicated by the fact that Coquery-Vidrovitch gives two different amounts for the Sultanats company. As the same author also notes, less than half of the money finally raised by a concessionaire like the Sultanats was ever transformed into fixed assets or even trade goods on the ground in Africa.

[2] J. Ballhaus, 'Die Landkonzessionsgesellschaften' in *Kamerun unter Deutscher Kolonialherrschaft*, H. Stoecker (ed.), East Berlin, 1968; K. Hausen, *Deutsche Kolonialherrschaft in Afrika*, Zurich, 1970, pp. 209, 312.

[3] Coquery-Vidrovitch, *Le Congo*, p. 49; H. Waltz, *Das Konzessionswesen im Belgischen Kongo*, Jena, 1917, pp. 259–75.

Ralph A. Austen and Rita Headrick

cash to increase their consumption of manufactured imports. The companies did not even keep the peace: their rapacious activities engendered costly African resistance. Even where profit rates were high, and for rubber they sometimes exceeded 100 per cent, the amount of capital actually accumulated was small given the inefficiency of production. Unlike the pre-colonial predatory states, the concessionaires repatriated their profits to Europe. This meant that Africans experienced only the negative aspects of the predatory economy. The governor of Gabon summed up the concessionary years: 'When [the company] leaves in 1923 – and we would be very guilty if we allowed a renewal or even an extension of its contract – nothing will remain of an almost thirty-year occupation. The company will leave the country much poorer than they found it and the people infinitely more miserable.'[39]

TRANSPORT INNOVATIONS

It was necessary for the state to take a more active role in the transport system, because private capital, even when given privileged access to equatorial resources, could not generate a viable economic base for the new colonies. This pattern was not at all unusual in colonial Africa; what made the equatorial case distinctive is the late start in such projects, their high financial and social cost, and the irrational distribution of effort.

The cheapest way to increase transport efficiency in the region was to build upon the existing river system with shipping and feeder roads. River navigation, however, was hindered by rapids and seasonal shallows. The building and use of roads in the forest were hampered by excessive rain, shortages of African labour, and the absence of pack or draught animals due to tsetse flies. The concessionaires never constructed roads, though some companies put steamers and motor vessels on the rivers. A specialised transport and trading firm, Messageries Fluviales, provided a reasonably efficient service on what had been the most active pre-colonial water route, the Zaire and Ubangi river stretch between Malebo Pool and Bangui.[40]

The importance of roads, even in tsetse zones, increased once motor vehicles were available. The German government of Cameroun built 500 kilometres of primary and secondary roads by 1914. These were vastly expanded under the French mandate. In AEF virtually nothing was done until the 1920s, when the energetic governor of Ubangi-Shari, Lamblin, constructed a network of 3 800 kilometres throughout the savanna zone. The shadow of concessionary strategy still hung on, however, and many surviving companies refused to invest in vehicles and still used coercive methods to recruit human porters.[41]

39 Lt-Gov., Gabon, to Gov-Gen., AEF, 13 May 1919.
40 Coquery-Vidrovitch, *Le Congo*, pp. 281–4.
41 *Ibid.*, pp. 193–4; Kalck, *Histoire centrafricaine*, vol. III, pp. 322, 324, 384–5.

Road construction always took second place to the building of railways for imperial strategists, but the equatorial lines were undertaken relatively late. The Germans completed the Nordbahn, running 160 kilometres from Douala to Nkongsamba, in 1911. Their Central line was halted at Eseka, 180 kilometres south-east of Douala, when the First World War intervened; in 1927 the French continued it another 160 kilometres to Yaoundé and Mbalmayo. In AEF the 515 kilometres of the Congo-Ocean railway from Brazzaville to Pointe-Noire was begun in 1921 but completed only in 1934. Although three railways of this size may not seem excessive for such a large region, they represented a heavy burden upon local resources in inverse proportion to their rationality. Most rational and least costly was the Cameroun Nordbahn, which was privately financed, with government guarantees, and built without trouble. It provided almost immediate profits from the rich produce and high populations of the volcanic Mungo valley. The Cameroun Central Railway traversed forest zones and therefore took more time to build, and cost dearly in both money and lives. It tapped an area which unexpectedly became a major centre of African export production and thus proved viable.[42] The Congo–Ocean was built through a terrain of forest and rugged hills at an immensely greater expenditure of public funds and African life. Up until independence this railway experienced difficulty in covering its annual running cost, and became really profitable only for a brief period in the early 1960s when linked to new mining enterprises.[43]

The railways were designed not for internal market growth but to connect export regions of the interior with oceanic ports. Yet even this logic could not justify the expenditures on the Cameroun Central and the Congo–Ocean, which were intended, among other things, to provide competition between colonial powers. The Central line was aimed not at Cameroun itself but at an eventual *Mittelafrika* which the Germans hoped to achieve by connecting equatorial Africa to German East Africa. The main purpose of the Congo–Ocean was to establish a *voie fédérale* as an artery of the hopelessly artificial AEF. Transport costs between the Atlantic and Chad or Ubangi would have been lower through Nigeria or Cameroun, or even by way of the long-existing Belgian Congo railway to Malebo Pool. But the French turned down Belgian offers to participate in rebuilding the Matadi–Léopoldville line.

The French decision to parallel the Belgian line instead of building elsewhere had repercussions within AEF. The alternative route proposed,

42 F. Baltzer, *Die Kolonialbahnen mit besonderen Berücksichtigung Afrikas*, Berlin, 1916, pp. 67–78; Rudin, *Germans in the Cameroons*, pp. 238–43; Hartmut Schömann, 'Der Eisenbahnbau in Kamerun unter Deutsche Kolonialherrschaft', Ph.D. thesis, East Berlin, 1964; René Costédoat, *L'Effort français au Cameroun*, Besançon, 1930, pp. 162–72.
43 Gilles Sautter, 'Notes sur la construction du chemin de fer Congo–Océan 1921–1934', *Cahiers d'études africaines*, vii, 2, 1967, 219–99; Virginia Thompson and Richard Adloff, *The Emerging States of French Equatorial Africa*, Stanford, Ca., 1960.

from Libreville to Ouesso, on the Sangha river, and Bangui was never built, and Libreville, though the capital of the most productive colony, remained completely isolated. Administrators in Gabon and later politicians agreed with the Annual Report of 1931: 'The day when, after thirty years of hesitation, they chose ... the Brazzaville–Ocean route, at that moment whether they wanted to or not, they detached Gabon from French Congo.'[44] Gabon's leaders remained bitter that the revenue from their timber helped pay for the new railway while their colony was left without a transportation network.

PRODUCTION FOR EXPORT

The immediate reward of investment in roads and railroads, according to orthodox development theory, should be increased production of commodities for the world market. In particular, the removal of transport barriers ought to allow small-scale producers already involved in some degree of market exchange to increase their production. The classical case is the West African colonial economy.[45] A similar analysis is sometimes applied to equatorial Africa and at first glance seems valid. After the railways were built, peasant crops, such as palm-oil and palm-kernels, cocoa, coffee and cotton, did become major exports from Cameroun and AEF.

A closer examination, though, suggests that the modes of export production deviated from the spontaneous market response which was supposed to occur. Instead Cameroun production was controlled not by small farmers but by Europeans or African planters and indigenous chiefs using coerced labour. Peasant cash-cropping was even less market-induced in the AEF savanna where the government itself forced people to plant cotton, in part to justify the infrastructural investment.

In the same way, the location of export production can only partially be explained by the new transport systems. In Cameroun the fertile crescent is rather neatly defined by two railways. In AEF the evacuation of cotton would have been impossible without the new roads and railway. Yet the major export region of AEF was Gabon, which lay entirely outside the railway network and had almost no roads. The territory through which the railway itself ran, Moyen-Congo, exported less than any other part of the federation. Though production along the line increased as people settled near the stations and grew food for the cities at both ends, it was not until the 1950s that a significant African export commodity, timber, was developed in Moyen-Congo.

The reason why orthodox development theory is inadequate in the

44 ANDOM 4 (1) D 37.
45 Anthony G. Hopkins, *An Economic History of West Africa*, London, 1973, esp. pp. 165, 192–8.

equatorial case is that it is based on the assumption that the major factor holding back export production is a bottleneck in the transport system. Moving goods was certainly a problem and continued to be so even after the railways were built, but equally important, in contrast to West Africa, was a persistent weakness of indigenous market response. The French tended to blame this situation on an innate lack of enterprising spirit among local African populations, thus justifying their use of coercion. André Gide, a colonial critic, wrote: 'It is understood that the native never knows the real value of anything. In this whole region there is no market, no supply or demand . . . not a single native owns anything but his wives, his herds, and perhaps some bracelets or spearpoints. . . . No object, no clothing, no cloth, no piece of furniture – and even if he had money, there is nothing for sale which could tempt him.'[46]

This explanation ignored certain demographic and historical factors and the lessons that Africans had learned from their experience of the slave-trade and the concessionary companies. Low population densities had inhibited the development of the thriving markets so characteristic of West Africa; nevertheless, many groups in pre-colonial equatorial Africa had engaged in long- and short-distance trade of impressive proportions. Then massive slave-raiding had battered the economy of much of the savanna. More destructive still, however, was the imposition of colonial rule, which disrupted old trade networks and led to the concession years when Africans discovered that they would not benefit from export production, since their small wages were quickly collected as taxes.

It was initially impossible to have an 'open economy' based on peasant production, because of the concessionary companies. The large commercial firms which operated in West Africa were effectively blocked. Production change did not arise from the presence of merchants acting as intermediaries between the world market and African producers. Even after the monopolies were eliminated and West African-based conglomerates expanded into Cameroun and AEF, they never achieved the dominance they enjoyed in West Africa. Instead, various combinations of political coercion, imported capital and the narrow concentration of export production led to the growth of enclaves.

The most obvious enclave was the timber industry of Gabon, which provided the biggest single source of exports for AEF from the 1920s. At first, timber entrepreneurs, some of whom were Africans, received concessionary rights to designated forest areas. The larger European firms required state cooperation in recruiting labour to cut *okoumé* logs and haul them to rivers. But because the logs floated down the rivers, the industry could operate without state transport investments and with less onerous demands for labour than ivory- and rubber-gathering firms. By 1940 the

46 André Gide, *Voyage au Congo*, Paris, 1927, p. 130, also translated by Dorothy Bussy as *Travels in the Congo*, New York, 1937.

timber companies were investing in their own sophisticated cutting and hauling equipment, thus reducing further their labour needs and foreshadowing the still more capital-intensive enterprises which would dominate Gabon after the Second World War.[47] Undertakings such as these are the purest enclaves since their linkages to the local economy are so limited. Elsewhere in the region, new forms of export production had a wider social and economic impact.

During the 1890s, at a time when it was granting gathering monopolies to concessionary companies, the German government of Cameroun allocated extensive land areas around Mount Cameroun and along the Mungo valley to Europeans intent on creating large-scale plantations. Unlike other private enterprises in the early decades of colonial exploitation, these plantations attracted substantial sums of capital from merchant firms active in the region as well as from financial and industrial groups in the metropole. The results were a solid series of efficiently managed enterprises, well-endowed with processing equipment, roads, harbour facilities, ships, and even a narrow-gauge railway connecting the plantations to the ports of Tiko and Victoria.[48]

The West Cameroun plantations eventually expanded the territorial market economy, in this case by demonstrating the viability of cocoa. At first there was a period of disruption in which thousands of forcibly recruited plantation labourers died and aspiring African cocoa-growers were suppressed. By the last years of German rule it had become obvious that cocoa could be cultivated by Africans with little capital, and European planters began to concentrate on oil-palms, Hevea rubber and bananas, which required more intensive cultivation, and the integration of processing and transportation.[49] During the mid-1920s and early 1930s a second cycle of European plantation began, this time combined with efforts to encourage some independent African cultivation. Until the late 1930s the French government continued to favour European planters in the most prosperous region of the Mungo valley. In 1946, however, the legal abolition of forced labour eliminated their advantage and Africans began to dominate the new area of coffee production and even made major inroads into the cultivation of bananas.[50]

The Africans who first took up cash crops in Cameroun were not peasant

47 Guy Lasserre, 'Okoumé et chantiers forestiers du Gabon', *Cahiers d'outre-mer*, viii, 29, 1955, pp. 119–60.
48 Marc Michel, 'Les Plantations allemandes du Mont Cameroun, 1885–1914', *Revue française d'histoire d'outre-mer*, lvii, 2, 1969, 183–213.
49 Sanford H. Bederman, *The Cameroon Development Corporation*, Bota, 1968; Mark W. DeLancey, 'Health and Disease on the Plantations of Cameroon, 1884–1939', in *Disease in African History*, Gerald W. Hartwig and K. David Patterson (eds.), Durham, N.C., 1978, pp. 153–79.
50 Richard A. Joseph, *Radical Nationalism in Cameroun: Social Origins of the U.P.C. Rebellion*, Oxford, 1977, pp. 120–3; Pierre Kalck, *Central African Republic: a Failure in Decolonization*, Barbara Thomson (trans.), New York, 1971, pp. 64–5.

growers but planters who created their own enclaves on the basis of existing advantages. The earliest successful cocoa-growers were Duala traders, who employed slave dependants to set up plantations along the rivers they had previously used for commerce. During the 1920s the major cocoa-growing area shifted south-east to Yaoundé, and government-appointed chiefs dominated the enterprise using the compulsory labour of their subjects. In contrast to these early entrepreneurs, the Bamileke planters who competed against Europeans in the upper Mungo valley were immigrants who began their careers as wage labourers or petty traders and then sought to acquire landholdings belonging to local élites or Europeans.[51]

Planting enterprises began to shift to smaller-scale operations by the mid-1930s through a combination of government action, the effects of the depression and migration. The Duala cocoa-planters survived the German abolition of slavery, their political conflict with both colonial governments, and rejected the opportunities of white collar and urban *rentier* careers. The depression, however, and competition from European planters undercut their paid labour force, and they abandoned their farms for purely urban undertakings. The chiefs in the southern cocoa regions became a source of political embarrassment to the French when depression conditions made their activities particularly oppressive. Once economic recovery began, reforms were introduced to cut down the most powerful African rulers and allow commoners to cultivate cash crops on their own land. The immigrant Bamileke were able to acquire small farms which they operated through a variety of family, sharecropping and cooperative arrangements very different from the concentrated model of early European plantations. Peasant agriculture in the fertile crescent of Cameroun can thus be viewed as a West African-type market response growing out of an earlier enclave system.

The comparable sector of the AEF economy, the village-produced cotton from the Ubangi and southern Chad savannas, must be explained along completely different lines. Here the government took virtually all initiatives and remained, in effect, proprietor of an enterprise only nominally in the hands of African growers and European merchants.[52]

AEF cotton production, like the concessionary system which it sought consciously to replace, was modelled upon policies in the Belgian Congo.

51 Ralph A. Austen, 'Slavery among coastal middlemen: the Duala of Cameroon', in *Slavery in Africa: Historical and Anthropological Perspectives*, Suzanne Miers and Igor Kopytoff (eds.), Madison, Wisconsin, 1977; Jane I. Guyer, 'Head Tax, Social Structure, and Rural Incomes in Cameroun 1922–1937', *Working Papers* NS No. 3, African Studies Center, Boston University, 1979; Joseph, *Radical Nationalism*, pp. 141–8.
52 Cabot, *Le Bassin*, pp. 171–89; Coquery-Vidrovitch, *Le Congo*, pp. 473–9; Eric de Dampierre, 'Coton noir, café blanc', *Cahiers d'études africaines*, i, 2, 1960, pp. 128–46; Ulrich Stürzinger, 'Baumwollbau im Tschad', Ph.D. thesis, Zurich, 1979; Weinstein, *Eboué*, pp. 85–99.

The character of commercial agriculture on both sides of this border, in contrast to the cocoa and coffee economy of Cameroun, derived from the fragile local savanna ecology. Permanent tree crops could not easily be grown there, and even an annual crop such as cotton placed great strain upon the soil. Yet cotton was promoted because it was seen as a vital industrial raw material which France otherwise had to import from foreign areas.

Cotton production began hesitantly owing both to opposition from surviving concessionaires and fears among administrators about its effect on Africans. By the 1930s it picked up momentum, but the crop always remained the product of coercion rather than of cultivator incentive. At first, as in Cameroun, chiefs compelled their subjects to work on collective fields, using both militiamen and specially trained *boys-coton* to add more sophisticated persuasion. From the late 1930s cotton was grown on individual fields but with chiefs still acting as supervisors and marketing intermediaries. To ensure that the cotton crop was purchased, the government divided the producing zones among several buying firms. Each of these enjoyed not only a monopoly of the local market but also a guaranteed return on expenses, no matter what the difference between local and resale prices.

To African growers the rationale of this system was clear. They were producing *le coton du commandant*, a crop which the government wanted in order to generate tax revenues. Their continuing distaste for the crop even after the Second World War was embodied in the slogan of the first Chadian political party: 'No more cotton, no more chiefs, no more taxes.'[53] The buying firms gained a secure but never impressive profit. Unlike the large West African merchant firms, they could not add significantly to these gains by expanding the import of consumer goods because the producers remained so poor. As for metropolitan cotton manufacturers, they turned out to be more concerned with using the colonies as markets for their shrinking exports than as a source of the then over-abundant raw material.[54] The cost of transporting cotton 2 000 kilometres by road, river and finally rail to the Atlantic was too great to allow reasonable remuneration to the growers; the cost of bringing in cloth was too great to sell it at a price that people could afford.

If Africans, cotton companies and the French textile industry gained little by this scheme, why then did the government underwrite the production system? A small part of the answer lies in the strategic desire to create an autonomous source of cotton. AEF, though, produced only a small percentage of French needs, unlike Mozambique, which became the

53 Robert Buijtenhuijs, *Le Frolinat et les révoltes populaires du Tchad, 1965–1976*, The Hague, 1978, p. 69.
54 Jacques Marseilles, 'L'Industrie cotonière française et l'impérialisme colonial', *Revue d'histoire économique et sociale*, liii, 213, 1975, 386–412.

major supplier of Portugal.[55] There was also the hope that cotton might increase in value, thus contributing more revenue to the state. Yet perhaps the real motivation was an inchoate feeling that something had to be done to end the economic stagnation of AEF, something which would neither simply diminish unrenewable resources nor be so coercive and monopolistic that it was intolerable to Africans or to protesting European merchants. In economic terms the entire enterprise made little sense, but it fitted the logic of imperial strategy.

PAYING FOR THE COLONIAL STATE

Although the aim of metropolitan government had been to minimise public expenditure in equatorial Africa, the results turned out to be very different. The military and administrative apparatus of the state was expensive, and so were the transport and social services. The cost of these services had to be met from metropolitan subsidies and loans or from taxes generated by production in Africa. During the German period, Cameroun received generous metropolitan support since Germany was a rich country which put high strategic value upon its few colonial possessions. This picture changed markedly once France took over. An ambitious programme drawn up in 1921 for the entire French overseas empire failed to get legislative approval. The depression led to even more far-reaching plans which were fully realised only after the Second World War. From 1931 major loans were made to the colonies, of which Cameroun received only a small portion. Cameroun remained essentially self-sufficient through the inter-war years, an impressive feat in terms of current colonial values but a sometimes painful one for the African population.[56]

AEF, by contrast, never achieved solvency. Even the penurious French governments of the 1920s and 1930s had to provide subsidies with which to run public health campaigns and improve transportation. In addition, there were much larger sums disbursed as loans for the Congo–Ocean railway, for medical facilities and for urban development. In reality, AEF could never meet the debt payments through its own revenues, so that the largest single item on each budget from 1926 was a subsidy for servicing the loans.[57] Support of this kind did not relieve the colony of pressure to generate income locally from head taxes and customs duties.

55 Marseilles, 'L'Industrie cotonière', 410–12; Thompson and Adloff, *Emerging States*, pp. 174–5.
56 Catherine Coquery-Vidrovitch, 'L'Impérialisme français en Afrique noire: idéologie impériale et politique d'équipement 1924–1975', *Relations internationales*, vii, 1976, pp. 265–7; Poquin, *Relations économiques extérieures*, p. 188; Suret-Canale, *French Colonialism*, p. 274.
57 Boulmer Inspection Mission, 'Emploi de la dotation exceptionnelle de 20 millions – loi du 14 mai 1930', no. 77. ANSOM A.P. 3131; Afrique Equatoriale Française, Haut Commissariat, *Annuaire statistique*, vol. I, *1936–1950*, pp. 186–7.

The equatorial finance system, which emphasised head taxes, led to a controlled economy, with the government dictating which products were to be grown or gathered by Africans to pay their tax assessments. Frequently the major goal of productive activity was to generate money for taxes, and the government was unconcerned about how much disposable income Africans were left with. In a more liberal economy most revenue came from customs duties on the imported goods that Africans chose to buy. In British West Africa customs duties were generally the only form of taxation. The French, however, like the Portuguese, did not trust the free market to generate sufficient taxes. In AEF, with its economic and demographic problems, such pessimism may have been justified. Cameroun, however, probably could have been operated more effectively on a British West African model. Nevertheless, in all of equatorial Africa the incentive for the French to increase the import trade was limited since most goods did not come from France.[58]

The tax burden varied. In German Cameroun taxation did not weigh too heavily. Although the rates were relatively high, they could be met without great difficulty by the assessed population, which included only adult males.[59] Under French mandate rule, however, all indications point to a much greater tax burden, in effect a direct appropriation of African wealth by the government. High taxes can partly be explained by the loss of the West Cameroun plantations to Britain and the difficulties of raising loans for a territory whose international status remained insecure. This policy was doubly costly to the local population during the mid-1920s, when the Central Railway extension was being built. After proposed metropolitan grants failed to materialise, local taxes, now on both men and women, were raised considerably. The surpluses were placed in a reserve and invested in French government securities at relatively low interest rates. Thus not only did Camerounians pay the entire cost of this transport investment but also advanced significant sums to the metropole to cover other colonial expenses, such as the continuing deficits of AEF.[60]

In AEF head taxes were harder to raise because of the sparser population and the difficulties in expanding export production. None the less, strenuous efforts, including the use of force, were made to collect taxes from men and after 1909 from women. Although lower than in Cameroun, taxes in AEF were higher than in the more prosperous French West Africa, and imposed a far greater burden on the population. The orientation towards a confiscatory rather than a liberal economy was

58 Guyer, 'Head Tax', 5–6, AEF, *Annuaire statistique*, 276.
59 Karin Hausen, *Deutsche Kolonialherrschaft in Afrika: Wirtschaftsinterressen und Kolonialverwaltung in Kamerun vor 1914*, Zurich, 1970, pp. 193–6; Rudin, *Germans in the Cameroons*, pp. 338–45.
60 League of Nations Permanent Mandates Commission, *Minutes* 3 (1923), pp. 34–8; 9 (1926), pp. 79–82, 90.

exacerbated by the tendency of surviving concessionary companies to pay for commodities by barter or with tax tokens rather than cash. This practice, which continued into the 1930s, reinforced the image of export goods as a form of tribute rather than an exchange commodity. Even when the AEF government succeeded in monetising the rural economy and freezing or even reducing the tax rates, the poor returns for cash crops provided little disposable income.

The depression years of the early 1930s represented a high point in the use of direct taxation to support government revenues in Cameroun. In AEF the ratio of taxes to incomes became ruinous. The recovery of export values in the later 1930s, coupled with an unchanged tax rate, brought improved conditions for African populations in Cameroun. In AEF the terms of trade improved markedly during the later 1930s; however, this shift benefited Africans very little. Imports destined for Africans still remained at a low level; less than one-half as many yards of cotton *per capita* entered AEF as entered Cameroun.[61] Moreover, AEF had been placed under a partial protective tariff, forbidden by the Cameroun mandate, which hit directly at the consumer market. Between 1934 and 1938 an average surcharge of just over 5 million francs was placed on foreign goods.[62]

By the end of the 1930s the economy of equatorial Africa was sufficiently in hand to provide a basis for stable continuity. For the metropole this was a minimal achievement, since France drew little benefit from the region. Africans, though most remained poor, at least saw the decline in living standards reversed. Along with political and economic stabilisation came demographic stabilisation, due to the end of violent upheaval and to the work of the health services.

SOCIAL EFFORTS : THE HEALTH SERVICES

As the French government began to assume more direct political and financial responsibility for equatorial Africa, investments in the human resources of the colonies became imperative. The fruit of this effort was the development of a health service intended to arrest the decline in population, and the creation of a school system aimed at producing literate employees for government and business. Before the Second World War, it was the medical service which got the lion's share of social-welfare benefits. In 1925, 8·4 per cent of the AEF budget was devoted to health, while

61 Coquery-Vidrovitch, 'L'Impérialisme', 264–7; AEF, *Annuaire statistique*, 267–9; Cameroun, *Rapport annuel 1937*, p. 80.
62 Catherine Coquery-Vidrovitch, 'L'Afrique coloniale française et la crise de 1930', *Revue française d'histoire d'outre-mer*, lxiii, 1976, no. 3–4, esp. 393–4; AEF, *Annuaire statistique*, 186–7, 265.

education received 1·4 per cent; by 1940, these percentages had gone up to 15·6 and 2·3 respectively. In comparative terms, AEF and Cameroun had a higher percentage of expenditures devoted to health and a lower percentage for education than either French West Africa or Indo-China.[63] The priority given to health in both AEF and Cameroun had an importance beyond budgetary figures and beyond the need to guarantee sufficient labour, for the work of the health services, and particularly the campaign against sleeping sickness, took on the aspect of a crusade. Self-interest was forgotten, and the humanitarian and scientific aspects of the work allowed France a certain measure of pride both at home and abroad. At last something other than scandal was coming out of equatorial Africa.

The story of the health services was closely tied to the murderous epidemic of sleeping sickness which began at about the same time as the European occupation. Sleeping sickness is a parasitic disease caused by the protozoa called trypanosomes which invade first the bloodstream and then the cerebro-spinal fluid. The name of the disease comes from the final comatose state of those who are not treated. Tsetse flies, the vector of sleeping sickness, also carry animal forms of trypanosomiasis, which make it impossible to keep work-animals in many regions. The West African variety of human sleeping sickness in Cameroun and AEF, known as Gambian sleeping sickness, differs from the more virulent East African form in that wild animals do not serve as a reservoir of the germ. Thus the epidemic was not caused by ecological changes involving game, cattle and bush as in East and southern Africa. Rather, the outbreak seems due to a greater movement of people following European penetration.

The French felt responsible for spreading the disease in AEF by connecting parts of the territory which had previously been isolated. Governor-General Gabriel Angoulvant expressed current opinion in his dispatch to the Minister of Colonies: sleeping sickness 'had followed a path parallel to our colonization, it is written all over that our *tirailleurs*, our porters, our houseboys, have disseminated it . . . we have been the principal agents of propagation. . . . These facts create a special obligation toward the affected population.'[64] At the turn of the century sleeping sickness was found along the caravan route from Loango to Brazzaville, and along the Congo, Ubangi, Sangha and Alima rivers. The epidemic reached its apogee in the late 1920s when it attacked southern Chad. Even with regard to severe epidemics Cameroun was more fortunate for, despite the very high contamination rates, the disease was largely confined to a few regions.

Although the epidemic began before the 1880s, few measures had been

63 AEF, *Annuaire statistique*, 188–9, 200–3; France, Union française, *Annuaire statistique d'outre-mer*, vol. II, 1939–49, 488; S. Abbatucci, *Public Health Services in the French Colonies*, Geneva, 1926; Raymond Leslie Buell, *The Native Problem in Africa*, vol. II, New York, 1928, pp. 208–9, 222, 358.
64 Gov-Gen., AEF, to Minister of Colonies, 22 Sept. 1917, ANSOM A.P. 3250.

taken by the First World War. The researchers of the Pasteur Institute in
Paris were part of the international scientific community working on this
mysterious disease, which had killed 200 000 people in Uganda and was
ravaging the entire Zaire basin. An investigating team, paid for by the
government, the Paris Geographic Society and the concessionary companies, had charted the progress of the disease in AEF in 1907–08. Their report

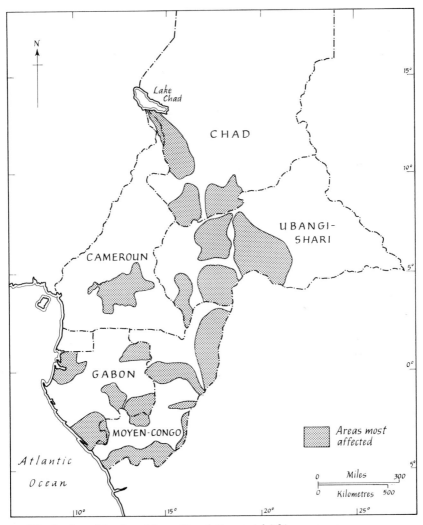

2:5 Distribution of sleeping sickness, French Equatorial Africa, 1900–40
Major sources: 'Notice pour la carte chronologique des principaux foyers de la maladie du
sommeil dans les états de l'ancienne fédération d'Afrique Equatoriale Française', *Bulletin de
l'Institut des Recherches scientifiques du Congo*, i, 45, 1962; Eugène Jamot, 'La Lutte contre la
maladie du sommeil au Cameroun', *Annales de l'Institut Pasteur*, 48, 1932, 484.

provoked little response from Parliament.[65] Two factors which combined to change this apathy were the acquisition of Cameroun and the construction of the Congo–Ocean railway. What counted in the politics of colonialism were appearances, and it looked as if the French takeover of Cameroun had resulted in drastic cutbacks in health services. The Germans had taken their time in providing medical care, but their final accomplishments were impressive. Now, under the French, the number of doctors had fallen by half and equipment was in short supply. The French worried both about their international reputation and, to a lesser extent, about the attitudes of Camerounians toward their rule.[66]

In AEF, meanwhile, recruitment had begun for the Congo–Ocean railway, and it seemed that no Africans would be left to build it. The 1924 report of the Pasteur Institute of Brazzaville predicted that soon 100 000 people would be afflicted with sleeping sickness and 25 000 of these would die each year. The report continued: 'The depopulation of AEF, even if it does not always show up in the official censuses, is indisputable. Porterage, famine and other reasons . . . have been used to explain this, but sleeping sickness, and it alone, could suffice.'[67] Accounts of whole villages disappearing, together with photos of living cadavers in the last stage of the disease, at last attracted the attention of the French legislature.

The publicity about sleeping sickness resulted in a preoccupation, almost an obsession, with the disease, which had consequences both favourable and unfavourable for the people of equatorial Africa. French subsidies and loans were advanced for a serious campaign against sleeping sickness from the late 1920s. In addition there was an intense scientific interest in methods of prevention and cure; graduates of the colonial medical school sought positions in Cameroun, with its model programme, and doctors posted to AEF, unlike administrators, did not feel that they had been banished to a backwater.[68] In consequence, people in rural areas received better medical care because mobile units were sent out to regions affected by the disease. Thus there was less top-heavy concentration of medical resources in urban centres and labour compounds than in most colonies. The emphasis on one

65 Gustave Martin, A. Leboeuf and E. Roubaud, *Rapport de la mission d'études de la maladie du sommeil au Congo français (1906–8)*, Paris, 1909; J. Laigret and Maurice Blanchard, 'La Maladie du sommeil en Afrique Équatoriale Française de 1908 à 1924', annexed to Institut Pasteur, Brazzaville, *Rapport annuel 1924*, located at Institut Pasteur in Paris; Eugène Jamot, 'La Lutte contre la maladie du sommeil au Cameroun', *Annales de l'Institut Pasteur*, xlviii, 1932, 481–539.
66 Gustave Martin, *L'Existence au Cameroun: études sociales, études médicales, études d'hygiène et de prophylaxie*, Paris, 1921, pp. 478–83; *Koloniale Rundschau*, 15 Dec. 1925, quoted in Tanon, 'Il faut sauver l'Afrique noire', *L'Afrique française*, xxxvi, 1926, 160.
67 Laigret and Blanchard, 'Maladie du sommeil', pp. 125–6; 'Rapport au Président de la République Française suivi d'un décret créant un service spécial de la trypanosomiase en Afrique Équatoriale Française', 18, Jan. 1928, France, Ministère des Colonies, *Bulletin officiel* 28, pp. 63–4.
68 Interview with Pierre LeStrade, Nice, France, 24 Jan. 1979. Dr LeStrade served in AEF in the late 1930s.

disease, however, led to a distortion in the health services. Regions without sleeping sickness got little attention, and less dramatic but equally serious problems were almost ignored. Very little effort was put into digging wells and supplying villages with clean water, potentially the most beneficial of all measures; yet wells would have kept people away from tsetse-infested river banks.

Considering the constant worry about the size of the population, the near-absence of maternal and infant care and the lack of a sustained campaign against venereal disease are both surprising. Studies in the past twenty years have shown that an overwhelming proportion of female sterility was due to lesions and Fallopian tube blockages caused by gonorrhea.[69] AEF doctors had long warned of the pernicious effects of venereal disease and of the need for continuing surveillance, especially among soldiers, the militia, and the servants of Europeans who were known to spread infection.[70] The initiation of special maternal and child care programmes in the mid-1930s was part of the shift towards more comprehensive policies. The efforts began on a very small scale, and by 1937 AEF still only had ten maternity clinics and two centres devoted to child care in contrast with fifty-seven centres for sleeping sickness. Cameroun had more facilities with fifteen maternity clinics and twenty-two paediatric clinics.[71] By that date in the Congo, the Belgians had begun a well-funded effort to cut down maternal and infant mortality by visiting expectant mothers and young children.[72]

The 1930s vision of what a health service should be was more fully implemented after the Second World War, when the blueprints were accompanied by an influx of development funds. The organisation to combat sleeping sickness was transformed into a multi-purpose service against many endemic diseases, and medical care throughout AEF and Cameroun was upgraded. The most remarkable feature of the post-war medical services was the growth of pre-natal and infant care as indicated by dramatic increases in numbers of specialised personnel, pre-natal consultations and hospital births. The post-war period was also marked by a great building programme. Though too much money was devoted to constructing show-case hospitals (the new Brazzaville General Hospital

69 Jeannel, *Stérilité en République Gabonaise*; Retel-Laurentin, *Infécondité chez les Nzakara*.
70 Gabon, *Rapport annuel 1924*, ANDOM 4 (1) D 28; Services Sanitaires, Gabon, *Rapport annuel 1933*, Pharo; Services Sanitaires, AEF, *Rapports annuels 1933, 1934*, Pharo; Services Sanitaires, Moyen-Congo, *Rapport annuel 1931*, Pharo.
71 Maurice Blanchard, Directeur du Service de Santé des Colonies, 'L'Oeuvre sanitaire de la France en Afrique Equatoriale', 1941, 15, ANSOM 3250; Cameroun, *Rapport annuel 1937*, 111.
72 Services Sanitaires, Afrique Occidentale Française, *Rapport annuel 1933*, ANSOM, Fond Guernut, B-14; for the Belgian Congo see the published annual reports from 1930 of the Fonds Reine Elisabeth pour l'Assistance médicale aux indigènes (Foréami), Brussels; also G. Trolli, *Historique de l'assistance médicale aux indigènes du Congo Belge: nouvelle méthode adoptée par Foreami, résultats obtenus*, Brussels, 1935.

alone absorbed one-fifth of all funds), the tradition of mobile medicine for rural areas was maintained.[73]

Health care in Cameroun and AEF was almost entirely provided by the government, and public health doctors were military officers. This differed from British, Belgian and Portuguese colonies, where substantial health contributions were made by missionaries, often subsidised by the government and incorporated into the public health system, or by company hospitals. In AEF the government insisted that practitioners have a French diploma, thus discouraging foreign doctors and nurses. The few foreign mission establishments were often not issued with medical material, so that Africans would not get the impression that government services were inadequate. Albert Schweitzer, in his hospital at Lambarene in Gabon, offended many officials and doctors by maintaining neutrality during the First World War and by employing Dutch, German and Swiss aides.[74] The official health service itself, however, was hard pressed to find sufficient personnel, and employed Russian emigré physicians. Though given the same responsibilities as the French doctors they were designated 'hygiénistes'. Cameroun, being a mandate, had a more liberal policy, yet there were only a dozen mission doctors throughout the 1930s and the national origin of their diplomas was carefully noted in reports to the League of Nations.

The real backbone of the health service was the African male nurse. In 1921 Dr Eugène Jamot, who designed the sleeping-sickness campaign, described how illiterate Africans could be trained to be auxiliaries. They were to do far more, however, than search for trypanosomes in blood samples. By 1938 there was one doctor for every 50 000 inhabitants of AEF but one male nurse for every 5 000 inhabitants.[75] They manned dispensaries in towns and villages, diagnosed illnesses, prescribed drugs, performed minor surgery and delivered babies. Their activity went far beyond what the laws permitted, and when accidents occasionally reached official notice, directives went out reminding the personnel of the regulations.[76] The nurses provided what little stability there was in a system where doctors were continually off on circuits through their territory or transferred to other posts.

At first nurses were trained by doctors on the job in hospitals and clinics. More formal programmes were organised at the Pasteur Institute in Brazzaville for nurses destined to serve on the sleeping sickness teams. The

73 Afrique Equatoriale Française Haut Commissariat, *L'AEF économique et sociale 1947–1958 avec l'aide du FIDES* (hereafter *FIDES*), Bobigny, 1959.
74 See dossier on Schweitzer, ANSOM A.P. 662.
75 Eugène Jamot, 'De l'Utilisation des moyens naturels de l'Afrique équatoriale pour la lutte contre la maladie du sommeil', *Annales de médecine et de pharmacie coloniales*, xix, 1921, 85–92; Blanchard, 'L'Oeuvre sanitaire,' p. 8.
76 See, for example, Dimpault Inspection Mission, 'Inspection générale des services sanitaires et médicaux', no. 34, 22 June 1933, 12–15, ANSOM A.P. 3133.

course was fairly rudimentary, and included the study of weights and measures, use of a microscope, recognition of sleeping sickness symptoms and, for better students, the taking of blood samples and giving of injections.[77] Many nurses were recruited from the ranks of the militia, were former domestic servants of Europeans, or had done a brief stint in a village school. Only a few were fully literate. In Cameroun higher-level medical training became available in 1932 with the opening of one school to train nurses and another for the higher grade of *aides de santé*, open only to graduates of the Ecole Supérieure at Yaoundé. In the late 1930s advanced courses were also instituted at the General Hospital in Brazzaville. In AEF, where higher education came late, a large proportion of the first generation of political leaders were male nurses.

The mobile teams which specialised in sleeping sickness tracked down every carrier of the disease in order to eliminate the parasite with drugs. This plan of attack differed from the British campaign, which put more resources into trying to destroy the tsetse fly. The idea of dividing AEF and Cameroun into sectors, each with its roving team to combat the epidemic, belonged to Jamot, who served first in Ubangi-Shari and then lobbied for and directed the well-funded programme in Cameroun.[78] Jamot's career nearly ended when one of his zealous underlings gave overdoses of the arsenic-based trypanocicles which blinded 700 people. Even proper treatment was painful. Villagers greeted the teams with little enthusiasm and fled when they could. The teams were therefore preceded by militiamen who rounded up the population.[79] These quasi-military tactics of the 1930s contained the disease, and by the 1950s it was almost wiped out.

A specialised concern of French and German health services was the care of workers on European-run enterprises. Inspections of medical facilities, housing conditions and food rations took place on Cameroun plantations and in Gabon timber companies' camps. Mortality was high in the first years of the plantations when workers from high altitudes were brought to low-lying coastal areas and when beriberi caused by inadequate nutrition was frequent among loggers.[80] Though some companies had small infirmaries, industrial medicine never approached the scale that it reached in the Belgian Congo or in southern Africa, where a substantial proportion of the total medical care went to miners.

77 Institut Pasteur, Brazzaville, *Rapport annuel 1917*, 43–5, located at Institut Pasteur, Paris.
78 For contrasting views of this man, see Marcel Bebey-Eyidi, *La Vie et l'oeuvre médico-sociale en Afrique intertropicale française d'Eugène Jamot (1879–1937)*, Roanne, 1950, and Suret-Canale, *French Colonialism*, pp. 408–12.
79 Interviews with retired nurses and former sleeping-sickness patients, carried out from February to August 1979 in the Congo, Gabon and Central African Empire.
80 DeLancey, 'Health and Disease on the Plantations of Cameroon'; E. W. Suldey, 'Une Epidémie de béribéri au Gabon: considérations cliniques, thérapeutiques et prophylactiques', *Annales de médecine et de pharmacie coloniales*, 1922, pp. 176–85.

The building of railways always entailed a much greater loss of life than did similar enterprises in Europe. The Germans enforced strict hygiene regulations, and most African deaths occurred from construction accidents rather than disease. Mortality rates nevertheless reached 10 per cent. When the French extended the Central line, they used more forced and less volunteer labour. The local administrator responsible for railway construction dismissed the doctor who hindered their efforts by attempting to protect the population from sleeping sickness, and death rates increased.[81] The most notorious wastage of African life occurred in the building of the Congo–Ocean railway, where the French recruited massive numbers of workers without adequate plans to transport them to work sites, feed them correct and familiar food, clothe and shelter them properly or care for them when they were sick and injured. In the worst year 450 out of each 1 000 workers died. Although French organisation improved and fatalities declined, at least 16 000 men died, many times the number killed on the Belgian line across the river.[82]

It was only after the Second World War that most equatorial Africans felt the real benefit of Western medicine, as health stations multiplied throughout the territory and the ratio of doctors and nurses to population doubled. The vastly enlarged school population received hygiene classes, inoculations and some anti-malarial drugs. Not only the facilities but also the tone of health care was being modernised. Previously, Western medicine was either unavailable or obligatory; now Africans were freer to choose the terms on which they wanted treatment.

EDUCATION

The French believed that education for Africans was a dangerous drug, which should be dispensed in minute quantities to avoid untoward side-effects. Before the Second World War the goal was to train only as many Africans as were needed by the administration or commercial firms and to spread a smattering of French throughout the territory. The great fear, found in countless administrative reports, was of producing a useless class of educated unemployed. At times, in fact, the size of the incoming class in the few schools of secondary education was tied directly to anticipated openings for Africans in the administrative service. To this was added a definite prejudice against equatorial Africans and a general concurrence with the view published for the 1931 Colonial Exhibition that '... the cycle

---

81 Pierre Billard, *La Circulation dans le Sud Cameroun*, Lyon, 1961, pp. 47–9, 61–2.
82 Death rate from Dimpault Inspection Mission, 'Main d'oeuvre du Chemin de Fer Congo–Océan', no. 1, ANSOM A.P. 3134. Death toll from Sautter, 'Chemin de fer,' 269. Total mortality on the Belgian line was given as 1 800, with death rates of 8·8 per cent in the worst year. René J. Cornet, *La Bataille du rail: la construction du chemin de fer de Matadi au Stanley Pool*, Brussels, 1948, pp. 331, 340. These figures seem unbelievably low.

of evolution of the black race turns more slowly in equatorial Africa than in neighbouring colonies'.[83]

It was not surprising, therefore, that very little money was allotted for education. The Cameroun budget had half the percentage allocated for education in Togo, another mandate; the AEF percentage was half that of Cameroun.[84] For many years there was not even a seat devoted to education on the various territorial advisory committees. Because of these factors even the minimal goals of the administration were unmet. The schools did not provide enough literate Africans to satisfy colonial needs, especially in AEF, and there were too few school-leavers with sufficient education to hold responsible professional positions.

Despite the lack of official interest in education in both AEF and Cameroun, there was a startling difference in opportunity for schooling in the two territories because of contrasting policies towards missions. The anti-clericalism which swept through the French educational establishment following the Dreyfus affair was mutely echoed in AEF, but the colony was too poor to spurn entirely the help of religious organisations. The occasional manifestations of anti-church feeling derived less from general doctrines concerning the separation of church and state than from the fear that missionary work might unsettle the population. Foreign missionaries, usually Protestant, were accepted most grudgingly and occasionally were even expelled.

In Cameroun, on the other hand, because the French inherited a colony where missions were firmly installed, and because the mandate guaranteed free operation of religious institutions, missions were allowed a much greater role in proselytising and providing education through both French and vernacular languages. The result was that in 1953, when no other French African territory had more private than public school pupils, in Cameroun three times as many attended mission schools as government schools.[85]

Missionary activity in equatorial Africa began in the 1840s. The imposition of colonial rule involved a certain ecclesiastical scramble though not strictly along national lines. The American Presbyterians who had pioneered the Ogowe region in Gabon left as French rule in the interior was extended. The Americans feared that they would be drawn into secular activity as a result of newly promulgated decrees. Underlying this was the feeling that French opposition arose 'from a settled determination to drive us from the colony because we are foreigners rather than because we are

83 Julien Maigret, *Afrique Equatoriale Française*, Paris, 1931, p. 80 – volume published under the patronage of Commissariat général de l'Exposition Internationale de Paris.
84 Union Française, *Annuaire statistique*, vol. II; budget figures from 1929 and 1938, p. 488.
85 France, Direction de la documentation, *Notes et études documentaires*, no. 1896 (19 July 1954), 'L'Enseignement dans les territoires d'outre-mer et territoires associés, première partie', p. 11.

Protestant'.[86] They turned their stations over to the Evangelical Mission Society of France, under whose auspices Schweitzer arrived in 1913. The Germans remained favourable to American Protestant missionaries but would not admit French Catholics. They eventually allowed German Catholics as part of a general policy of reconciliation between the Protestant-dominated state and Catholic interests in the metropole.[87] French Catholic missions quickly installed themselves along with the French administration in the Congo. The Holy Ghost Fathers were in Loango and Brazzaville in 1883 and in Bangui in 1890. Despite various international accords guaranteeing free access to all missionaries, Protestant missions run by Swedes and Americans were never extended equal treatment.

In Cameroun the educational establishment of the missionaries was impressive even by 1914, when they had about 40 000 pupils in primary schools.[88] The missionary schools continued to flourish in the inter-war period, and the number of children enrolled more than doubled. The basic reason for this was the pressure on the government to expand and support mission education. There was a competitive spirit which was lacking in AEF where educational reports were filed away and control was valued above development. The French government in Cameroun was determined to show that it could run the colony as well as the Germans had, and it requested French missionaries, both Catholic and Protestant, to fill the rather large shoes left behind by the Germans. Educational statistics were scrutinised by the League of Nations, where comparisons were made with the British mandates. French Protestants were not eager to see Catholics replacing German Protestants, and encouraged the American Presbyterians to expand. Thus though the French government resented the wealth of American missions, and distrusted their politics, they were under both international and French Protestant pressure to allow them to operate and extend their sphere of influence. Finally, there was the large part played by Camerounians themselves, eager to proselytise and educate in new areas either under the auspices of established missionary societies or in separatist native churches. The Bulu in south Cameroun ran 'out-reach' programmes throughout Bulu and non-Bulu regions and the Grassfield missions expanded north into Muslim territory.[89] The resulting statistics on the eve

86 Paul Richard Dekar, 'Crossing Religious Frontiers: Christianity and the Transform-ation of Bulu Society, 1892–1925', Ph.D. thesis, University of Chicago, 1978, pp. 105–10, quotation from the Mission Meeting minutes.
87 Smith, *German Colonial Empire*, pp. 141–2.
88 Rudin, *Germans in the Cameroons*, p. 360; Hanns Vischer, 'Native Education in German Africa', *Journal of the African Society*, xiv, 1915, 123–41.
89 League of Nations Permanent Mandates Commission, *Minutes*, 3, 1923, pp. 28–9; 6, 1925, pp. 34–5; 13, 1928, p. 84; Jaap Van Slageren, *Les Origines de l'Eglise Evangélique du Cameroun*, Yaoundé, 1972, pp. 133–54; Joseph, *Radical Nationalism*, pp. 30–31; Dekar, 'Crossing Religious frontiers'.

of the Second World War were remarkable, with 11 000 students in official mission schools and 92 500 in 'non-recognised' schools using French or the vernacular. The mission primary school population grew slowly in the late 1940s and then exploded, so that by 1958 there were 275 000 pupils.[90]

State education, as opposed to mission education, began slowly under the German administration, which established more regulations than schools. At the end of the German period there were only four state primary schools, one in Muslim territory. An industrial and an agricultural school were also opened, showing German interest in practical education. The French government continued the German policy of relying on missions for early primary schooling, and encouraged them with subsidies to teach in the French language of the new coloniser. The government schools concentrated on providing upper-level primary education and on training students for administrative work, technical jobs in agriculture, medicine and public works.

Three aspects of government education in the inter-war period in Cameroun are worth noting. First, Cameroun was again far ahead of AEF in providing advanced education. The Ecole Supérieure de Yaoundé had no counterpart in AEF until the Ecole Edouard Renard opened fifteen years later. The regional and vocational schools in AEF were on a much smaller scale than in Cameroun. Secondly, although the upper-level education apparatus was impressive in Cameroun, the number of students who benefited was not. Between 1921 and 1937 a total of 680 students attended the Ecole Supérieure de Yaoundé but in 1937 only 118 pupils were beyond the third year of education.[91] Considering that by many standards Cameroun had the best education system of any French black African colony, these numbers appear all the more meagre. Finally, it must be emphasised that though the programme was modelled on French schools and had a heavily Europeanised curriculum, it did not lead to metropolitan diplomas. Cameroun kept its educational lead in the late 1950s, when 7 500 pupils were enrolled in secondary school and more than 200 scholarship students were in French universities. Inequality continued, however, between north and south and between boys and girls.[92]

In AEF the primary school population lagged behind Cameroun because public education had a low priority, subsidies to mission schools were small and irregular, and foreign missionaries were harassed.[93] The most serious problem was the law of 1929, which prohibited instruction in the vernacular for anything but religious purposes. Missions could no longer

90 Cameroun, *Rapport annuel 1938*, p. 104; Victor T. Le Vine, *The Cameroons from Mandate to Independence*, Berkeley, California, 1964, pp. 78–9.
91 Cameroun, *Rapport annuel 1937*, pp. 104–5.
92 Helen Kitchen (ed.), *The Educated African: a Country by Country Survey of Educational Development in Africa*, New York, 1962, pp. 513–25; Le Vine, *The Cameroons*, p. 78.
93 AEF, *Annuaire statistique*, pp. 70–71.

provide any kind of programme 'between catechismal instruction and a complete academic program. [The law] thus prevented thousands of pupils of existing bush schools, which taught some French, reading, and arithmetic, along with religion, to benefit from anything but religious instruction.'[94] Though missions eventually found ways to comply with these rules, they inhibited the growth of 'non-recognised' schools. The fear behind these decrees went beyond a xenophobic worry about anti-French propaganda to basic anxieties about control of the population. The governor of Ubangi–Shari acknowledged the beneficial work of the American Protestant mission, but then added, 'one can fear that the religious teaching directly inspired by the Bible cannot always be understood by the natives and that they may reach conclusions prejudicial to our authority'. Complaints were also voiced about Christian villages supported by Catholic missions which 'escape the authority of the regular cadres'.[95]

In AEF, state education until the mid-1930s was extremely limited, haphazard and vulnerable to economising measures. There were urban schools with a more extensive programme in the major towns, and village schools run by militiamen, untrained monitors or administrators and their wives in off-hours. In 1929 when the colony was supporting 488 metropolitan soldiers, only twenty-five European school-teachers could be afforded. In Ubangi plans to increase the number of European school-teachers from five to fifteen in 1932 were cancelled because of the depression. In 1929, the school-age population of AEF was about 400 000, but only 4 000 pupils were in state schools, and then with poorly-trained monitors and few books or supplies.[96]

Education began to change in 1935 under the reforming governorship of Joseph Reste. His reports no longer spoke only of control, authority, production quotas and labour recruitment. The railway was completed, and Reste realised that the administration had been hampered by its own short-sighted policies and its fear of educated Africans. The governor-general was not just motivated by the cost-cutting prospect of replacing high-priced European bureaucrats with cheaper African ones. He also recognised the legitimacy of increasing African aspirations and the desirability of creating an African professional class. In a report on proposed reforms Reste declared, 'There is in this colony not a single trained teacher, a single doctor, a single veterinarian, a single forestry agent,

94 David Gardinier, 'Education in French Equatorial Africa 1842–1945', *Proceedings of the Third Annual Meeting*, French Colonial Historical Society, p. 125.
95 Oubangui-Chari, *Rapport annuel 1932*, ANSOM, Fond Guernut B-38; Moyen-Congo, *Rapport annuel 1932*, p. 22, ANSOM, Fond Guernut B-40.
96 Maigret, *AEF*, pp. 137, 139; Boulmer Inspection Mission, no. 72; Gardinier, 'Education', p. 128. For a description and legalistic history of education in AEF see Pierre Gamache, 'L'Enseignement en Afrique Equatoriale Française', *L'Afrique française, Renseignements coloniaux*, xxxviii, 1928, 751–9.

a single agent in the agriculture department or public works, who is a native.'[97] He set out to change this state of affairs. He organised the Ecole Edouard Renard, opened in 1935, with courses in education, medicine, administration and commerce, but this was not the equivalent of a French secondary school. State primary education was also increased and improved, and by 1939 there were nearly 10 000 pupils, only 2 000 fewer than in Camerounian state schools.[98] Overall, however, Camerounians still had seven times more opportunity to go to school than the people of AEF.

After the Second World War the influx of development funds caused a remarkable expansion of education in AEF, and Congo and Gabon were catapulted to near the top of literacy rates for Africa. A full primary and secondary programme was instituted, serious technical schools were opened up, and scholarships were provided for university education in France. This new flourishing of educational opportunity was still on a weak base and gave uneven results. The rate of school enrolment reached 70 per cent in Congo but only 27 per cent in CAR, 8 per cent in Chad, and even less in the Muslim north. Even in 1958 there were only 4 500 pupils in secondary schools and 825 in technical schools; sixty-nine Africans had earned a complete baccalaureate the previous decade, and a mere thirty-four had gone on government scholarships to French universities.[99]

Throughout most of the colonial period, the educational system put limits on African advancement. The first African doctors trained in the region began their medical courses in 1937, but were not equivalent in education or privilege to metropolitan doctors.[100] Only by the eve of independence could equatorial Africans get a complete French secondary school education and qualify for a higher administrative post. Before the Second World War there were not enough European children to support a lycée to which *évolué* children might be admitted as in other French colonies. A very few equatorial Africans were sent on to the Ecole Normale William Ponty school in Senegal for training as government auxiliaries, and a still smaller number of Dualas paid the expense of schooling in Europe. Inadequate though the system was, it played a major role in creating the new social formations of the later colonial period.

NEW AFRICAN SOCIAL FORMATIONS

Compared to other colonial territories, equatorial Africa before the Second World War offered limited opportunities for African advancement.

97 'Note au sujet des réformes politiques et sociales envisagées pour l'AEF', no 1009, 12 July 1936, ANSOM, Fond Guernut B-41.
98 AEF, *Annuaire statistique*, p. 70.
99 FIDES, 76–9; Kitchen, *The Educated African*, pp. 419, 424, 429, 435; A. Le Rouvreur, *Sahéliens et Sahariens du Tchad*, Paris, 1962, p. 459.
100 Interview with Raymond Mahouata, first AEF physician, March 1979, Brazzaville.

Nevertheless, those individuals and groups who could gain some advantage played critical roles as mediators between the small cadre of European rulers and ordinary subjects, between the pre-colonial past and the post-independence future, and between independent status and a still-dominant external world.

For the colonial rulers the first set of African intermediaries were political auxiliaries, who were preferably chosen for their indigenous status. The pre-colonial societies of this region were by no means egalitarian, but they did lack powerful structures of political authority. The 'big men' systems of the forest had virtually none of the bureaucratic characteristics useful for European rule. Moreover, they were built upon commercial activities which competed directly with European interests and thus had to be destroyed.

The one area where a pre-colonial political system survived as a significant force was Adamawa, in northern Cameroun. Here the German and French régimes not only made use of established rulers but initially lent them support in controlling subordinate populations. Adamawa, however, was relatively isolated from the mainstream of colonial development, so that continuity with traditional leadership can be equated with a weakness of European economic and cultural influence.

The areas of more central concern to the Germans and French were either in the forest, where there were no strong states, or in savanna regions such as the Cameroun Grassfields, Ubangi and southern Chad with relatively small or recently established conquest states. African authorities were needed to assist with tasks which disrupted the existing order: collecting newly imposed taxes, enforcing colonial law, gathering commodities for concessionaires, growing cocoa or cotton and recruiting labourers. Some of the 'paramount chiefs' who were most effective had inherited their status; among them were Duala Manga Bell on the Cameroun littoral, Garega of Bali, and Njoya of Fumban in the Grassfields. Others, like Charles Atangana in southern Cameroun, and Angoula in Moyen-Congo, were, at most, village big men with dubious claims of descent.[101] In either case, the criterion applied was not 'legitimacy' but rather utility to the administration. When Duala Manga Bell resisted German policies and Njoya quarrelled with French administrators, they were stripped of their offices. Garega's son and Atangana had their

---

101 Austen, 'Duala vs. Germans'; Elisabeth M. Chilver, 'Paramountcy and Protection in the Cameroons: the Bali and the Germans, 1889–1913', in *Britain and Germany in Africa: Imperial Rivalry and Colonial Rule*, Prosser Gifford and William Roger Lewis (eds), New Haven, Connecticut, 1967, pp. 469–511; Claude Tardits, *Le Royaume Bamoun*, Paris, 1980, pp. 218–66; Jane I. Guyer, 'The Depression and the Administration in South-Central Cameroon', *African Economic History*, 1981, 67–79; Claude Robineau, 'Contribution à l'histoire du Congo: la domination européenne et l'exemple de Souanké (1900–1960)', *Cahiers d'études africaines*, vii, 26, 1967, 325–6.

authority drastically reduced when the Cameroun administration became worried about oppressive labour policies.

It would be wrong, however, to regard such figures as nothing more than instruments of the colonial state. The Germans, and even the French, were well aware of the abuses and discontent caused by government through raw force of arms, and they attempted wherever possible to install a civilian chief who was locally acceptable. On occasion even a resistance leader might be co-opted into such a role; Angoula only became paramount chief after he brought the population of his original village back from Cameroun, where he had moved them to avoid recruitment for the Congo–Ocean railway.

The chiefs recognised by the government made use whenever possible of traditional devices for retaining their positions. Some of them forged personal bonds with local administrators. Indeed, in a pattern borrowed from earlier relations between African and European traders, a few administrators married women from chiefly households.[102] The distinction between personal and political ties became blurred, as when a chief supplied manpower for a 'pacification campaign' aimed at a traditional enemy. The resources available to a chief in the new order remained quite limited. An individual European official did not remain long, and ties of personal obligation or political alliance could not always be secured with his successor. To stay in power, chiefs had to invest in the economic system that Europeans were creating and in Western education.

The combination of political office and economic entrepreneurship was not new. In the pre-colonial period organisations headed by forest big men could be considered commercial firms as easily as states. The establishment of colonial rule deprived these rulers of political authority over trade routes and installed transport systems based on railways, motorised vessels and lorries, which Africans could not hope to control. Africans therefore had to find their own niches in the European-dominated economy. The chiefs of the colonial era who most successfully dominated new enterprises were the remote Fulani lamidos of Adamawa who profited from an expanded cattle-trade and the commercial cultivation of ground-nuts. More short-lived was the position of Duala trading chiefs who became cocoa-plantation owners, and of other rulers who directed cash-crop cultivation. Their economic position was lost when the régime decided to encourage independent peasant cultivators. Even in Adamawa, the shift from ground-nuts to cotton after the Second World War allowed small farmers to escape the control of the lamidos. This form of commercial agriculture lessened the power of traditional élites, but the new family units of production were

102 Germany, Reichstag, *Stenographische Berichte*, XI Legislations Periode, 1905/06, Vierte Anlageband, No. 294, 3398, 3403–4; Weinstein, *Eboué*, p. 48.

too small to provide a direct means of upward mobility for the peasantry.[103]

Trade and commerce were only slightly more significant than agricultural activity in bolstering old élites or forming new ones. As the concessionary companies and trading firms replaced the big men and conquest rulers, Africans were left to operate as agents, brokers and retailers only beyond those points where Europeans themselves collected and distributed goods. This was petty capitalism at most, and African spheres were further restricted as the transport network expanded, government licensing systems became more effective, and Levantine immigrants took up middle-men functions. Even the itinerant peddlers and small shopkeepers were often Hausa from Nigeria. The French sometimes invited Hausa traders to settle in order to stimulate commerce.[104]

African business remained a small affair not just in the towns and villages but also in the cities. In Brazzaville and Libreville indigenous private enterprise was extremely poorly developed. The important stores and market stalls were owned by Europeans, Levantines or West Africans. In Chad the wealthiest Africans were from the Anglo–Egyptian Sudan, Nigeria or the Fezzan in Libya. Even in Douala, with its thriving commerce, only a few Duala businessmen attained major wealth, while the Bamileke, although progressing economically, were confined to small-scale undertakings. Some Bamileke entrepreneurs invested in lorries and taxis, but it is remarkable how few Africans entered the transportation field compared to elsewhere on the continent.[105] Though some groups improved their standard of living through agriculture and business, the surest path to advancement was through Western education. In commerce large European firms had reduced their dependence on Africans to supply export goods but now needed literate employees with accounting skills. In the public sector it was no longer chiefs but rather indigenous clerks, teachers and medical assistants who became the major intermediaries between Europeans and the subject population. The military often acquired a rudimentary education while in service.

In the early colonial period both the élites with Western education and the soldiers came from regions in British and French West Africa with a long history of European contact. These black expatriates continued to

103 Victor Azarya, *Aristocrats Facing Change: the Fulbe in Guinea, Nigeria and Cameroon*, Chicago, 1978, p. 82; Jean Assoumou, *L'Economie du cacao*, Paris, 1977, pp. 181–8; Jacques Champaud, *Mom: Terroir Bassa (Cameroun)*, Paris, 1973, pp. 32–51.

104 John A. Works, Jr., *Pilgrims in a Strange Land: Hausa Communities in Chad*, New York, 1976, pp. 179–80; Georges Bruel, 'Les Populations de la moyenne Sanga: les Pomo et les Boumali', *Revue d'ethnographie et de sociologie* I, 1910, 28.

105 Georges Balandier, *Sociologie des Brazzavilles Noires*, Paris, 1955, pp. 103, 110; Lasserre, *Libreville*, pp. 183–5; Works, *Pilgrims*, pp. 200–6; R. Diziain and A. Cambon, *Etude sur la population du quartier de New-Bell à Douala, 1956–62*, Recherches et études Camerounaises, no. 3 Spécial; Billard, *Circulation dans le Sud Cameroun*, pp. 212–15.

serve as clerks in European businesses, but the local educational systems were soon large enough to produce indigenous African cadres for government service. Nowhere in equatorial Africa did important conflicts develop between educated *évolués* and traditional chiefs. Chiefs and their families were often in the forefront of those acquiring Western education, thus reinforcing their position. The French even encouraged chiefs to send their children to school and occasionally built special institutions for them.

Educational achievement tended to follow ethnic lines rather than class lines. Coastal peoples such as the Duala and Bassa in Cameroun and the Mpongwe, Lari and Vili in AEF occupied many positions requiring literacy. This represented a continuity with the past. Groups which had been middlemen in pre-colonial trade now became middlemen as auxiliaries of the administration. A ranking developed based on proximity to European culture. Felicien Challaye, who accompanied the Brazza investigation in 1905, presents a caricature of this hierarchy: 'The Bandas call the Mandjias savage, the Yakomas call the Bandas savage, the Loangos [Vili] call the Yakomas savage, the Senegalese call the Loangos savage, certain whites call the Senegalese savage, and Maurice Barres [a contemporary right-wing French writer] calls us all barbarians. Only our Chinese cook maintains a polite and dignified indifference.'[106] The concentration of educational opportunity in the south-west of each colony (except Gabon where it was in the north-west) did not always reinforce pre-colonial patterns. In Chad the modern élites came from the cotton region which had most of the schools and a tradition of volunteering for the colonial army. The Muslim north, which had been politically dominant, lost ground. Muslims had little interest in enrolling their children in government schools with non-Muslim teachers, and the French would not modify their programme to a mixed Koranic–French curriculum.[107]

Ethnicity in equatorial Africa was more than just a determinant of educational opportunity. Certain occupations also became identified with specific groups: the Bamileke were the petty entrepreneurs of Cameroun and the Sara from the savanna of AEF became soldiers. Equally important, ethnic groups were to become the bases of protest movements against the colonial régime. These groups were not static. The same fluid religious and commercial processes which formed ethnicity in the pre-colonial past continued in the colonial period. To these were added intensified urban competition, occupational camaraderie, and mission experience which all served to delineate ethnic groups. The Sara in *tirailleur* army units and work brigades on the Congo–Ocean railway formed new relationships among themselves. The Lari, who were not mentioned as a distinctive entity at the

106 Challaye, *Le Congo français*, p. 89.
107 Buijtenhuijs, *Le Frolinat*, pp. 52–8.

time of colonisation, became the dominant ethnic group in Brazzaville. By being more cooperative with the French than the indigenous Tio and by seeking mission education, they became the major source of auxiliaries and domestic servants, migrating into Brazzaville at a greater rate than other Kongo-speaking peoples.[108] The Bamileke, also a new cultural category, emigrated to the Mungo valley and populated Yaoundé and Douala. Like other urban groups they formed voluntary associations to assist one another in competing for advancement. In Douala, Bamileke rotating credit associations were perceived by European businessmen as a threat to their own commercial positions.[109]

Although different peoples regularly brushed shoulders with one another, the cities also served to increase ethnic divisions. There were rivalries between native groups and immigrants, particularly in Douala and Libreville where the Duala and Mpongwe struggled to protect their economic and political position against the ultimately more numerous Bamileke and Fang. Occupational monopolies, housing patterns and voluntary associations all contributed to ethnic consciousness. This was true of older commercial cities, like Douala, where European businesses at the same time offered opportunities and competition for Africans, and it was true of new administrative cities, like Fort-Lamy (Ndjamena) where the vast majority of Europeans were government employees. Ethnic concentrations occurred both where improvised squatting confounded all attempts to rationalise the urban landscape, as in Libreville, and in cities like Brazzaville, where geometric African quarters were planned in advance of settlement.[110]

The more cosmopolitan aspects of urban life had a limited effect because the cities were so small. Before the Europeans arrived, the largest city in the whole region was Abeche, capital of Wadai in eastern Chad, with about 28 000 people. The population declined sharply following a series of natural disasters, and the city lost importance to Fort-Lamy, which became the focal point of routes through Chad. At the beginning of the Second World War, the largest city was Brazzaville with a population of 45 000. Libreville, the oldest French settlement and the capital and commercial centre of the richest of AEF's territories, seemed particularly small with 11 000 people in 1940 and only 28 000 at independence.[111]

Many other factors contributed to ethnic formations. The establishment of churches in which the language of worship and formal education was Duala, Bulu or Mbochi helped create a new culture consciousness through

108 Sautter, *De l'Atlantique*, pp. 475, 565–69.
109 Jonathan Derrick, 'Douala under the French Mandate 1916–1936', Ph.D. thesis, University of London, 1979, p. 402.
110 Derrick, 'Douala,' pp. 390–8; Lasserre, *Libreville*, pp. 16–19, 35–41, 206–31; Works, *Pilgrims*, pp. 93–129.
111 Samuel Decalo, *Historical Dictionary of Chad*, Metuchen, N.J., 1977, pp. 24–5; Donald G. Morrison *et al.*, *Black Africa: a Comparative Handbook*, New York, 1972, pp. 212, 243.

the missions. Religious proselytising often led to ethnic conversions, as people outside of core areas accepted the language and customs as well as the faith of the preachers. Ethnic solidarity also played a major role in political protest, since the class basis for such an action was insufficient before the Second World War. There was no concentration of labourers in work situations which would make them conscious of being part of a modern order and capable of organising within it. The relatively privileged railway workers were organised in informal friendly societies rather than in unions. The victims of recruitment for forced labour and other forms of socio-economic oppression had even less chance of protecting themselves. During the period of railway construction in both Cameroun and AEF, resistance usually took the form of migration. The most intense response to years of forced labour, concessionary company misrule and railways recruitment was the 1929 rebellion of the Baya people on the Cameroun–Ubangi border. This armed uprising drew international attention to the evils of local régimes, but the reforms achieved brought closer European supervision rather than greater autonomy.[112]

The Westernised élite as a class was neither large enough nor frustrated enough to protest vociferously about their position. A very small number were legally French citizens. Among the others few could meet the educational qualifications for senior jobs, and barriers of race and citizenship were less used than barriers of education. There were no professionals such as lawyers or journalists independent of the government. Occasionally, *évolués* would petition the government for better employment, or education, or preferential treatment in hospitals, but these efforts did not persist. Ultimately the only political activity which the colonial régimes seriously worried about before the Second World War emanated from the most Europeanised ethnic groups. These were led by *évolués*, not as representatives of their class but as ethnic leaders of the Duala in Cameroun and the Lari in Moyen-Congo.

The Duala had the longest and most serious history of anti-colonial protest, beginning with petitions to the Reichstag about the injustices of urban land expropriation, and continuing with complaints to the Versailles peace conference, the League of Nations and the French government. Their demands went beyond land issues to call for radical modernisation of Cameroun and an advance of its political status toward sovereignty. The popular base for these claims was strengthened by the formation of an independent Native Baptist Church. The church itself was essentially orthodox, but the sermons and hymns of its leader, Pastor Alfred Lotin Same expressed a longing for liberation from colonial rule.[113]

112 Thiéno Mouctar Bah, 'Karnou et l'insurrection des Gbaya: la situation au Cameroun 1928–1930', *Afrika Zamani*, iii, 1974, 105–61; Philip Burnham, '"Regroupement" and mobile societies: two Cameroon cases', *JAH*, xvi, 4, 1975, 577–86.
113 Richard A. Joseph, 'Church, State and Society in Colonial Cameroun', *International Journal of African Historical Studies*, xiii, 1, 1980, 23–32.

The political phase of the Lari movement, led by André Matsoua, was shorter-lived. Matsoua began his career as a rural mission catechist and then became a senior customs clerk in Brazzaville. After the First World War he went to Paris and entered the milieu of pan-Africanists demanding general reforms of the colonial empire. His attempts to organise in AEF in 1928 received support from the Lari, but also ended his active career. He was arrested, exiled, escaped, arrested again, and died in prison in 1942. Starting with Matsoua's arrest and stimulated by his death, the Matsouanist movement lost its secular character and turned into a Lari messianic cult linked with Kimbanguism among the related Kongo-speaking peoples of the Belgian Congo.[114]

Neither the Duala protests nor the Matsouanists really represented a challenge to French rule, both because of their unrealistic goals and because of their ethnic particularism. Matsouanism led to a withdrawal from the colonial system rather than an attempt to take it over. The Duala, on the other hand, sought broader Camerounian support against Germans only to have their leader, Duala Manga Bell, executed on the basis of evidence provided by Sultan Njoya of Bamun. The French were also successful in discrediting Duala demands as being the self-serving manoeuvres of a small population mistrusted by other Camerounian groups. Decolonisation, when it approached, was thrust upon the people of equatorial Africa and did not emerge from earlier well-articulated demands.

THE ERA OF DECOLONISATION

Until the 1930s France's policies towards its African colonies can be described as minimalist. Except in the area of basic transport infrastructure, investments were kept low and political involvement was reduced to the maintenance of a marginal bureaucratic régime. Under the impact of the world depression two changes occurred. First, the colonies rose to a significant position in the external trade and investment activities of France. Metropolitan economic planners now began to give greater attention to overseas territories as a potential shield against further crises in the world market. Second, colonialism, as practised up to this time in equatorial Africa, became politically and morally discredited. A new generation of administrators demanded reform, and the left-wing Popular Front government, which took office in France in 1936, offered support.[115] The two decades from the mid-1930s to the mid-1950s were thus the high point of French commitment to the African colonies. There were, however, serious contradictions in this new strategy. It rested primarily on the

114 Balandier, *Sociology of Black Africa*, pp. 389–472; Martial Sinda, *André Matsoua: fondateur du mouvement de libération du Congo*, Paris, 1977.
115 Catherine Coquery-Vidrovitch, 'Colonisation ou impérialisme: la politique africaine de la France entre les deux guerres', *Le Mouvement Social*, cvii, 1979, pp. 51–76.

external circumstance of French decline rather than on positive developments within Africa. Moreover, the neo-mercantilist urge to integrate the colonies more closely into the metropolitan economy was ultimately incompatible with the liberal impulse to grant local populations greater opportunities for running their own affairs.

During the 1930s the colonial reformers were given too few resources and the Popular Front government was too short-lived to do more than lay down the plans for a radically altered colonial policy. The Second World War brought increased hardships in Africa and political turmoil at home but also provided AEF and Cameroun with a unique moment of glory. Because of their peripheral location and the personal decisions of local French administrators, most notably Félix Eboué, the black West Indian governor of Chad, these territories were the only major French colonies to rally to the Free France of Charles de Gaulle against the collaborationist Vichy régime. The temporary prominence of the region meant that in 1944 the triumphant Free French chose Brazzaville as the site for a conference to announce a major liberalisation of France's relations with its overseas possessions. Even at this stage, the changes proposed did not envisage any sacrifice of imperial structure. 'Self-government' was explicitly excluded. Instead, the reforms aimed at creating more dynamic ties between the metropole and the tropical dependencies.

The end of the Second World War at last provided the conditions for serious change. France was in ruins, and its recovery appeared to depend upon the development of the franc zone as a self-sufficient economic system. The empire, now conceived of as the overseas section of a French Union, also had to be provided with institutions which lived up to the liberal promises of the Gaullists and their left-wing allies. These aims were met first by the 1946 constitution of the new Fourth Republic, which gave Africans citizenship, although not on an equal basis with the natives of France. Meanwhile, France launched a major series of development projects within the African territories under the extensive programme of FIDES (Fonds d'investissement et de développement économique et social des Territoires d'Outre-Mer).[116] By the late 1940s the new colonial policy was well under way. Soon afterwards, however, the contradictions in these policies made themselves felt, most tellingly in the external arena.

France did manage a very impressive economic recovery after the Second World War without any significant contribution from the colonies. The terms of international trade had turned against tropical raw materials so that French conservatives began to criticise investments in Africa as a wasteful public expenditure. At the same time, attempts by

---

116 D. Bruce Marshall, 'Free France in Africa: Gaullism and Colonialism', in Gifford and Louis, *France and Britain in Africa*, pp. 713–48; Jean Suret-Canale, 'The economics of French decolonisation', in Prosser Gifford and William Roger Louis, *The Transfer of Power in Africa*, New York, 1982.

Ralph A. Austen and Rita Headrick

France to retain political control over Indo-China and Algeria were destroying the Fourth Republic. The probable cost of maintaining similar hegemony in west and equatorial Africa, when neighbouring British territories were approaching self-rule, did not seem worth the benefits.

From about 1955 French strategy towards Africa therefore shifted again. Although the colonies were by no means to be precipitously abandoned, as some right-wing anti-colonialists urged, the connection, both economic and political, was to be more flexible. Instead of competing with other industrial powers through an autarkic French Union, France now joined the European Economic Community. This arrangement allowed the metropole to retain a privileged position in its present and former overseas possessions, but shared the right to trade and responsibility for development aid with other members of the Community. For equatorial Africa it is particularly significant that West Germany was the most active new partner. In politics, France now tried to pre-empt radical independence movements by offering limited power to malleable African leaders. The *loi cadre* reforms of 1956 gave internal territorial self-government; in 1958 new African republics were established within a French Community, and full formal independence came in 1960.[117] The parabolic movement of French strategy from intense concern for colonial empire to a relegation of Africa to the margins of metropolitan interest explains what happened in equatorial Africa between the depression and 1960. Developments within this region also helped determine the colonial attitudes of France.

THE ECONOMICS OF FIDES

The idea that neo-mercantilism could help to solve metropolitan problems while also improving the conditions of life for local populations was based on confidence in continued African economic growth. This belief was supported by the major export increases achieved during the late 1930s and surpassed during the period of massive investment after the Second World War. This growth occurred essentially within the range of products established during the 1920s. The gains following the depression came from increases in world demand, improved transport capacities within equatorial Africa and local population growth. Despite new financial resources, there was no qualitative transformation of the production base.

The major source of export goods from the Cameroun fertile crescent and Adamawa plateau as well as the AEF savannas continued to be peasant

117 Rudolf von Albertini, *Decolonization: the Administration and Future of the Colonies, 1919–1960*, Francisca Garvie (trans.), Garden City, N.Y., 1971, pp. 425–52; François Caron, *An Economic History of Modern France*, Barbara Bray (trans.), New York, 1979, pp. 216–17; Henri Burgelin, 'La Décolonisation et les relations entre puissances occidentales', in *La Communauté internationale face aux jeunes états*, Jean-Baptiste Duroselle and Jean Meyriat (eds), Paris, 1964, pp. 89–97.

farms. Some investment was directed towards increasing the efficiency of this sector. In AEF the French again took inspiration from the Belgian Congo, and attempted during the 1950s to group African cultivators into government-organised settlements called *paysannats*; the results were disappointing.[118] From 1937 onward provident societies were introduced throughout the rural districts. Mandatory payments by African members were combined, after 1946, with major contributions from aid budgets for local development projects. Although less oppressive than the *paysannats*, the provident societies appeared to Africans as an additional taxation system over which they had no control. External funding declined after 1958 and the societies left little impact. Despite increasing market participation and loans from provident societies, individual peasants made only minimal investments in their farms. Even cheap insecticides among Cameroun cocoa-growers became status symbols rather than implements for intensified production.[119]

In the first stage of post-war expansion the equatorial African economy seemed ready for medium-range enterprise of a type previously lacking. Many more Africans entered commerce, transport and timber-cutting, and European planters settled in southern Cameroun, the Niari valley of Moyen-Congo and the Ubangi savanna.[120] These activities became important in political terms, because they increased competition and friction between Europeans and Africans. From an economic perspective, however, they suffered particularly from the decline in export prices, and were overshadowed by the growing concentration of modern enterprises in state and private enclaves.

One such enclave was the Cameroon Development Corporation, formed in 1946 by the government of British Cameroun to operate the plantations confiscated from German owners and never returned to the private sector. In Gabon the timber industry became mechanised under the control of expatriate firms. At the same time, the new mineral sectors of manganese, petroleum and uranium in Gabon and of diamonds in Ubangi-Shari demanded investments beyond the capacities of African or European settler capital.[121] The finance and technology for these last enterprises, and also for an aluminium processing plant in Cameroun, came from public sources, and metropolitan or multinational corporations such as United

118 Stürzinger, 'Baumwollbau im Tschad', pp. 78–84; Thompson and Adloff, *Emerging States*, pp. 171–3.
119 Jane I. Guyer, 'The Provident Societies in the Rural Economy of Yaounde, 1945–1960', unpublished paper, African Studies Association Meetings, Philadelphia, 1980; Thompson and Adloff, *Emerging States*, pp. 168–71; Assoumou, *Economie du cacao*, p. 197.
120 Pierre-Philippe Rey, *Colonialisme, néo-colonialisme et transition au capitalisme : exemple de la 'Comilog' au Congo-Brazzaville*, Paris, 1971, pp. 476–92; Sautter, *De l'Atlantique*, pp. 639–714.
121 Bederman, *Cameroon Development Corporation*; Lasserre, 'Okoumé', 135–40; Rey, *Colonialisme*, pp. 469–75.

States Steel and the French aluminium firm of Pechiney-Ugine. Although the undertakings had a great impact on the local economy while under construction, when large amounts of labour and provisions were required, this phase was part of the deceptive boom created by the FIDES programme. Once installed, the enclave industries provided few links with African-based enterprises, and local profits were absorbed by the state. They did not provide the basis for economic growth.

The public capital invested in equatorial Africa during the last stage of colonialism was impressive. The FIDES funds were more generous than comparable aid in British West and East Africa. Although a larger absolute amount of this money was distributed to French West Africa than to Cameroun and AEF combined, the two equatorial territories received far higher rates of assistance *per capita*.[122] However, the FIDES package was a mixed one, involving some outright metropolitan grants, but also loans and matching expenditures which imposed a strain upon local budgets. Repayment of this debt was to come from the increased productive capacity generated by the funded projects. Export statistics indicate that such an increase did take place but not at a pace equal to the new financial burdens. The problems were partially structural. New transport projects were more costly than older ones which had used forced labour, and did not create as dramatic an impact on the economy as the first roads and railways. Secondly, the fever of development planning inspired many unviable projects, particularly those aimed at agriculture in AEF. Finally, when prices for equatorial African commodities began to decline, even increased quantities of exports could not cover imports. The result, as usual more severe in AEF than Cameroun, was a need for new taxation and subventions from the metropole. Thus at the moment of independence the equatorial African economy found itself living with an enlarged version of its old dilemma.[123]

THE SOCIAL BASE OF DECOLONISATION POLITICS

No episode of the equatorial African past has been so fully chronicled as the whirlwind of constitutional changes, party struggles and emerging nationalist leaders which swept across the region between 1946 and independence in 1960. These events appeared to represent a dramatic break with the old colonial order and to foreshadow even greater changes under fully democratic African régimes. Several decades later, however, this

122 M. Younes *et al., Les Investissements d'origine locale et d'origine extérieure dans les pays francophones d'Afrique tropicale 1946–1960*, Paris, 1964, pp. 159–60.
123 Philippe Hugon, *Analyse du sous-développement en Afrique noire: l'exemple de l'économie du Cameroun*, Paris, 1968, pp. 61–104; Samir Amin and Catherine Coquery-Vidrovitch, *Histoire économique du Congo 1880–1968*, Paris, 1969, pp. 55–64; Thompson and Adloff, *Emerging States*, pp. 358–60, 400–3, 445–8, 495–6.

period appears as a brief exercise in electoral politics, bracketed on both sides by authoritarian rule. Despite mass involvement in public life during the last colonial decade, there are similarities with the restricted political systems which preceded and followed it.

Attempts at political reform were begun in the late 1930s amid liberalising economic and social policies. Africans were allowed broader participation in territorial administrative councils. In AEF, a small electoral college was instituted in 1937 to choose the African members. In Cameroun, political reform in the mid-1930s led to a shift of government patronage from powerful chiefs, like Atangana, to more 'traditional' village chiefs. Reforms slightly increased African participation in administration, but did not lead to autonomous political activity or organisation. The administrative councils had no legislative power. The 'traditional' rulers installed in place of the powerful chiefs were less able to meet Europeans on equal terms.[124] All Africans holding new or enlarged roles were there because Europeans had chosen them. None had a strong enough base to wrest concessions or privileges from the administration, and no effective African leadership emerged in the local and territorial councils.

External ideological influences were also weak. The colonies were fairly isolated, and despite government paranoia, only a small amount of 'subversive' material came in from metropolitan, pan-African, Comintern or pro-German sources. The only non-ethnic groups to emerge in post-war politics were founded by the authorities themselves. In 1938, in order to counter German designs on the mandate, educated youths were recruited to a propaganda organisation called Jeunesse Camerounaise Française (Jeucafra). While it did essentially what the French wanted, it also managed to insert a few pleas for reform into declarations of loyalty. More significantly, it served as a meeting ground for future political leaders. Similar organisations were fostered by Eboué as governor-general of AEF during the Second World War.[125]

The 1946 constitution radically altered the rules for politics. Under its provisions Africans lost their subordinate status as subjects. Disabilities such as the *indigénat* legal system and the *corvée* labour obligations were abolished, while the right to elect representatives to territorial assemblies and to Paris was guaranteed. At first the number of Africans allowed to vote was restricted to only 100 000 in AEF; a separate electoral college was limited to individuals previously holding French citizenship, mainly local Europeans. The franchise was extended in stages until virtual universal suffrage arrived in 1956.

124 Guyer, 'Depression and Administration'; Buijtenhuijs, *Frolinat*, pp. 60–62.
125 Joseph, *Radical Nationalism*, pp. 40–44, 351–3; Elikia M'Bokolo, 'French colonial policy in Equatorial Africa in the 1940s and 1950s', in Gifford and Louis, *Transfer of Power*.

Political progress throughout the years of declonisation was determined by the interplay of four forces: the metropole, the colonial state, the white settlers and the politicised Africans. The role of the metropole involved initiating constitutional change, usually in response to pressure outside equatorial Africa. The colonial state carried out the reforms while also serving as an anchor against loss of metropolitan control. White settlers sought to protect their economic position and to capture some of the new political power devolving on the colonies. Finally, politically conscious Africans, acting within newly created parties, were the focus of the new system.

The metropolitan parties which advocated colonial reform hoped to increase their influence with rising indigenous leaders. From 1944 French socialists and communists formed study groups and branches of their respective metropolitan political and trade union organisations. The Gaullist and Catholic party representatives were less successful, because they were too conservative and sometimes identified with right-wing settlers. Local colonial governments made alliances with African groups who showed strength in the elections, but also tried to ensure the success of their favourites by manipulating voting. The authorities encouraged settler politics to limit African emancipation claims but settlers often provoked African groups into radical anti-colonial postures.

The prominent role played by the local European community was unusual in colonies without a long tradition of white settlement. Most of the whites were newcomers. Some had recently bought farms for ranching or growing tropical products or had started small urban enterprises. The majority were involved with the development projects of FIDES as administrators, technicians, foremen and skilled workers, and probably did not intend to remain permanently. Under the dual electoral college system these Europeans had their own representatives on territorial councils as well as in Paris. They used these platforms to call for a delayed enfranchisement. The settlers diminished in importance as the inevitability of independence became apparent. Yet non-indigenous politicians sought office as representatives of African constituencies and in AEF were appointed cabinet ministers by African heads of government. In 1957 one-fifth of Moyen-Congo deputies were Europeans, and in Ubangi one European was placed on each roll of MESAN (Mouvement pour l'Evolution de l'Afrique Noire), the local party which won all three seats. Even more unusual was the election of Hector Rivierez, a well-connected West Indian lawyer who had never set foot in Ubangi, as that territory's representative in the French Senate. Chad came close to attaining independence with a former administrator, also a West Indian, as its premier.[126]

---

126 Kalck, *Histoire centrafricaine*, vol. IV, p. 515; Jean Michel Wagret, *Histoire et sociologie politiques de la République du Congo*, Paris, 1963, p. 92.

European influence was greatest, however, when exercised behind the scenes, supporting African politicians. Even Africans who had successfully defeated government-supported or settler-backed candidates soon found themselves surrounded by Europeans offering advice, overseas contacts and financial assistance. These *eminences blanches* often played divisive roles, stirring up rivalries to ensure their own personal or political position. A socialist tract from Pointe-Noire was quite bitter: 'A small number of whites, living in this country, saw the *loi cadre* only as a practical way to raise their standard of living and social status. Before they were negrophobes, now they have become negrophiles.'[127] Though European supporters played active roles, especially in AEF, ultimately what counted was winning African votes. The mobilisation of support occurred through newly legalised socialist and Catholic trade unions, and through youth and student organisations, veterans' clubs and associations of traditional rulers.

The trade unions should have been a major political force but in AEF they had limited success in recruiting and holding members. Neither Ubangi nor Chad had any industries, ports or railways. In Gabon, the largest single group of salaried industrial workers were hard to unionise because they were employed by timber companies on scattered sites. Moyen-Congo was different, and many transport, construction and government workers were unionised, though the labour organisation purposely distanced itself from electoral politics and its leaders refused to enter government. Union organisers were incapable of reaching the tremendous numbers of unemployed and semi-employed who had recently flocked to the cities. Brazzaville had swollen to 100 000, and Moyen-Congo had a larger proportion of its population in cities than any country in tropical Africa.[128] The FIDES boom had attracted people to the urban centres, but many of their jobs were on temporary construction projects. Added to this was the problem caused, paradoxically, by the unusually high rate of school attendance; many of the job-seekers had high aspirations based on only one or two years of education. These frustrations exacerbated ethnic tensions and led to several sets of deadly urban riots. In Cameroun, there was less structural imbalance than in Moyen-Congo. Though Douala was slightly larger than Brazzaville, the ratio of urban to rural population was more balanced. Trade unions were also more effective, and Camerounian syndicates and farmers' organisations in both

127 *Ibid.*, pp. 70–1.
128 *Ibid.*, pp. 123, 208–9; René Gauze, *The Politics of Congo–Brazzaville*, Richard Adloff and Virginia Thompson (trans. and eds), Stanford, California, 1973, pp. 51–4; John A. Ballard, 'Four equatorial states', in *National Unity and Regionalism in Eight African States*, Gwendolyn M Carter (ed.), Ithaca, N.Y., 1966, pp. 284–7; A. M. O'Connor, *The Geography of Tropical Africa*, Oxford, 1971, p. 162.

British and French zones chose to play political roles and often affiliated themselves with parties.[129]

Political leaders thus sought support from the new trade unions and organised their parties around the ideological principles of metropolitan or West African parties. Initially, it was sufficient to appeal to the socialist views of the élite, the pro-Gaullist sentiments of the war veterans, or the advantages which chiefs gained by supporting the administration. As more people were enfranchised, and as the stakes grew higher, both politicians and voters fell back on the security of ethnic solidarity. In Chad, the Parti Progressiste Tchadien began as a national party, but ended up as a Sara one, and Chad, despite attempts to retain Muslim support, advanced toward independence 'with a political class divided along a religious cleavage'.[130] In Moyen-Congo, the Lari ended their boycott of elections to vote for their compatriot, Abbé Foulbert Youlou, who presented himself as Matsoua's heir. In Gabon, the Fang were secure enough in their ethnic majority to allow competition among rival politicians.

The central issue of decolonisation politics was whether African leaders could become independent of European patronage and ethnically defined constituencies. The most ambitious political movements in equatorial Africa, the UPC (Union des Populations du Cameroun) in Cameroun[131] and Barthélémy Boganda's MESAN in Ubangi-Shari, tried to do this.[132] The UPC had a major non-ethnic base in the *évolués* of Jeucafra and in the communist-affiliated trade-union confederation. Outside the major urban areas it also built up a network of local committees, although ultimately its strength was concentrated among three ethnic groups of the fertile crescent, the Bamileke, Bassa and Duala.

MESAN was the creation of a single man, Boganda, who as an ordained priest was one of the few Africans with a secondary education in all of Ubangi. Boganda was selected to run for the French National Assembly by the church hierarchy but later built his own political base through contacts as a mission teacher and with an organisation of lorry drivers. Boganda's messianic style was suited to a territory with a tiny élite and continuing crude exploitation by white colonists. Despite the fortuitous origin of its border Ubangi was the most unified of all equatorial states because of its

129 O'Connor, *Geography*, p. 164; Joseph, *Radical Nationalism*, pp. 253, 258; Victor T. Le Vine, 'The Cameroun Federal Republic', in *Five African States: Responses to Diversity*, Gwendolyn M. Carter (ed.), Ithaca, N.Y., 1963, pp. 293, 297–303; Ballard, 'Four states', p. 284.
130 Philippe Frémeaux, 'La Rébellion tchadienne', unpublished memoir, Université de Paris I, 1973, p. 30, quoted in Buijtenhuijs, *Le Frolinat*, pp. 72–3.
131 Jean-François Bayart, *L'Etat au Cameroun*, Paris, 1979, pp. 46–101; Willard R. Johnson, 'The Union des Populations du Cameroun in rebellion: the integrative backlash of insurgency', in *Protest and Power in Black Africa*, Robert I. Rotberg and Ali A. Mazrui (eds), New York, 1970, pp. 671–92, Joseph, *Radical Nationalism*.
132 Ballard, 'Four states', pp. 261–6; Kalck, *Central African Republic*, pp. 71–117; Kalck, *Histoire centrafricaine*, vol. IV, pp. 477–593.

good roads, its Sango lingua franca, and its lack of ethnic, religious or regional cleavages.

At the time of their emergence, both the UPC and MESAN had a reputation for radicalism among French administrators. In reality it was the tactics of local governments in allying themselves with reactionary settler groups which radicalised these parties. The UPC deserved its reputation more, since at an early date it demanded independence and reunification with British Cameroun. The UPC and its labour-union allies also severely criticised the French economic role in Cameroun and retained ties to their original communist sponsors in France. However, there was little socialist content in the UPC's vision of an independent Cameroun, and the party is best seen as a radical nationalist movement.

The radical mystique of the UPC was enhanced by its decision in 1956 to engage in terrorist violence. It was the only party in the region to do so. The UPC did not win any seats in the first Cameroun elections because the government used every device at its disposal to defeat it, from promoting alternative parties, to Catholic church propaganda, to rigging elections. The UPC sponsored coordinated demonstrations in 1955, was banned and went underground. Its subsequent guerrilla tactics were no match for French troops, who crushed the movement by the end of 1958. The administration also mobilised the Muslim north and the Beti peoples against it. About 6000 people died in the rebellion, yet the French ultimately agreed to a form of decolonisation in line with the party's demands.

The tragedy of the UPC was that other Camerounians viewed it as a threat rather than as a model of modernisation. It was one of the few parties in equatorial Africa independent of European direction, but it proved unable to attract a sufficiently multi-ethnic constituency on the strength of its nationalist platform. The French did not create the anxieties felt by the northern Muslim leaders or by the *évolués* and by peasants of the southern fertile crescent concerning UPC domination, but by playing on these fears France assured itself of close ties with the new rulers of Cameroun.

French moves against Boganda were less serious than those aimed at the UPC. The church hierarchy and the administration opposed Boganda when he proved more outspoken than expected, and they were distressed by his marriage to a Frenchwoman. Then in 1951 he was arrested but only held for a day. This provided the obligatory martyrdom which led to Boganda's winning an overwhelming majority in the National Assembly election. By 1954, when the UPC had not yet embarked upon its violent phase, Boganda had already come to terms with the French. MESAN never even took on a left-leaning appearance. Boganda had been associated with the Catholic party rather than the communists, and continually expressed a desire to assimilate French culture. In economic terms Boganda considered himself a champion of the peasantry, and during his brief period as Ubangi's prime minister he initiated, with the collaboration of French advisers, a scheme to increase cotton and coffee production by African smallholders. This proved to be a costly disaster which discredited MESAN in the eyes of the rural population. Boganda's most consistently radical position was his fight to maintain the unity of AEF and even make it the base for a United States of Latin Africa. His dream lives on in the choice of 'Central African Republic' for the post-colonial name of the most isolated of the equatorial territories. Once established as the leader of Ubangi, Boganda did not conceal his dependence on Europeans and West Indians for virtually all government functions. After his sudden death in a plane crash in 1959, his successor, David Dacko, was the candidate favoured by Madame Boganda, by the French high commissioner and by the European business community of Bangui.

The failure of radical nationalism in equatorial Africa was a victory for France. The impressive feat was achieved despite the tactical error of backing local European groups in the early phase of decolonisation. By the mid-1950s administrators realised that long-term French goals would not be threatened by the African leaders emerging through the electoral process. Many of these leaders, who began their careers with strong anti-colonial demands, now sought an accommodation with France which would assure continued aid. The states of equatorial Africa came to formal independence not just under pro-French governments, but with stronger political and economic ties to the former metropole than to one another.

The Camerounians were successful in absorbing most of British Cameroon, and their president, Ahmadou Ahidjo, was a representative of both the Muslim north and the modern élite. The economic advantages of Cameroun in the colonial period were maintained after independence by policies which increased agricultural exports, extended the railway system, and began light industries.

In AEF, independence prospects were more troubled. The French had never overcome the difficulties of integrating physically or economically the vast territory they had placed under one governor-general in Brazzaville. The post-war political reforms had discouraged the formation of wide political parties and strengthened local interest groups. AEF could not survive the centrifugal forces. Gabon's desire to be rid of the poorer colonies and the fear in Moyen-Congo that Boganda had designs on the north of the territory, were enough to assure the break-up of the federation. Only heavy French pressure could have kept AEF together, but the French were satisfied with four weak, dependent states.

The economic difficulties of the colonial period, the lack of labour in Gabon, the lack of markets for industrial products and the expense of transport to inland colonies were exacerbated as the internal borders of AEF became international boundaries. Customs, monetary and political agreements between the states were insufficient to prevent nationalist economic policies and guarantee the free movement of people across frontiers.

CONCLUSION: THE LEGACY OF COLONIALISM

This chapter began by listing the goals of colonial powers as the economic hopes for markets and raw materials and the political hopes for prestige and by 1982 it was remarkable how well France had achieved these goals. This outcome would have been hard to predict before the Second World War. The economic potential of the territories seemed most limited, and the early policies destroyed much of what there was. There was almost no assimilation and much to alienate the population from France.

After the Second World War France finally invested sufficient money and energy to cement bonds. By ensuring that the successor states remained in the franc zone, forging intimate ties with African political leaders, and continuing large-scale foreign aid, France assured itself a dominant position in its former colonies. Paradoxically, there have been more French people and more French trade in these territories after decolonisation than there were before. With the exception of Gabon, equatorial Africa is still not of strategic economic importance, but the former metropole has raised its international standing by maintaining influence over the region.

The hardship which colonial rule imposed was replaced after the Second World War by a general increase in material well-being and social opportunity. The chances of healthy survival were now increased, oppressive labour exactions were ended, manufactured consumer goods became available, and schools were established even in remote rural districts, although the cost of this advance was not only continued external dependency but also new threats to internal stability. Equatorial Africa is a classic example of rising popular expectations outstripping increases in productive and organisational capacity. This is most evident in the problems of employing and sometimes even feeding the rapidly increasing urban populations. Ethnic and regional loyalties became based on larger units than in the pre-colonial period, but cleavages between groups had deepened. People now thought of themselves, before all else, as Bulu or southerners or Muslims. Added to these divisions was the emergence of new social classes with much larger disparities in wealth than before. There were real barriers between those educated early enough to step into the highest government positions, a larger group of poorly paid state employees, and the rural and urban masses. AEF remained distinctive even among African states for its lack of an indigenous entrepreneurial class. In Cameroun, the unusually dynamic private sector of the southern region became identified with threats of Bamileke ethnic domination and was thus held in check by official policy.

The colonial legacy of equatorial Africa manifests itself most obviously in the financial indebtedness and political instability of post-independence régimes and their resulting dependence upon aid, and occasional armed intervention, from France. In apparent contradiction to this continued Western dominance, the new rulers have pursued internal development along extraordinarily diverse paths, ranging from open or planned capitalism, to Marxism–Leninism, Islamic militancy and even Bonapartist monarchy. In the Chadian case, Islamic domination represented a reversion to the pre-colonial order. The other choices, however, reflect ideologies and strategies introduced to Africans by Europeans at different points in the colonial era. After two decades of independence it is still not clear which, if any, among them will finally lead towards broad economic growth and integrated national communities.

CHAPTER 3

Rural society and the Belgian colonial economy

BOGUMIL JEWSIEWICKI

The force of colonialism deprived African societies of choice. Because their industrial revolution was imposed upon them, they were not spared its social cost, nor were they able to exercise political control over it. Colonisation was not a minor accident, nor was it a radical and illogical break with the past. The modern history of rural societies in Central Africa contains both new departures and elements of continuity. Colonial economic 'development' inevitably created inequality, as does all industrial development, but its magnitude was particularly pronounced. The formal unification of territories whose boundaries had been artificially determined created conflicts of unprecedented violence and tenacity. This situation further exacerbated problems created by colonial development itself. The rural peoples of Zaire were doubly victims of this process. As Africans, they were considered irrational, which justified their being taken in hand by the coloniser; and as peasants, their traditional way of life justified their subordination to the interests of 'modernisation'.

The late-nineteenth-century socio-political and economic units of Central Africa both welcomed the coloniser and opposed him. Ecological, economic, social and political relationships all affected the response. The rural societies of the Zaire basin were not empty-handed when they met the missionary, the merchant, the soldier, the businessman. They reacted in accordance with their own specific structures, and not only in terms of the industrial world that they were to enter. The transformation imposed by colonisation was never able totally to destroy the constantly changing patterns of the Central African world. Thus, the articulation of Central Africa with the Western economy has been a lengthy, two-way process of adaptation.

The second half of the nineteenth century saw a sudden rise in Western demand for gathered and hunted materials, principally ivory and rubber. Many historians consider this to have been a mercantile period. This judgement is true only in so far as it emphasises the direct articulation of

Central Africa with the Western world. The Swahili agents from the east coast were also very much part of this alien penetration, as were the Muslim peoples of the north.

The African response radically increased the working population engaged in the extraction of these products and in their transport. Agricultural change was also needed in order to ensure foodstuffs for the labour force, which could no longer be self-reliant. Demographic patterns, which had previously evolved to allow an efficient occupation of the natural environment, were profoundly affected. New political structures, both states and more fluid social stratifications, also developed to meet the challenge. This included the intensive exploitation of resources, the control of traffic, the appropriation and consumption of surplus and the accumulation of manpower. The effects of external intervention were least felt in the heart of the Zaire basin, where human occupation and transformation of the eco-system had made the smallest impression.[1]

THE DIRECT CONTROL OF AFRICAN RESOURCES, 1885–1910

In the 1870s and 1880s European agents, including merchants, explorers, missionaries and state representatives, were integrated into local political activity. They accomplished their political and economic objectives by manipulating local conflicts. At first, their wealth and their firepower made them attractive allies rather than dangerous adversaries. Several African political leaders, among them Tippu Tip, the leading Swahili merchant and political leader in the Zaire basin, Ngongo Lutete of Tetela, Ngaliema of the Tio and Semio of Azande, thought that they could use Europeans to their own advantage, only to be abruptly and brutally eliminated.

The changing demands of the Western market for raw materials and the competition between colonial powers led to the formation of colonial states. The conquest and perpetuation of these states, designed to take over the region's economic resources, had to be financed locally. This created the vicious circle of colonial administration. It began in 1885 with the birth of the Congo State, a semi-private state which was the personal possession of King Leopold II of Belgium. More even than the other colonies of Central Africa, it was based on the violent exploitation of natural and human resources. Even before 1885, the expeditions of exploration had in part been financed by ivory-dealing. After failing to attract private Belgian and international sources of capital, the Congo State in 1890 declared itself to be the owner of all natural products of the forest. Already in 1885, it had seized so-called 'vacant' land not directly occupied by Africans. The state

1 B. Jewsiewicki, 'Lineage Mode of Production: Social Inequalities in Equatorial Central Africa', in *Modes of Production in Africa: the Precolonial Era*, D. Crummey and C. C. Stewart (eds), Beverly Hills, California, 1981, pp. 93–114; J. Vansina, 'Lignage, idéologie et histoire en Afrique équatoriale', *Enquêtes et documents d'histoire africaine (Edha)*, iv, 1980, 133–55.

was incapable, however, of directly exploiting and managing the production of rubber and ivory; it resigned itself to indirect management.[2] The two principal Leopoldian concessionary companies, Abir and Anversoise, were created in 1892, and in the following year they received, as did the Domain of the Crown, almost exclusive development rights for the central Zaire basin. Under the concessionary system, the state gave over to the companies for a pre-determined period of time exclusive

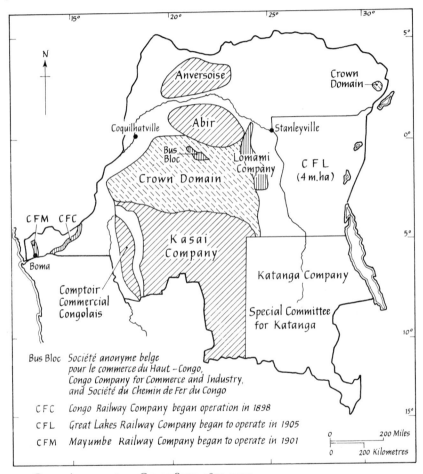

3:1 Concessionary system, Congo State, 1892–1905

2 For this period see numerous articles by the specialist Jean Stengers, and a bibliography in his chapter in *Reappraisals in Overseas History*, P. C. Emmer and H. L. Wesseling (eds), Leiden, 1979; for a general discussion of the causes of partition, see B. M. Ratcliffe, 'The economics of the partition of Africa: methods and recent research trends', *Canadian Journal of African Studies (CJAS)*, xv, 1981, 3–31; a recent general account of the Leopoldian period is L. H. Gann and P. Duignan, *The Rulers of Belgian Africa 1884–1914*, Princeton, N.J., 1979.

development rights. These included the sole right to purchase products from Africans, who were obliged to furnish them solely to the concessionary company. The state granted each company unhindered effective control, and itself became a business associate of the concessionaires. Business was accomplished through a system of pillage. A network of European agents, assisted by African auxiliaries, used force to acquire products and were remunerated according to the yield obtained. The atrocities of the system were revealed in the Congo Reform Campaign led by Britain. The cost in human lives for each ton of rubber was certainly very high. The destruction of economic and social life, the dismembering of political structures and the change in demographic patterns were even more important consequences of this system.[3]

After initial success the profitability of the concessionary system declined for several reasons. The average yield of a rubber tree was half a kilogram of latex, and an acre of forest generally contained only six trees.[4] Gradually, this resource began to be used up. Even more important, the pool of workers who could be coerced into gathering the thinly scattered crop diminished. Resistance increased, and revolts broke out, as in Mongala. A political challenge to Leopold II caused him to modify the system, and, in 1906, three industrial companies were created with the aid of Belgian and international capital.[5] They were to play a key role in the future Congo colonial economy, which was oriented toward mining. By 1907 the Congo State took over the activities of the principal concessionary zones, with the exception of Katanga, and the system was dismantled.

The taking over of the Congo by Belgium in 1908 was a necessary condition for the massive intervention of public and private Belgian capital. Until this time, the great Belgian financiers had been reluctant to interest themselves in the Congo. The weak Congo State had therefore been obliged to turn to international capital to finance the administration of the area. In 1891 the Katanga Company, a chartered company, had been created to explore and develop the far south, and from 1900 to 1910 the administration of its land was put in the charge of the Special Committee for Katanga. An African Great Lakes Railway Company was created in 1902 and entrusted not only with the construction of a railway network but also given certain public powers and vast land grants in the east. The same pattern was used in 1911 for creating the Huileries du Congo Belge, a Lever subsidiary. During the Leopoldian era in Zaire history, the Congo State gained half of its revenue by dealing in the shares of its concessionary

3 See *Les Sociétés de la forêt équatoriale*, special issue of *Edha*, iv, 1980.
4 F. Goffart, 'Concessions caoutchoutières du bassin du Congo', *Revue générale*, 1908, 238, and 'La Mise en valeur du Congo', *Revue générale*, 1907, 40–55, 265–77.
5 Union Minière du Haut-Katanga for Katanga copper mines development; Compagnie du Chemin de Fer du Bas-Congo au Katanga, for construction of a railway from Katanga to the lower Congo; and Compagnie Internationale Forestière et Minière, which discovered and developed the diamond mines of Kasai.

companies. Only 10 per cent of income came directly from the Crown domains, the profit from which was mostly used to finance the activities of the Crown in Belgium. Rubber and ivory, which had contributed 60 per cent of the total value of exports in 1890, were responsible for 95 per cent of the total in 1900. Rubber accounted for 84 per cent of this figure, but in the long run the system destroyed itself by destroying its own resources of men and rubber trees.[6]

In the Leopoldian period, one principal characteristic of the Belgian colonial system became apparent. The state favoured large companies with itself as a stockholder, and this state–capital alliance was used to open a communications network including, for example, the Matadi–Kinshasa railway. Companies also mobilised African labour and received guaranteed profits. They represented a mortgage on tax revenue. The state also assisted in amalgamating private companies into large conglomerates.[7]

It is impossible to speak of a Leopoldian agricultural policy. Some attempts were made to explore local resources and to introduce European agriculture and animal husbandry. Some amateurish efforts to cultivate coffee, cocoa and cotton largely failed. Extraction from the African rural economy remained the basis of the first generation of colonial activity. It was only during the First World War that palm products and minerals replaced ivory and rubber as the principal exports of the Congo.

AGRICULTURAL POLICY AND COLONIAL INDUSTRIALISATION

The most important change to occur when Belgium took over the Congo colony was the introduction of a monetary economy in the villages. This facilitated the collection of the new head taxes introduced between 1910 and 1912. Palm products were sold for cash, and workers were recruited for wages. The money-based economy, however, still did not spread quickly to the entire country. Additional measures, including village foodstuff production for workers and cotton-growing, were both designed to speed up rural incorporation into the colonial economy.[8]

The First World War tested the productive capacities of 'traditional' African agriculture. The Belgian Congo was heavily involved in the military campaigns against German Africa, and the regions east of the Lomami were obliged to furnish great amounts of foodstuffs and numbers of porters. Local agriculture was simultaneously responsible for the supply of food to the mine-workers of Katanga and to railway construction gangs.

6 R. Harms, 'The end of a red rubber: a reassessment', *Journal of African History (JAH)*, xv, 1975, 73–88.
7 J. P. Peemans, *Le Rôle de l'Etat dans la formation du capital au Congo pendant la période coloniale (1885–1960)*, Louvain, 1973, mimeographed; and the shorter version in P. Duignan and L. H. Gann (eds), *Economics of Colonialism*, vol. iv of *Colonialism in Africa 1870–1960*, Cambridge, 1975, pp. 165–212.
8 See A. Delcommune, *L'Avenir du Congo belge menacé*, Brussels, 1919.

In 1917 compulsory cultivation of cotton and rice was undertaken on an experimental basis. Each able-bodied adult male was required to cultivate a fixed amount of these plants, and the harvest was bought from him at a guaranteed rate. From the point of view of the administration, these experiments were a success.[9]

At the beginning of the 1920s another important change occurred. Large amounts of Belgian capital arrived, and large companies further outstripped the small enterprises. The Congo Cotton Company (Cotonco) created in 1920 with participation of the state and the great Belgian holding company, the Société Générale de Belgique, are good examples.[10] Legal limits were enforced on small businesses during the 1920s, and African businesses were the first to pay the cost.[11] However, the Belgian Congo still had no agricultural policy. The intervention of European capital was essentially limited to the processing and sale of exports, such as palm products and cotton. As far as foodstuffs were concerned, European farmers had failed. Only in the production of coffee and in animal husbandry did they play a small but significant role. The production of foodstuffs thus remained in African hands, and its regional commercialisation remained within the framework of a free market.[12]

In the 1920s several experiments in 'modernisation' were attempted in African agriculture. These included a cooperative movement, an extension of the transportation network for cotton cultivation, the development of palm-groves, and some limited local support for a rural African bourgeoisie. In Katanga, a rejection of the idea of native reserves led to a liberal attitude to African agriculture. Simple manual machines and private ownership of land were encouraged. The policy was aimed at nourishing Katanga industrial workers without hampering their recruitment.[13] The rural economy of Kasai Province was based on palm-oil and cassava production for the urban market in Léopoldville, while that of Equateur Province was based on harvesting copal and palm-nuts. The Brussels officials responsible for colonial agriculture favoured compulsory crop-growing. Other interests preferred a free market with both African

9 Mulambu-Mvuluya, 'Cultures obligatoires et colonisation dans l'ex-Congo belge', *Cahiers du CEDAF* (Centre d'Etudes et de Documentation Africaine), 6–7, 1974.
10 J.-L. Vellut, 'Le Zaire à la périphérie du capitalisme: quelques perspectives historiques', *Edha*, i, 1975, pp. 114–51.
11 Mboyo Mutuana Malungu, 'La Politique de l'administration envers le commerce africain au Katanga d'après l'inventaire d'une collection provenant des Archives Régionales du Shaba (1910–1960)', M.A. thesis, Lubumbashi, 1972–3.
12 B. Jewsiewicki, 'Le Colonat agricole européen au Congo belge, 1910–1960: questions politiques et économiques', *JAH*, xx, 1979, 559–71.
13 B. Jewsiewicki, 'Unequal Development: Capitalism and the Katanga Economy', in *The Roots of Rural Poverty in Central and Southern Africa*, R. Palmer and N. Parson (eds), London, 1977, pp. 317–44; J.-L. Vellut has a different opinion in 'Développement et sous-développement au Zaire: notes préliminaires pour une perspective historique', in *La dépendance de l'Afrique et les moyens d'y remédier*, V. Mudimbe (ed.), Paris, 1980, pp. 161–7.

agriculture and a European plantation sector. The two models coexisted.[14] Basically, however, the central administration was preoccupied with the mining industry, the export revenues of which overtook that of plant products after 1915. Priority, therefore, was given to railway construction and worker recruitment.

The economic crisis of the 1930s profoundly changed the colonial economy. International markets were modified, Belgian investments were reduced, workers returned to the villages, the volume and value of mineral exports dropped, and the exports of natural products increased. The system of compulsory planting was extended in the Belgian Congo, as in so many other Central African colonies. Processing and marketing became the monopoly of European companies. The free agricultural market for rural African producers disappeared. By 1934–1935 the administration exercised direct control over African village production.[15]

Agricultural policy in the 1940s sought to increase local consumer markets and the buying power of farmers, at the same time moving away from direct compulsion.[16] Europeans withdrew progressively from direct agricultural production and marketing and concentrated more on the profitable processing business. African soil had become exhausted, and villages deteriorated. In spite of these conditions, African agriculture, now indirectly controlled, continued to produce raw materials and city foodstuffs outside the capitalist mode of production.

Experiments in official support for peasant production had been considered in the 1930s but became official policy in the 1950s. Parcels of land were assigned to families who were required to follow a pre-established crop rotation, a system called the *paysannat*. The state sponsored cooperatives and organised the production of African perennials such as palm products, coffee and Hevea rubber for processing by a local European entrepreneur. In the 1950s, the production of coffee by small African farms received the support of the administration, which wanted to encourage the birth of an African rural middle class. Yet although the form changed, European administrative management continued to dominate African agriculture.

DEMOGRAPHY AND SOCIETY

Where high population densities occur in Central Africa, they are the result

14 B. Jewsiewicki, *Agriculture itinérante et économie capitaliste*, vol. I, Lubumbashi, 1975; for a good example see Congrès Colonial National, *Compte rendu des séances*, 4ᵉ session, Brussels, 1935.
15 Jewsiewicki, *Agriculture itinérante*, pp. 184–206; for price evolution see J. P. Peemans, *Diffusion du progrès et convergence des prix: Congo-Belgique*, Louvain, 1970.
16 *Plan décennal pour le développement économique et social du Congo belge*, Brussels, 1949, pp. xii–lxiii.

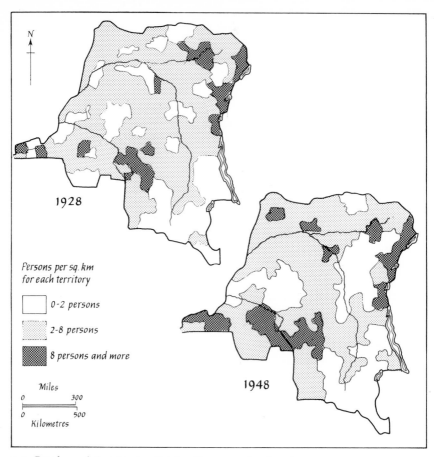

N

*Persons per sq. km
for each territory*

☐ *0-2 persons*

▨ *2-8 persons*

▮ *8 persons and more*

Miles
0   300
0   500
Kilometres

1928

1948

3:2   Rural population density, Belgian Congo, 1928 and 1948

of a slow demographic increase over a long period of time.[17] Accumulation probably resulted from an efficient use of the environment and the adaptation of social relations. Sometimes high population density corresponded to a heavy concentration on good agricultural land, as in eastern Zaire; but in other areas, as in the central basin, the opposite situation occurred; here agricultural land was scarce and the population tended to cluster where it could survive. Agriculture was never able to play a dominant role in the pre-colonial food system of the basin.[18] The demographic structures were so rooted in the past that even the great socio-

17 We have no reliable evaluation of population, see Sabakinu Kivilu, 'Les Sources de l'histoire démographique du Zaire', *Etudes d'histoire africaine*, vi, 1974, 119–36. The Randles hypothesis is not proven; see 'La Civilisation bantou, son essor et son déclin', *Annales: Economies, Sociétés, Civilisations*, xxix, 1974, 267–81.
18 B. Jewsiewicki (ed), *Contributions to a History of Agriculture and Fishing in Central Africa*, special issue of *African Economic History*, vii, 1979. See also Map 3:2 of this chapter.

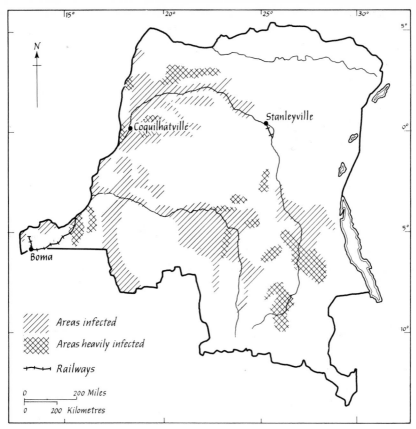

3:3 Distribution of sleeping sickness, Belgian Congo, 1912

economic upheavals of the nineteenth and early twentieth centuries were incapable of erasing them. Recent changes may even have increased existing disparities.

Nineteenth-century emigration and the rupture of societies contributed to the on-going demographic transformation. The violent economic and political reorganisation of the northern savanna under the impact of expanded Sudan–Egyptian trade moved rather than destroyed the region's dense population.[19] In the eastern Zaire basin, and in the Kivu, Rwanda and Burundi regions, heavy population densities persisted. Even the disruptions of the Atlantic slave-trade did not destroy the demographic potential of northern Kasai. Early colonial expansion had a disastrous impact on the lower Zaire region. High densities were none the less re-established when porterage, railway construction, and sleeping sickness

19 D. Cordell, 'Dar al-Kuti: a History of the Slave Trade and State Formation on the Islamic Frontier in Northern Equatorial Africa', Ph. D. thesis, Madison, Wisconsin, 1976, to be published by Wisconsin University Press.

ceased to take their toll. The economic development of this region was facilitated by the permanence of the rural demographic landscape, by the diversity of its resources and the adaptability of its social life. Colonisation brought about certain modifications, such as the regrouping of villages along paths of communication, but scarcely any fundamental change. During the early colonial occupation, however, the rubber and ivory business did cause a definite demographic crisis. It struck, more severely, and with more lasting effect, in the less-populated regions, particularly the equatorial forest, Kwango and Kwilu, thus stressing their demographic fragility.

In the field of health, sleeping sickness and the Spanish influenza epidemic of 1918 profoundly affected the demographic situation.[20] The epidemic diseases coincided with the declining ability of local societies to be self-sufficient in food production. At the same time, the temporary abandonment of villages, long-distance porterage and the intensive recruitment of workers all provoked the spread of disease and the deterioration of hygiene. Diseases spread along paths used by migrant workers and soldiers, along navigable waterways and in commercial centres. African communities which had recently settled to trade along waterways were either destroyed or dispersed. Medical services arrived slowly, and were almost entirely oriented towards the struggle against these two great epidemics.[21] Some concern for a balanced diet for colonial workers was felt in the 1920s, but only in 1940 did such matters become the subject of scientific research.

In the mid-1920s, a crisis in the availability of workers caused a census to be taken. A policy of conservation and reproduction of the labour force was envisaged. Demographic study showed that the zones of low density had a low birth-rate and a fragile or negative rate of growth. On the other hand, heavily-populated zones had a tendency towards growth. Although certain pathogenic factors of recent origin, such as venereal disease, were in part responsible for negative growth, disease relating to changed sexual behaviour was less important than the relationship between society and ecology. Subsistence economies were based on a fragile equilibrium. The balance was frequently adjusted between agriculture, hunting, fishing and the gathering of fruits and vegetables. When destroyed, this balance could not be restored since it was incompatible with the demands of the colonial economy. Colonial policies which were designed to overcome population loss were sometimes counter-productive. Administrators mobilised labour when it should have been engaged in the harvest. The cultivation of single

20 This epidemic killed 5 per cent of the African population and only 2 per cent of the European population of the Congo; see Royaume de Belgique, *Documents Parlementaires, Chambre des Représentants, session 1920–21*, no 441, p. 19.
21 We lack a history of medical services in the Belgian Congo; R. J. Cornet, *Bwana Muganga: hommes en blanc en Afrique noire*, Brussels, 1971, is apologetic.

food crops predominated over that of several, which would have resulted in a more balanced diet. The zones in which cassava became the principal food developed low birth-rates. In order to forestall famine and to create a trade in foodstuffs which would meet the needs of salaried employees, the administration encouraged and often imposed the production of cassava. Its high productivity was well known, and its cultivation released African workers for employment elsewhere. The high domestic labour requirement for its preparation and its low nutritional value were not considered.

Agricultural populations were unevenly integrated into the colonial world. Those situated outside the early colonial gathering economy and

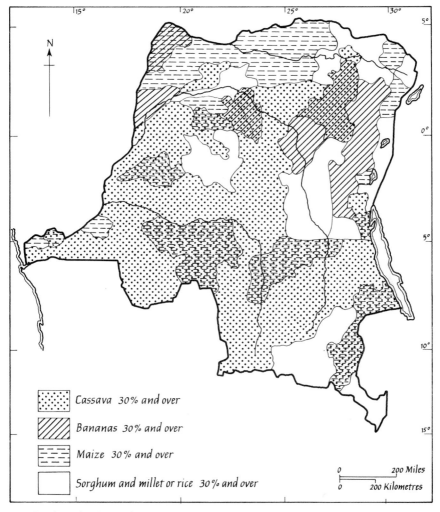

Cassava 30% and over

Bananas 30% and over

Maize 30% and over

Sorghum and millet or rice 30% and over

0   200 Miles

0   200 Kilometres

3:4 Food production, Belgian Congo, c. 1950

mining zones were incorporated into the system in large numbers only in the 1920s. The eastern Kasai populations were brought in only when the Bukama–Port Francqui railway opened in 1928. Integration into a market economy was much more rapid along the lines of communication, both in Katanga and in the lower Congo. Not all societies suffered nutritional deficiencies. It is true that Africans lost their poultry and small animals to Europeans, but their place in the local diet had been relatively minor.[22] In spite of colonial economic and social pressures, agricultural populations did preserve some control over their working hours and their diverse food production. Despite frequent appearances to the contrary, the colonial administration did not attempt to kill the milch-cow which Africans represented.

COLONIAL TERRITORIAL REORGANISATION

Of the five zones[23] into which the Zaire basin was divided in the late nineteenth century, only the river zone was kept almost completely within the political territory of the Congo State. The other zones, penetrated by the Swahili, the Luso-Africans, the lower Zaire traders and the northern *jallaba* traders, respectively, were dismembered by rival colonial states, by the use of military force, administrative coercion and economic manipulation. From the 1890s, the contemporary political and cultural groupings, the kingdoms and empires of the nineteenth century were dismantled in order to partition Central Africa among the colonial powers. Colonial intrusion was the second great shock for such rural societies, within fifty years. Many of the regional cultures, which were in the process of becoming embryonic national ones each with its vernacular language, political system and commercial practices, were destroyed.[24] Local decentralising tendencies were used, treason was encouraged and assassination employed to eliminate important political leaders. Leaders of basic social groups survived, but the colonial state nevertheless created a political void. It was filled by both black and white adventurers, who used armed bands to terrify the population into submission. This was the fate both of the zones delegated to concessionary or chartered organisations and of those areas administered by the state.

Political confusion and social fragmentation lasted until 1910. Territorial reorganisation was not attempted until 1918. The state, however, still remained weak, and its place was taken by missionaries, commercial

22 During the 1920s and 1930s big game was exterminated by professional hunters hired by European companies in order to supply meat to its workers; see Archives Africaines, Brussels, *Questionnaire aux employeurs, 1927.*
23 B. Jewsiewicki, 'Une Conception d'histoire économique et sociale du Zaire moderne', *Likundoli: Enquêtes d'Histoire Zairoise*, ii, 1974, 206–7.
24 Mumbanza mwa Bawele, 'L'Histoire des peuples riverains de l'entre Zaire-Ubangi', Ph.D. thesis, Lubumbashi, 1981.

groups, African auxiliaries and poor whites, all trying to create their own 'little empires'.[25] The disappearance of the concessionary companies brought little relief. The administration tried but failed to be omnipresent, its efforts hampered by the rapid turnover of poorly-qualified personnel, by lack of financial resources and by difficulties in communication. Economic production continued thanks to systematic banditry, in which the state remained an accomplice. In particular, its activities included the recruitment of workers for railway construction. Between 1910 and 1920 mining production was concentrated in the north-eastern corner of the country and in southern Katanga. In Kasai, palm products were brought by way of navigable waterways.[26]

Slowness of transportation and difficulty of communication made centralised administration of the country impossible. When Belgium had gained control of the Congo, these difficulties had resulted in the division of the colony into four zones, administered by vice-governors. Each region, with the exception of the equatorial one, combined known mineral resources with agricultural production. Each one possessed an autonomous transportation network connected with the 'national way' along the Zaire river. In 1920–1921 Governor-General Lippens awarded substantial autonomy to each region from the administrative capital in Boma.[27] This was made possible by the arrival of an increased number of qualified civil servants, by the reform of the army and by the massive influx of Belgian capital. This provincial autonomy, however, was contrary to the fundamental tendency of Belgian capital to be concentrated in three holding companies. Although these did not immediately opt for administrative centralisation, the government quickly came to realise that it was necessary for economic control of the colony.

During the economic crisis of the 1930s, centralisation was re-imposed from the new capital in Léopoldville. Opposition to centralisation was overruled, and the four vice-governments were replaced by six new provinces which were no longer economically autonomous. Katanga, having lost the Lomani region, was now more closely bound to the central government. The old Orientale province lost Kivu and Maniema (now reorganised as a separate Kivu Costermansville Province). These had previously been the regions with the strongest tendencies towards autonomy.

25 J.-L. Vellut speaks of armed bands; see his *Un Exercice d'histoire sociale: à l'ouest du Lualaba 1915–1930*, Lubumbashi, 1973, mimeographed.

26 J. Stengers, 'La Belgique et le Congo, politique coloniale et décolonisation', in *Histoire de la Belgique contemporaine 1914–1970*, Brussels, 1974, pp. 391–440; J.-L. Vellut, 'Les Belges au Congo (1885–1960)', in A. d'Haenens (ed.), *La Belgique: sociétés et cultures depuis 150 ans*, Brussels, 1980, pp. 260–5.

27 See M. Lippens, *Notes sur le gouvernement du Congo, 1921–1922*, Ghent, 1923; also *Notre politique coloniale*, Brussels, 1928; he was the first important Belgian politician to become a Governor-General of the Congo.

3:5 Administrative subdivisions, Belgian Congo, 1926 and 1933, and Zaire, 1981

A new 'African' territorial organisation also appeared during the 1930s. Although apparently based on traditional societies, it actually reflected the new lines of communication and the new economic centres of gravity. The region to the east of the Lomami river, including the former Swahili zone and Katanga, was based on elements of cultural unity dating from the end of the nineteenth century. Between 1910 and 1930 a basic economic unity developed out of the need of the mining economy for foodstuffs and men. The growth of a national river–rail system from Stanleyville to Elisabethville replaced the Rhodesian rail network as the carrier of exports and contributed to integration. The spread of the Swahili language, and later the Kitawala religion,[28] along the rivers and railways resulted in a distinctive urban culture. The European population of this zone also acquired a regional unity, embracing both company employees and farmers.

The north-western forest and northern savanna zones were structured by a network of waterways and savanna roads, which were developed in the 1930s by the Uele railway company. The northern economy evolved first through the gathering of ivory, rubber and copal, and then, after 1920 through cotton and wild palm products into a plantation economy. By the end of the 1930s the cultivation of palm and rubber trees replaced gathering. The dominant vernacular language was Lingala, which spread widely through its use by the administration and the missions.

Lower Congo formed a semi-autonomous commercial and agricultural zone within the colony. Its economy particularly attracted migrant Angolans. Cultural unity was manifested by the use of the Kikongo language. This unity came to be reflected both in the religious vitality of Kimbanguism[29] from 1921 and in the politics of the 1950s.

Kwango-Kwilu and Kasai were a buffer-zone during the colonial period, even though they possessed a certain autonomy. Before the colonial partition, Kasai had been an integral part of the Luso-African zone in Central Africa. During the colonial period, however, it was constantly torn, both economically and politically, between Katanga and Lower Congo. Its labour force and foodstuffs were bitterly disputed by these two economic areas, after the Bukama–Port Francqui railway was put into service. This situation was responsible for the extroverted character of the Kasai economy.[30] It led to the dispersal of Kasai peoples throughout the colony. Kiluba became their vernacular language, and Luba their ethnic identity outside the region. The internal tensions which led to the Luba-Lulua conflict of 1959–1960 resulted in the creation of the two Kasaian administrative units of present-day Zaire. This division roughly

28 See chapter by Vellut below.
29 *Ibid.*
30 Tshundolela Epanya, 'Politique coloniale, économie capitaliste et sous-développement au Congo belge: cas du Kasai (1920–1959)', Ph.D. thesis, Lubumbashi, 1980.

corresponds to the line of demarcation between Katanga and Lower Congo influences. The intensive economy of Kasai, based on agriculture, cotton, foodstuffs and diamond-mining, was never a full counterweight to these external pressures.

The influence of the great companies on cotton, palm products and mining is difficult to trace exactly on the map. They were clearly engraved, however, on the minds of the people. The boundaries between missionary congregations, especially between Catholic and Protestant zones, were also very clearly established in social space. They profoundly affected rural history through conversion, teaching and the spread of certain vernacular languages.[31] Comparable new African social and cultural forces were even less visible to the colonial eye. The most obvious was the influence of religious movements in three large regions: in the east, Kitawala dominated; in Lower Congo and in Equateur region, Kimbanguism was most important; and in Kwango-Kwilu-Kasai, 'traditional', non-Christian religions persisted.[32]

LAND, WORK AND CAPITAL

The analysis of rural economies and societies involves both the relations of production and technological changes. During the colonial period a real separation of producers from the means of production and the destruction of their rural social environment occurred. This brought about the creation during the 1940s of an almost unlimited supply of labour at subsistence wages. The technological changes, however, were minor in terms of rural, non-capitalist production, and in some cases they were non-existent. The African peasant entered the colonial period with the hoe, and he came out of it with the hoe.[33] A considerable number of new plants were introduced, but the technology remained unchanged. The 'modernisation' effort was

---

31 Mumbanza mwa Bawele, 'La Contribution des Zairois à l'oeuvre d'évangélisation et la prospérité des établissements missionnaires: la Mission catholique de Libanda (1933–1960)', *Etudes d'histoire africaine*, vi, 1974, 225–74; M. D. Markowitz, *Cross and Sword: the Political Role of Christian Missions in the Belgian Congo 1908–1960*, Stanford, California, 1973; A. Gaspar, 'Assimilation and discrimination: Catholic education in Angola and the Congo' in *African Reactions to Missionary Education*, E. H. Berman (ed.), New York, 1975, pp. 54–74; G. Samba, 'Tolérance religieuse et intérêts politiques belges au Kibali-Ituri (1900–1940)', *Etudes Zairoises*, 1973, 92–112; B. A. Yates, 'The origins of language policy in Zaire', *Journal of Modern African Studies*, xviii, 1980, 257–79.
32 J. Vansina, 'Les Mouvements religieux kuba (Kasai) à l'époque coloniale', *Etudes d'histoire africaine*, iii, 1971, 155–87; J. Vansina, 'Lukoshi-Lupambula: histoire d'un culte religieux dans les régions du Kasai et du Kwango (1920–1970)', *idem*, v, 1973, 51–97; see also Munayi Muntu-Mouji, 'Le Mouvement kimbanguiste dans le Haut-Kasai 1921–1960', Ph.D. thesis, Aix-en-Provence, 1974.
33 M. Klein (ed.), Introduction to *Peasants in Africa: Historical and Contemporary Perspectives*, Beverly Hills, California, 1980, p. 25, quoting W. Rodney, *How Europe Underdeveloped Africa*, London, 1972, p. 239.

essentially directed toward export crops for industry. Even more important, the same production techniques were used in a variety of new environments. This brought heavy pressures to bear on the land and on society. The extent of arable land diminished, whereas pressure caused agricultural production to increase. Land alienated to capitalist agriculture represented only a small part of the territory, but it was often in the best and most accessible areas.[34] Agricultural industries, such as palm-oil plantations, deprived itinerant agriculturalists of the important natural resources of the forest.[35] This was true on the large concessions, and even more on the small ones.

The Catholic missions and individual colonists chose the richest parcels. The rush of colonists to densely populated Kivu at the end of the 1920s quickly created a typical 'colonial peasantisation'.[36] The regrouping of villages in official locations and the imposition of a market economy brought about increased pressure on attractive land. Commercial cultivation was most profitable closest to the roads. Elsewhere transportation of the harvest to a point of sale quickly became a thankless task. The real price which a peasant received for the harvest was sometimes lower than the market value of the days he had spent transporting it. In certain isolated regions, peasants sometimes cultivated fields according to directives which they had received, but they left them unharvested since they had not been specifically directed to harvest them and it was unprofitable on their own account. Head taxes and the monetisation of social relations such as bridewealth and fines nevertheless often forced people to sell their crops for cash at any prices. At the same time, government restricted local small-scale processing of certain types of agricultural products such as rice or palm fruits, and Africans were forced to sell them as raw materials.[37] After 1935, road construction brought rural communities into closer contact with markets. The burden of transportation was lightened, and village locations were stabilised, but the local road construction effort had been placed on the rural communities. The over-exploitation of land, especially in cotton-growing areas, became so acute in the late 1940s that even the cotton companies considered turning to free peasant production. The director-general of the Agricultural Institute himself reported in a confidential note to the Provincial Council at

34 See as far back as 1939, G. Malengreau, 'Le Régime foncier dans la société indigène', *Congo*, ii, 1939, 40–6.
35 M. Merlier, *Le Congo de la colonisation belge à l'indépendance*, Paris, 1963, offers a very good analysis; see also P. Demunter, *Masses rurales et luttes politiques au Zaire: le processus de politisation des masses rurales au Bas-Zaire*, Paris, 1975.
36 E. Sosne, 'Colonial peasantization and contemporary underdevelopment: a view from a Kivu village', in *Zaire: the Political Economy of Underdevelopment*, G. Gran (ed.), New York, 1979, pp. 189–212.
37 Jewsiewicki, *Agriculture itinérante*, pp. 167–94.

Stanleyville on the dangers of soil exhaustion.[38] African agricultural production was little improved by research; for years, any such research was oriented towards plantation agriculture and export crops. Only after the Second World War did the Agricultural Institute concern itself with the peasant production of foodstuffs.

THE DESTRUCTION OF SHIFTING AGRICULTURE

For a long time African agriculture was considered to be barbaric and simplistic. The profound rationality of shifting agricultural techniques of production was not understood by Europeans, who were convinced of their own technological superiority. Land had traditionally been renewed by lengthy fallow periods and only occasionally with organic fertilisers. This had important consequences for landed property and agrarian structure. Contrary to European belief, itinerant agriculture was better suited to the constraints of population need, available land, the labour force and relations of production. From the point of view of social relationships the rationality of shifting agriculture was evident.[39] It preserved a supple relationship between lineage or clan groups and villages. It was adapted to the interrelated activities of hunting, fishing and food-gathering.

By the middle of the nineteenth century the development of commercial and military activities related to the changing pattern of external demand intensified the local use of resources such as cultivated land and intensively managed ponds. Such activities increased the demand for labour. This resulted in the development of domestic slavery, in social inequalities and in family ownership of ponds and cultivated land. By investing work in a piece of land, an individual and his legal heirs often received exclusive rights to its use. Shifting agriculture among the Azande was varied, rich and complex and was a good example of the potentialities of the system. The sophistication of their labour organisation through 'clients' created, by the end of the nineteenth century, a surplus of foodstuffs for military expeditions.[40]

It was colonisation which modified shifting agriculture and brought a backward movement and a simplification of techniques. Traditional intensive agriculture disappeared when colonial production took over the land and forcibly transferred part of the labour force to the capitalist sector. The same fate affected intensive forms of food-gathering and fishing. Compulsory cultivation ruined the equilibrium of shifting agriculture.

38 F. Jurion, 'L'Organisation de l'agriculture indigène: note pour le Conseil de Province de Stanleyville, 14 May 1945', in Archives de la Division Régionale des Affaires Politiques du Haut-Zaïre, Kisangani.
39 P. De Schlippe, *Shifting Cultivation in Africa: the Zande System of Agriculture*, London, 1956.
40 D. Lloyd, 'The Precolonial Economic History of the Avongara-Zande c. 1750–1916', Ph.D. thesis, Berkeley, California, 1977.

New plants, new agricultural calendars and new crop rotations which took no account of local situations destroyed the complex and delicate balance. Passive resistance, the refusal of all innovation and working to rule constituted the best protection for exploited populations.[41]

PRIMITIVE ACCUMULATION AND THE FIRST STAGE OF COLONIAL 'MODERNISATION', 1910–1933

A regression in agricultural flexibility was the curious legacy of modernisation. The administration transformed rural societies into vast work camps rationally managed to meet exterior needs. Man became a labouring and reproductive force. The misery of the peasant was the basis for the political 'stability' of the colonial and post-colonial governments. It ensured the articulation of the colonial economy with the world economy.

In order to understand the role of agriculture and of peasant society in Belgian colonial production, it is necessary to study the local mechanisms of primitive accumulation. By the time when the Leopoldian predator-state gave way in 1908 to the Belgian colony, the best-quality rubber and ivory resources had been extracted. They were replaced by a new exploitation of African agriculture. From 1910 to 1933, the 'liberal' phase gave rise to several sometimes contradictory policies. Five enormous concessions were granted to the Congo subsidiary of Unilever, and many smaller ones to other agro-commercial companies. The company benefited from a monopoly on buying local products, which it then processed. It was legally required to develop its concession by establishing man-made plantations and processing installations. A commercial monopoly and the urgent need to develop the African monetary economy during the 1920s in order to gather taxes allowed concessions to escape from government control. In 1920, cotton companies received monopoly control over purchases of cotton grown by Africans in their own zones. In return, the companies were to establish ginning facilities and to create a network of roads. The principal company involved was Cotonco.

In 1928 the colony and the private consortium of Empain created a Kivu National Committee to manage land holdings, exploit forests and develop transport. When Belgian agricultural colonists thronged into Kivu, the colony alone was incapable of 'rationally' allocating resources and settler land. A para-statal organisation was therefore set up on the model of the Katanga Special Committee to protect the interests of big capital in the region beyond the territory of the Great Lakes Railway Company.[42]

41 'The poorer you look the better you are protected against exploitation' was the principle of all under-privileged people; see F. Braudel, *Civilisation matérielle, économie et capitalisme, XVe–XVIIIe siècles, I Les structures du quotidien: Le possible et l'impossible*, Paris, 1979, pp. 44–5.
42 E. Mendiaux, 'Le Comité National du Kivu', *Zaïre*, 1956, 803–15, 927–64.

Collaboration between the state and capital had only begun. Its development required proof that cotton and other export crops could be cultivated by Africans. Large-scale capital needed guaranteed supplies of raw materials, and so the system advanced to compulsory cultivation. Weaknesses in the infrastructure delayed the development. Major railways, including the Bukama–Port Francqui and the Great Lakes railway, were completed at the beginning of the 1930s, but the rural road network was constructed only after 1935 by rural community labour. Meanwhile, labour shortages increased the cost of porterage. The administration always gave priority to labour supplies for the mining sector and railway construction, yet the African cultivator lay at the base of the industrial economy.

In Katanga, attempts to introduce small-scale settler agriculture failed. Only a few small and medium-sized European plantations survived during the 1920s, due to high food prices. Settlers and planters were not encouraged, and from 1921 priority was given to large-scale agricultural capital which bought and processed African produce.

Despite the introduction of compulsory cultivation, much African agriculture remained a free market activity. The purchase of foodstuffs remained for the most part in the hands of small merchants. The concentration of salaried employees in urban and industrial centres, like Léopoldville, Elisabethville and Kilo-Moto, raised the price of foodstuffs. African agriculture responded positively, though its capacity was limited. Commercial African agriculture was restricted mainly to Katanga and the Léopoldville region. Some primitive accumulation began locally in Kasai and in north Kivu, where certain chiefs persuaded their subjects to cultivate cotton and coffee. Some initial agricultural and commercial capital was accumulated by cooperatives, but that direction was not encouraged by the administration.

In industrial Katanga, the administration hesitated in choosing between two rural policies. One was to establish native reserves on the South African pattern; the other was to create 'model' villages. The village alternative was preferred. New populations of immigrants from regions considered to be over-populated, such as Rwanda, were to be settled under European surveillance. They were to produce foodstuffs and serve as a pool of industrial labour. In rural areas model villages were established with local populations. Simple machine presses and gins were locally introduced in Katanga and in Orientale Province to free rural labourers for the industrial centres. In those regions a few cooperatives and even experimental savings banks were established. They allowed some local accumulation by chiefs, but were fundamentally intended to further integration into the European-ruled economy.

THE RURAL ECONOMY AND THE INDUSTRIAL SECTOR, 1933–1950

By 1928 it was clear that only an over-all strategy could align African agriculture with the needs of the evolving colonial capitalist economy. In order to resolve critical manpower needs, fight the cost of foodstuffs and support commercialisation of agricultural products, it was necessary to harness the rural economy to European capitalism. In Katanga a few colonial dissidents favoured proletarianisation. The majority of white society, as well as the government, were opposed to the idea of a black proletariat or a black middle class. Measures directed against small businesses began to eliminate the small middle class. The administration began in 1928 systematically to plan the exploitation of African rural societies.

After the world economic crisis, state intervention became effective in the rural sector, when rapid centralisation of the administration, the return of unemployed industrial workers to their villages, and the ruin of small white businesses created conditions in which state management could emerge. Compulsory cultivation and buying monopolies became widespread. In this way, the state guaranteed the necessary cotton, rice and palm-kernel supplies to the factories. Near the urban areas informal monopolies purchased all foodstuffs.[43] The Kasai market, which had been opened by the Bukama–Port Francqui railway in 1928, provided a good example of colonial agricultural action.[44] Local economic consultative committees and the administration planned agricultural needs and fixed agricultural prices. The minimum purchase price, determined to protect the producer, was never exceeded by monopoly buyers. Head taxes, special tax rates and all kinds of fines drove people to sell agricultural goods and labour at any prices. For all practical purposes, the official freedom to sell one's harvest was effectively eliminated. The peasant had no alternative but to sell his produce at the minimum price, or to leave the village and sell his labour. 'Freedom' was carefully controlled by passbooks and work contracts. A peasant who chose the city could remain there only while he was employed. If he lost his job, he had to return to his village. During the 1930s, separation of producers from their means of production came about in the Belgian Congo without permanent proletarianisation. The pain which the system inflicted on rural societies was clearly identified by the reported reluctance of the 'natives' to grow uneconomic crops.

From the colonial perspective, the system devised in the 1930s 'worked'. The Congo survived the world depression thanks to a significant increase in agricultural exports. Peasants produced export crops and foodstuffs at one

43 Kalulambi Pongo, 'Le Problème vivrier du Katanga: les Commissions vivrières et la planification agricole au Kasai 1946–1954', M.A. thesis, Lubumbashi, 1977; also Tshundolela Epanya, 'Politique coloniale'.
44 H. Nicolai and J. Jacques, *La Transformation des paysages congolais par le chemin de fer, l'exemple du BCK*, Brussels, 1954.

quarter of the previous price.[45] They were also forced to construct local feeder roads in order to facilitate further capitalist penetration of the rural economies.

The war effort of 1940–1945 ruined the land and exhausted the people of the Belgian Congo.[46] Emigration became the obvious sign of a situation which had become intolerable for the rural population. It was henceforth impossible to maintain the usual forms of rural production. The *paysannats* seemed to offer one kind of solution. They brought some public investment in infrastructure and hygiene. Truly agricultural forms of support, such as fertiliser, mechanisation and cooperative development, occurred only in a few pilot regions. To many, the *paysannat* seemed to be little more than a sophisticated form of agricultural bondage since it completed the process of separating the peasants from their land. Compulsory cultivation was replaced by new forms of constraint and directives which were even more rigid for the peasant. Members of the *paysannats* were settled on plots chosen by an agronomist, but often, due to the lack of specialists, it was an administrator who made the choice. In many cases, this parcelling out of the land did not take into account customary property rights. Peasants were thus randomly dispossessed of their land. The technological benefits which should have followed this agrarian reform did not occur. Some increase in agricultural production took place, but the lot of the peasant was scarcely improved. In fact, peasants became even more dependent on the power of the state's agents.[47]

In some sectors of the colonial economy, producer cooperatives were established. The newly-introduced African plantations of Hevea rubber were one example. This system avoided the necessity for salaried employees, and shifted the risk of price variations to African producers of raw latex. Its processing and marketing remained in European hands. In spite of violent opposition by the white colonists, the production of coffee underwent a similar Africanisation.[48] Some African coffee-growers managed to create viable plantations and even began to develop their own processing facilities. This middle-class minority took advantage of

45 Jewsiewicki, 'Unequal Development', pp. 335–7; see also Map 3:4.
46 Tshibangu Kabet, 'L'Effort de guerre 1940–1945 en territoire de Likasi: ses incidences socio-économiques', M.A. thesis, Lubumbashi, 1971–2; M. Lovens, 'L'Effort militaire de guerre, au Congo belge (1940–1944)', in *Cahiers du CEDAF*, 7–8, 1975; J. Stengers, for the Académie Royale des Sciences d'Outre-Mer (Brussels), is editing an important book on this period.
47 O. Tulippe and J. Wilmet, 'Géographie de l'agriculture en Afrique centrale: essai de synthèse', *Bulletin de la société belge d'études géographiques*, ii, 1964, 301–73; H. Beguin, *La Mise en valeur du Sud-Est du Kasai*, Brussels, 1960; J. Wilmet, *Systèmes agraires et techniques agricoles au Katanga*, Brussels, 1963; the bibliography by B. de Halleux *et al.*, *Bibliographie analytique pour l'agronomie tropicale: Zaire, Rwanda, Burundi*, Brussels, 1973–7, 3 volumes, is very useful.
48 Tshibanda-Mbwebwe, 'Aux Origines de l'introduction des cultures de café et de thé en milieux indigènes du Kivu (1953–1955)', *Likundoli: enquêtes d'histoire zairoise*, ii, 1974, 181–90.

European institutions to accumulate capital through small-scale business and advance their cause through access to African chiefly power. A lack of agricultural credit, however, delayed such developments until the very end of the colonial period. African land ownership under written law was too limited to allow the breakthrough of a true rural middle class.[49] Only in the last decade of the colonial régime did government opposition relax. In the 1950s, however, so-called 'reforms' worsened relations between African producers and European merchants. The reform of cotton policy enforced from 1949 to 1951 provided exemplary proof. Henceforth, though partially protected against price fluctuations, peasants found themselves providing a disguised credit to the cotton companies through a trading board COGERCO.

SOCIAL STRUCTURES AND CLASS CONSCIOUSNESS

In colonial society, the separation of races obscured all other relationships of inequality. In 1933 the Minister of Colonies insisted that 'anything which might diminish the prestige of the White Man in the eyes of the Black must be carefully avoided'.[50] Colonial crimes attracted colonial punishments:

> On 9 March 1931 I arrested one Konka, Leonard, whose words compromised public tranquillity and the stability of our institutions at Kole.... He made natives believe that in a few months they would become 'whites' ... and those in European service would remain black, thus encouraging them to quit service. I was obliged to chain the detainee for spreading the rumour ... that he would return to Heaven whence he came.[51]

The official ideology of colonisation established a line of demarcation between 'civilised' and 'savage', not between white and black. The assimilation of Western culture, its ways of life and its ideology was presented as the natural escape from the new inequality. On it rested the symbolic power of Boula Matari, the 'rock-breaker', which the colonial state represented.[52] Yet this cultural division of colonial society was never accepted by white society; whites preferred to practise racial and biological segregation.

The city and its 'modern' world were the source of civilisation, while the

49 B. Jewsiewicki and Muhima Faradje, 'Les Planteurs individuels de Bobandana', *Likundoli: archives et documents*, ii, 1974, pp. 125–68; for a different opinion see P. Harroy, 'Développement rural et acculturation', *Bulletin de l'ARSOM*, 1979, 185–96.
50 Minister of Colonies P. Tshoffen to the Governor-General, Brussels, Sept. 1933, p. 2, in Archives Régionales du Shaba, Lubumbashi.
51 'Rapport sur la conduite du nommé Konka Léonard, Kole, 9 mars 1931', in Archives du CND, Mbandaka.
52 J. Crokaert, *Bula Matari ou le Congo belge*, Brussels, 1929. On Boula Matari languages (vernacular languages such as Lingala) see Yates, 'The origins of language policy'.

rural areas remained a 'traditional' world, the world of dupes. A 1931 decree gave a special status to the African urban centres. The awareness of this inequality increasingly influenced the behaviour of peasants. Rural emigration increased. Education, especially that provided by urban schools, began to be considered as a means of social progress. After the Second World War numerous adolescents were sent to live with their urban relatives. In this way they could continue their education in the hope of making a place for themselves in the 'civilised' world.[53] This tendency increased even as white society rejected the claims of the 'detribalised' Africans to equality.

The perception of inequality corresponded to an economic and social reality. It reproduced the dominant ideology, assured the continued exploitation of the rural world and perpetuated white domination. The 1930s saw the emergence of the peasantry as a class, albeit one without class organisation, and African peasants developed the first signs of a class consciousness. They manifested collective attitudes which, in spite of regional and ethnic differences, expressed the same view of the relations of production and of exploitation.[54] This peasant consciousness was particularly expressed in the Bushiri rising of 1944 which promised an end to miseries and an access to riches. Bushiri claimed to be sent by God to save the black race.[55] The colonial judicial authority, worried by the effectiveness of this ideology, advised that 'revolts occurring in any corner of Congo have reverberations that are more general and profound than formerly; repression should be carried out with sufficient violence to instill the necessary intimidation'.[56]

The growth of class awareness did not proceed smoothly. In the 1950s, ground was lost as the colonial state manipulated power to retard the consolidation of peasants as a social class. Administrative constraints subjected a rural world to a capitalist economy. For this reason the state favoured the formation of a false social consciousness based on the myth of

53 For a modern history of education in the Congo, see *Etudes d'histoire africaine*, vi, 1974, G. Feltz (ed.); also his, 'Un échec de l'implantation scolaire en milieu rural: le cas de la Lulua et du Katanga central de 1920 à 1960', *CJAS*, xiii, 1980, 441–59; B. A. Yates, 'Shifting goals of industrial education in the Congo 1878–1908', *African Studies Review*, xxi, 1978, 33–48; D. de Failly, 'Histoire de l'enseignement agricole au Congo', *Cahiers congolais de la recherche et du développement*, xii, 1970, 100–33.
54 B. Jewsiewicki, 'Political consciousness among the African peasantry in the Belgian Congo', *Review of African Political Economy*, xix, 1980, 23–32; Mulambu Mvuluya, 'Introduction à l'étude du rôle des paysans dans les changements politiques', *Cahiers economiques et sociaux*, viii, 1970, 435–50.
55 The Bushiri rising in Masisi-Lubutu region, Northern Kivu, in the first half of 1944 was the second important rural revolt after the Kwango rising of 1931. In colonial Zaire it was the bloodiest revolt and its political significance has been very important. We have no good analysis of this; M. Lovens, 'La Révolte de Masisi-Lubutu (Congo belge: janvier–mai 1944)', in *Cahiers du CEDAF*, 1974, no. 3–4, offers a good description.
56 Note from Procureur Général Devaux, Elisabethville, 29 Jan. 1945, 7, in Archives du Parquet Général, Lubumbashi.

modernity, progress and technological civilisation. Education was associated with 'civilised' status; but in order to become more educated, one had to cease to be a native. The black peasant was doubly excluded as native and as a cultivator.

The 'native' in the dominant ideology of the Belgian Congo was rooted in a particular culture, not in a general one as was a white. Particularism was maintained through customary courts and traditional political titles. The learning of French was restricted to urbanised Africans. It was feared that the teaching of French as a common language in rural areas might facilitate the formation of a peasant class. All natives were tied for life to their group of ethnic origin. Paradoxically, the economic and administrative territory of the colony was progressively unified after 1920, while 'indigenisation' simultaneously divided people into small cultural units. The assimilation of 'registered' Africans was slowed down.[57] All Africans were excluded from credit, from private ownership of land and from the right to hire employees. The birth of a black middle class was nipped in the bud. At the same time, traditional leaders were turned into servants of the state. The rural world was administered by a native chief, with a native tribunal and a complementary native tax system. Migration was controlled by passes in order to limit movement and to prevent a villager from moving from one *chefferie* to another. The restrictions were designed to impede flight from taxation, and from obligatory cultivation or roadwork. Even the most successful salaried employee who escaped from his chiefdom was sent back there if he lost his job, and thus became 'undesirable' in the city. The burdens of village life in Katanga during the Second World War were vividly described in a colonialist's account:

> Villages are not merely empty because of mine recruitment but because the Black wants to flee. Finding a job among Whites is an escape from a birthplace which has become odious. The reason is cotton, which the Blacks hate. . . . It ties them so they cannot attend palavers, collect debts, mourn old aunts. . . .
>
> When a private employer complains of bad faith, laziness, low yields or desertion, administrators reply, 'Treat them better, pay more, avoid these difficulties.' Yet government itself employs classic methods of cotton production contrary to this advice: a few weeds in the plot – the whip; a couple of square yards unplanted – a fine. . . . Cotton pulverises

57 From Leopoldian Congo to the 1920s educated Africans, soldiers and others permanently working for Europeans could ask to be inscribed on a 'registered natives' list and become subject to written rather than customary law; see C. Young, *Politics in the Congo*, Princeton, N.J., 1965; on the *évolués* see R. Anstey, 'Belgian Rule in the Congo and the Aspirations of the *évolué* class', in L. H. Gann and P. Duignan, *Colonialism in Africa, 1870–1960*, vol. II, Cambridge, 1970, pp. 194–225.

native customs. ... In compulsory planting all risks are borne by the Black: drought, ravages, caterpillars, locusts, flood, barren soil, world price fluctuations, everything is against our savage. ... Yet the Black must subsist ... millet, sweet potatoes, oil palms, beans, tobacco all require further labour. ... And what about fishing and hunting, for our man cannot live on cassava and peanuts alone?[58]

PEASANT RESISTANCE

Peasant action generally took the form of a refusal to conform. Common interests took shape against Belgian and white domination. This consciousness spread through both traditional and Christian religious movements; the content of the message was freedom from oppression. The objective was rather the destruction of the existing colonial society than the construction of a new order. A positive programme was lacking even in the Christian-oriented movements, and only the spiritual message of a black God brought some hope. Traditional methods of control were attempted over fortune and misfortune, through cures, divination and protection against evil. The popular message proposed to sweep away this miserable world and await the return of the golden age of the ancestors. The colonial government reacted against what it perceived as anti-colonial ideas. Efforts to maximise use of African working time and to integrate people into the colonial institutions led to a laborious struggle against traditional cultural rites, such as initiation, dances, divination and the casting of spells. From the colonial perspective these practices represented defiance.

Collective manifestations of peasant political consciousness occurred in the 1920s. During the revolt of Maria Nkoi in the southern Zaire basin, the *Djermanis*, or Germans, were expected to liberate blacks from the Belgian yoke. There were other movements whose universality appealed to all Africans. They were inspired by a Christian universal message of a black God. This was an important element in the rejection of the idea of European racial superiority.

The integration of local culture into new cults facilitated the spread both of Kimbanguist and of Kitawala Christianity. Their growth followed the traditional techniques for the expansion of religious movements. Their strength in the face of colonial repression was decentralisation, diversity of leadership and flexibility of practice. Their social function included the struggle against sorcery and the purification of society. Their ideological message enabled their followers to resist the symbolic impact of colonial power. As God was black, racial segregation was not inherent, but had been

---

58 B. Geldhof to M. Schwennicke, Manono, 15 May 1943, Archives de la sous-région du Tanganyika à Kalemié.

created by men. The anti-racial message of Kitawala was the clearest and most radical. Unlike Kimbanguism, Kitawala directly denounced all forms of colonial authority as the work of Satan. Only the authority of the church leaders and elders was legitimate. The ideological message had been turned against the colonial power. Even an anti-clerical Minister of Colonies, L. Franck, expected the church to make good workers in Congo as it did in Belgium.[59] This reversal of religion can be seen as a profoundly tragic mental estrangement. Africans were obliged to resort to the very instruments of colonialism in order to resist it effectively.

The messages of Kimbanguism and Kitawala took root during the 1930s. Other forms of awareness also became apparent after 1931. The rapid decrease in European population during the depression spread rumours throughout the country. They foretold a Belgian withdrawal, an American takeover and the return of *Djermani* liberators. People went to the railway stations to watch whites leave the Congo. They were said to be taking with them the souls of dead Africans who would serve as workers in Europe. In hospitals for blacks it was believed that black people were killed and their souls sent to Mputu (or Europe) to produce merchandise for Africa. The message of 'Tupelepele' was the ideological inspiration of the Pende revolt of 1931. This claimed that whites had stolen the riches of the ancestors for their own profit. Blacks would regain them when society was purified and reconciled with the ancestors. This refusal to recognise the superiority which whites claimed was an important element of the growing awareness of colonial exploitation.

Passive resistance to the orders of administrators, missionaries and other whites grew with the new awareness.[60] Escape and non-cooperation provoked 'police operations', so more passive opposition was tried. Cottonseed was boiled before being sown. The roots of coffee trees were cut underground. Infertile ground was chosen for the planting of compulsory crops. People fled into the forest in the face of a census or a medical team. They refused European medicine. They maintained initiation rites and dances.[61] The approach of a white man revived bitter memories. In 1938, a Katanga labour recruiter visited a Kasai village but the

59 L. Franck, 'Quelques aspects de notre politique indigène au Congo', in *Etudes de colonisation comparée*, Brussels, 1924.
60 B. Jewsiewicki, 'La Contestation sociale et la naissance du prolétariat au Zaire au cours de la première moitié du XXᵉ siècle', *CJAS*, x, 1976, 47–71.
61 For other aspects see R. E. Smith, 'L'Administration coloniale et les villageois: les Yansi du Nord du Bulungu, 1920–1940 (Zaire)', in *Cahiers du CEDAF*, 1973, no 3; also his 'A case study of economic competition in the Kwilu, Zaire, 1920', *Anthropos*, lxxiii, 1978, 497–514; J. Vansina, 'Les Kuba et l'administration territoriale de 1919 à 1960', *Cultures et développement*, iv, 1972, 275–325; T. Yogolelo, 'La Politique indigène au Congo belge et ses problèmes: cas de l'organisation politique et administrative du Bulega (1910–1930)', *Likundoli: Mélanges*, 1976, pp. 148–80; E. Bustin, *Lunda under Belgian Rule: the Politics of Ethnicity*, Harvard, 1975; Bishikwabo Chubaka, 'Deux Chefs du Bushi sous le régime colonial; Kabare et Ngweshe (1912–1960)', *Etudes d'histoire africaine*, vii, 1975, 89–111.

people fled at his approach, reminded of an occasion seven years previously when an administrator had burnt the settlement.[62]

During the 1920s, the administration endeavoured to increase the power of the 'customary' chiefs and limit the political role of missions and companies. Opposition to a recognised chief could take one of three forms: the manipulation of historical traditions might disprove his legitimacy; discreet collective sabotage could bring doubts about his authority; and he could be challenged by sorcery. The traditional mechanism for the solution of conflicts had been the break-up of groups. This became increasingly difficult when the administration forced fugitives to return to their registered villages. Although police operations enabled the administration to control the situation to the advantage of the recognised chiefs, it was unable to eliminate passive resistance and sorcery, which was probably more important than power relationships. The rural success of syncretic movements and their widespread conversions were linked to the struggle against sorcery. Meanwhile, the position of the recognised customary authorities remained very ambiguous. This situation eventually led to a break between them and the peasants.

The peasants were not the only Africans to experience a growing awareness and new identity. In 1944, the mutiny of African soldiers in Kasai and Katanga sought better recognition for their services.[63] At the same time African bureaucrats demanded special élite treatment to distinguish them from the 'savages' and to integrate them into the colonial middle class. These manifestations remained isolated before the rebellions of 1964, and economic improvements stabilised the situation in the countryside during the 1950s. The rural exodus was easily absorbed by an expanding industrial base. The road system facilitated law enforcement. A horizontal racial and ethnic solidarity buried the nascent class consciousness. The peasantry served as the political battleground in which different interests in the black bureaucracy sought support. When mobilised by the anti-colonial slogans of the late 1950s, it was the peasantry which enabled the élite to seize control of the state.

After the Second World War, the syncretic religious movements, notably Kitawala, became more radical. Their leaders were more frequently recruited from rural areas. At the same time, sorcery and anti-sorcery movements declined. Colonial repression played only a secondary role in this process. As long as it remained a publically recognised means for deciding conflicts, sorcery could be practised in secret. Repression, instead

62 See Cloutier to the Département MOI, letter no. 39, 8 Nov. 1938, Archives de la direction du personnel, Gécamines, B1 D 53.
63 J.-L. Vellut, 'Le Katanga en 1944: malaises et anxiétés dans la société coloniale', forthcoming in a volume on the Second World War to be published by the Académie Royale des Sciences d'Outre-Mer (Brussels). I am grateful to the author for the opportunity to consult this paper.

of stamping it out, encouraged it. The fact that it seems progressively to have become a private matter is deeply significant in the evolution of social relations. The estrangement which individuals experienced was radical. It changed the social universe of family and village.[64]

DAILY LIFE

As early as the 1920s, the Belgian administration in the Congo tried to intervene in the daily life of villages. It attempted to improve hygiene. It struggled against polygyny, sorcery and independent religious movements, but above all it acted out of economic motivation. Before the creation of 'native' tribunals, administrators were also judges.

Even missionaries imposed judicial sentences. Missionaries, merchants, recruiters, agronomists and doctors all might intervene in village society by using persuasion, money or threats. Certain missionaries even tried to change matrilineal societies to patrilineal forms.

When the programme of obligatory cultivation was extended in the 1930s, the colonial administration moved to a new stage of 'rationalisation' in everyday life. In his village the black was deemed to waste precious time, so dancing was prohibited, except on Saturday night and on Sunday. Social life was attacked through the imposition of a six-day week with an eight-hour working day. The principal objective of rural education and of evangelisation was the teaching of the industrial rhythm of work and discipline. Villages began to live according to the rhythm imposed by the administration. During the Second World War, the annual minimum work required of a peasant was doubled to 120 days. Firm deadlines and frequent inspections were imposed on agricultural work. Even a Belgian colonial administration was incapable of controlling everything, however. Many orders had no effect because people quickly learn how to evade, pretend and postpone. After 1940, African auxiliaries gained considerable power; deception now required the acquiescence of the auxiliaries.

The effect of the Second World War on rural family budgets was dramatic, as illustrated at Likasi (then Jadotville) between 1938 and 1944.[65] In order to ensure the purchase of this material minimum, it was necessary in 1938 to sell 190 kilograms of maize. By 1944, the same peasant had to

---

64 See C. Mushagasha, 'Note sur la dynamique d'une mission du Kivu: Nyangezi (1906–1929)', in *Etudes d'histoire africaine*, vii, 1975, 125–35; Bishikwabo Chubaka, 'Rôle socio-politique de la mission du Bugweshe (1921–1945)', *Likundoli: enquêtes d'histoire zairoise*, vii, 1974, 191–203; R. Ceyssens, 'Mutumbula, mythe de l'opprimé', *Cultures et développement*, vii, 1975, 483–550; W. McGaffey, 'The West in Congolese experience', in P. D. Curtin (ed.), *Africa and the West: Intellectual Responses to European Culture*, Madison, Wisconsin, 1971; C. Turnbull, *The Lonely African*, London, 1963; M. Douglas, *The Lele of the Kasai*, London, 1960.
65 Compiled from Tshibangu Kabet, 'Effort de guerre'; and Jewsiewicki, *Agriculture itinérante*.

HOUSEHOLD NEEDS (EXPRESSED IN CONGOLESE FRANCS)[66]

	1938	1944
tax	42	73
trousers	20	50
shirt	25	60
used jacket	25	50
blanket	30	125
kitenge cloth	48·50	140
Total	190·50	498

sell 431 kilograms. This total did not include the purchase of tools, social and judicial expenses, traditional or modern medical care or pleasure items like tobacco or beer. Both social and material forms of life had become based on money. This evolution was due both to the pressures of the dominant economy and to administrative and missionary action. The generalisation of cash payments for fines and bridewealth, the increased use of European cloth, the campaign against nudity, all worked to impose the use of money in daily life. Since the acquisition of money did not take the same social routes as the acquisition of traditional wealth, internal power relationships were radically disturbed. The income of a chief from participation in tax collecting had once assured him of a dominant economic position in his village. The rapid deterioration of the buying power of the Congolese franc during the war, however, reduced his wealth compared to villagers actively engaged in the monetary economy. Chiefs became the lower civil servants of the colonial administration, incapable of defending their internal position except through repression in the name of the white man. Polygyny had previously constituted a productive investment in the agricultural labour of a wife; but under pressure from the missions, chiefs were encouraged to become monogamous. A decree of 1948 limited polygamy's prestige by excluding those who practised it from the 'civilised' world. Only conspicuous consumption remained as a means of affirming social position.

CONCLUSION

The atomisation of social groups in favour of the nuclear family and the separation of the producer from the means of production are inherent in the process of primitive accumulation. The colonial transition could lead only to the colonial method of production and to the incorporation of a dependent Congo economy into the industrialised world. In certain places radically new societies were created in urban and industrial centres. In the majority of cases, however, change tortured, modified and upset existing

66 *Ibid.*

societies but did not destroy them. Contrary to the general belief, it did not bring local societies closer together. In fact, wider regional cultures were sometimes destroyed in order to facilitate colonial domination. The supply of products and labour to meet foreign requirements was thereby accelerated.

The Zairian peasantry[67] constituted the basis of the colonial system. Its size and its place in the colonial system of production were important. Rural production, whose direct contribution to exports varied considerably, assumed two principal functions. It was responsible both for the reproduction of human resources and for the formation of colonial public capital. Rural income, manipulated by the state through taxes, customs and trading boards, was necessary for the development of the colonial infrastructure. The peculiar 'state capitalism' of the Belgian Congo arose specifically from the exploitation of African cultivators. The state had appropriated all land which was deemed vacant in 1885, a measure which enabled it to appropriate the gathered products of the land, ivory and rubber. This gathering economy saved the Leopoldian state from bankruptcy. After about 1930, the state took control of African agricultural production. This was equivalent to judicial expropriation of the land cultivated by Africans. The colonial state thus came to regulate land use, to dictate commodity prices and to impose certain monopolies. In this way, thanks to the destruction of African social structures, the colonial state became able to manipulate African labour. The effective ownership of all resources had thus been transferred from African political systems to colonial state and capital.

67 This is no place to discuss the very important 'peasantisation' literature in African studies, but see Klein (ed.), *Peasants in Africa*.

CHAPTER 4

Mining in the Belgian Congo

JEAN-LUC VELLUT

Zaire is the world's largest producer of cobalt, supplying sixty per cent of the mineral. It is also the seventh world producer of copper. It is the number one world producer of industrial diamonds. Mining activity is thus the fundamental basis of the Zaire economy. In 1979, the mineral sector supplied more than eighty per cent of export earnings, sixteen per cent of GDP and about seventy-thousand workers' salaries.

– Le Monde, 23 November 1980

The Belgian Congo mining economy began in Katanga, an area of old iron and copper mines, dating from about the fifth century A.D. Traditional mining was done by means of shafts from which malachite, an easily converted, high-grade ore, was extracted. Copper crosses and ingots were widely traded across the savanna region south of the rain-forest, for example to Angola, where Katanga copper was so valued that the Portuguese tried to export it to Brazil in the early nineteenth century. Production became highly specialised and included such techniques as wire-drawing.[1]

Early European expeditions into the centre of Africa were less attracted by copper, however, than by rumours of gold, an incentive that brought several expeditions to Katanga from 1884, the year before the establishment of the Congo State. It was only by coincidence, however, that Katanga found itself included within the borders of the State. By the stroke of a pen on a map Leopold II annexed the region. His unilateral action was motivated more by a desire to acquire territory than by the attraction of then unknown underground wealth but the region was remote from the main communication systems on navigable waterways, and the State's first expeditions to Katanga were delayed. It was not until

1 M. S. Bisson, 'Copper currency in Central Africa: the archaeological evidence', *World Archaeology*, vi, 3, 1975, pp. 276–97; E. Roger, 'L'Évolution de la métallurgie du cuivre au Katanga', *Comptes rendus du Congrès Scientifique*, Elisabethville, 1950, Brussels, Comité Spécial du Katanga (CSK), 1950, pp. 129–68, esp. pp. 130–33.

126

1891 that the most important gold expedition was organised as a cooperative venture by the State and by a private company involved in trading and transport in the Congo.[2] This tradition of collaboration between the State and private firms continued throughout the colonial period. In the same year, a subsidiary company was created, the Compagnie du Katanga, which obtained a vast land concession from the State. Its concession covered one-third of the 'empty lands' in Katanga and was to prove immensely profitable.

In spite of high expectations the gold expeditions were disappointing. One of them located copper deposits, but they were considered unminable at the time and for Belgians Katanga remained 'a God-forsaken land'. Only several years later did interested groups gain formal control of the various mining regions. Once established, however, these industrial groups, through various forms of association with the State and the Catholic church, made up a power bloc which profoundly changed the course of history in Central Africa.

PROSPECTING AND PARTITIONING[3]

There were three distinct waves of prospecting in Belgian Africa. The first dated to the Leopoldian period when British companies, with English-speaking personnel, American, Australian and South African, were more important than Belgian ones. Indeed, the first systematic prospecting in Katanga was set in motion by Cecil Rhodes, who had long believed in the region's mining potential. A plan to merge the British South Africa Company with the Katanga Company and to share mining revenue was mooted but fell through. It was, however, one of Rhodes's partners, Robert Williams, who opened prospecting in the region. His 1899 Tanganyika Concessions Company explored Northern Rhodesia's mining resources and began negotiations with the Katanga Company. The prospecting rights had by then been transferred to a 'Special Committee' merging the concessionary rights of the State and the Company, with respectively two-thirds and one-third of the voting rights. In 1900 and 1902, agreements

2 J. Strengers, 'Leopold II et la fixation des frontières du Congo', *Revue belge des questions politiques et littéraires*, 1963; and 'Le Katanga et le mirage de l'or', forthcoming in *Mélanges H. Brunschwig*, Paris. My thanks go to Professor Stengers for permission to consult this contribution.

3 The discussion here relates to the era when standard prospecting systems were in operation (wells, trenches, gauging of rivers and so on). In fact, the divisions took place at this juncture, and not in the course of later prospecting campaigns, which, after the Second World War, had recourse to systems using geophysics and geochemistry; L. Calembert and P. Evrard, 'Prospections et exploitations minières', *Livre Blanc de L'Académie Royale des Sciences d'Outre-Mer (l'ARSOM)*, Vol. III, Brussels, 1963, pp. 1061–84. Since 1955, the Central African Museum at Tervuren has been publishing a *Bibliographie géologique du Congo Belge et du Ruanda-Urundi*, the first volumes of which comprise a retrospective bibliography of mine-prospecting.

between Tanganyika Concessions and the Committee were signed, giving the majority of future revenue to the 'Special Committee' but leaving Williams freedom to prospect and finance the mines.

Throughout the colonial period, the Katanga Special Committee remained the concessionary authority in Katanga, and it held shares in every mining business established there. This might appear to have been in violation of the mining laws of the State, which reserved ownership of underground resources, and the granting of prospecting and mining rights, to itself. Yet the stance taken in mining conformed to the earlier handling of monopolies in ivory and rubber: the State granted concessions in return for revenue.

The Union Minière du Haut-Katanga, founded in 1906 as a compromise between Leopold II and Williams, was the show-piece among the new mining firms. By that time the Belgians had slowly overcome their scepticism of Katanga's mineral wealth while Tanganyika Concessions systematically charted ancient African copper-workings. Feasible development of these deposits merely required a rail to link Katanga with the South African system. The new company, which aimed to exploit copper and tin deposits, was floated by Williams and the Société Générale, Belgium's main financial holding company, with the Katanga Committee receiving a large block of shares. Gradually the Société Générale became preponderant, especially from 1928 when it acquired control of the Katanga Company.[4] In the management of the company, the Katanga Committee always relied on the judgement of the representatives of private capital.

It was not only in Katanga that the State granted extensive authority to private interests. It also sought to attract the powerful 'Empain' corporation to the Congo with a large concession in the east based on profit-sharing with the State. The concession was intended to bring Empain to build railways in eastern and north-eastern Congo and in 1902, the corporation did float the Great Lakes Railway Company which became a concessionary authority with rights of exploration. Further north, in 1903, Australian prospectors had located gold deposits. This development should have profited Leopold's Crown Domains, which had previously relied on ivory and rubber along the Zaire and Kasai, but which now received exploitation rights over the gold mines. Direct state supervision of the Ituri basin deposits, however, produced only indifferent results. The development of diamond-mining also linked the colonial state with private mining corporations. Forminière was established jointly by the Société Générale and two American concerns in 1906 with a diamond-mining concession in which the state held a one-half interest. In a late attempt to counteract the tendency of the Société Générale to monopolise Congo

---

4 S. E. Katzenellenbogen, *Railways and the Copper Mines of Katanga*, Oxford, 1973.

mining, another firm, Géomines, was founded in 1910, with a view to prospecting tin in eastern Katanga. Like Forminière, it was fortunate to locate mining deposits in its estates.

The creation of giant mining companies opened a second wave of prospecting, more systematic in character. After Belgium annexed the Congo in 1908, the new régime did not interfere in the large mining concessions which had been granted by Leopold II. Almost everywhere, old concessions were respected or even enlarged, as with the Great Lakes concession which, from 1921, encompassed Maniema as far as Nyangwe. In this area a third wave of exploration began in the late 1920s. The railway concessionaire opened the region east of the Lualaba river to public exploration at a time when gold and tin prices were rising, and by 1932 it had issued 2 500 gold and tin prospecting permits. Prospectors tramped

4:1 Mining zones, Belgian Congo

   Source: U.S. Department of the Interior, *Mineral Resources of the Belgian Congo and Ruanda-Urundi*, Washington, D.C., 1947.

through forests, dug shafts, probed and sifted river gravel, and claims were staked out as new deposits were uncovered. The Société Générale did not occupy a dominant place in this new mining area; instead, several minor concerns obtained concessions, and control of the eastern tin region remained decentralised. In general, the Belgian Congo's mining policy respected much of the spirit of the old State policy. Concessionary authorities and mining companies, representing both official and private interests, remained under the actual management of private capital.

On a continental scale, the importance of the Congo's mining zones was considerable. In 1934 investment in the Belgian Congo represented 11·7 per cent of all foreign investment in sub-Saharan Africa, with mining and transport investment being preponderant.[5] By the beginning of the 1950s mining production represented over 20 per cent of the Belgian Congo's GNP.[6] One must keep in mind, however, that the Congo mining industry was diversified, and that it was integrated into an export-oriented economy that also emphasised a variety of agricultural products. This fact contrasts the Belgian Congo with Northern Rhodesia, where by 1950 copper made up more than 96 per cent of exports. The continental importance of Central Africa's mining regions nevertheless failed to match that of South Africa. On the eve of the Second World War the Transvaal gold mines alone employed twice the work-force of the combined Belgian Congo and Northern Rhodesia mining zones.

THE 'PORTFOLIO-STATE' AND THE MINING COMPANIES

By holding large blocks of shares in the mining companies, the colonial state became, in the words of a Belgian senator, a 'portfolio-state'. In 1935 Governor-General Ryckmans exclaimed, 'Thank heaven we have the mines!'[7] It is not an exaggeration to say that the colonial edifice was built on mining revenue. It is difficult, however, to calculate accurately the mining receipts which included dividends from state-held shares, a tax on profits, royalties, tariffs and direct taxes. Furthermore, smelting, together with power stations and a chemical industry, also enhanced the contribution of mining to the economy. In exchange for taxes the companies tried to impose maximum demands on the state and to minimise

5 South Africa (43%), the two Rhodesias (8%) and the Belgian Congo (11%) together represented 62% of private capital invested at this time in Africa south of the Sahara; Frankel, quoted by Lord Hailey, *An African Survey*, Oxford, 1938, p. 1318.
6 Data calculated from the *Annuaire statistique de la Belgique et du Congo Belge*, the 'Rapports annuels sur l'industrie minière du Congo Belge et du Ruanda Urundi' published, from 1949 onwards, in *Annales des mines de Belgique*. Attempts at a national accounting system in the Congo described in 'Quelques considérations sur le développement de l'économie congolaise de 1920 à 1954', *Bulletin de la Banque Centrale du Congo Belge et du Ruanda-Urundi*, March 1958, pp. 99–108.
7 He proceeded in moralising vein: 'three kilos of gold pay us in taxes the equivalent of a religious nurse's salary'. *Conseil de Gouvernement*, 1935.

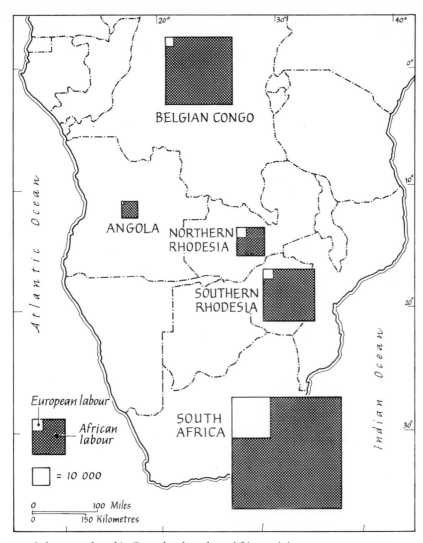

4:2 Labour employed in Central and southern African mining zones, 1937–1939

Note: South Africa (1939)   464 359 (incl. 52 693 Europeans)
Northern Rhodesia (1939)   24 900 (incl. 2 700 Europeans)
Southern Rhodesia (1938)   90 886 (incl. 3 116 Europeans)
Angola (1937)   8 697 (incl.   160 Europeans)
Belgian Congo (1939)   157 250 (inc. 2 250 Europeans)

Sources:
Congo: U.S. Department of the Interior, *Mineral Resources*. Angola: communication from W. G. Clarence-Smith. N. Rhodesia: C. Perrings, *Mineworkers*. S. Rhodesia: communication from I. Phimister. South Africa: F. Wilson, *Labour in the South African Gold Mines, 1911–1969*, Cambridge, 1972. For the data above, I wish to thank W. G. Clarence-Smith, C. Perrings, I. Phimister and C. van Onselen for their help.

its legal rights. Mining interests expected the state to create a favourable industrial environment, to provide access to manpower and to ensure low-cost food supplies. Governor Ryckmans commented on the early 1930s mining boom in Maniema:

> When the crisis of the depression struck, European initiative succeeded in locating, prospecting and developing the rich new Maniema basin. Now it asks only that we [the state] handle the recruitment and sustenance of the work-force. It will take care of the rest.[8]

The companies expected prospecting and mining concessions to be granted in large blocks to well-capitalised companies. Their argument was that only in this manner could prospecting be carried out systematically, production be mechanised and labour be rationally allocated.[9] Companies resisted state interference in their investment policy, in their use of profits and in their development decisions. Government representatives on company boards had little influence.[10] Only in 1938 was the colonial government able to overcome the opposition of mining interests and create its own geological department. Before then, mining problems were seldom discussed in the Government Council. This consultative assembly, which was entirely composed of appointed members, met in the capital, Léopoldville, far removed from the mining centres of Kasai, Katanga and Orientale.

At the beginning of the Second World War demand for metals from Britain and the United States put the colonial government in a difficult situation. The mining inspection agency was undermanned, and the administration had no production statistics. Although it tried to transform its role into a more active one, company power was maintained and state intervention in production remained minimal.[11] Acting on their own initiative, the Congo mining companies put themselves on a war footing

---

8 *Conseil de Gouvernement*, 1935.

9 This argument was developed in more detail by M. Robert, 'Du rôle économique de l'administration coloniale dans le développement des colonies', *Etudes administratives*, I, 1935, 374–9; see also G. Moulaert, 'De la politique minière', *Bulletin de l'Institut Royal Colonial Belge (IRCB)*, xiv, 3, 1943, 528–53. Both seek to entrust numerous offices to the state while simultaneously limiting its rights.

10 J. Renkin in 1921, quoted in the Sap Report, *Documents parlementaires*, Chamber, 1927–8, no. 236, 16. In 1933 the Leyniers Report stated: 'in reality, government does not play a significantly influential role in any of these societies. ... Apart from a few rare exceptions, the delegates [of the State] are no sooner appointed than they are absorbed, if that is the right word, by these societies. Most of the time they plead the cause of the societies where they are "delegated" at the Colonial Ministry.' The report denounced 'a continuous pressure on the part of the business world on the controls of the Colony, in Belgium and Africa.' *Documents parlementaires*, Senate, 1932–3, no. 70, 5, 7–8.

11 L. Cahen, 'Contribution à l'histoire du rôle des pouvoirs publics dans l'effort minier de guerre du Congo Belge (1940–45)', forthcoming in a collective work prepared by the ARSOM in Brussels and devoted to the history of the Belgian Congo during the Second World War. My thanks to Mr Cahen for permission to consult this article.

and increased the strategic output of industrial diamonds, tin and cobalt. Through a network of new subsidiaries in the United States, they retained, during the war, effective control over production, refining and marketing for their American customers. In a famous episode, the Union Minière delivered to New York a supply of radium and uranium before Belgium was occupied by the Nazis. These foreign contacts reinforced the autonomy of the companies in relation to the Léopoldville administration. Even after 1945, the state still had insufficient technical competence or political will to influence mining and industrial development.

At the root of the influence wielded by Belgian companies was the high level of financial concentration that characterised the Congolese economy. In 1933 a Belgian parliamentary commission estimated that four conglomerates controlled 75 per cent of the capital of the colonial companies. The Société Générale alone accounted for more than 60 per cent of all private investment in the Congo.[12] This concentration was also shown in the close personal ties linking companies in each conglomerate. The Jadot–Cousin–Gillet 'clan', helped by three engineering classmates from Louvain University, built the colonial section of the Société Générale into an 'empire'. An interlocking network of management indicated the power of this exclusive group: by 1937 a mere twenty-eight people held 400 board seats in colonial companies.[13] In the years between the world wars, close personal links also existed between governments and company directors. The same names repeatedly appeared in ministerial cabinets and on company boards. When provincial governors lost their position in a 1933 administrative reform, most of them promptly re-surfaced on the boards of colonial companies. These linkages existed also at the lowest levels of administration, where the ranks of colonial civil servants were a ready recruiting ground for private companies. Civil servants frequently found employment with a company operating in their own administrative district, often to the detriment of government interest. In 1929 the Government Council was therefore not surprised when Katanga's two largest firms, Union Minière and the railway company, offered to finance the state's 'secret information agency'.

The strength and cohesiveness of private and public ties in the great Belgian colonial show-piece surprised observers in the 1930s. In 1934 a Brussels socialist newspaper published an in-depth story on the activities of the Société Générale. It described the company's 60 000 African workers and denounced 'the imperialist, careerist and profit-oriented atmosphere created by the Société's representatives'. It also criticised an atmosphere which at best was characterised by unrelenting work, but at worst was selfish, uncivilised and soulless.[14] Similar criticism was voiced in

12 Leyniers Report, *Documents parlementaires*, Senate, 1933–4, no. 85, 35.
13 *Mines coloniales*, Aug. 1937, 108.
14 *Le Peuple*, Brussels, 4–6 Feb. 1934.

parliament. In this climate of doubt the government proposed to limit industrial development, and devote more attention to the modernisation of African agriculture, especially by means of developing more intensive forms of culture by individual African landholders. These plans were only half-heartedly endorsed by the administration, but they were enough to disarm the critics of unrestrained capitalist development in the Congo.

The notion of a Belgian 'national interest' was central to the collaboration of state and companies. The state lent extensive support to the Belgian element in the mining sector. In 1927 it obliged the companies to recruit Belgian nationals at all levels of management. The same agreement required the export of most products to Belgium, and preference for Belgian industrial supplies.[15] This was in reaction to the early condition of mining, when foreign prospectors and engineers had played the leading role. Until the 1920s the fourth of July, anniversary of the United States Declaration of Independence, remained the great public holiday in Tshikapa, the diamond capital. In Katanga, where English and South African working languages long prevailed, there was a tenacious struggle for influence between 'Belgians and Anglo-Saxons' after 1910, and particularly after white South African workers tried to organise a union in 1920.[16]

National struggles also affected financial control. In 1921, for example, when the resources of the Tanganyika Concessions were tied up in the construction of the Benguela railway, the Union Minière succeeded in reducing its rival's holding of stock from 45 to 16 per cent. On the great Copperbelt the Zaire section was thus placed under firm Belgian control, whereas the Rhodesian slope was controlled by multi-national firms without direct participation by the Rhodesian colonial government. By contrast, in Kasai the Société Générale did extend its influence beyond the frontier into Angola and helped to establish the Diamang company. The Générale retained a considerable interest in Angolan diamond-mining throughout the colonial period.

Another dominant force in the Congo mining zones was the Catholic church. It played a particularly important role in 'stabilising' the work-force. Each of the chief mining concerns adopted at different times a policy of 'stabilisation' towards company workmen and their families. These measures were especially applied to more highly-trained personnel. The companies subsidised Catholic religious bodies in order to provide educational instruction for its newly settled labour force. Their task was to inculcate respect for discipline, work and authority. The missions also

15 T. Heyse, 'De l'évolution de la politique de concessions au Congo', *Etudes administratives*, I, 1935, pp. 380–91.
16 B. Fetter, *The Creation of Elisabethville, 1910–1940*, Stanford, Ca., 1976; B. Jewsiewicki, 'Contestation sociale au Zaïre (ex-Congo Belge). Grève administrative de 1920', *Africa-Tervuren*, xxii, 1976, 57–66, especially 64.

undertook the education of workers' wives and children. A mission-educated wife from Kasai came to be the highest aspiration of the new urbanised work-force of the Union Minière. The prototype for this collaboration between companies and missions evolved in Benedictine 'model camps' run for the Union Minière.

The power which controlled the Congo mining industry was thus made up of several components whose characteristic traits distinguished it from the Rhodesian Copperbelt. In the Belgian Congo financial and political authority were more coherent and more authoritarian. Management decisions were made at the top and based on rigorous criteria of efficiency. Informal arbitration and high-level planning maintained this coherence. In Northern Rhodesia, by contrast, ownership and management were more divided. The state held no shares in the companies, and there were no privileged relationships between companies and church. In Northern Rhodesia the companies had a much larger contingent of white workers, who were able to resist the pressure of employers. Ironically, this may have given the colonial régime in Rhodesia a more liberal political character. These various factors – political, economic, social – combined to give increased durability and resilience to colonial boundaries.

TECHNOLOGY AND CHANGE IN THE MINING ECONOMY[17]

Social or political factors cannot alone explain the historical development of Congo's mining industry. Indeed, technological changes determined the limits within which political and social choices were made. In order to remain competitive on the world market, mining concerns had to keep up with technological innovation and push for increased productivity. Technological advance was in turn affected by economic and social constraints. World metal markets go through sluggish periods, and these business cycles help us to explain why technical progress was marked at certain times but was delayed in other circumstances. The size, competence and cost of the available work-force also influenced the choice of development techniques. These variables may be traced region by region, with due attention to the peculiarities of each mining sector. The history of copper, for example, is different from that of tin or diamonds. There are, however, similarities in the collective history of the mining industry in the

17 General accounts: E. Prost, *La Métallurgie en Belgique et au Congo Belge*, Liège, 1936; A. Marthoz, *L'Industrie minière et métallurgique au Congo Belge*, Brussels, Académie Royale des Sciences Coloniales, 1955. Good monographs on metallurgy in the sphere of the CSK in *Comptes rendus du Congrès Scientifique*, Elisabethville, 1950, vol. III, Mining and Metallurgical Commission, Brussels, 1950. Various societies have published monographs on the history of techniques on their sites: Symetain, *Maniéma, le pays de l'Etain*, Brussels, 1953; Union Minière du Haut Katanga (UMHK) 1906–56, *Evolution des techniques et des activités sociales*, Brussels, 1957.

Congo. Indeed, the same stages of technical development can be traced everywhere, although the rhythm varied from region to region.

During the first phase, site installation and road construction were carried out by primitive methods. Thus early mining development was confined to rich deposits requiring a minimum of excavation. Ore concentration was carried out manually with shovels, wheelbarrows and wooden sluices. It was only for copper that any substantial metallurgical equipment was installed from the beginning.

In a second phase, mechanised operations became more important, in particular for excavating and concentrating ore, while new metallurgical installations were built for refining copper, cobalt and tin. Through this period, important stages of production were still based on manual labour. By the end of the Second World War, however, several mining industries were about to enter a new technical phase. By that time, mineral resources had been more systematically mapped, and it was known that ore reserves were among the richest in the world. Important foundries and refineries had been developed, both in the Congo and in Belgium.[18] Yet the exploitation of Congolese resources was still in its beginning, as was shown by an inadequate production of electric energy. The country's immense hydro-electric potential had hardly been tapped, and the large-scale exploitation of mineral reserves awaited new initiatives. It was after the war that a third phase of mechanisation and an upsurge in the production of electric energy took place. The old, less profitable operations like alluvial gold-dredging were gradually abandoned.

The social repercussions of this technical evolution were considerable. In the first stage of mining there was a massive, indiscriminate mobilisation of labour. Organising the labour force meant transporting migrant workers from villages to mines. The state played a decisive role in implementing and justifying this labour shuttle. At this stage the work-force was unskilled. Villagers became excavators, porters and wood-cutters for limited periods.

During the second phase, an effort was made to reduce the industrial labour force. Skilled labour now proved necessary. The management sought a permanent, 'stabilised' work-force with wives and children living in permanent compounds near the mines. For the mining companies, it was a stage of social investment. The state and some industrial managers also began to realise the need to safeguard rural society from the effects of excessive large-scale recruitment. According to colonial ideology, the countryside should become a labour reservoir, and a storehouse which could supply industrial workers. An agrarian policy was needed to ensure

18 Most of these refineries belonged to 'the empire of the *Générale*'. The metallurgy of non-ferrous metals employed 9 917 workers in Belgium in 1938, and 7 885 in 1947. The most important sector, zinc, did not depend primarily on imports from the Congo. *Annales des mines de Belgique*, 1950, p. 113.

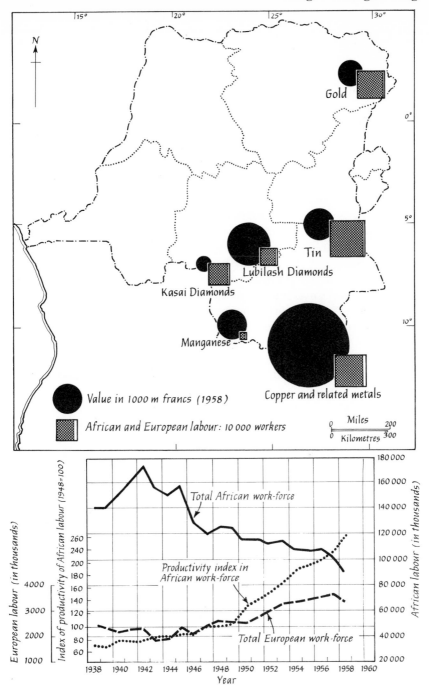

4:3 Labour productivity, Belgian Congo, 1958
Table 4:1 Mine labour in the Congo, 1938–1958
Source: A. Vaes, 'L'Industrie minière du Congo et du Ruanda-Urundi', *Annales des Mines de Belgique*, 1959, 1119.

137

the reproduction of African labour in the framework of the village economy. During this phase, which lasted through the 1920s, the division of labour between industrial and agricultural sectors was not yet clearly marked. Even though part of their labour force may have been permanent, the companies continued to seek temporary migrant workers from local societies. The standard of living of these 'auxiliary workers' was generally lower than that of their 'stabilised' counterparts. These temporary workers were particularly numerous in 1924 and during the following years, as they were required for road construction and large-scale transport of materials for building compounds.

The third phase of technical development was characterised by high productivity and a reduced labour force. In 1938 Géomines proudly announced to its shareholders that its mechanisation programme would allow the laying-off of 30 per cent of its African personnel. Between 1942 and 1958 industry-wide evolution brought about a 50-per-cent decrease of African labour, while productivity rose almost four-fold.[19] At the same time, the European labour force increased by 48 per cent, so that the proportion of African workers to Europeans fell dramatically, particularly for highly mechanised operations. Even with this decline in the African work-force, however, the ratio of Europeans to Africans remained much lower than elsewhere in southern Africa. A systematic reduction of the 'native' labour force was the consensus policy of the mining and metallurgy commission meeting at Elisabethville (Lubumbashi) in 1950. It was symbolic of the success of that policy that the colonial period should have ended with the inauguration in 1960 of a fully automatic plant for the electrolytic production of copper. All phases of production were supervised and corrected from a central control room in the plant.[20]

COPPER AND GOLD, DIAMOND AND TIN : INDIVIDUAL PROFILES

Although the mining industry evolved as a whole, individual mining zones developed in different ways, as is shown by their widely differing rates of productivity. The copper zone was always the show-piece. It had the most highly developed mechanisation, the most diversified metallurgy, and a social policy that came to be considered the prototype for colonial endeavour. The first great turning-point in the history of copper came with attempts to exploit low-grade oxide ores in 1918. Steam-shovels, first introduced in 1914, made bulk excavation mechanically possible.

19 A. Vaes, 'L'Industrie minière du Congo Belge et du Ruanda-Urundi en 1958', *Annales des mines de Belgique,* Nov. 1959, 109–22. The evolution of productivity is well illuminated by F. Bezy, 'Changements de structure et de conjoncture de l'Industrie minière du Congo, 1938–1960', *Notes et documents,* Léopoldville, Institut des Recherches Economiques et Sociales, 1961.
20 J. Gouverneur, *Productivity and Factor Proportions in Less-Developed Countries: the Case of Industrial Firms in the Congo,* Oxford, 1971, p. 65.

Production changes also affected the preparation of the ore. It was necessary to improve fusion processes, and smelting and refining required cheap energy. The answer was found in Southern Rhodesia (Zimbabwe), where the exploitation of the coal deposits of Wankie began in 1906. This permitted the construction of modern ore-treatment and metal-processing plants. An integrated rail transport system began in 1912, when trains hauling copper from Katanga to Beira returned with Rhodesian coal and coke. The interdependence of coal and metal was responsible for the close links between the Katangan and Rhodesian industrial complexes, and, in these circumstances, Belgian national considerations had to yield to economic necessity. At the same time the Union Minière did acquire large capital holdings in the Wankie colliery.[21]

In the 1910s American engineers sought to apply new leaching processes to operations in Katanga, and the Union Minière decided to build a gravity-fed smelter. This smelter began operating at Panda, near Likasi, in

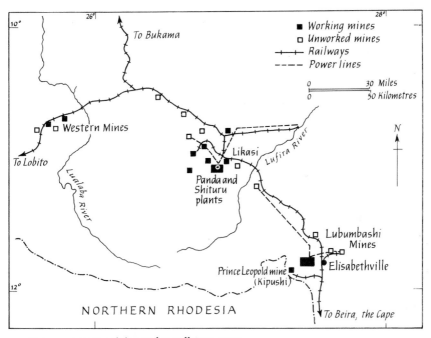

4:4 Katanga copper-mining and metallurgy, 1937
Source: *Revue universelle des mines*, March 1937, 115

21 In 1929, the Wankie collieries were producing approximately 1 200 000 tons, roughly a quarter of which was supplied to the UMHK. M. Robert, *Le Centre africain*, Brussels, 1932, p. 143. In 1959, the UMHK was claiming 580 000 shares at 10 shillings each tied up in the stock of Wankie Colliery, *Recueil Financier*, Brussels, 1959, Vol. III, p. 2810. Katanga's coal requirements were considerably reduced when the production of electrical energy was developed in the 1950s. With the functioning of the new dam on the Lualaba, Katanga began exporting electrical energy to Rhodesia.

1921, despite the copper-market slump. The great investment decisions to step up capacity were made in 1924–1926, after which the Likasi region became the heart of strip-mined oxide-ore transformation. During the years 1925–1928 three new plants were built. At the same time construction of a dam at Lufira was undertaken, and by 1929 it supplied the region with cheap electric energy which made possible the operation of an electrolysis plant. In 1929 the cluster of industrial installations at Likasi included a sulphuric acid plant, an iron and steel foundry, and a mining community of 1 200 Europeans and 4 500 Africans. Within ten years the complex began processing ore from the western areas of Katanga. Another quite separate sector of Union Minière activity was the processing of sulphur ores from Kipushi. This was a shaft mine, developed after 1935. The Kipushi concentrates were refined at Elisabethville.

Copper exploitation entered a new phase after the Second World War. Another dam was constructed on the Lufira in 1950 and two more by 1957 on the Lualaba. These dams produced electric energy which allowed the extension of production in the western sector at a time when the central mines were becoming exhausted. This period was also marked by a diversification into other metals. World market conditions and low-cost energy made this possible.

Manganese was one of these new developments. It profited from the expansion of American steel-works after 1949. The Katanga Railway Company decided to tap one of its western concessions, and a subsidiary began production in 1950.[22] Within a few years this source produced about 8 per cent of the non-communist world production. In 1959, the Lualaba power stations began supplying energy to produce ferro-manganese alloy for special steels. This highly mechanised operation did not face problems of labour recruitment, unlike works where manual labour still played an important role.

The zinc industry also developed on the basis of cheap energy and cheap labour. In 1948 the Union Minière instigated an association of Belgian zinc refineries which set up a zinc foundry at Likasi. Production began in 1953, forging a new alliance, and division of labour, between the Belgian non-ferrous metals industry and the Congo mining industry.[23] Unrefined cobalt production had developed before the war, when the Union Minière

22 At the same time, large American groups concerned with the metallurgy of iron started to exploit the manganese beds of Gabon and Brazil. In 1949, it was estimated in Belgium that the production costs of iron-manganese in Kolwezi might amount to only a ninth of the market price obtained in Anvers. I. De Magnée, 'Réflexions sur l'avenir de l'industrie minérale congolaise', *Revue de l'Université de Bruxelles*, Feb.–April 1949, 203–11. For a historical account of the exploitation by *BCK-Manganèse*, see L. Autenne, 'L'Exploitation du manganèse à Kisenge', *L'Industrie katangaise, réalisations et perspectives*, Elisabethville, 1961, pp. 263–79.
23 Discussions for certain sectors in Conseil Professionnel du Métal, *Avis sur l'évolution des rapports entre les industries congolaise et belge de l'étain, du zinc, et du cuivre*, mimeographed, no place of publication, 1958.

had the lion's share of world production. By 1945 on-site refining became possible at the Shituru electrolysis plant, and exports of locally refined cobalt rose.

The labour policy of both the Union Minière and the Rhodesian Copperbelt companies was strongly influenced by technical developments.[24] During the first phase, the large Union Minière work-force required extensive expatriate supervision, but from 1920 the percentage of Europeans declined as duties were handed over to African personnel. On the Congo slope of the copper field, it was the accepted policy of the colonial power bloc to discourage the hiring of expensive European labour likely to take root and to call in question the existing hierarchy. The Belgians therefore favoured the training of cheap African labour, and from 1926, the Union Minière encouraged long-term, three-year contracts in Katanga. This did not apply, however, to the entire labour force. In the wake of the crisis in the early 1930s, for example, the company regularly brought in external labour furnished by contractors. This contract labour was relatively well paid, though its housing and living conditions were poor. The labourers enjoyed an atmosphere of freedom that contrasted with the regimentated life style that prevailed in the mine compounds. Casual labour was especially used whenever manually operated sites were expanding. In 1948 the Union Minière still listed 6 500 externals, as against 23 234 regular employees.

The use of a temporary work-force was practised longer and on a broader scale in other mining zones, especially in the eastern gold and tin industries. Gold-mining was noted for the long survival of its 'manual' phase; it had the largest, worst-paid, and often worst-treated labour force. After the Belgian annexation of 1908, the state continued to expand gold-mining operations. Both Kilo and, later, Moto cast bullion, which was sent as crude gold for refinement in Belgium. Mining techniques remained primitive until 1920, and basic equipment was built of wood locally. Dams were constructed by manual labour, and porterage long remained the method of transport. After 1920, however, as state administration was tightening its control over the region, the Kilo–Moto mines began constructing roads and compounds, improving equipment and organising supply channels.

In order to exploit low-grade gold deposits, changes were introduced in the organisation of labour, either through the intensive use of low-cost labour, or by mechanising certain operations. In the 1920s gold-dredging was conducted by teams of a dozen men paid by the piece,[25] and placed

---

24 C. Perrings, *Black Mineworkers in Central Africa*, London, 1979.
25 'Payment for piece-work has produced remarkable results. Relevant teams of workers manage to double their work. ... A man wielding a shovel has achieved a daily output of 8 to 10 cubic metres in the barren parts and of 3 to 4 cubic metres of lode gravel. This is the

(continued overleaf)

under the supervision of an African 'capita'. Between 1924 and 1933 the number of team-operated sites rose from 546 to 1259. One European supervisor controlled about twenty sites initially, but by the 1930s the responsibilities of the capita increased, and European supervision was reduced to one controller for thirty, or even fifty sites.[26] Mechanisation followed prospecting on the great rivers, the Shari, Kibali and Ituri. Electric dredges began gravel extraction on the Shari in 1926 and on the Kibali in 1933, using local hydro-electricity, but, on the whole, mechanisation became important only when shaft-mining required crushing and smelting processes. Shaft-mining took on some importance in the late 1920s, and after the Second World War finally replaced the exhausted alluvial gold.

Working conditions in the gold industry forced the mine administrators to resort to a gigantic labour force. At the beginning of the Second World War, the gold-mining work-force of 90 000 made up nearly 40 per cent of the country's total mine labour. For best results, employers divided labour into rival groups of regular employees, working under contract, and auxiliary workers. The auxiliaries were poorly-paid, occasional workers whom site-bosses could hire or fire as the need arose. They were paid a lower rate, with food or premiums.

The diamond-fields, like the gold-fields, were in two quite distinct zones. In the west, the Kasai tributaries were manually mined by digging shafts and trenches. This required an abundant supply of cheap labour. Methods were very different in the east. In the Bushimaie valley the industrial techniques of mass mining became viable when a market opened for very small diamonds to be used in machine tools. The Kasai concessionaire was itself instrumental in developing the commercialisation of industrial diamonds in Europe and America. From 1938, it then undertook an extensive programme of mechanisation. The growth of diamond-mining gave a definite boost to the Belgian city of Antwerp which, since the end of the nineteenth century, had been the centre of the world diamond industry. It had first processed diamonds from South Africa and Namibia, but Kasai diamonds experienced a great upsurge in the 1920s.

The Congo tin deposits were the last mineral zone to be worked. Demand for tin, previously produced only on a small scale, was high in 1926, and several prospecting expeditions were launched. It was only after 1934, however, that tin-mining really expanded. In scattered deposits

(25 *continued*)
peak yield of the native digger'; G. Moulaert, 'Les mines de Kilo–Moto', *Congo*, 1926, 155–90, especially 182. A detailed description of work on site is to be found in R. Monty and R. Anthoine, *Manuel d'exploitation des gisements aurifères au Congo Belge*, Liège, 1927.
26 G. Moulaert, 'Les Exploitations minières de Kilo–Moto et de la Province Orientale', *Congo*, 1935, 1–31, especially 8.

which were too small to be worked mechanically, mining was at first done manually, using sluices along the waterways. Elsewhere, low-grade but extensive deposits were mined by machine. Manono mine developed modern equipment and a foundry to produce tin on site; this contrasted with regions such as Maniema, which remained essentially manual until the 1950s. In several cases, and particularly in the 1930s, operations were not far above the verge of profitability, but even unprofitable producers had a market from 1934 through the Congo quota on the world tin market. In Maniema profitability was sought during the 1930s by artificial curbs on labour costs. The scale of labour recruitment, both for infrastructure and for mining, was huge. It was estimated in 1933 that one million people, men, women and children, were involved in road-building, mine-digging and the supply of food during the Maniema mining boom.[27] From that point of view, the tin industry lagged fifteen or even twenty-five years behind the companies of industrial Katanga. As late as 1938 very few companies in Orientale and Kivu provinces had a permanent labour force settled around their mines. Since, at that time, tin-ore reserves had not yet been systematically prospected, most companies were still uncertain about the durability of their operations and postponed the 'stabilisation' of their labour force.[28]

THE HINTERLAND OF THE MINING ZONES

Mining development was determined by the organisation of huge exchanges. Both men and food had to be extracted from agrarian societies and channelled to the mining zones. The result of this organised transfer of labourers and food supplies was the establishment of rural areas attached both economically and socially to the mining economy. Although they were planned by the colonial power, these areas were shaped at every stage of their existence by African societies themselves. These societies were not intimidated into passive submission by the colonial conquest. Peasant society, because of its geographic distribution, its material culture, its historical heritage, its sense of identity, actively helped to determine the development and underdevelopment of the regions tapped by the mining basins. On the map of the Congo, one can follow the installation of these organic areas that linked peasant and industrial societies. Throughout

27 *Conseil colonial*, 27 April 1934, 527. The business ventures in question were expecting the colonial administration to lend its support to the recruitment of temporary labour. The irrational exploitation of the mining-bed of the Maniema was attributed to the lack of coordination between producers in the absence of adequate financial concentration. M. van de Putte, 'L'Évolution du marché de l'étain', *Bulletin IRCB*, 1931, 208–26; P. Fontainas, 'La Question de l'étain et le Congo Belge', *Bulletin IRCB*, 1931, 227–9.
28 H. Léonard, 'Les Mines du Congo et les problèmes que l'exploitation pose aujourd'hui', *Bulletin IRCB*, 1938, 78–99.

Congolese mining history these areas were the crucible of work experience and of new social divisions. The work experience reflected not only a way of life on the mine sites and in the workshops and compounds; it also concerned change undergone by agrarian societies on the edge of the mining zones.

The political boundaries in the Belgian Congo were arbitrary, unlike the first boundaries between territories tapped by the Central African mining zones. The nature of African societies guided the activities of recruiters and food procurers. Their first task was to establish a resource map indicating the distribution of population, potential food supplies and natural communication routes. Ecological considerations were also important. Employers learned quickly that an intolerable mortality rate could result from mixing, in one compound, groups from different disease zones. One divide formed between areas where recruitment for Transvaal mines was conducted, and areas where workers were recruited for the Katanga or Rhodesian mines.[29] In the north-east, the Kilo–Moto mines were also divided between Kilo which, for some of its sites, recruited in the high country around the lake and the Nile–Zaire watershed, and Moto, which recruited in the low-lying west. As late as 1936, attempts to recruit in Rwanda for Moto failed when acclimatisation proved impossible. It proved similarly impossible for high-altitude Katanga to recruit in low-lying Maniema.[30]

Restrictions on labour mobilisation also arose from the material culture of African people. In the early mining period, the companies subjected workers to a composite food ration according to supplies and costs. In Katanga the local Sanga-Lamba diet of maize and cereal porridge was adopted. At Moto, the workers' diet was banana, maize and sweet potato. Forminière used cassava as a staple diet familiar to its Luba miners. Company physicians gradually modified these basic, monotonous, low-protein diets.[31] Only in the 1920s, however, did health and sanitation come to be considered primary factors in increasing company profits. Local cultural factors also shaped early recruitment policies. Savanna and woodland peoples frequently found that the difficulty of ensuring adequate food supplies between harvests was compounded by natural catastrophes

29 As from 1913 the Transvaal mines broke off their recruitment north of 22° latitude south; Perrings, *Black Mineworkers*, p. 30.
30 'Recruits from Orientale Province have less racial resistance.' In spite of this, the rejection rate of recruits at the medical inspection was very high. Réunion UMHK–Gouvernement, 6 Oct. 1927, Archives Service du Personnel Gécamines (henceforth GCM), C8/039a.
31 For a table of 25 diets in force with the main employers, see E. J. Bigwood and G. Trolli, 'Problème de l'alimentation au Congo Belge', extract from the *Rapport du IIe Congrès International de la Société Scientifique d'Hygiène alimentaire, Paris, 25 octobre 1937*, Brussels, 1937, p. 39.

such as locusts.[32] These frequent times of famine and scarcity had traditionally been times of emigration. Now they became the labour recruiter's opportunity, as the availability of food at the mines was an important incentive to recruits.

Diet was not the only legacy of African society on the mines. As early as 1920, Forminière succeeded in adapting the ancient Luba tradition of agricultural colonisation. The firm embarked on a large-scale programme of settling African colonists on new farmlands to produce company food.

Although African culture provided the framework of the new mining communities, it must be realised that the state and the companies quickly shaped conditions to meet their need for efficiency. The careful planning of policy gradually replaced improvisation. Where mining operations were located near large rural populations, as in the Moto region, the back-and-forth oscillation of migrant workers continued, and neighbouring rural populations provided the greater part of company food supplies. By contrast, in cases where the mines were removed from farming and population centres, organisation became more elaborate and expensive. From one technical phase to the other, the mining zones gradually became better established. A regular migratory flow came to feed the nucleus of stabilised population, and an established trading network came to handle the commercialisation of food produced by African agriculture. Gradually, colonial policy in the mining zones matured.

As each potential labour hinterland was identified, the state and the companies set up an initial network of porterage trails and, wherever possible, river boats. This network was then slowly replaced by roads and railways. Between 1910 and 1931, three main railways divided Katanga into complementary zones. The industrial, commercial and administrative region became more densely populated, although the vast rural expanse had only minor commercial and administrative outputs linked by rail, road or trail. Within this zone the traditional pattern of scattered villages was destroyed. The population was forcibly relocated along the new communication networks dictated by the administration.[33]

The first attempts to recruit workers along the new routes were often violent. This was particularly the case in Kilo–Moto, where in 1919 the situation was dramatic. The workers were destitute and ill fed. Harsh treatment was commonplace. The Moto mine manager announced in 1920

32 A.I. Richards, *Land, Labour and Diet in Northern Rhodesia*, Oxford, 1939, p. 35. L. Mottoulle alludes to the famines and scarcity of food at the end of the nineteenth and the beginning of the twentieth century in 'L'Alimentation des indigènes au Congo Belge', Institut Colonial International, 24th session, Rome, 1939, 268.
33 H. Beguin, 'Chemins et agriculture en Afrique centrale', *Bulletin de l'ARSOM*, 1962, 1050–71, esp. 1050. Geographers are unanimous about the disastrous consequences of clustering along the roadsides from the point of view of the rational use of a village's best land; J. Wilmet, *Systèmes agraires et techniques agricoles au Katanga*, Brussels, ARSOM, 1963, 67–8.

that profit ran highest when the whips cracked loudest. This conscription quickly met fierce resistance. Between 1905 and 1923, Lendu country was in almost constant upheaval. The only relief was the proximity of the Uganda border, which permitted desertion and escape.

In Katanga, only a fraction of the labour force readily accepted mine-work on short-term contract. European recruiters and their African assistants scoured the countryside, making arrangements with chiefs, with strongmen, with contractors, with capitas and with outpost administrators, to procure a semi-captive labour force. These conscripts often included client dependants, victims of private vendettas and paupers. In the 1910s, it was not uncommon to send the recruits to the mines of Katanga in columns with ropes tied around their necks.[34] Compulsory recruitment divided

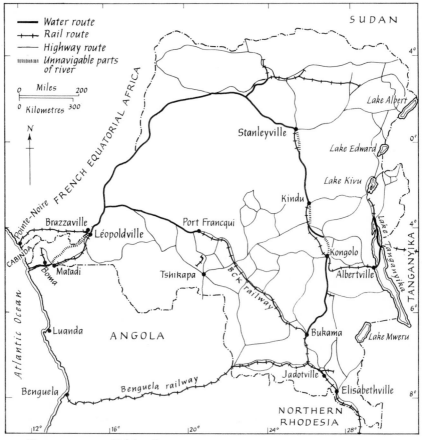

4:5 Transport system, Belgian Congo

34 F. Dellicour, 'Les Premières Années de la Cour d'Appel d'Elisabethville, 1910–23' in *Les Propos d'un Colonial Belge*, Brussels, undated, p. 19.

village society into antagonistic groups riddled with mutual hostility, with accusations of witchcraft and with terrorist activity. As late as 1927, the Maniema mining boom caused particularly violent recriminations over the payment of conscription bonuses to chiefs.[35]

The first stage of recruitment was characterised by competition among merchants, food buyers, recruiting officials and private contractors. They roamed vast territories, irrespective of political boundaries. For example, in the Kilo–Moto region, Greek, Afrikaner and Goanese merchants came in from the Sudan, Kenya and Uganda. In Katanga, too, national boundaries were less important than roads to labour recruitment. Until about 1924 most Union Minière labour was recruited in British-administered Luapula and Lozi country. However, as the need for unskilled labour grew rapidly during the construction phase of expansion on the mining sites, recruitment had to become surer and more efficient. The mines also sought lower wages and reduced rates of mortality and desertion. The first step was to reduce dependence on Rhodesia, and to recruit within the Congo, where the full cooperation of the colonial state was available.[36] State support became indispensable in funnelling labour into the mining zones. Only where government gave priority to agricultural production were mining concerns hampered in seeking conscripts. Even Kilo–Moto, with its reputation for harsh treatment and low pay, sought state aid, though not without repeated disagreement with the local administration.[37] In 1936 the Moto gold mines still sought state cooperation in recruiting 1 800 workers annually in the Uele region. Despite the goodwill of the state, the Katanga employers never gained a labour monopoly for their recruitment agency, which they had patterned on the South African Witwatersrand Native Labour Association. Labour demand was consistently high enough and varied enough to prevent the formation of a united front and the full success of an employers' union.

The colonial administration gradually became more reluctant to use conscription for the benefit of employers. It was felt that such practices would finally disrupt the way of life in the villages. Yet rural communities had to conform to European norms of production, and the administration played a decisive part in bringing about this transformation. From their perspective, the traditional way of life in the villages, the time-honoured

35 People talked of 'Maniema's penal servitude'; *Conseil colonial*, quoted by *Mines coloniales*, Sept. 1937; see also *Conseil colonial*, 1934, 567.
36 'We want to make sure that we will not lose the benefit of our Congo natives on which, through our government, we will always have more pressure than on foreign natives,' 1923, a director of the UMHK, quoted by Perrings, *Black Mineworkers*, p. 60.
37 It is true that the mine managers did not baulk at direct recourse to the Colonial Ministry, on the pretext that the state owned society: 'if there is not a well-intentioned state administration, the mines will produce less and yield less to the State', *Comité de Gestion de la Régie au Ministre des Colonies*, 3 Oct. 1925, Archives of Kilo–Moto, Brussels (courtesy of Bakonzi Agayo).

organisation of labour, conveniently appeared outmoded, and communities which lived on their own land were regarded as 'underemployed'. They were required to pay tax or tribute. Indeed, as seen by the villagers, migrant labour was another tax to be paid by farmers. Returning from their contract, recruits found they had lost access to cultivated land. They often also failed to make cash savings. Former contract workers tended not to resume farming but took supervisory positions in the villages as capitas, tax collectors or policemen. The scale of rural disruption was documented concerning Orientale province in a 1935 report which catalogued the devastating effect on village life of successive levies of short-term auxiliary workers.[38]

In Katanga the final onslaught on traditional village life occurred in 1920–1925, in the wake of massive recruitment for copper and tin. In those years, a network of routes, shelters and acclimatisation camps was established. The Luba region became the key area for new recruitment. The head of Union Minière's personnel department borrowed the hunters' enthusiastic terminology to depict 'the fertile plains between the Lomami and the Lubilash where one finds plentiful, strapping, Baluba who can be used as workers in mining operations'.[39]

By the 1920s, however, it was no longer possible to conscript workers regularly in Katanga. In the Kasai region, moreover, Forminière never resorted to recruitment by force, as it had quickly succeeded in becoming the centre of a movement between employment offices and the Luba colonisation sites around Tshikapa and the Bas Congo-Katanga railway. In 1936 the company estimated that some 200 000 persons yearly were passing the physical tests of the medical service, thus enabling management to keep at 18 000 the number of workers at the mine sites.[40]

Large-scale labour migrations involved feeding. In the north-east, particular difficulties were apparent in the gold mines, far removed from village markets. A state of anarchy prevailed until 1920, when Afrikaner and Belgian settlers began to produce food and carry provisions bought in African markets. In 1924 Kilo cultivated nearly 1 000 hectares of maize and beans. In addition to feeding the workers, these crops brought prices down. In Moto, where the neighbouring region was more populated, local markets were sufficient to feed the widely dispersed labourers.

Forminière had an efficient policy of provisions for diamond workers. At first, company farms furnished provisions. From 1912, the company settled African farmers in the sparsely populated neighbouring regions, and within twenty years this internal colonisation amounted to several hundred

38 Col. A. Bertrand, *Rapport de la Commission de la main-d'oeuvre, Province Orientale,* Brussels, 1931, 192–3.
39 Union Minière Haut Katanga, *Evolution des techniques et des activités sociales,* Brussels, 1956, pp. 213–14.
40 Provincial Commission of Labour, Lusambo, 6–7 April 1936, GCM, B5/D15.

thousand people and supplied 25 000 workers as well as low-cost food for the mines.[41] One key to success was the magnificent road system built in Tshikapa by American engineers. It was along these roads, maintained compulsorily by the colonial subjects, that the uniform company villages were situated. Favoured workers were installed by the company, and in a few years the new villages became magnets for the population of the region. The economic success of cassava production stimulated their growth. A fundamental explanation for success, however, lies in the history of the immigrant Luba peasantry. In the hinterland of Forminière sites, a feeling of common identity was reinforced both by company policy and by the influence of the local Catholic missions, which the company financed.[42]

In Katanga, the problem of importing supplies into the mining region was altogether greater. In the early stages of development, although Robert Williams had not succeeded in completely monopolising the supply of provisions, Katanga had, nevertheless, depended on Rhodesian agriculture. National policy, however, was self-sufficiency and the linking of the province with the north.[43] In Elisabethville it was at first thought that any formula which would assure African food producers of regular revenues would discourage them from going to work in the mines. To minimise this danger, and for political reasons, it was decided to encourage Belgian settlement on the Rhodesian frontier. A settlement project was undertaken between 1911 and 1914, but it failed. In the early 1920s consideration was still given to following the Rhodesian model, by creating African reservations and thus clearing land for European development. The project met with hostility both from Africans and from colonial authorities. In fact, the period was marked by much improvisation. In Katanga, one can trace the story of a grain boom in the Sakania region. The boom arose between 1916 and 1922 along the rail line to Northern Rhodesia as a result of the ban on the import of Rhodesian food, and ensuing price increases in Katanga. Plantations sprang up in Sakania, and farmers moved to hamlets near new sorghum fields. A modest prosperity, indicated by more generous payments of bridewealth, spread through the region. The excessive sale of crops and the intrusion of labour recruitment caused famine to break out in 1926. A decline followed.

41 P. Miny, 'Ravitaillement du personnel indigène et cultures vivrières dans la zone d'action du Kasai de la Société Internationale Forestière et Minière du Congo', *Ve Congrès International d'Agriculture Tropicale, Anvers, juillet 1920*, Brussels, 1930, 603–9.
42 Chalux, *Un an au Congo Belge*, Brussels, 1925, pp. 199–228; L. Franck, *Le Congo Belge*, Brussels, 1930, Vol. I, p. 271 (the villages of Forminière were established on a 'tribal' basis). Tshund'Olela Epanya insists on the social divisions in the heart of the Forminière hinterland, and on the tribal dimension these contradictions assume, 'L'Impact de la Forminière sur les populations Bakwanga', *Zaïre–Afrique*, ivc, Kinshasa, 1975, 349–62.
43 G. De Leener, *Le Commerce au Katanga: influences belges et étrangères*, Brussels–Leipzig, 1911, p. 141.

Similar failures were not exceptional. They did not deter the administration or the firms from relying on African agriculture, but they wanted it to be strictly regulated. In fact, by the 1920s the need for planning industrial development and rural production was felt throughout the Congo. In 1924, a director of the Société Générale expressed his fears that the resilience of rural society was running out: 'Blacks must have the means to live, to provide future labour, and to reproduce their race.'[44] A few years later, joint commissions of government and business worked out a division of population into economic zones. Each zone would engage in a specific activity while remaining capable of reproducing its labour force. This policy was reinforced during the depression, although pressure on recruitment eased. In 1935 Governor-General Ryckmans reaffirmed administration policy: 'the mines should not be a dead zone where only misery makes recruitment possible, yet care should be taken not to allow cotton growing where food for the mines is the priority'.[45]

As early as the end of the 1920s, for some mining regions at least, migratory labour patterns were so well established that recruitment was often unnecessary. A rural exodus had been triggered which met the fluctuating demand for temporary labour and swelled the ranks of the stabilised compounds. The Union Minière was the pioneer, stimulated as it was by a desire to build a 'national' hinterland independent of Rhodesia. From 1926 the company had turned towards a policy of labour reserves. It considered two possibilities: either to develop artificial creations of the company, or to develop reserves out of traditional society. Attempts to follow the first line meant in practice to reproduce the Forminière 'colonies',[46] but they were abandoned in the depression. Reserves based on traditional agriculture became the norm, and employment offices were established in Lomami and Rwanda. To ensure future reproduction and regeneration, the Union Minière actively intervened in the life of its remote new labour hinterlands. Periodically it allowed certain areas to reconstitute themselves by slowing down employment extraction. In its protected regions, the company encouraged the monogamous marriage of workers. It funded prosperous Catholic missions. It planned the development of commercialised agriculture in cooperation with the government. It sought especially to maintain an equilibrium between prices for agricultural products and income from salaried work.

The mobilisation of African agricultural production for colonial

---

44 P. Fontainas, 'La Colonie: déterminantes économiques', *Bulletin de l'Institut des Sciences Economiques*, Louvain University, March 1930, 201–16, especially 211.
45 *Conseil de Gouvernement*, Léopoldville, 1935.
46 As the instigator of the project wrote, the example of Forminière showed that it was possible to change African society: 'gradually the natives, grouped hygienically along the roadsides, will understand that it is in their interests either to cultivate their local land or to work down the mine', Land archives of Shaba, Lubumbashi, 611–14 (L. Mottoullel's report, 21 Sept 1927).

purposes was a constant preoccupation of the administration. The system took away from the peasant free choice in production and free access to markets. Buyers grouped together to impose long-term reductions in the price to the producer. Only near cities did commercial freedom continue to function. Elsewhere a double servitude of labour supply and low-priced production prevailed. Two structural factors combined to influence prices: compulsory production often led to an excess supply, while marketing monopolies aggravated the decline in prices.[47] In 1929 Kilo–Moto signed an agreement with a firm which brought together Belgian and Greek commercial interests linked to the Sudan. This company acquired the food monopoly for the Kilo gold mines. It also monopolised the sale of consumer goods to some quarter of a million inhabitants in the region. The agreement contained the usual opportunities for corruption or exploitation, because the manager of the mines was also an administrator of the commercial company.[48]

In other regions, the monopoly was more discreet, although just as effective. In Katanga, Kasai and Maniema, the bulk of the provision trade gradually came under the control of Interfina, a member of the Société Générale group. In several regions, the territorial administration depended on Interfina trading posts to guarantee economic activity, and to generate enough reserve to ensure the success of tax collection. Mining companies themselves built flour-mills to cut costs and take away the processing of grain from African household enterprise. After 1935, the flour industry in Katanga depended entirely on the Congo, not Rhodesia, for supply. This radical transformation of Katanga's economic geography was linked to the opening of the railways to Kasai in 1928 and to Angola in 1931.

The consequence of labour migration, rigged marketing and the levying of rural recruits for public works was a deterioration of village nutrition, both in quantity and in quality.[49] This contrasted with the industrial zones where rations were progressively improved, though nutrition among workers' wives and children long remained unsatisfactory. Progress in

47 A study of the evolution of agricultural prices in the Congo is available, but it is on a macro-economic level, province by province and at five-yearly intervals. Here, a gradual reduction in agricultural prices for provisions can be observed. J. P. Peemans, *Diffusion du progrès et convergence des prix: Congo-Belgique 1900–1960*; Louvain–Paris, 1970, p. 434. For an historical analysis, a more sharply defined grid is required. B. Jewsiewicki has collected precise data in 'Histoire de l'agriculture africaine dans l'ancienne province du Katanga', *Enquêtes et documents d'histoire africaine*, 1, 1975, Louvain, 55–113. See also his contribution to R. Palmer and N. Parsons (eds), *The Roots of Rural Poverty in Central and Southern Africa*, Berkeley and London, 1977.
48 Monopoly of the SHUN, low purchase prices and 'exorbitant' selling prices documented in Bertrand, *Rapport de la Commission*, 197–8. Debate between A. Bertrand and Moulaert on this topic in *Essor colonial et maritime*, Brussels, 4–18 Feb. 1934. See also 'Les "Grandes Figures Coloniales": le Général Moulaert ou l'Art de Démissionner', *Les Cahiers socialistes*, Brussels, July 1947, 89–91.
49 'Those living in the native environment are inadequately fed.... Blacks are undernourished', Bigwood and Trolli, 'Problème de l'alimentation', 1937, 16.

meat production was partly responsible for the improvement in the quality of industrial rations. During the 1920s, stock-breeding became important in the mining zones. In cattle-raising, by contrast with agriculture, capitalist organisation of production prevailed. Indeed, some important Belgian financial interests lent their support to the establishment of stock-breeding in the mining hinterlands.

In the long run, the need for strict administrative supervision of the mining hinterlands was mitigated by technological change and social evolution. As was seen earlier, from the end of the Second World War the mines reduced their labour demands. The new development of manganese mining in western Katanga illustrated the new relationship between company and hinterland. From the outset, the work-force was limited to a mere 700 men who could be recruited around the company headquarters. In ten years, however, 20 000 people had settled in the vicinity of the mining site, and the company took charge of social services in the neighbourhood. In this case, there had been no need for a systematic intervention in a vast hinterland. Gestures of goodwill aimed at ensuring good local relations were limited to the immediate neighbourhood.

At a period when the mining industry was entering a new stage in its development, there were alarming signs for the future of rural society. The formation of colonial capital had mobilised the resources of peasant societies of the Congo. While there had indeed been a transfer of resources based on agriculture, this movement had not led to radical changes in agricultural productivity. The formation of capital in this sector had been limited to such matters as road-building and scientific research on new crop varieties. There had not been any general development of the rural economy. In a society which was ruled by colonial planners, there was no free peasantry, and there was also no class of owners who could have unified lands, invested in them, and transformed agricultural production. In ruling colonial circles, however, there was a growing awareness that underdevelopment was gradually submerging the rural hinterland of the industrialised regions.[50]

MINING COMPOUNDS AND AFRICAN TOWNSHIPS : PRELUDE TO THE FORMATION OF SOCIAL CLASSES

Throughout the history of the Belgian régime, new forms of social consciousness developed in the Congo. As in every colonial society, the colonised majority acquired a sense of identity in the face of the foreign presence. This diffuse feeling played a decisive role in restricting the extent of European influence. In this instance, however, there was no united front

50 *Bulletin du Centre d'Etudes des Problèmes Sociaux Indigènes (CEPSI)*, 3, Elisabethville, 1946–7, 1–3.

of the colonised against the colonisers. For a long time Congo societies did not have a common political language with which to oppose the domination of the colonial power. Alliances and solidarity, rivalries and contradictions were formed through individual experience, and primarily through work practices. The organisation of work led to fundamental cleavages in African society under colonial rule.

Until the early 1950s, the Congo economy was marked by the preponderance of traditional agriculture. The vast majority of people continued to belong to production systems in which the organisation and techniques of work were essentially African. Changes there came only slowly. At the same time, throughout the country, in urban centres and even in large villages, foreigners set up new systems of production. The new production techniques and new job definitions and functions contrasted with traditional work norms. The tasks of mine and plantation labourers, of clerk, soldier, or railway worker had been defined by the white employer. They were an extension into Africa of structures which had developed in industrial Europe. The distinction was not always absolute, because industrial workers were sometimes reintegrated into their original village community, especially in the case of migrant labour. Nevertheless, it can be shown that a fundamental division pitted those who worked in jobs defined by Europeans against the rural poor, the *Bashenzi*,[51] the 'left-overs' of colonial growth.

This broad division covered a number of areas of social conflict where finer divisions can be traced. They can be followed in village societies[52] and in new work situations. The latter can be explored, first from the perspective of the employers, as they defined the characteristics of the social classes they wished to create in Africa, and later from the perspective of the industrial worker himself, the situation in which he found himself, his perceived interests, his allies and his conflicts. This experience involved both industrial traditions and the African heritage.

'GOOD HEALTH, GOOD SPIRITS AND HIGH PRODUCTIVITY'

This motto was set forth by the Union Minière in 1927,[53] and it embodied the belief that only combined action, touching body and spirit, would succeed in forming an efficient working class. In 1935, a director of Forminière described the task of all the great mining companies of the Congo:

The production chief supervises the training of his black worker ... the

---

51 From the Swahili word *washenzi*, an insult used by the colonial world to put down the 'barbarians from the bush'.
52 See chapter by Jewsiewicki: above.
53 Service order of the Union Minière in *Revue juridique du Congo Belge*, 15 March 1927, 141–5.

compound chief watches over the discipline of his personnel during work and ... the missionary ... instils into child and adult precepts of morals and hygiene. The doctor cures and prevents illness. All instruct and raise the black man. ...[54]

The first concern was health. High mortality among first recruits had shown that, without socialised medicine, companies could not bear the cost of maintaining a work-force. As often happened in Congo history, American experience was called upon. In 1919, a Belgian doctor invoked the Panama precedent where hygiene had been the prerequisite of a stable coloured labour-force working under white control.[55] This utilitarian idea permeated the medical literature of the Belgian Congo of the 1920s. The functioning of humans had to be improved. The individual had become a unit of production, a tool.[56]

The first step to health was the reduction of mortality in the compounds. This was done first of all by admitting only robust and healthy individuals. The doctor was asked to develop a sharp eye, in order to reject medically unsuitable recruits. The procedure was cruel, because the weakest recruits had to find their way back to their villages unaided.[57] In the short term, epidemics and chronic illnesses were reduced. Katanga nevertheless suffered heavy mortality during the Spanish influenza epidemic.[58] Endemic diseases, climate, deficient nutrition and miserable working conditions all took their toll. Accidents were also frequent among workers unfamiliar with new tasks and tools. Work in mud and in water sluices was particularly dangerous. It brought on sores and ulcers. In the early years, workers were often worked until exhausted, and legal safeguards were ignored. 'It is often at the hospital that the results of excessive demands on labour and poor work conditions manifest themselves', observed a Union Minière doctor.[59] Before mechanisation, work on the mines was

54 A. Cayen, quoted by G. Hostelet, *L'Oeuvre civilisatrice de la Belgique au Congo, de 1885 à 1945*, Vol. I, Brussels, IRCB, 1954, 246–7.
55 A. Boigelot, *Rapport sur l'hygiène des travailleurs noirs, 1918 à 1919*, Brussels, 1920.
56 The publications of doctors from the Union Minière (Mouchet, Van Nitsen, Mottoulle) constitute the principal source for the history of social medicine in Katanga from the 1920s onwards. The published material relating to the other mining zones is considerably less, but see Dr Gillet, 'Que font les sociétés minières pour l'hygiène des noirs au Congo Belge?', *Bulletin de l'Association pour le perfectionnement du matériel colonial*, April 1929, 108–21.
57 It was a frequent event to find someone half-dead on the road, a wreck from Katanga's Labour Exchange; Second De Leeuw Mission Report, 1925?, Lubumbashi Archbishopric Archives, IIE13.
58 The 1918 epidemic resulted in 1 179 deaths in the contingent of workers from the Katanga Labour Exchange. Katanga's Governor to the Governor General, Elisabethville, 11 Sept. 1919, in J.-L. Vellut, *Les Débuts du marché du travail au Katanga – Documents tirés des Archives du Shaba* (photocopies), p. 13.
59 L. Mottoulle, *Politique sociale de l'Union Minière du Haut–Katanga pour sa main-d'oeuvre indigène*, Brussels, 1946, p. 14. In 1928 a report by Dr Mouchet pointed out some 'regrettable' instances where sites were still demanding a working week of 7 days, or days of 10 or even 14 working hours; see J.-L. Vellut, *Les Débuts*, p. 215.

commonly regarded as the most dangerous and exhausting of industrial occupations.

In the 1920s, housing, hygiene and nutrition were also denounced as factors in excessive mortality. In 1918, a small camp in Kambove housed 236 men, 30 women, and 9 children, piled on platforms. About half a square metre was allowed per person.[60] In large company compounds, this over-crowding disappeared gradually in the 1920s, but housing conditions long remained miserable in small enterprises. In 1928, Union Minière officials still complained that labour contractors were less affected by the death of their workers than if they had been slave-owners.

During the period of migrant labour, the Katanga mines adopted the policy of compound construction from the Rand, though mortality remained much higher until 1918. When part of the labour force was stabilised, the companies built family camps, and housing became progressively more comfortable. By the 1930s stabilised workers had far better housing than in the neighbouring townships, where conditions long remained very poor. As late as 1950, Bukavu, with 10 735 African inhabitants, had only eight water fountains and no public showers nor toilets.[61] Only in the last ten years of the colonial régime were large investments granted to improve life in the towns.

It was in the compounds and in the adjoining townships that the colonial companies wanted to form the core of a working class. Depending on the evolution of each mining zone, the split between temporary and permanent labour did not occur at the same rate, but gradually all important enterprises formed a stabilised labour-force. They tapped this resource, just as they tapped their capital to develop their self-sufficiency. A hierarchy developed in the new working-class population. Specialised tasks and advanced job-training began early in the Union Minière, but by the 1950s it had spread even to the tin-mines, with spectacular results. In those years, visitors were impressed by the greater degree of specialisation among African workers of industrial Katanga than that in South Africa or Rhodesia.[62]

The hierarchy among stabilised workers widened still further the gap between them and non-permanent, auxiliary workers. It was carefully maintained by differences in salary, clothing and housing. The working class of the Congo thus developed as a fragmented class. In some cases, the privileges for the favoured part of the labour-force represented a costly social policy for the mining companies, though all did not provide services

60 Dr Boigelot, 'Rapport au Vice-Gouverneur Général sur le camp des recrutés de la Bourse du Travail du Katanga', Elisabethville, 21 June 1918, in J.-L. Vellut, *Les Débuts*, pp. 26–32.
61 F. Gevaerts, 'Le Problème de la construction d'habitations à bon marché pour les indigènes de Costermansville', *Bulletin du CEPSI* (Centre d'Etudes Politiques et Sociales Indigènes), Elisabethville, 12, 1950, 183–98.
62 B. Davidson, *The African Awakening*, London, 1955, pp. 121–3.

on the same scale. Until the late 1920s many functioned with only a minimal medical service; by 1925, the 20 000 gold-mine workers had only two doctors. As the number of doctors and hospital beds increased, urban mortality was gradually reduced to rates as low as in industrial countries. The road was long, but the 1929 infant mortality of 315 per thousand in the Union Minière fields was brought down to 58 per thousand by 1955.[63] Mortality among workers was decisively reduced between 1926 and 1932. In the townships, however, outside the sphere of mine health-care, infant mortality remained very high.[64]

The creation of an 'industrial race' required the imposition of discipline. In the early period, order prevailed by means of external constraint. Discipline was imposed through blows, shouts and insults.[65] In the 1920s, however, open violence gave way to group discipline and strict regimentation. The employers wished to encourage self-imposed discipline among African workers. In 1951 a tin company used the teachings of Loyola and Baden-Powell as an inspiration for moral discipline among the working class. In all mining compounds, only Catholic missionaries were permitted to impose this climate of moral discipline without which, it was felt, there could be no good working-class environment. Union Minière explained the Catholic mission in 1931: 'There are two authorities in our camps, the compound head, responsible for discipline maintenance, and the teacher–preacher responsible for morals and learning. The two must always be seen to be in agreement before the natives.' In the programme of the companies and the church there was a naïve confidence in the virtue of work and discipline. A Benedictine official in Elisabethville rejoiced that the factory hooter had replaced the thousand-year-old howling of leopards and hyenas.[66] On the whole, the colonial feeling was one of optimism. In 1924 Belgians proudly heard a visiting South African minister comment on

63 L. Mottoulle, 'Mortalité infantile, mortinatalité, et natalité chez les enfants des travailleurs UM (camps industriels)', *Bulletin médical du Katanga*, vii, 1, 1930, 7–15; Union Minière du Haut Katanga, 1906–56, *Evolution des techniques*, p. 318. After the beginning of the 1930s, the death-rate of the workers from the Union Minière was lower than that registered in the mines of Southern Rhodesia. C. van Onselen, *Chibaro: African Mine Labour in Southern Rhodesia, 1900–1933*, London, 1976, p. 50. Until then, the death-rate in Katanga had been higher than in Rhodesia or South Africa.
64 A doctor practising in Lubumbashi shortly after the Second World War observed that the health standards of the 'little nucleus watched over and cared for by an army of agents from the Union Minière' were moving from strength to strength. Meanwhile, the situation for the majority remained unchanged, particularly as regards infant mortality. Dr P. Vos, *L'Enfer katangais: Lubumbashi 1946–1949*, Brussels, 1973, especially p. 264.
65 In 1918 the foremen in the Lubumbashi foundry presided over the work with a stick or a whip at the ready. J.-L. Vellut, *Les Débuts*, p. 84. The reaction was one of amazement when, around 1926, Dr Mottoulle introduced sanctions against those Europeans who beat Africans on the UMHK sites.
66 J. Plissart, 'Quelques Considérations sur les centres industriels du Katanga et leur conquête spirituelle', *13ème Semaine de Missiologie de Louvain*, 1935, 136–47, especially 139.

their 'contented blacks, well-dressed, well-fed, laughing and singing'.[67] Companies tried to attach prestige to mining so that each worker would become 'an agent of spontaneous publicity bringing back from his leave a few brethren envious of his success'.[68] The aim was to organise happiness in minute detail. Even the workers' marriages were arranged under the auspices of the companies, often through the missions. In this authoritarian climate[69] there was no place for social confrontation. At Union Minière, when 'his' workers went on strike in 1941, the 'native personnel' head was 'sickened by the attitude of the labourers and regretted that shots had not been fired and that two or three hundred had not been killed'.[70]

SOCIAL CLASS DEFINED BY MEN LIVING THEIR OWN HISTORY

In colonial townships and in the mining compounds, which were neither city nor countryside, social groups were formed. They shared a common experience of being tied to capitalist production in either a transitory or a permanent way. Workers, craftsmen, independent entrepreneurs, office employees, each became aware of their identity, although more often as interest groups than as classes.[71] Strikes, however, were special moments when workers became aware of themselves as a whole entity. Several examples of worker action occurred despite legal prohibitions. In 1920 Moto gold-miners went on strike. In 1924, the Great Lakes Company railway workers went on strike, and the company granted a pay rise to those who refused to join in. In 1926 striking Matadi dock workers doubled their wages. In 1931, Luba workers of Union Minière demonstrated against stringent camp discipline. Bukavu, Lower Congo, Léopoldville, all saw numerous examples of worker action in the 1940s. But the 1941 strike by African workers of Union Minière was the greatest demonstration of worker consciousness in the colonial period.

When workers demonstrated for pay increases in Elisabethville in 1941, troops panicked and opened fire, leaving forty-eight dead and eighty wounded. The massacre created a gulf between soldiers and civilians in the Katanga capital. Despite concessions by the company, the strike failed to

67 Quoted in A. Bertrand, 'La Main-d'oeuvre indigène dans la Colonie', *Revue universelle des mines*, Liège, 15 May 1924, 198–207, especially 203.
68 E. De Leeuw, 'L'Agglomération indigène de la Géomines', *Comité Special du Katanga, Comptes rendus du Congrès Scientifique*, Elisabethville, 1950, Vol. VI, 119.
69 Some even refer to totalitarianism; B. Fetter, 'L'Union Minière du Haut-Katanga, 1920–1940: la naissance d'une sous-culture totalitaire', *Cahiers du CEDAF* (Centre d'Etudes et de Documentation Africaine), Brussels, 6, 1973.
70 Mottoulle, 'The day of the strike, 6 Dec. 1941, at Likasi,' *Grèves 1941–1942*, Vellut Papers, African Archives, Brussels.
71 For an initial general view of Zaire's class-consciousness during the colonial period, see B. Jewsiewicki, 'La Contestation sociale et la naissance du prolétariat au Zaïre au cours de la première moitié du XXème siècle', *Canadian Journal of African Studies*, x, 1, 1976, 47–71.

restore to workers the erosion of wages which wartime cost of living had brought.

Several factors explain why worker action was sporadic. Only after the Second World War were Congo workers legally allowed to form unions. Even then they were hindered by the authoritarian tradition of the colonial power, as well as by their own divisions. Fragmentation was caused by ethnic divisions, and by a hierarchy of qualifications. After the Kipushi incidents of 1931 Union Minière perfected a strategy which depended on trusty workers maintaining discipline in the camps. This invidious division was heightened by the more basic one between permanent workers and the reserve army of auxiliaries and migrants. These old rivalries played an important role in the conflicts which exploded in the rebellions that followed independence. It was among semi-proletarianised workers that the most virulent radicalism erupted. This was most acute in the countryside and the small towns.

Even though open conflict was not common, worker power asserted itself slowly, often silently. During the depression employers had been powerful enough to force a salary decrease of 40 per cent, but after the Second World War pressure from the workers led the administration to lift the ban on some union activity. Initially employers and the state tried to retain control of African unions, but worker pressure became too strong in the 1950s.[72]

Congo clerical workers developed a group identity, almost a class consciousness, from an early period. They were continuously torn, however, between sectional interests and the desire to unite in common cause with the rest of the African population. As early as the 1920s, a few educated Congolese in Belgium had adopted a 'nationalist' tone and denounced forced labour, low salaries, backwardness of education and the absence of all political rights.[73] Later, however, ambiguity prevailed, as was shown by the sectional tone of letters from African readers published in the Elisabethville press in 1934, or again by a group of clerks in Luluabourg in 1944. Protest alternated with collaboration. The privileges gained came to distinguish the évolués from the masses.

Despite their privileges, clerks were strongly aware of the racism which permeated colonial society in the 1920s. A high government employee remarked in 1923 that:

blacks have before their eyes the disdain, nay hatred, with which most

72 This is explained partly by trade-union pressure and partly by minimum-wage legislation. J. L. Lacroix, *Industrialisation au Congo: la transformation des structures économiques*, Paris–The Hague, 1967, p. 67. Lowering of wages during the crisis: *Comité Régional du Katanga*, 1932, p. 35.
73 F. Bontinck, 'Mfumu Paul Panda Farnana, 1888–1930', in *La Dépendance de l'Afrique et les moyens d'y remédier*, Acts of Congress of African Studies in Kinshasa, edited by V. Y. Mudimbe, Paris, 1980, pp. 591–608.

Europeans, especially the new social classes, treat old servants; they are described as *Macaques*, as Europeanised caricatures of men, and contrasted to good Africans who remain in the shadow of the banana tree.[74]

Racist practices in the Belgian Congo were as much a question of attitudes and custom as of legal discrimination. They discriminated against mulattos as well as against Africans. In the 1920s, racism spread with the growth of indirect administration, which led to a closing-off of African society. At that time it was unusual for Congolese to be allowed to travel abroad, and contact with foreign anti-colonial circles was only sporadic. Support could also not be expected among Belgian leftists. The Belgian political left was only mildly interested in colonial questions. In the 1920s their opposition to the colonial régime was sporadic. Indeed, condemnation of the hegemony of the large companies in the colonial economy came as much from the right as from the left. Despite this abstention, the humanitarian tradition, so alive under Leopold II, never completely died, and in 1930 it obtained the creation of a commission to investigate the question of compulsory labour in the Congo.

For a short period in the late 1920s, Belgian communists showed much interest in the Congo. At a theoretical level, the party leaders discussed industrialisation and proletarianisation in the colony. Their analysis often adopted a sterile and inflexible position with which to challenge rival movements. In practice, party propaganda reached only a few hundred Congo sailors who frequented Antwerp. Militants supported a Congo crew strike in 1930,[75] but generally the Belgian communist party was weak. This weakness of the left was even more striking in the Congo itself. There was no alliance between white and black proletarians in a colonial society. Colour created an almost unbridgeable gap.[76] After 1945 some branches of Belgian unions were organised in the Congo, but such organisation had no deep roots among African salaried workers. They expressed their identity in another cultural context.

74 *Comité permanent du Congrès Colonial National*, Brussels, 1923, 553. The perpetrator of this intervention, de San, had represented the 'iron hand' in the repression of the Kimbanguist movement in 1921.
75 This item of news was reported by a radical South African newspaper, *Umsebenzi*, on 27 June 1930 ('White workers support black sailors and demand Independence for the Congo') in B. M. Kanku, 'Les communistes belges face au problème de la révolution au Congo Belge (1929–1931)', *Likundoli: enquêtes d'histoire zaïroise*, Lubumbashi, I, 1972, 1, 18–25, especially 23.
76 In 1929, when a socialist journalist, A. Wauters, invited the white and black workers to form an alliance, the colonial press pointed out to him that the white artisan, since he is able to dress in white like everybody else, to have his own servants and to enter into a relationship with the lesser agents from the administration and from the societies, tends to assume middle-class values. J. Lhomme, 'Prolétariat blanc et prolétariat noir', *Essor Colonial et Maritime*, 29 May 1930.

Colonised society usually avoided open conflict with colonial power, yet it protected itself in other ways from the weight of colonial authority. An important strand in the social history of the Congo is the history of a new urban, African culture, over which the coloniser never gained complete control. Before the 1950s, the standard of living in the urban centres of the Congo was miserable, yet an urban culture developed with its leisure occupations, its games and customs. It was the women, much less numerous than the men, who introduced luxuries, fashions, ostentation, into the colourless cities. Football was played in Elisabethville from the 1920s. In Kinshasa, bars with 'orchestras' began to multiply after the First World War, provoking indignation on the part of missionaries and African religious movements alike.[77] Drug abuse was another source of official worry. Everywhere in the cities local beers were brewed, alcohol was distilled and hemp was sold, despite all efforts by the authorities to control the traffic. Urban life was the subject of African painting and song. This popular culture was rooted in the early towns, but sometimes it carried the heritage of the pre-colonial past, though always reinterpreted and renewed.[78]

Ethnic identity is a case in point. It quickly became inseparable from the life of the urban centres, and indeed it was the key to the new social consciousness. Groups expressed ethnic loyalties by sharing customs and laws, kinship rules, language and history. The ethnic identities of the colonial period, however, were different from those of the past. They were always linked to the colonial state, unlike the old ethnic feeling which ignored colonial divisions. In Elisabethville the first urban associations were village associations. By 1925 new associations were created, sometimes for a satirical purpose. The Lubumbashi compound had ten regional associations calling themselves 'Belgian' – for example, the 'Baluba Belgians' or the 'Kabinda Belgians'. Their officers were given titles such as governor, district commissioner and bank director.[79] The gradual emergence of effective colonial frontiers meant that no pan-Bemba or pan-Lunda movement developed in Central Africa. The Bemba of the Congo and those of Northern Rhodesia evolved separate identities; so did the Lunda of the Congo and those of Angola. In every case, however, ethnic

---

77 The *maringa* dance-halls were generally found only in the urban centres of the Lower Congo, but towards the end of the First World War the 'bad dances' spread over the whole area. J. Cuvelier, 'Les Missions Catholiques en face des danses des Bakongo', *Africanae Fraternae Ephemerides Romanae*, Rome, June 1939, pp. 143–70. Kimbangu ordered his followers to forgo these dances and to abstain from alcohol. D. Feci, 'Vie cachée et vie publique de Simon Kimbangu', *Cahiers de CEDAF*, Brussels, 9–10, 1972, 40.

78 For the most recent period, see J. Fabian, 'Popular Culture in Africa: Findings and Conjectures', *Africa*, xlviii, 4, 1978, 315–34.

79 B. Fetter, 'African Associations in Elisabethville, 1910–1935: their origins and aims', *Etudes d'Histoire Africaine*, vi, 1974; notes of the Lubumbashi camp overseer on the 'les Belges' organisations, 20 Aug. 1928, GCM, Lubumbashi, C8/D13.

identity appeared as a new form of consciousness, neither totally class-based
nor totally cultural in character. Within the territories defined by colonial
borders, new land-tenure systems and new divisions of labour developed.
These sharpened feelings of ethnic identity. The Kasai Luba came to be
associated with jobs in the administration, on the railways and in industrial
Katanga. The Kongo of Kinshasa protected their interests against
immigrants from the middle Zaire river, so much so that ethnic loyalty
became associated with new social threats and opportunities. In the social
history of the Congo, solidarity of 'brothers' was usually stronger than
solidarity of 'class'. It was founded on new myths, new identities and also
on new judicial practices.

Gradually colonial authority began to see problems in encouraging such
divisions. In Elisabethville the church, which had tried to encourage ethnic
identity and regional organisations, soon preferred to create professional
organisations.[80] After some hesitation Union Minière based its camp
organisation on ethnic mixing. The company wanted to breed a new 'tribe'
of workers, the Tshanga-Tshanga, with the idea of mixing people of
different ethnic origins. The army also mixed recruits from different
regions. The mutiny which broke out in the army camps of Luluabourg,
Elisabethville and Jadotville in 1944 was attributed to negligence in
following this policy. On those occasions, panic in the administration
revealed the vulnerability of the colonial giant. This giant had crushing
power and a cohesive leadership, but it was temporarily helpless whenever
colonised society gave rein to its deepest aspirations. The powerful anxieties
of Africans were effectively presented in the language of utopia, of
millenarianism, of fantasy and of bitter social criticism.

CONCLUSION

An impression of fragility thus dominates colonial history. This is a
paradoxical conclusion to the story of a powerful material empire. This
empire was born from the confiscation of Leopold II's Congo State by
Belgian high finance and industry. It was born from the ties that these
economic powers developed with the colonial state as it gradually took
shape after the annexation by Belgium in 1908. It was moulded by the
conjunction of economy, politics and the Flemish Catholic revival. These
powers fused in a colonial monolith which exuded the image of Boula

---

80 The experiment in establishing clusters 'according to race' was re-staged in Elisabethville
in 1926, but was soon abandoned as the associations proved difficult to control. In 1932 there
were three professional associations: businessmen, small farmers and clergy. An association
for skilled workmen and artisans was envisaged, B. Thoreau, 'Les Oeuvres sociales à
Elisabethville', *Rapport à la 10ème semaine de Missiologie de Louvain*, 1932, 208.

Matari, the 'colonial hero', who wanted to be feared for his strength and admired for his wealth.[81]

This empire did have a durable influence on the economy and society of Zaire. The history of the mining sector shows how the empire multiplied production capacities, transformed social relations and radically moulded new aspirations. Even during the colonial period, however, the survival of the African heritage and the new popular culture kept imperial influence at a distance. The fragility of this influence became visible only with hindsight. The rapid erosion of the material culture inherited from the Belgians bears witness to this. So, too, does the silence which has fallen on an age now rapidly receding into the past. An observant visitor recently noted 'how surprising it is already that so little of Belgium remains in the minds of the people.... Most of those under thirty had heard nothing about Belgians from their parents or their grandparents.'[82]

81 *Boula Matari* (the 'rock-breaker') was the eponymous hero of Belgian colonial power. J.-L. Vellut, 'Matériaux pour reconstituer l'image du blanc au Congo Belge, 1900–1960', *Stéréotypes nationaux et préjugés raciaux aux XIXème et XXième siècles*, Louvain-la-Neuve, 1982, pp. 91–116.
82 V. S. Naipaul, 'A New King for the Congo', *New York Review of Books*, 26 June 1975, 19–25, especially 22. French translation in *Le Débat*, Paris, 8 Jan. 1981, 20–49.

CHAPTER 5

Capital accumulation and class formation in Angola

W. G. CLARENCE–SMITH

Portuguese colonialism has generally been seen as a case apart. Many English-speaking authors argue that Portugal was a poor, underdeveloped country, which participated in the 'Scramble for Africa' only for reasons of humiliated national pride. In Africa it hoped to revive faded imperial glories. Portuguese rule, so the argument runs, was therefore inefficient and backward.[1] This picture has both distorted the reasons for Portuguese colonialism and exaggerated its ineptitude. The Portuguese had deep economic motives in their search for colonies, and the forms which their rule took were remarkably similar to those prevailing in the Belgian Congo and French Equatorial Africa. The relative backwardness of Portuguese society did introduce some variation in the colonial pattern, but the similarities are more striking than the differences.

THE SCRAMBLE FOR AFRICA AND ITS AFTERMATH, 1875–1910

From the mid-1870s, Portuguese manufacturers, wholesale traders and shippers became increasingly dependent on heavily protected colonial markets. Portugal's slow economic growth had been hampered throughout the early and mid-nineteenth century by British 'free trade imperialism', which aimed to keep Portugal and its colonies as captive markets for British goods and services. The problem became acute in the mid-1870s, when the capitalist world entered a long period of recession. Industrial over-production led to cut-throat competition for markets. European nations responded to the crisis by putting up tariff barriers against foreign goods and by attempting to acquire new protected markets outside Europe.[2] Portugal was no exception. Indeed, the restricted size of the home market and the backward state of the economy made the country

1 See especially R. J. Hammond, *Portugal Africa, 1815–1910, a Study in Uneconomic Imperialism*, Stanford, California, 1966.
2 J. F. Munro, *Africa and the International Economy, 1800–1960*, London, 1976, ch. 3.

163

particularly vulnerable in times of slump. The textile and wine industries of northern Portugal and the traders and shippers of Lisbon rapidly became powerful pressure groups for imperial expansion.[3] Portugal thus took an active and aggressive part in the 'Scramble for Africa' in order to defend vital economic interests, and not, as has often been alleged, in order to indulge in some nebulous imperial nostalgia. This is not to say that there were no ideological motives for imperial expansion. Ideology, however, can only properly be understood in relation to the economic forces in play.

The weak Portuguese state was no match for the other European powers in Africa. It had to struggle to hold areas already within the Portuguese trading orbit in West-Central Africa. At the Berlin conference of 1885, Portugal lost all hope of controlling the lucrative trade of the Zaire estuary. Even in territories nominally awarded to Portugal, the Cabinda enclave and the south bank of the Zaire, the regulations of the new 'Congo Free Trade Zone' prevented any country from imposing tariffs of a protectionist kind. The harshest blow came in 1890. Under pressure from Cecil Rhodes and Scottish missionaries in Malawi, the British delivered an ultimatum to Lisbon to withdraw from the Central African plateau between Angola and Mozambique. There was, however, some compensation in the following year. In an agreement with the Congo State, Portugal acquired what is now north-eastern Angola, even though the Portuguese had not originally laid claim to this area.[4]

Within the area left to Portugal as a protected market – that is, Angola south of the Loge river – the tariffs of 1892 established strong protection for metropolitan goods and services. Goods produced in Portugal, exported from a Portuguese port and carried in a Portuguese ship paid only 10 per cent of the import duties imposed on foreign goods, from a foreign port and transported in a foreign vessel. Intermediary tariffs were created for foreign goods exported from Portuguese ports under the Portuguese flag.[5] The tariffs of 1892 resulted in a profound transformation of the patterns of Portuguese trade with Angola. In 1890, only 2 per cent of Angola's cotton textiles were made in Portugal, whereas in 1898 this proportion had risen to 75 per cent.[6] The Portuguese had cornered the market in plain white cotton cloth and had made great advances in the sale of dyed cloth. Many Portuguese factories were set up or reorganised specifically for the Angolan textile market.[7] A sharp, temporary trade slump in Angola at the turn of

3 J. Capela, *A burguesia mercantil do Porto e as colónias, 1834–1900*, Oporto, 1975; J. Capela, *O vinho para o preto*, Oporto, 1973; V. Alexandre, *Portugal no século XIX*, III, *Origens do colonialismo português moderno, 1822–1891*, Lisbon, 1979.
4 Hammond, *Portugal and Africa*, chs 3–5; E. Axelson, *Portugal and the Scramble for Africa, 1875–1891*, Johannesburg, 1967.
5 H. de Paiva Couceiro, *Angola, dous annos de governo*, Lisbon, 1910, p. 364.
6 T. de Carvalho, *Les Colonies portugaises du point de vue commercial*, Paris, 1900, pp. 90–1.
7 J. Capela, *O imposto de palhota e a introdução do modo de produção capitalista nas colónias*, Oporto, 1977, p. 57.

the century resulted in a major crisis in the cotton mills of northern Portugal.[8] Strong pressures from metropolitan manufacturers contributed to the closing down of two small but prosperous cotton textile factories, which had been established in southern Angola in the 1860s.[9] Cotton cloth was by far Angola's most valuable import, but the Portuguese also sold wines, spirits, foodstuffs and miscellaneous manufactured goods to the colony.[10]

Wholesale traders and shippers based in Lisbon gained at least as much as manufacturers from the tariffs. Their operations in Angola had already been protected by earlier tariffs in 1880. At that time, the British consul in Luanda castigated the tariffs as being 'favourable only to the monopolising interests of Lisbon merchants'.[11] Protection was increased in 1892, and the merchant princes of Lisbon became ever more dependent on the artificially stimulated transit trade to and from the colonies. In the five years 1909–1913, 72 per cent of Angola's exports by value were sent to Lisbon to be re-exported, while only 12 per cent were sent directly to foreign ports.[12] The Empresa Nacional de Navegação, set up in 1881 to benefit from concessions offered to Portuguese shipping companies on colonial routes, rapidly came to dominate Portugal's struggling merchant navy. In 1914, Portugal's merchant fleet had a gross tonnage of 73 000 metric tons, of which 63 000 belonged to the Empresa Nacional de Navegação.[13]

Although the Portuguese bourgeoisie was keen to trade with Angola, it was much more reluctant to invest in the colony. The amounts needed to build railways or start mines and plantations in remote areas were very great, and the risks were extremely high. The major Portuguese investor in the colonies was the Banco Nacional Ultramarino, founded in 1864, with a monopoly of colonial banking which was periodically extended. The bank was closely linked to the merchants and shippers of Lisbon, and was reluctant to do more than lend money to Angolan entrepreneurs. During each economic crisis, however, the bank was forced to take over land which had been pledged as security for loans. Often, the bank could not find buyers for such land. In 1902, the bank thus reorganised its major landholdings in Angola as a separate company, the Companhia de Cazengo. This was the colony's largest producer of coffee, but it was more of a worry than an asset, in view of the generally depressed price of coffee on the world market.[14] The other large Portuguese investor, the Luanda

8 F. Pimentel, *Investigação commercial na província de Angola em 1902–1903*, Oporto, 1903, preface.
9 J. M. Cerqueira de Azevedo, *Angola, exemplo de trabalho*, Luanda, 1958, pp. 322, 433.
10 J. Mesquita, *Dados estatísticos para o estudo das pautas de Angola*, Luanda, 1918.
11 British Parliamentary Papers, C. 3968, Luanda trade report, 1882.
12 Mesquita, *Dados*, pp. 25–7, 84.
13 R. de Sousa, 'A renovação da frota mercante portuguesa', *Actividade Económica de Angola*, xxxix, 1954, 9–90.
14 Banco Nacional Ultramarino, *Relatórios*, Lisbon, annually from 1865.

Railway Company, also had a difficult time. This company was set up in
1885, with a share capital of £600 000. A further £1 890 000 of loan capital
was raised on the London money market. Low coffee prices made the
railway unprofitable, and the company avoided bankruptcy only because
of government subsidies.[15]

The Portuguese bourgeoisie preferred to take the safe option of acting as
an intermediary for wealthy foreign capitalists in colonial ventures. Foreign
investors were compelled to set up companies which were legally
Portuguese and had a majority of well-paid Portuguese directors, often
retired politicians.[16] In Angola, the most important of these companies was
the Benguela Railway Company, founded in 1902 to link the copper-mines
of Katanga to the sea. The share capital of £3 million and the loan capital of
£9 million was raised almost entirely in Britain. There were considerable
initial financial and technical problems, so that the railway reached the
central highlands of Angola only in 1910, and was completed to the
frontier of the Belgian Congo until 1928.[17] Other speculative railway and
mining companies set up by foreign investors found that mineral and other
resources did not warrant major investment.[18]

The highly protectionist economic system imposed on Angola was
strongly resented by the local bourgeoisie and petty bourgeoisie in the
colony. The settlers argued that protectionism and monopolies were
stifling the economic development of Angola and diverting trade to
neighbouring territories. Angolan traders alleged that the 1892 tariffs made
trade goods twice as expensive in Luanda as in the Congo Free Trade
Zone.[19] The settlers also argued that high import duties on tools and
machinery, artificially high shipping costs, expensive credit and
prohibitions on local industries were preventing the colony from
developing its true economic potential. Going on to the offensive, the
settlers claimed that Portuguese entrepreneurs were simply being
encouraged to produce inefficiently at the expense of the public.[20] The
settlers were few in number, however, and politically impotent. The
election of the handful of colonial deputies to the parliament in Lisbon was
usually cynically manipulated by the government to ensure the victory of
candidates with no interest in the colonies.[21]

Angolan traders actually did quite well during these years, in spite of
their woeful protests. The high cost of trade goods was offset by the ready

15 Portugal, Ministério das Colónias, *Pareceres e documentos sôbre a questão de Ambaca*, Lisbon, 1919.
16 G. Papagno, *Colonialismo e feudalesimo*, Turin, 1972, pp. 141–51.
17 S. Katzenellenbogen, *Railways and the Copper Mines of Katanga*, Oxford, 1973.
18 W. G. Clarence-Smith, *Slaves, Peasants and Capitalists in Southern Angola, 1840–1926*, Cambridge, 1979, pp. 17–18; Azevedo, *Angola*.
19 F. Frazão, 'Os tecidos nacionaes nos mercados da Africa portuguesa', *Portugal em Africa*, primeira série, Vol. 3, Part 3, 1896, pp. 300–1.
20 Couceiro, *Angola*, pp. 182 and 359–72, for a concise summary of the settlers' views.
21 A. de Seixas, *Uma opinião baseada em factos*, Lisbon, 1889, pp. 82–3.

availability of fire-arms and spirits. The Portuguese authorities were slow, hesitant and inefficient in enforcing international agreements to ban or restrict the sale of these commodities to Africans. Colonial authorities in neighbouring territories complained of the influx of fire-arms and spirits from Angola, but to little avail. There was no lobby of employers to warn of the dangers of rapidly spreading alcoholic addiction. Traders merely found that addiction increased the pressures on Africans to sell rubber and other commodities. The army had some misgivings about the growing arsenal of fire-arms accumulating in the independent African polities, but such objections were partially met by a prohibition on the sale of technologically advanced weapons.[22] The traders had one other major advantage; the government turned a blind eye on the lucrative export of slaves to the cocoa plantations of the Portuguese island colony of São Tomé in the Gulf of Guinea.[23]

The export trade of Angola surged forward and became increasingly dependent on a single commodity, wild root rubber. Total exports from Angola south of the Loge river were worth an average of £340 000 a year in the decade 1867–1877.[24] In the 1900s, they averaged £820 000 a year, at a time when the value of the pound had changed little. Wild rubber accounted for 35 per cent of exports in 1895 and 77 per cent in 1910. Coffee prices were depressed for most of the period, but coffee remained the colony's second most valuable export. By the 1900s, however, the export of slaves to São Tomé had become roughly as valuable as coffee exports, though slaves did not appear in official export statistics.[25]

Planters fared worse than traders in these years, although the distinction between traders and planters was not always clear when settlers combined the two occupations. The uncertainty of coffee prices badly affected the Cazengo plantations. Sugar-cane appeared to provide a solution to the difficulties of planters for a short while. Sugar-cane was distilled into a fiery spirit known as *aguardente*, which was bartered for rubber and other commodities. This activity flourished in the 1890s, as the 1892 tariffs reduced the competition from imported foreign spirits. Then, in the 1900s, the distilling of *aguardente* was restricted by the government, under the pressure of other European powers and the Portuguese wine and spirits lobby.[26] By 1911, when the distilling of *aguardente* was finally prohibited, the Angolan plantation sector was in a state of crisis.[27]

22 J. de Azevedo Coutinho, *A questão do alcool de Angola*, Lisbon, 1910.
23 J. Duffy, *A Question of Slavery*, Oxford, 1967.
24 G. Pery, *Geographia e estatística de Portugal e colónias*, Lisbon, 1875, p. 358; J. Alves Roçadas, *La Main d'oeuvre en Angola*, Lisbon, 1914, p. 22.
25 Mesquita, *Dados*; slave exports calculated on the basis of numbers given in Roçadas, *La Main d'oeuvre*, and prices in Clarence-Smith, *Slaves*, p. 31.
26 Coutinho, *A questão do alcool*.
27 Great Britain, Foreign Office, *Annual Series*, 4903, 1912.

Angolan planters also faced an uncertain labour situation. By the law of 1875, slavery was to come to an end throughout the empire within three years. But the government was both unwilling and unable to pay compensation to slave owners. In the ensuing confrontation, the authorities adopted a compromise solution. A legal façade of indentured labour was instituted to satisfy international opinion. Beneath the façade, employers continued to own their labourers as chattels. At best, the state enforced some improvements in the treatment of slaves, who were paid a small wage. But the settlers were left in the uneasy position of having only a tacit and unofficial approval of slavery, which could be revoked at any time. Moreover, the price of slaves rose rapidly, owing to the insatiable demand for labour from São Tomé. In the mid-1870s, an adult slave was worth between £3 and £5 on the coast; by 1905, the price had reached £20 to £30.[28] As a result, adult slaves came to be reserved mainly for São Tomé, and Angolan planters had to make do with children.[29]

The planters agitated for a system of forced labour. Unlike slaves, forced labourers could be laid off in times of slump. But forced labour entailed a degree of control over African societies which the colonial state, by and large, did not exercise at this time. The 1899 decree legally instituted compulsory labour for all the colonies, but it could not be implemented in Angola before 1910. Only in the hinterland of Luanda was forced labour of any significance, and it tended to be monopolised by the state and the railway company. Forced porterage was, however, imposed wherever the Portuguese had an effective presence, and it was a major source of friction between Portuguese and Africans. In the hinterland of Luanda, a peculiar system developed whereby militia troops were requisitioned for labour duties and handed over to private employers.[30]

In spite of the problems of the plantation sector, bitter conflicts over land erupted in these years. Old and complex disputes between the Mbundu and the planters in the Cazengo and Golungo Alto districts ebbed and flowed according to the price of coffee on the world market and the incidence of natural disasters.[31] South of the Kwanza river, new coffee plantations were carved out in the lush and fertile Amboim highlands in the 1890s, during a brief boom in coffee prices. Revolts and punitive expeditions resulted from this process.[32] In the far south there was interminable friction over land and cattle. In the 1880s, Boer and Madeiran settlers took over the best lands in the Huila highlands and forcibly expropriated African cattle. Cattle were exported live to São Tomé or employed in the flourishing transport-riding

28 Clarence-Smith, *Slaves*, pp. 30–32.
29 M. Martins Contreiras, *A província de Angola*, Lisbon, 1894, p. 90, n.2.
30 Roçadas, *La Main d'oeuvre*; Couceiro, *Angola*, pp. 217–23.
31 M. A. Fernandes de Oliveira (ed.), *Angolana, documentação sobre Angola, I, 1783–1883*, Luanda, 1968, pp. 337–8, 357, 403–4, 415–16, 684–6; see also chapter by Jill R. Dias in *The Formation of Angolan Society*, F. W. Heimer (ed.) (forthcoming).
32 R. Pélissier, *Les Guerres Grises*, Orgeval, 1977, p. 329.

business, which the Boers initiated in response to the chronic shortage of porters to carry rubber to the coast.[33]

The settler population expanded during the rubber boom, and became more socially stratified. The white population rose from some 3 000 at the end of the 1860s to about 13 000 early in the first decade of the twentieth century.[34] Immigrants were mostly interested in making a quick fortune and returning home, but many found themselves bound to their new country by persistent poverty. The continuing influx of exiled convicts, usually taken from the lowest strata of Portuguese society, contributed to the formation of a 'poor white' population, though some of the convicts became wealthy and respectable.[35]

The Angolan bourgeoisie was drawn increasingly into the economic orbit of Portugal. Wholesale trade south of the Loge river continued to be dominated by local import–export houses, but the rapid expansion of the rubber-trade led to a general dependence on credit from Lisbon financiers.[36] Some metropolitan concerns became directly involved in trading in Angola, and one Portuguese textile firm tried to cut out middlemen by sending representatives to deal with Africans in the depth of the bush.[37] Successful local traders repatriated profits to Portugal, and themselves retired to Portugal when they could afford to do so.[38]

Profits were not all repatriated, and Angolan capitalists began to invest more in directly productive activities. Land was cheap and readily available, and slaves provided a moderately secure source of labour. Fortunes were made when the prices of *aguardente*, coffee or dried fish were high, but Angolan entrepreneurs waited in vain for a boom similar to the cocoa boom in São Tomé.[39] The high risks involved in such enterprises led to a great concentration of capital in a few hands. By 1910 the plantation sector and fishing were effectively controlled by half-a-dozen family firms and by the Banco Nacional Ultramarino.[40]

These changes in the Angolan capitalist class are well illustrated by the career of its most prominent member, António de Sousa Lara. Born in northern Portugal in 1849, Sousa Lara emigrated to Brazil at the early age of twelve. He began as a humble employee in São Paulo state, but rapidly set up in business on his own account. When disaster struck, in 1873, Sousa Lara fled to Angola to avoid his creditors. He started afresh and rapidly

33 Clarence-Smith, *Slaves*, pp. 44–6 and 82–4.
34 G. Lefebvre, *L'Angola, son histoire, son économie*, Liège, 1947, pp. 77, 80. Figures are rare and suspect.
35 G.J. Bender, *Angola under the Portuguese, the Myth and the Reality*, London, 1978, ch. 3.
36 A. Bastos, *Monographia de Catumbella*, Lisbon, 1912, pp. 35–6.
37 Pimentel, *Investigação*, pp. 115–16.
38 A. de Lemos, *Nótulas históricas*, Luanda, 1969, pp. 156–7; J. de Mattos e Silva, *Contribuições para o estudo da região de Cabinda*, Lisbon, 1904, pp. 65–7.
39 Contreiras, *A província*, pp. 12–17, 60–1.
40 Couceiro, *Angola*, pp. 259–60.

became one of the most important traders in the colony. In the 1890s, he took up sugar-cane planting near Benguela. He made a great deal of money out of distilling *aguardente*, and was one of the few Angolan planters with the capital resources and foresight to convert his estates from *aguardente* to sugar production in the 1900s. In 1905, his agricultural holdings were converted into a joint-stock company, with a capital of £125 000. In the late 1920s, Sousa Lara retired to Portugal and became the president of the influential Associação Comercial de Lisboa.[41]

Beneath the colonial bourgeoisie, Angola had a much larger petty bourgeoisie, dominated by small traders. The well-established petty-trader community was reinforced by an influx of poor Portuguese immigrants, lured into the colony by the hope of making a quick fortune in the rubber-trade. With little or no starting capital, small traders borrowed heavily from coastal merchants at high rates of interest. Many thus became debt peons. They were compelled to buy their trade goods and sell their rubber at the warehouses of their creditors, who manipulated prices in such a way that the initial debt could never be paid off. One of the ways of breaking out of this debt trap was to obtain an official post in the interior, usually by paying a bribe. Many lucrative possibilities for exploiting Africans, and rival traders, then opened up. The abuses generated by this trader-official system were responsible for destructive outbursts of protest.[42]

Small farmers and fishermen moved to the south. Official settlement programmes attempted to convince other European powers of Portugal's 'effective occupation'. In the early 1880s, the government welcomed 300 Boer trekkers from the Transvaal and gave them lands in the Huíla highlands. Further Boer immigration brought nearly 2 000 Boers to Angola by 1910. About the same number of illiterate and poverty-stricken Madeiran peasants were shipped to the Huíla highlands at government expense to counter-balance and assimilate the foreign community. At the same time, a current of spontaneous immigration brought several hundred poor fishermen from southern Portugal to the rich fishing grounds and healthy climate of southern Angola's coast. A few Boers became wealthy transport riders and hunters, and a handful of Portuguese prospered as fishing entrepreneurs. However, most of the southern whites remained a classic petty bourgeoisie, owning their means of production and employing only family labour. The poorest among them fell into debt with the coastal merchants or were reduced to the position of proletarian wage-labour.[43]

The third section of colonial society consisted of employees, mainly in government service. This was the bastion of the old 'creole' or 'Euro-

41 Companhia do Açúcar de Angola, *Companhia do Açúcar de Angola, 1920–1940*, Lisbon, 1940.
42 Clarence-Smith, *Slaves*, pp. 47–8; Pimentel, *Investigação*.
43 Clarence-Smith, *Slaves*, ch. 4.

African' élite. After the abolition of the Atlantic slave-trade, they had preferred the security of government employment to the risks of trading and planting. These creoles found their position in the bureaucracy increasingly undermined by competitors from Portugal. As the administrative system was slowly reformed and extended, formal education became the key to the best jobs. In spite of the existence of the episcopal seminary, it was almost impossible to obtain a proper secondary education in Angola. Sending children to be educated in Portugal or Brazil was very expensive. At the same time, the wave of social-Darwinist thought then engulfing Europe affected Portuguese attitudes towards creoles of mixed or African blood. The creoles fought back against discrimination

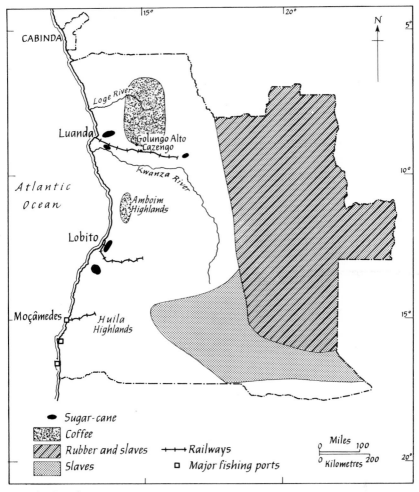

5:1 The Angolan economy, c. 1910

through newspapers and pamphlets. Although this press campaign has been described as a form of proto-nationalism, it was rather the swan song of the old multi-racial slaving élite in Angola.[44]

At the bottom of colonial society were the slaves, whose lot improved slightly in spite of their lack of freedom. The legal abolition of slavery in the late 1870s was a meaningless charade. Slaves simply had to go through the formal process of 're-contracting' themselves to their masters every five years. Slaves were bought from African dealers and immediately contracted. The colonial authorities did, however, enforce certain regulations, which improved the condition of slaves. In addition to food, shelter and clothing, masters were obliged to pay a token monthly salary of £0·13 for men and £0·08 for women. Many masters did not pay in full, or paid in kind, or paid in bonds redeemable only at their own store, but payment of some kind did become fairly general. The authorities also restricted the use of torture, which had regularly been inflicted on slaves.

Slave conditions varied widely, but the worst conditions were to be found in the southern fisheries. Slaves were dumped in a desert environment, with no fresh food and brackish drinking water. The work was strenuous and unfamiliar, and could be very dangerous. Many diseases were spread by the poorly treated fish fed to the labourers. Men heavily outnumbered women, who were employed only for the lighter work of drying and salting. Conditions were very different in the northern coffee plantations. Women and children predominated in the labour-force. The diet was deficient, but slaves could augment it by cultivating a small plot. Escape from the coffee plantations was far easier, and masters were obliged to be more humane. Slave resistance in Angola generally took the form of flight. There were also a few slave rebellions in the 1870s and 1880s, and runaway slaves often became 'social bandits'.[45]

African societies retained a very considerable degree of autonomy until about 1910. The Portuguese mounted occasional punitive expeditions and exercised a loose suzerainty, but the amount of territory directly controlled by the colonial authorities was small, probably not more than a tenth of the total land area of the colony. Tribute was sporadically and irregularly demanded from vassal chiefs until 1896, when it was abolished. Taxation was introduced in the form of hut tax in 1906, but it was only slowly and cautiously extended beyond the colonial nucleus.[46] Portuguese trader-officials in the interior relied on slave soldiers, unreliable militia forces, and the threat of punitive expeditions in order to exercise a precarious and

44 D. L. Wheeler and R. Pélissier, *Angola*, London, 1971, pp. 93–108; M. A. Samuels, *Education in Angola, 1878–1914*, New York, 1970.
45 Clarence-Smith, *Slaves*, pp. 31–2, 35–41; Pélissier, *Les Guerres Grises*, pp. 330–32; D. Birmingham, 'The coffee barons of Cazengo', *Journal of African History (JAH)*, xix, 4, 1978, 523–38; Contreiras, *A província*, pp. 58–67; Companhia Agricola do Cazengo, *Relatório do anno de 1902*, Lisbon, 1903, pp. 17–19.
46 Couceiro, *Angola*, pp. 222–3.

fluctuating authority. Most of the time, they had to cooperate with African chiefs.[47]

Social banditry flourished in the indeterminate zones between colonial society and the autonomous African polities. Africans robbed of their lands, deserters from the colonial army, escaped slaves and fugitive head-porters joined together in loosely organised bands. They operated from natural guerrilla territory, such as the hilly Ndembu jungle near Luanda, the forests of Amboim, and the dense, thorny thickets of the southern Huila highlands. Wandering traders bartered fire-arms for the booty of their raids and acted as spies and informers. This was not a form of proto-nationalism, as has sometimes been argued but, rather, social banditry. The bandits sought to expel invaders and restore the traditional order of society. Much of this bandit activity, however, had no clear social motives, and African villagers often suffered as much at the hands of bandits as did settlers.[48]

The inequalities between autonomous African societies were sharpened by the rising tide of the export trade. Some prospered and expanded. The Zombo in the north seized the opportunities provided by the new Matadi railway in the Belgian Congo to become the most active traders in the Kongo zone. The trade of the coastal Sorongo groups simultaneously declined. In Luanda's hinterland, the collection of wild coffee and the rubber-trade brought prosperity to some Mbundu peoples, but left others out in the cold. The greatest rubber and slave middlemen were the Ovimbundu peoples of the central highlands, whose trading caravans ranged as far east as Lake Tanganyika. In eastern Angola and neighbouring parts of the Belgian Congo, the industrious Chokwe spread rapidly as collectors of rubber and as hunters of elephants. In the far south, the prosperity of the Ovambo was based on the export of slaves and cattle to São Tomé. In contrast to the pockets of prosperity, other African societies declined and became the victims of the resurgent slave-trade. The great Lunda empire, straddling north-eastern Angola and the western Belgian Congo, collapsed under Chokwe pressure.[49]

African societies in the late nineteenth century and early twentieth century were affected by a crippling succession of natural disasters. The causes of this atypical cumulation of ecological catastrophes are not known, but they may have been linked to increased mobility consequent on the export trade and colonial expeditions. The 1870s were years of severe drought, interspersed with flash floods, which hit northern Angola particularly hard. Smallpox epidemics followed in the 1880s and 1890s, again particularly in the north. Then an appalling outbreak of human sleeping sickness devastated the north at the turn of the century. Mortality

---

47 Pimentel, *Investigação*.
48 Clarence-Smith, *Slaves*, pp. 85–8; Couceiro, *Angola*, pp. 59–60.
49 Details scattered through Pélissier, *Les Guerres Grises*.

rates were so high in the fertile Zaire and Kwanza valleys that some regions came to be known as the 'lands of death'. The colonial authorities began campaigns against both sleeping sickness and smallpox in the 1900s, but it is not clear whether the eventual decline in mortality was in fact connected with treatment. In the south, locusts and smallpox were followed by an outbreak of rinderpest, a highly contagious disease of cattle and game, which almost wiped out the cattle population between 1897 and 1899. In 1915 and 1916, the south was ravaged by a drought and a famine, which seem to have been the worst ever recorded in the colony. In 1918, Spanish influenza decimated the enfeebled survivors. These natural disasters were made worse by the serious spread of alcoholic addiction.[50]

In successful African societies, over-all prosperity was often accom-

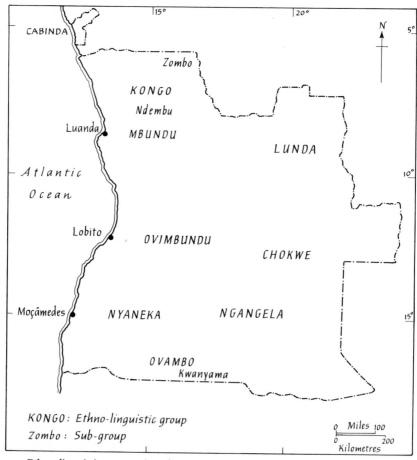

5:2 Ethno-linguistic groups, Angola

50 J. R. Dias, 'Famine and disease in the history of Angola, c. 1830–1930', *JAH*, xxii, 1981, 349–78.

panied by rapid social stratification and increased exploitation. In Ovamboland, there emerged a military clique of raiders, who ruthlessly seized cattle and slaves from their own people as well as from others.[51] Among the Ovimbundu, wealthy traders sold their junior relatives to the São Tomé slavers, usually in payment for a debt. They also intensified the use of slaves in local agricultural production, in order to produce food for the great trading caravans. Slave labour was similarly a notable feature of African coffee cultivation and collection in the hinterland of Luanda.[52] Chokwe society, in contrast, appears to have remained decentralised and

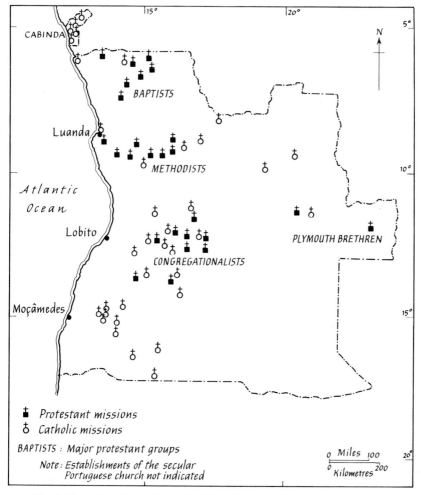

5:3 Distribution of mission stations, Angola, early twentieth century

51 Clarence-Smith, *Slaves*, pp. 74–82.
52 See chapters by W. G. Clarence-Smith and J. R. Dias in *The Formation of Angolan Society*, Heimer (ed.).

fairly egalitarian, in spite of its astonishing expansion in eastern Angola.[53]

In ideological terms, the most striking development in African societies came from the spread of Christian missions, though conversions were limited in this period. The French Holy Gost Fathers entered the colony in force in the 1870s and gained a virtual monopoly of Catholic mission enterprise. Protestant missions were dominated by English-speaking groups: Baptists in the northern Kongo region, Methodists in Luanda and its hinterland, and Congregationalists in the central highlands.[54] Early Christian converts were frequently the victims of the trade boom. The Ngangela turned to the Holy Ghost Fathers for protection against slave raiders. In Ovambo and Ovimbundu societies, slaves and oppressed commoners were often those most receptive to the message of the gospel. Powerful African chiefs were interested in missionaries as intermediaries with the colonial authorities and as sources of information and technical progress.[55]

By 1910, Angola was fast becoming an anachronism in a sub-continent where commerce with African societies had become subordinate to the labour demands of mines and plantations. There was practically no mining in Angola, and the small and declining plantation sector was worked with slave-labour. The export economy depended on the barter of trade goods for the wild rubber produced by autonomous African societies. Political power was only sporadically exercised by the colonial state within the arbitrary boundaries defined in the chanceries of Europe. There was no attempt to produce a flow of cheap migrant labour through taxation, compulsion or land alienation. It needed a radical political upheaval for the protected industries and monopolies of the metropolis to relax their profitable grip on Angola and allow more widespread colonial development.

THE FIRST REPUBLIC, 1910–1930

Tentative reforms were introduced into Angola in the 1900s, but no systematic changes in colonial policy were implemented until the triumph of the republican revolution in Portugal in 1910. The new régime was ideologically inspired by positivist rationalism. It drew its support from the urban petty bourgeoisie, which resented the domination of the country and its empire by a small clique of monopolists in league with foreign interests. The main thrust of the republic's colonial policy was thus to initiate a more rational and efficient exploitation of the empire, which would benefit a wider spectrum of Portuguese society. This was summed up in a change of

53 J. C. Miller, 'Cokwe trade and conquest in the nineteenth century', in *Pre-colonial African Trade*, R. Gray and D. Birmingham (eds), London, 1970, pp. 175–201.
54 Samuels, *Education*, ch. 4.
55 Clarence-Smith, *Slaves*, pp. 89–93; Samuels, *Education*, ch. 4.

name. The 'overseas provinces' became colonies in name as well as in fact. At the same time, the republicans had a paternalistic concern for their African subjects, and wished to administer them more efficiently.[56]

The new régime acted cautiously in the delicate matter of reserving colonial markets for metropolitan interests, and in this sphere, as in others, it was distracted by participation in the First World War. In the 1920s, however, the stifling level of protectionism was radically reduced. The effects of this were both rapid and complex. On the one hand, Portugal's share of Angola's import trade fell drastically. In the years 1913–1918, 60 per cent of Angola's imports by value came from Portugal.[57] Between 1924 and 1929, this proportion fell to 35 per cent.[58] On the other hand, Angola's imports roughly trebled in real terms over this period, so that Portuguese exports to Angola actually increased in absolute figures.[59] Over-all calculations also conceal strong variations between sectors. Portuguese wine exports surged ahead, stimulated by the final prohibition in 1911 on the distillation of local *aguardente*, although exports of cotton textiles tended to stagnate.[60]

In the service sector, the republic continued to protect Portuguese concerns, but it strongly encouraged greater competition among Portuguese companies. The monopoly of the Empresa Nacional de Navegação over colonial shipping was broken, and by the 1920s there were three companies competing for colonial routes.[61] Similarly, in the banking sector, the Banco Nacional Ultramarino lost its monopoly in Angola, although its rival went into liquidation in 1926.[62] Another ephemeral competitor collapsed almost as soon as it was formed, in a sensational scandal over forged bank notes.[63] The Banco Nacional Ultramarino itself met difficulties in the hyper-inflation of the 1920s. By 1930, it had pulled out of Angolan banking altogether and handed over its operations to a state-owned organisation, the Banco de Angola.[64]

The creation of the Banco de Angola was part of a wider phenomenon, the large-scale investment of public funds in Angola. This was partly due to financial and administrative decentralisation, long promised by the republicans and finally implemented in the 1920s. The parsimonious

56 A. de Oliveira Marques, *História de Portugal*, Vol. II, *Das revoluções liberais aos nossos dias*, 5th ed., Lisbon, 1978, chs 12, 14.

57 H. Meyer, *Das portugiesische Kolonialreich der Gegenwart*, Berlin, 1918, p. 38.

58 G. H. Bullock, *Economic Conditions in Angola*, London, Department of Overseas Trade, 1932, pp. 38–9.

59 A. Monteiro, *O problema das transferências de Angola*, Lisbon, 1931, figures scattered throughout text.

60 A. de Almeida Teixeira, *Angola intangível*, Oporto, 1934, pp. 353–5, 364–5.

61 Sousa, 'A renovação'.

62 J. Ferreira Pinto and Velloso de Castro, *Angola: notas e comentários de um colono*, Lisbon, 1926, pp. 199–200; Monteiro, *O problema*, p. 45; D. da Cruz, *A crise de Angola*, Lisbon, c. 1928, p. 66.

63 A. Alves Reis, *O Angola e a Metropole, dossier secreto*, Lisbon, c. 1926.

64 F. P. da Cunha Leal, *Subsídios para o estudo do problema do crédito em Angola*, Lisbon, 1930.

caution of the colonial ministry was replaced by an ambitious programme of public borrowing, initiated by the first pro-consular High Commissioner, Norton de Matos. By 1928, Angola's consolidated debt had risen from virtually nothing to £5·5 million. Had the money been spent wisely on projects which increased production and revenue, this debt would have been tolerable. But Norton de Matos squandered much of the money on ambitious but unrealistic schemes. The financial shambles was made worse by rampant inflation imported from Portugal, and Angola was practically bankrupt by 1930. The positive effect of public spending was in communications. The Luanda state railway and port were extensively reconstructed, and the Moçâmedes railway was extended to the Huíla highlands. A network of dirt roads was built for lorries, which took over from head-porters and ox-wagons in the 1920s. Road-building, however, owed as much to forced labour as to public investment.[65]

Portuguese private investment grew markedly after the First World War, although colonial theorists complained that the flow was too small and too speculative. Colonial companies tended to be under-capitalised and poorly organised. The stock-exchange euphoria which went with inflation and easy credit encouraged speculation. There were, nevertheless, about £2 million invested by private Portuguese concerns in the colonies by the end of the 1920s.[66] The Banco Nacional Ultramarino was still dominant outside the banking sector, but it changed the nature of its investments in Angola. The bank sold its controlling interest in the Companhia de Cazengo and acquired a wide variety of minority share-holdings in other companies. It remained the major source of colonial credit in Angola until its dissolution as a local banking concern at the end of the 1920s. Most important of all was its function as a comprador agent for foreign companies.[67]

The Société Générale de Belgique was the main foreign investor in Angola from the 1910s. This gigantic banking and industrial conglomerate, a kind of precocious multi-national corporation, dominated the economy of the Belgian Congo. Many of its Angolan ventures were extensions of its activities in Belgian territory. Its Congo diamond company exploited the diamonds of north-eastern Angola from the late 1910s through a sister company, the Companhia de Diamantes de Angola, Diamang. Diamonds became Angola's most valuable export by the end of the 1920s, and Diamang became the largest single employer in the colony.[68] The Société Générale also bought shares in the Benguela railway and invested in a large number of agricultural, mining and service

65 Pinto and Castro, *Angola*, pp. 31–7; R. T. Smallbones, *Economic Conditions in Angola*, London, Department of Overseas Trade, 1929, p. 9.
66 C. Cya, *Economia affricana, le colonie portoghesi*, Florence, 1936, p. 66.
67 See Reports of BNU.
68 Munro, *Africa and the International Economy*, p. 135; A. Brandão de Mello, *Os diamantes de Angola*, Luanda (?), 1925.

companies. In all these operations, the Banco Nacional Ultramarino and other Portuguese concerns acted as 'front men', so as to avoid nationalist criticism of a foreign company infiltrating Angola on such a scale.[69]

Angolan settlers welcomed reduced protection and increased investment, but the policies of the republic initially intensified an already serious economic crisis. The root cause of the slump was the collapse of the price of wild rubber on the world market. By 1913 cheaper and better plantation rubber from South-East Asia had conquered the market.[70] The republic added to the crisis by banning the slave-trade to São Tomé and prohibiting the distillation of *aguardente*. A third blow came in 1911, when slavery was abolished without compensation. Nor could the new authorities immediately provide an alternative flow of tax-induced labour or forced labour, as Portuguese control over African societies was still so weak. The advent of the republic in Angola was thus marked by a wave of bankruptcies and considerable settler discontent.[71]

The slump of 1911 was short-lived. After the First World War, there was a period of rapid commercial expansion. By 1929, Angola's exports in real terms were worth two-and-a-half times as much as in 1911.[72] The recovery was partly due to diamond exports, which made up a quarter of the total value of exports in 1929. Coffee and maize accounted for a third, and palm products, sugar, fish, cattle and wax made up most of the rest. About 40 per cent of total exports came from the African peasant sector, and African peasants produced most of the foodstuffs consumed in Angola.[73]

The structure of commerce changed in Angola in the 1920s. Sales for cash became more frequent, as taxation was imposed on Africans. Traders became labour recruiters, as forced labour replaced slavery. Fixed stores along roads and railways replaced the wandering backwoodsmen of earlier years. Lorries and trains made possible a trade in high-bulk and low-value products such as maize.[74] By 1929 there were some 4000 white retail traders and 150 wholesale merchants in Angola.[75] Traders still came to Angola to make a fortune and go home. Although traders were less frequently appointed to official posts, they maintained close relations with officials in rural areas.[76]

The recovery of local entrepreneurs was favoured by rising commodity prices and by new land and labour policies. Slavery was effectively replaced by compulsory labour, once colonial rule had finally been imposed in the

69 Bullock, *Economic Conditions*; Katzenellenbogen, *Railways*, p. 114.
70 R. Hobson, *Rubber, a Footnote to Northern Rhodesian History*, Livingstone, 1960, p. 3.
71 Arquivo Histórico Militar, Lisbon, Secção 2, Divisão 2, Pasta 14, Documento 31 (provisional classification 1975), Report of the head of espionage services, 31 March 1915.
72 Monteiro, *O problema*, pp. 38, 41, 48, 61–2.
73 Teixeira, *Angola intangível*.
74 J. d'Almeida Mattos, *O Congo português e as suas riquezas*, Lisbon, 1924, pp. 66–9.
75 Smallbones, *Economic Conditions*, p. 20.
76 Pinto and Castro, *Angola*, pp. 19–20.

1910s. The effect of the new labour system on African societies is considered below, but one should note that it was not without its problems for the Angolan entrepreneurs it was designed to help. The corruption of petty officials favoured large companies with funds for bribery and political influence. Employers faced continuing competition from São Tomé and illegal, but tolerated, labour migration to neighbouring territories. Coerced labourers, on six-month contracts, had poor incentives and few skills. Labour productivity was thus even lower than under the old slave system.[77] In its land policy, the republican régime claimed to balance the needs of African peasants and capitalist producers. In practice, it set aside a mere 98 square miles as 'native reserves', and granted 1 805 square miles as land concessions to farmers and planters.[78] Many of these concessions were highly speculative in nature, and only a small part of the land was actually put under cultivation.[79]

Within the white settler population, social differentiation became more striking. At one end of the scale, the three 'sugar barons' gained control of all sugar production and much of the exports of coffee and palm products. At the other end, illiterate and ragged whites, especially in the south, succumbed to the burden of debt and unemployment and lived by begging. In between, the small rural traders were no longer so predominant. There was an influx of white employees, who were often rewarded with colonial sinecures for loyal service to the republican cause. By the late 1920s it was estimated that there were roughly as many white employees as white petty traders in the colony.[80] The over-all white population grew from 13 000 in 1913 to nearly 60 000 in 1931.[81]

The position of Africans and *mestiços* in colonial society became more uniform. The creole élite was decisively thrust downward into lower-paid jobs in the colonial bureaucracy, as the republic increased the educational qualifications required and created a special service for those locally recruited.[82] In contrast, the ex-slaves moved upward in society. Old-established slave families did not return to their societies of origin when slavery was abolished. They became an urban labour aristocracy, trading their scarce skills for better wages. In some cases, they were able to become independent petty-bourgeois producers, as artisans, fishermen or small farmers.[83]

77 *Ibid.*, pp. 109–16, 470.
78 Bender, *Angola*, p. 148.
79 Cruz, *A crise*, pp. 22–3, 56; J. M. Norton de Matos, *A província de Angola*, Oporto, 1926, pp. 255–9.
80 J. C. Rates, *Angola, Moçambique, São Tomé*, Lisbon, 1929, especially pp. 107–8.
81 Lefebvre, *L'Angola*, pp. 77, 80.
82 M. A. Samuels, 'A failure of hope: education and changing opportunities in Angola under the Portuguese Republic', in *Protest and Resistance in Angola and Brazil*, R. Chilcote (ed.), Los Angeles, 1972, pp. 53–65; see also chapter by D. L. Wheeler in the same volume.
83 Clarence-Smith, *Slaves*, p. 42.

The great majority of Africans still lived outside colonial society, but they were systematically subjected to colonial rule by the new Portuguese régime. For them, these were difficult years of transition, marked by high levels of violence. Fertile land was to be given up, regular taxes were to be paid and a flow of cheap labour was to be ensured. In order to impose such requirements, the republicans organised systematic military campaigns, which met with violent resistance. By the 1920s, however, only the remote and thinly populated eastern plains held out against the newly invigorated colonial drive.[84]

The republicans intended to employ the standard African mechanism of taxation in order to stimulate the supply of labour, but they rapidly fell back on a system of forced labour. The strong commercial lobby strenuously opposed any restrictions on African commodity production. As long as Africans could meet their tax obligations by marketing produce, taxation did not compel Africans to work for the very low wages paid by employers.[85] The Portuguese were unwilling to make the kind of decision adopted by the British, whereby some colonies were reserved for commercial interests and others for capitalist production. The Portuguese therefore chose to subject Africans to a legal obligation to work for wages, which could be applied flexibly so as to meet the needs of both traders and planters. Africans were allowed to choose their employers. Contracts were for a maximum of six months, with employers obliged to provide food, shelter and clothing, in addition to a minimum wage. Part of the wage was paid at the end of the contract in the labourer's home area. In addition to this kind of contract labour, the state could demand unpaid forced labour on public works. Forced labour was also the penalty for a wide variety of criminal offences, notably the non-payment of taxes.

The new labour system did not always follow the legal patterns established in Lisbon. Officials, who were paid low salaries at a time of rising inflation, accepted bribes in return for agreed numbers of labourers. African policemen and headmen rounded up the men arbitrarily, even ones who had paid their taxes and fulfilled their labour obligations. Every kind of trick was used by employers to extend contracts illegally and to withhold pay. Working conditions very rarely corresponded to the provisions of labour regulations. Brutality was widespread. The corruption of officials was compounded by the ignorance of labourers, who had no idea of their legal rights. State labour fell heavily on women, who built the network of dirt roads, often with their own tools.[86]

The tax system was equally vitiated by corrupt officials. Hut tax was reintroduced into Angola in 1906, and was imposed systematically after

84 Pélissier, *Les Guerres Grises.*
85 Pinto and Castro, *Angola*, pp. 95–6, 109–11.
86 E. A. Ross, *Report on the Employment of Native Labour in Portuguese Africa*, New York, 1925.

1910.[87] Commodities accepted in lieu of cash included cattle, rubber, wax and ivory, and officials manipulated prices in their own favour. Tax collectors received a share to stimulate their zeal. In 1913, district officers received 10 per cent, tax collectors 5 per cent, compilers of tax-lists 10 per cent, and African headmen 4 per cent. Nearly a third of the tax was thus legally appropriated.[88] In the 1920s, the hut tax was replaced by a poll tax, payment in kind was forbidden and the percentage entrusted to local officials was greatly reduced. Many abuses persisted, but the Ross Report noted that taxation was less of a grievance in Angola than in Mozambique. Some officials refused payment in cash and insisted on contract labour as the only source of tax payment. The tax system also increased the dependency of African producers on Portuguese traders. As peasants became indebted through tax obligations, they were forced to sell commodities to their trader-creditors at artifically low prices.[89]

Land alienation, although a source of bitter grievance, was much more localised than demands for tax and labour. The 1919 regulations, nominally designed to protect African communal farmers, effectively led to wholesale spoliation. Only in 1927 were the needs of 'slash-and-burn' agriculture recognised, by guarantees to Africans of four times the land actually cultivated.[90] By the mid-1930s, 2 per cent of Angola had been granted as concessions, in a country where only 3 per cent of all land is really fertile.[91] Land alienation was naturally concentrated in those few favoured spots: in the coffee lands of Cazengo and Amboim, on the central highlands and along the new railway lines. Natural stands of Kongo oil-palms were also subjected to seizures in the 1920s. Complaints about land-law violation and warnings of African resentment were swallowed up in the corrupt administrative apparatus.[92]

The new administration was not only corrupt, but also arbitrary, brutal and incompetent. Colonial administrators from Lisbon had no knowledge of local conditions and were moved around too frequently to gain any. They were therefore manipulated by their subordinates, often sergeants in the colonial army who had married into prominent African lineages.[93] In more remote areas, officials were still recruited among petty traders, who were usually above the law, unless a non-Portuguese, especially a

87 J. M. Norton de Matos, *A situação financiera e economica da província de Angola*, Lisbon, 1914, p. 19.
88 Arquivo Histórico de Angola, Luanda, Códices 32–1–33 and 5–5–20, Report of Financial Inspector, 1914.
89 Matos, *A província*, pp. 264, 276; Ross, *Report*, pp. 8, 14, 20, 24, 49, 59.
90 René Pélissier, *La Colonie du minotaure, nationalisme et révoltes en Angola, 1926–1961*, Orgeval, 1978, p. 153.
91 Portugal, Ministério das Colónias, *Primeira conferência económica do império colonial português*, Lisbon (?), 1936, Vol. I, p. 319.
92 Ross, *Report*, p. 21; Matos, *A província*, pp. 255–9.
93 Arquivo Histórico de Angola, Luanda, Códices 32–1–33 and 5–5–20, Report of Financial Inspector, 1914.

missionary, took up the case. Corporal punishment was the rule, and contacts between the administration and its African subjects were marked by a high degree of violence.

Actual violence to Africans was not generally applied by European officials, but by black collaborators. These *cipaios* or policemen were brought in from other areas, and had no kinship links with the local population. Many were criminals, who enlisted to escape a sentence for their misdeeds. They were practically unsupervised, and many engaged in profitable trading activities. There was no appeal against the *cipaios*, who 'grossly abuse their authority for the purposes of lust, spite or extortion'. Once the last resisters had been disarmed, the rifles of the uniformed *cipaios* represented the power of the colonial state in the remote bush.[94]

Headmen also became collaborators of the administration. Chiefs of large African states were deposed in the campaigns of conquest, and headmen became the lowest rung of the new hierarchy. They were paid a small salary and received part of the tax gathered in their area. They were exempted from paying any taxes themselves, and were not subjected to contract labour. They could settle minor disputes but were not allowed to impose fines. Headmen were intended to benefit from traditional legitimacy, but their power clearly derived from their colonial status.[95] Although headmen were generally neither legitimate nor popular, they were not feared and loathed like the *cipaios*. Headmen were often the richest Africans in their area, producing cash crops or owning large herds of cattle.[96]

As the colonial system began to bite, Christian missions became important to Africans. Once the great rebellions had been suppressed, Africans had only missionaries to protect them from the administration. The missionaries also offered economic advantages. They were a source of seeds, tools, agricultural advice and even land. For the more talented, mission education was the normal avenue to employment in the colonial bureaucracy. The missions themselves employed Africans in responsible positions, as pastors, priests and catechists, although the Africanisation of the higher levels of the hierarchy was slow. In more general terms, the missionaries offered an ideological possibility for Africans to reconcile themselves to military defeat and the realities of colonial life.[97] By 1940, the first official figures show that 741 145 Angolans had become Catholics and 286 182 had become Protestants.[98]

The picture given so far is somewhat deceptive; it fails to bring out the

94 Ross, *Report*; Mattos, *O Congo*, p. 111.
95 Matos, *A província*, pp. 262–75.
96 See for instance, J. Statham, *Through Angola, a Coming Colony*, Edinburgh, 1922, pp. 152–3.
97 T. M. Okuma, 'The Social Response of Christianity in Angola, Selected Issues', Ph.D., thesis, Boston University, 1964.
98 A. Costa Valdez Thomaz dos Santos, *Angola, coração do império*, Lisbon, 1945, p. 100.

uneven impact of colonial rule and the regional variation in African response. The pressures of taxation, forced labour and land alienation varied widely from one area to another, and even within a single region.[99] Angola was still far from being a uniform social formation. Colonial conquest imposed the hegemony of the colonial state, but it did not create a single society out of the many societies over which the Governor-General in Luanda ruled. It is thus necessary to look more closely at the different regions of Angola.

In the Kongo zone of the north, the republicans characteristically tried to impose the new colonialism with insufficient force. They provoked a massive rebellion, which took place from 1913 to 1915. Falling rubber prices, increased taxation and arbitrary labour recruitment were the main causes. The republicans were also, incidentally, unable to manipulate the complex traditional politics of the Kongo kingdom. The rebellion spread far beyond the heartland of the old Kongo kingdom, however, to areas long hostile to the pretensions of the Kongo monarchy. Not all Kikongo-speakers were involved, but the rebellion was far-ranging and its suppression proved difficult.[100]

In the 1920s, the contrast between the two parts of the Portuguese Kongo province was strong. The northern Cabinda enclave was not involved in the rising and became the economic centre of the province. The Cabinda Company possessed 140 000 hectares of fertile land, of which 1 500 were under cocoa, 700 under coffee, and 700 planted with oil-palms. Other plantation companies were active, as were African peasant producers, and Portuguese traders drained off produce from adjacent areas in the Belgian Congo and French Moyen-Congo. Prosperous Cabinda imported unskilled contract labour and exported voluntary skilled labour to the rest of Angola. The distinctiveness of the enclave was further emphasised by its proud creole élite, its noble titles and the predominance of Catholics amongst the Christian population.

South of the Zaire river, the picture was different. Few plantations were successful. The export economy depended on coffee and palm kernels collected from wild bushes and trees by local Kongo and sold to Portuguese traders. The pressures of labour recruitment for Cabinda and São Tomé led to a drift of population towards the Belgian Congo. Along the Matadi–Léopoldville railway, Kongo from Angola became a large community. They were often employed by Portuguese traders, who dominated retail commerce in this part of the Belgian Congo. The powerful Baptist church also straddled the frontier, and Protestants became more numerous than Catholics. English and French were currently spoken.[101]

99 Mattos, *O Congo*, p. 92.
100 Pélissier, *Les Guerres Grises*, ch. 9.
101 Mattos, *O Congo*.

The Mbundu zone of north-central Angola was rocked by two major rebellions. The hilly Ndembu jungle had long been a centre for bandit activity. In 1913, a hut-tax rebellion broke out, which was not subdued until a campaign of particular brutality was mounted by Portuguese irregulars between 1918 and 1919. An even more serious explosion of violence occurred in the Amboim highlands in 1917 and 1918. The major grievance was the arbitrary expropriation of coffee land, and 130 white men, women and children were killed. The vengeance wreaked by white planter militias presaged the massacres of 1961 in the northern coffee zone.[102]

After the campaign of suppression, the Amboim highlands were transformed into major coffee plantations, using the wide tracts seized from the 'rebel' population. Belgian capital played a crucial role, and helped to develop the world's largest coffee plantation. Portuguese interests built a private railway from Porto Amboim and founded a new shipping line to serve the coffee plantations.[103] The remnants of the local population proved insufficient for the labour needs of the plantations, and Ovimbundu contract labour was brought in from the central highlands. Amboim became a plantocracy where planters mixed brutality with paternalism in a closed and regimented world, only penetrated with difficulty by outsiders.[104]

North of the Kwanza, African societies evolved very differently. Coffee plantations stagnated, perhaps because transport costs were higher than in Amboim at a time of uncertain coffee prices. Coffee production remained in the hands of African peasants, who still collected the beans from wild bushes as well as cultivating them.[105] Outside the coffee zones, new resentments were reinforced by old class divisions. According to one villager in the 1920s: 'Twelve years ago, when there was slavery, the slaves had all the hardships, while the free negroes were not badly off. Now we are all slaves.'[106]

The central highlands constituted the one major region in Angola where there was no rebellion against the Portuguese in the 1910s. In part, this was because the Ovimbundu had already been thoroughly intimidated by the campaign of 1902, but it also reflected the rapid and successful adaptation of the Ovimbundu to the new conditions. When the rubber-trade collapsed and the slave-trade was banned, the Ovimbundu intensified the production of maize. In the 1920s, Ovimbundu maize became the colony's second or third export. The Benguela railway provided transport to the coast, and

102 Pélissier, *Les Guerres Grises*, chs 10, 13.
103 Companhia do Amboim, *O Amboim, região privilegiada de Angola*, Lisbon, Anuário Comercial, 1924; A. Brandão de Mello, *Angola: monographie historique, géographique et économique*, Luanda, 1931, p. 96.
104 C. Carneiro, *O Amboim*, Lisbon, 1947, for a rather romanticised picture.
105 A. Lisboa de Lima, *L'Angola et la crise*, Brussels, 1933, pp. 105–6.
106 Ross, *Report*, p. 20.

colonial maize received protection on the Portuguese market. Since production was of low-grade maize for pig-fodder, profit margins were low. White farmers were not attracted by the crop, and land alienation did not become a serious problem. The Ovimbundu could easily pay their taxes by selling maize in a broad swath of territory on either side of the railway. Contract labour prevailed only in fringe areas.[107] At the same time, the Ovimbundu reoriented the use of their slaves. Some were used to extend maize cultivation, while others were sent to perform the labour obligations of their masters.[108] Although many Ovimbundu had grievances, there was a clear contrast between the abject misery of Luanda's hinterland and the conditions on the central highlands.

In the far south, it was taxation which sparked off the major rebellion of 1914–1915. The Portuguese had to organise the largest military expedition to be sent to Angola before 1961, for the southern rebellion coincided with a German assault from South-West Africa. The Germans surrendered to South African forces before the Portuguese arrived. The Africans of southern Angola, including the still-independent Kwanyama state, were crushed in the middle of a terrible drought and famine. As the south recovered, the Kwanyama turned from slave-raiding to cattle-raising, and southern Angola became an important source of hides for the Portuguese market. Some poor Ovambo commoners worked as herdsmen for the rich cattle-owners, but most preferred to migrate to the mines of South-West Africa. Many were also compelled to labour in Angola, notably in the southern fisheries.[109]

It was in the sandy eastern plains that the imposition of taxation and the collapse of the rubber- and slave-trades were most strongly felt. The eastern peoples lacked any commodity to replace rubber and slaves, although wax did something to fill the gap. It was when the credit structure collapsed that the situation came to a head. European traders, themselves heavily in debt to coastal merchants, demanded payment from their African debtors. People unable to pay killed a few white traders in 1917 and refused to pay taxes. The Portuguese sent an ineffectual punitive expedition, but they had the greatest difficulty in pinning down their elusive foes. The Ovambo had a chief who could be captured, a capital which could be entered in triumph, and a professional army which could be mown down with Maxim guns. The eastern peoples, by contrast, were scattered in autonomous villages over a vast and inaccessible area; they were well armed and trained in warfare after decades of slave-raiding. Colonial campaigns therefore

107 H. Pössinger, 'Interrelations between economic and social change in rural Africa: the case of the Ovimbundu of Angola', in *Social Change in Angola*, F. W. Hiemer (ed.), Munich, 1973, pp. 32–52. Pössinger is somewhat unreliable for historical detail, but presents the best overall picture.
108 G. M. Childs, *Umbundu Kinship and Character*, London, 1949, p. 42; Ross, *Report*, p. 31.
109 Clarence-Smith, *Slaves*, pp. 81–2 and epilogue; R. Pélissier, *Les Guerres Grises*, ch. 17.

dragged on well into the 1920s.[110] Where taxes were imposed, people drifted into Northern Rhodesia and the Belgian Congo, sometimes as migrant labourers but mainly as permanent settlers. Others went to work on the diamond-fields of north-eastern Angola, which employed some 6 000 unskilled labourers.[111]

In two decades, Angola had become similar to the other colonies of Central Africa. International capital commanded the heights of the mining and plantation economy, while local settlers consolidated their position in agriculture and fishing. The colonial state more or less controlled the territory internationally allocated to it, and extorted labour and taxation in a rather erratic and brutal fashion. Communications were modernised, and settled agriculture was slowly replacing raiding, hunting, collecting and caravan-trading. The local colonial oligarchy enjoyed certain political and legal freedoms, and had become almost as white and racist as elsewhere in Central Africa. Slavery had finally been eradicated, and the sale of alcohol and fire-arms was closely regulated. Portugal could participate in the International Colonial Exhibition of 1931 as a full and equal member of the dubious fraternity of colonial powers.

THE SALAZARIST ERA, 1930–1961

The rise to power of António Salazar began with an army *coup* in 1926. The military leaders were divided about their aims, and some only wanted to 'cleanse' the democratic system. It was the world economic depression which allowed Salazar, a lecturer in accountancy, to consolidate his position in the government. He established a 'new state' modelled on Mussolini's Italy, but managed to avoid the fate of Italian fascism by remaining neutral in the Second World War. Salazar's support came initially from Portugal's southern landowners, major industrialists, and northern peasants, who had been alienated by republican anti-clericalism and rural neglect. The church was another pillar of the régime, but Salazar's relations with the army were ambivalent. He allowed the army considerable autonomy, while simultaneously increasing the power of para-military forces under his direct command.[112]

Salazarist colonial policies had both ideological and economic motivations. On the one hand, Salazar employed a delirious colonial rhetoric to encourage a virulent nationalism. This was to be the cement for the uneasy class coalition which underpinned his régime. The colonies were the living link with past glories, and valueless fortresses like Ajúda, in French Dahomey, were retained like museum pieces. On the other hand,

---

110 Clarence-Smith, *Slaves*, pp. 95–6; Pélissier, *Les Guerres Grises*, chs 11, 16.
111 Rates, *Angola*, pp. 55–6.
112 Marques, *História*, ch. 13; D. Porch, *The Portuguese Armed Forces and the Revolution*, London, 1977, ch. 1.

Salazar turned to the colonies for a solution to the economic crisis of the 1930s. Reliance on colonial markets and raw materials was in vogue in the 1930s. The peculiarity of Salazar's 'colonial pact' was that it survived long after other powers had abandoned the idea.[113]

The first strand in Salazar's colonial economic policy was the restoration of protected markets. Tariffs and exchange regulations favoured Portuguese products, notably textiles, although Salazar did not return to the excessively high protectionism of the 1890s. Angolan imports from Portugal stabilised at around 50 per cent during these decades. Cotton textiles, wine and foodstuffs were supplemented by Portuguese beer and cement in the 1930s, and by chemical and metal products in the 1940s, thus reflecting the slow but steady diversification of Portuguese industry. Motor vehicles, railway equipment, coal, petrol and many kinds of machinery were obtained from foreign sources.[114] Commerce and shipping continued to be protected, and the merchant navy was renovated in the 1950s for operation on protected colonial routes.[115]

In addition to practising traditional protectionism, Salazar began systematically to exploit Angola's raw materials. Half of Angola's exports were for consumption in Portugal, especially raw sugar, raw cotton, maize, hides and oil-seeds. It is often asserted that Portugal obtained these commodities cheaply, but the situation was more complex. In the 1930s, and again in the late 1950s, Portugal was obtaining colonial raw materials at prices above those on the world market. Salazar was pursuing two separate policies, one of lowering the cost of raw materials, and the other of providing stable prices for colonial producers.[116] The other half of Angola's exports were not involved in this domestic pricing. Diamonds, most of the coffee, sisal and fish products were sold abroad to earn foreign exchange. In 1931, it was decreed that all foreign exchange gained in exports was to be deposited with a government agency in Luanda, which then allocated it to importers. In 1948, a single foreign-exchange fund for Portugal and its colonies was set up in Lisbon. Thereafter, the substantial Angolan trade surplus subsidised Portugal's chronic trade deficits.[117]

Although Salazar was said to have been hostile to foreign investment, his attitude was in reality ambivalent.[118] Xenophobic attacks on privileged interests were balanced by efforts to attract more foreign capitalists to

113 Marques, *História*, ch. 14.
114 F. O'Meara, *Report on Economic and Commercial Conditions in Angola*, London, Department of Overseas Trade, 1937; D. Fynes-Clinton, *Portuguese West Africa, Economic and Commercial Conditions*, London, Board of Trade, 1949.
115 Sousa, 'A renovação'.
116 Portugal, *Primeira conferência*, Vol. I, p. 27; Fynes-Clinton, *Portuguese West Africa*, p. 13; J. P. Pontes and N. Santos, 'O têxtil e a inserção internacional da economia portuguesa', *Economia e Socialismo*, iv, 43, 1979, 37–49.
117 F. O'Meara, *Report*, pp. 2–3; Fynes-Clinton, *Portuguese West Africa*, pp. 17, 24.
118 A. K. Smith, 'António Salazar and the reversal of Portuguese colonial policy', *JAH*, xv, 4, 1974, 653–67, for the view that Salazar was hostile to foreign capital.

invest in the colonies in the 1930s.[119] The bankruptcies of the great depression led foreign companies to take over important sectors of the Angolan economy.[120] Diamonds and cotton concessions were largely controlled by the Société Générale de Belgique, while another Belgian corporation, the Hallet group, consolidated its hold over Angolan coffee plantations. The Cabinda Company also fell into Belgian hands.[121] The aim of Salazar was not to keep foreign capital out, but to strike a better bargain with foreign investors. The stable and authoritarian 'new state' proved a more efficient broker than the transient governments of the republic.

In the 1940s and 1950s, the state was pressed by the Portuguese oligopolies to take a harder line with foreign capital. The Spanish Civil War and the Second World War were times of great prosperity for Portuguese industry, which profited from neutrality in both conflicts. At the same time, the disruption of transport to Africa lowered the profits of colonial trade. With surplus capital in hand, the oligopolies began to think for the first time of investing in the colonies. Between 1937 and 1943, Salazar enacted a complex set of laws and decrees to determine that certain types of property could be held only by Portuguese nationals. In the colonies, these laws particularly affected the plantation sector.[122] Portuguese houses recovered both coffee interests and the Cabinda Company from Belgian control.[123]

Even more striking was the relaxation in the 1940s of the ban on colonial industrialisation, as the oligopolies began to finance import-substitution industries. This process was directed at the African mass market, and not, as often alleged, at the settler luxury market. Cheap cotton textiles, hoes, and other simple iron tools were the first goods to be produced. In the late 1950s, the emphasis shifted towards intermediary goods for local productive activities. Bulky goods which were expensive to transport came high on the list, notably cement, tyres, jute sacking and petro-chemicals.[124]

The state took an active role in improving economic infrastructures. The colonial development fund of 1938 financed the widening of the Moçâmedes railway and improvements to the port of Luanda. With the introduction of regular development plans in 1953, the emphasis shifted to

119 Cya, *Economia*, p. 57.
120 A. S. Gonçalves, 'O crédito de fomento em Angola', *Boletim da Associação Industrial de Angola*, iv, 15–16, 1953, 8–9.
121 Bullock, *Economic Conditions*, pp. 27–8 on the Société Générale; Cya, *Economia*, p. 102.
122 J. da Costa Oliveira, *Aplicação de capitais nas províncias ultramarinas*, Lisbon, 1961, pp. 12–14.
123 A. Castro, *O sistema colonial português em África (meados do século XX)*, Lisbon, 2nd edn, 1978, pp. 14, 132–4; Companhia de Cabinda, *Relatório e contas*, Lisbon, 1955, p. 12.
124 Azevedo, *Angola*, especially pp. 326–30, 434–9.

hydro-electric stations. A network of air transport was also established. Most of the funds for these projects were generated inside Angola, or took the form of loans from Portugal. Little direct aid was involved. Cheap forced labour continued to underpin the public works programme.[125]

Foreign capital was welcomed in high-risk, costly and technologically advanced sectors of production. Thus the Belgian Petrofina company took over petroleum prospecting and began production near Luanda in the mid-1950s.[126] Foreign capital was also allowed in other sectors, but only if it was associated with Portuguese firms. The Banque de Bruxelles took a half-share in the Banco Comercial de Angola, set up in 1957 after long negotiations. The new bank rapidly acquired a stake in a wide variety of enterprises.[127] Belgian capital continued to maintain a quasi-monopoly of foreign investment, perhaps because Salazar had few qualms about a small neutral state like Belgium, whereas he feared the intentions of great powers.

The Angolan bourgeoisie was hit hard by the 1930s depression, but it blossomed once again after the war. The rise in coffee prices from the mid-1940s led to a sustained planting boom. The coffee lands of North Kwanza became a new El Dorado. Poor immigrants were able to obtain land concessions and benefit from cheap forced labour. Coffee required little specialised knowledge or equipment, and was a hardy plant which grew wild in the area. Immigrants, unlike their African competitors, gained preferential access to credit and markets. By the end of the 1950s, a new class of small planters had sprung up, determined to hang on to its prosperity whatever the hostility of local Africans.[128] Some of the profits were invested in expanding production or in local industries, but most continued to be repatriated to Portugal and invested in metropolitan real estate.[129]

The white community in Angola expanded and contracted with the economy. In the 1930s, government departments and companies cut back strongly on employment. Indebted self-employed traders, farmers and fishermen lost their means of subsistence. Some poverty-stricken whites begged on the streets, while others were repatriated.[130] The over-all evolution of the white population is shown overleaf:

---

125 *Ibid.*, pp. 123, 110–11, 200–11; Castro, *O sistema*, pp. 38–9; Fynes-Clinton, *Portuguese West Africa*, pp. 5–6.
126 *Boletim da Associação Industrial de Angola*, ix, 34, 1958, 26.
127 H. Lopes Guerra, *Angola, estrutura económica e classes sociais*, Luanda, 1975, p. 46. The date, 1950, given by Guerra is incorrect. My thanks go to Jean-Luc Vellut for information on Belgian companies.
128 Pélissier, *La Colonie*, pp. 454–67.
129 Castro, *O sistema*, pp. 169–71; Guerra, *Angola*, pp. 52, 153, 156–64.
130 J. de Sousa e Faro, *Angola como eu a vi em 1930–1931*, Lisbon, 1932, p. 22; Portugal, *Primeira conferência*, Vol. I, p. 334.

TABLE 5:1

WHITE POPULATION OF ANGOLA[131]

1920	20 700	1940	44 038
1927	42 843	1950	78 826
1931	59 493	1960	172 529

Some whites found their El Dorado in Angola, but the most striking characteristic of the white community was its poverty. The deeply rooted white poverty of the south was only slowly ameliorated. Lack of land, indebtedness, archaic production techniques, alcoholism, malnourishment,

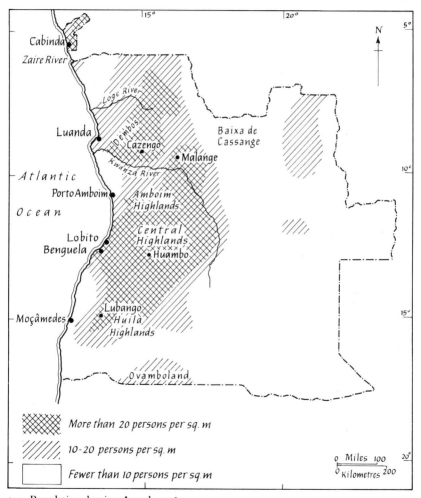

5:4 Population density, Angola, 1960

131 Lefebvre, *L'Angola*, pp. 77, 80; Bender, *Angola*, p. 20.

illiteracy and cultural isolation made the recuperation of southern whites as difficult as that of the Afrikaner 'poor whites' in South Africa. In the towns, white unemployment was a great problem, made worse by high rates of illiteracy. In 1960 up to 20 000 unemployed whites lived off charity, the sale of lottery tickets, illegal activities and the earnings of their African wives and concubines. Even the employees of Luanda, often considered the luckiest of whites, lived a hard life. The cost of living was high, and salaries were modest. Some white-collar employees earned less than white dockers. Bachelors lived in small hostels, where alcoholism and prostitution were serious problems. Employees in the private sector were better paid, but they worked very long hours.[132]

The effects of this persistent poverty were a paradoxical mixture of radicalism and racism. There was a strong feeling of egalitarianism and solidarity in the white community, born of a sense of exploitation. Some whites, like working-class radicals in Algeria, went so far as to join the clandestine communist party. But radicalism generally went together with a virulent racism. Newly arrived immigrants were provided with a shelter and some source of income, often at the expense of Africans. Skin colour was used as much as possible to gain advantage, and the discourse of whites was as racist as that prevalent in South Africa and Rhodesia. The political impotence of the settler population prevented the promulgation of any overtly racist legislation. The mixture of poverty, radicalism, solidarity and racism accounted for the hysterical determination of the white community not to give in to African nationalist demands in 1961, in strong contrast with attitudes in the Belgian Congo.

The African and *mestiço* petty bourgeoisie was thrown into crisis by the late 1950s, largely because of white immigration. The depression of the 1930s had virtually cleared the creoles out of their remaining positions in the productive sector of the economy. Only a few hundred freehold coffee-planters survived the intense pressure of their white rivals. The overwhelming majority of the 26 000 *mestiços* and 30 000 'assimilated Africans' worked in the bureaucracy or in skilled and semi-skilled occupations. They faced growing competition from white immigrants, desperate for jobs and filled with a sense of racial superiority.[133] Wage differentials based on skin colour were frequent, up to four-fold in the docks.[134] By 1961, Luanda had become a flash point of racial tension. The MPLA (Movimento Popular para a Libertação de Angola) emerged in the late 1950s to defend creole interests.[135]

---

132 Castro, *O sistema*, pp. 150, 181–6, 203; Lefebvre, *L'Angola*, pp. 81–110; Reis Ventura, *A nova Angola*, Luanda, 2nd edn, 1959, pp. 106–15, 131, 187; P. Anderson, 'Portugal and the end of ultra-colonialism', *New Left Review*, xvi, 1962, 101–2.
133 F. W. Heimer, *Der Entkolonisierungskonflikt in Angola*, Munich, 1979, pp. 51–6, 67–81.
134 Castro, *O sistema*, p. 182.
135 J. Marcum, *The Angolan Revolution*, vol. I, 1950–62, Cambridge, Mass., 1969.

The MPLA also enjoyed support among the urban working class, which was growing fast and becoming more proletarianised. The black population of Luanda grew from 46 000 in 1940 to 155 000 in 1960, with most migrants coming from the Mbundu hinterland.[136] Some were under contract, but increasingly they came to stay with their families. In 1942, the government encouraged firms to employ stabilised proletarian labour on the Belgian model. Efficient firms themselves moved towards labour stabilisation, since the cheapness of migrant labour was outweighed by its low productivity.[137] By 1961, black proletarians were a force to be reckoned with, and they were as discontented with their wages and conditions as the creoles.

Outside the colonial nucleus, Africans were affected in contradictory ways by the slump of the 1930s. On the one hand, the demand for land and labour fell away; many employers went bankrupt, and nearly all those who stayed afloat reduced their work-force and took land out of cultivation. On the other hand, conditions at work became harsher, as employers cut their costs.[138] As crop prices fell, Africans found it hard to pay their taxes. Opportunities for migrant labour abroad shrank. Africans thus moved away from centres of authority, and the value of the poll tax fell markedly.[139]

The return of colonial prosperity in the 1940s brought back conditions similar to those of the 1920s. Forced labour became widespread once again, though purged of its most brutal features. Employers offered bribes of £1–2 sterling per labourer, and local officials rounded up the requisite number of labourers. Contracts were for a year, to be followed by six months' rest. Wages, mainly paid at the end of the contract, were a little over £2 sterling a month. Food, shelter, clothing and medical assistance were to be provided by the employer. The standard diet was scarcely nutritious: 500 grammes of cassava flour a day, together with three or four dried fish, often rotten, and a little palm-oil. Contract labourers regularly spent their meagre wages on ground-nuts to complete their diet.

Contract labour was supplemented by casual labour hired on a daily basis, especially on small farms. At peak times in the agricultural year, much of this labour-force was made up of women and children. Women received 1 *escudo* a day, or £0·40 a month. Women were still those most affected by unpaid forced labour demands for public works, such as road-

136 R. Ladeiro Monteiro, 'From extended to residual family: aspects of social change in the musseques of Luanda', in *Social Change in Angola*, F. W. Heimer (ed.), Munich, 1973, pp. 213–14.
137 J. Ferreira, *Província de Luanda*, Coimbra, 1945, pp. 136–8; Castro, *O sistema*, pp. 193, 201–2.
138 J. do Couto Rosado, *Companhia agrícola de Cazengo*, Lisbon, 1945, p. 81; Azevedo, *Angola*, p. 406.
139 Associações Económicas de Angola, *Considerações sôbre o problema das transferências de Angola*, Lisbon, 1932, pp. 53–4; O'Meara, *Report*, pp. 3–4.

building and -repairing. In 1957, more than 25 000 people worked for the state under these conditions. Penal labour was frequently still imposed by the courts, especially for tax-defaulters.

In 1956, Portugal finally signed the international forced-labour convention and brought in new regulations. The news spread rapidly through Angola, and some workers refused to sign contracts until they were brought under control. The major employers in the colony, the diamond-mines and coffee plantations, were exempted from the new labour protection regulations, and forced labour on public works continued. Under the new regulations, 1 300 labour recruiters obtained official licences and fanned out through the colony. Every kind of underhand method was used to sign up African contract workers, and officials were still prepared to put pressure on recalcitrants. Although conditions at work may have improved slightly, the 1956 regulations failed to satisfy the expectations they aroused. By the late 1950s, rural labour was as discontented as urban labour in many parts of the colony.[140]

One colonial grievance was very specifically located in Angola. This was forced cotton cultivation in the Baixa de Cassange, which contained a little under 200 000 people. Forced cotton cultivation had been introduced in 1926, but it was only widely imposed in the 1940s. Cotton cultivation zones were exempt from contract labour; instead, all the inhabitants had to cultivate a hectare or so of cotton. Cotton concessionary companies provided seed, supervised planting, gave technical advice and provided insecticides. The companies then bought the crop at fixed prices set by the government. This rigid system was much disliked by the people of the area, partly because food crops tended to suffer, but mainly because of the large amount of labour involved for small and uncertain rewards. Cotton prices were set very low, and no account was taken of the various natural calamities which affected the harvest. Africans responded to the system by clandestine emigration, and minor outbreaks of violent protest occurred in the 1950s. The bad season of 1959–1960, with its excessive rains and a plague of insects, set the scene for the bloody rising of 1961.[141]

Land alienation in the northern coffee zone was another bitter but localised grievance. The area under coffee cultivation doubled in the 1950s. Some land was seized from Africans by openly violent and illegal means, but most of the time the settlers seem to have remained within the letter of the law. Africans had neither the money nor the expertise to register land rights or to fight for them in the courts. Land alienation was doubly galling, as dispossessed landowners could be declared vagabonds and thereby forced to work on what had been their own land. As in the Baixa

140 Castro, *O sistema*, pp. 89, 105, 110, 130–1, 145–6, 150, 155–6, 182, 187, 193, 196–8, 408.
141 Pélissier, *La Colonie*, ch. 11.

de Cassange, emigration and isolated outbreaks of violence preceded the great explosion of peasant resentment in 1961.[142]

The land problem in the centre of Angola and in parts of the south was of a different nature. White settlers took up little land, but rapid population growth, soil erosion and unequal family access to land created severe pressures. The Ovimbundu expanded outwards, but were unable to find enough fresh lands for their needs. The central highlands became the main labour reservoir of the colony, and men migrated because of economic pressures rather than administrative coercion. The greatest social tensions related to rural credit, which tied men to traders who acted as labour recruiters. The lack of any major upheaval in the central highlands in 1961 may indicate that land shortage and rural debt, unlike land seizures and forced cultivation, were not perceived to be the fault of the colonial system.[143] In the south, colonial cattle ranches disrupted traditional patterns of cattle transhumance, but the major stresses were caused by population growth in an ecologically marginal area. The Ovambo in particular were driven to migrate in search of work, going to South-West Africa rather than to centres of employment in Angola.[144]

The east, too, was quiet in 1961, under the close domination of the diamond company. Diamang encouraged labourers to bring their families to settle permanently in the mining zone, offering them land and agricultural assistance. The soils were poor and fit for little more than subsistence production, but the company guaranteed to buy up any surplus produce. By 1957, about two-thirds of the 21 000 mine labourers were local residents. Diamang ran its own police, schools, hospitals, roads, airports, power stations, shops and cattle ranches, and there were no rival employers. Salaries were a little above the Angolan average, and the social services provided by the company were incomparably better than those elsewhere in the colony. In particular, the company eradicated sleeping sickness over a wide area. Diamang also provided training for skilled and better paid jobs. In effect, Diamang imported from the Belgian Congo that particular mixture of technocracy, autocracy, paternalism and social Catholicism which was such a marked feature of the great Belgian corporations.[145]

A small minority of Africans consolidated their position as rich peasants or kulaks. In the 1950s there were 30 000 Africans producing coffee for the market, of whom about a tenth were well off. A few hundred of these coffee kulaks had made the transition to full capitalist farming, owning land in private freehold tenure and employing contract labour. Elsewhere,

142 *Ibid.*, ch. 12; Castro, *O sistema*, especially pp. 127–8.
143 Pössinger, 'Interrelations'.
144 Clarence-Smith, *Slaves*, epilogue; C. A. Medeiros, *A colonização das terras altas da Huíla*, Lisbon, 1976.
145 Companhia de Diamantes de Angola, *Companhia de Diamantes de Angola, breve notícia sobre a sua actividade em Angola*, Lisbon, 1963; Castro, *O sistema*, pp. 155–6.

kulaks were still working communal lands with family labour, though rights to land in the central highlands were moving towards a system of *de facto* private property. The wealthier maize producers were buying bicycles, radios, sewing machines and even cameras, as a testimony to rural prosperity. A few thousand Africans produced sisal for the market, and some southern pastoralists owned hundreds of head of cattle.[146] There is no indication that the kulaks were collaborators with the Portuguese; indeed,

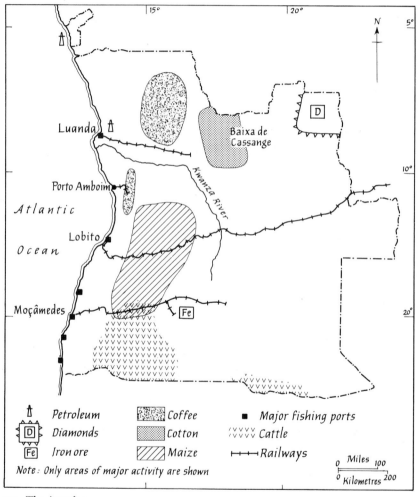

5:5 The Angolan economy, c. 1970

146 Castro, *O sistema*, pp. 112, 118–20, 127–9, 142, 181, 196, 202; Pélissier, *La Colonie*, pp 457–67; Clarence-Smith, *Slaves*, p. 103.

it can be argued that their rising expectations sometimes made them the spear-head of anti-colonial protest.[147]

Rural frustration was intensified by the heavy hand of an authoritarian administrative system, unchecked by humanitarian influence from the metropolis. Unlike other colonials, Africans could not count on the press and left-wing parties of the metropolis to defend their interests. Only a few courageous individuals tried to break through the dense web of censorship and repression. Portuguese administrators remained petty dictators, frequently meting out corporal punishment to their African subjects. As before, it was the hated African *cipaios* who actually administered beatings. Corporal punishment was often ordered on the simple denunciation of a white employer or trader, and Africans had no effective legal possibilities of redress.[148]

The only intermediaries between the administration and the people were the Christian missions, which flourished as never before. In the 1960 census, 49 per cent of Angola's black population registered as Catholic, and 17 per cent as Protestant. Even if the figures for Catholics were inflated, Angola was one of the most Christianised colonies in Africa. Nowhere was this process more advanced than in the central highlands, where one distinguished anthropologist had great difficulty in finding any 'traditional' Ovimbundu left at all. Education did not keep pace with conversion, however, and only 6 to 7 per cent of African children attended school. Health facilities were similarly undeveloped and in rural areas were left to the missions, which received a small subsidy.[149]

The Protestants formed harassed but very vital sub-cultures in Angola, and they were to play a part out of all proportion to their numbers in the liberation struggle. Salazar distrusted Protestant missionaries, and suspected them, not without reason, of instilling anti-Portuguese ideas in the minds of their converts. Protestant Africans found it particularly hard to obtain assimilated status and a job in the bureaucracy. The non-recognition of Protestant marriages was often used to refuse assimilated status to Protestants. Many Protestant Africans were thus channelled into kulak farming, particularly in the north and centre of the colony. In Luanda, the Methodists were in a different situation. Their prestigious secondary school was attended by a mixture of up-country Mbundu mission children and the offspring of the Luanda élite. Many of the Protestant Africans who were educated in this school became assimilated Portuguese citizens and played a leading role in the MPLA opposition to colonial rule. The divisions between different Protestant groups and the

147 W. G. Clarence-Smith, 'Class structure and class struggles in Angola in the 1970s', *Journal of Southern African Studies*, vii, 1, 1980, 109–26.
148 Castro, *O sistema*, especially pp. 176–7.
149 Okuma, 'The Social Response'; A. Edwards, *The Ovimbundu under Two Sovereignties*, London, 1962.

wider division between Catholics and Protestants had deep roots in Angola by the 1950s. They were probably more important than ethnic differences.[150]

The Protestants were not the only religious group to be persecuted for their beliefs. The 1950s witnessed the modest development of African independent churches, spilling over from the French and Belgian Congos. By 1961, 50 000 Angolans were members of independent churches. The Kongo and the Chokwe, in frontier areas, were those most affected. Two major groups were the Lassy church, active in Cabinda, and the Toko church, which split off from the Baptist church. Independent movements generally preached a passive withdrawal from the white man's world, instructing their adherents to obey the constituted authorities. The response of the Portuguese was unnecessarily heavy-handed, since the independent churches did not pose any real political threat. By deporting members of the Toko church to other parts of Angola, the authorities merely broadened the base of what had been originally a narrowly Kongo movement.[151]

CONCLUSION

By 1961, social tensions were high in Angola, and it needed only a spark to set the whole fabric of colonial society alight. Forced labour, land alienation, forced cultivation, racial animosity and religious persecution formed a potent combination of grievances. The spark was provided by the rapid decolonisation of Africa, and in particular by events surrounding the independence of the Belgian Congo in 1960. It has often been asserted that the Portuguese were caught completely unaware by the uprisings in 1961, but this is far from the truth. The authorities had become increasingly worried by the internal and external threats to Portuguese sovereignty. In 1957, the Policia Internacional de Defesa do Estado (PIDE) a 'secret' political police, was brought into Angola for the first time. It wrought havoc in the ranks of urban opponents to Portuguese rule but found difficulty in penetrating the countryside. In 1959, army reinforcements were sent from Portugal because of the situation in the Belgian Congo. It was the scale and the bitterness of the 1961 risings which took the Portuguese by surprise. Censorship and political authoritarianism had made the government particularly ignorant of the realities of life in Angola.[152]

If the Portuguese underestimated the power of despair, the liberation movements failed to understand the determination of their colonial masters

150 L. Henderson, *Angola, Five Centuries of Conflict*, Ithaca, N.Y., 1979, pp. 145–60, 217–22.
151 Pélissier, *La Colonie*, ch. 4.
152 *Ibid.*, pp. 322–30.

to resist. The poverty of Angolan whites was a key factor in local resistance to the 'winds of change'. However, the determining factor in 1961 was that the colonies were still vital to powerful sectors of the Portuguese bourgeoisie. This dependency had long ceased to be important in the more developed countries of Europe.[153] In political terms, a neo-colonial solution was not viable, owing to the weakness of the non-white petty bourgeoisie. Equally important, the ideological practice of the Salazarist régime had become so dependent on colonial mythology that it was impossible for Portugal to let go of even the smallest and most unprofitable of its colonies without the régime itself being threatened.

153 E. Rocha, 'Portugal, anos 60: crescimento económico acelerado e papel das relações com as colónias', *Análise Social*, xiii, 51, 1977, 593–617.

CHAPTER 6

The political economy of East-Central Africa

LEROY VAIL

The white man has brought wealth along with his other gifts, and this
wealth is free to all who will work.
— Blantyre, Nyasaland newspaper editorial, 1900[1]

I'm working in hunger;
The owners are full.
It's a bad sign!
It's a bad sign!
— Mozambique work song, 1975[2]

Anger and sadness are constant companions of the student who explores the
history of the people of Mozambique, Malawi and Zambia over the past
century. During this period, the overriding fact of their existence has been
their inexorable subjugation to the demands of various forms of capitalism.
The history of this process, which resulted in the erosion of the village
household economy and a declining quality of life, is a dolorous tale. One
must guard against identifying colonialism, imposed in the 1890s, with the
growth of capitalist relations. The region's involvement with the world
capitalist economy began well before the imposition of formal control by
the imperial powers of Europe, and continues today, long after the end of
empires. Although of cardinal importance, the colonial state and its policies
were the logical consequences of a set of changes already well-advanced by
the 1890s. These had already brought profound economic and social
restructuring of African societies in the region. In order to begin to assess
the political economy of colonialism in East-Central Africa, then, one must
turn back to the middle of the nineteenth century.

1 *Central African Times*, Blantyre, 17 March 1900.
2 Song sung in Lomwe by Armindo Francisco and Manuel Ahipetela, of Mulevala,
Mozambique, at Muidi compound village, Luabo, Mozambique, 9 Aug. 1975.

SOCIAL DISINTEGRATION IN THE NINETEENTH CENTURY

The changes that set the stage for the establishment of formal colonial rule throughout East-Central Africa were complex. One of these changes originated in South Africa. In the 1810s the Zulu state under its great leader Shaka began expanding against its neighbours, using revolutionary military technology and strategy. The result was a tremendous social and political upheaval in the Natal and Transvaal areas in the 1810s and 1820s. This came to be known as the *mfecane*, the 'crushing of people', or the *difaqane*, 'the hammering'. From this event there arose groups of refugees, known variously as Gaza, Kololo, Ndebele and Ngoni, who were equipped with the new and highly effective military technology and tactics

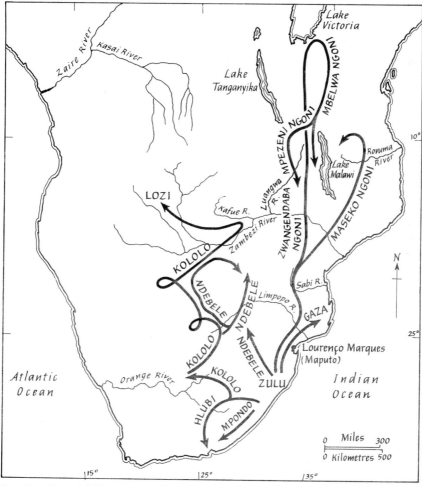

6:1 East-Central Africa: nineteenth–century migrations after the *mfecane* and *difaqane*

201

which Shaka had developed. These groups moved northwards across the Limpopo river, attacking and raiding as they went. For three decades their marauding disrupted the people of Mozambique, Zimbabwe, Malawi, Zambia and Tanzania, reaching even the shores of Lake Victoria. More important, they exposed wide areas to their innovative technology and principles of organisation. In self-defence many peoples emulated the outsiders. This led to a general militarisation of South-Central and East-Central Africa and a great increase in the level of insecurity in the region.[3]

A second outside influence interacted with the first, resulting in further dislocation. This was the spread of mercantile capitalism from the east coast of Africa in the form of a trade in slaves, ivory, cloth, beads, guns and gunpowder. For centuries there had been a modest slave-trade along the East African coast, but the nineteenth century witnessed a remarkable increase in demand. The first surge occurred along the coast of Mozambique and in the Zambezi valley. Britain had outlawed trading in slaves by its subjects in 1807, but because it was seeking trade concessions in Brazil, it did not press Portugal to take similar action. Since the Portuguese-held areas north of the Equator had already been 'slaved out', the still-legal Portuguese trade shifted to new markets along the Mozambique coast. This coincided with a massive increase in demand for slaves to work the rapidly expanding sugar plantations of Brazil. Ships soon began arriving in Mozambique's ports in search of human cargoes.[4] Over the next three decades this legal trade grew steadily, utilising the already existing Portuguese *prazo* estates in the Zambezi valley as conduits through which slaves from the interior were funnelled down to the coast.

After three decades of expansion, the Portuguese responded to new British pressure in the early 1840s and outlawed the slave-trade. The trade continued none the less, even expanding to meet fresh demands for slaves in Cuba, the islands of the Indian Ocean and in East Africa, as well as in Brazil itself. In Mozambique, the business moved from Quelimane and Mozambique Island to secluded coves and estuaries. Slavers traversed northern Mozambique, Malawi and eastern and northern Zambia to draw new areas into the pattern of trade.[5]

In addition to the growing demand for slaves, there was also an active demand for ivory. Long valued in India, China and Europe for ornaments, ivory's value increased greatly after 1850 when it came to be used for billiard balls and piano keys among Europe's expanding middle class.

3 For a detailed discussion of the groups that left South Africa for the north and the migration routes, see John Omer-Cooper, *The Zulu Aftermath*, London, 1966.
4 The development of this slave-trade is discussed at considerable length in Leroy Vail and Landeg White, *Capitalism and Colonialism in Mozambique: a Study of Quelimane District*, London, 1980, pp. 16–41, 85–7.
5 For a full discussion of the slave- and ivory-trades, see Edward A. Alpers, *Ivory and Slaves in East Central Africa*, London, 1975, as well as his 'Trade, state and society among the Yao in the nineteenth century', *Journal of African History (JAH)*, x, 3, 1969, 405–20.

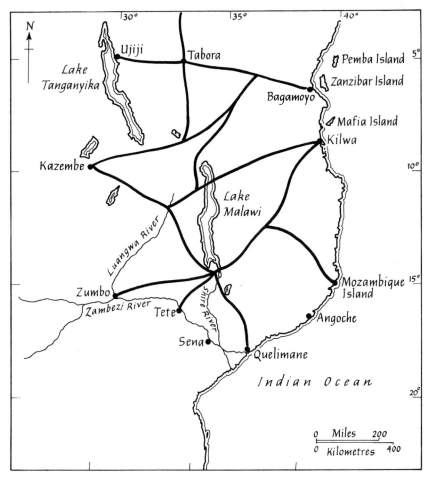

6:2 Trade routes in East-Central Africa in the mid–nineteenth century

Hunters and traders followed the depleted herds of elephants deeper into the interior, bringing more of the region's people into contact with the corrosive force of mercantile capitalism.[6] The ivory- and slave-trades became intertwined in a complex web of routes and business dealings that gradually drew the various parts of the region into an economic unit with focal points at the coastal ports of Quelimane, Kilwa, Zanzibar and Bagamoyo.

With the passing decades, traders moved westward in increasing numbers, and their activities brought change to the pre-capitalist societies of the interior. The traders sought alliances with local leaders who could

6 On this point, see Geoffrey Kay's seminal *Development and Underdevelopment: a Marxist Analysis*, London, 1975, especially pp. 95–105.

supply ivory and slaves. As market values became increasingly important, social and economic stratification became pronounced. Chiefs, hunters and raiders augmented their power. Of deeper consequence, the region experienced the emergence of strong societies with well-developed élite groups that could mobilise military force against weaker neighbours. Aggression became a way of life for many of them.[7] The strong preyed upon the weak and fought amongst themselves. This lust for gain, coupled with the ever-growing militarisation of the area, turned societies into grotesque parodies of their former selves, and insecurity became rampant. Of Malawi in the 1850s it is remembered that 'the villages were small and isolated from one another. There was a constant pouncing on people to catch them as slaves. It was unsafe to go even a quarter mile from one village to another'.[8] Children became an especially valued commodity in these insecure times.

Contact with the disruptive slave- and ivory-trades also caused profound ecological changes. Throughout the lightly wooded plateaux of the region, the ideal settlement pattern had been one of households sprinkled evenly over the arable land. The people followed land-extensive agricultural systems which demanded light inputs of capital and labour. Exhausted land regenerated itself through long periods of fallow. These systems were important in East-Central Africa, where high infant-mortality rates, long periods between bearing children, and periodic epidemics kept available labour power scarce and demand for foodstuffs low. A low population density was the key to making such a system work effectively. The yield was then 'far higher in terms of crop weight per unit of direct and indirect' labour than was possible in more intensive systems.[9]

Such an agricultural system could not survive the raiding and insecurity that the ivory- and slave-trades brought to the region. People withdrew from the countryside and huddled together in newly established stockades and fortified villages, or fled to more secure areas, seeking patrons who could protect them. As early as the 1820s and 1830s areas of Mozambique were reported as depopulated, with fields abandoned and with unproductive bush infested by wild animals and tsetse fly.[10] The slave-trade also removed the most important human resource, thereby diminishing the productive capacity of an area already suffering labour shortages. This new pattern of settlement spread inland with the trade,

7 For accounts of societies such as the Ndebele, the Lozi, the Lunda of Kazembe, the Bemba, see chapters by Reefe, Smith and Beach in volume one.
8 I. Mwale, quoted in Margaret Read, *The Ngoni of Nyasaland*, London, 1956, p. 88; see also Frederick Cooper, *Plantation Slavery on the East Coast of Africa*, New Haven, Connecticut and London, 1977, p. 240, where the author notes that most slaves used on the clove plantations were drawn from the Malawi area.
9 Ester Boserup, *The Conditions of Agricultural Growth: the Economics of Agrarian Change under Population Pressure*, London, 1965, pp. 70–2.
10 Vail and White, *Capitalism and Colonialism in Mozambique*, p. 28.

attended by declining productivity. People still recall that in those days of destruction and insecurity 'agriculture was at its lowest ebb. In the days of the Ngoni wars people feared going into the fields because they did not want to be captured.'[11]

The general decline in productivity and in soil fertility was capped in the 1890s by a set of ecological disasters of almost Biblical intensity. The first of these was the appearance of an insect which had crossed the Atlantic from Brazil in 1872, the South American sand jigger (*Pulex penetrans*). This swept across Africa, reaching East-Central Africa in the early 1890s and arriving on the coast of Mozambique a few years later. The people did not know how to deal with this unfamiliar pest when it burrowed under the skin to lay its eggs. Widespread loss of limbs from infection and gangrene resulted, with many cases of blood-poisoning also occurring. In some instances whole villages were wiped out.[12] Almost simultaneously, a plague of red locusts appeared, destroying crops between 1894 and 1896.[13] Immediately afterwards, the great rinderpest epidemic swept through the region, killing both wild game, an important source of protein, and cattle, the basis of people's wealth.[14] One by one, the disasters of the 1890s mounted, weakening the people and rendering them susceptible to a widespread smallpox epidemic, a drought and finally to a savage famine between 1900 and 1902.

By the end of the nineteenth century most societies of East-Central Africa had undergone, in just a few decades, a range of revolutionary changes. People were left peculiarly vulnerable to the new forms of capitalism then making their appearance in the form of the 'scramble for Africa'. It was largely for this reason that imperial control was imposed without effective resistance by East-Central Africans.

CAPITALISM FROM THE SOUTH

During the nineteenth century East-Central Africa's orientation had been firmly towards the east coast, but in the 1890s it fell under the magnetic pull of the Witwatersrand's gold industry. The discovery of diamonds at Kimberley in 1867 and of gold on the Rand in 1886 had transformed a South African economy hitherto based upon pastoralism and agriculture.

---

11 O(ral) T(estimony). Chilobe Phiri, Chilobe village, Lundazi district, Zambia, 1 May 1974.
12 For a detailed discussion of this process among one important Central African people, see Leroy Vail, 'The making of the "Dead North": a study of Ngoni rule in northern Malawi, c. 1855–1907', in *Before and After Shaka: Papers in Nguni History*, J. Peires (ed.), Grahamstown, 1981; also Helge Kjekshus, *Ecology Control and Economic Development in East African History: the Case of Tanganyika, 1850–1950*, London, 1977, pp. 134–6.
13 *Ibid.*, pp. 138–40.
14 For a discussion of the tragic impact of rinderpest upon southern Africa, see Charles van Onselen, 'Reactions to rinderpest in Southern Africa, 1896–7', *JAH*, xiii, 3, 1972, 473–88.

Instead, it became an economy based on industrial growth. The new industries, particularly the mines, required large numbers of manual labourers at low cost. As South Africa was chronically short of manpower, industrial leaders looked to the north. Mobilisation of labour required direct political control, for workers from north of the Limpopo river were no keener to journey far from their homes to work for small wages than were South Africans. Large-scale industrial capital thus required a transformation of relations with East-Central Africa through imperial expansion.

A second impulse to imperial domination over the region stemmed from the growing belief that the survival of European capitalism depended upon linking it with a politically overt imperialism. The depression of 1873 had curtailed the European economy sharply and encouraged the growth of neo-mercantilist notions of closed economic systems underpinned by colonial empires. Portugal had long claimed a band of territory across Africa from Angola to Mozambique. Throughout the 1870s and into the 1880s it was ruled by men who attempted to attract capital investment to its colonies, believing that it would strengthen their hand in their endeavours to retain the empire against rival claimants. The efforts were not notably successful. Portugal was joined in its African preoccupations by Leopold of Belgium as well as by French and British interests. The growing concern with Africa led to the Berlin conference of 1884–1885. Portugal's leaders became convinced that their earlier record was unconvincing and decided to pursue more aggressive policies in East-Central Africa. This occurred precisely when the Rand's mines were being developed, and the need for black labour was acknowledged. Thus Portugal and the southern mining interests were rivals in their desire to control the area.

At this point a third factor made itself felt. In 1887, after more than a decade of short money supply on European markets, investment capital became available in excess of what could be utilised at home.[15] The growing European bourgeoisie had large savings and was willing to risk them on the stock market.[16] This change in the money supply occurred just as the Rand's mines were becoming established. In the years before 1914 some 4 per cent of all capital invested by major European countries in their dependencies or spheres of influence overseas went to finance these mines.[17] The conjunction of interest in East-Central Africa as a potential source of labour and minerals and the availability of surplus European capital resulted in the founding of several large companies. These carried the forces of capital and colonialism into South- and East-Central Africa and accelerated the region's transformation by the world capitalist system.

15 S. B. Saul, *The Myth of the Great Depression, 1873–1896*, London, 1969, p. 17.
16 Robert V. Kubicek, *Economic Imperialism in Theory and Practice; the Case of South African Gold Mining Finance, 1886–1914*, Durham, N.C., 1979, p. 30.
17 *Ibid.*, p. 22; see also chapter by Phimister below.

In the 1880s, that old institution, the chartered stock company, had been revived by European governments eager to extend imperial control into far-flung corners of the world without using metropolitan taxpayers' money. The marriage of private money and public administration was attractive but it was also filled with profound contradictions.

The first company chartered for the area was the British South Africa Company, founded in October 1889 at the instigation of a group of London financiers and with the full support of Cecil John Rhodes. This South African politician and gold and diamond magnate was eager to extend his power and influence northwards into what are today Zimbabwe and Zambia, in search of both minerals and labour.[18] The British South Africa Company proceeded to extend its control over these countries. In January 1891, with Rhodes's financial backing, the British also seized control over the British Central Africa Protectorate, later Malawi, thereby forestalling a Portuguese attempt to annex the area.

Rhodes's expansionism threatened Portugal's very presence in Mozambique, and in 1891 it chartered the Mozambique Company to balance Rhodes's British South Africa Company. This company had administrative rights over the area between the Sabi and Zambezi rivers. In the same year Portugal also chartered the Niassa Company to govern the two northern districts of Mozambique, Cabo Delgado and Niassa. In 1892, most of Quelimane and Tete districts were leased to a set of private companies, the largest of which was the Zambesia Company.[19] In two years South- and East-Central Africa was thus divided up. Only the Mozambique Island district of Mozambique and the British Central Africa Protectorate were not ruled directly by agents of private capital. Even in areas administered by the state, the interests of investment capital were uppermost in administrators' minds, and 'effective occupation' required economic growth based on outside capital.

The European imperialists faced considerable obstacles in making actual their theoretical powers despite the neat political divisions made in Europe, and despite African weakness after decades of social erosion and ecological decline. The issues involved were clear: in order to establish an economy oriented to the needs of capital, all facets of African independence had to be curtailed. Resistance to colonialism was often linked to the slave- and ivory-trades, which provided centralised groups with guns and other commodities independently of European industrial capital. As Lewis Gann has written:

---

18 For a discussion of Rhodes's motives in expanding his interests north of the Limpopo river, see I. R. Phimister, 'Rhodes, Rhodesia and the Rand', *Journal of Southern African Studies* (*JSAS*), i, 1, 1974, 74–90.
19 For a discussion of these companies, see Leroy Vail, 'Mozambique's chartered Companies: the rule of the feeble', *JAH*, xvii, 3, 1976, 389–416; and Vail and White, *Capitalism and Colonialism in Mozambique*, pp. 113–20.

[N]o European settlement could take place for the direct exploitation of the country. . . . The slave trade was not only immoral and cruel. As the commandant of the British South Africa Company's police in North West Rhodesia put it succinctly, it also constituted an 'iniquitous abduction of valuable labour'.

A system of slave labour could not exist side by side with a system of wage labour. The European mine managers and railway engineers needed African labour. However, they did not want to 'own' Africans and keep them to their dying days. They did not want women. They wanted adult African labourers for limited periods, working for wages and bound to them by contract.[20]

Throughout the 1890s, therefore, and into the early years of the twentieth century, the imperialists strove to end the slave- and ivory-trades and to gain direct access to African labour through war, police action and fraudulent treaty-making. In Mozambique the turning point came in 1895, when the powerful Gaza people in the south were overcome. This put a large number of well-trained soldiers under the control of the Portuguese. They used them as mercenaries in the conquest of the rest of the colony. By 1902 most of Mozambique was secure, although some remote areas resisted domination for another fifteen years.

The British in British Central Africa (Nyasaland) were more fortunate than the Portuguese. Many people, internally disunited, harassed by decades of slaving, and oppressed by their own ruling élite welcomed the British as harbingers of peace. Those who did not share this assessment were gradually defeated. Chiefs were tolerated as long as they did not interfere with the flow of labour to the new European plantations on the Shire Highlands. When they impeded the establishment of the new economy by curtailing the availability of labour, they were attacked and defeated.

Cecil Rhodes sent agents northward to forestall Leopold II's attempt to seize control of Katanga. He failed to acquire Katanga, but did obtain most of the area between the Zambezi and Katanga, including mineral rights over land claimed by Lewanika of the Lozi. In 1891 Britain and Portugal concluded an agreement that largely defined their colonial boundary. In the same year Leopold II's agents seized Katanga without touching Rhodes's claims. Thus within two years the British South Africa Company had gained international recognition of its claims north of the Zambezi. Once secure, the company temporarily abandoned the area and turned to consolidate its hold on what is now Zimbabwe, charging the Commissioner of British Central Africa, Harry Johnston, to look after its territories north of the river.

---

20 Lewis Gann, 'The end of the slave trade in British Central Africa, 1889–1912', *Rhodes-Livingstone Journal*, xvi, 1954, 40.

Only at the end of 1895 did the company resume responsibility for the area which in 1897 was named Northern Rhodesia. The company struck into the territory from two directions. One lay through the Zambezi valley and British Central Africa. The company's agents were aware that they had to be careful of the Ngoni state of Mpezeni, the Lunda state of Kazembe, and especially the fearsome Bemba kingdom, which had established an economy based upon raiding for slaves and ivory and selling them to Swahili traders from the east coast. Adopting policies which Johnston had used to good effect in British Central Africa, the company gained the adherence of people raided by the Ngoni, the Lunda and the Bemba by posing as their protector, and defeated one by one the groups which would not yield to persuasion alone. By 1899 all the peoples of north-eastern Rhodesia were under company control.

The second line of advance was from South Africa through Southern Rhodesia and Botswana and towards Lewanika's Lozi state. Lewanika by this time was aware that the Portuguese were pressing upon him from the west, while the British were advancing from the south. In response he increased the size of his kingdom to gain a bargaining advantage. Without direct access to arms, however, he had no opportunity to survive as an independent ruler. In 1900 he formally recognised the inevitable, and yielded effective control over his territory to Rhodes's company. It was an option preferable to Portuguese rule.

By 1902, when the end of the Anglo–Boer war signalled the beginning of economic expansion throughout southern Africa, virtually all the region had been occupied by the British, the Portuguese or private companies. The slave- and ivory-trades were at an end. The people were in the process of being disarmed, and their access to gunpowder was curtailed. The area was ready for direct capitalist exploitation. Although each of the territories developed along unique lines, all had one characteristic in common: they were oriented away from the merchants of the east coast and towards the industrial complex that was fast growing on the Witwatersrand. To accomplish this, there was a rapid mobilisation of labour from the rural households and the creation of a complex network of labour migrancy.

TOWARDS LABOUR MIGRATION

The economic exploitation of East–Central Africa at the turn of the century was shaped by the often contradictory tendencies in patterns of capital investment throughout South- and East-Central Africa. On the one hand, the area seemed an unlikely place for extensive capital investment. Immense stretches were in the deep interior and difficult to reach. Roads and railways did not yet exist, and most rivers were not navigable. Draught animals could not be used because of the presence of tsetse fly. Hence, almost everywhere, every form of manual labour was carried out by people. Although valuable minerals had been eagerly sought, few were found. Finally, the soil was not generally so fertile or the climate so salubrious as to make the area obviously better suited for farms and plantations than other parts of the world. It appeared that the ideal function for the area from a capitalist perspective would be as a labour reserve for the industries of the south. Yet despite its glaring disadvantages, plantation owners and adventurers, mining prospectors and traders, missionaries and settlers soon arrived in the area.

As a result, an extremely spotty pattern of economic activity emerged, with certain areas witnessing the establishment of mines, railways, plantations, farms and settlements. All rivalled the south in their pressing need for immense numbers of cheap labourers, yet they were marginal creatures, insufficiently capitalised and inefficient, and hence unable to pay the sort of wages which would attract the labour they needed. It was obvious to all government officials, whether English or Portuguese, that this labour had to be forced out of the rural households quickly and made available at low cost to the new ventures if they were to survive. Furthermore, local administrations needed money, and they decided to use taxation as a tool to attain both objectives.

It was not enough that labour be mobilised. Throughout southern Africa investors and their agents felt that the creation of a fully proletarianised working class had to be avoided. Instead, they wanted to use migrant labourers, hired for specific periods of time under contract. They were men who would leave their homes and journey to their places of work, either as 'voluntary' workers in search of money to satisfy tax obligations and other requirements, or, under various schemes of recruitment, as forced labourers. The migrant was paid enough for his survival and for taxes, while the migrant's wife and family were expected to sustain themselves by marginal agriculture, maintaining a home to which the migrant returned regularly to beget children and to which he would ultimately retire. The cost of reproducing the labouring population was thereby transferred from the capitalist sector to the village. This effectively meant that villages were subsidising the establishment of capitalist enterprises throughout the region. Employers had the use of the workers at the height of their physical well-being, but escaped the costs of health services and retirement benefits which would have become their responsibility had labour been fully proletarianised. Moreover, by recruiting labour across political boundaries, employers avoided the cost of schools, hospitals and other publicly funded facilities that ordinarily would have been met by taxation.[21] In effect, the

---

21 For an outspoken statement of this point of view by a Rand capitalist in 1905, see Shula Marks and Stanley Trapido, 'Lord Milner and the South African State', *History Workshop*, No. 8, 1979, 71–2.

costs were transferred to outside governments which, because of an over-all lack of economic activity, could provide them only by taxing the migrants themselves on their return home.

Migrant labour had other, less obvious advantages. Throughout southern Africa labour was recruited under contracts which rendered the workers criminals if they evaded the terms of their obligations. The force of law could be brought to bear against such problems as shirking and absenteeism. Migrant labour was also malleable. Although locally recruited workers could evade the employer's control by fleeing to nearby villages where they could lose themselves among friends and relatives, the migrants had nowhere to go. All, whether married or single, lived communally in labour compounds, isolated from the surrounding community and easily subject to employers' supervision and police control. Within the compounds a hierarchical system of 'boss boys' and 'capitaes' kept the workers under a quasi-military discipline. As a further safeguard against the growth of proletarian consciousness or protest, the compounds were ethnically segregated, with inter-compound rivalry in such ethnic skills as dancing being actively encouraged by employers. The ultimate guarantee of both profit and labour control was that the migrants should continue to regard themselves as rural villagers rather than industrial workers.[22]

The migrant labour system that developed in southern Africa, with its advantages of mobilisation and control, had two great drawbacks. First, recruitment of contract labour was expensive. Wages in many areas were far too low to attract 'voluntary' workers. Labour was often therefore physically coerced, and employers had to pay handsomely the men who forced it. Secondly, and more difficult to deal with, there was an over-all shortage of labour. As the mines and plantations and transport companies were expanded, intense competition for labour grew. Compounding the problem for the capitalists was a growing awareness by the area's administrators that the incessant draining of manpower from the villages threatened their very survival. To limit this threat, governments gradually tried to regulate labour recruitment. This politicised the process, involving employers in extensive lobbying to ensure labour supplies independent of any so-called 'law' of supply and demand. It was within this framework of private capital competing for migrant labour and of colonial administr-ations acting as arbiters that the various territories of East-Central Africa began to take on distinctive characteristics. Yet the political economies of all of them were dominated by the realities of labour migrancy.

22 For an illuminating discussion of the compound system as it existed in Southern Rhodesia, see Charles van Onselen, *Chibaro: African Mine Labour in Southern Rhodesia, 1900–1933*, London, 1976, pp. 34–73.

Leroy Vail

MOZAMBIQUE: ENCAPSULATED EXPLOITATION, 1890–1919

Mozambique perhaps best illustrates the uneven and often contradictory pattern of economic activity that came to typify East-Central Africa. Here different administrations highlighted the basic contradictions of the colony. In the far south, the area from the Maputo river to the Sabi river was under uneasy state control in the 1890s, and large numbers of its men were drawn to work on the Rand's mines. In the area north of the Sabi and south of the Zambezi, Mozambique Company authority was gradually imposed. European activity took the form of unsuccessful prospecting for diamonds and gold, and of the construction and maintenance of transport services between Rhodesia and the port of Beira. Company officials taxed the people by levies of beeswax and ivory, which they then sold on the world market. In the far interior, in Tete district, which the Zambesia Company administered, a little prospecting constituted the European presence, while the Niassa Company's activities were so slight that the slave-trade continued well into the twentieth century.[23] A combination of initial undercapitalisation and a financial strategy of spinning profits through speculative stock-jobbing ensured the neglect of any possible investment opportunities in all these areas. The one section of Mozambique which did experience substantial capitalist economic activity was the lower Zambezi valley. In the period between 1890 and 1905 a group of companies established a tenuous plantation economy based on sugar and copra on the long-moribund *prazos*. This activity was almost the only Portuguese sign of 'effective occupation' outside the cities of Lourenço Marques and Beira.

The people of the lower Zambezi valley had initially responded to market demands for ground-nuts, sesame seed and other vegetable products and, in the 1880s, had established a flourishing peasant economy. This production met the desires of international trading companies, but was viewed by government officials as an obstacle to the development of plantations. Throughout the 1890s the Mozambique authorities sought to restrict such commodity production and force people to work on the new estates. A series of legal measures furthered this policy. In 1892 the government increased export duties at the very time when world prices were declining, making it less profitable to grow cash crops. In 1893 it put restrictions on Indian merchants who had been the middlemen. Another step was taken when government increased taxes, intending to drive more people to work for European interests. Later in the decade independent marketing was curtailed. In 1899 the Portuguese carried the process a step further when they promulgated a new labour code that required that 'all inhabitants of the Portuguese overseas provinces shall be subject to the moral and legal obligations of attempting to obtain through work the

23 See Vail, 'Mozambique's Chartered Companies', 397–401.

212

means of subsistence which they lack and improve their social condition'.[24] Local authorities were given the power to fix the length of time that people would have to work. The code applied generally to all males between the

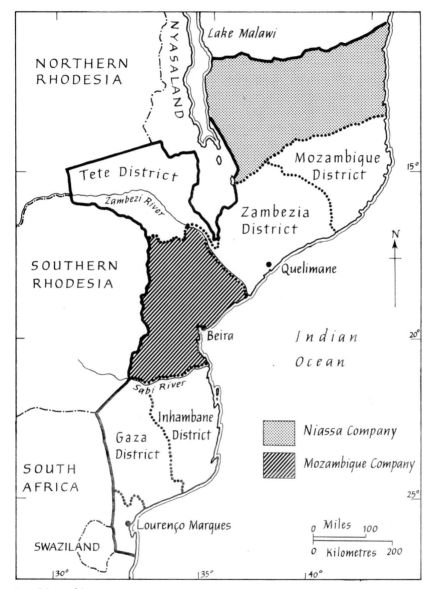

6:3 Mozambique, c. 1920

24 J. M. da Silva Cunha, *O trabalho indigena: estudo de direito colonial*, 2nd ed., Lisbon, 1955, pp. 147–8.

ages of fourteen and sixty.[25] By 1901 African export production had almost ceased, and the people had been turned into a reservoir of plantation workers.

During the 1890s another consumer of Mozambique's labour-power was rapidly increasing its demand. The development of deep-level gold-mines on the Witwatersrand resulted in labour demands, which by 1899 had risen to 97 000 men. The mineowners sought cheap labour beyond the Transvaal borders, in southern Mozambique. By 1897 half of the workers came from this area.[26] The Portuguese government felt that this outflow of labour would benefit Mozambique only if it could be regulated. Labour costs were rising around Lourenço Marques due to the emigration of workers to the Rand, and this impeded the establishment of local industries and plantations.[27] Control would overcome the local shortages and provide government revenue.

The Anglo-Boer war of 1899–1902 gave the Mozambique authorities the chance for which they had been looking. Alfred Milner, the British vice-regal agent in South Africa, keenly wanted cheap labour supplies to reconstruct the gold-mines, so that they could provide the base for a buoyant post-war economy in the Transvaal. In 1901, even before the war's end, he concluded an agreement in which the Witwatersrand Native Labour Association (WENELA) was given monopoly recruiting rights in all parts of Mozambique under direct state administration. This decision resulted in a scramble for the colony's labour as various interests sought to ensure their access to adequate supplies at lowest cost. Mozambique was turned into a set of closed labour reserves where people were not free to sell their labour, but were disposed of by the authorities.

In the south, WENELA had direct access to the large population of Lourenço Marques, Gaza and Inhambane districts. Further north the Mozambique Company argued that all its people were needed locally to gather rubber, to work at the port of Beira and on the railway to Rhodesia, to labour in the new mines, and to staff the sugar estates on the south bank of the Zambezi. It therefore prohibited all recruitment for work beyond its borders. To prevent labour leakage by men seeking higher wages elsewhere, it imposed severe penalties for anyone caught trying to escape from its territory.[28] North of the Zambezi, in Quelimane and Tete districts, a constellation of small companies re-invigorated the ancient *prazo* system and enjoyed advantages regarding labour. In effect, the *prazos* were legalised private labour pools on which the companies could draw in

25 See Vail and White, *Capitalism and Colonialism in Mozambique*, pp. 134–6, for a more complete discussion of the labour code of 1899.
26 Sheila T. van der Horst, *Native Labour in South Africa*, London, 1942, pp. 127–36.
27 J. Mousinho de Albuquerque, *Moçambique, 1896–98*, reprint of 1899 ed., Lisbon, 1934, pp. 144–50.
28 P(ublic) R(ecord) O(ffice), London. F.O. 63/1449, Hale to Secretary, Transvaal Chamber of Mines, 6 Feb. 1902; Consul General, Lourenço Marques, to Milner, 10 March 1902; Arnold to Miller, 22 April 1902.

lieu of tax payments. Two large and populous areas of Quelimane district did, however, remain under state control, and were thus included in WENELA's recruiting area under the terms of the 1901 agreement. Moreover, certain of the *prazo* companies, instead of developing plantations, chose to export labour through their own recruiting contracts with enterprises elsewhere in Africa.

The competition for labour between those who wished to use it locally in Zambezia and those who sought to profit from its sale elsewhere grew bitter. As certain companies expanded their plantations, their labour needs could not be satisfied by levies within their own *prazos*. In the first fifteen years of the century, these productive companies sought to enlarge their labour supply by acquiring new *prazos* and by diverting to their own plantations labour previously exported.

One may gain an insight into the way in which the system worked by looking at the *prazo* area of lower Zambezia in some detail. The economy was based on three crops: sugar, coconuts and sisal. One man, an Englishman named J. P. Hornung, dominated sugar production on a set of *prazos* which he used as the base of a closed economic system typical of Mozambique until the 1930s. By 1912 he administered, policed, levied taxes and controlled the labour supplies over some 14 000 square miles of territory. He also monopolised trade through 100 shops. In addition, he drew labour from a slice of territory under the Mozambique Company. By 1914 he was producing 29 000 tonnes of sugar, making his the largest industry in Mozambique. The various governmental restrictions upon trade in African-produced goods had long before sacrificed peasant agriculture to the interests of the *prazo* companies. This meant that along the Zambezi people had to work for Hornung to satisfy the law, to pay their taxes and to obtain necessities such as cloth and hoes.

The initial reluctance to work for the companies was overcome by an increase in compulsion. People well remember the *chicote* whip made from hippo hide that was used to get the early plantations into operation.[29] In the area of the Boror Company, women were forced to dig large irrigation channels without pay, the company asserting that such work was for the public welfare.[30] Such exploitation went beyond brutality. It was structural also. By levying taxes in kind as well as in labour, the companies comandeered the best foods produced by the people. Taxes were demanded in rice, for example, and this was used to feed workers. The people were 'given' the food that they themselves had produced. Tax was also levied in the form of raw alcohol, which was then distilled and returned to the workers as pay. Children employed by the Madal

29 O.T. Group interview, Macuse, Mozambique, 1 Sept. 1977.
30 Francisco Xavier Ferrão de Castello Branco, 'Relatorio dos Investigações a que precedeu o Secretário dos Negócios Indígenas . . . de maio de 1908', *Relatórios e Informacões: Annexo ao 'Boletim Oficial'*, *Anno de 1909*, Lourenço Marques, 1909, p. 244.

Company were paid five litres of rotgut spirits per week.[31] The use of alcohol as currency contributed mightily to the high incidence of alcoholism and formed an intrinsic part of the oppressive company system. The law guaranteed that the companies could determine prices of goods exchanged in their stores, thus allowing them to cream off extra profits through astute pricing.

The *prazo* regulations provided the coconut companies with the perfect self-sustaining mechanism. Rents due to the state, management salaries, dividends for shareholders and local overheads were all underwritten by expropriating from the people first their coconuts, then their trees, and then their labour. Payment was in items taken from the people in the first place. This policy allowed the companies to accumulate the capital needed for large-scale expansion. The companies extended their interests into other areas of business becoming profitable agents for international firms. Expansion also involved setting up new sugar and coconut plantations and searching for new crops that might be grown in their drier inland areas. The ideal crop was found in sisal, and large plantations devoted to it were established in the hinterland. This discovery brought to a head the over-all problem of labour supplies, as the company *prazos* were unable to obtain all the labour that they required. Increases in production came to an abrupt halt in 1915, and output stagnated thereafter.

It was at this point that the basic illogicality of the *prazo* system was demonstrated, for although the successful *prazo* companies were being starved of labour, other *prazo* companies were exporting people. A key weakness of the system was the fact that the largest populations dwelt on *prazos* where little economic activity occurred. The authorities administering these populations, the state and the Zambesia Company, were eager to make their control remunerative, and therefore sold to the highest bidder. The first purchasers of this labour were the gold-mines of the Rand, profits from which were more certain than those of local agriculture. By 1903 WENELA recruiters were at work on the state lands as well as in the Zambesia Company's *prazos*, paying the proprietors a capitation fee five times as high as the annual tax. Between 1903 and 1907 several thousand men were sent from the Tete and Quelimane districts to the south despite excited protests of the production-minded companies in the area.

The initial drain to the Rand was increased in 1908 by the export of people to São Tomé, where cocoa production was threatened by the curtailment of labour recruitment in Angola. Scandals over slavery in Angola had led to an international boycott of São Tomé cocoa, and the plantations sought a new source of labour.[32] In Mozambique the São Tomé planters turned to *prazos* without plantations, renting three densely

31 *Ibid.*, p. 223; O.T. Group interview, Macuse, Mozambique, 1 Sept. 1977.
32 P.R.O., F.O. 367/46, Memorandum of a meeting between William Cadbury and São Tomé Planters, 4 Dec. 1907.

populated areas and contracting further labour from the state. After 1908 15 000 men and women were sent to São Tomé, and despite reforms, few returned home. Although there was a shortage of labour in Zambezia, pressure from powerful São Tomé planters in Lisbon persuaded the Portuguese government to give them precedence over foreign-owned plantations in Zambezia.[33]

In the early days of Portuguese administration the people tended to flee beyond the reach of the *prazo*-holders. With the passage of time, the companies and the state developed more efficient police forces to keep the people within their respective borders. Heavy penalties for attempted escape were imposed, and places of refuge became less numerous. Refugees went as far as British territory, where conditions were better, though not marvellous. The most striking single example of such flight occurred in 1917 and 1918, when thousands of people fled the brutalities of the Mozambique Company and settled in Nyasaland and Northern Rhodesia.[34]

The steadiest drain of people came from the two northern districts of Cabo Delgado and Niassa. The governing Niassa Company, under the control of the South African mining house of Lewis and Marks, remained economically feeble. It refused to invest in a sound economic infrastructure and restricted its efforts to establishing a series of military posts, from which its police periodically raided people for taxes, goods and labour. The company's territory was a mosaic of controlled zones around military posts, and large independent areas. WENELA was given recruiting rights in 1903, but met energetic resistance until 1909. By the time the company gained control over the area, recruitment for the South African mines had been ended because of the high mortality rate suffered by northern miners. The company negotiated to send workers to the *prazos* of Zambezia and the mines and railways of the Belgian Congo. Once the male population had gone, local exploitation fell upon women and children. A visitor to the area remarked in 1914 that 'so far as natives are concerned, this is a land of blood and tears, where the most brutal ill-treatment is no crime and murder merely a slight indiscretion'.[35] When resistance succumbed to the company's forces, people fled as refugees to Tanganyika or Nyasaland. More than 100 000 reached Nyasaland by 1919. The Niassa Company atrocities rivalled the more widely-publicised disgraces of King Leopold's

33 Speech by A. A. Freire d'Andrade, 21 Dec. 1910, encl. in P.R.O., F.O. 367/234, Villiers to Grey, 27 Dec. 1910. A. A. Freire d'Andrade, who made this decision, was in later years rewarded with a directorship of one of the largest of the São Tomé plantation companies.
34 For a discussion of the events preceding this mass migration, see A. F. Isaacman, *The Tradition of Resistance in Mozambique*, London, 1976; for a discussion of migrations within Mozambique, see Vail and White, *Capitalism and Colonialism in Mozambique*, pp. 169–71.
35 P.R.O., C.O. 525/59, Hemming to Bostock, 7 Feb. 1914, encl. in Bostock to MacDonnell, 25 Feb. 1914, encl, in MacDonnell to Grey, 9 Mar. 1914.

Congo, of Angola, and of São Tomé. Its rule created an enclave of enduring desolation and poverty in northern Mozambique.

In the years before 1919 Mozambique was divided into a complicated set of encapsulated economic zones administered by private companies or state officials. All shared one characteristic: the exploitation of the people for the sake of profit. Gradually, the improvement of administrative structures, the increased use of police and the closing-off of possible havens ensured that labour would be more efficiently exacted. In the years prior to the First World War, there was a steady erosion of the vitality of the rural household. The draining of village workers continued the dissolution of rural societies that had begun in the days of the slave- and ivory-trades.

NYASALAND: UNCERTAIN PRIORITIES, 1891–1919

The British Central Africa Protectorate, like all colonies, was concerned to find a source of revenue to pay for its administration. The policies of the 1890s were remarkably similar to those across the border in Portuguese Mozambique. The Protectorate's first commissioner, Harry Johnston, was aware that the prices of peasant-produced commodities were declining on the world market. He felt that, as the protectorate was far inland and as transport costs were high, it would be difficult for goods such as oil seeds to be grown profitably. In his mind, economic prosperity depended upon the development of European-run plantations on the fertile Shire Highlands, in the southern part of the Protectorate. Although some missionaries argued that economic prosperity lay in African peasant cultivation, the colonial administration disagreed, viewing settler interests as economically paramount. Only through state support could European plantations produce high-value commodities that could bear the transport cost to the world market. State intervention emulated the practice in Mozambique, and ceded large tracts of land to plantation companies and settlers with the right to extract labour in lieu of rent. This *thangata* system became the main grievance of Nyasaland's people.

The labour that could be mobilised by *thangata* was inadequate for plantations where every type of work was done by hand. To stimulate a flow of labour from beyond the Shire Highlands area, while incidentally raising revenue, the state taxed the people. In 1892 a hut tax of six shillings was imposed.[36] Although this was reduced to three shillings in 1894, this was still an extraordinarily high figure for a country with limited employment opportunities. Over time the three-shilling figure proved inadequate in driving people to employment, and the tax was again raised to six shillings unless a person could produce a certificate that he had

36 For a detailed discussion of tax policies and practices in Nyasaland, see Colin Baker, 'Tax collection in Malawi: an Administrative History, 1891–1972', *International Journal of African Historical Studies*, viii, 1, 1975, 41.

worked for a European for at least thirty days, in which case he paid three shillings.[37]

Settler views were eloquently expressed in their local newspaper: 'The work needed for the regeneration of the African is hard, honest labour, work as makes horny hand and strengthens sinews. Work not for luxuries, and only while the fancy pleases, but work under the stern lash of necessity.'[38]

The state knew what it had to do, and its agents undertook to coerce labour from the villages. One officer of the Protectorate administration described the method when he wrote home to his mother:

I got some goats by looting, so I get fresh milk and the natives bring me fresh fish every day. One chief has to bring me 200 men to work for nothing, & he brings some every day, but he has to bring a lot more yet. The hatred on his face when I tell him he has to bring more still or I'll make war on him is intense, but he's got to do it, or I'll burn all his villages and crops down.[39]

Such assiduous execution of the forced-labour policies of government provoked widespread resistance in 1900.[40] It was only in 1904, however, that the British government in London, apprehensive about possible rebellions in Central Africa and the exposure of scandalous practices, forbade direct coercion.[41] Despite this ban, administrators continued to burn villages as a means of collecting taxes and mobilising labour for the Shire Highlands.

The state also acted like any Mozambique *prazo*-holder in refusing to allow the recruitment of labour within the Protectorate for work abroad. It attempted to prevent men from seeking higher wages in Southern Rhodesia or the Rand by sending police patrols to seal the borders.[42] Despite all efforts, the Shire plantations failed. The planters could not have chosen a worse moment to establish coffee plantations. Between 1890 and 1898 the world price for coffee declined by 50 per cent, and Brazilian growers were driven to dumping sacks of beans into the sea.[43] The attempt

37 *Ibid.*, p. 49.
38 *Central African Times*, 12 Aug. 1899.
39 M(alawi) N(ational) A(rchives). The Francis Garden Poole Papers. F. G. Poole to his mother, 14 Aug. 1897.
40 M.N.A., J 1/2/1, 'H.M.C.B. & C.G. to C.J.O., 1900–1901', Nunan to Manning, 16 Feb. 1901. See also Z(ambian) N(ational) A(rchives). BS 1/97, which has much evidence on this practice in north-eastern Rhodesia.
41 P.R.O., C.O. 525/12, Sharpe to Hynde, 17 March 1906, encl. in Sharpe to C.O., 19 March 1906.
42 *Central African Times*, 11 Nov. 1899, letter of the Acting Deputy Commissioner Pearce to the Chamber of Agriculture and Commerce, 27 Oct. 1899; Z.N.A., BS 1/97, 'Restrictions Placed on Skilled Natives from leaving B.C.A., 1901–1903', Beaufort to Codrington, 22 April 1903, encl. in Codrington to the Commissioner of British Central Africa, 24 April 1903.
43 John Iliffe, *A Modern History of Tanganyika*, Cambridge, 1979, p. 128.

to produce coffee in British Central Africa died under the combined impact of low prices, high transport costs, drought and disease.[44]

Despite this failure, the Protectorate government did not abandon its hopes of future success. One problem had been competition between planters and the transport companies which served British Central Africa,

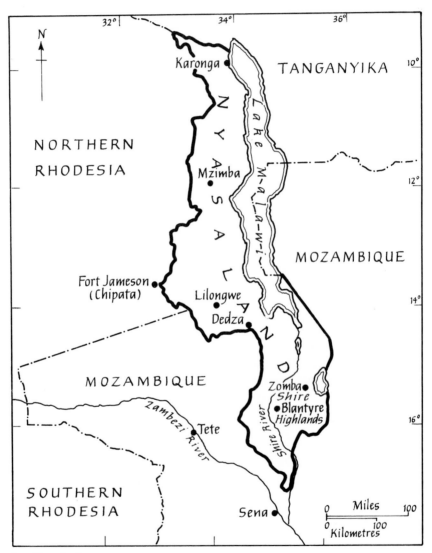

6:4 Nyasaland

44 For a description of the phases of agricultural production in the Protectorate, see C. A. Baker, 'Malawi's Exports: an Economic History', in *Malawi Past and Present*, G. W. Smith, B. Pachai and R. Tangri (eds), Blantyre, Malawi, 1971, pp. 88–113.

Lake Malawi and the regions of Lakes Mweru and Tanganyika, which needed large numbers of baggage porters. The demand for such labour seriously threatened the planters since transport companies paid higher wages. For many years they therefore pressed the government to build a railway that would free tens of thousands of workers. The government was slow to act, but in 1903 decided to guarantee the construction of a railway by granting to a private railway company 3 200 acres of prime land for every mile completed. The decision was a great portent for the country's history.

The failure of coffee had resulted in a temporary abundance of labour in 1903, and the state had permitted WENELA to recruit people for work on the Rand. In return, it insisted that European agricultural produce should be allowed duty-free access to the lucrative Transvaal market. When the planters decided to try their hand at tobacco and cotton, and when the building of the new railway created a local demand for labour, the government abruptly ended WENELA's recruiting operations.[45] The state once again followed Mozambique's lead, and enacted laws which strengthened the plantocracy's hold over its people. In 1907, when the name of the Protectorate was changed to Nyasaland, the planters were given seats on the colony's legislative council and a voice in its government. The plantations nevertheless remained resolutely inefficient.

The high tax-rate, and the brutalities of forced labour on a much-weakened social fabric, drove Africans to become migrant labourers. They were not willing to work locally, however, when wages were higher everywhere else in southern Africa. By going to an area where the pay was higher, one worker earned enough to pay several men's taxes, hence permitting more men to be at home at any one time. A whole village would raise the money to send a man away and keep him there until he began to earn a wage. Men took turns as the village wage-earners and tax payers. This strategy partially frustrated the state's efforts to mobilise labour for local needs. It also helped maintain the vitality of the village household. People who had received some education at the Scottish mission schools were well aware that the protectorate offered them no opportunity for advancement. At the end of one mission school debate in the early 1900s, for example, the students voted 78–2 in favour of leaving Nyasaland after receiving their diplomas.[46] These educated people, mostly from the northern part of the country or the Shire Highlands, aided their fellows to emigrate from the Protectorate as covert 'voluntary' labourers.[47] So bad were conditions in Nyasaland that many educated

45 P.R.O., C.O. 525/2, Sharpe to C.O., 16 Aug. 1904.
46 P.R.O., C.O. 525/35, Memorandum of Charles Casson, encl. in Casson to Deputy Governor, 17 Nov. 1910.
47 *Ibid.*, Casson to Deputy Governor, 17 Nov. 1910.

migrants went as skilled labourers to the Mozambique *prazos*, where they formed a labour élite.[48]

Prosperity continued to elude the European plantations, and cotton did not alleviate the state of crisis. Survival was ensured by the arrival in Nyasaland of Lomwe-speaking refugees from Mozambique in the years after 1898. These people, known locally as 'Anguru', fled from the *prazos* or the rule of the Niassa Company. Between 1900 and 1903 between 15 000 and 30 000 settled in one district alone.[49] In later years they continued to arrive in Nyasaland in response to pressures in Mozambique. As refugees in a strange land, they enjoyed no local position, yet were subject to the host country's tax requirements. The planters recognised an opportunity inherent in their plight, and offered them permission to settle on the estates in return for a period of *thangata* labour. In 1912 the state forbade the immigrants from settling on Crown land, thereby compelling them to accept the *thangata* arrangement. The Lomwe had become the planters' *akapolo*, their 'domestic slaves'. The Lomwe were trapped, with no rights of residence and no chance of more remunerative employment, no education and no access to patronage. Furthermore, they were tolerated only as long as they furnished their landlords cheap labour when it was most burdensome to provide, during the rainy season. With *thangata* labour the planters increased the acreage of tobacco from 1 000 acres in 1905 to 21 000 acres in 1921. They also grew cotton and created the tea industry, which became firmly established in the 1920s and 1930s.[50]

The resentment that the *thangata* system generated on one of the estates was the principal cause of the Chilembwe rising of January 1915. The uprising has been widely hailed as a forerunner of anti-colonial nationalism, because its leader, the Reverend John Chilembwe, was a member of the well-educated African élite.[51] The majority of his supporters, however, were Lomwe refugees, and the rising may be considered less a forerunner of Malawian nationalism than a local revolt of badly exploited, landless immigrants. With the revolt's failure, the Lomwe found themselves permanently trapped on the plantations. What the state had striven to accomplish in the 1890s by forcing labour out of the Protectorate's central and northern districts was ultimately achieved through reaction to the violence of the Mozambican authorities and the realities of *thangata*.

In effect, the arrival of the Lomwe enabled the Protectorate to be turned into a gigantic labour reserve. Once the government realised that the

---

48 P.R.O., C.O. 525/32, Notes by Charles Casson, encl. in Wallis to C.O., 21 July 1910.
49 C. Baker, 'A note on Nguru immigration to Nyasaland', *The Nyasaland Journal*, xiv, 1, 1962, 41.
50 P.R.O., C.O. 525/44, Manning to C.O., 2 Oct. 1922.
51 For the basic history of the rising, see George Shepperson and Thomas Price, *Independent African*, Edinburgh, 1958.

planters had secured access to Lomwe labour in the Shire Highlands, it radically altered its attitude towards the Protectorate's other African inhabitants. It came to view the people who dwelt in the central and northern parts of the country as 'surplus' to the country's needs, and therefore fit to be sent abroad as recruited labour. The administration decided to experiment with various labour recruitment schemes so as to ensure the collection of taxes. The state sponsored the recruitment of 'surplus' labour for the sugar plantations of Mozambique, for the Rand gold-mines, for Southern Rhodesia's mines and farms, as well as for work in Northern Rhodesia.[52] So enthusiastic did its officers become in marketing the Protectorate's people that in 1908 they suggested a scheme to supply Kenya with labourers.[53] Within twenty years the government had turned the country into a labour pool upon which capital throughout southern Africa could draw. The people of the north still recall the startling realities:

> A hut tax of three shillings was introduced in 1906. That year the people paid the tax, but when taxes were demanded again in 1907, the people rebelled, saying, 'Should we pay taxes a second time? No!! That cannot be so!' ... It was after the tax rebellion that the government sent Reuben, MacDonald and Pickford to burn the huts of those who refused to pay.
>
> There was wailing ... villages were burned in Embangweni here, in Engalweni, everywhere. The main complaint was against the system of taxation, which was very bad in those days. The defaulters were often treated badly. Even if they were girls, they were tied up with ropes and beaten with the *sjambok*. The people had to emigrate to Southern Rhodesia. There was no money in this country, so the people had to walk all the way to Rhodesia.[54]

Still the government was not wholly satisfied while there were people living in the south or along the shores of Lake Malawi who might be used to produce local export commodities. The government therefore sought to build a third segment of the economy.

Britain had long purchased its cotton from American growers. At the end of the nineteenth century, however, world demand exceeded production, and the British cotton industry went through a hard period. In mid-1902 British manufacturers established the British Cotton Growing Association one of whose aims was to increase cotton production in the British empire. The association felt that the future of Nyasaland was well

52 Z.N.A., BS 1/97, Administrator, N. E. R. to Commissioner, British Central Africa, 24 April 1903; BS 1/33, British South Africa Company to Codrington, 21 Dec. 1907; P.R.O., C.O. 525/19, Pearce to C.O., 9 Oct. 1907; C.O. 525/23, Knipe to Manning, 11 Jan, 1908, encl. in Manning to C.O., 17 Jan, 1908; C.O. 525/24, Sharpe to Crewe, 14 September, 1908.
53 P.R.O., C.O. 525/23, Sharpe to Harris, 2 June 1908.
54 O. T. Councillors of Inkosi Mzukuzuku, Embangweni, Mzimba district, Malawi, 16 Sept. 1971.

suited to cotton and cotton seed was distributed in parts of the country. Production spread, and in 1909 the Protectorate established an agriculture department specifically to foster African cotton. From 1910 it began to coerce people into growing cotton wherever feasible. By so doing it pushed areas of the country, especially in the south, towards a peasant economy, initially oriented towards cotton but later diversifying into rice, tobacco, ground-nuts and miscellaneous foodstuffs. In the Shire valley, where transport costs were low, people showed enthusiasm for cotton-growing as an alternative to migrancy. Production expanded considerably when Sena-speaking refugees migrated into the area from Mozambique, thereby giving peasant landholders access to willing cotton field-hands, in exchange for permission to settle on the land. An African version of the *thangata* system developed.

There was great inhibition about the development of a 'peasant alternative' in Nyasaland. The state was willing to aid settlers with legislative concessions, but refused to protect African planters. They were left to the mercy of settlers and Indian merchants whose cartels conspired to lower prices for peasant produce. The system was similar to the Mozambique closed economies. In 1910, for example, plantation companies purchased African-grown cotton for one penny per pound and resold it in England at ten pence per pound with a clear six pence profit for their 'service'; even state officials were disgusted.[55] Despite structural discouragements, the state's reluctance to aid African agriculture, and the vagaries of the weather, many Africans preferred to grow crops rather than emigrate. By 1920 government officers acknowledged that such agriculture might provide the basis for a healthy economy.

NORTHERN RHODESIA : COMPANY MISRULE, 1898–1924

In the late 1890s, the British South Africa Company's main concern was the embryonic mining economy of Southern Rhodesia. When it did turn its attention to its territories north of the Zambezi, it was somewhat uncertain as to what to do with the immense stretch of land. Although Alfred Milner, in delineating British interests throughout southern Africa in 1899, had specified that the areas north of the Zambezi river were not to be used for European settlement, the company was less certain.[56] It hoped that these areas might support a mixed economy, with copper-, lead- and zinc-mining complemented by cattle-ranching and rubber and cotton plantations.[57] Yet problems with transport, disease and competition from

55 P.R.O., C.O. 525/32, Sharpe to C.O., 15 March 1910.
56 Ian Henderson, 'Labour and Politics in Northern Rhodesia, 1900–1953: a Study in the Limits of Colonial Power', Ph.D. thesis, University of Edinburgh, 1972, p. 11.
57 Philip Lyttleton Gell Papers, Hopton Hall, Wirkworth, Derbyshire, England: British South Africa Company. BSA 8/94, Codrington to Gell, 24 June 1903; BSA 9/109, Codrington to Gell, 3 March 1904.

Southern Rhodesian producers frustrated all the early experiments at diversifying the economy. By 1910 the company reluctantly agreed with Milner's assessment, concluding that the 'greater part of the country is not ... ripe for European settlement at the present time, and ... it should be developed through the native inhabitants of the country'.[58] Unlike the situation in Nyasaland and Mozambique, where local plantations were from an early date able to influence state policies, in Northern Rhodesia no such powerful influence appeared. In 1911 there were only 250 Europeans in North-Eastern Rhodesia, while in North-Western Rhodesia, where a small settler community had grown up along the railway line that had been constructed from Southern Rhodesia to the mines, there were only 1 200 settlers.[59] They led a haphazard existence, eking out their living by a mixture of farming, transport riding, hunting and serving as recruiters of African labour. The company was hostile to the expansion of such marginal and unproductive European settlers. It was apprehensive that abuses of the local people might lead to a popular uprising like the 1896–1897 revolts in Southern Rhodesia.[60] Company policy therefore was to restrict Europeans to the mines and the farms they already held.

Northern Rhodesia, however, was not useless to the company merely because it was unsuitable for European settlement. It had people, and human labour was a much-valued commodity throughout southern Africa. In 1898 there was a severe labour shortage in Southern Rhodesia, where local people were unwilling to abandon cash-crop production and turn to work in the new mines. To solve this problem the company's administrator in North-Eastern Rhodesia decided to impose a hut tax specifically to stimulate a flow of labour southwards to Southern Rhodesia.[61] Northern Rhodesia's role as a labour reserve for Southern Rhodesia grew after 1908, when European farming expanded.

The principal means by which the state mobilised people were, as elsewhere, taxation and coercion. The company rounded up gangs of men, brought them to the administrative centres, and handed them over to the Rhodesian Native Labour Bureau, which marched them south. Officials burned huts and grain stores, and made free use of the whip to get their quota of men.[62] The response was widespread resistance, especially in

58 Gell Papers. BSA 10/5, Northern Rhodesia. *Report on the Administration of North-Western and North-Eastern Rhodesia*, London, 1910, p. 8.
59 Z.N.A., BS 2/35, 'Miscellaneous Files, 1911: Outletters, High Commissioner', Vol. II, Census Report, encl. in Wallace to Gladstone, 14 July 1911.
60 Marilyn Y. Jones, 'The Politics of White Agrarian Settlement in Northern Rhodesia, 1898–1928', M.A. thesis, University of Sussex, 1974, pp. 1–9.
61 Z.N.A., A 2/12, Codrington to the Manager of the North Charterland Exploration Company, 7 Sept. 1898, as cited in William Rau, 'Mpezeni's Ngoni of Eastern Zambia', Ph.D. dissertation, University of California at Los Angeles, 1974, p. 295.
62 Z.N.A., BS 2/10, 'In Letters, High Commissioner, 1910', Crewe to Selborne, 20 Jan. 1910, encl. in Selborne to Acting Administrator, N.W.R., 15 Feb. 1910; see also van Onselen, *Chibaro*, pp. 104–5.

southern and central districts, where people could sell tobacco and cattle to obtain their tax money.[63] Violent resistance was overcome by force of arms, but the brutality was counterproductive and did not drive people 'to seek work on their own initiative';[64] it merely caused Africans to risk robbery, attack and starvation in the wilderness in preference to recruitment.[65]

The state's assault on the people's way of life was complex and has been generally over-simplified. The basic process was repeated throughout East-Central Africa, but it is particularly well documented for Northern Rhodesia. One facet of the state's over-all strategy was, as in Mozambique, to deny people alternatives to wage labour. When the Ngoni of Mpezeni were defeated in 1898, for example, their herds of cattle, which constituted their principal form of wealth, were seized, and many were sent to Southern Rhodesia to replenish herds depleted by rinderpest. The impoverished Ngoni had no choice but migrancy.[66] Where people lived by hunting and selling ivory, the company forbade it.[67] Where they produced salt to sell, the company suppressed its manufacture.[68] The right to make tools from local iron was taxed out of existence.[69] And where people sought to grow foodstuffs to meet their tax obligations, the company stopped them. The remark of one company official in North-Western Rhodesia is typical:

> As regards the extra money which will fall into the hands of the natives of Kasempa District, I am personally persuaded that it will not ultimately benefit them. The Bakakoudi who inhabit this district are of exceptionally fine physique and are said ... to be the most satisfactory mining natives of which this province can boast. The total wages per annum which can be earned by a miner is admittedly greater than the sum of money which a native agriculturalist can hope to win in the course of one year. Consequently it would seem to be better policy to encourage the energies of the Bakakoudi in the direction of mining rather than agriculture.[70]

63 Z.N.A., BS 2/33, 'Miscellaneous Files – Out Letters, 1910', encls. in Wallace to Selborne, 12 March 1910.
64 Z.N.A., KSK 1/1/1, 'Correspondence – Administrator & Department of Native Affairs, 1902–1906', Coxhead to Hughes, 24 Aug. 1904.
65 See also Z.N.A., BS 2/35, 'Miscellaneous Files, 1911: Out Letter, High Commissioner', Vol. II, Hazell to Supt. of Native Affairs, 13 June 1911.
66 J. A. Barnes, *Politics in a Changing Society: a Political History of the Fort Jameson Ngoni*, 2nd ed., Manchester, 1967, pp. 93–6.
67 O.T. Village Headman Chilundu, Chilundu village, Lundazi district, Zambia, 8 May 1974; O.T. Chilobe Phiri, Chilobe village, Lundazi district, Zambia, 1 May 1974.
68 Z.N.A., KSD 7/1/1, Annual Report for Mpika District, 1909/10; also KSD 4/1, 'Mpika District Notebook', Vol. I.
69 Personal communication, Joseph Mtisi.
70 Z. N. A. BS 2/33, 'Miscellaneous Files – Out Letters', Acting Administrator to Selborne, 12 March 1910.

African agriculture continued only where it benefited European interests, as in the southern part of the country, where produce was either sold to Europeans or grown in share-cropping arrangements.

In Northern Rhodesia, as in Mozambique and Nyasaland, the state tampered with the rural economy in ways that upset the ecological balance, and as time passed the rural areas became less viable, and their people came to be more dependent for their survival on wages earned in labour migrancy. Perhaps the root of government policy lay in its attitude towards land and settlement patterns. The insecurity brought about by the nineteenth century's militarism and the slave- and ivory-trades had impelled the people to seek security in a host of scattered, stockaded villages. Given the ecological realities of the area's soils, such concentrations of people were highly abnormal. With the return of more peaceful conditions, people sought to return to their older, more congenial and economically rational settlement pattern. As one official noted in 1904:

> The Natives are, now that they have no fear of war or raids, everywhere breaking up the larger villages into smaller settlements. .... One good result of this spreading out is that the food supply is better. Gardens are the principal consideration in selecting a new site. I do not think that as a rule the idea is to avoid taxation.[71]

This dispersal of the people, though suitable for agriculture, pleased neither chiefs and headmen nor the new company officials. The power and the prestige of the chiefs in the nineteenth century had depended on the number of people under their control, and this was greatly facilitated by having the people dwell in large, consolidated villages.[72] The company wanted the people to continue to live in large villages, even in times of peace, to ease administration and reduce costs. Compliance required some forceful tactics.[73] This quick reversion to the late nineteenth century's abnormal pattern of large settlements prevented efficient methods of food production being used precisely when large numbers of male labourers were absent. The rural areas were deprived of the labour needed for shifting cultivation, and in 1910 a company official noted that 'the area under cultivation was very much smaller than usual – probably in consequence of the absence of so many of the able-bodied men in Southern Rhodesia'.[74]

71 Z.N.A., KSK 1/1/1, 'Correspondence – Administrator and Department of Native Affairs, 1902–1906', Report on Native Affairs for the quarter ending 30 June 1904.
72 See Z.N.A., BS/31, 'Report of Capt. Close', encl. in Bertie to British South Africa Company, 3 May 1899.
73 Z.N.A., KST 3/1, 'Lundazi District Notebook', Vol. I, 'Account of an Indaba of 17 Aug. 1908'; also KDG 5/1, 'East Luangwa District Notebook', Vol. I, 'Account of an Indaba of 31 March 1908'. In one district the average number of huts in a village leaped from 14 to 45 in a single year; KSD 7/1/1, 'Mpika Annual Report, 1906/07'.
74 Z.N.A., KST 4/1/1, 'Annual Reports – Lundazi, 1903–1933', Report for 1910/11.

The daily realities of colonial control, labour migrancy and village consolidation, interacted with the natural disasters of the 1890s to precipitate an ecological collapse. Fields and gardens deserted in the nineteenth century and pasture emptied of cattle by the rinderpest epidemic reverted to bush. The compulsory consolidation of the villages and the general shortage of male labour caused these areas to remain unused. At the same time, wild game made a rapid comeback, much aided by colonial legislation. Company officials naturally mistrusted Africans with guns as a potential danger to a weak and scattered administration. Futhermore, sports-minded officials felt that African wild animals should be protected to ensure their survival as a species and their availability for hunting trips by European aristocrats. In 1897 the British Central African Protectorate set up its first game reserve and promulgated restrictive game laws which were later adopted in Northern Rhodesia. In 1900 a conference was held in London to discuss strategies to protect African wildlife, and this gave international sanction to the ideal of the conservation of animals in Africa.[75]

For the people of East-Central Africa these decisions meant several things. First, the laws prohibiting hunting and trapping and forbidding the sale of guns and gunpowder to Africans were promulgated at the very time when their cattle and other animals had been decimated by the rinderpest. This cut off a traditional source of protein.[76] Nutritionally, the people were worse off in 1900 than they had been in 1890. Second, during the long African dry season, the people had hunted for both food and ivory, keeping the animal population in check. With the establishment of gun and game protection laws, however, the wild animals began to multiply rapidly, filling the now under-used land. Predators, especially lions, so terrorised people that they became reluctant to venture far from the villages. This exacerbated problems of soil fertility in agricultural system that required long periods of fallow.[77] Throughout East-Central Africa in the early years of the century officials reported great depredations of elephants and bush-pigs.[78] Time and again, when they toured the villages, the main complaint they heard was about the ravages of wild animals, yet they remained deaf to pleas for guns to hunt and for permission to build huts in the gardens to frighten animals off.[79] The conservation problem was complicated in large

75 P.R.O., F.O. 881/7395, 'Protection of Animals in Africa Conference, 1900'.
76 O.T. Group interview with Chief Chitungulu and councillors, Chitungulu village, Lundazi district, Zambia, 12 May 1974.
77 Z.N.A., KST 4/1/1, 'Annual Reports – Lundazi, 1903–1933', Report for 1908/9, among others.
78 Elephants were the greatest pest because of their high fertility and annual growth rate of 5 per cent; elephants were naturally drawn to crops of millet and maize because of their sweetness; the absence of adult men as hunters and restrictions on guns encouraged elephants to dwell in closer proximity to people.
79 Z.N.A., KSD 7/6/1, 'Tour Reports – Mpika, 1907–1924', Report for Oct. 1912; also BS 1/131, 'Report by the Administrator of North-Eastern Rhodesia for the two years ending 31 March 1905'.

areas of Northern Rhodesia by a government decision in 1907 to forbid the use of *chitemene* agricultural systems. *Chitemene* involved lopping off tree branches and carrying them to gardens, where they were burnt. The fertilising ash ensured a heavy crop of millet in the first year and fairly good yields in succeeding years. The company was horrified at this 'waste' of trees and by a system which impeded the control 'of natives and collection of hut-tax'.[80] The banning of *chitemene* led to a sharply reduced food supply as soils were too poor to produce adequate crops without an infusion of ash fertiliser. The company soon noted with satisfaction that there was no difficulty in obtaining labourers from areas in which *chitemene* had been banned.[81]

The regulations against *chitemene* were withdrawn when the people seemed on the verge of revolt; but while they were enforced, they encouraged the spread of tsetse fly to areas previously immune.[82] In order to survive, tsetse requires a light bush covering, which gives it the shade to breed, and wild animals, upon whose blood it feeds. When government regulations encouraged the spread of bush and wild animals they facilitated the spread of the tsetse fly and of sleeping sickness. As early as 1903 one official wrote regretting 'very much to have to report the serious fact that this pest is increasing most alarmingly. This without any possible doubt, is due to the great increase in big game, notably the rhinoceros, the elephant and the buffalo'.[83] The spread of tsetse fly and sleeping sickness occurred widely and further impoverished the people when it appeared in areas where it had hitherto been unknown and killed their cattle.[84]

The decline of the Northern Rhodesian rural economy through the impact of labour migrancy and ecological decay greatly accelerated in the period between 1914 and 1922. Tsetse and sleeping-sickness continued their advance.[85] Wild animals continued to multiply, bringing further destruction to fields and grain stores. In the western part of the colony an outbreak of bovine pleuropneumonia in 1915 destroyed the basis of the Lozi economy. This disaster, coupled with drought, resulted in labour

80 *Report of the Directors of the British South Africa Company for the Year Ending 31st March 1907*, London, 1907, 71; Z.N.A., KSD 4/1, 'Mpika District Notebook', Vol. I.
81 Z.N.A., KSD 7/1/1, 'Annual Reports, Mpika', Report for 1907/8.
82 See Leroy Vail, 'Ecology and history: the example of eastern Zambia', *JSAS*, iii, 2, 1977, 138–40.
83 Z.N.A., KTQ 2/1, 'Chinsali District Notebook', Vol. I.
84 Z.N.A., BS 1/131, 'Report for the Two Years Ending 31 March 1905'. Also KST 4/1/1, 'Annual Reports, Lundazi, 1903–1933', reports for all years between 1907 and 1910; KTQ 2/1, 'Chinsali District Notebook', District Travelling Report, 24 June 1909, among many reports. For Nyasaland, see the *Nyasaland Sleeping Sickness Diary*, xii, 1910, 10, encl. in Z.N.A., BS 1/98, 'Sleeping Sickness – Correspondence with Commissioner, Zomba'. Z.N.A., KTQ 2/1, 'Chinsali District Notebook', report on tsetse fly for 1903.
85 Z.N.A., KST 4/1/1, 'Annual Reports, Lundazi District, 1903–1933', and KDG 5/1, 'East Luangwa District Notebook', Vol. I, for many examples.

migrancy on a scale previously unknown and a missionary wrote that the
situation:

> has deeply affected the life of the natives around our Station, as most have
> been compelled to leave their homes and seek work in the South, in
> order to get money for their tax and for their personal needs ... even
> small boys have, in many instances, left the country and deserted school
> to look for work.[86]

The First World War brought the final dénouement to the first phase of
colonial exploitation in East-Central Africa. The war constituted 'the
climax of Africa's exploitation: its use as a mere battlefield'.[87] To fight the
Germans in nearby Tanganyika, the British organised an army. In 1916 the
British were joined by the Portuguese, and campaigns ranged over
Northern Rhodesia, Mozambique and Tanganyika, adversely affecting
these territories as well as neighbouring ones. To supply goods and
ammunition to the army, the men of East–Central Africa were called up to
serve as carriers called *tenga-tenga*. Between the start of the war in August
1914 and March 1917, more than 270 000 men were conscripted from
North-Eastern Rhodesia alone, with large levies from Nyasaland,
Mozambique and North-Western Rhodesia as well. This immense demand
drained labour from the villages as never before, still further injuring the
vitality of the already-ailing rural economy. War also required food, and
cattle and foodstuffs were forcibly diverted to the war effort. The
cumulative effect was famine.

The suffering endured by the *tenga-tenga* carriers had a profound impact.
Malnutrition, disease, exhaustion and violence all exacted their toll, as the
carriers wandered through the East African wilderness in defence of
capitalism and colonialism. In the last half of 1917, the official death-rate in
the carrier corps was 2 per cent per month, and the rate of 'wastage', which
included disabilities, illness and desertion, stood at 15 per cent per month.
Deaths from dysentery, malaria and pneumonia were common, and
carriers who attempted escape were summarily shot by their officers as
examples.[88] The tragedy did not end with the war. Upon demobilisation,
the exhausted and malnourished remnants returned to their shattered
homes. Bubonic plague and sleeping sickness appeared in many areas, and
in 1918 the great Spanish influenza epidemic swept through the region,

---

86 Quoted from sources in the Zambian National Archives in Laurel van Horn, 'The
agricultural history of Barotseland, 1840–1964', in *The Roots of Rural Poverty in Central and
Southern Africa*, Robin Palmer and Neil Parsons (eds), London, 1977, p. 156.
87 Iliffe, *Modern History of Tanganyika*, p. 241.
88 *Ibid.*, p. 250. For a discussion of the situation in Nyasaland, see Melvin Page, 'The war of
Thangata: Nyasaland and the East African Campaign, 1914–1918', *JAH*, xix, 1, 1978,
87–100. The impact of the war upon Mozambique has never been assessed from the point of
view of the African people, but fragmentary evidence suggests that they suffered far more
than did the people of the neighbouring territories.

carrying off thousands of weakened people. As a *coup de grâce*, inflation immediately after the war sent prices soaring, and the company doubled the hut tax from five to ten shillings. People were once again forced to clothe themselves in skins and bark-cloth.

The days of British South Africa Company misrule in Northern Rhodesia were drawing to an end. For many years the company had been concerned with high administrative costs, and in the post-war period it sought to shed its governmental responsibilities. In 1923 self-government was granted to the white settlers of Southern Rhodesia, and in 1924 the company transferred its authority in Northern Rhodesia to the British Colonial Office, retaining for itself the territory's mineral rights. Pleased to rid itself of Northern Rhodesia, the company could be content: in twenty-five years, the company had shattered the rural economy and ensured a pattern of continuing labour migration to other parts of Africa from an impoverished and dispirited country which was firmly a member of the southern African regional economy.

MOZAMBIQUE, 1919–1960: THE REVOLUTION OF ANTÓNIO SALAZAR

In many ways Mozambique was worse affected by the First World War than were Nyasaland or Northern Rhodesia. Although the British territories suffered the demand for *tenga-tenga* carriers and for food, they did not experience much actual fighting. After Portugal declared itself an ally of Britain and France in early 1916, however, a German army at once invaded Mozambique and conducted prolonged campaigns there. The transformation of the country into a battlefield involved not only demands for *tenga-tenga*, but also the expropriation or destruction of crops by warring armies. There was widespread famine. Death was common, with the estimates of those killed reaching 50 000. South of the Zambezi, in Mozambique Company territory, recruiting of carriers and road-building crews precipitated the great Makombe rising of 1917, with some 60 000 people fleeing company rule after the revolt was put down.[89] After the war Mozambique suffered the Spanish influenza epidemic. For a country whose main resource was population, the war had been acutely devastating.

Considerable changes marked the post-war period in Mozambique. Prices of commodities rose, triggering a demand for sugar, copra and sisal in the Zambezi area. In the far south and the western highlands of the Mozambique Company's territory, some Portuguese settlers began to produce maize, fruit and cattle in imitation of South Africa and Southern Rhodesia. Economic buoyancy in the British territories exacerbated the

89 Barry Neil-Tomlinson, 'The growth of a colonial economy and the development of African labour: Manica and Sofala and the Mozambique Chartered Company, 1892–1942', in University of Edinburgh, Centre for African Studies, *Mozambique*, Edinburgh 1979, p. 12.

tensions in labour-depleted Mozambique. Employers strove both to protect their labour supplies and to increase the amount of time that each man worked in a year. Violence and coercion increased yet again. Political strife also broke out among various groups of capitalists, and contributed in 1926 to the fall of the republican régime in Lisbon and the rise to power of António Salazar in 1928.

Before 1919 Mozambique had been divided into two great labour pools. The area south of the Sabi river was an adjunct of the South African economy, and the north was controlled by the 'northern interests' which represented mostly British capital. After the First World War Mozambique was given a large measure of self-government, and this neat division was challenged. A group of vocal Portuguese settlers found their plantation agriculture hindered by a lack of cheap labour, for most men worked in the mines of South Africa. They aimed to curb this drain of manpower, and the new administration, sympathetic to a struggling petty bourgeoisie, decided to curb South African influence.

The government might have been successful in restructuring the economy and changing the patterns of labour migrancy had it enjoyed a sound economic and fiscal base. But it was not in a legal position to influence the country's economy in any substantial way, since the Mozambican economy of the 1920s was largely in the power of the Banco Nacional Ultramarino. This private bank enjoyed great powers as the bank of issue for currency in the colonies and was beyond the effective control of either the Portuguese or the Mozambican government. The bank, for its own reasons, followed policies that resulted in both inflation and stagnation, occasioning much social and political unrest.[90] When undermined by the bank, the government sought economic support on international money markets, but whenever a loan was nearly concluded, the South African government blocked it. The government attracted a constant barrage of settler criticism, as did foreign interests which so obviously dominated Mozambique. The clamour, coupled with the bizarre actions of the bank as it ruined the country's economy, demonstrated the failure of colonial self-government.

While South African interests, foreign capitalists and the local Portuguese petty bourgeoisie squabbled amongst themselves as to who would control the country, the pre-war patterns of domination continued, with South Africa and the 'northern interests' both expanding their influence. As usual, the burden fell upon the African population. In the far north the Niassa Company continued its exploitations under a new British owner, the Union Castle Steamship Company. In 1924 a British official accurately noted that the situation in the company's area was 'one of actual slavery under cruel and barbaric conditions'.[91] On the *prazos*, plantation

90 Vail and White, *Capitalism and Colonialism in Mozambique*, pp. 202–5.
91 P.R.O., C.O. 525/109, Long to C.O., 15 Feb. 1924.

companies expanded their sugar, coconut and sisal plantings, and the state intervened to supply more labour. The erosion of the rural household accelerated, and a South African visitor noted that a:

> native works here all his life under horrible conditions to buy scanty clothing for his wife and daughters. The men and boys can rarely afford proper clothing, and a small piece of rag, insufficient for decent covering, represents on a prazo, the reward allowed a native for the labours of a lifetime.[92]

In the Mozambique Company territory the state sought to compel people to work for twelve months at a time, but met insuperable resistance. Instead it imposed forced labour on six-month contracts and made up the short-fall by importing men from north of the Zambezi. By 1926, 108 000 people were working under labour schemes, 40 per cent of them migrants from beyond the company's territory.[93] The trend to longer labour contracts was by now pronounced.

While compulsion provided much labour, it also attracted unwanted international attention to conditions within the Portuguese empire. The League of Nations was concerned with stamping out the remnants of slavery in the world, and in 1925 Professor E. A. Ross published for its attention his *Report on the Employment of Native Labour in Portuguese Africa*. This was caustically critical. It created a furore in Lisbon, for its publication coincided with publicity on the subject of South African efforts to gain the port of Lourenço Marques. The Portuguese feared that the report might even result in their colonies being taken away.[94] The Portuguese ruling élite concluded that Angola and Mozambique needed to be taken in hand. Economic crises, social and political strife and scandals were undermining the fabric of empire. Conditions in Portugal were scarcely better, with strikes, inflation, and political disorder causing the British Ambassador to remark in 1925 that:

> all educated Portuguese realise only too well the deplorable position into which their country is sinking, but instead of taking steps to remedy it, they cry feebly for a Mussolini or a Primo de Rivera to save them.[95]

Portugal's Mussolini was soon to appear in the person of António Salazar.

In May 1926 a military clique, some of whose members openly espoused fascism, overthrew the republican régime of Portugal. The new government moved speedily to re-define its relationship with the colonies. The effective end of the international gold standard in 1914, the disruption

92 'Report on Native Labour Conditions in the Province of Mozambique, Portuguese E. A.', *South African Labour Bulletin*, ii, 2, 1975, 22.
93 Neil-Thomlinson, 'The growth of a colonial economy', p. 13.
94 P.R.O., F.O. 371/11094, Minute of Villiers, 19 Nov. 1925.
95 P.R.O., F.O. 371/11933, 'Annual Report for 1925', by Sir Lancelot Carnegie.

of the world economy caused by the First World War, and the confusion created by alternating periods of growth and recession in the early 1920s had combined to make Europe's economy far more sluggish than it had been in the pre-war years. To protect their enfeebled domestic industries, European states abandoned old principles of free trade and fell back upon the protection offered by high tariffs. The colonial powers, deeply in debt to the United States, sought to conserve their scarce dollars by utilising their empires as sources of commodities that would otherwise have to be purchased with dollars.[96] When Portugal's new leaders came to power, they were unhappy with the striking lack of commerce between the colonies and the metropole. The republic had preferred to buy in the cheapest markets, and had declined to embrace a system of imperial preference in colonial trade; its industries could also not compete with British and German manufactures in colonial markets. In 1926, for example, only 11 per cent of colonial imports were from Portugal, while the colonies exported only 21 per cent of their products to the metropole.[97] The new government sought to improve the situation by re-establishing central direction of the colonies from Lisbon. It decided that the interests of the white petty bourgeoisie in Mozambique were expendable. Black workers on the Rand would be more profitable to Portugal than a settler community. The government therefore abandoned the attempts to reduce South Africa's influence, and concluded a convention which permitted the annual recruitment of 80 000 mine workers.

In mid-1928 António Salazar became Finance Minister. He was able to exploit the severe economic depression in Portugal to obtain virtually dictatorial powers for his office, using them to establish his 'New State', modelled on Mussolini's Italy. Freedom of speech and of political association were curtailed and opposition muted. Salazar formulated a colonial programme to benefit the metropolitan Portuguese bourgeoisie. First, he felt it essential that the state authority be unquestioned throughout the empire and therefore terminated the charter of the Niassa Company in 1929. He next moved against the *prazo* companies, cancelling their powers in 1930. The Mozambique Company had powerful friends in London and Lisbon, and its charter was allowed to run its course and expire in 1942. In 1930 Salazar's Colonial Act moved towards a consolidation of the empire by asserting that the role of the colonies was simple: 'to produce the raw material and sell it to the Mother Country in exchange for manufactured goods'.[98] Protectionism was to provide metropolitan capitalists with

96 J. Forbes Munro, *Africa and the International Economy, 1800–1960*, London, 1976, pp. 124–6.
97 Domingos da Cruz, 'A evolução comercial da metropole e das colónias, I', *Boletim Geral das Colónias*, No. 39, 1928, 61.
98 António de Oliveira Salazar, *Doctrine and Action: Internal and Foreign Policy of the New Portugal, 1928–1939*, London, 1939, pp. 303–4.

secure markets, with sources of cheap raw materials, with foreign exchange and with places for investment. The final stage in the process of integrating the colonies to metropolitan bourgeois interests came in 1937, when the laws of the corporative state were extended to the colonial empire.

Salazar's vision of the state's role was not limited to unquestioned sovereignty over the colonies and the protection of Portuguese interests. His state was highly interventionist, accepting the need for capitalism, yet also asserting that the state must undertake close supervision to prevent abuse. This interventionism took the form of laws, employers' guilds, marketing boards, workers' organisations, quota systems, fixed prices and other manifestations of corporativism. Further, Lisbon strictly limited the powers of the colonial governments, even in such areas as health, education and public works, specifying that Portugal's needs came first. In short, the colonies were actively to support the burden of economic recovery in Portugal. Salazar carried his changes in Mozambique further. He decreed that the country had been allowed to drift for too long, and that a bureaucratic revolution was essential to oversee the establishment of corporativism. In the 1930s a small army of bureaucrats was posted to Mozambique and paid for by the local tax-payers who were subjected to vigorous tax-collecting campaigns.

The scandals over alleged Portuguese 'slavery' disturbed Salazar, and he determined to end abuses. In 1928 and 1930 laws established legal protection of workers, curtailed irregularities in the recruitment of labour, particularly for private estates and industries, and provided for social-welfare programmes. The legal edifice was impressive but was little more than a false front hiding a stark reality. Although legally free to choose to work or not to work, a person had to pay taxes. Controls established under Salazar prevented free peasant agriculture, so the ordinary person had little choice other than to work as a migrant labourer for at least six months a year. Once the Mozambican economy began to revive in the early 1940s the law was constantly violated by government officials anxious to meet the labour needs of the planters.

The basic attitudes of the Salazar régime towards Mozambique can be well illustrated by looking at the decision to foster cotton production in the colony. During the 1930s the Mozambique economy had faltered. Production of coconuts, sugar and sisal declined, and labour appeared, in government eyes, to be underemployed. Towards the end of the 1930s Portugal therefore decided to implement a cotton-growing scheme to supply Portugal's mills. In the 1920s a cotton expert had declared that almost all Mozambique was 'marginal or sub-marginal cotton territory', and predicted that cotton would have but a small future in the country.[99] He did point out, however, that cotton grown by Africans under European

99 Colónia de Moçambique, *O Algodão em Moçambique*, Lourenço Marques, 1928, p. 28.

supervision might be profitable because of its low overhead costs. The Portuguese took up the suggestion and instituted a notorious system of cotton concessions.

The country was divided into zones, each of which was granted to a concessionaire who had the right to monopolise cotton produced in that area. The people were legally obliged to grow cotton and sell it to the concession-holder at a price fixed by the state. By the late 1930s almost everyone was growing cotton, whether they lived on land suitable for the crop or not. This led to abuses, and people resisted growing a crop for which they were paid almost nothing after six months' hard work. Since Salazar had ordered Mozambique to produce cotton, the bureaucrats had no choice but to meet the quota. Terror and threats once more made Mozambique a land of tears and travail. The situation became especially bad in the 1940s when the economy expanded to meet the demands of the Second World War. As a neutral nation, Portugal could sell to both sides, and took advantage of the demand for sugar, sisal, tea and copra. The result was a labour shortage, as the people were caught between the demand for cotton and the expanding market for primary products. To resolve the problem, in October 1942 the governor-general redefined African obligations to work, specifying that all able-bodied men between the ages of 18 and 55 had to work six months a year, and ordering government officials to 'assist' people to obtain such work. To ease the pressure on male workers, the burden of growing cotton and rice, a new compulsory crop, was often shifted to the women. Salazar had declared that his government was firmly against 'everything which may minimize or divide or break up the family',[100] yet when the imperatives of capitalist accumulation became crucial his government quickly forgot its scruples and moved to meet capital's requirements.

The situation rapidly worsened after October 1942. The number of men recruited by the government leaped at once, and the number of hectares under cotton increased by 50 per cent in a single year. Men chosen arbitrarily by their chiefs were forced to work successive six-month contracts. Bribery of officials was rife. Welfare provisions were ignored. Abuses of every kind were commonplace. Although forced labour continued into the 1970s, it was the compulsory cotton and rice schemes that produced the greatest abuses. Assaults, confiscations and violence against women were all common, and to this day the word for 'cotton' evokes an automatic response from the people: 'suffering'.[101] A vivid

100 Salazar, *Doctrine and Action*, p. 26.
101 See Leroy Vail and Landeg White, '"*Tawani, Machambero!*"': forced rice and cotton cultivation on the Zambezi, 1935–1960', *JAH*, xix, 2, 1978, 239–63, for a discussion of the forced cotton-growing scheme. For a parallel in Belgian Central Africa see the chapter by Jewsiewicki above.

memory of the rice concession scheme recalls the general atmosphere of the times:

> A long time ago we used to work for Ruy. We didn't work for him by our own choice. It was a punishment. . . . A big garden was worked by only one woman. If you did not do very much, they came and beat you very hard. There was no fooling around. The children at home would stay the whole day without being fed. If the birds ate the rice that you had been given to plant, they beat you saying, 'While the birds were eating the rice, where were you?'[102]

The underlying licence for this situation was Salazar's utopian vision that bureaucratic edict could solve any problem. He believed that the district governor, in cooperation with other officials, could study tables of wages and taxes, of labour available and labour needed, official food prices and peasant production figures, and simply manipulate one against another to produce the desired harmony of interests. But it was a vision that constantly eluded implementation, for there were too many incalculables: droughts, diseases, floods, fluctuating commodity markets, and the number, competence and integrity of the officials themselves. When anything went wrong, it was the people who bore the brunt of increased pressure. This overt violence was made even worse by famine caused by the diversion of male labour towards plantation agriculture and female labour towards rice and cotton production. Throughout the 1940s food shortages were common, and people were forced to use the small amounts of money they obtained to purchase grain imported from Angola.

The period before 1960 was one in which Salazar's 'reform' of the state structure revived the abuses of earlier times. The old divisions of the colony were ended, former laxness was replaced by rigour, and people suffered accordingly. They resisted, but their resistance was sharply limited by the omnipresent threat of terror, and to survive one had to compromise. By the late 1950s, Salazar's revolution was deemed successful, and Lisbon and Lourenço Marques formulated plans for new development. These included settling Portuguese smallholders, building public works such as the Cabora Bassa dam, and modernising industry and agriculture in order to reduce labour demands. Change, however, came too late. In the north active discontent was coupled with new taxes and attempts to stifle cash-crop production. The people's leaders organised a mass movement, copying techniques used over the border in Tanganyika by Julius Nyerere. In June 1960 the Portuguese agreed to meet members of the movement for discussions at the town of Mueda. Such a large crowd came that the Portuguese officials panicked, and ordered troops to fire. Five hundred

102 O.T. Luis Chaaze, Mathilde village, Chinde, Quelimane district, Mozambique, 13 Nov. 1976.

people were allegedly killed. The Mueda Massacre initiated four years of unrest in northern Mozambique. It also stimulated organised resistance which in 1962 culminated in the formation of the Frente de Libertaçao de Moçambique (Frelimo) and the long guerrilla struggle.

NYASALAND, 1919–1953 : THE BRITISH EMPIRE'S 'CINDERELLA'

By 1919, the government of Nyasaland had decided that encouragement of local peasant production would provide the base for a healthy economy, something which had proven so elusive in the Protectorate's first thirty years. This required an infrastucture of roads to the rural areas and produce markets. Agricultural advice was required if people were to grow new and improved crops. Veterinary and cattle-dipping services were likewise needed. Plans were formulated, but none was implemented by 1930 since the government found itself without the necessary money. The reason for the administration's poverty was curious, yet real. The colonial state required a degree of power if its plans were to be realised, but power lay in London, not in Nyasaland. This was shown clearly in 1919. The First World War had eroded the old structures of international finance and trade, and much of the world seemed open for American economic penetration. Britain protected its trading position in East-Central Africa by moving energetically into Mozambique. It arranged for a British firm to purchase the shares of the Niassa Company, and it supported the construction of a railway from Beira, the capital of the Mozambique Company's territory, to the Zambezi.[103] This railway, passing through bleak and largely empty land, was clearly destined to be uneconomic, and therefore needed some official guarantee before capital could be raised. Without any consultation with the Nyasaland government, the imperial government in London, to gain influence in Mozambique, assigned the obligation of guaranteeing the railway's dividends to the Nyasaland government.[104] Nyasaland, already deeply disadvantaged by its links to South Africa and Southern Rhodesia, was having a new chain fashioned, to link it with Mozambique.

The implications of this decision were not lost on local Europeans, and their newspaper accurately asserted that:

> the agreement seems to us to be entirely one-sided and we thus see the extraordinary position that we are to be taxed to construct a railway in a foreign country and for the benefit of a foreign chartered company. The worst feature, however, is that this burden of taxation for these railways

---

103 The background to this discussion is in Leroy Vail, 'The making of an imperial slum: Nyasaland and its railways, 1895–1935', *JAH*, xvi, 1, 1975, 98–103.
104 P.R.O., C.O. 525/85, Read to Barstow, 18 Aug. 1919.

in foreign countries will hamper us in the development of our own country.[105]

Such complaints fell on deaf ears. The governor's arguments that the people of Nyasaland were becoming increasingly restive over high taxes and the small number of services that they received in return were also ignored. His complaints that all attempts to develop peasant agriculture in Nyasaland would prove abortive unless the burden of the railway was removed failed to move London. Nyasaland entered upon what a later governor termed the 'Times of Starvation'.[106]

The protectorate functioned on the so-called 'half-and-half principle'. This meant that when the country had a budgetary deficit, the imperial Treasury loaned it money at 7 per-cent interest. When it had a budgetary surplus over £275 000, half of the surplus had to be applied to the liquidation of past debts. Nyasaland had already taken loans from Britain to finance the local war effort, and the new indebtedness incurred for the railway meant that it was now impossible for the government to achieve the surpluses necessary to end Treasury control and develop peasant agriculture. The economy continued to be shaky throughout the 1920s. The railways were granted an effective transport monopoly, and at once raised freight rates. Tobacco could bear the new rates, but rice, maize or ground-nuts could not, so peasant crops were ruled out. Only cotton continued relatively successfully until 1924. More and more acres of European estates were placed under tea, a high-return commodity that benefited from *thangata* labour. By 1932, 12 600 acres were planted. One African success was fire-cured tobacco. In the central districts people enthusiastically turned to the production of tobacco in the early 1920s as an alternative to labour migrancy. Even this one bright spot vanished when, in 1927–1928, prices collapsed because of over-production, and did not recover until the late 1930s.

The final blow to Nyasaland's plans for African agriculture came in 1928 when the British government, to stimulate the British steel industry before the elections of 1929, decided to construct the world's longest bridge to span the Zambezi in Mozambique. The responsibility of paying for the bridge was placed upon the frail shoulders of Nyasaland, thereby continuing the policies that had brought some of the worst rural conditions in the colonial world. Nyasaland had become a slum, and the Conservative Colonial Secretary, Lord Amery, bluntly wrote that Nyasaland's:

social services, particularly sanitation, education and technical services are at a scandalously low ebb. The death rate is disgraceful. The

105 *The Nyasaland Times*, 29 April 1920.
106 See Leroy Vail, 'Railway development and colonial underdevelopment: the Nyasaland case', in *The Roots of Rural Poverty*, Palmer and Parsons (eds), pp. 370–4.

inhabitants are emigrating. Owing simply to present poverty everything in Nyasaland is below the standard of other African colonies.... In present circumstances this African Cinderella cannot pay for the necessities let alone raise money for bridges and railways.[107]

The coming to power of a new Labour government in England in 1929 signalled a decisive but temporary change in London's attitude towards Nyasaland. To complement the decision to build the Zambezi bridge the Colonial Office decided to implement plans for peasant agriculture, if only to give the railway something to carry. The new Colonial Secretary wrote to the Treasury:

It is recognized that any power which takes responsibility of governing uncivilised races should, in the words of the Covenant of the League of Nations, 'apply the principles that the well-being and development of such peoples forms a sacred trust of civilization.' In this duty British control has failed ... [I do] not intend to suggest that the administration of Nyasaland can be brought up to the standard of the Belgian Congo or French Madagascar, but the Protectorate should be at least maintained in a condition to avoid grave public discredit which would attach to His Majesty's Government both in this country and abroad should the present scandalous state of Nyasaland attract attention.[108]

The Treasury briefly abandoned its former insistence upon fiscal rectitude, granted interest-free loans, and encouraged the expansion of African cash-crop production.

The harsh realities of the depression and the fall of the Labour government rapidly tarnished the promised new era. Prices for primary products fell, the railway increased freight rates, and the British government terminated development projects. Only tea-planting showed much sign of life during the 1930s. Maize-growing was vetoed lest it compete with European-grown maize from Kenya and Southern Rhodesia. Tax collecting faltered.[109] The European community declined.[110] An alternative to the aborted peasant production was needed. When in 1923 the white electorate of Southern Rhodesia voted for self-government, the settlers looked northward for a sphere of influence to exploit. They came to view both Northern Rhodesia and Nyasaland, from which migrant workers could not be recruited for mines of South Africa after 1913 because of the high death-rate there, as their own labour reserves. By 1933 an official at the Colonial Office could comment that 'Nyasaland

107 P.R.O., T 161/742/S.28446/4, Amery to Churchill, 8 July 1928.
108 P.R.O., C.O. 525/137, Bottomley to Treasury, 11 April 1930.
109 P.R.O., C.O. 525/154, Hall to Cunliffe-Lister, 12 June 1934.
110 P.R.O., C.O. 525/149, Minute of F. Green, 28 March 1933.

is within the Rhodesian orbit and is indeed claimed by Southern Rhodesia as part of their future domain'.[111]

Southern Rhodesian ambitions distressed some sensitive Protectorate officials who felt that the interests of the 'Protected' should be considered. The Chief Justice, for example, worried, 'why should any territory wish to join with Nyasaland? The only answer could be: "To get the benefit of Nyasaland's plentiful, good, and cheap labour". Did that not mean making the Native a pawn in the game?'[112] The answer to his rhetorical question was obvious, but the Protectorate government hesitated only briefly. In 1934 the Chief Secretary made a speech in which he said that either there would be money to encourage peasant production, or the people would have to be sent off to work.[113] The government decided to export its people, and in late 1934 a Southern Rhodesian firm recruited 100 workers.[114] The die had been cast.

Throughout the region the economic situation was changing in the early 1930s. South Africa's abandonment of the gold standard caused the price of gold to rise, so it became profitable to work mines that hitherto had been considered uneconomic. The development of anti-pneumonia drugs again permitted the recruitment of men from north of latitude 22°. 'Tropicals' were thought to be especially suited to the high temperatures of the deep-level mines. A report published in Nyasaland caused embarrassment to the British government, so vividly did it describe the destruction of the rural household. The report noted that labour migration 'brought misery and poverty to hundreds and thousands of families and that the waste of life, happiness, health and wealth was colossal'.[115] It suggested that migration be controlled and revenue fed back into the rural areas to stop the erosion of family life. The administration agreed, and decided to emulate Salazar's Mozambique in regulating recruitment for the south. At once there was conflict over whether Nyasaland labour should be monopolised by Southern Rhodesia, or whether South Africa would receive a share. Southern Rhodesia's Prime Minister Huggins knew where his interest lay:

> We do not consider conditions on the Rand superior, except from the ignorant natives' point of view; that is to say, he gets higher wages in exchange for which he gets higher mortality rate, higher sickness rate;

111 P.R.O., C.O. 525/148, Minute of F. Green, 25 March 1933.
112 Report of a meeting of the East African Group of the Overseas League, in *East Africa*, 25 Jan. 1934.
113 Speech by Mr Hall, Chief Secretary to the Nyasaland Government, reported in *East Africa*, 25 Jan. 1934.
114 P.R.O., C.O. 525/155, Hall to Cunliffe-Lister, 31 Aug. 1934; see also M.N.A., S2/4 II/31, Minute of 20 Aug. 1934.
115 *The Report of the Committee Appointed by His Excellency the Governor to Enquire into Emigrant Labour, 1935*, Zomba, 1936 (Lacey Report).

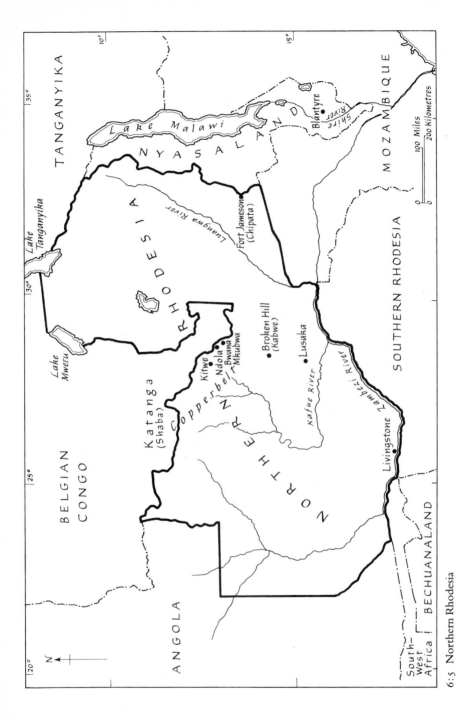

6:5 Northern Rhodesia

the Native learns vicious habits and unnatural methods of living there, whereas here he lives a more natural life, but on a smaller wage.[116]

The Nyasaland government decided in 1938 that it could accommodate both countries.

During the Second World War Nyasaland's people worked throughout southern Africa's regional economy. Tens of thousands went to Southern Rhodesia and the Rand; some went to the copper-mines of Northern Rhodesia or the gold-fields of Tanganyika; educated men took positions of responsibility in these countries as well as in the Belgian Congo and Mozambique. To take their place in the local economy, new groups of Lomwe-speaking people from Mozambique arrived, fleeing the harshness of the Salaza government cotton campaign and providing labour for expanded plantations. Using such labour, European settlers enjoyed some success. Tea production, for example, rose in value from £60 000 in the early 1930s to about £2 million in the early 1950s. African production of peasant cotton and tobacco recovered after the 1930s, but crops began to suffer from land shortages.[117] All in all, there was little change in the condition of Nyasaland, and in 1944 the Governor wrote to London to complain that conditions there were 'a disgrace'.[118] By this time the administration had long since abandoned plans to foster peasant production and had accepted the position of Nyasaland as a labour reserve for the rest of central and southern Africa. It seemed only sensible to permit political reality to follow economic reality. In 1953 Nyasaland was joined to Southern Rhodesia as part of the Federation of Rhodesia and Nyasaland.

NORTHERN RHODESIA, 1924–1953 : COPPER AND SOCIAL CHANGE

At the beginning of the 1920s Northern Rhodesia seemed little more than an isolated backwater of the British Empire. A sparse population of little more than a million people was scattered across an area of almost two million square kilometres. The British South Africa Company's governmental apparatus was tiny, and its main concern was the collection of taxes and the flow of labour to Southern Rhodesia. The state supported no schools, and there were almost no medical facilities available. Only a few roads existed, mostly near the railway, and goods were transported on the heads of porters in most areas.

The country's internal economy was dominated by a small community of European settlers who lived along the railway from Southern Rhodesia

116 P.R.O., C.O. 525/173, Huggins to Stanley, 23 Dec. 1937, and in Stanley to Harding, 24 Dec. 1937.
117 W.J. Barber, *The Economy of British Central Africa: a Case Study of Economic Development in a Dualistic Society*, London, 1961, pp. 81–3.
118 P.R.O., C.O. 525/197, Richards to C.O., 2 Feb. 1944.

to the mineral deposits of Broken Hill (Kabwe) and Bwana Mkubwa, and in a small eastern enclave around Fort Jameson (Chipata). These settlers numbered about 3 500. In 1924, when the British Colonial Office succeeded the company as the administrator of the territory, the settlers were given five seats on the newly established Legislative Council. In the years before 1919 the settlers had prospered modestly by selling maize and cattle to the mines of Katanga.[119] They either grew maize themselves or had share-cropping African tenants, or purchased the crop directly from African producers. After the First World War they suffered economic reverses when Southern Rhodesian competition caused the price of maize in Katanga to plummet, and by the time the Colonial Office took over the territory a vocal settler community was seeking state protection.

Areas beyond the line-of-rail remained labour reserves where men found money to pay taxes by emigrating. Labour migrancy became a basic way of life. By the early 1920s, the colony's African societies were extremely fragile, undermined by the laws and regulations of the pre-war period and by the heavy demands of the war itself. They needed respite if they were to recover. The first governor of Northern Rhodesia under the Colonial Office, however, was Sir Herbert Stanley, a man whose government experience had been in South Africa and Southern Rhodesia and who strongly believed that the colony's future lay in the growth of European agriculture. His Northern Rhodesia was meant to become a 'white man's country'.

If settlers were to be attracted, Stanley believed, land would have to be cleared of its African inhabitants. Three land commissions were established to identify European areas and create 'Native Reserves' to which Africans could be removed. Most land set aside for European settlement was along the line-of-rail, but good land in the eastern and northern parts of the country was also cleared of people in the late 1920s. The division of territory between Europeans and Africans was also intended to produce labour for local European enterprise. This had been largely lacking up to then, as the African people preferred the higher wages of Katanga or Southern Rhodesia. The Native Reserves reduced opportunities for independent cultivators and share-cropping tenant farmers since the assigned land was inferior in quality and deliberately crowded in population. People were therefore driven to work for local wages in order to survive. As the General Manager of the North Charterland Exploration Company commented during hearings to establish a 10 000-square-mile set of Native Reserves in areas it controlled in the east: 'It would be politic to procure Reserves on the basis of the bare subsistence of the Native, giving

---

119 Much of this material derives from Ackson M. Kanduza, 'The Impact of Railway Rates and Customs Agreements on Settler Farming in Northern Rhodesia–Zambia, 1910–1939: the Case of Maize and Cattle Farming', M.A. thesis, University of Zambia, Lusaka, 1979.

an allowance for that only, assuming that the policy of the country is to encourage European development.'[120]

Ironically, however, it was not the European settler who was the main beneficiary of this division of the land. Competition from Southern Rhodesia, coupled with a railway pricing policy that favoured Southern Rhodesia over Northern Rhodesia, gradually eliminated Northern Rhodesian producers from the Katanga market.[121] In the east the tobacco industry collapsed in 1927, and many settlers abandoned the area. The land they had cleared remained vacant, and reverted to bush known as 'the silent land'. Wild animals and the tsetse fly invaded, bringing sleeping sickness which spread death to the overcrowded reserves.[122] The profound deterioration of the reserves during the 1930s was summed up in a complaint to a government official in 1937: 'We were moved from our homes ... that Europeans might come to live there. No Europeans have come and soon there will be none of us left here. If we stay here we shall know that the Government has destroyed us.'[123] Because of the reverses suffered by European agriculture in the 1920s, Governor Sir James Maxwell reversed the policies of his predecessor and decided after all that Northern Rhodesia was not to be a 'white man's country'. Maxwell's vision, however, was wrong, and changes already taking place were destined to make Northern Rhodesia very much a white man's country, albeit not of the type previously foreseen.

During the First World War British leaders had recognised the desirability of obtaining raw materials from the empire which 'ought to be capable in any emergency of being independent in respect of the supply of every essential commodity'.[124] Northern Rhodesia was the only part of the empire with untapped copper reserves, and in 1922 the British South Africa Company reformed its mining laws to allow the granting of mining concessions.[125] American, British and South African capital began to flow in. By 1928 deposits of profitable ore had been discovered along the upper Kafue river, which became known as the Northern Rhodesian Copperbelt. By 1930 four mines were being developed, Roan Antelope and Mufulira with American capital, and Nkana and Nchanga opened by the Anglo American Corporation of South Africa.

Just as the new industry was being established, the great depression

120 Z.N.A., ZP 1/1/5, 'Evidence Presented to the North Charterland Exploration Company Commission on Native Reserves', evidence by Bruce Livingstone.
121 Kanduza, 'Railway Rates and Customs Agreements', pp. 45–117.
122 Leroy Vail, 'Ecology and history', 143–51.
123 Z.N.A., SEC/NAT/363, 'Tour Report No. 3/1937, Petauke District'.
124 Cd. 9035, *Final Report of the Committee on Commercial and Industrial Policy After the War*, London, 1918, p. 29.
125 Much of this information is derived from a Ph.D. dissertation by Chipasha Luchembe, University of California at Los Angeles, forthcoming.

struck the world economy. The copper companies quickly organised a cartel, which stabilised the prices and permitted the industry to survive. Production rose from 5 465 tonnes in 1929 to 143 501 tonnes in 1935, and copper became the dominant economic force in the country, leaving European agriculture far behind:

TOTAL VALUE OF NORTHERN RHODESIAN DOMESTIC EXPORTS (£ STERLING)

	Minerals	*Non-minerals*
1913	52 000	143 000
1929	557 000	262 000
1935	4 492 000	176 000

Source: S. H. Frankel, *Capital Investment in Africa*, Oxford, 1938, p.212.

By 1938 copper and other minerals counted for 97 per cent of the country's domestic exports, and copper production rose to 213 000 tonnes to meet demand generated by the threat of another war in Europe.

Economic growth of such magnitude radically reshaped Northern Rhodesia to meet the needs of the mines. One beneficiary of the growth was the European settler community. By 1930 the 22 000 African and 4 000 European mine workers required 300 000 bags of maize and other foodstuffs. The state sought to protect the settlers from Southern Rhodesian competition, and in 1935 passed a Maize Control Ordinance which guaranteed that a Marketing Board would purchase all maize produced in the country. This, intended as support for the settlers, also provided a market for African-produced maize, particularly in the southern province. In this case, as well as in others where transport facilities were available, an African peasantry was established which no longer needed to migrate.

The rapid expansion of the Copperbelt during the depression altered the patterns of labour relations within the colony. Given the large amounts of capital at their disposal, the mine-owners could have created a highly capitalised industry requiring relatively few skilled workers. Because of the depression and the large numbers of unemployed men laid off by retrenchment in Katanga and Southern Rhodesia, the owners decided to prefer an industry based on cheap, unskilled labour. This decision marked a great new departure in East-Central Africa in general and in Northern Rhodesia in particular. Until then, the whole area had been, with certain local exceptions, a labour reserve. Suddenly an industry modelled on the Witwatersrand gold industry had been created, and with it came the social, economic and political tensions found in South Africa. For specialised work the companies recruited Europeans both from Europe and from South Africa. Many of them brought racial prejudices against black Africans, and racial separation was applied on the economic level. European workers were paid the high salaries considered necessary to keep them in Africa and provided with fringe benefits and amenities. African workers were considered migrants whose proper homes were in the village and were paid low rates, housed in unsanitary compounds and fed an unbalanced diet. Marked material disparities and open racial animosity provided the focal point for African discontent with colonial realities.

Discontent with taxation, labour migrancy, racial discrimination, structural exploitation, governmental neglect, poor African education and inadequate health had long been voiced throughout East-Central Africa. In northern Nyasaland the Scottish Presbyterian missionaries did establish an impressive educational system based at Livingstonia, and thousands of Africans were educated, some to high standards. As they could find no opportunity for employment at home, they emigrated to areas throughout South and South-Central Africa, experiencing the many-faceted reality of class oppression and racial discrimination. As early as 1912 some of these men organised themselves to seek colonial reform. Throughout the 1920s and 1930s 'Native Associations' were set up in Nyasaland, and 'Welfare Associations' in Northern Rhodesia. They fought for African rights within the context of a reformed colonial system. In an area divided by a multiplicity of languages and customs, where social horizons were frequently bounded by the village or chiefdom, the message of these educated men was strikingly new. All Africans, regardless of language, religion, ethnic affiliation or custom had a common duty to oppose colonial oppression. One of the migrants from Nyasaland told his Northern Rhodesian audience in 1932 that the time had come 'for African to uplift African'.[126]

This feeling soon centred on the Copperbelt, for it was here that oppression and exploitation appeared most clearly. In 1935 the Northern Rhodesia government increased taxes for mine-workers. It was startled by the African response. All workers, ranging from educated clerks from Nyasaland to the lowest-paid underground miners, united in strike action for better pay and improved amenities. Violence broke out, and at the Roan Antelope Mine government forces killed six strikers and wounded seventeen. The government appointed a commission of enquiry which laid bare the workers' grievances. In subsequent years, however, neither the mine-owners nor the state did much to redress the grievances. For the state, African workers were rural people, and it would be wrong to make mining areas permanently attractive. The mining companies saw no reason to raise wages or improve living facilities so long as unemployed men were seeking jobs.

In 1936 the European mine-workers formed the Northern Rhodesian Mine Workers Union, which in 1937 was recognised by the mine-owners.

---

126 Z.N.A. KDB 4/2/2, 'Welfare Associations – Livingstone', Minutes of 5 March 1932, speech by Daniel Soko.

Since neither the mine owners nor the state desired a stabilised African work-force, and since African labour turnover was consequently very high, European miners monopolised the best jobs and entrenched themselves behind a colour bar based on that existing in South Africa. This meant that no Africans were permitted to compete for jobs with Europeans. A formal colour bar was added to the apparatus of colonialism in Northern Rhodesia.

In 1940, after the outbreak of the Second World War, the white miners successfully struck for a 5 per-cent pay rise and increased overtime payments. Seeing the advantage of such a strike, 15 000 African workers struck on 28 March 1940. Once again violence broke out, and once again government forces fired on the strikers, this time killing thirteen and wounding seventy-one. Once again a commission of enquiry was held, and once again the government was surprised at the workers' grievances. The grievances of low pay and poor conditions were now compounded by dissatisfaction with the colour bar and the fact that Africans could not advance upwards to white-held jobs. By 1940 many African workers refused to consider themselves rural people temporarily sojourning on the mines. They were permanent mine-workers and wanted opportunities for promotion. The lines of opposition were drawn between unionised European workers and increasingly militant African workers, while the government and the mine-owners looked nervously on.

During the war years, Europeans entrenched themselves politically as well as economically, by seeking seats on the Legislative Council. European workers were seen as crucial to the success of the wartime copper industry, and the government was unwilling to challenge them. By the end of the war their power and influence had much increased, yet they realised that their position in Northern Rhodesia was far from secure while the area was under the Colonial Office. They therefore sought political allies in Southern Rhodesia, where government was firmly committed to the colour bar and white supremacy and coveted Northern Rhodesia's mineral wealth. During the 1930s Southern Rhodesia's desire for amalgamation with Northern Rhodesia increased with rising copper production. London recognised that Southern Rhodesia considered both Northern Rhodesia and Nyasaland to be part of its sphere of influence.

By the end of the Second World War it was clear that the colonial arrangements of the pre-war era could not last. The weakness of Britain, the hostility of the United States to formal empires that might exclude American trade, the growth of British opinion favouring decolonisation, and increased agitation for independence in other colonial areas led to a quickening of political awareness in the British sphere of Central Africa. Nationalist leaders began to abandon their demands for reform and call for freedom.

In Nyasaland Africans had organised the Nyasaland African Association.

This organisation represented the interests of the fairly prosperous and well-educated élite who wanted greater participation in governmental affairs. They saw the often-discussed amalgamation with Southern Rhodesia as the worst possible development. 'We totally refuse to amalgamate,' they declared, 'until we have been given at least ninety-nine percent of the rights we are entitled to enjoy in the administration of our own country.'[127] Although opposition to amalgamation developed into a mass nationalist movement in the later 1950s, its earliest manifestations were élitist.

It was in Northern Rhodesia that opposition took on the character of a more broadly-based movement among African mine-workers. In 1948 a new African union was started, the Shop Assistants Union, with Kenneth Kaunda as one of its organisers. Other unions followed, and in 1949 they were joined together to form the African Mineworkers Union under the leadership of Lawrence Katilungu. It soon had a membership of some 20 000 men. Meanwhile, the élitist Welfare Associations of Northern Rhodesia had followed their Nyasaland counterparts and created a Federation of African Societies of Northern Rhodesia. This was to be an umbrella organisation for Africans throughout the country. As in Nyasaland, the issue that catalysed African opinion was the question of amalgamation with Southern Rhodesia. Africans were bitter from their experience of the colour bar on the Copperbelt, and the last thing that they wanted was its general extension to all areas of life within the country. No matter how sensible a proposal for amalgamation might be from an economic point of view, it was politically unacceptable to Africans.

Amalgamation seemed a real threat. Northern Rhodesia's wealth and Nyasaland's labour were seen as necessary for Southern Rhodesia's economic growth. Northern Rhodesian whites wanted the protection from rising African aspirations that union with Southern Rhodesia would afford. The governors of all three territories shared European sentiments, while in London official opinion saw such a scheme as economically sensible. A united British Central Africa would attract the capital needed for economic growth more readily than would three separate territories. By 1948 a wide spectrum of non-African opinion generally accepted that some type of union would occur. Local Europeans launched a campaign to achieve union as soon as possible.

Africans also campaigned, led by such élite leaders as Nyasaland's Hastings Kamuzu Banda, then resident in Britain, and Northern Rhodesia's Harry Nkumbula. Their principal concern was to halt the spread of the colour bar, an essentially political matter of importance to educated men and skilled workers. The nationalist leaders gave little immediate thought

127 Quoted in Robert I. Rotberg, *The Rise of Nationalism in Central Africa: the Making of Malawi and Zambia, 1873–1964*, Cambridge, Mass., 1966, p. 190.

to African cultivators. Their campaign was an attack on colonialism rather than an alternative vision of society. This fact shaped the later nationalist movements in both Nyasaland and Northern Rhodesia, and resulted in the long continuation of many of the structures of colonialism and a neglect of rural peasants. In 1953, however, despite African opposition, the British government agreed to the creation of the Federation of Rhodesia and Nyasaland, thereby encouraging the growth of mass nationalism in Nyasaland and Northern Rhodesia.

CHAPTER 7

Zimbabwe: the path of capitalist development

IAN R. PHIMISTER

The path of capitalist development in colonial Zimbabwe can best be understood by analysing conflict between capital and labour. It is also important to consider how the long association of international capital with settler colonialism changed in the course of struggle to secure conditions in which capitalism could flourish.

CONQUEST AND SPECULATION, 1890–1902

> The relationship between a good or bad sharemarket on the one side and a British Colony in the stage of tender infancy on the other is to be studied, if anywhere, in this country of Rhodesia. Rhodesia is a country which, almost avowedly is intended to be built up, or at least forced upward, by aid of gold mining and land dealing on the £1 share limited liability principle.
>
> – *Rhodesia Herald*, 14 September 1898

The immediate genesis of colonial Zimbabwe followed the discovery of gold on the Witwatersrand in 1886. A mixture of poor luck and faulty judgement left Cecil Rhodes's Gold Fields of South Africa Company on the fringes of the first Rand boom. The consequences of this, together with the threat seemingly posed to British supremacy by the magnitude of the gold discoveries, combined to drive Rhodes's 'pioneer column' northwards in 1890 in search of a 'Second Rand'.[1] Thus rooted in the complex strategies of British imperial hegemony and of mining capital, the Chartered Company[2] adventure rested on an alliance between inter

---

1 See R. Robinson and J. Gallagher, *Africa and the Victorians*, London, 1961; I. Phimister, 'Rhodes, Rhodesia and the Rand', *Journal of Southern African Studies (JSAS)*, i, 1974.
2 Rhodes's B(ritish) S(outh) A(frica) Company was granted a Royal Charter on 29 October 1889 authorising it 'to make treaties and promulgate laws as well as to maintain a police force and undertake public works'; see P. Mason, *The Birth of a Dilemma*, London, 1958, p. 128.

national capital and settler colonialism. The latter was the junior but indispensable partner.

At first, it was confidently assumed that the settlers would be very junior partners indeed. The legendary riches of Ophir had long been rumoured to lie between the Limpopo and the Zambezi, and it was thought that as soon as 'several new Johannesburgs'[3] had been discovered, their development would necessarily be in the hands of large capital. For its part, the Chartered Company did not seek direct involvement in production. As the primary representative of financial and speculative capital, the BSAC set the terms of entry and sought to hold the ring for the operations of industrial and merchant capital. It aimed to provide an administrative and transport infrastructure, but would otherwise take its profits in the market through share-holding in other companies.[4] Under the newly-framed mining law, 50 per cent of the shares of any company were claimed for the Chartered Company, leaving Rhodes to exult to his London Board that the system was 'an enormous thing', as it 'practically means ... we ... shall get half the minerals in the country'.

Initial exploration in Mashonaland, however, produced little to cheer about. Although systematic mining work was severely handicapped by lack of equipment and by intermittent and expensive communication with the south, prospectors quickly established the poverty of local gold-fields. When this impression was confirmed by visiting experts, the territory slid swiftly into an economic depression.[5] Only two mining companies were floated in 1892. With little fresh capital entering the territory, the Chartered Company found its original capitalisation of £1 million ludicrously inadequate for the task before it, and was saved from collapse only by a 'monthly subsidy from De Beers and other friends'.[6] Cash expenditure was slashed, leaving what remained of the civil administration heavily dependent on settler magistrates, field cornets and voluntary forces.[7] In its place a system of extravagant land concessions was used to reward companies and individuals for past services and to encourage speculative interest in Mashonaland.[8]

The resulting highly combustible mixture of settler and speculative interests was soon ignited by a clash with the Ndebele near Fort Victoria in July 1893. Even as news of the incident caused Chartered shares to fall

---

3 The phrase is Eric Walker's, *A History of Southern Africa*, London, 1964, p. 429.
4 J. S. Galbraith, *Crown and Charter*, Berkeley, Ca., 1974, p. 122.
5 'At present everything is stagnation. Economy the order of the day in every household. The whole concern has the appearance of [an] enormous bladder unduly inflated and suddenly pricked. One might say that the experts were the people who have pricked it'; H. Mss. BO 11/1/1, Borrow to father, 26 Nov. 1891. All file references are held in the National Archives, Zimbabwe.
6 Walker, *Southern Africa*, p. 426.
7 T. O. Ranger, *Revolt in Southern Rhodesia*, London, 1967, p. 60.
8 Galbraith, *Crown and Charter*, pp. 278–80.

rapidly, its outcome in favour of the company suggested the possibility of a cheap confrontation with Lobengula, the Ndebele ruler. After momentary hesitation, Rhodes and Jameson raised settler columns on the promise of land and mining claims yet to be won, and set out to manufacture a war for the seizure of Matabeleland.[9] As Jameson well knew, 'the getting Matabeleland open would give us a tremendous lift in shares and everything else. The fact of its being shut up gives it an immense value here and outside.'[10]

The BSAC basked in unaccustomed favour and prosperity for roughly two years after the end of the war. Within months of the conquest, it was reported that 'a sum of over half a million has . . . been subscribed in cash by independent Companies'. As this trend accelerated in 1895, the number of development companies in the country rose to about two hundred, while on the Bulawayo stock exchange, Chartered shares changed hands at £8 17s 6d. Much of the boom was speculative, not industrial, in character. Although partly based on overestimation of the region's mineral resources, it was intimately dependent on the Rand boom of 1894–1895. The close association of the two sharemarkets allowed the local boom to continue undisturbed even after the failure of Matabeleland to disgorge a major gold-field.[11] It was a market where insiders made money, where visitors were cynically informed that 'when output begins speculation ceases'[12] and where for 'nine months of each year the development of auriferous Mashonaland is gravely performed by cable and telegraph'.[13]

Rhodes and his associates had in the meantime come to a more sober appraisal of the country's gold prospects, although they continued to encourage and sustain the boil and froth of speculative capital. A visit in August–September 1894 by Consolidated Gold Fields' famous mining expert, John Hays Hammond, had emphasised that the real whereabouts of the 'second Rand' lay in the deep levels of the Rand itself and not in the very different quartzite reefs of Matabeleland and Mashonaland, where extensive development work was necessary to establish their values.[14] The BSAC therefore passed fresh legislation in 1895 which aimed to encourage industrial as opposed to purely speculative capital in the mining industry. In

9 *African Review*, 8 July 1893 and following issues. See especially J. R. D. Cobbing, 'The Ndebele under the Khumalos, 1820–96', Ph.D. thesis, University of Lancaster, 1976, pp. 353–70; P. Stigger, 'Volunteers and the profit motive in the Anglo-Ndebele War, 1893', *Rhodesian History*, ii, 1971, 11–23.
10 Cited in Ranger, *Revolt*, p. 94.
11 There was considerable speculation in land; by 1899, 9.3 million acres were held by companies. See R. H. Palmer, *Land and Racial Domination in Rhodesia*, London 1977, pp. 34–8.
12 H. C. Thompson, *Rhodesia and Its Government*, London, 1898, p. 48.
13 *Rhodesia Herald*, 16 March 1894.
14 J. H. Hammond, *The Autobiography of John Hays Hammond*, 2 vols., New York, 1935, Vol. I, pp. 276–8.

this way they hoped to nudge companies into continuous development of their properties.

Tied to this tentative encouragement of industrial capital were further attacks on African economic and social organisation. The essential purpose of the company state was to provide the minimum conditions necessary for the more or less orderly accumulation of capital. Thus, the company had lost little time in the struggle to assert its authority over those Shona polities it could reach, most infamously through the para-military police patrols of 1892.[15] Much less haste was evidenced in the narrowly economic sphere, where the search for gold and the speculative obsessions of the colonists and companies generated only small and sporadic labour needs. Indeed, the primary tendency at that time was for some African communities to sell more and more foodstuffs to the settlers.

Then, as hopes of rich gold discoveries in Matabeleland flared and flickered, both the BSAC and the settlers turned to a more thoroughgoing looting of the 'natural economy' of the Shona and Ndebele. Between October 1893 and March 1896 anything from 100 000 to 200 000 cattle were seized from the Ndebele; forced labour became widespread; and the collection of hut tax, first imposed 'illegally' in May 1893, was stepped up after imperial sanction was received in 1894.[16] Its collection was 'arbitrary and irregular, appearing more like the levy of a tribute than the collection of a civil tax', as marauding bands of Native Department levies despoiled villages and districts of their crops and livestock.[17] The struggle to drive Africans into wage labour was very largely left to the future. Neither the interests of speculative capital nor the extremely limited resources of the company state required a profound transformation of indigenous social formations.

As a result, African polities, although becoming less autonomous, could still readily muster the political and social cohesion necessary to resist the colonial net settling unevenly over them. The particular advance of the mining-settler frontier provided some Shona and Ndebele with ample cause to resist, without significantly detracting from their capacity to fight. Opportunity was presented by the Jameson Raid, which denuded Chartered territory of police and troops. In March and June 1896 the Risings began. They persisted in various areas until near the end of 1897, and were crushed only with the assistance of a British army and at the cost of thousands of lives and hundreds of thousands of pounds.

The combined effect of the Raid and the Risings on the infant mining industry was disastrous, as the flow of investment capital evaporated along with the value of Rhodesian mining and development company shares.

15 Ranger, *Revolt*, p. 64.
16 Cobbing, 'Nbedele under the Khumalos', pp. 372–82; Galbraith, *Crown and Charter*, p. 325.
17 Ranger, *Revolt*. p. 77.

This collapse of the speculative bubble forced the BSAC to try, much more seriously this time, to foster genuine mining activity. In short, the new situation was to be one in which the large capitalist 'should be encouraged, but only as a mining and industrial factor, not as a speculator pure and simple'.[18] For this, railway transport was essential. Although it had previously resisted settler clamour for years, the Chartered establishment now authorised the speedy completion of rail communication with the coast and later the construction of branch lines to the major mining districts. Encouragement of a different sort came from a belated attempt to enforce the provisions of the 1895 Mines and Minerals Act and end the speculative holding of thousands of mining claims. In September 1898 the mining industry entered a new phase when the Geelong, soon to be joined by other mines, began a regular output of gold. Until that point, Southern Rhodesia's capitalist mining industry had produced less than 7 000 ounces of gold, but in 1899 alone over 65 000 ounces were won, and by 1902 annual production had climbed to nearly 200 000 ounces.

No sooner had the mining industry clambered precariously to its knees, however, than it was once more threatened, this time by the outbreak of the South African War in October 1899. Railway communication with the south was disrupted. As transport and mining costs went up and the financial resources of nearly all companies were stretched to breaking-point, it became increasingly difficult for the industry to sustain its existing top-heavy structure. Large sections of it were moribund, paralysed by the conflicting need to confiscate claims and curb speculation without frightening off fresh capital. Such working capital as there was tended to be completely inadequate, and incompetent management was rife. Most companies were overcapitalised through speculation, through reservation of shares for the Chartered Company and through the practice of floating subsidiary companies to raise extra cash.[19] Above all, however, the war precipitated a major crisis between mining capital and black labour.

Once the mines had begun the slow process of moving away from share-market dealing to actual production, profitability came to depend crucially on abundant supplies of cheap labour. As early as 1895, provincial labour bureaux were formed, along with a central compound in Bulawayo to direct the flow of labour to the mines. This first initiative failed because of heavy financial losses and the impact of the Risings. A second attempt was made in 1899, when the Labour Board of Southern Rhodesia was established, again in two provincial sections. It supplied more than 6 000 workers to Matabeleland mines in the last six months of 1899 and, together

18 *Rhodesia Herald*, 23 Feb. 1898.
19 See variously, LO 4/1/2. Report by the Commissioner of Mines for year ending 31 March 1898; C. T. Roberts, *The Future of Gold Mining in Mashonaland,* Salisbury, 1898; A1/5/5, Wilson Fox to Earl Grey, 26 Oct. 1903; *Financial Times*, 16 April 1902; *Rhodesia*, 13 Jan. 1900; J. H. Curle, *The Gold Mines of the World*, London, 1902, p. 105.

with the huge contingents of forced labour provided by the Native Department,[20] undoubtedly was instrumental in the fall in average mine wages from almost 40 shillings per month in 1897 to 22 shillings by early 1900.[21] During the same period the size of the produce market open to black agriculturalists was restricted by companies sending some food supplies up from the south by rail.

The war stopped this practice, and made forced labour itself somewhat more problematic by leaving the mining industry dependent on peasant grain production. Africans who could 'trade their grain at a considerable profit'[22] were unwilling to work on the mining industry's terms, and obliged employers to look elsewhere for their needs. As the Chartered Company administration then lacked the means to tap northern labour reservoirs and to contain the high desertion rate, it instituted a desperate and exotic search for indentured labour in the Red Sea area, and, rather more predictably, for Indian and Chinese workers. None of the schemes was successful. The industry's problems ballooned when, in swift succession, the Labour Board collapsed under the weight of excessive administrative charges and provincial rivalry, and the British Secretary of State for the Colonies barred Native Commissioners from direct involvement in labour recruitment.

Lack of labour affected the mines in two main ways. If they were not forced to close down completely, plants were run well below capacity. This pushed up working expenses and eroded profitability,[23] while cash wages rose in order to attract and retain what labour was available. Wages increased to roughly 30 shillings per month in March 1901 and to just over 40 shillings a year later.[24] Attempts by the industry to reverse the process were met with strike action. In fact, most mines 'could not afford to run the risk of adopting a reduced scale of wage, as the margin of profit was so small that it did not allow of their running the risk of stopping the battery'.[25] As mines closed and profits fell, sentiment in the London money market hardened:

> The argument of the thinking man in the City is this: 'You have in Rhodesia say ten mines trying to produce gold and pay dividends ... [but] ... not one of these ten milling companies has been able to run for

20 C. van Onselen, *Chibaro: African Mine Labour in Southern Rhodesia 1900–1933*, London, 1976, pp. 78, 80.
21 I. Phimister, 'History of Mining in Southern Rhodesia to 1953', Ph.D. thesis, University of Rhodesia, 1975, p. 110.
22 *Report of the Chief Native Commissioner, Matabeleland, for the year ending 31 March 1901*, p. 10.
23 BSAC, *Information as to Mining in Rhodesia, 1902*, p. 172; *Financial News*, 1 May 1902.
24 Phimister, 'History of Mining', p. 110.
25 A3/18/30/23, extract, General Manager of the Mashonaland Agency Ltd, Bulawayo, to the Secretary, London, 19 Feb. 1902.

twelve months without having to hang up the whole or some part of their [crushing] stamps for want of labour to keep the mill going, and development ahead of the mill. ... Show me that the labour can be obtained and then we will see about the capital.'[26]

The London headquarters of the BSAC concurred, and later stressed that 'want of money for the mines has been induced by want of labour'.[27]

The mining industry's crisis magnified its discontent with the rule of the BSAC. At the start of 1902 all of the candidates returned from the mining province of Matabeleland in the Legislative Council elections opposed the continuation of the Chartered administration. The BSAC was also attacked in the widely read *Mining Journal*, which argued that 'mining adventurers have certainly been deterred by the extortionate system of royalties', and offered the shrill prediction that 'if any gold discoveries were made which precipitated a rush into Rhodesia no free mining community would submit without bloodshed to the exactions of their present landlord'.[28]

The opposition baton now passed to a different segment of the tiny settler society. Quite apart from variously felt economic grievances, an emotional link tying many settlers to the BSAC had snapped with Rhodes's death in March 1902. This accentuated speculation about Southern Rhodesia's political future. In August, a mass public meeting of the Bulawayo Debating Society had as its motion the abrogation of the BSAC's charter. Prominent 'independent' settlers castigated the company's economic policy favouring big companies, especially those doing nothing to develop the country, and the motion was carried with acclamation.[29] These aims threatened the entrenched position of large mining companies, who hastily proclaimed that although the community's grievances were serious, they were 'capable of remedy' under the existing system. Fearful of unrestricted competition from the Rand for labour supplies, the Rhodesia Chamber of Mines warned that 'annexation to either the Transvaal or the Cape would have a disastrous effect on the progress and prosperity of Rhodesia'. It concluded that the mining industry would be 'best maintained and fostered under the Charter until the white community has increased to such an extent as to enable it to demand self-government'.[30]

When the directors of the BSAC arrived on a tour of inspection in

26 *Rhodesian Times*, 15 March 1901; cited in van Onselen, *Chibaro*, p. 78.
27 A1/5/6, Wilson Fox to Milton, 12 March 1904.
28 Cited in E. Lee, 'Politics and Pressure Groups in S. Rhodesia, 1898–1923', Ph.D. thesis, University of London, 1974, p. 63.
29 *Ibid.*, pp. 65–6. By 'independent' is meant those not directly employed by large companies.
30 H. Mss. RH2/1/1, Rhodesia Chamber of Mines, minutes, 29 Aug. 1902; cited in Lee, 'Politics and Pressure Groups', p. 66.

September 1902, they found an 'embittered country'.[31] Even if large mining capital shied away from ending Chartered Company rule, it was still anxious for concessions. The economies which it had implemented, along with the post-war depression generally, had created a new constituency of unemployed prospectors and miners discharged by contractors. They, too, turned to the company for redress.[32] Commerce was also depressed, and even the minuscule white agricultural interest which had benefited from the wartime exclusion of southern foodstuffs now complained angrily about high railway rates. Major demands put to the directors thus focused on the mining law's restrictions, on the old and vexatious question of the percentage of shares reserved for the BSAC, on the high cost of living and on the small number of elected Legislative Council members.

Most of these demands in fact were conceded. The conjuncture of mining capital's labour crisis, its unwieldy structure and manifest unprofitability,[33] and the growth of wider settler opposition to company government left the directors with little choice. Legislation was revised to allow small mines to work for a profit without being floated as companies; the company's percentage of shares in large companies was formally reduced from 50 to 30, and railway rates were adjusted and reduced in some instances. The directors also agreed to raise the number of elected Legislative Council representatives to equal the number of nominated members. It was a move deliberately designed to defuse the more extravagant settler political movements and to associate influential white residents in the economic and legislative policies of reconstruction.

RECONSTRUCTION AND THE RISE OF DOMESTIC CAPITAL, 1903–1922

I see no objection [to making it a Native Reserve] as the area in question, which is practically a conglomeration of kopjes with very small cultivable valleys in between, is infested with baboons and is only traversable by pack animals.

– F. W. Inskipp to P. S. Inskipp, 23 February 1915

The concessions made by the BSAC at the end of 1902 were welcomed by the settlers and even by Rand mining houses. Sir Aubrey Woolls-Sampson confided in a Bulawayo interview that 'the views of the Rand people have changed about Rhodesia. . . . We are opening up offices here on a bigger scale . . . and other houses are sending men up. I think you will see things move.'[34] Confidence had begun to return, and it was thought that

---

31 L. H. Gann, *A History of Southern Rhodesia*, London, 1965, p. 208.
32 P. F. Hone, *Southern Rhodesia*, London 1909, pp. 264–6.
33 See S. H. Frankel, *Capital Investment in Africa*, London, 1938, p. 157; T2/29/59/1, Summary, Cash dividends paid by Rhodesian companies, 7 Jan. 1920.
34 *St James Gazette*, 4 March 1903.

the mining industry 'had begun to turn the corner'. [35] Instead, it turned out to be whistling in the dark. In January 1903 the Chartered Company's London manager warned that 'the only talk on the market at the present moment is the question of Native Labour. Everyone has got the blues.' By May, markets were 'as dull as ditchwater', and in June there was 'a very severe slump in the Markets, determined partly by the American position and partly by the labour position in South Africa. If only the second could be settled there would be a speedy revival.'[36] Rhodesian mining shares, already vulnerable because of their past record, lost their uncertain support and the territory plunged back into depression.

It became obvious that, without support from London, more far-reaching changes and concessions would be necessary to see the industry through the depression. Through its own initiatives and in response to pressure from the mines, the Chartered administration began pruning and shaping the industry's structure both to the contours of Southern Rhodesia's particular geological constraints and to the reality of competition from the Rand. In short, it began the reconstruction of the mining industry. At the same time, the sharemarket slump confirmed the urgent need for state intervention to secure conditions for the accumulation and reproduction of capital. The largely episodic looting of the 1890s was thus superseded by the initiation of a two-pronged assault on the black inhabitants of Central Africa, through intensified labour recruitment and through renewed attacks on their landholdings and participation in produce markets.

The earlier concession made to small mines was broadened in 1904 and again in 1914, and resulted in a rapid increase in their number. By 1905 there were already seventy-six small mines each producing under 1 000 ounces of gold annually; by 1907 their number had more than trebled. In many respects, the extremely low capitalisation of this mining petty bourgeoisie was ideally suited to working the smaller quartz reefs, as these 'great hustlers' could readily 'flit from one property to another'.[37] Their extremely low working costs were firmly grounded on minimal expenditure on African wages and working conditions. This, together with maximum use of legally entrenched rights to wood and water for mining purposes, enabled smallholders to win gold more cheaply than almost all larger mines.[38]

At first, the pattern was for smallworkers to follow large, financially exhausted companies from whom they leased property. But this stage soon gave way to one in which they owned the mines they worked. Where

35 Hone, *Southern Rhodesia*, p. 261.
36 See A1/5/4, Wilson Fox to Milton, 23 Jan. 1903; 1 May 1903; 12 June 1903.
37 *Financial Times*, 17 Feb. 1909.
38 For further discussion, see I. Phimister, 'The reconstruction of the Southern Rhodesian gold mining industry, 1903–10', *Economic History Review*, xxix, 1976, 469–74. See also the description in Hone, *Southern Rhodesia*, p. 272.

smallworkers could prove the size and profitability of their mines, these were sold to large companies. Capital was now following smallworkers. An essential function of smallworkers had become that of paving the way 'for capital to come in on a surer basis than it did in the earlier stages of the country's history'.[39] This was an important structural relationship between domestic and international mining capital, and did much to mitigate the speculative and uncertain character of quartz reef gold-mining.

Alongside the emergence of hundreds of small mines occurred a marked strengthening in the position of many large company mines. Management and machinery costs were reduced, capitals were reconstituted on more modest lines, and in 1907 the BSAC agreed to substitute a sliding scale of royalties on output for its 30 per-cent shareholding in individual companies. Much less success attended efforts to cut railway rates and the price of coal, but, in any case, the vital consideration for all mines was the supply and cost of black labour. On the Rand, labour accounted for 50 to 70 per cent of total working costs,[40] and the proportion was greater still in Southern Rhodesia where the small scale of most mining operations militated against widespread mechanisation.[41] Cost minimisation in this crucial sphere was multi-faceted. Not only had black labour to be cheap, but adequate and regular supplies had to be ensured and labour had to be utilised as profitably as possible.[42]

The urgency of the situation was not lost on mining capital and the state, and within months of the sharemarket fall the Rhodesia Native Labour Bureau was formed. Its recruiting net was quickly cast and, at various times, fell over much of Northern Rhodesia, as well as drawing on labour from parts of Nyasaland and Mozambique. By supplying the minimum labour needs of the mines – that is, an annual average of more than 11 000 workers between 1906 and 1911 – the bureau significantly contributed to the regular and increasingly profitable mining of gold ore. Lowly paid '*chibaro* boys' undercut other workers; and the bureau both excluded the Rand from certain recruiting areas and directed labour to local mines rather than towards Rand mines. Also, by providing labour for capitalist agriculture, it greatly tightened the squeeze on peasant producers and accelerated the process of proletarianisation.[43] As all of these measures began to improve the supply of labour, so at last the mines were able to reduce wages, most drastically in 1906 and 1907.[44]

39 *Report of the Secretary for Mines for the year ended 31 December 1909*, p. 1.
40 W. J. Busschau, *The Theory of Gold Supply with Special Reference to the Problems of the Witwatersrand*, London, 1936, p. 38.
41 *Rhodesia Herald*, 2 Dec. 1910.
42 F. A. Johnstone, *Class, Race and Gold*, London, 1976, p. 20.
43 See especially van Onselen, *Chibaro*, pp. 103ff.
44 *Rhodesia Chamber of Mines Annual Report for the year ended 31 March 1906*, p. 4; NB6/1/19, Compound Inspector, Division I, report for year ending 31 March 1907. For the use made by the mines of skilled black labour, see Phimister, 'History of Mining', pp. 111–12, 135–6.

Expenditure on African housing, diet and medical attention was, if anything, even more ruthlessly minimised. For many years black workers built their own accommodation on almost all mines. The only exceptions were the *chibaro* barracks erected on large mines, and the housing provided by some of the bigger companies after 1920. The 'frequently squalid' dwelling conditions endured by the majority of black workers were neither temporary nor accidental. On the contrary, they constituted an integral aspect of mining capital's cost-minimisation strategies to secure the profitability of otherwise doubtful enterprises. Food, too, was an obvious target for cost-conscious employers. The modest diet scale introduced by the state in 1908 and fractionally revised upwards in a series of stages to 1935, when it stabilised, never made much demand on the industry's generosity. At four pence per day it cost slightly less in 1944 to feed a single black worker than it did in 1908. Nor was the diet scale ever nutritious enough on its own to maintain workers' health. Instead, miners supplemented their rations where they could with purchases from the local store, from neighbouring villages, and by hunting and fishing expeditions. Poor diet and squalid accommodation in turn led directly to a high death- and sickness-rate, particularly during the reconstruction of the mining industry between 1903 and 1910, but also extending well beyond that date. At a conservative estimate, pneumonia and scurvy, and to a lesser extent tuberculosis, miners' phthisis, dysentery, influenza and syphilis, altogether claimed the lives of an estimated 33 000 black miners between 1900 and 1948.[45]

For mining capital, driving to profitability along a road littered with the broken and diseased bodies of black workers, the results of reconstruction were certainly gratifying. Over-all profitability was achieved, and the rising volume of dividends attracted substantial investment from Rand mining houses. After 1903 the number of mines increased dramatically, and the value of gold output almost trebled to over £2.5 million in 1910. By then the industry was producing virtually as much in a single year as it had done in the entire pre-reconstruction period. Both output and dividends continued to rise for the next six years, until overtaken by wartime inflation.

The economic predominance of gold-mining was not to be challenged for another thirty years or so, but in 1910, as reconstruction drew to a close, a new commodity entered the balance sheets when tobacco accounted for one per cent of Southern Rhodesia's exports. In its own way, the growth of capitalist agriculture at this time was as remarkable as developments on the

45 For fuller discussion and the evidence on which this paragraph is based, see van Onselen, *Chibaro*, ch. 2; and Phimister, 'African labour conditions and health in the Southern Rhodesian Mining Industry, 1898–1953', in I. Phimister and C. van Onselen, *Studies in the History of African Mine Labour in Colonial Zimbabwe*, Gwelo, 1978. See also *Report of the Secretary, Department of Mines and Public Works, on Mines*, 1937, 8.

mines. The Chartered Company had begun with the same policy in agriculture as in mining: 'the principle in both cases being to encourage flotations of companies, and the consequent introduction of large capital into Southern Rhodesia, which the British South Africa Company considered would more rapidly develop the resources of the territory than the smaller capitals of individual settlers'.[46] Huge areas were alienated to the ubiquitous 'development' companies, but, without 'effective occupation' clauses, land was simply held as a speculative asset. In 1899 there were fewer than 250 white 'farmers' actually on the land, most of whom devoted their energies to trading and transport-riding.

From that point, however, small settler capital began gradually expanding agricultural production. The reasons for this transformation lay in the combined impact of three events between 1897 and 1902: rinderpest and other cattle diseases, the arrival and extension of railway communication, and the South African War. The devastation wrought by successive cattle diseases and the strict quarantine measures imposed to contain them made transport-riding generally impossible. It had already been made less attractive by the advent of the railway, which for the first time put major domestic markets on the farmers' doorsteps. At that very moment the war excluded competition from South African agriculture and pushed up prices for grain and other foodstuffs. The number of occupied farms increased from about fifty to one hundred and fifty to well over three hundred in 1903, and went on rising as 'a steady influx of men with small capital and a large capacity for work ... [occupied] farms all over the country.'[47]

Many of the newcomers planted maize, with the result that production rose dramatically. In 1914, when more than 2 000 farms were occupied by whites, maize production totalled some 634 000 bags. Tobacco, too, experienced an impressive beginning, with production surging upwards. The result of this expansion of prices and markets was wholly predictable. Maize output, together with peasant production, soon filled the country's tiny internal market, with the result that its price fell by 30 to 50 per cent between 1903 and 1912.[48] When maize spilled over into export markets, it found prices even less to its liking. Tobacco's advance went a little further, but retreated more precipitously when prices collapsed following saturation of the available markets for Turkish and Virginian leaf in 1911 and 1914 respectively.[49]

Settler agriculture was to wrestle inconclusively with the problem of external markets for another generation. It had also to limit peasant competition and to procure labour on favourable terms. Nevertheless, its

46 Hone, *Southern Rhodesia*, p. 197.
47 *Rhodesia Herald*, 26 Oct. 1906.
48 G. Arrighi, 'Labour supplies in historical perspective: a study of the proletarianisation of the African peasantry in Rhodesia', *Journal of Development Studies*, vi, 1970, 215.
49 F. Clements and E. Harben, *Leaf of Gold*, London, 1962, pp. 63–77.

first priority was to win recognition for itself as a legitimate sphere of economic activity. The Rhodesia Agricultural Union objected to existing legislation, which expressly subordinated agricultural to mining interests. It pressed for reduced railway rates; argued that state assistance for agricultural research and to the industry generally was too small, grudging and sporadic; and fought for improved titles to land at lower prices. These grievances coincided with the campaign mounted by mining capital against the percentage of shares reserved for the BSAC. In 1907 the company once more bowed before settler pressure, for the very pragmatic reason that none of the big agricultural companies had made a profit in 1906.[50] Settlers therefore comprised the cutting edge of productive agricultural enterprise. The BSAC reorganised its governmental form and policies along lines more acceptable to the interests of white farmers and producing mines by conceding a majority to elected members in the Legislative Council and by separating administrative and commercial revenues. Mining companies were helped by the removal of the company's right to 30 per cent of their shares, and the company administration committed itself to improved land titles and their promotion through a newly established Estates Department.

The company recognised that its economic interests, as well as those of capital in general, lay in encouraging the expansion of settler agriculture. This made inevitable further attacks on African production structures to curb peasant competition and increase the flow of labour. After a half-hearted attempt to press the land companies into releasing some of their possessions, the state concentrated on African holdings. Provision for African reserves had first been made with the infamous Gwaai and Shangani reserves. After the Risings, at the insistence of the Imperial Government, a further 24·8 million acres were hastily put aside for black occupation. From 1908 onwards, the Chartered administration steadily chipped away 500 000 acres of the best of this land, and after the report of the Native Reserves Commission of 1914–1915, excised a further million acres from the reserves. As far as possible, the boundaries of the reserves were redrawn to exclude richer soils, higher rainfall and easy access to markets.[51]

What the state may have missed with one hand it tried to take with the other. The doubling of hut tax in 1904, which lifted the African contribution to state revenues to 41 per cent, was followed by a spate of fresh levies and taxes between 1908 and 1914. In 1909, Africans living on so-called unalienated land had to pay rent to the Chartered Company; even higher fees were exacted from the tenants of white farmers; dog tax was introduced in 1912; and in 1914 an ordinance made cattle dipping, at 1 to 2 shillings per head, compulsory 'in any area where this was the wish of the

50 Lee, 'Politics and Pressure Groups', p. 83.
51 For full discussion, see Palmer, *Land and Racial Domination*, chs. 3–5.

majority of [white] farmers'. By 1923 three-quarters of all African-owned cattle were being dipped.[52]

These actions to strengthen the position of capital were not, however, just handed down by the state, but were shaped and infused by a shifting balance of forces and interests, and by a process of struggle. Although some Chartered Company officials looked forward to the day when the reserves would disappear, the actual extent of the state offensive against their size and location was defined by two major considerations. One, of course, was the economic interest of the mines and farms. Where elements in the mining industry had once favoured a proletarianised and stabilised black work-force, the lesson of reconstruction had been firmly in favour of migrant labour. With its labour force rooted in the rural areas, mining capital paid only the costs of single workers and was not responsible for looking after their families. Later on, when conditions deteriorated in the reserves, the mines were able to effect labour stabilisation largely on their own terms. Because settler agriculture frequently competed with African producers for markets, it certainly wanted the reserves to be small and distant, but it did not want them eliminated. Its pronounced vulnerability to fluctuating prices and its seasonal demands for workers strongly favoured migrant labour. The second, and dominant, consideration was that armed resistance would be provoked by the complete confiscation of African-held land. It was certainly this need to guard against a repetition of the Risings which induced the imperial authorities to hover more or less watchfully in the background.

Nor did the state offensive succeed in transforming all Africans into labour migrants when they were not rural cultivators and into rural cultivators when they were not migrants. Although administrative measures oppressed all blacks, their impact was influenced by the process of differentiation already well under way in African rural areas. The uneven development of capitalism since 1890 had encouraged peasant production to the point where, in 1903, Africans received about £350 000 from the sale of grain, livestock and other produce. As the reconstruction of the mining industry proceeded, they were able to supply the hundreds of markets which sprouted across the countryside. It was a process which sometimes accentuated and sometimes initiated differentiation between strata and between areas. Although thousands bought ploughs, only a few could afford to invest in carts and wagons for the transport of produce; where proletarianisation was advanced, as in the Victoria region by 1914, it had scarcely started in Belingwe district twenty years later.[53] Almost certainly

52 Arrighi, 'Labour supplies', 210; Palmer, *Land and Racial Domination*, pp. 89–90, 98.
53 See Phimister, 'Peasant production and underdevelopment in Southern Rhodesia, 1890–1914, with particular reference to the Victoria district', in *The Roots of Rural Poverty in Central and Southern Africa*, R. Palmer and N. Parsons (eds), London, 1977, pp. 255–67; P. Zachrisson, *An African Area in Change. Belingwe 1894–1946*, Bulletin of Department of History No. 17, Gothenburg, 1978.

it was the poorer peasants who were least able to absorb the state's demands and who were further marginalised in this period.

Inside the mining industry itself, the state and mining capital cooperated closely through 'a web of coercive labour legislation, designed to regulate the mobility of black labour and stabilise employment under contract'. In the resulting compound system, remarkable for its pervasiveness and brutality, class struggle assumed distinctive features. Black workers characteristically confronted exploitation in the shadows, 'in the nooks and crannies of the day-to-day work situation'.[54] Their techniques of resistance were similar to those once developed by slaves in the southern states of North America: 'Side by side with ordinary loafing and mindless labour went deliberate wastefulness, slowdowns, feigned illness, self-inflicted injuries, and the well-known abuse of livestock and equipment.'[55] Every one of these devices found early expression on Southern Rhodesian mines. On the Red and White Rose Mine, for instance, where conditions were appalling, black miners in 1899 staged an effective 'go slow' which drove the management to frustration. Nor were these tactics ever relinquished as weapons in the years before 1948.[56]

The highly unequal terms of struggle were rendered more uneven still, as *chibaro* and 'voluntary' foreign workers undercut local miners and 'denationalised' the labour force, and as more and more Ndebele and Shona workers were squeezed on to the labour market. Whereas striking workers on the Camperdown Mine in 1901 could successfully block an attempt to reduce their wages, the expanding labour supply subsequently allowed capital to enforce wage cuts despite strikes on the Bonsor and Ayrshire mines in 1905 and 1909. Wages were again reduced during the First World War. Shortly thereafter conflict ensued when the soaring inflation rate coincided with a temporary labour shortage brought about by wartime demands for peasant produce and by the devastating impact of the Spanish 'flu pandemic. There were strikes and unrest at Wankie colliery between 1918 and 1921; a strike at the Globe and Phoenix in 1918; unrest at the Bushtick Mine in 1920; and a boycott of mine stores at Shamva also in 1920. However, as the slack in the labour market was rapidly taken up by foreign workers, the mines were able to hold wage increases far below the rise in the cost of living.[57]

54 The quotations are drawn from C. van Onselen, 'Worker consciousness in black miners: Southern Rhodesia, 1900–1920', *Journal of African History (JAH)*, xiv, 1973, 245, 249. For discussion of the compound system, see van Onselen, *Chibaro*, chs 5 and 6.
55 E. D. Genovese, *The Political Economy of Slavery*, New York, 1967, p. 74, cited in van Onselen, 'Worker consciousness', 249.
56 See Phimister, 'African worker consciousness: origins and aspects to 1953', in Phimister and van Onselen, *African Mine Labour in Colonial Zimbabwe*.
57 This paragraph is based on van Onselen, *Chibaro*, pp. 219–24; Phimister, 'History of Mining', pp. 123, 134, 318–19; and J. M. Mackenzie, 'Colonial labour policy and Rhodesia', *Rhodesian Journal of Economics*, viii, 1974, 13.

In the immediate post-war period, the large companies were also locked in conflict with white miners who had parlayed the wartime shortage of their skills into improved conditions and trade-union organisation. At the end of 1919, white workers successfully struck for a 25 per-cent wage increase and a 48-hour working week, but over-reached themselves the following November when they demanded a further 20 per-cent rise in wages. Mining capital proceeded to organise itself in the Rhodesia Mine Owners Association, and took advantage of division in union ranks and the ebbing of the skilled labour shortage not only to reject union demands but also to follow up a strike at Shamva with a general lock-out during February–March 1921. It ended with union capitulation and eventual collapse. Even as the companies celebrated their victory over white labour with wage reductions in 1922 and again in 1923,[58] the struggle for political control of Southern Rhodesia was under way.

In 1916, settler political quiescence had been disturbed by a substantial increase in railway rates, which had doubled the rate on grain cargoes. Tempers were then fully aroused by company proposals to amalgamate Northern and Southern Rhodesia, an arrangement which settlers feared would foreclose political options when the BSAC charter expired. In 1917 a Responsible Government Association (RGA), which demanded self-government, grew swiftly from the moment of its foundation. It enjoyed close links with organised agriculture. Much more damaging, indeed terminal, to the Chartered administration was the 1918 Privy Council decision in favour of Crown ownership of the land. At a stroke, the company lost its most valuable commercial asset. As a result it decided to stop subsidising administrative deficits,[59] which henceforth would have to be covered locally.

This decision had 'a tremendous impact'[60] on settler politics and politicians, who argued that if 'the country is to be administered on its own resources and credit . . . it might as well have the management of its own affairs'.[61] In the 1920 elections, the RGA, representing a loose and heterogeneous coalition of 'farmers, trade unionists, small traders, women, Dutch nationalists and perhaps junior civil servants' swept to victory over the representatives of large capital who, with the BSAC, looked to union with South Africa to safeguard their interests.[62] The newly elected Legislative Council members promptly petitioned the Imperial authorities to grant Responsible Government, but were obliged to jump through another hoop before their request was met. In the referendum of

58 See I. Phimister, 'White miners in historical perspective: Southern Rhodesia, 1890–1953', *JSAS*, iii, 1977, 187–206.
59 Lee, 'Politics and Pressure Groups', pp. 150–63, 189.
60 *Ibid.*, p. 196,
61 *Rhodesia Herald*, 18 Oct. 1918; cited in Lee, 'Politics and Pressure Groups', p. 196.
62 Lee, 'Politics and Pressure Groups', p. 210.

November 1922 the RGA again emerged victorious after a bitter contest in which the 'reptile press, the influence of the Chartered Company, the machinations of the non-Rhodesian capitalists and politicians, with their local satellites, have all been against us. We have had no friends, but the "man in the street".'[63]

THE COMPROMISE OF THE SETTLER STATE, 1923–1930

> I cannot quite get over the fact of the huge profits the Trusts make out of the tobacco which we are trying to grow out here by the sweat of our brows, or perhaps I should say the natives'. . . . The fact of Directors of the Trusts dying multi-millionaires . . . makes one wonder if they ever think of where all their money came from and how it is that a few crumbs from their groaning tables are not let fall to enable the growers in Rhodesia, or in other parts of the world for that matter, to make a bare living.
>
> — Fletcher to Newton, 9 March 1929

Although international capital initially viewed the referendum result and Southern Rhodesia's assumption of Responsible Government with considerable apprehension, its fears soon evaporated. It became clear that the alignment of domestic interests in the 1920 elections against large capital had been a vote against the Chartered administration and not one unreservedly in favour of Responsible Government. Agriculture, for example, although strongly against the BSAC in 1920, had split by 1922. The majority, comprising ranchers and tobacco planters for whom the South African market was essential, voted for union; others, primarily maize farmers, wanted Responsible Government. And not only was the domestic bourgeoisie itself fragmented, but also its electoral ties with organised white labour were tenuous and easily disturbed, making it extremely vulnerable to the deliberate process of penetration instituted by large capital from 1923 onwards.[64]

The constitution, moreover, was hedged about with safeguards. These were designed to 'protect rights of capital, prevent discriminatory legislation against Africans without Imperial sanction, and stop Southern Rhodesia from passing laws incompatible with the more general interests of the Imperial connexion'.[65] In short, the settler state was a carefully crafted compromise between the interests of local and metropolitan capital. As the dependent partner, the settler state was obliged to accept constitutional provisions which limited initiatives that might disturb the orderly accumulation of capital. Together, these factors produced a

63 H. Mss. CO8/1/3, Coghlan to Mrs B. Buller, 21 June 1921.
64 Lee, 'Politics and Pressure Groups', pp. 216–49; D. J. Murray, *The Governmental System in Southern Rhodesia*, Oxford, 1970, p. 207.
65 L. H. Gann and M. Gelfand, *Huggins of Rhodesia*, London, 1964, p. 62.

thoroughly conservative successor to the Chartered state, so much so that 'the average [Legislative Council] session of the 'twenties resembl[ed] more a well-conducted shareholders' meeting than a national convention'.[66]

Most of the shares were held outside the colony. The social formation inherited by the settler bourgeoisie in 1923 was remarkable for the degree of dominance exerted by a few big companies. Southern Rhodesia's railway system was owned by the BSAC; its only colliery was a BSAC subsidiary; its chrome industry was effectively in the grip of one company, as were its asbestos mines; gold-mining became increasingly dominated by a handful of large, company-owned mines. Although investment by large capital was much less prominent in agriculture – exceptions being the citrus industry and to some extent beef cattle – its predominant position in world markets gave it the whip-hand over small capital.

On various occasions when the settler state was prevailed upon to stand with domestic interests against large capital, it invariably emerged from such confrontations rumpled, perhaps clutching a tatty agreement which on close inspection revealed yet another compromise in favour of big capital. For example, protests by farmers and miners over high railway rates encouraged the government to institute a commission of enquiry in 1924. But the ensuing Railway Act of 1926 left BSAC ownership and profits essentially intact. There was a further clash in 1928 when the railways refused to construct a branch line in the Umvukwes region which would have benefited small, independent producers to the detriment of the Chrome Trust, with whom the railways were linked through the BSAC. For once, the state was able to play off the Chrome Trust against another large chrome company which was prepared to put up money for the branch line, and Rhodesia Railways were forced to give way. The victory was nullified soon afterwards, however, when the Chrome Trust swallowed up its rival, and with monopolistic conditions restored, rates on the branch line were manipulated to the disadvantage of the remaining small mines.

Apart from this brief interlude, international capital was left in unchallenged possession of base mineral mining. Southern Rhodesia's chrome and asbestos output was dominated by multinationals whose control on a world scale of production and marketing allowed them to influence prices and make production decisions without reference to their host countries. For much of the 1920s, for instance, it suited the Chrome Trust to expand its Rhodesian activities to the point where the colony accounted for over half of the world's production in 1929. Three years larer, production slumped to 8 per cent of the world total because of the depression and because the Trust's production strategies changed in order to eliminate a regional competitor. For some time past, a rival grouping had been expanding production in southern Africa, and the Trust utilised

66 *Ibid.*, p. 68.

the contraction in the world market caused by the depression, along with its access to chrome production and supplies outside Africa, to 'shut out' its rival's chrome. By early 1932 enough pressure had been exerted, and the Trust bought up the opposition. During this entire exercise, the settler state sat powerless to intervene, beyond denunciations in the Legislative Assembly of those 'who control in Rhodesia every other form of life, who control the chrome, the copper and the asbestos, and will subject those people engaged in those industries to desolation because it suits their market manipulations'.[67]

Experiences in agriculture were equally unhappy. In broadest outline, white agriculture comprised a mass of small, undercapitalised farmers around a core of big concerns, either individually or company owned. Throughout the 1920s and early 1930s this mass of small farmers tended to 'rush' from crop to different crop in search of elusive riches. This phenomenon imparted an extraordinary volatile element to the volume of production and aggravated the highly uneven productivity of the sector as a whole. Indeed, white farmers seemed destined to share the fate of the biblical swine of Gadarene, until the state was persuaded eventually to provide safety nets for those who successively hurled themselves over the 'cliffs' of cattle, cotton, tobacco and maize.

In the early 1920s the need to find cattle export markets had become urgent. A large and fairly indiscriminate wartime demand which had helped cattle owners build up an export trade gave way in 1921–1922 to depression and falling prices, which hit Southern Rhodesian ranches particularly heavily because most of their animals were low grade. The colony's small domestic market was quite unable to absorb significant numbers of cattle, and as the surplus grew, so prices were further depressed. Ranchers initially tried to market surplus cattle by mobilising local capital in cooperative ventures. A canning factory was set up in 1919 near Umtali, but went out of business within three years because of the familiar problem of undercapitalisation and because of inability to compete on external markets dominated by international capital. A second attempt, made in 1921 when a cooperative Meat Producers' Exchange aimed to secure 'fair' prices by limiting supplies and bypassing the middlemen who infested the important Johannesburg market, was aborted through the shadowy actions of the Imperial Cold Storage Company (ICSC).[68]

As a result, ranchers turned to the state for help, and ironically the state extended an invitation to the ICSC to come in by the front door. Sensitive to charges that its policy was 'equivalent to handing over Rhodesia, bound hand and foot, to the mercies of interests that ... in other countries are

67 See I. Phimister, 'The structure and development of the Southern Rhodesian base mineral industry, 1907–Great Depression', *Rhodesian Journal of Economics*, ix, 1975, 82–4; *Southern Rhodesia Legislative Assembly Debates*, 17 April 1931, col. 737.
68 I. Phimister, 'Meat and monopolies: beef cattle in Southern Rhodesia, 1890–1938', *JAH*, xix, 1978, 401–4.

269

regarded as the enemies of cattle producers'[69] the settler government tried hard to interest other large companies in a proposal to establish a meat-freezing industry in the colony, but with no success. Southern Rhodesia's remoteness from the major world meat markets and its limited number of generally poor-quality cattle held little attraction for established American and British multinationals. Instead, the colony had to settle for the ICSC which, although of overwhelming regional importance, was insignificant outside southern Africa. Even then, it was only coaxed into Southern Rhodesia by an agreement, confirmed in 1924. Among other benefits, it received a ten-year monopoly over the export of frozen and chilled meat, and a guarantee that if in any year its profits fell below 10 per cent of its capital, the state would make up the difference to a maximum of £15 000. After a short honeymoon, the agreement began to break down over a provision calling for the development of exports to higher-priced but more discerning overseas markets. The settlers could not maintain regular supplies of quality cattle, and as the ICSC could not compete with international muscle, losses began to mount. In 1929, despite a state-funded export bounty in support of bids for overseas contracts, the company still lost money. The cattle industry was as far from lucrative export markets as it had been at the start of the decade.

By this time, the plight of tobacco-planters was desperate. Their traumatic experience really began in 1924, when Rhodesian tobacco was favourably received at the Wembley Empire Exhibition in London. Prices and prospects went higher still when, in July 1925, Britain increased imperial preference on tobacco by 50 per cent, causing Southern Rhodesian growers to turn their backs on the South African market and concentrate on meeting what they thought was Britain's huge demand. With prices in 1925 and 1926 far in excess of low production costs, white farmers abandoned cotton- and maize-growing for the 'leaf of gold':[70] 'all eyes turned on tobacco. Every farmer one meets talks about it and very handsome profits have been made or are anticipated being made as a result of this year's crop.'[71] The industry's expansion was startling. Acreage planted with Virginian leaf rose from 7 000 in 1924 to an estimated 60 000 in 1928, and involved 987 planters.[72]

The bubble was not long in bursting. 'In retrospect,' admitted the industry's chroniclers, 'there is something almost pathetic about a group of ingenuous and isolated farmers sitting in their rustic high-ceilinged boardroom in the village which was Salisbury, blundering confidently into

69 *Bulawayo Chronicle*, 15 Sept. 1923.
70 Clements and Harben, *Leaf of Gold*, pp. 90–1, 96–7.
71 H. Mss. NE1/1/6, Leggate to Newton, 18 June 1926.
72 S1180/4(14), Imperial Economic Committee, Tobacco Enquiry, 9 May 1928, Summary of a Discussion on the Marketing of Southern Rhodesian Tobacco; Clements and Harben, *Leaf of Gold*, pp. 98–9.

the vortex of international financial and political interest. Visitors told them their tobacco was good; they were learning the art of growing it; there seemed no logical reason why they should not be able to sell it.'[73] The gigantic crops of 1927 and 1928, most of which was very poor quality, proved virtually unsaleable on the British tobacco market, where the dominant companies, interlinked with American interests, found it neither feasible nor desirable to use Empire leaf on so large a scale. As the industry teetered on the brink of total collapse, the Southern Rhodesian state was forced to come to the rescue of the planters' export company, the Tobacco Warehouse, with over £500 000, in order to pay off merchant-bank loans and to put at least some cash in growers' pockets. Many planters nonetheless faced ruin, and by 1930 700 of them had abandoned the industry. Production fell as once more domestic interests lay prostrate before international capital.

The helping hand extended to the tobacco-growers was economically and politically unavoidable, but it was also exceptional. Other supplicants were grudgingly assisted or ignored, as when the state refused to act on the annual resolutions of the Rhodesia Agricultural Union calling for controlled production and compulsory marketing of maize. Although responsible to a settler electorate, the Southern Rhodesian government had to consider the economic, political and ideological interests of other classes and groups, and did not simply preside over an unrestricted process of domestic accumulation. On the contrary, the state sought to contain the antagonistic relations engendered by the unceasing struggle to secure the conditions necessary for the operation of capitalism.[74] Through segregationist policies the colonial state tried to bridge the gap between the economic interests of mining and agricultural capitals and the social and political conditions necessary for the undisturbed working of the system and the making of profit. It thus continued to discriminate against African rural areas, most notoriously with the Land Apportionment Act of 1930, which froze the reserves in a structurally subordinate position, while simultaneously setting in motion policies intended to blunt the most immediate contradictions which had become apparent in the meantime.

The general deterioration of the reserves in the early 1920s, accelerated by the post-war slump in grain and livestock prices and by severe drought in 1922, sufficiently alarmed the state for 'developmental' policies to be introduced. From 1924, black agricultural demonstrators were trained at Domboshawa and Tjolotjo schools. In the same year a Native Trust Fund, supported mainly from dipping fees, was established for the improvement of cattle and agriculture generally, and in 1926 the post of 'Agriculturalist

73 Clements and Harben, *Leaf of Gold*, p. 102.
74 See B. Jessop, 'Recent theories of the capitalist state', *Cambridge Journal of Economics*, i, 1977.

for the Instruction of Natives' was created.[75] As these initiatives coincided with rising commodity prices after 1924, the next five years saw a modest recovery in the reserves. More than 700 000 bags of maize were harvested in 1929, and the fact that almost 200 000 bags were marketed 'threatened to become a serious problem' for settler farmers.[76]

The fruits of recovery, though, were unevenly distributed. In the late 1920s overcrowding, overstocking and soil erosion became evident in the reserves, and increasing numbers of local people, particularly Shona, became labourers, many taking jobs in poorly paid white agriculture. At the other end of the scale, cattle ownership was becoming concentrated in fewer hands, and those who could turn the vagaries of reserve geography to good account became market gardeners supplying the towns.[77] It was here that the impact of the state's agricultural advice was clustered. Instead of 'raising the level of agriculture throughout the Reserve', agricultural demonstrators tended to form class alliances with the rural élite, thereby imbuing 'a few natives with the idea of money-making', and effectively becoming 'the farm managers of a few enterprising and money-seeking plot owners'.[78]

The state also moved to contain the revolution being wrought by capitalism on the fabric of African society. Emerging class antagonisms and aspirations were delayed and blurred by the gradual implementation of policies designed to prop up the disintegrating social cohesion of the reserves: 'encouraging Africans to move into the reserves thus became for many native Commissioners a means by which to slow down the break-up of the tribal system and to hinder the growth of potentially hostile political movements'.[79] By defining and supporting 'traditional' rulers, as, for example in the Native Affairs Ordinance of 1927, and by modifying and codifying African customary law, the settler state tried to channel African hopes and grievances into 'tribal' outlets very largely controlled by the state itself.

Political legitimacy so narrowly defined could not accommodate the independent initiative of the Ndebele National Home Movement (later the Matabele Home Society) for a restored kingship in a consolidated 'national home'. Nor could it meet the modest grievances of the tiny black petty-bourgeoisie voiced through the Rhodesian Bantu Voters' Association and the Rhodesian Native Association.[80] It was unrelentingly hostile to other,

---

75 Zachrisson, *Belingwe*, p. 190; Palmer, *Land and Racial Domination*, p. 202.
76 *Report of the Chief Native Commissioner for 1929*, p. 4.
77 M. C. Steele, 'The Economic Function of African-owned Cattle in Southern Rhodesia, 1914–1943', unpub. 1977, p. 7; *Report of the Chief Native Commissioner for 1929*, p. 4.
78 *Report of the Chief Native Commissioner for 1932*; cited in Zachrisson, *Belingwe*, 210.
79 Palmer, *Land and Racial Domination*, p. 145.
80 For full discussion, see T. O. Ranger, *The African Voice in Southern Rhodesia*, London, 1970, chs 4–5; Palmer, *Land and Racial Domination*, pp. 151–3, 226–7.

more dramatic challenges which the state and capital faced from millenarianism and trade unionism in the late 1920s. In rural Mashonaland, specifically in areas shaken by the boom and collapse of the tobacco industry, the Watch Tower movement gained an enthusiastic following through its efforts to 'restructure demoralised rural society' and through its predictions of the imminent overthrow of white oppression. However, it was speedily intimidated by police and military patrols, and its foreign preachers from north of the Zambezi were deported.[81] The Industrial and Commercial Workers' Union (ICU), established in Southern Rhodesia in late 1927, proved rather more resilient and survived the early deportation of its leader, Robert Sambo. It rooted itself successfully in the Bulawayo location, where it began articulating the diverse grievances of the urban working class, the rural areas, and its petty-bourgeois leadership.

In fact, the most serious challenge to capital accumulation in this period was not spearheaded by Watch Tower or the ICU, but grew directly out of changed conditions in the gold-mining industry. In 1925 the post-war premium on the price of gold was removed, and from that point Southern Rhodesia's gold output fell steadily. The most important reason for this was that as mines were worked deeper in the 1920s, the cost per ounce tended to rise, either through a falling-off in the value of the deposit with depth, or because it became more expensive to mine the deeper levels. When the mines applied their time-honoured solution to rising costs by maximising output and cutting expenditure on labour, they stirred up widespread strike action by black workers. For once, black miners enjoyed a relatively strong bargaining position, because African cash-cropping in Nyasaland and the expansion of other sections in the Southern Rhodesian economy had made the supply of labour tight. Between December 1925 and October 1928, there were at least ten strikes on various mines, including one on the large Shamva Mine which did much to rattle settler complacency, as workers resisted cuts and fought for increases. Beyond victimising identifiable leaders and trying to ensure that wages generally did not rise, there was little that mining capital and the state could do. Without wage reductions, production declined accordingly, until by 1929 the amount of gold produced was smaller than in 1907.[82]

OPPRESSION AND EXPLOITATION INTENSIFIED, 1931–1939

It is difficult to conceive of a principle more inequitable or dangerous than that of deliberately paying to the better-off producers of a State more for a product than is paid to less well-off people in the same State for the identical product. It is the antithesis of assistance according to

81 Ranger, *African Voice*, pp. 203–15.
82 Phimister, 'History of Mining', pp. 125–9, 137–9.

need and of the universally acclaimed principle of raising rather than
depressing the lower classes.
– Report of the Native Production and Trade Commission, 1944

Southern Rhodesia's economy was already low in the water when the
Great Depression broke across the world economy at the start of the 1930s.
The national income, never very large, fell from £13.9 million in 1929 to
£8.7 million in 1931 as commodity prices plummeted and markets
shrivelled.[83] Thousands of black miners lost their jobs when chrome and
asbestos mines cut back on production, while in capitalist agriculture:

> a chain of circumstances . . . [had] placed the industry in a very precarious
> position, and unless a certain measure of relief is applied immediately a
> collapse on a large scale must be faced. . . . The cotton failure, followed
> by the tobacco débâcle, has forced a large number of farmers to produce
> maize, and is the principal reason why there has been an increase in the
> acreage under that crop.[84]

At the time this warning was sounded, maize had fallen from 10 shillings to
8 shillings a bag on external markets, and over the next twelve months the
price virtually halved again.[85] In the same period, cattle exports met 'a
disastrously low market', and the gloom was completed when an outbreak
of foot-and-mouth disease brought all meat exports to a halt. During
1931–1932 the fortunes of the cattle industry were at their lowest ebb. All
live exports were banned, and South Africa even refused to allow the
transit through its territory of chilled or frozen beef, which led to a
growing surplus and further depressed prices.[86] Farms went out of
production, and farmers constituted the largest single group of white
unemployed.

This desperate situation evoked a prevaricating response from the
government, then under the tepid leadership of H. U. Moffat. Only after
the government began shedding seats in by-elections did a somewhat half-
hearted Maize Control Act and a Cattle Levy Act find their way on to the
statute books. Developments in South Africa drew the Southern
Rhodesian state a little further down the path of intervention and control,
when it was obliged to follow the South African example and pass a Dairy
Industry Control Act. The administration also responded to South Africa's
imposition of a quota on duty-free Rhodesian tobacco by establishing a
Tobacco Control Board to distribute the quota amongst planters.[87] None

83 *Report of the Committee of Enquiry into the Protection of Secondary Industries in Southern Rhodesia*, 1946, p. 9.
84 S1193/C6c, General Manager, Farmers Co-op. Ltd to Minister of Agriculture, 24 Feb. 1930.
85 Murray, *Governmental System*, p. 73.
86 Phimister, 'Meat and monopolies', 410–11. The direct quotation comes from H. Mss. DO1/1/1, Downie to Fletcher, 1 April 1931.
87 Murray, *Governmental System*, pp. 77, 81–2.

of these measures did much to lift the Depression or to reverse the government's waning political fortunes. Its purchase of mineral rights from the BSAC for £2 million in 1933 positively inflamed a growing opposition which, loudly proclaiming its hostility to monopoly interests, went on to win the election of September 1933. To the outgoing administration it seemed as if victory had gone to 'the underdogs, the down and outs and all those with little stake in the country'.[88]

Although the victorious Reform Party programme called for a state Reserve Bank, the development of secondary industries and opposition towards foreign monopolies, the party umbrella sheltered interests of very different persuasions. Some, such as commerce wedded to free enterprise, had no interest in the party programme, with the result that the Reform Party quickly began to break up. By October 1934, majority elements in the Reform and recently defeated Rhodesian parties had come together in a United Party under the avowedly pragmatic leadership of Godfrey Huggins, and in November elections routed the radical rump of the Reform Party. The Reform Party claimed, with pardonable exaggeration, that the 'Rhodesian "Establishment", consisting of the senior ranks of the civil service, the chambers of commerce and of mines, the agricultural and show societies, the Salisbury Club, backed by Argus Press and the Anglican hierarchy, was back in power'.[89] However, this did not mean unconditional capitulation to metropolitan imperialism. Huggins was not prepared to confront imperialism, but he was willing to take certain measures in support of settler interests.

The first of these were in agriculture where an Amended Maize Control Act, favouring small white farmers against both large-scale growers and peasant producers, was passed in 1934. Control over tobacco production was extended through the Reserve Pool Act of 1934 and particularly by the Market Stabilisation Act of 1936 which established a Marketing Board to organise the compulsory sale of all tobacco through licensed auction floors and buyers, and to advise the government on quotas for the protected markets.[90] The beef cattle, dairy, pig and cotton industries were also drawn within the ambit of the state, until by 1937 'of the principal agricultural products from European farms only poultry and eggs remained outside the system of control'.[91]

This network of control boards and subsidies enjoyed mixed results. Settler maize production was stabilised and undoubtedly saved from catastrophe. Tobacco output, stimulated by Britain's policy of giving preferential prices to empire products, expanded steadily from a weight of

88 H. Mss. DO1/1/4 Leggate to Downie, 13 Sept. 1933; cited in Gann, *History of Southern Rhodesia*, p. 296.
89 Gann, *History of Southern Rhodesia*, p. 311.
90 Murray, *Governmental System*, p. 85.
91 *Ibid.*, p. 86.

5·5 million pounds in 1930 to hover around the 20-million-pound mark for most of the decade. The cattle industry though, despite regular infusions of subsidy support, continued to decline. Exports remained consistently uncompetitive on the world market and usually failed to recover their costs of production. Many ranchers drew the appropriate conclusion and abandoned the struggle entirely. Between 1925 and 1938 'anything from one million to two million pounds sterling' was 'lost or withdrawn' from the industry, and the number of white-owned cattle fell from about 992 000 in 1932 to about 735 000 in 1937. As it was mainly the larger producers who left the industry and further blunted its competitive marketing edge, the remaining small ranchers were heavily dependent on continued subsidies. This development, as well as concern over the financial losses of the past, and mounting dissatisfaction with the practices of the Imperial Cold Storage Company, induced the state to cut its losses and expropriate the freezing works. In 1938, after bitter arbitration proceedings, the refrigeration plant and works were taken over by the newly established Cold Storage Commission. Monopoly control of the meat industry now rested with the state.[92]

In the gold-mining industry, settler interests initially seemed to be carrying the day. The uneven impact on the colony of the Depression meant that even as the profitability of most primary products contracted, so those of gold-mining boomed. Millions of tons of previously unpayable ore were made profitable by two developments. Firstly, workers formerly employed in agriculture and on base mineral mines, together with people forced from the reserves, had to take the only work going, which was on the gold-mines. Secondly, the price of gold rose when Britain abandoned the gold standard in September 1931. With abundant labour and a higher gold price, the obstacles which had blocked cost minimisation and output maximisation in the previous decade disappeared. Gold output jumped from 532 111 ounces in 1931 to 814 078 ounces in 1938, while the number of mines quadrupled within three years to over 1 600 in 1934. Virtually all the new producers were smallworkers, 90 per cent of whom mined less than 500 ounces annually. Nonetheless, the contribution of small mines to the total gold output went up to about 30 per cent in 1936, not much below that of the large mines whose relative importance had declined significantly since the late 1920s.

The shift in favour of smallworkers was both cause and consequence of changed state policy towards the mining industry after 1933. Smallworkers, irritated by the Moffat administration's negative attitude, had swung behind the Reform and later the United Party in 1933–1934. Thereafter,

92 For maize, tobacco and cattle statistics, see H. Weinmann, *Agricultural Research and Development in Southern Rhodesia, 1924–1950*, Salisbury, 1975. For the cattle industry, see Phimister, 'Meat and monopolies', 411–12. The direct quotation comes from *Report of the Committee of Enquiry into the Economic Development of the Colony*, 1939, p. 21.

the inflated numbers and economic importance of smallworkers ensured that political power was deployed to consolidate their particular interests within the mining industry. A wide range of state services was instituted, most notably the construction of a state-financed Roasting Plant at Que Que for the treatment of refractory sulphide ores, and the provision of regular cheap power through the Electricity Supply Commission. A Government Loan Fund gave still more help to smallworkers, most of whom were anyway exempted from special taxation imposed on the gold-mining industry as a whole. In short, the policy 'amounted to a concerted effort to rebuild the gold mining industry on the basis of a partnership between government and small workers'.[93]

It was also a policy which ran out of momentum by 1937. By this time it was apparent that there were limits to how far the state would go in pursuit of settler interests. International capital was sometimes verbally assailed and pressed on to a defensive posture, but nothing else was done. Although at the time of his brief flirtation with the Reform Party Huggins had asserted that 'whilst the Rhodesian Party looks at the people through the eyes of the big financial organisations, the Reform Party looks at the big financial organisations through the eyes of the people',[94] in later years he steadfastly averted his gaze from the most prominent monopolies entrenched inside the colony. Chrome- and asbestos-mining remained in the firm grasp of monopoly capital, as did coal and the railways. No positive action was taken to foster secondary industrialisation; nor did Southern Rhodesia push very hard to improve its constitutional position in the imperialist chain.[95] Settler interests, located in mining and agriculture, sought to improve their bargaining position, not to transform the nature of the transaction by questioning dependency as such. Consequently, 'in the late 1930s, after nearly two decades of self government, the country had a typically colonial economy with no industrial sector apart from the railway workshop and small firms engaged in wholly subsidiary activities'.[96]

All the measures affecting the relationship between local and international capital would have come to little more than shuffling the seating arrangements on a sinking ship if capital as a whole had not been able to re-establish its overall buoyancy. As settler ideology became even more sharply segregationist, further burdens were added to the black peasantry and working class. Under various control and levy acts, African cattle-owners and maize-growers were manipulated and taxed in order to subsidise the earnings of white ranchers and farmers. The Cattle Levy Acts of 1931 and 1934 imposed a levy on the slaughter of all cattle for domestic consumption in order to pay a bounty subsidising exports almost

93 Murray, *Governmental System*, p. 136.
94 *New Rhodesia*, 27 Aug. 1932.
95 On this latter issue, see Gann and Gelfand, *Huggins*, p. 101.
96 G. Arrighi, *The Political Economy of Rhodesia*, The Hague, 1967, p. 36.

exclusively owned by whites.[97] Because the levy proved difficult to collect, an additional tax on all cattle was introduced in 1934. This fell most heavily on African cattle-owners because, while some white ranchers found ways of evading it, 'those living in reserves will hardly know that there has been such a tax, by reason of the fact that they have built up a reserve dipping fund from which the tax will be paid'. Although one or two eyebrows 'came to be raised at the ethics of collecting the African contribution from what ... [were] "trust funds"', Huggins protested that Africans 'would prefer an indirect to a direct form of stock tax "unless ill-intentioned people or agitators stir them up"'. The tax, however, proved unpopular with white ranchers and was dropped after one year in favour of a slaughter levy. Although this change decreased the cash burden on the African peasantry, it simply increased the cattle burden. Both prices and the size of the market fell as butchers 'passed on their levy deductions to the African by offering lower prices', and tried to minimise the impact of the levy by only buying heavier and higher-quality stock.[98]

Similarly, the general impact of the Maize Control Acts of 1931 and 1934 depressed prices paid to Africans in order to subsidise the return received by white farmers. Whereas the average price per bag paid to African producers between 1934 and 1939 fluctuated from 1s 6d to 6s 6d, white growers over the same period received an average price of over 8s per bag.[99] One immediate effect of control was to weaken 'the African's ability to meet rent, tax, dipping fees and other monetary obligations and charges'.[100] From Matabeleland it was reported that people in the Insiza district 'have been accustomed for years to obtain revenue for taxes by sale of mealies, and this undoubtedly [is] going to hit them hard' – an opinion which was echoed at the other end of the country by the Native Commissioner for Umtali, who blamed the 'delayed collection of tax' on 'the extension of the Maize Control Act to this district'.[101]

No less immediate, however, was the stimulus which the successive Acts imparted to peasant production and 'competition'. Output rose unsteadily from approximately 750 000 bags in 1930 to touch the million-bag mark by 1936. The percentage of African sales both to total African production and

97 Africans theoretically gained from bounties, too, but in practice were excluded since throughout the 1930s there was no system for weighing and grading their stock. See C. Keyter, 'Beef control in Southern Rhodesia, 1931–1938, and its significance to African rural underdevelopment', unpub. 1978, p. 13.
98 This account of the Cattle Levy Acts, including the direct quotations, is based on Keyter, 'Beef control in Southern Rhodesia'.
99 Keyter, *Maize Control in Southern Rhodesia 1931–1941: the African Contribution to White Survival*, Salisbury, 1978, p. 28.
100 Keyter, *Maize Control*, p. 20.
101 S1542/M2, Native Commissioner, Ft. Rixon, to Superintendent of Natives, Bulawayo, 29 July 1934; *ibid.*, Report by the Native Commissioner, Umtali, in Chief Native Commissioner to Minister of Native Affairs, 7 Feb. 1935; both cited in Keyter, *Maize Control*, p. 20.

to total sales increased significantly: in the first instance from 23·5 per cent in 1930 to 43 per cent in 1936; and in the second, from 14·8 per cent in 1930 to 23·9 per cent in 1936.[102] These trends partly reflected the spread of the money economy in the rural areas, but they also expressed the general compulsion exerted by falling prices to produce more to maintain existing incomes. Here, too, not everyone could respond equally because transport costs were deducted from the fixed prices obtainable at Control Board depots, and so control gave an added twist to existing patterns of rural differentiation. In 1936 the Chief Native Commissioner thought that 'the present system of Maize Control was a contributory factor to the tendency to abandon settlement in the remoter Districts and crowd in to the towns and mine markets'. It was, he observed, 'especially noticeable with advanced Natives'.[103] By 1937 the Native Commissioner for Mazoe was reporting an 'almost 100 per cent increase in the area under maize', and in 1938 the Chief Native Commissioner confirmed that the 'production of maize in central districts appears to be increasing'.[104] The contrast with outlying regions was striking. Districts such as Belingwe, Sinoia and Nuanetsi saw important markets disappear, and their inhabitants forced into the labour market if they could not diversify their crops.[105]

For much of the 1930s this was a market where the balance of class forces moved firmly to the side of capital. White workers, already vulnerable to the overtures of capital, were ensnared and disarmed through the Industrial Conciliation Act of 1934. For the black population in general and labour in particular, the climate of repression worsened even further. Through the Sedition Act of 1936, the state tried to halt the 'spread of subversive and seditious propaganda and literature in the Colony',[106] and in their place offered more wholesome fare concocted by the Native Department in association with the *Bantu Mirror* and other publications.[107] The Industrial and Commercial Workers' Union was infiltrated by spies, its meetings monitored and its organisers harassed. It was quickly defeated and expelled from the tightly controlled mine compounds, and when it attempted to develop a rural constituency, its leaders were barred from the reserves.[108] In the same year that the ICU expired, the Native Registration Act of 1936 compelled every male African in the towns to have 'in addition to his *situpa* [registration certificate], the following: a pass to seek work in the town; a

---

102 Keyter, *Maize Control*, p. 25.
103 S1215/1090/246, 'Maize Growers Conference', Salisbury, 8 Sept. 1936. See also S987/2, 'Memorandum on Maize Control' by E. R. Jacklin, Chairman, Maize Control Board, Oct. 1942.
104 *Reports of the Chief Native Commissioner*, 1937, 1938; cited in Keyter, *Maize Control*, p. 22.
105 Zachrisson, *Belingwe*, 198; Keyter, *Maize Control*, p. 23.
106 *Southern Rhodesia Legislative Assembly Debates*, 23 April 1936, col. 1022.
107 See the extensive correspondence contained in S1542/L11.
108 Van Onselen, *Chibaro*, pp. 214–18; Palmer, *Land and Racial Domination*, pp. 227–8.

certificate to show that he was employed within the town; a certificate signed by a Native Commissioner to the effect that he was earning a living in the town by lawful means; if employed outside the town, a written permit from his employer; a visiting pass'.[109] By these means, the 'distribution of the total African labour supply between the different capitalist sectors . . . was not mainly left to the law of supply and demand . . . [as the Act] tightened up the Pass Law and effectively contributed to the maintenance of a wage structure whereby the white farmers constantly paid unskilled labour lower wage rates than other employers'.[110]

In all of this, the hand of the state and capital was immensely strengthened by the flood of unemployed released by the impact of the Depression on the rural areas of Central Africa and by the contraction of capitalist agriculture and base mineral mining. Surviving farmers, for example, were able to pay labourers only 14 shillings per month in 1932, and in some areas pushed payment down to 8 shillings per month by 1934.[111] On the gold-mines, where expansion secured the economic salvation of the settler state, profitability was realised through unremitting assault on the cash wages of black workers. In the early 1930s, average monthly wages fell by almost 30 per cent. For capital, enjoying 'the cheapest black labour probably in the British Empire',[112] the reward was a 'very remarkable and indeed unprecedented growth in the National Income from 1932–39',[113] up from £9·6 million to £21·5 million.

INDUSTRIALISATION AND CLASS STRUGGLE, 1940–1948

> STRIKE! Meeting on Tuesday of the African Workers Voice Association. . . . Come and join for your benefit, your children and grandchildren. Forward we go and Backwards never. FIRE!!
>
> – Strike notice, 1948

The expansion of gold-mining began to falter as the cost of black labour moved slowly upwards once the supply slackened after the Depression. At the outbreak of the Second World War the state nonetheless imposed a tax on the increased price of gold as a contribution to the colony's war effort. This tax, together with the inflation unleashed by the war and the rising cost of labour, were important causes of the huge drop in gold production between 1940 and 1945. Over the same period, the number of mines decreased from 1 477 to 732. As the greatest number of casualties were smallworkers, the large mines began to recover their predominant

---

109 R. Gray, *The Two Nations*, London, 1960, p. 154.
110 Arrighi, *Political Economy*, p. 32.
111 W. J. Barber, *The Economy of British Central Africa*, London, 1961, p. 204.
112 *African World Annual*, 1934, 173.
113 *Report of the Commission of Enquiry into the Mining Industry of Southern Rhodesia*, 1945, p. 22.

7:1 Southern Rhodesia, c. 1950

position. In 1945 large mines produced over 46 per cent of the total gold output and ten years later, over 60 per cent. Gold was becoming more like chrome- and asbestos-mining as a preserve of international capital, but whereas the war and its aftermath precipitated an absolute decline in gold production, strategic base minerals, particularly chrome, experienced both rising prices and demand.[114]

The growing importance of international capital in the mining industry reinforced the tentative 1939 *rapprochement* between the United Party and the Chamber of Mines, and found concrete expression in post-war state policy. After a commission of enquiry, special taxation which had most affected the biggest mines was removed, and other measures favouring large capital were introduced. This resulted in an accelerated decline of

114 Phimister, 'History of Mining', pp. 161–4, 171–3.

smallworkers, who were powerless to prevent a series of state actions all of which adversely affected them: 'in 1947 prospecting grants were discontinued; in 1948 the miners training school was closed; in 1949 the Electricity Supply Commission was reorganised, the hidden subsidies to smallworkers removed, and charges fixed on an economic basis'.[115] The new climate was one in which, 'where there was conflict between the interests of smallworkers and those of mining companies, the latter tended to be favoured'.[116]

These developments were in complete contrast to those in agriculture, where the fortunes of settlers, specifically tobacco-planters, were soaring. During the war, the rising price of tobacco leaf was followed by a somewhat shaky rise in the volume of production, due to still rude growing techniques and to limited fertiliser supplies. However, irrespective of its quality, the tobacco could be sold, and, for 'the first time since tobacco had been commercially planted in Rhodesia, every grower was making money'. From 1946, however, some of the planters began making fortunes as the pattern of demand, determined by Britain's own dollar shortage which limited its ability to buy American crops and the huge sterling balances accumulated by various countries during the war, favoured the Southern Rhodesian market. The price of tobacco leaped upwards from 20 pence per pound to an average of over 32 pence per pound, at which level it 'brought a profit of over 100 per cent to the efficient grower'. In 1946 tobacco exports beat gold into second place for the first time. In subsequent years tobacco increased its lead as the acreage planted, the number of growers and production all boomed.[117]

The extraordinary demand for Southern Rhodesian tobacco placed the large British manufacturers in an increasingly uncomfortable position. Starved of dollars, they were unable to fill their customary requirements from American markets, and turned reluctantly towards Southern Rhodesia and its inflated tobacco prices. Negotiations were opened in which British capital, through its Tobacco Advisory Committee, admitted that it was 'desperate' for Rhodesian leaf, but argued that 'it was insupportable to pay the average price of 59 pence a pound, which had been reached at the opening of the Rhodesian auctions. Such a price paid on the floors meant that Rhodesian tobacco landed in Great Britain at 75 pence compared with 45 pence for American and 33 pence for Canadian leaf, both of which were then generally superior in quality to the Rhodesian product.' A compromise was suggested to the planters in which the manufacturers agreed to purchase a significant proportion of the annual crop in return for lower prices. The effective choice was 'of exploiting

115 Murray, *Governmental System*, p. 158.
116 *Ibid.*, p. 157.
117 This and the next two paragraphs are drawn from Clements and Harben, *Leaf of Gold*, pp. 130, 133–4, 136–7, 140.

Britain's difficulties by demanding grossly inflated prices which would bring rich rewards in the short run, or of securing ... a permanent and substantial share of the British market'.

After some hesitation and with much suspicion, the planters committed themselves to the latter course. In the London Agreement of December 1947, the big tobacco companies undertook to buy 46 million pounds at an average price of 29–30 pence per pound, 'reviewable and renewable' every year for the fifth year ahead, thereby creating the stable market conditions for future spectacular increases in production. War and the decisive weakening of British imperialism thus secured in a decade the market which had eluded the best efforts of Southern Rhodesian growers in the previous forty years.

The movement towards tobacco cultivation during the war was so pronounced that Southern Rhodesia lost its previous self-sufficiency in basic foodstuffs. The state, faced with its commitment to feed Empire forces and Italian prisoners of war, as well as with the difficulties of trading in wartime, hastily converted the existing control boards into marketing boards to oversee the supply and distribution of agricultural produce.[118] Most important of all, it began rethinking its position in regard to black cultivators as a source of surplus production. These deliberations increasingly came to be made in the context of two developments. The war-induced growth of secondary industry generated not just an expanding demand for labour but also a need for a stabilised work-force, and eventually a wider and deeper internal market. As a second factor, the reserves continued to deteriorate, and declining yields and eroded soil were made to support an impoverished and marginalised population. These conditions completely overshadowed the state's conservation and extension advice programme, which was slowly consolidating a small but distinct class of middle and upper peasants.

Comprehensive recommendations by the 1944 Native Production and Trade Commission of Enquiry that:

> the maximum benefit both for the state, and for the natives, from Native Agriculture and Animal Husbandry can only be obtained by compulsory planned production whereby a statutory body should be empowered to direct what crops, acreages and areas should be planted and what livestock should be kept to enforce good husbandry conditions, and to control the distribution and marketing of the consequent products[119]

were largely accepted and implemented. Compulsory marketing at fixed prices was extended to cover all important African-grown crops. The

118 Murray, *Governmental System*, pp. 101–2.
119 *Native Production and Trade Commission,* p. 36; cited in Murray, *Governmental System,* p. 305.

production of cotton and, later, Turkish tobacco for export, was encouraged, and the state fought to control the peasant production process by activating those sections of the Natural Resources Act of 1941 which empowered Native Commissioners to 'depasture stock, give orders on methods of cultivation, prohibit the cultivation of land, and control water'.[120] Money to pay for these ambitious schemes was raised by the Native Production and Marketing Development Act of 1948, which imposed a 10 per-cent levy on all African-marketed crops and cattle. The entire drive to intensify commodity production in the reserves culminated in the 1948 Native Reserves Land Utilisation and Good Husbandry Bill, which proposed to replace the existing system of land tenure with a 'hybrid tribal–capitalistic system of individual holdings and communal grazing', in which good husbandry practices would be enforced under threat of dispossession.[121]

The attempt to transform the African rural areas was fundamentally rooted in the shift of the colony's economy towards secondary industry. Although the roots of this sector stretched back in some instances to the 1890s and to the First World War, it expanded substantially only when imperialism was convulsed by crisis during the Depression and the Second World War, and imports from the advanced capitalist countries were slashed. Commerce, cut loose from the metropole, added its voice to the industrialists' clamour for sympathetic state treatment, and in 1940 an Industrial Development Advisory Committee was formed. Two years later the state nationalised and expanded Southern Rhodesia's tiny iron and steel works. It also established a cotton-spinning industry, Huggins explaining that 'if private capital is prepared to function, we want to preserve the freedom and initiative of private enterprise, but if that enterprise fails in any way, or if the industry is not established, then the State must step in if we are to progress'.[122] However, the speech effectively marked the end of a phase, not a beginning. The colony's industrialists strongly opposed nationalisation, and the state subsequently retreated from an interventionist stance. Even the purchase of the railway system in 1947 was part of an infrastructural policy to establish 'a basis on which private enterprise can then build its own industry',[123] and was certainly not part of a coherent attack on external monopoly control.[124]

120 Murray, *Governmental System*, p. 305.

121 *Ibid.*, p. 306; M. Yudelman, *Africans on the Land*, Cambridge, Mass., 1964, p. 119. See also R. W. M. Johnson, 'African agricultural development in Southern Rhodesia: 1945–1960', *Food Research Institute Studies*, iv, 1964, 165–223.

122 *New Rhodesia*, 4 Dec. 1942.

123 *Southern Rhodesia Legislative Assembly Debates*, 23 June 1949, col. 1953; cited in Murray, *Governmental System*, p. 187.

124 This section is based on Murray, *Governmental System*, pp. 177–8; Gann and Gelfand, *Huggins*, pp. 159–60, 195–7.

With or without state intervention, industrial expansion in the 1940s was impressive.

INDEX OF VOLUME OF PRODUCTION

Year	Agriculture	Mining	Secondary industry
1938	100	100	100
1939	91	98	102
1940	116	103	121
1941	113	99	132
1942	137	100	146
1943	129	92	160
1944	132	87	186
1945	160	81	221
1946	155	77	253
1947	172	74	267
1948	209	81	291

Source: *Survey of Rhodesian Industry, 1954*

The wartime interruption of competition from overseas was complemented by a massive expansion of the domestic market through the siting of the Imperial Air Training Scheme in Southern Rhodesia.[125] After 1945, demand was sustained by the doubling of the black urban population to about 200 000 by 1956, and by an influx of white immigrants which drove the settler population up from about 80 000 in 1945 to about 125 000 in 1950.[126] Factories increased in number from 299 in 1938 to 473 in 1948, and over the same period their gross output grew from £5·1 million to £25·8 million.[127] By 1950, manufacturing was second only to settler agriculture as a source of the colony's income.

Aggregate figures, though, conceal the stages through which this process passed, as well as the nature of the industrialisation. During the war itself, the pace of industrialisation was relatively modest, and was confined to concerns using local raw materials, particularly food-processing. From 1946 industrial expansion quickened, only to falter almost immediately in 1947 and 1948 as the return of foreign competition cut into internal and export markets.[128] Many settler 'factories' were little more than extended workshops, characterised by small outputs, an extremely low capital-to-labour ratio, and by low productivity.[129] They were vulnerable to competition and takeover by international capital in the post-war phase of imperialism. In fact, foreign capital, drawn primarily from Britain and

125 Gann and Gelfand, *Huggins*, p. 153.
126 *Official Year Book of Southern Rhodesia*, 1952, p. 130.
127 *Economic and Statistical Bulletin of Southern Rhodesia*, 21 June 1951.
128 A. G. Irvine, *The Balance of Payments of Rhodesia and Nyasaland, 1945–1954*, London, 1959, p. 325.
129 *Report . . . into Protection of Secondary Industries*, pp. 21, 23.

South Africa, did not so much penetrate as overwhelm local industries and the economy generally. Annual foreign investment, which totalled £13·5 million in 1947, doubled itself in 1948, and was almost as much again in 1950 when it peaked at over £50 million.[130] Foreign capital was distributed more or less evenly between the public and private sectors of the economy,[131] and both contributed mightily to the shouldering of local capital well into the wings of the industrial stage in the late 1940s and early 1950s.

The general failure of local capital to resist takeover by international interests was determined not by size and market competitiveness alone. It was also hurt at the point of production, where intensifying struggle by the black working class began to exert upward pressure on wages and conditions of employment. Those smaller capitalists who opposed measures aimed at selectively stabilising the work-force and improving housing conditions found the state relatively unsympathetic. They were brusquely told by Huggins that if they could not afford the expenditure, they ought to go out of business.[132] It was, however, advice which rang hollow for black workers enmired in the urban squalor of Bulawayo and Salisbury locations. For them capital's internal differences were marginal, if not irrelevant. It was brutally clear that the real struggle was between capital and labour.

The wages of the vast majority of urban Africans remained well below the poverty datum lines calculated in the 1940s, and lagged far behind the 140 per-cent rise in the cost of living between 1939 and 1947.[133] One survey conducted between 1942 and 1943 found that the average minimum monthly wage needed to maintain a married couple with two children was £4 15s 0d. This made no allowance for tax, education, medicine, travelling or amusements. However, only 8·8 per cent of married Africans earning cash wages alone received that amount or more.[134] Although some workers managed to make ends meet through the barter system known as *tswete*,[135] for most people conditions were desperate. At the same time, more critical and assertive voices were raised against the job colour bar and the settler state. One letter to the press pointed to the contradiction between the British Empire's struggle against Nazi racism and the prevailing

---

130 C. H. Thompson and H. W. Woodruff, *Economic Development in Rhodesia and Nyasaland*, London, 1953, p. 173.
131 C. Stoneman, 'Foreign capital and the reconstruction of Zimbabwe', *Review of African Political Economy*, xi, 1978, 64.
132 Gann and Gelfand, *Huggins*, p. 178.
133 For details, see Gray, *Two Nations*, pp. 210–19; D. Clarke, 'The underdevelopment of African trade unions in Rhodesia: an assessment of working class action in historical perspective' unpub. 1974, p. 10.
134 Gray, *Two Nations*, p. 211.
135 N. Shamuyarira, *Crisis in Rhodesia*, London, 1965, p. 99. Shamuyarira was describing Harare African township in the early 1950s. See also L. Vambe, *From Rhodesia to Zimbabwe*, London, 1976.

attitude of the Southern Rhodesian Government towards its black subjects.[136] Other letters later on took comfort from the new constitution in the Gold Coast (Ghana), which gave Africans a majority in the Legislature, and from India's impending independence:

> Let us boldly demand our rights from the Government, [wrote Leopold Takawira,] such as proper Franchise ..., payment and appointment based on individual qualification and ability rather than on colour or race, recognition of African trade unions. ... We live in a country flowing with milk and honey ... but are dying of starvation and malnutrition, we live in a country nominally under-populated but are suffering because of overcrowding in our Reserves. Where is then democracy for us?[137]

Strikes had occurred intermittently during the war, but the first major explosion was the railway workers' strike in October 1945. Although actual concessions eventually won by the strike were limited, its broader implications and consequences were enormous. 'The Railway strike,' exulted Jasper Savanhu, 'has proved that Africans have been born. . . . Africans realise as never before that united they stand and divided they fall. . . . We have found ourselves faced by a ruthless foe – exploitation and legalised oppression by the white man for his and his children's luxury. . . . The days when a white man could exploit us at will are gone and gone for ever.'[138]

Within one week of the ending of the railway strike, a Bulawayo African Workers' Trade Union, later renamed the 'Federation', was established. Savanhu was its president. In quick succession Bulawayo's building trade, bakeries, garages, general stores, chemist shops, milling factories, breweries, and its drivers, messengers, and engineering and foundry workers were all unionised, and affiliated to the Federation.[139] Independent unions also sprang up, and the process was repeated in Salisbury where, among others, the Reformed ICU was resuscitated by Charles Mzingele in June 1946. Frequent mass meetings and demonstrations were held in the main urban locations, as strikes and unrest spread all over the colony, at various times involving Bulawayo municipal workers, Wankie miners, engineering workers, senior school pupils and labourers in brickworks, construction firms and textile companies. This militant phase ended with a major organisational split when, early in 1947, the African Workers Voice Association was founded in Bulawayo by Benjamin Burombo 'for the benefit of the workers'. The Federation, said

136 *Bantu Mirror*, 25 Jan. 1941.
137 *Ibid.*, 19 July 1947.
138 Cited in Gray, *Two Nations*, p. 319.
139 This section on the General Strike is drawn from Phimister, 'Class struggle and industrialisation in Zimbabwe: the 1948 General Strike' (in preparation).

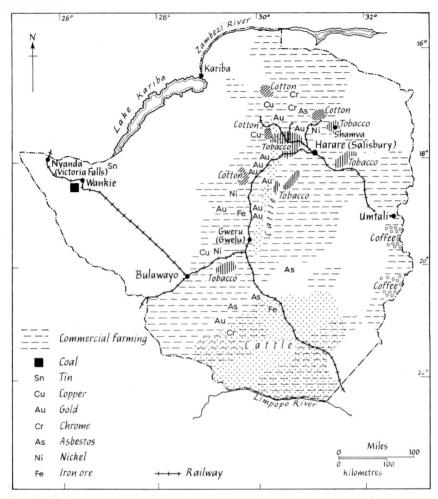

7:2 Zimbabwe

Burombo, 'concerned itself only with rich men and big business propositions. It is not interested in the common working class.'

For the remainder of 1947, although strikes continued to erupt, especially after meal and meat rations were cut because of drought, organised labour devoted its attention to unsuccessful attempts to heal the breach in its ranks. It was intently concerned with the deliberations of the Labour Board, which had been set up to arbitrate between management and labour on the railways. The award, published at the beginning of 1948, recommended wage minima based on various grades, overtime payment, recognised holidays and better housing.[140] Although accepted by the

140 Clarke, 'Underdevelopment of African trade unions', p. 10.

288

railways, the award was swiftly rejected by other employers and just as quickly seized on by unions as a reference point for their own demands. In February, the Federation and the Workers Voice both called for a national Labour Board to consider black wages generally, while in Salisbury, Mzingele, speaking for the RICU, condemned the prevalent attitude of capital 'that the development of this Colony has to be carried out at the expense of the African with no regard to his right as a consumer of any produce he is sweating to produce'.

Unrest and strike action once more intensified, and by early April 1948, in the absence of any significant concessions by capital, Bulawayo workers decided to take matters into their own hands. At gatherings called by unions to counsel delay and caution, crowds 'yelled that they had waited too long and now was the time for action', and shouted down official speakers. On 13 April at a meeting called by the Workers Voice Association and attended by 'practically every native in Bulawayo', the result was the same: 'native leaders got up in succession and tried to calm the mob. The mob would not listen, but started shouting "Sit down, we are going on strike tomorrow". . . . the meeting broke up in complete confusion and disorder and the town natives went streaming back to their places of residence shouting "Chia, Chia."'

The next morning, Bulawayo's white residents awoke to the sounds of pickets enforcing the strike throughout the city. It spread unevenly to other centres in the colony during the last weeks of April, drawing in most urban workers, including domestic servants, and many miners. Although the state lost little time in mobilising army and police forces, in general it reacted cautiously, and no lives were lost. A number of economic concessions were made by the state and capital as a result of the strike, but its real and lasting significance lay in its impact on the consciousness of black and settler alike. It symbolised a new era in which the arena and form of class struggle had been transformed by urbanisation and the growth of secondary industries.

CONCLUSION

For much of the first sixty years of colonial Zimbabwe's history, international capital and settler colonialism shared an essential community of interests in the manner in which the black majority were oppressed and exploited. While settler and metropolitan interests fought constantly over the size of their respective shares, this was never confused with the primary need to cooperate in securing the conditions for the satisfactory operation of the capitalist system. As the initial emphasis was on mining and agricultural produce for export, the economic imperatives of capital demanded and obtained cheap labour from rural areas economically and politically shaped by the colonial state. Africans were wanted only as migrant labourers whose permanent homes were in the so-called reserves.

In the 1940s, the ties between settler and international interests encountered a number of problems. Settler capital increasingly was confined to farms and mines critically dependent on the maintenance of cheap labour structures. International capital, on the other hand, became largely associated with the rapidly expanding secondary industrial sector. This sector needed to stabilise part of its labour force so that workers could learn to operate factory machinery. Secondary industries also wanted to expand the local African market for their products and gain access to the neighbouring markets of Northern Rhodesia (Zambia) and Nyasaland (Malawi). It was now more difficult to reconcile the needs of settler capital with those of the ever more powerful industrial sector. This was especially so because of African trade-union organisation and strikes. New methods of co-opting some African workers, or at least their leaders and members of the middle class, had to be found. The 'partnership' of Federation was one of several such strategies. It was rejected as, first, different settler political parties and, later, black nationalists fought for control of the state. Only the struggle and war of the 1970s were to underline the fundamental need to change it.

CHAPTER 8

The northern republics, 1960–1980

CRAWFORD YOUNG

The year 1960 was one of triumph for nationalism in Africa. The New Year was greeted by independence for Cameroun; before it ended, sixteen other states followed into the sunlight of political sovereignty, including five of the seven that will serve as focus for this chapter. Two decades later, it is not easy to recapture the mood of fresh and unspoilt hope that accompanied the end of the long colonial night. The political structure of colonial rule had crumbled, without the harsh and bitter armed struggle that occurred on the southern rim of Central Africa. With such victories in hand, surely many more could be anticipated in the years ahead. A life more abundant was within reach. The new state could redesign the warped colonial economy, and direct its resources towards the satisfaction of the urgent needs of its population. Or so it seemed to citizens, leaders and observers in the euphoria which attended the sudden dissolution of formal colonialism. In the northern tier of Central African states, seven countries set out on the quest to fulfil this promise: Cameroun, Gabon, Congo, Central African Republic (CAR), Zaire, São Tomé e Príncipe, and Equatorial Guinea.[1]

Even before the year 1960 was out, events in Zaire had made manifest the potential hazards which lay ahead: within a fortnight of independence, the army had mutinied, senior European administrators in most areas had fled, the richest province had seceded, and the most powerful external forces in the world rushed to turn the situation to their advantage. As time went by, more of the difficulties confronting the new states came into view: the persistence of neo-colonialism, the constraints of dependency, the gap between available resources and popular expectations. By the 1970s more

---

1 The wholesale change of place-names in Zaire (formerly Belgian Congo) poses difficult problems. Current designations will be used throughout, with former names in parentheses on first encounter. Thus 'Congo' refers to the People's Republic of the Congo, with Brazzaville as its capital. Further confounding analysis is the difference in designation for the Zaire river since President Mobutu of Zaire declared the name to be changed. In Brazzaville, it is still the Congo river. Arbitrarily, we refer to the Zaire river.

TABLE 8:1

CHRONOLOGICAL OVERVIEW, 1960–1980

Year	Zaire	Cameroun	Congo	C. African Republic	Gabon	Equatorial Guinea	São Tomé e Príncipe
1960	Independence; mutiny; Katanga secession; Lumumba ousted	Independence; Ahidjo	Independence; Youlou	Independence; Dacko	Independence; M'ba		
1961	Lumumba murdered; Adoula government	Unification with W. Cameroun					
1962	—	—	—	—	—	—	—
1963	Katanga secession ended		Youlou ousted; 'trois glorieuses'; Massemba-Débat succeeds			Autonomy	
1964	Rebellions; Tshombe government	UPC uprising withers			M'ba ousted; French restore him		
1965	Mobutu *coup*						
1966	Mercenary mutiny	Single party		Bokassa ousts Dacko			
1967	Mercenary mutiny; OAU summit				M'ba dies; Bongo succeeds		
1968			Ngouabi ousts Massemba-Débat			Independence; Macías Nguema	
1969			Marxist-Leninist state				

chilling possible outcomes became clear, such as the systematic perversion of the state into a predatory instrument of its ruler. This occurred both in Equatorial Guinea and in CAR and, in certain respects, in Zaire. Independence provided an opportunity which colonialism could never offer, of collective effort to better the lives of the citizenry; yet the achievement of sovereignty brought only a possibility of a new departure, not the assurance of success.

CONTINUITIES AND DISCONTINUITIES

In certain respects continuity from the colonial patterns of evolution stands out. This is probably most marked in the two states which have experienced the most placid political evolution, Cameroun and Gabon. The territorial units created by colonialism did experience some

Year	Zaire	Cameroun	Congo	C. African Republic	Gabon	Equatorial Guinea	São Tomé e Príncipe
1970	—	—	—	—	—	—	—
1971	—	—	—	—	—	—	—
1972	—	—	—	—	—	—	—
1973	—	—	—	—	—	—	—
1974	Copper price breaks						
1975	Crisis begins; Angola invasion						Independence; Marxist–Leninist state; President, Manuel Pinto da Costa
1976	—	—	—	—	—	—	—
1977	Shaba I 'rebellion/ invasion'		Ngouabi assassinated; Yhombi–Opango succeeds	Bokassa crowned 'Emperor'			
1978	Shaba II 'rebellion/ invasion'						
1979			Sasso Nguesso ousts Yhombi–Opango	French oust Bokassa; Dacko restored		Macias Nguema overthrown, executed; Obiang succeeds	
1980	—	—	—	—	—	—	—

adjustment, but within a logic dictated by colonial boundary concepts. The administrative federation of French Equatorial Africa had been, to all intents and purposes, dismantled by the 1956 Loi-Cadre, which fixed political evolution at the level of the four component territories. The French-administered Cameroun was enlarged in 1961 by unification with the southern half of the British Cameroons, till then attached to Nigeria. New concepts of citizenship and nationality were firmly tied to these national units. The only serious challenge to this principle, the secession of mineral-rich Shaba (Katanga) in 1960, was crushed by the international community, through the United Nations.[2]

2 The best analysis of this episode is Jules Gérard-Libois, *Katanga Secession*, Madison, Wis., 1966.

Much of the basic framework, public doctrine and structure of the colonial state was retained as well. The apparatus was swiftly Africanised, but its routines and habits possessed a strong conservative force. The command style of the regional administration persisted, as did its insistence on bureaucratic dominion over the population.[3] Even where the novel institution of a political party existed alongside the state bureaucracy, its object of *encadrement* of the people made it essentially an auxiliary of the administration, not a popular competitor to it. Even where, as in Zaire, there were sharp discontinuities and a dislocation of the state apparatus, bureaucratic rejuvenation under the Mobutu régime followed colonial patterns.

Political independence in itself had no impact on economic arrangements. The continuities in this domain were particularly marked in the four states formerly under French rule. The retention of a common currency, the CFA franc, incorporated into the franc zone, showed the tendency of economic structures to persist. Even after a decade of official Marxism-Leninism in Congo, the primacy of the French business community was immediately apparent to the most casual visitor to Brazzaville.

Over time, there was some evolution. Zaire in particular had two phases of major confrontation with colonial capital: in its nationalisation of the copper giant, Union Minière du Haut-Katanga, in 1967;[4] and its ultimately disastrous Zairianisation campaign of 1973–1975.[5] Also, in a phase of apparently imminent prosperity, at the beginning of the 1970s, a major effort was made to secure new investment from non-Belgian sources. Some new multi-national capital appeared in Congo, Gabon and Cameroun, but the former coloniser remained the most important external economic factor.

At the same time, there were significant elements of discontinuity with the colonial past. The acquisition of sovereignty did create for the nations a new status in the international realm. They became members of an emerging African concert of states. This fell well short of the pan-African dream, but it played a significant part in continental affairs and in defining African orientations towards the rest of the world. They also became part of the Third World and non-aligned movement in international politics, with an anti-imperial public face and a common demand for a more equitable world order. Non-alignment was, of course, very differently understood in Congo and in Gabon. It was a radical anti-imperialism in

3 For an eloquent account of what he terms the 'preceptoral state' in Cameroun, see Yamvu Makasu, 'Political Learning: a Study of the Effects of Social Relations upon Political Knowledge, the Case of Ayos, Cameroon', Ph.D. thesis, University of Wisconsin, Madison, 1980.
4 Kamitatu Massamba, 'Problématique et rationalité dans le processus de nationalisation du cuivre en Afrique Centrale: Zaire (1967) et Zambie (1969)', Ph.D. thesis, Institut d'Etudes Politiques de Paris, 1976.
5 Michael G. Schatzberg, *Politics and Class in Zaire*, New York, 1980, pp. 121–52.

Congo. In Gabon it was a patina lightly concealing an underlying set of privileged associations with the former metropole. New and important international actors became part of the web of external affiliations and influences. For much of this period the United States became the primary external sponsor of successive régimes in Kinshasa. China became important in Congo in the 1960s, and in Zaire in the 1970s. The Soviet Union, as a global power, established a diplomatic presence everywhere, and developed a strong presence in Brazzaville, especially in the 1970s. Even a small state like Cuba became a familiar part of the matrix of Central African international linkages. It influenced Congo in the 1960s, Equatorial Guinea in the 1970s, and was an invaluable military ally of the MPLA government in Angola to the south.

8:1 The northern republics

In the post-independence years, a growing differentiation appeared among the states of northern Central Africa. Though there had been significant differences in the texture of the colonial experience in these countries, imperial rule had many common features. By 1980, the range of variation was much greater than would have been forecast at the hour of independence. Régime ideologies ran the gamut from the official Marxism-Leninism espoused by Congo since 1969 and São Tomé e Príncipe since its independence in 1975, to the multinational corporation-dominated capitalism of Gabon, or the more domestically focused market economy of Cameroun. Whereas only Zaire had a mineral-based economy before independence, Gabon and Congo and even CAR later came to depend upon petroleum and mining. Equatorial Guinea and CAR experienced prolonged and destructive periods of rule; the ravages of a personal tyranny were particularly severe in Equatorial Guinea. Zaire, which for a time prospered under the apparent stability of the Mobutu régime, fell victim to a spiralling crisis after 1975. This produced a steady decline in national income and, more important, an extraordinary mass impoverishment. Cameroun, on the other hand, enjoyed a degree of stable rule and moderate economic expansion which few would have hoped for in 1960. Gabon, on the basis of an externally oriented mineral economy, moved from being a relative colonial backwater to having the second highest *per capita* income in Africa. Although the figure is deceptive, the contrast with the economic distress of Zaire, or the delapidation of Equatorial Guinea, was none the less striking. Thus, in 1980 the political, economic, and social landscape was far more diverse than it had been in 1960.

THE DECOLONISATION SETTLEMENTS

The shift in French policy from resistance to co-option of African nationalism was embodied in the 1956 Loi-Cadre. It provided for territorial autonomy and was, in terms of its own objectives, reasonably successful. The early colonial rule in Congo and CAR (then Ubangi-Shari) had been as harsh and exploitative as any. African traditions of resistance were well-rooted, yet the actual battle for political independence was relatively mild. It was sharpest in Cameroun, where the most assertive nationalist movement of the 1950s, the Union des Populations Camerounaises (UPC), did initiate tactics of direct confrontation in 1955. However, the UPC leadership was out-manoeuvred by a combination of repression and the cultivation of alternative African leadership.[6] The UPC

6 For an informed journalist's account, see Georges Chaffard, *Carnets secrets de la décolonisation*, 2 vols., Paris, 1965–7; also Willard Johnson, *The Cameroon Federation*, Princeton, N.J., 1970; Victor T. LeVine, *The Cameroons from Mandate to Independence*, Berkeley, Ca., p. 964.

was dissolved, and its guerrilla resistance became the object of vigorous military action over the next decade. The *maquis* resistance was effectively stigmatised as a mainly Bamileke movement, and the colonial administration gave encouragement to other African parties through the new institutions of territorial autonomy. Although the moderate and reassuring Ahmadou Ahidjo emerged by 1958 as a prospective premier, his party, the Union Camerounaise (UC), had important parliamentary rivals. In 1960, however, independence came in cooperation with France.

In Gabon, Congo and CAR, politicians such as Léon M'ba, Abbé Fulbert Youlou and Barthélémy Boganda,[7] who had earlier been critics and adversaries of the French administration, found satisfying status in the new roles as territorial leaders. With the door to autonomy open, the major issue in the final colonial years was the rivalry between African contenders for power. Also of some significance was the future of the administrative federation on which French colonial rule had been based. The 1958 referendum on the constitution of the Fifth Republic, presented as a plebiscite on membership in the French Community, was overwhelmingly won everywhere in equatorial Africa. It was supported by all major political figures. The transition from the autonomous affiliation with France to official independence in 1960 came unexpectedly. Developments in West Africa[8] rather than popular clamour in Gabon, Congo or CAR determined the outcome.[9]

The presumption shared by all, however, was that an intimate French connection would remain. This was somewhat less pronounced in Cameroun, which soon after independence was reunited to the formerly British-administered West Cameroon. The territory, as a UN mandate, had never been so fully incorporated into the French state as were the 'colonies' proper. But Cameroun faced the still-substantial UPC *maquis*, which could be defeated only with French military assistance.

After independence, some significant ties between the states were sustained. Only Congo favoured the retention of the framework of the pan-territorial Afrique Equatoriale Française (AEF). The reasons are obvious enough. A large part of the Congolese colonial economy was built on servicing the administrative federation. Gabon in particular was

7 Boganda, the most charismatic of the equatorial African politicians, perished in a plane crash in March 1959; David Dacko succeeded him as leader, and first prime minister after independence.
8 Mali sought by 1960 *de facto* independence through full transfer of those sovereign attributes reserved for France in 1958 (defence, foreign policy, higher education, currency, justice). When President de Gaulle gave way on this demand, President Félix Houphouët-Boigny, till then the most intransigent spokesman for retention of a French umbrella of sovereignty, suddenly reversed his stand and demanded the same status for Ivory Coast. When this occurred, formal independence for all the African territories then under French rule necessarily followed.
9 For details on the final pre-independence years, see Virginia Thompson and Richard Adloff, *The Emerging States of French Equatorial Africa*, Stanford, Ca., 1960.

adamantly opposed to remaining within a larger framework. There was a long-standing conviction that Gabon resources were diverted into building the infrastructure of Congo; the mineral prosperity of the territory would go much farther when shared only among its small population. A customs and currency union was nevertheless created in 1966 to include Cameroun and AEF.

The decolonisation formula in Zaire was far more precarious. The political openings for African participation under French dominion had no Belgian parallel in any sphere. By 1952, Belgian administration had begun a cautious reform programme, the ultimate goal of which was the creation of a Euro-African commonwealth permanently joined to Belgium. Until 1957 this was assumed to be decades away. Meanwhile, from 1956, political nationalism became visible, and the leisurely time-tables of the colonial administration were overtaken by events. A pivotal event, symbolic of the entire process, was the rioting in Kinshasa in January 1959. This formless, largely spontaneous assault on the symbols of domination in the capital revealed the vital energy of protest and accumulated frustration. It also presaged the inability of political structures to capture, direct and channel mass disaffection. In the tumultuous final months of Belgian rule, political movements sprang up across the country, mainly on an ethnic or regional basis. The once omnipotent administration lost its control over key areas of the country. By late 1959, Belgium faced the alternatives of negotiation with the nationalists, on the basis of their demands for immediate independence, or a problematic and politically unthinkable intervention by the metropolitan army.

The basis for independence, on which nationalists and Belgians came to agreement in January 1960, was the acceptance of a virtually immediate transfer of sovereignty on 30 June 1960. A new set of representative political institutions, including a parliament and provincial assemblies, was to be created from scratch. These bodies would choose the leadership. The crucial instruments of the colonial order, the administration and the army, would remain for a transitional period under Belgian domination. On the eve of independence, only three of the top 10 000 public servants were African, and none of the 1 000 army officers.[10]

This gamble quickly failed. The time was far too short for the political parties to create a solid organisational basis for themselves.[11] Their bitter electoral competition intensified mutual fears of regional or ethnic domination. The result was a parliament, the theoretical fount of authority,

10 Thorough accounts of decolonisation in Zaire may be found in René Lemarchand, *Political Awakening in the Congo*, Berkeley, Ca., 1964; Paule Bouvier, *L'Accession du Congo Belge à l'indépendance*, Brussels, 1965; Crawford Young, *Politics in the Congo*, Princeton, N.J., 1965.
11 Herbert Weiss argues convincingly that the parties themselves were swept along in a wave of radical rural protest which all but engulfed them; *Political Protest in the Congo*, Princeton, N.J., 1967.

which was badly fragmented. The largest party, the Mouvement National Congolais of Patrice Lumumba, held only 33 of 137 seats. A precarious compromise divided executive power between the two most conspicuous leaders, with Joseph Kasavubu becoming President, and Lumumba Prime Minister. These flimsy structures were shattered by the army mutiny against its white officers only five days after independence. For the first five years of independence, Zairian politics were dominated by the painful legacy of an aborted decolonisation.

Equatorial Guinea and São Tomé e Príncipe were not affected by the great wave of decolonisation in 1960. They were both small and isolated. The authoritarian régimes of the occupying powers, Spain and Portugal, were themselves insulated from the ascendancy of anti-colonial forces elsewhere. In the Portuguese case, the state ideology of the Salazar régime made the colonies a core component in the national claim to status. Spain briefly enunciated a similar doctrine, but this belated assimilation was abandoned in 1963. The way was opened for political advance on a pattern which was assumed to yield a post-colonial state closely bound to Spain, on the neighbouring francophone pattern. Francisco Macías Nguema had begun his career as a Spanish protégé. His flawed and paranoiac political personality soon turned a neo-colonial Spanish appendage into the object of his personal tyranny.

São Tomé achieved independence through the collapse of the Portuguese colonial state, and following the remarkable success of revolutionary movements in Guiné-Bissau, Mozambique and Angola. Armed struggle was impossible on the small island domain, but an exiled nationalist leadership was in close contact with other liberation movements, especially in Angola. The post-colonial régime succeeded to power with a set of perspectives akin to those of Guiné-Bissau or Mozambique, even though the direct experience of liberation combat was absent.

PATTERNS OF SOCIAL CHANGE

The post-war years in most of the region were ones of accelerating social change. Relative prosperity and the beginning of major public investment in education and amenities had brought some rise in living standards, and awakened hopes for further advance. Educational development had been particularly rapid in Congo, which by 1960 had the highest literacy rates in francophone Africa. Whereas in 1939 there were only 21 895 primary students in all of French Equatorial Africa, by 1959 75 per cent of primary-age Congolese were in school.[12] Not long after independence, universal primary education had almost been achieved in Congo. Gabon, Cameroun

12 Thompson and Adloff, *French Equatorial Africa*, pp. 278, 292.

and Zaire also had swiftly expanding educational systems. In Zaire, where primary education had become general in the 1950s, comparable expansion of the secondary network occurred in the 1960s and 1970s. In 1960 only 135 students completed secondary school, but by 1978 there were 40 000 pupils in the last year of secondary instruction, though only 17 per cent passed the state examination.[13] The number of Zairian teachers rose from 37 000 in 1960 to 230 000 in 1978.[14] CAR, Equatorial Guinea and São Tomé were much less touched by the educational revolution. In 1960, the Central African Republic had a single secondary school, with only three candidates passing the first part of the French baccalaureate examination.[15]

Nevertheless, the swift enlargement of the scholastic infrastructure had important consequences. One of the most direct was to accelerate the process of urbanisation. Young people generally had to journey to town to find post-primary educational opportunities. There were then few appropriate rural careers for those who finished school. Urban growth, which had been very gradual until the Second World War, occurred with phenomenal speed. Congo and Zaire, in particular, were well on their way to becoming predominantly urban countries. In 1972, 42 per cent of the Congo population lived in towns larger than 25,000.[16] Kinshasa, which had only 191 000 inhabitants in 1950, had more than 2 million by 1980. Matadi and Bukavu, which had only 18 000 in 1950, recorded populations of 110 000 and 135 000 respectively in 1970. Kikwit swelled from 13 000 in 1958 to 112 000 in 1970. Many large towns tripled in size.[17] The capital cities experienced particularly dramatic growth. Resources also tended to be concentrated there. In Kinshasa, two-thirds of the post-independence investment projects were situated in the capital, which accounted for 53 per cent of cement consumption, and 30 per cent of all wage payments.[18] By 1980 Libreville had become a jumble of elegant new high-rise buildings and Bangui was a prime centre for public expenditure.

The structure of urban populations was also changing in significant ways. Many more persons considered the town as their permanent abode, and increasing numbers of young Africans were born in the city; 21 per cent of the Kinshasa population was under five years of age in 1967.[19] In many cases, the level of formal employment opportunities was stagnant. Much of the burgeoning population drew an insecure sustenance from an

---

13 *Zaire* (Kinshasa), 18 Sept. 1978.
14 International Bank for Reconstruction and Development, *Zaire: Current Economic Situation and Constraints*, Washington, D.C., 1980, p. 67.
15 Pierre Kalck, *Central African Republic: a Failure in Decolonization*, New York, 1971, p. 115.
16 Hugues Bertrand, *Le Congo*, Paris, 1975, pp. 77–90.
17 'Les résultats du recensement de la population 1970 au Zaire', *Etudes Africaines du Centre de Recherches et d'Informations Socio-Politiques* [CRISP], T. A. 140, 1972.
18 Banque du Zaire, *Rapport Annuel 1974*, pp. 228–9.
19 Léon de St Moulin, 'Kinshasa', *Revue Française d'Etudes Politiques Africaines*, lxix, Sept. 1971, 51–6.

enormous informal sector of petty trade, personal services, artisan vocations, prostitution and even crime. The sex ratios were also changing, and the former heavy male predominance faded, as young women abandoned the countryside for the questionable opportunities of the towns. By 1970 women formed more than half the population of Kananga (Luluabourg), the second-largest Zairian city.[20]

CLASS FORMATION

Urbanisation, education and, especially, political independence brought rapid change to class structures. Before independence, the cleavage which transcended all others was between European and African. This was most striking in colonial Zaire, the only one of the equatorial states where the white population was substantial. On the eve of independence, the European community numbered 110000 in Belgian Congo, in contrast to just under 10000 in Congo, 5000 in CAR amd 4600 in Gabon. The far greater wealth of Zaire brought a striking affluence to this European community, which received almost 50 per cent of the total wage payments in 1959. Elsewhere the colonial élite also reserved economic privileges for itself. In CAR, Africans were excluded from the only profitable export crop, coffee, until late in the 1950s. They were instead compelled to grow cotton, of which two-thirds of the value was taxed, while the administration guaranteed profits to the European ginning and exporting companies.[21] In Congo and CAR commerce was mainly in the hands of European trading houses which were the lineal descendants of the notorious concessionary companies of the early colonial era.

African opportunity for achieving privileged status was slender. In Zaire, this opportunity came primarily through the priesthood; there were 500 African clergy by 1960. The first graduating class from the newly established university emerged only in 1958, and was mainly European. Zairian traders encountered a barrage of blocking mechanisms, and were, in the phrase of a Zairian sociologist, 'subsistence merchants'.[22] Brazzaville had no equivalent of the famous Ecole Normale William Ponty in Dakar, whose graduates served as teachers, administrators and doctors throughout former French West Africa. Although there were senior black functionaries, many – like the famous wartime Governor-General, Félix Eboué – came from the West Indies.

Libreville, Douala and São Tomé did have significant clusters of Westernised African and mulatto élites. Libreville and its coastal environs

20 Nzongola Ntalaja, 'Urban Administration in Kananga', Ph.D. thesis, University of Wisconsin, Madison, 1975, p. 94.
21 Kalck, *Central African Republic*, pp. 84–6.
22 Mukenge Tshilemalema, 'Businessmen in Zaire: Limited Possibilities for Capital Accumulation under Dependency', Ph.D. thesis, McGill University, Montreal, 1974.

had been under French rule since 1839. Its colonial society bore some resemblance to the four old communes of Senegal. A coterie of professional Africans, who partly accepted the assimilation mystique, could point out that coastal Gabon had been French longer than Nice and Savoy.[23] Douala, as a coastal mercantile state, was also an early base for trade and mission activity, which had brought social promotion for some. In colonial times, the Bamileke had become an intensively mobile group, and dominated much of the retail commerce of southern Cameroun, even spilling into Gabon. In São Tomé, centuries of Portuguese domination had produced a substantial Afro-Portuguese creole community. But these small enclaves of modest African success were the exception rather than the rule. Privilege and wealth, for the most part, were the preserve of the Europeans.

Political sovereignty did add new dimensions to the class structure. Although in most instances it did not eliminate the European group, over time whites were mostly displaced from the state apparatus itself, though in several states a few high-placed advisers exercised important influence. The conquest of the political kingdom, though it did not bring control over the economy, did force open a pathway to status and wealth through high political and bureaucratic office. By a process first noted by Fanon and Dumont,[24] a state bourgeoisie quickly took its place alongside the previously dominant foreign estate.

The power, status and income derived from the state could readily be invested in private economic ventures. Premier David Dacko, of CAR, urged his deputies to buy French coffee plantations in the early 1960s. 'Every day,' he told one writer, 'I tell our growing élite not to be ashamed of becoming the bourgeoisie, and not to be afraid of getting rich, provided they do not forget people who are in less fortunate positions than themselves.'[25] This pattern became most highly developed in Zaire during the Mobutu years, when the leading members of a politico-mercantile class acquired great wealth. Accumulation on this scale involved both legitimate business and alternative mercantile activities such as smuggling and traffic in foreign exchange. These illicit transactions generally required state favour and immunity from prosecution. Success required either high office or close ties with those near the summit.[26]

In the early years of independence, when fiscal pressures were generally less severe than they later became, there was a strong tendency to expand the apparatus of the state, and hence the openings for the developing state

23 Thompson and Adloff, *French Equatorial Africa*, p. 351.
24 Frantz Fanon, *The Wretched of the Earth*, New York, 1963; René Dumont, *L'Afrique Noire est mal partie*, Paris, 1962.
25 Kalck, *Central African Republic*, p. 117.
26 David J. Gould, *Bureaucratic Corruption in the Third World*, New York, 1980; J. P. Peemans, 'The social and economic development of Zaire since independence: an historical outline'. *African Affairs*, lxxiv, 295, April 1975, 148–79.

bourgeoisie. This reflected the pressure to find employment outlets for the growing flood of secondary and college graduates, particularly in Congo. The new political class had pledged to its electorate an increase in public amenities, especially education and health. Supply of these basic services implied personnel to provide them. The most dramatic illustration of this growth was in Congo, where state personnel expanded from 3 969 in 1960 to 36 354 in 1972.[27]

Although the state itself was the prime engine of class formation, some exceptions should be noted. In Cameroun, the Bamileke predominance in commerce was independent of the state. The concentration of the UPC dissidents in the Bamileke zone had placed this dynamic group in an ambiguous relationship to the régime. Though some leading Bamileke figures occupied high governmental posts, the Bamileke mercantile class was not a mere auxiliary to the state bourgeoisie. In Equatorial Guinea the blood-stained tyranny of Macías Nguema was destructive of both the state and the African middle class. In Congo, the socialist state ideology placed some constraints on the parallel economic ventures of the state bourgeoisie. There were important differences in the degree to which corruption was tolerated as a mechanism for conversion of power into wealth. Zaire is the extreme case on one end of the spectrum. President Mobutu himself, in two speeches before huge crowds in Kinshasa, appeared to treat theft of public resources as a natural part of the social order. On 1 May 1974, he enjoined his audience to 'steal cleverly, little by little, and invest your money in Zaire'.[28] On 4 January 1975, he told his listeners that, 'you who have stolen money and put that money into houses here in Zaire, and not abroad, I congratulate you on putting your money into those houses and those houses will remain yours because you have improved our land'.[29] Congo and Cameroun had higher standards of probity in the operation of the state.

The foreign estate, meanwhile, retreated to the economic realm. Overall, its numbers remained stable. In Cameroun, Congo and CAR, the size of the European community was approximately the same in 1980 as it had been in 1960. In Zaire, it shrank from its 1959 peak to about 50 000, mainly concentrated in Kinshasa and in the mineral zones of Shaba. In 1968, the expatriate sector still accounted for nearly 50 per cent of the private sector wage fund.[30] In Gabon, the European community grew more numerous, drawn in by the phenomenal development of oil, manganese and uranium, and their subsidiary ventures. In Equatorial

27 Bertrand, *Le Congo*, p. 255.
28 David J. Gould, 'Disorganization Theory and Underdevelopment Administration: Local "Organization" in the Framework of Zairian National "Development"', annual meeting, African Studies Association, Houston, Texas, Nov. 1977.
29 Transcript of speech, 1 Feb. 1975, in Kinshasa.
30 Peemans, 'Zaire since independence', 168.

Guinea, the small Spanish community fled the country during the Macías years, but was poised to return in 1979.

European capital, technology and cadres were crucial to the operation of the mineral sectors where post-independence foreign investment was concentrated. This basic fact was not altered either by nationalisation or by the availability of African university graduates. In Congo, despite sustained efforts to acquire effective control over the forest industry, two-thirds of the 1978 output came from four French companies. In Gabon, a small minority of the managerial cadres of the oil, manganese and uranium companies were nationals; COMILOG, the manganese combine, had only 50 Gabonese executives amongst its 3 500-person work-force in 1972, after twenty years of operation.[31] The nationalised copper firm in Zaire continued to rely heavily on expatriate personnel. Whereas the numbers of Zairian cadres rose rapidly (from nil in 1960 to 1 135 of 2 479 in 1974), the European personnel had withdrawn into the technological core of the enterprise.[32] Zairians were concentrated in the administrative, personnel and public-relations services. In the late 1970s Kisangani had 650 resident Zairian university degree-holders, but the one productive enterprise in town, a French textile mill, included no Zairians among its forty-five executives.[33]

The new foreign estate was not necessarily the same as the colonial white population. Precise figures are lacking, but one may reasonably argue that, everywhere, the majority of Europeans had arrived since 1960. Few had any interest in putting down long-term roots. For the corporate managers and high-level technical assistants, work in equatorial Africa was a highly remunerative interlude in a work career based elsewhere. There remained some long-term residents such as operators of small factories, merchants and missionaries. These had learnt that involvement in local politics carried more risks than gains. Their successes in operating in Marxist-Leninist Congo as well as capitalist Gabon taught the foreign estate that it could survive comfortably under almost any kind of régime, except one as capricious and unpredictable as that of Equatorial Guinea.

The importance of foreigners to the economy gave them considerable leverage in their dealings with the state. This was most conspicuously so for the multi-national firms involved in mineral exploitation. The absolute dependence of the state on the fiscal revenues and foreign exchange derived from minerals made all régimes circumspect in their dealings with foreign capital. In effect, any action which compromised the revenue base of the state undermined the economic foundation of the state bourgeoisie.

31 Yves de Schaetgen, 'L'Economie gabonaise', *Revue Française d'Etudes Politiques Africaines*, XC, June 1973, 67–94.
32 GECAMINES, *Rapport Annuel*, 1974.
33 Benoît Verhaegen, 'Universities, Social Class, and Economic Dependency', Conference on Higher Education and Political Change in Africa, Bellagio, Italy, Aug. 1978.

The foreign estate had another quite important impact upon the pattern of domestic stratification. It served as a reference point of consumption for the dominant political and bureaucratic group. Not all foreigners lived sumptuously. A contingent of teachers and missionaries lived in quite modest circumstances, but the more visible whites generally drew higher pay and maintained a more opulent life-style than they could have afforded in their home countries. Senior African personnel in the state and private sectors expected quite naturally that career success would be capped by access to comparable wealth. In the beginning, this assumption was rooted in a response to the pervasive racism of the colonial era. Privilege was tied to pigmentation. In 1952, France adopted the administrative statutes known as the Loi Lamine Guèye, which aligned salary scales and perquisites of ranking African functionaries with those of their European counterparts. An analogous act was adopted at the last minute by the Belgians in 1959. What began as a justifiable reaction to racism became, by subtle degrees, an entrenchment of privilege.

Both the foreign estate and the state bourgeoisie became permanent categories, even though there was considerable turnover in the individuals who composed them. In the case of the foreign estate, this was because of the transitory nature of their African residence. For the state bourgeoisie, especially the political segment of it, there was considerable insecurity for those who had reached the top by arduous struggle. Loss of political office, especially when incurred through disgrace, could mean financial ruin and seizure of assets. In Zaire the state bourgeoisie was virtually a service class whose opportunities for the consolidation of wealth depended on the good graces of the presidency. The needs and interests of the state bourgeoisie as a whole weighed heavily in the policy equation. At the same time its individual members were held in considerable personal insecurity.[34]

The petty bourgeoisie was in an even more precarious situation. Wealth did not accrue to teachers, subordinate employees of the state, clerks in the private sector, rank-and-file members of the security forces. A generation before, a significant fraction of the same group had gained social promotion from decolonisation. No similar opportunity was likely to recur. They were too far down the hierarchy to occupy positions of power. In the 1950s this group had been poor but had stood at the top of the African status hierarchy. After independence they lost most status.

At the lower end of the social hierarchy, the ranks of the regular wage-earners remained stagnant. After independence economic change accentuated this tendency. The extraordinary surge in national income in Gabon was little reflected in new opportunities for wage employment. Modern oil and manganese operations require few employees. The Zaire

---

34 Schatzberg, *Politics and Class*, captures particularly well the ambiguities and fluidity of the process of class formation in Zaire.

copper-mines employed 31 597 persons in 1974, fewer than in the 1920s, but produced several times the volume of copper.

Workers became a direct political force in Congo. In three days of street demonstrations the highly politicised youth and workers brought down the neo-colonial régime of Fulbert Youlou in 1963. Since 1969 the ideology of 'scientific socialism' has stressed that the working class is the social basis for the ruling party. In fact, the labour movement has continued to be a turbulent element in the complex factional politics of Brazzaville. Its social force was illustrated in the 1974 figures of the International Labour Organisation, which showed Congo second only to oil-rich Libya in the minimum wage increases.[35] Rising real wages have also reached the small cohorts of Gabon and Cameroun workers. In Zaire, by contrast, wage-earners have experienced a large deterioration of their well-being. According to figures published by the labour movement, urban real wages in 1976 stood at only 26 per cent of their 1960 level.[36] Deterioration has accelerated since that time.

The peasant sector has not been a beneficiary of independence, with the partial exception of Cameroun. Among the equatorial states, only Cameroun has pursued a consistent rural strategy and accorded priority to the agricultural sector. It had no mineral alternative till oil production began in 1980. By the 1970s governments realised that agricultural output, marketed through official channels, was either stagnating or declining. Major sums of precious foreign exchange had to be allocated to food imports. In Zaire this expenditure reached $300 million.[37] In Gabon, a once promising cocoa development withered away. In both São Tomé and Equatorial Guinea, cocoa output fell to less than half pre-independence levels. In Congo, the 1971 salaries of the state agricultural service exceeded cash returns to the peasants, yet production had declined.[38] In Zaire, some real prices dropped to a fifth of their 1960 level. Only the output of coffee, an especially remunerative crop, increased significantly.[39] In CAR, a momentary surge was followed by a decline in the export of coffee and cotton. These dreary figures obviously relate to the scale of rural exodus.

ETHNICITY

The changing nature of the class structure was accompanied by a rise in new forms of politicised ethnicity. These had a substantial impact upon

35 Susumu Watanabe, 'Minimum wages in developing countries: myth and reality', *International Labour Review*, cxiii, May–June 1976, 353.
36 Union Nationale des Travailleurs Zairois, *Position concernant la politique des salaires*, Kinshasa, 1977.
37 Crawford Young, 'Zaire: the unending crisis', *Foreign Affairs*, lvii, 1, Fall, 1978, 169–85.
38 Bertrand, *Le Congo*, pp. 188, 256; in the later 1970s, performance improved for some crops, notably rice and ground-nuts.
39 Guy Gran (ed.), *Zaire: the Political Economy of Underdevelopment*, New York, 1980, p. 5.

political and social interaction. Earlier chapters have expressed the historically fluid character of ethnonyms. During the colonial period, several social processes enlarged the scope and changed the meanings of ethnic categories. Missionaries who gave standardised written form to languages played one part; so did European administrators, who simplified social reality by imposing ethnic classifications. The rise of towns brought important new social arenas within which group identification and loyalty became important. Colonialism brought very uneven economic and social development. Some groups were well located with respect to schools, wage employment, communications and towns, whereas others were isolated. A growing appreciation of ethnic competition took hold, and with it a sense of resentment by some and of social advantage by others. The rise of ethnic associations in towns, and the availability of published ethnic 'knowledge', diffused stereotypes which gave new structural and ideological resources to the expression of group identities.[40]

Ethnicity was a familiar phenomenon, but neither emergent nationalists nor external observers attached decisive importance to it until the eve of independence. The crucial social cleavage was the racial one, dividing all Africans from all Europeans. In the decade before independence several developments escalated the ethnic rivalries. Urban centres suddenly became major agglomerations. The consciousness of social competition was much more intense in these confined social arenas. An educated generation began to use the newly crystallised ethnic categories in a more self-conscious way. Such was the origin of the Zairian Alliance des Bakongo (ABAKO), which sought to unite Kikongo speakers.

The politicisation of ethnicity became especially important in the late 1950s. This was triggered by the sudden and unanticipated pace of emancipation. Until the middle 1950s, political independence was unthinkable in São Tomé and Equatorial Guinea, decades away in Zaire, and likely to occur within some form of French framework in the remaining states. But quite quickly the situation changed. Decisions had to be made in the political arena at a time when Europeans dropped out of the picture as significant elements in the competition. All of a sudden, a new issue engaged the politically active. The succession to power might be exercised to the advantage of some ethnic communities and to the detriment of others. Independence was very hard to imagine. Its prospect evoked the highest of hopes, but also inchoate fears of possible domination by other groups. When ethnic polarisation was most pronounced, as in Zaire, Congo and Cameroun, the final months of colonial rule were marked by mingled anticipation and anxiety. It was in such an atmosphere that Brazzaville, in February 1959, experienced the worst riots in its history, when the northern M'Bochi were pitted against the southern Kongo and Lari.

40 For an introduction to the considerable literature on this theme, see Crawford Young, *The Politics of Cultural Pluralism*, Madison, Wis., 1976, and works cited therein.

The politicisation of ethnicity went furthest in Zaire, where it pervaded the campaign in the independence elections of March 1960. Most parties openly mobilised an ethnic or regional clientele. It was also of great importance in Congo, where the battle for power was a closely balanced struggle between north and south, and in Cameroun, where fear of the dynamic Bamileke was widespread. It was least visible in CAR, where a single nationalist movement emerged behind the charismatic figure of Boganda, and in 1959–1960 remained united even after his death. There was no open competition in São Tomé, where the major ethnic division was between landholding creoles (and Portuguese) and immigrant plantation workers. In Equatorial Guinea politicisation generally was very slight, but the small Bubi community on Bioko (formerly Fernando Po) feared domination by the mainland Fang. Their premonitions proved to be well justified under the Macías régime.

The realisation of the potentially harmful force of politicised ethnicity made a strong imprint upon post-independence conceptions of political order. The political élite gained the widespread conviction that unitary political formulas were indispensable. The genie of ethnicity, if allowed out of the bottle, had the destructive potential of rending the very fabric of the state. Thus it had to be carefully contained and rendered harmless. Open appeals to ethnic solidarity were everywhere considered illegitimate. National unity was an imperative.

Central African societies rapidly assimilated a contemporary concept of the nation–state. A crucial goal was 'nation-building', or 'national integration'. From a culturally complex social collectivity, the state undertook the task of working toward a self-conscious national community. Ethnicity, of course, would not disappear, but it would be transcended by a collective consciousness of an historically and ethically superior nature. The aspiration embodied in the official slogan of the ruling Union Nationale Camerounaise (UNC) speaks for a common aspiration: 'one leader, one party, one country'.

The elimination of overt electoral competition did not in itself bring about the disappearance of ethnicity, although it made it less politically visible. Ethnicity continued to affect the web of faction and alignment in clandestine ways. In Congo, the 1969 military *coup* which brought Marian Ngouabi to power was not just a change of face in the presidency, but a shift of regional gravity from south to north. Since that time, Kongo and Lari have played only a peripheral part. In Zaire, the inner core of the Mobutu régime has a marked Equateur and Lingala character. In CAR, Bokassa, as support dwindled, relied increasingly on his own Ngbaka group, which was less than 5 per cent of the population.[41]

41 Kalck, *Central African Republic*, p. 14, notes that the Ngbaka and other Ubangi valley groups, who collectively numbered fewer than 5 per cent of the population, occupied 60 per cent of the civil-service posts in the 1960s.

THE DIFFICULT CHALLENGE OF INDEPENDENCE

The challenges confronted by the new states were awesome. The 'revolution of rising expectations' was very real, and it affected all categories of people. The emergent state bourgeoisie expected to accede to a level of well-being approximating that of the foreign estate. Foreigners relinquished political power but expected to maintain their economic standing. Young people emerged from the schools stirred by the liberating message of nationalism. They desired career and leadership opportunities to which they felt entitled through their formal scholastic qualifications. Rural communities were promised schools, dispensaries, safe water supplies and roads. All of this required far more resources than were immediately at hand.

The threat of excessive expectations was compounded by the precarious ethnic nature of the national community. The Zaire crisis in 1960 and attempted secession by two regions underlined the dangers. So also did serious ethnic rioting in both Congo and Zaire in 1959–1960. The integrity of territorial units could not be assumed. If disunity threatened, external influences might give it ready encouragement, as happened in Shaba.

After independence, the limitations of the state in confronting these challenges became apparent to the more lucid leaders. Kanza Nsenga, a minister in the Lumumba government, later put the matter eloquently in an account of the turbulent summer of 1960:

> Though we sat so comfortably in our sumptuous official cars, driven by uniformed military chauffeurs, and looked as though we were ruling this large and beautiful country, we were in fact ruling nothing, and a prey to whatever might happen.[42]

In Cameroun, the UPC *maquis* was far from defeated. While the independence festivities took place, skirmishing occurred not far from the gates of the capital. The survival of independent Cameroun was visibly dependent upon muscular French support, both through direct military aid, and through the tracking of UPC exiled leaders by the French intelligence services.

It did not take long to discover the phenomenon of economic dependency. External resources, in the form of aid, loans and investments, narrowed the gap between needs and funds. But the funds available were less than the needs, and often carried disagreeable conditions. Investors insisted on tax holidays which denied to the state an early return. The state, faced with the immediate pressures of its own payroll, had difficulty in generating public investment capital. Foreign borrowing had narrow limits and, as Zaire discovered in the 1970s, great perils. It is necessary to

---

42 Thomas Kanza, *Conflict in the Congo*, Harmondsworth, 1972, p. 151.

examine how these dilemmas were resolved, what formulas were available to grapple with intractable problems, what pathways could be followed.

THE SCIENTIFIC SOCIALIST PATHWAY

In terms of official ideology, the most radical experiments occurred in São Tomé and Congo. In centuries past, São Tomé had a crucial influence on the region, as a sugar estate and slave entrepôt. It then became a colonial backwater, exporting cocoa grown with conscripted Angolan labour, with some Mozambicans and Cape Verdians as well. São Tomé was not affected in the 1950s by the large settler influx into Angola and Mozambique. Nor did it experience on the same scale an exodus of human and physical capital after independence in 1975. Independence was nevertheless accompanied by a sharp drop in cocoa production, which no doubt reflected the difficulty of adapting the colonial structure of exploitation. It became necessary, in particular, to secure labour by wage incentives alone. The new régime of the Movimento de Libertação de São Tomé e Príncipe (MLSTP), did not emerge out of a liberation struggle. Its ideological option for scientific socialism was the product of the quest for a liberation philosophy amongst the revolutionary movements which challenged Portuguese rule on the mainland. The Angolan option was particularly influential since the São Tomé élite shared a common intellectual milieu with the Movimento Popular da Libertaçao de Angola (MPLA) leadership. The microcosmic dimensions of this insular state, and its cocoa mono-economy, offered few opportunities for the application of Marxist-Leninist doctrine. The 1980 Human Rights report of the US Department of State noted the near-absence of political prisoners[43] and remarked upon the peculiar intimacy of politics in a tiny state where everyone knew everyone else among the élite.[44]

The Congo road to scientific socialism was rather different. The post-independence régime of Fulbert Youlou was a perfect example of a neo-colonial polity. Although remarkably servile to French political and economic interests, it was swiftly corroded by venality and became an embarassment not only to its internal supporters but also to its French sponsors. It could not withstand the pressure from young workers in the capital. In August 1963 street disorders could not be crushed, but President de Gaulle was not willing to use his 'Africa' intervention forces to save the

43 An important exception was former Prime Minister Miguel Trovada accused of plotting a *coup* and arrested in 1979 in UN premises; several persons were charged with conspiracy in 1979, and placed on trial; verdicts ranged from twenty-four years in prison to acquittal.

44 US House of Representatives, Committee on Foreign Affairs, and Senate, Committee on Foreign Relations, *Country Reports on Human Rights Practices for 1979*, submitted by Department of State, 4 Feb. 1980; for one of the rare pieces on this micro-state, see Laurie S. Wisenberg and Gary F. Nelson, 'São Tomé and Príncipe: mini-state with maxi-problems', *Africa Report*, xxi, 2, March–April 1976, 15–17.

régime. France stood by during the 'trois glorieuses' while the Youlou régime crumbled in the face of the militant urban disaffection.

The new Massemba-Débat régime endeavoured to define a radical alternative to neo-colonialism. It adopted the political language and structural forms of the most self-consciously left-wing régimes of the day, especially of Ghana, of Guinea and of Mali. The divisive force of ethnicity and the dangerous antagonism pitting north against south were contained within a newly created national party, the Mouvement National de la Revolution (MNR). What to the radical youth had been the demeaning pro-Western alignment of Youlou was supplanted by diplomatic affiliation with an aggressively anti-imperial cluster of African states. There was an earnest quest for an alternative to openly avowed neo-colonialism.

The change of perspective was most visibly reflected in the diplomatic field. Symbolic anti-imperial discourse at the United Nations was a response to the need for a legitimate conception of the state among urban youth, workers and intelligentsia. Nor was it all merely rhetoric. In two ways the new political orientation of Congo had a major impact on Central African history. It influenced both Angola and Zaire.

In the long run, the most crucial change was the willingness of radical Congo to provide an operational base to the Angolan MPLA. When Youlou fell, the MPLA was at its historic low point, torn by factionalism, demoralised, denied the pan-African recognition attributed to its rival, and excluded from facilities in Zaire; it faced bleak prospects. Massemba-Débat at once extended to the MPLA a right to operate from Congo. This base was contiguous to the Cabinda enclave where a rejuvenated MPLA soon undertook its first new campaign. It was also close enough to Angola to be useful. Congo, therefore, ensured the survival of the movement as a force in Angolan liberation politics. Subsequently, during the civil war of 1975, Congo also played a critical role as a transit point for Soviet arms and Cuban troops. Without that support the political outcome in Angola might have been different.[45]

The second foreign impact of the Congo 'revolution' was upon Zairian politics. The change of régime in Brazzaville enabled a segment of the Lumumbist opposition to cross the river and launch a movement of revolutionary insurrection. Training camps for insurgents were established on Congo territory.[46] They had little effect, however. In subsequent years,

45 This conclusion emerges from Basil Davidson, *In the Eye of the Storm: Angola's People*, Garden City, N.Y., 1972; see also John Marcum, *The Angolan Revolution*, Vol. I, Cambridge, Mass., 1969.

46 For a documentary record of the political instruction at this camp, assisted by Chinese advisers, see *Les Cahiers de Gamboma, instructions politiques et militaires des partisans congolais (1964–1965)*, Brussels, Centre de Recherches et d'Informations Socio-Politiques, 1965; on the Zaire rebellions, see especially Benoît Verhaegen, *Rébellions au Congo*, 2 vols., Brussels, 1966, 1969; Robert Rotberg and Ali Mazrui (eds), *Protest and Power in Black Africa*, New York, 1970, pp. 968–1011.

Congo, despite its ideological differences with Zaire, became circumspect about permitting the use of its territory for armed action. The risk of reciprocal sanctuary for Brazzaville dissidents was too obvious.

Another aspect of the Congo search for a radical alternative was an active opening towards the socialist camp. The Soviet Union, Cuba and China all became diplomatic partners. Initially, there were hopes that the communist countries might offer economic assistance to reduce Congo dependency upon established colonial circuits. The Chinese did build a textile factory, and some modest Soviet aid eventually came, but it soon became clear that the battle against dependency could not be won on this front. Diplomatic exchange with communist states did, however, sustain an image of vigorous anti-imperialism.

The expansion of a socialising economic sector was also undertaken. Import–export trade came under state management, and state marketing monopolies were created for agriculture and forestry. There was a partial takeover of oil-palm plantations and the sugar industry. Petroleum distribution networks also passed into state hands. Plans were laid to create a new socialist industrial sector of parastatal factories. By and large, the enterprises which came into state hands were the least profitable French undertakings, which may explain the relative lack of resistance to the thrust of nationalisation.

The socialist régime in Congo encountered growing political difficulties. Although it never experienced the complete loss of public support which had brought the collapse of Youlou, neither did it master the turbulence of the urban popular sectors. Brazzaville politics were an effervescent compound of volatile elements. Ideology was one area where the endless fractionalism of the left found full expression. The youth and labour movements were ideological hot-beds where segmentation was constant and debate passionate. Regionalism and ethnicity played their part. Pointe Noire, the city of the Vili, was a social universe of its own. The disadvantaged north resented the Lari-Kongo predominance in the top ranks of the state apparatus. With Brazzaville such an international ideological battle-ground, major embassies recruited their own clients and supported factional organisers in need of lubrication. The would-be radical state was in constant need of French assistance, and constantly constrained by its participation in the franc zone. These compromises with imperialism were harshly judged by the ideological factions. This compound of conspiracy and intrigue required qualities of consummate statecraft to allow politicians to remain in office, let alone to fulfil radical promises.

In 1968, the Massemba-Débat experiment was ended by factionalism in the army. The Brazzaville para-commando unit had come under the control of a popular northern officer, Marian Ngouabi. Massemba-Débat attempted to balance this by forming two paramilitary units outside the army, one linked to the youth movement, and the other to a party militia.[47] The army watched with growing dismay as these Cuban-trained units grew to army size and received material perquisites. The ensuing *coup* was far from bloodless, and the final assault on 300 party militia left 100 dead.

Seizing power was one thing, but exercising it, in the super-heated political climate of Brazzaville, was something else. Although Ngouabi had been a political moderate, the imperatives of statecraft soon led him to embrace the ideological left, and to declare Congo to be a People's Republic, guided by Marxism-Leninism.

The ambiguities of the People's Republic were several. Ngouabi's innermost convictions had not changed as much as his public discourse. As a newly self-proclaimed Marxist-Leninist, 'Ngouabi not only mastered the jargon, but also the Byzantine intricacies of developing a radical dialectic while holding centrist positions and purging the true militants in the political system'.[48] With the military as its ultimate power base, the régime was not really prepared to grant full hegemony to a Leninist party. Ngouabi also replaced southern political predominance with unmistakable northern control of the major organs of state and party.

The new ideological idiom in Congo did not suffice to co-opt the youth and labour movements. Though these organisations were formally part of the party structure, the régime could not impose full control. In 1974 a student leader had the audacity to use the party congress to decry the 'neo-colonial character of the state'. Ngouabi dissolved the student union, and threatened ringleaders with military conscription.[49] In 1976 the trade unions threw down the gauntlet by calling a general strike. Ngouabi excoriated the strike leaders as 'opportunists, situationists, and bandits'.[50]

The party experienced periodic convulsions and purges in which membership grew and fell. Its ability to broker succession crises in 1977 and in 1979 gave some evidence of its institutionalisation. In 1977, after Ngouabi's assassination,[51] the party was able to serve as the selection mechanism for a military successor. Two years later, in a surprising assertion of party supremacy, the Central Committee removed one officer-president and replaced him with another northern officer. The same blend of public radicalism and private moderation continued.

47 The best treatment of military politics and Congo factionalism is Samuel Decalo, *Coups and Army Rule in Africa*, New Haven, Conn., 1976; and Carl G. Rosberg and Thomas M. Callaghy, *Socialism in Sub-Saharan Africa: a New Assessment*, Berkeley, Ca., 1979, pp. 231–64.
48 Decalo, *Coups and Army Rule*, p. 164.
49 *Africa Contemporary Record, 1974–75*, London, pp. B576–7.
50 *Ibid.*, 1976–7, p. B493.
51 The circumstances of his assassination have never been fully elucidated; former President Massemba-Débat was executed as an alleged author of the conspiracy and theories abound. The coincidence of his assassination with the 'Katanga gendarme' incursion into Zaire fuelled speculation about international dimensions. The atmosphere of endemic conspiracy helped lend plausibility to quite diverse explanations.

The reshaping of the Congo political economy to conform more closely to ideology raised two critical obstacles. The first was the mediocre performance of the public sector. The new socialist cement, textiles and matches factories were a disappointment. In arrogant contrast, the French logging industries continued to cream off forest produce. The ineffective state corporations required annual subsidies of four thousand million CFA francs;[52] Ngouabi imputed their shortcomings to 'imperialism allied to the apathy of administrators . . . corruption and embezzlement'.[53]

A second, and related, difficulty arose from the rapid expansion of the state itself. The civil service and the state corporations each hired one-quarter of all wage employees. Pressure to employ school-leavers led to over-staffing. The state thus found itself confronted with a constant fiscal crisis to meet its wage bill. The inflationary expedient of printing money was excluded since the state had no central bank under its own control and was a member in the Central African common currency zone. All energies of statecraft were thus consumed by the search for revenue. This gave leverage to potential investors. Offshore oil was the most important bait, but hope was also placed in a potash-mine.

The health and stability of an incumbent régime became increasingly tributary to its oil revenues. Some oil was produced in the 1960s, and substantial production began in 1972 in time to benefit from the oil price surge of 1973–1974. This brought relative harmony to the political sphere. Subsequently the price dropped, and production levels were not sustained; by 1976, the state was back in its fiscal impasse. Factional conflict increased until the 1979 price surge. Output again increased and brightened the political atmosphere.

The pattern of politics in Congo, and the ideological options of successive régimes, can be understood only in the context of the pressures to which the society was subject. The politicised youth culture, the weight of the urban sector, the overdeveloped state apparatus, the visible persistence of much of the colonial economy and the new multi-national mineral sector: all of these subjected any leadership to intense and contradictory pressures. The peculiar blend of revolutionary ideology and supple policy is a subtle form of statecraft which has transcended the endless web of factional intrigue and brought positive returns to the society. Whatever the flaws of the successive régimes since 1963, a moment's retrospective glimpse provides a reassuring perspective. The crass exploitation and brutalities of the concessionary companies, the institutional privilege reserved to the foreign estate in the years of reformed colonialism, the lamentable inadequacy of the Youlou neo-colonial régime, all suffice to convince that the present is at the very least a marked improvement on the past.

52 Rosberg and Callaghy, *Socialism in Sub-Saharan Africa*, p. 260.
53 *Africa Comtemporary Record 1976–77*, p. B493.

CAMEROUN: NATIONAL UNITY AND THE LIBERAL ECONOMY

Among the equatorial states Cameroun stands out for its stability. For two entire decades after independence, President Ahmadou Ahidjo ruled. Cameroun lacks the Western paraphernalia of weekly pulse-taking opinion polls, but the apogee of national consensus behind the Ahidjo formula was probably reached in the earlier rather than the later 1970s. The persistence of the régime stands out, along with its relative absence of articulated opposition. Small exiled factions in Europe maintained that the apparent solidity of the régime reflected only the effectiveness of the police and the prisons. A pronounced continuity in the bureaucratic and authoritarian style of governance which had characterised the colonial state did maintain the instruments of repression. Repression alone, however, is not a satisfying explanation for the relative effectiveness of the Ahidjo régime.

In 1960 the future of Cameroun seemed singularly precarious. UPC guerrillas operated not far from the capital. Ahidjo had an uncertain electoral majority, and some bitter enemies. The country had only a moderately prosperous agricultural base, and no immediate prospect of mineral wealth. And yet the Ahidjo régime was able over time to consolidate its power, to create by patient manoeuvre and negotiation a single national party, to incorporate West Cameroun, and to manage competently the country's development within a market-economy framework.

The two most obvious challenges were to overcome the cultural divisions within the country and to eliminate the UPC guerrilla insurrection. The cleavages confronting the polity were of several orders. The Muslim far north, at the eastern end of the Fulani state-building zone of the nineteenth century, was much less affected by the colonial economy and its agencies of social mobility than was the south. The impending end of colonial rule brought inevitable fears of domination by the mainly Christian élite of the south. Within the south, a gulf of distrust and suspicion separated the highly mobile Bamileke from all other groups. The Bamileke, as traders, teachers and administrative personnel, were found everywhere in southern Cameroun, and the visibility of their success was jarring. In Douala, at the time of independence, Bamileke were believed to account for 70 per cent of the professional posts, 30 per cent of the civil service positions, 60 per cent of the traders, and 80 per cent of the artisans.[54]

The integration of two territories with four decades of different colonial experience added yet another strain. The former French mandate of East Cameroun was by far the largest of the two components; yet special accommodation had to be made for West Cameroon, with its attachment

54 Johnson, *The Cameroon Federation*, p. 50.

to English as the administrative language. As colonial political party development occurred in different frameworks, the party systems were entirely separate.

The UPC uprising had begun in 1955. Initially the major activity was in the Bassa area, near the coast, but after the 1958 death of the major *maquis* leader, Ruben Um Nyobe, action there had gradually diminished. Thereafter, the UPC guerrilla movement was a fragmented and decentralised set of bands, concentrated in Bamileke country. Their activity consisted of sporadic attacks against local government installations. Independence eliminated their most important argument, and the guerrilla UPC was a fading force by 1960. Its decline, however, is much clearer in retrospect than it was at the moment of independence.[55]

At the hour of independence Ahidjo presided over a very disparate coalition. His own party, the Union Camerounaise, had won only 34 per cent of the votes in East Cameroun in the final pre-independence balloting of 1956. It was an alliance of groups representing the five northern districts, and had no base in the south. Five other parties competed for the southern vote, including a legal wing of the UPC which in 1959 broke away from the guerrilla and exile factions. The tenuous situation of Ahidjo in the early independence months was demonstrated by the large (40 per-cent) negative vote in February 1960 on a constitutional referendum. There appeared to be a very real possibility that Ahidjo would be defeated in legislative elections to be held in April 1960.[56]

Ahidjo quickly demonstrated the skills which made him a commanding figure for the next two decades. With a finely tuned combination of coercion and co-option, he progressively unified the political realm. The UPC, already shaken by factional dispute and military defeats, was offered amnesty and legality, for those willing to abandon the *maquis*. Those declining the invitation were subjected to intensified military pressure, with continuing French assistance. In November 1960, the exiled leader, Felix Moumié, was poisoned in Geneva, an assassination in which many saw the hand of French intelligence services. In October 1961, after unification with West Cameroon, the remnants of the UPC *maquis* lost a sanctuary across a border which had bisected their zone of ethnic support. By 1964, the guerrilla resistance had all but ended.

On the political front, the Union Camerounaise reinforced its leading role in the April 1960 voting, raising its percentage of the ballot from 34 to 45 per cent. The several southern parties in East Cameroun began to rally to the Ahidjo movement. At the next parliamentary election the Union

55 Richard Joseph, *Radical Nationalism in Cameroun*, Oxford, 1977.
56 Useful sources on post-independence Cameroun politics include Jean-François Bayart, 'L'Union Nationale Camerounaise', *Revenue Française de Science Politique*, xx, 4, Aug. 1970, 681–716; Victor T. LeVine, *The Cameroon Federal Republic*, Ithaca, N.Y., 1971; Marcel Prouzet, *Le Cameroun*, 1974.

Camerounaise swept 93·5 per cent of the East. The process of political unification was then completed in 1966, when the main surviving party in English-speaking West Cameroon accepted fusion into a single national party, the Union Nationale Camerounaise. Although initially the UNC preserved the fiction of being a coalition of political groups, its component parts soon dissolved. A parallel process occurred on the legal front. Though West Cameroon had been induced to accept unification on the promise of a federal structure, in 1972 a new constitution was promulgated which transformed the country into a unitary state. As one observer put it, 'Cameroun, torn by civil war, threatened with dislocation, surrendered itself to [Ahidjo], as Rome had given itself over to a dictator'.[57]

In the first two decades of independence, the stability and unity of Cameroun thus hinged upon the talents of its president. Taciturn, withdrawn, quite lacking in personal charisma, Ahidjo had initially seemed an unlikely candidate for such a role. Yet these very qualities, joined to a prudent statesmanship and canny political sense, proved to be elements of strength. His father was a Fulani of middling status, and his mother was from a non-Islamic northern group. Because he was not tied to the Fulani aristocratic or clerical class, he could be relatively acceptable to the south. Because he had northern antecedents, even if he lacked high customary status, he could quieten Fulani fears of southern domination.

The subdued and cautious policies pursued by the Ahidjo régime mirrored the political personality of the president. While retaining the reality of close cooperation with France, Ahidjo eschewed the image. Doctrinal debates on development held little attraction. The state-controlled market economy of the post-war era persisted without major alteration. Patient, prudent, consistent economic policy within a stable framework paid undeniable dividends. While Cameroun could not boast the growth rates of oil- and mineral-rich countries, diversified agricultural expansion brought a modest but significant improvement in well-being to the rural areas. The neo-colonial ransom paid for capitalist development was less obvious in Cameroun than in Gabon or Ivory Coast. The European population did not increase after 1960, and foreign enterprise and technicians did not become so conspicuous.

GABON: MINERALS AND MULTI-NATIONALS

Gabon also followed the capitalist path, and shared with Cameroun a record of political stability. In other respects the contrasts were more striking than the similarities. With a *per-capita* income over $3 000, Gabon had become a remarkably wealthy state by 1976.[58] The aggregate figures

---

57 Bayart, 'L'Union Nationale Camerounaise', 715.
58 *World Bank Atlas*, 1978, p. 14.

conceal, however, an economy whose wealth is heavily concentrated in a mineral sector under multi-national management, and whose rural sector stagnated. The mineral boom, which made Gabon an extroverted economy, with a revenue-rich state and an impoverished peasantry, really began only after independence. The old colonial economy had been based upon forest products. Oil production started in 1957, and became substantial only in the 1960s. Manganese ore was first exported in 1962, and uranium mines went into operation in 1961.

A curious form of political economy emerged from the mineral bonanza. The mines and oil-wells themselves were models of the enclave economy. Few Gabonese were employed in these operations, and their link with the local economy was small. The raw materials left the country unprocessed. The state, however, received unusually high royalties and export taxes. State revenues expanded ten-fold between 1960 and 1973; by 1970, Gabon state expenditures were more than twice those of Togo, which had four times the population.[59] The affluence of the state explained the political stability that Gabon enjoyed in the 1970s. The state could afford generous treatment for its public servants and political cadres. It could also ensure basic amenities, particularly schools and dispensaries, in the rural sector. In the 1970s, the régime of Omar Bongo sustained its political monopoly without significant challenge.

Potential opposition was well aware of the formidable political resources which affluence placed in the hands of the incumbents, and of the French support for the régime. With its commitment to nuclear energy, France placed high strategic value on Gabonese uranium, not to mention its financial stake in petroleum and manganese ventures. Gabon had a defence treaty with France, which maintained an intervention force in the country. In 1964 President Léon M'ba was overthrown, and French troops intervened at once to reinstate him. Throughout the 1970s there was no doubt that the same service would be provided to President Bongo if required. Confronted with such obstacles, opposition was a singularly unpromising form of participation, when contrasted to the attractions of cooperation.

Political quiescence was not always so marked. In the 1950s, when electoral politics were introduced, competition was intense before Léon M'ba emerged as the dominant figure. In his youth, M'ba had been considered a dangerous agitator and rusticated to Ubangi-Shari for thirteen years. In 1946, he briefly participated in the Libreville Groupe d'Etudes Communistes,[60] but by 1960 he had developed close ties with the French.

Until 1963, the M'ba government continued to face pressure from its pre-independence adversaries, led by Jean Aubame. The 1964 military

59 De Schaetgen, 'L'Economie gabonaise', 67–94.
60 Brian Weinstein, *Nation-Building on the Ogooué*, Cambridge, Mass., 1966, p. 170.

coup, which briefly installed Aubame in power, and the French intervention which crushed it, were crucial turning points. Gabon soon thereafter became a one-party state. By the time of the death of M'ba in 1967, visible opposition had all but disappeared. Bongo, a hand-picked successor, assumed power without incident, and faced little subsequent challenge.

TYRANNY AND ITS COSTS: CENTRAL AFRICAN REPUBLIC AND EQUATORIAL GUINEA

The Central African Republic and Equatorial Guinea illustrate another, quite different, experience since independence. In both instances, the vagaries of politics placed the fortunes of the state in the hands of singularly deficient leaders. By a relentless logic, as the inadequacies of the president became manifest, so his political base narrowed. In a downward spiral fuelled by paranoia, the ruler lashed out with increasingly capricious force at an ever-growing pool of enemies. In the process, the public purposes of the state all but disappeared. The government apparatus served only the immediate whims of the leader. What remained of the perverted state was little more than a predator upon society. Public calamities on this scale were quite unanticipated at the time of independence. The stagnant polity had been foreseen, but not the terrifying tyranny which emerged in Equatorial Guinea.

The Central African Republic of Jean-Bedel Bokassa fell well short of Equatorial Guinea as an exemplar of decay. Initially Bokassa's power seizure was welcomed, and his first years in office showed some positive results. When he took over on New Year's Day 1966, the Dacko régime was both politically and economically bankrupt. Bokassa held out the hope of a new beginning. For a number of months, the technocrats in the administration were given a free hand, and cotton, coffee and diamond production appeared to be on the rise. However, the contradictory caprice of Bokassa began to cast its shadow over the polity.

Tragedy was inscribed in Bokassa's childhood. His father was killed by the French, and his mother committed suicide. He was then raised by Catholic missionaries. Bokassa had twenty-three years' service in the French army, with combat experience in Indo-China; he rose to the rank of captain and won fifteen decorations. Even as Chief of State, he proudly maintained his French citizenship, conscientiously performing his civic duty to participate in the presidential elections. He was thus able to offer his ultimately embarrassed patron, President Giscard d'Estaing, not only generous tributary offerings of diamonds, but also his vote. From this background one may understand some of his peculiar traits: his extraordinary dedication to France, his constantly reaffirmed desire to embellish ties of personal clientage with Paris, and the extravagant replication of French imperial splendour at his Napoleonic-style self-coronation as 'Emperor' in 1977. At a cost of $22 million, or one-third of the 1977 budget, French rococo ceremonial was reproduced, from the caparisoned horses and vintage wines to the ermine robes and gold-inlaid throne. Napoleon, after all, had once been a corporal.

The utter inadequacy of Bokassa as a ruler had become clear long before the comic-opera coronation. By the late 1960s, plot and conspiracy were suspected on all sides. In 1969, he quite suddenly executed his number two man, Colonel Banza. In a fit of pique over inadequate deference and subsidies from Paris, he suddenly expelled French technicians in the same year and brought diamond-mining to a halt. 'Scientific socialism' was discovered as a sacred text, and a top-level mission dispatched to Moscow to explore what capital returns might flow from this ideological conversion. It returned empty-handed, and scientific socialism vanished as quickly as it had appeared.[61]

In the 1970s, the capricious rule of Bokassa took a growing toll of state and society. As the governmental apparatus became demoralised, state services eroded. In turn, the productive infrastructure dwindled, as cotton and coffee production began to fall. Cotton output dropped from a record 58 700 tons in 1969–1970 to 10 300 tons in 1977–1978; coffee slipped from 12 600 tons in 1964–1965 to 10 000 tons in 1977–1978. A substantial fraction of the diamond output passed directly into the hands of Bokassa, to finance his imperial household. After the coronation, the Emperor spent much of his time in a palace retreat some distance from the capital. His armed forces were converted into an imperial guard, and were primarily recruited from his own Ngbaka ethnic group. Functionaries feared taking important decisions, which might bring down upon them the unpredictable and possibly lethal wrath of the ruler. Yet the Emperor had such a limited understanding of a modern political economy that the state was constantly at risk to some costly new whim.

It was finally the schoolchildren who set in motion the train of events that swept away the Bokassa régime. In January 1979, a sudden decree appeared requiring all school pupils to purchase new school uniforms bearing Bokassa's name and effigy. It was widely known that the Emperor's family owned the textile plant supplying the uniforms. At the same time, an increasingly severe erosion in the real incomes of even the relatively well-paid echelons of the bureaucracy made this imposition unendurable. The children dared what their elders could only secretly admire, and erupted in street demonstrations. The Ngbaka imperial guard retaliated brutally, and many children were killed. In April 1979, several dozen adolescent demonstrators were murdered in prison, with Bokassa personally participating in some of the shootings. The Ngbaka quarter of

61 Kalck, *Central African Republic*, pp. 167–74.

Babgui became subject to nocturnal assaults with such rudimentary weapons as spears and lances. The troops redoubled their vengeance.[62]

The shock wave produced by these atrocities soon engulfed the Emperor. While African diplomatic etiquette normally precluded public criticism of other independent African states, the powerful evidence that Bokassa was not only responsible for, but a participant in, these abhorrent deeds internationalised the issue. A commission of African jurists was constituted to investigate the tragedy and was chaired by a Senegalese magistrate. In the summer of 1979 it published a stinging report which, beneath the antiseptic formulations imposed by protocol, was an unmistakable indictment of the Emperor. Gifts and fervent pledges of francophonic fealty were now of no avail. France stepped in to depose Bokassa in October 1979, and reinstalled his predecessor, Dacko. CAR was not as devastated as Uganda or Equatorial Guinea. None the less, the damage to polity and society was extensive, and recovery would take years, even if a régime so visibly imposed by Paris could somehow escape the blemish of its origins and achieve a degree of legitimacy.

The costs of unrestrained personal rule by a sanguinary tyrant were most fully exposed in Equatorial Guinea. This micro-state, of less than 11 000 square miles, was utterly devastated by the eleven-year dictatorship of Francisco Macías Nguema. At the time of independence, it had achieved a modest prosperity. On Bioko Island, cocoa was grown on Spanish-owned plantations worked by Nigerian contract labour. Forest products were exploited on the mainland where 89 per cent of the population dwelled.

Macías Nguema had served the Spanish administration as a clerk, and received a secondary education in Spanish schools. A tranquil neo-colonial relationship was envisaged, with the small, predominantly mainland African élite accommodated in the political structure, and the Spanish forestry companies and cocoa plantations flourishing as before.[63] These comfortable assumptions were soon shattered. Macías Nguema as president was quite a different individual than when a clerk. He became obsessed by suspicions of conspiracy, and the execution block and the dungeon became the prime instruments of statecraft. Within a few years, ten of twelve members of his cabinet had been liquidated, and two-thirds of parliamentarians disappeared. Nor was terror confined to the upper echelons of society; during his decade in power, an estimated 50 000 persons, out of a total population of 280 000, are believed to have been killed, and another 50 000 fled into exile in neighbouring Cameroun and Gabon.[64]

The constitutional institutions hastily erected just before independence

---

62 For thoroughly documented accounts, see *Le Monde*, 22 Sept. 1979, 25 Feb. 1980.
63 René Pelissier, *Etudes hispano-guinéenes*, Paris, 1969; Suzanne Cronje, *Equatorial Guinea: the Forgotten Dictatorship*, London, 1976; *Le Monde*, 29–30 Aug. 1979.
64 *West Africa*, 3294, 8 Sept. 1980, 1731; *Africa Contemporary Record*, 1978–9, pp. B551–7.

disappeared at once. The apparatus of the colonial state shrivelled not long afterwards. Most of the skilled personnel, Spanish and Guinean, departed. What remained of the state was a quite personal instrument, whose inner core was linked to Macías Nguema by kinship ties. The palace guard was augmented in the 1970s by a Cuban detachment. Macías Nguema also received some Soviet support, in return for port facilities to service the Soviet surveillance and trawling fleets and unrestricted fishing rights.

These were not the only power resources. Lacking institutions, Macías Nguema turned to manipulating the occult. He fostered with apparent success the popular belief that he had supernatural powers; one version held that he could transform himself into a lion and consume any transgressor.[65] In the final era of the régime, Christian rites were forbidden and the sole authorised cult was adulation of the president. When he was finally overthrown in 1979 by his nephew, Obiang Nguema Mbasaka, he was sentenced to death, but local troops refused to shoot him. The execution had to be carried out by Moroccan soldiers, brought in by the new régime as its own palace guard. The Cuban guards had been expelled in 1977 by Macías Nguema in a fit of rage because they had ridiculed the magical rites he performed.[66]

By the end, the decomposition of the state was well-nigh total. Civil servants and security forces were no longer paid. State receipts from the dwindling sales of cocoa and timber went directly into the presidential treasury. Cocoa exports had shrivelled from 40 000 to under 4 000 tons annually, while timber production dropped from 300 000 to 50 000 tons.

The Macías years saw a holocaust. The recuperative powers of a society thus devastated would be tested in the 1980s. With an economy in ruins and its pool of national talent drained, the successor régime turned to the outside for survival. A praetorian guard of 200 Moroccans provided the inner core of security for the state. Links were re-established with the former metropole; and in 1980 250 Spanish civil servants played key roles in all ministries.[67] Recently discovered offshore oil held some promise of new revenues, but years would be required to pay the ransom of the Macías era.

THE RISE AND DECLINE OF THE MOBUTIST STATE IN ZAIRE

By far the most important of the equatorial states in size, population and resource potential was Zaire. Its pivotal significance was metaphorically expressed by the observation President Mobutu borrowed from Frantz Fanon: 'Africa is shaped like a pistol, with Zaire as its trigger housing.'[68]

65 *West Africa*, 3294, 8 Sept. 1980, 1731.
66 *Ibid.*
67 *Africa Confidential*, xxi, 15 Oct. 1980, 6.
68 Mobutu Sese Seko, speech to the UN General Assembly, 4 Oct. 1973.

The scale of Zaire gave rise to a widely shared conviction that the country was endowed by destiny for leadership. Global strategies in West and East alike perceived much higher stakes in the political outcome of decolonisation in Zaire than in the smaller states. Periods of instability and crisis gave rise to extensive international involvement.

The first five years of independence were dominated by the immediate dislocations of a failed decolonisation. The First Republic was then swept away on 24 November 1965, when the army high command installed Mobutu Sese Seko[69] as president. Until 1973, the new régime appeared in many respects to have achieved a striking success in bringing stability and strength to an enfeebled state. After 1974, however, the Second Republic also became engulfed in crises, although ones of a different character. The pattern of events in Zaire held little warrant for the premise that history is an unfolding design of human progress.

The initial political breakdown in 1960 had four interrelated phases: the army mutiny, the flight of expatriate functionaries, the secession of the mineral-rich regions, and the collapse of the constitution and the political coalition in Kinshasa. All occurred within two months of independence. The consequences were many. The state lost effective control over regional administration, over the security apparatus, over much of the fiscal base and over mechanisms for legitimate adjustment of political conflict. External involvement was far-reaching. A UN peace-keeping force was the most potent armed body in the country until 1964. The former metropole, the major powers of West and East, and the mining interests, all intervened as well.[70]

The mutiny of the army against its exclusively European officer corps began on 5 July at a garrison near Kinshasa. Owing to the excellent communications network, and to the atmosphere of hostility and distrust, the insurrection of the ranks spread like wildfire throughout the country. Within a few days, nearly all the white officers had fled, except in Shaba. The new Lumumba government desperately tried to contain the situation by placing the army in the hands of some former non-commissioned officers. It was at this point that Mobutu, a journalist in Lumumba's party, and who had served from 1950 to 1957 as a non-commissioned officer, became Chief of Staff.

The flight of European state employees followed at once. The dissolution of the colonial army and the pent-up racial frustrations led to a

---

69 In 1971 all Zairians were required to abandon the Christian forenames which usually accompanied mission baptism in favour of postnames of Zairian origin; the new names are utilised here.

70 The most valuable single source for the early years of independence is the series of documentary yearbooks published by the Centre de Recherches et d'Informations Socio-Politiques from 1959 through to 1967 (*Congo 1959* to *Congo 1967*); for a comprehensive bibliography, see Edouard Bustin, 'Congo-Kinshasa: Guide Bibliographique', *Cahiers du CEDAF*, 3–4, 1971.

number of assaults and more widespread public humiliation of whites by mutinous soldiers. These incidents multiplied into an avalanche of lurid rumours, provoking a psychosis of panic. Only in Shaba did most European functionaries remain at their posts. To grasp the impact of this exodus, it is important to recall that, on the eve of independence, the public service had 10 000 executives of whom only three were Zairian.[71] The state, at the hour of its gravest crisis, was suddenly stripped of its senior cadres.

In the face of this dislocation of the pillars of the state, and of its administration and security forces, the richest province, Shaba, declared its separation from the republic on 11 July 1960. The European community in this Copperbelt region had long agitated for autonomy from the centralising claims of Kinshasa. The provincial African leadership, representing the southern part of Shaba, had its own resentments against the social hegemony of the Kasai Luba in the province. In addition, the mining giant, Union Minière du Haut Katanga, was fearful of the vaguely radical nationalism of Lumumba and his followers. The disarray elsewhere in Zaire offered the opportunity to put into operation a secession scheme which had been contemplated for some time.

The Shaba region accounted for about half of state revenue and 70 per cent of mineral production; its loss appeared a mortal blow to Zairian hopes for a prosperous and expanding economy. In the following month, there was another severe setback, when the diamond–mining region of Kasai, homeland of the Kasai Luba, also declared its independence. In this instance, separation was triggered off by the exclusion of the main Luba political movement from both national and provincial power. Luba fear was accentuated by widespread physical assaults on migrants who had taken up residence in other parts of Zaire during the colonial period. Luba who believed themselves persecuted on all sides saw Kasai secession as the price of survival.

These sudden and explosive events sent shock waves throughout the world. Elsewhere in Africa, the Shaba secession appeared as a frontal assault by imperial interests on African nationalism. The transparent role of European interests and of the mining company in abetting the secession was ample proof that sordid manoeuvres were afoot whose ultimate aim was the subversion of African independence. Defeat of the secession was a life or death matter, not only for Zaire, but for Africa.

Political breakdown in Zaire became complete at the beginning of September, when the laborious compromise by which Kasavubu and Lumumba shared authority as president and prime minister came unhinged. Kasavubu suddenly dismissed Lumumba on 5 September, opening a constitutional crisis with Lumumba's fluctuating parliamentary

71 INCIDI, *Staff Problems in Tropical and Subtropical Countries*, Brussels, 1961, p. 174.

majority. Ten days later, army Chief of Staff Mobutu 'neutralised' both figures and installed a caretaker régime. In this period of total confusion, Kasavubu and Mobutu received decisive support from the American intelligence service. Soviet efforts to provide aid to the Lumumba group proved ineffectual. The key UN personnel on the spot at the moment of crisis favoured the Kasavubu side. Lumumba was placed under arrest. By the beginning of November his followers had abandoned hope of immediately regaining power in Kinshasa, and regrouped in their regional bastion at Kisangani. Lumumba himself made a spectacular escape, but was intercepted *en route* to Kisangani. The Kinshasa authorities delivered him to Shaba, where he was murdered in January 1961.[72]

The Lumumbist group, which believed that its leader had been illegally stripped of the premiership, established its own government in Kisangani and claimed to be the legitimate authority for the country. A fraction of the unruly army rallied to them, and by early 1961 a loose Kisangani authority was established over the north-eastern quadrant of the country. This rival Lumumbist government based its appeal both upon constitutional arguments[73] and on the conviction that the true heritage of nationalism was preserved in their régime. These claims enjoyed support from the socialist bloc, and the radical camp of African states.

Thus at the beginning of 1961 the prospects for Zaire seemed bleak indeed. The country was divided into four fragments: two, Kinshasa and Kisangani, affirmed that their authority covered the entire territory; and two, the Luba state and Shaba, asserted their independence. The Lumumba murder left a legacy of bitterness among his following, and became a *cause célèbre* throughout the world.[74] Kinshasa was supported by the West, Kisangani by anti-imperial Third World and communist states, and Shaba by the mining interests and by some circles in Belgium. The United Nations, which held the ring through its peace-keeping force, was given an ambiguous mandate. The United Nations tended to regard Kasavubu as the primary repository of constitutional legitimacy, but its daily policy was affected by an on-going political struggle within the organisation in New

72 On the UN role, see especially Rajeshwar Dayal, *Mission for Hammarskjold*, Princeton, N.J., 1976; also Cathryn Hoskyns, *The Congo since Independence*, Oxford, 1965; Arthur M. House, *The UN in the Congo*, Washington, D.C., 1978. On American policy, see Steven Weissman, *American Foreign Policy in the Congo 1960–1964*, Ithaca, N.Y., 1974.

73 Kasavubu based his action on Article 22 of the provisional constitution, which empowered the president to 'name and revoke' the prime minister. Although this may seem clear enough, the act at once plunged the country into a constitutional impasse, as a prime minister required a parliamentary majority, which only Lumumba could obtain at that juncture.

74 For documentation on the CIA role in plotting the assassination of Lumumba in the fall of 1960, though not performing the actual murder, see US Congress, Senate, Select Committee to Study Government Operations with Respect to Intelligence Activities, *Interim Report: Alleged Assassination Plots Involving Foreign Leaders*, 94th Congress 1st Session, 20 Nov. 1975.

York. Zaire itself was thus splintered and helpless, at the vortex of an international combat between global forces for which the country was simply one arena among many.

Over the next two years, Zaire edged away from the brink of destruction. In August 1961, a compromise régime reunited the Kinshasa and Kisangani governments under Cyrille Adoula. The Luba state was reabsorbed into the national polity, and there remained only the Shaba secession to eliminate. After indecisive negotiations and manoeuvring, the United Nations finally subdued the secessionist régime by force in January 1963. The threat to survival appeared to fade.

One of the costs of reunification was a wholesale fragmentation of the six colonial provinces. The process was governed by a large measure of ethnic self-determination and the personal ambitions of local faction leaders. Although the creation of new provinces in 1962 and 1963 momentarily diminished the intensity of regional conflict, the twenty-one new units were soon paralysed in their turn by factional battles.

The social peace of 1963 proved short-lived. The Lumumbist faction felt itself short-changed in the Adoula government, and went into opposition. In August 1963 a change of régime in Brazzaville opened the possibility of sanctuary, and some of them crossed the river to launch a revolutionary challenge to the Adoula régime. Others, particularly Pierre Mulele in Kwilu district, began to organise rural insurrection. By March 1964, armed rebellion had spread to the border regions of the eastern frontier.

By 1964, the UN peace-keeping force was being withdrawn, and the insurgents faced only the poorly disciplined national army and its demoralised and disaffected units. The Mulele *maquis* was contained in Kwilu, but rebel bands in the east snowballed as the national army crumbled without resistance. In August 1964, the Lumumbist fief of Kisangani was seized, and a revolutionary republic proclaimed. The insurgent forces drove government forces out of approximately one-third of the national territory.

The insurrection was not a single movement, but several simultaneous revolts loosely united in their attachment to the symbols of the Lumumbist heritage. The structures were loose-knit, and the revolutionary régime in Kisangani never really governed its domains. It reflected a profound disappointment with the reality of independence, and with the betrayal of campaign promises by the political class. The youths who rallied to the insurgent bands externalised a bitter anger towards Kinshasa, politicians, civil servants, teachers, and their Belgian and American external allies. In captured towns, where concentrations of white-collar personnel were found, thousands of executions occurred. The rebellions were a vast, turbulent, formless social protest which applied spontaneous and violent sanctions to those symbolising the perceived evils of an independence which had failed. A 'second independence' was needed to right these wrongs, but the fragmented structures and factionalised leadership of the rebellions made this dream impossible.

The shock of the rebellions brought dramatic change in Kinshasa. Adoula was ousted in July 1964 in favour of Moise Tshombe, who had led the Shaba secessionist state from 1960 to 1963. In exile, Tshombe had paved the way for his spectacular return by fostering the impression that he could end the rebellions by negotiation. Remarkably, he initially enjoyed enthusiastic favour in Kinshasa.[75]

Tshombe had no success in his overtures to the insurgents. He turned to a military solution, drawing on his Shaba strategy of recruiting white mercenaries for his army. Mercenary units, and some Belgian military personnel, were hastily assembled. By September 1964 columns were mounted to recapture the lost terrain. The national army, with its mercenary auxiliaries, advanced toward the insurgent capital. The rebels retaliated by interning several hundred Belgian and American hostages. On 24 November 1964 this led to a partly successful Belgian–American parachute rescue operation in Kisangani.[76] On the same day, the mercenary-led column reached Kisangani, and the rebel leaders fled into exile. This proved a fatal blow to the insurrections, though insurgent pockets remained for years, and one continued resistance on the eastern frontier into the 1980s.

The Belgian–American intervention in Kisangani provoked a new surge of anger in Africa. The operation was judged to be an arrogant interference in Africa. It was noted that foreign white victims of the civil war were the main objects of concern. The episode was further seen as a Western salvage of Tshombe, the symbolic leader of the Shaba secession and accomplice in Lumumba's murder. After the Kisangani affair, significant external support began to flow to the rebels from the Soviet Union, China, Algeria and Egypt, passing through Sudan and Tanzania. In 1965, the legendary Ernesto 'Che' Guevara spent several months with 200 Cuban combat veterans fighting alongside the Zairian insurgents.[77]

The rebellions, though ultimately unsuccessful, revealed the fragility of the First Republic's institutions and the weakness of the political order. The national fabric was further threatened in 1965 by a bitter presidential struggle between Kasavubu and Tshombe. A new 1964 constitution required that parliament and the provincial assemblies designate a new president in 1965. In the fluid mosaic of factions and parties, each candidate

75 On the Tshombe experience, see Ian Colvin, *The Rise and Fall of Moise Tshombe*, London, 1968; Moise Tshombe, *Quinze mois de gouvernement au Congo*, Paris, 1966.
76 About one hundred of approximately one thousand hostages were killed during the rescue operation; *Congo 1964*, Brussels, 1965, p. 410.
77 Maurice Halpern, in John Seiler (ed.), *Southern Africa since the Portuguese Coup*, Boulder, Colo., 1980, p. 31; Guevara told an interviewer shortly before his death in 1967 in Bolivia: 'The human element failed. There was no will to fight. The leaders are corrupt. In a word, nothing could be done.'

had enough votes to block the other. This impasse provided the pretext for the army high command to install General Mobutu as president.

Parliament was summoned to ratify the *coup*. By unanimous vote, it surrendered itself to the proposed new order. Implicit intimidation played some part in their docile submission, but this was far from the only factor. The harrowing experiences of the First Republic had persuaded a broad spectrum of Zairian opinion that their political order was fundamentally flawed. With the powerful and centralised colonial state as their point of comparative reference, the élite saw the weakness of the post-independence state as an insuperable obstacle to development. The proliferation of provinces, most of them paralysed, was generally conceded to be a failure. The high cost of heavily politicised ethnicity was evident to all. This was blamed on the multiplication of parties, whose leaders found ethnic affinity the most efficient basis for creating clients. For those in white-collar strata, the potential for class violence demonstrated by the rebellions was terrifying. Many had been forced to flee for their lives, or to hide in the forests for weeks on end.

In the first five years of Zairian independence the damage to the economy was substantial. Although the mines and large European enterprises continued operation, rural marketing networks were hard hit. Wage employment and national production declined. Only a relatively small group of bureaucrats and politicians, who had won sudden promotion from modest clerical posts to well-remunerated leadership roles, gained real benefits from independence.

In the same years a high order of external involvement in Zairian affairs had become entrenched. International participation in Zairian affairs was firstly a political phenomenon. Hammarskjöld had believed that the United Nations was uniquely suited to benevolent, disinterested intervention in situations of turmoil. Although the UN role was in many respects creditable, the Zaire experience shattered the vision of the United Nations as suited to such ambitious tasks. In addition to its political concerns, Belgium had $1 billion of investment to protect in Zaire. The other major actors – the United States, France, Britain, the Soviet Union – had few economic stakes of consequence at that stage. Zaire was above all the unwitting arena for yet one more episode in the global cold war.

Most Zairians came to view the First Republic as a veritable Hobbesian state of nature. In justifying his power seizure, Mobutu invoked the widespread currency of the term 'Congolisation' to connote chaos and anarchy. If generalised disorder and insecurity were to be seen as the most critical problem, then the Hobbesian remedy of a Leviathan state becomes perfectly comprehensible. Using the colonial state heritage of centralised, bureaucratic, authoritarian rule, Mobutu promised a new order founded upon a strong, unitary, depoliticised régime. Such a project initially commanded overwhelming assent.

The first step was to dismantle the political structures of the First Republic. The thirty-nine parliamentary parties were suspended, and ultimately dissolved. The number of provinces was progressively reduced to eight, and the chief officers were converted from premiers, representing local assembly majority, into prefects who served at presidential pleasure. All autonomy was removed from the provinces which became, as in colonial times, simply administrative subdivisions.

When politicians were cut off from their local base of support, a substantial fraction of them were co-opted into positions of authority in the new régime. At the political summit, Mobutu assigned important responsibilities to a circle of First Republic politicians who had played key roles in the Adoula years. Ranking military officers, through whom he maintained political control over the security forces, also had significant influence. So also did a group of young university-trained intellectuals, who entered the political arena only in the mid-1960s. Several who were reputed to hold radical views were brought on to the presidential staff. This skillfully executed process of co-option played no small part in the rapid consolidation of power by the Mobutu régime.[78]

In 1967, Mobutu took the first steps towards creating a new infrastructure for his régime. A new constitution was adopted, confirming the unitary state and vesting decisive power in the presidency. At the same time, a single national party, the Mouvement Populaire de la Révolution, was launched, as an instrument of fostering support and legitimacy.

On the economic front, a well-executed programme of stabilisation in 1967 finally brought hyperinflation under control, and gave some coherence to the disorderly budgetary procedures of the First Republic. By 1968 there was a new mood of optimism as the GNP exceeded the pre-independence levels for the first time. National finances appeared under control, a settlement of the colonial debt was within view, and the foreign trade account was in healthy balance.

In June 1967 the last major focus of political opposition was removed, when former Prime Minister Tshombe, who in exile maintained connections with the white mercenary leaders, was kidnapped. His small aircraft was pirated to Algeria where he died in prison two years later. Mercenary elements, supported by some troops from the Tshombe region of Shaba, mutinied in 1966, and again in 1967. They were finally eliminated from the armed forces.

The full acceptance of the Mobutu régime into the African family of nations was symbolised in 1967 by the convening of the Organisation of African Unity annual summit in Kinshasa. Mobutu had been controversial, because of his close American associations and his purported role in the

78 On the early Mobutu era, see Jean-Claude Willame, *Patrimonialism and Political Change in the Congo*, Stanford, Ca., 1972.

death of Lumumba. Most African states, however, were eager to see the 'Zaire crisis' removed from the OAU agenda, so that the more urgent problem of liberating the white redoubts to the south could be faced. Benediction was thus bestowed upon the new régime by the rest of Africa as an additional testimonial to the consolidation of its power.

The nature of the régime changed in important ways during the 1967–1974 period. The President increasingly achieved a personal ascendancy over the political class. The national figures who were at first the primary collaborators in the Mobutu entourage were systematically ousted. Some were permitted to construct lucrative commercial empires, although others went into exile. The once-assertive radical intellectuals on the presidential staff either accepted more subdued roles or went on assignments abroad. The council of ministers, and the ruling political bureau of the MPR, were shaken up at least once a year. Few persons remained for long periods in office. The crucial criteria were fidelity to the President and adroitness in the execution of the presidential will. There was no longer any possibility of an autonomous power base; high office was a transit hostel for courtiers.[79]

By the early 1970s power had become thoroughly personalist and patrimonial. All crucial decisions were made by the President. By the early 1970s, 20 per cent of the operating budget, and a larger fraction of the capital budget, was processed directly through the presidential account. The rewards for faithful service were very great. In 1974, a member of the political bureau earned over $5 000 per month in addition to generous perquisites. The opportunities for illicit gain were even greater, and were an integral part of the system.[80]

Official ideology reflected the growing personalisation. While the régime initially spoke of 'authentic Zairian nationalism' as its creed and invoked the Lumumbist heritage, by 1974 Mobutism was officially declared to be state doctrine. 'Deviationism' was a crime proscribed in the constitution. A revised constitution in 1974 gave textual expression to the remarkable concentration of personal power. The President was declared to be the chief presiding officer over the party, the executive, the legislature and the supreme court. In effect he appointed the members of all of these bodies, as well as officers of the regional administration.[81] The régime had reached its pinnacle. Its authority was unchallenged within and without.

---

79 For descriptions of the system by leading Zairian political figures, see Cléophas Kamitatu, *La Grande Mystification du Congo-Kinshasa*, Paris, 1971; Kamitatu Massamba (Cléophas), *Le Pouvoir au portée du peuple*, Paris, 1977; Daniel Monguya Mbenge, *Histoire secrète du Zaire*, Brussels, 1977.
80 Exhaustive documentation on corruption in Zaire is found in Gould, *Bureaucratic Corruption in the Third World*.
81 André Durieux, 'Nouvelle Réforme constitutionelle au Zaire', *Revue Juridique et Politique*, xxix, 2, April–June 1975, 163–81.

An era of rapid economic expansion appeared at hand. A rendezvous with abundance was pledged for 1980.

The strategy for achieving these grandiose visions was essentially founded upon the exploitation of energy and mineral resources with the assistance of foreign capital. The government had acted swiftly in 1966 to extinguish the claims of Belgian colonial corporations to mineral rights over nearly half the total land surface.[82] Zaire sought a diversified set of foreign investors: American, Japanese, German, French, British and others. The mineral endowment of Zaire was enticing. For a time, there was a stampede of purveyors of contracts, loans, consulting services and mining projects. The biggest scheme of all was a copper-mining venture which ultimately required over $1 billion of investment. This required an equivalent infrastructure investment by the Zairian state for a new dam on the lower Zaire at Inga, and a 1 700-kilometre direct-current transmission line to Shaba.[83]

The perils of this economic strategy lay in heavy reliance on foreign loans and contract services. Actual equity investment proved to be quite modest, and much of this went into assembly plants and small factories such as car assembly-lines, flour mills, tyre and textile plants, which operated on the basis of imported materials. Other actual investments – for example, by Gulf Oil – were made on terms exceptionally unfavourable to Zaire. In the 1970–1974 period, Zaire rapidly built up a huge external debt, and acquired plant heavily dependent upon imports. This was destined to operate below capacity whenever foreign exchange was in short supply.

The foreign capital base of the development programme in the economic sphere was accompanied by a somewhat differently conceived thrust for African political leadership. Mobutu sought to shed his image as an American client through a diplomacy oriented more to the Third World. His travel programme was remarkable. In 1973 he spent no fewer than 150 days out of the country, visiting twenty-six different states. There was a spectacular *rapprochement* with China in 1972, symbolised by a $100 million Peking credit line for rural development. Mobutu played an active role as mediator of African crises, and became more vocal on southern African issues.[84]

In its first decade, the Mobutu régime appeared to have a number of remarkable achievements to its credit. After 1974 the picture altered dramatically. The country was plunged into a profound crisis, accompanied by massive pauperisation, renewed hyperinflation, decomposition

82 *Echo de la Bourse*, Brussels, 24 Aug. 1970.
83 For illuminating detail on this project, see US Senate, Hearing before the Subcommittee on International Finance of the Committee on Banking, Housing, and Urban Affairs, 96th Congress, 1st Session, *U.S. Loans to Zaire*, 24 May 1979.
84 Crawford Young, in Seiler, *Southern Africa*, pp. 195–212; Jeanninck Odier, 'La Politique étrangère de Mobutu', *Revue Française d'Études Politiques Africaines*, cxx, Dec. 1975, 25–41.

of the state and demoralisation of the population. During the 1975–1980 period, there was a steady decline in the national income. Externally, the state was in virtual receivership, with a swiftly rising debt which by 1980 exceeded $5 billion. Zaire was reduced to periodic mendicant negotiations with its external creditors and with the International Monetary Fund, in order to secure momentary reprieves from international foreclosure. The dreams of prosperity and grandeur had become a nightmare of impoverishment and despair.

Some of the causes of Zaire's decay were external. In 1974–1975 the price of copper fell from a historic high to a nearly all-time low. Rising oil and food prices took their toll. In 1975, the best export route for Shaba minerals, the Benguela railway, was closed by the Angolan civil war. The exchange value of Zairian exports in 1975 was half what it had been in 1970.[85] These were tremendous blows to a developing economy.

Self-inflicted damage contributed to the scale of the crisis. On the external front Zaire, in partnership with the United States and South Africa, entered the Angolan civil war. It supported the FNLA, which had been closely tied to Kinshasa throughout the guerrilla years. Several Zairian battalions were committed to this campaign. After advancing close to Luanda, they were routed by Cuban and MPLA forces. This intervention not only demoralised the Zaire army, but cost Mobutu much of his hard-earned diplomatic status in Africa.

An effort in 1973–1975 to 'Zairianise' the economy by seizing the assets of foreign shopkeepers, of plantation owners and of a number of Belgian enterprises, quickly turned to disaster. The businesses affected were turned over to private Zairian 'acquirers'. The political class thus received, by patrimonial distribution, title to a broad swathe of the economy. This exercise was justified as 'economic independence', but those outside the privileged circle of beneficiaries viewed it as a sordid class action by the political bourgeoisie.[86] Worse, the 'acquirers' proved generally unable to manage their new enterprises, and a massive dislocation of the commercial economy coincided with the copper price-crash.

The crisis laid bare certain weaknesses of the Mobutu state. Internally, the patrimonial state had degenerated into institutionalised corruption. The diversion of public resources into private channels as a mechanism for sustaining the loyalty of subordinates permeated the system. The state required enormous resources to sustain itself, and consumed in 1974 no less than 59 per cent of the GNP. Yet in the later 1970s, its capacity effectively

85 Banque du Zaire, *Rapport Annuel*, 1979; International Bank for Reconstruction and Development, *Zaire*.
86 Schatzberg, *Politics and Class*, pp. 121–52; Michael G. Schatzberg, 'The State and the Economy: the "Radicalization of the Revolution" in Mobutu's Zaire', *Canadian Journal of African Studies*, xiv, 2, 1980, 239–57; Edward Kannyo, 'Political Power and Class-Formation in Zaire: the "Zairianization Measures, 1973–75"', Ph.D. thesis, Yale University, 1979.

to deliver public services declined.[87] Meanwhile, the country appeared locked externally in a hopeless cycle of debt and dependency. The copper and energy gamble of the early 1970s proved disastrous. Most of the projects for which the external debt had been incurred had slim prospects of generating enough revenue to relieve the crushing mortgage upon the future of the society.[88]

The Mobutu régime somehow survived, through a shrewd manipulation of the diplomacy of dependency, co-option and coercion. A growing world consciousness of global resource shortages gave new importance to Zairian cobalt and copper. Western economic interests increased their loans, contracts and investments. The strategic rivalry with the Soviet Union intensified after the Angolan civil war, and the Soviet–Cuban intervention in Ethiopia in 1978. Mobutu was thus able to present his régime as the sole alternative to chaos or worse. When remnants of the old 'Katanga gendarme' units invaded Shaba from Angolan bases in 1977 and 1978, foreign troops quickly came to the rescue. A widespread conviction took hold that the West was committed to maintaining Mobutu in power at all costs. With such powerful support, opposition seemed unavailing.

Internally, co-option remained a potent instrument. The capacity of the régime to salvage its erstwhile adversaries was quite exceptional. Each new list of ministers or political bureau members contained its dramatic surprise inclusion of personalities widely believed to be hostile to the régime. Coercion assured that no overt opposition within the country was visible. The external opponents, divided by personal rivalry and factional intrigue, found their ranks regularly depleted by those who, despairing of an effective challenge to the régime from Brussels or Paris, chose the path of cooperation.

FINAL REFLECTIONS

In a number of respects, the two decades of independence left a far more differentiated set of nation-states in northern Central Africa than one might have forecast in 1960. Although these states were subject to a common set of constraints in their interaction with international markets and with industrial powers, each was none the less a political galaxy of its own. The peculiar chemistry of each political arena yielded national configurations which appear quite distinctive: the institutionalised yet ambiguous scientific socialism of Congo; the surprisingly stable though authoritarian market economy of Ahidjo in Cameroun; the extroverted, mineral state of Gabon dominated by multi-nationals; the crippled giant of Zaire; the

87 For more extensive detail, see Young, 'Zaire: the unending crisis'.
88 The contributions to Gran, *Zaire*, offer a sombre assessment.

prostrate states of Central African Republic and Equatorial Guinea ravaged by personal tyrannies.

The experience of these two decades suggested several problems concerning their political evolution. There was, to begin with, the question of the state. Not only was its prefectoral command style unaltered, but its rapid expansion pressed hard against the outer limits of the society's resources, especially in Congo and Zaire. Part of the dynamics of state expansion reflected the response to popular demand for 'amenities', especially schools. The new costs of 'sovereignty' also figured, with more expensively equipped security forces and diplomatic networks. Large and often deficit-ridden parastatal sectors contributed to the fiscal crisis of the state. In some instances, particularly CAR, Equatorial Guinea and Zaire, the competence and integrity of the state were corroded by predatory and corrupt régimes. The urgency of state revenue and foreign-exchange needs enhanced the leverage of foreign creditors and investors, and focused development resources upon mineral projects rather than on the rural economy.

Around the apparatus of the state the political and bureaucratic bourgeoisie was emerging as the dominant class. Uncertainties remained as to whether this group would become a closed social category, transmitting its status across generations. Also unclear were the long-term linkages which this class would develop with external forces and with the lower internal social strata. In the early years of independence, considerable mobility remained, especially through the educational system, while reversals of political fortune brought a turnover in the composition of the state class.

A widespread decay of the rural sector posed a serious threat. Hyper-urbanisation and costly food imports were but two of the consequences. Only Cameroun was an arguable exception to the general conclusion that the peasantry had failed to benefit from independence. The full implications of the widespread demoralisation of rural society were not yet clear twenty years after independence.

The intersection of class with ethnic and regional tensions posed continuing problems. Régimes learned to contain and even smother ethnicity through the elimination or careful control of open political competition. The underlying cleavages were not thereby removed, and could reappear at moments of political crisis.

The increasing importance of mineral exploitation in most of the equatorial republics reinforced the dependency on foreign capital, technology and personnel. Large increases in oil production were anticipated in the 1980s. Such development could improve state revenue flows, but the enclave nature of petroleum exploitation remained. Political non-alignment or the radical anti-imperialism of Congo and São Tomé e Príncipe did not overcome the harsh realities of economic dependency.

The euphoria which greeted independence had long since vanished by 1980. Prosperity was far more difficult to achieve than independence. Only patient, sustained effort could bring a better life within grasp. The margin for miscalculation was narrow, and the perils of the peripheral state numerous. The equatorial experience in these decades demonstrates that progress is possible, but that it is by no means ordained by history.

CHAPTER 9

Settlers and liberators in the south

DAVID BIRMINGHAM AND TERENCE RANGER

A turning point occurred in the liberation of Africa in 1948. Far to the west of Central Africa, in the British colony of the Gold Coast, a new and active Ghanaian nationalism began to stir. Quite suddenly, across Africa, the name of Kwame Nkrumah began to be heard. The black people of West Africa began to demand new rights, new freedoms, new dignity. Occasionally they made their demands riotously. Normally their request was peaceful, thoughtful and modest. In the aftermath of a world war which had been partly fought in defence of human rights, their case could not be denied. Under the eye of the new United Nations Organisation, constitutional steps were taken to give self-government and independence to the colonial peoples of West Africa.

In the same year 1948, a quite different development occurred on the southern frontier of Central Africa. In the far south colonised peoples lost ground in their quest for independence. The white settlers of South Africa, aggressively calling themselves 'Afrikaners' and 'Nationalists', insisted that they too wanted more power and more autonomy. In 1948 they won that power through a colonial-style election in which few black Africans could vote. White power was set for a revival and began to sweep north. It was on a collision course with the new black nationalism born in West Africa.

The crunch between black nationalism and white power developed along a frontier which ran right across the middle of Central Africa. In the north the republics of 1960 were established in nearly peaceful cooperation with the retiring metropolitan administrators. Flags were designed, presidents were elected, anthems were sung and the new neo-colonial instruments of economic intercourse were laid down. In the south these steps did not take place. The decade of the 1950s was not used to prepare the ground for a new type of Afro-European relationship. On the contrary, white settlers, metropolitan governments and international business corporations consolidated their domination over African land, African minerals and an African work-force.

The first step in the northward spread of white power came in 1953 when the white, self-governing Rhodesian régime in Zimbabwe (then called Southern Rhodesia) succeeded in gaining control over its two northern neighbours. Most of the colonial authority which Britain had exercised in Zambia (Northern Rhodesia) and Malawi (Nyasaland) was transferred to a new federal government in Salisbury the colonial city known to Africans as Harare. This government planned to use the labour force of Malawi and the copper revenue of Zambia to build up the industrial and agricultural economy of Zimbabwe's white settlers. This dramatic white capture of two Central African countries was approved by Britain in return for slender guarantees of African advancement. Some further education was offered to the privileged few, and a voters' roll was recognised for the literate black middle class. By comparison with West Africa, however, the countries bordering the Zambezi basin did not appear to be moving towards black independence despite all the talk of partnership.

The second step in the consolidation of white power in the southern half of Central Africa came on each flank of the new British federation. In the west and in the east Portugal began, for the first time, to send large numbers of white immigrants to its colonies. Portuguese peasants who had previously preferred Brazil were induced to sail to Angola and Mozambique. By the late 1950s the numbers reaching Angola were approaching 10 000 each year. Many did not expect to stay for life, but all expected to be given job preferences, tax advantages and colonial privileges, until they had saved enough to return home. These white workers were powerful opponents of black nationalism. Far from uniting with black labour jointly to improve their economic prospects, white labour sought to exclude black rivals from preferred fields of semi-skilled and white-collar employment. White immigrants aspired to move rapidly into small business activities and to exclude traditional African entrepreneurs.

The third stage of southern advance in Central Africa was more subtle. In July 1960 the Shaba mining province of southern Zaire decided to secede from the new republic and preserve its copper wealth for itself. This 'Katanga secession' apparently received significant covert support from the south. A copper-mining republic, amenable to the interests of financial corporations, would be valued for itself as well as for the protection it could afford to the northern flank of the British sphere in Central Africa. The collision between north and south became focused on the Copperbelt. War broke out, and the world community lined up in partisan support. The crucial decision, however, was made by the United States of America. The new president, Kennedy, decided that America's long-term strategic and economic interests would best be served in this instance by supporting the black political republics rather than the white financial corporations.

It took two years to turn the tide of white advances in Central Africa. All the might of the United Nations, funded largely by the United States, was not enough to bomb the rebel province back into submission. By the time all the necessary compromises had been made the tide was strongly flowing the other way. Black nationalism had become vocal, indeed militant, throughout the southern belt. The two-year 'Katanga war' in Zaire had proved costly, unnecessary, and counter-productive to white interests. Over the next ten years a whole series of much more violent and protracted wars broke out all along the borders of Central Africa and South Africa.

The first war of liberation was fought in Angola. The most visible antagonists were the rural black peoples of the north and the east opposed by a large expeditionary force from Europe. The less visible participants were the neighbouring nations, the super-powers, and increasing numbers of local conscripts, black and white, who were enrolled into the colonial army. It will be chronicled below how this war went through many stages, and a chaotic colonial débâcle, before a semblance of national unity was restored in the late 1970s. Two other wars followed in a similar pattern, in Mozambique from 1964 and in Zimbabwe from 1972. In each case a military stalemate was reached, with nationalist irregulars in control of much of the countryside and colonial or settler armies in command of the towns and strategic highways. Negotiated settlements in 1975 and 1980 led to a more orderly political transition than in Angola and to a significant degree of economic continuity.

From 1960 the southern states of Central Africa went through a generation of tension between town and country which was perhaps as significant in its power of social transformation as the struggle over political liberation. An early manifestation of this tension occurred in Zaire. There the early 1960s saw a rapid and serious erosion of rural economic standards. Peasants, small farmers and country-dwellers rose up in violent anger against the swelling ranks of school-leavers in the towns. Protests led to much-publicised killings, to severe political disruption, and to an economic dislocation which further reduced the marketing opportunities of rural producers. Frightened refugees and ambitious seekers of opportunity added to the growth of urban population. Unemployment and food shortages faced peoples with golden expectations of the fruits of independence. Only an authoritarian régime similar to the colonial police-state built by the Belgians could survive in the 1960s.

Similar rural discontent occurred in all the southern states of Central Africa. The great coffee rebellion of 1961 in Angola was triggered off by falling prices, delayed wages, land alienation and the continued immigration of ill-paid conscripts from the south. As the resulting war drew on it became critical for Portugal to avoid a mass rural rebellion in the Angolan central highlands. The worst excesses of labour extraction were moderated, and economic policies of positive rural development were experimentally initiated in the last years of the war. Ironically, the rural anxieties of the highlands became more severe after Portuguese power had begun to wane. The conflict between town and country was grafted on to the 1975 war of foreign intervention. It brought an element of bitter civil war to the already distressed state of the country.

Mass unrest in the rural areas came rather later to Mozambique. In the early 1970s, however, the narrow strip of settler country between Zimbabwe and the sea saw the large-scale flight of young men from the villages, where they feared conscription into the colonial army or preventive custody in harsh political camps. Rural discontent provided the climate in which Central Africa's most successful armed political movement, Frelimo, effectively brought Portugal to its knees. The virtual defeat of the colonial army in Mozambique, and the collapse of its morale in 1974, was the turning point in the retreat of white power.

It was not only in Portuguese territories that rural populations gained new political muscle. In Malawi protest against continued domination by the Salisbury federal government led to a crisis in 1959 which effectively brought down the federation and convinced Britain that government by consent was the only viable way to maintain its influence in Central Africa. Malawi was therefore allowed to evolve autonomous political institutions. This independence of Malawi was reluctantly followed by the logical granting of independence to Zambia. The ability of Zambian political leaders to win rural support was, however, severely tested in the process. The urban community had a different set of aspirations, and many rural peoples sought a new future through religion rather than politics. The millenarian movement of Alice Lenshina seemed to many northern Zambians to offer a surer future than the customary path of late colonial politics. Although politicians in Zambia never had to launch a full-scale war to subdue the countryside, the conflict between modernisers and traditionalists was nevertheless to remain a source of tension.

It was in Zimbabwe that the slow mobilisation of rural discontent was carried to the greatest lengths. The original nationalist leaders were men of the colonial middle class with town constituencies. When their expected path was blocked by the challenge of settler power and settler independence in the early 1960s, it took nearly a decade for the broad peasantry to steel itself to the possibility of a long guerrilla war. It eventually did so, however, as the country's eastern border was gradually opened by nationalist military operations in Mozambique. There followed a seven-year war, in which people were more radically affected than in any other war of liberation. Refugees fled across the borders. Young men were signed up in two nationalist armies and one colonial one for long periods of service. Cultivators were uprooted and camped in wire hamlets under insanitary conditions. Fear percolated through the country to the very borders of the cities. However, the rural population, once mobilised, held to its demand for land, for change, for freedom of opportunity. Zimbabweans created political parties rather different from the old parties of the 1960s which had inherited their legacies with little questioning of the values and structures of colonial society. The new parties contained young men who believed that independence meant change. This new radicalism, and its confrontation with the entrenched political and economic realities of southern Central Africa forms the focus of this final chapter.

ANGOLA AND THE PORTUGUESE, 1961–1975

The first southern country to be affected by new visions of freedom was Angola. The high point in the formal decolonisation of Africa occurred in 1960, and the news spread rapidly. Three events in that year showed that most European powers had decided to grant flag independence to their black tropical colonies. The first in significance was the granting of what had once been called 'dominion status' to Nigeria, Africa's most populous country. This sequel to the freedom which Kwame Nkrumah had gained for Ghana in 1957 was also the forerunner of British East African decolonisation over the next four years. The British policy of withdrawing formal colonial authority and maintaining economic, cultural, educational and military ties with the new African nations was also adopted by France, in the same year, 1960. The turn-around of French colonial policy had been faster than the British one. It was spurred in 1958 by the refusal of Guinea, led by Sekou Touré, to accept the integration of Africa into a multi-national Greater France. Finally the third event of 1960 was the even more sudden decision of Belgium to create an independent republic out of the Belgian Congo. All three of these events, but especially the Belgian abdication in Congo, had a swift impact on southern Central Africa in general and on Angola in particular. When the crunch of southern decolonisation occurred, the wars that broke out were of far greater destructiveness than any of the conflicts which had accompanied tropical decolonisation further north. Even the Mau Mau war in Kenya and the civil war in Cameroun had been limited in comparative scope. The conflagration all along the border of South Africa outstripped in duration, if not in intensity, even the seven-year war of Algerian independence where white resistance had reached a scale of brutality previously matched only in the European domestic wars of the 1940s, and never before in Africa. It is these southern wars of liberation in Angola, in Mozambique and in Zimbabwe which need to be explained and chronicled. They represent a dark epilogue to colonial rule in Central Africa.

The main conflict between black and white rule in the 1960s focused on two wars of liberation, in Angola and Mozambique. In 1960 farming was still the dominant experience of many black Mozambicans and Angolans.

For some peasants farming was still a free enterprise, presenting a choice of how to use one's own land in one's own time, but such freedom had become scarce. Opportunities for independent farming had been severely restricted in Mozambique from the earliest days of colonial conquest. By 1960 a large number of Angolans had also been mobilised by the colonial economy and deprived of full use of their land. Farming no longer provided many freedoms. It had become an ill-paid chore on someone else's land, or a marginal, intermittent occupation between stints of deep mining or town servitude.

The history of farm labouring on the colonial estates of Portugal's African empire is best captured in the few literary works that have been published. Honwana, in his Mozambique essays, relives the muscular agony of weeding maize that his children will never eat, the burning minutes of noon-day sun before the overseer calls the dinner break, the horror of a society without natural justice.[1] Mondlane, in a more academic style, described how a few hundred landlords owned nearly half of Mozambique's fertile land, how the wealth produced on these prosperous holdings was transferred to Europe, and how the Portuguese colonial government ploughed the minimum back into schools, roads and clinics.[2] In 1960 Mozambique was ready to burst into flames, but Angola erupted first.

The Angolan war broke out in January 1961. It started in a small way, completely unnoticed by the world outside. The roots of distress, however, were deep and the expectations of freedom were boundless. The war began in the cotton fields of the Kwanza and Kwango basins, and along the Luanda line-of-rail. For several decades the Portuguese had been trying to produce cotton in this zone of agricultural marginality, but cotton was a risky, low-profit crop. It therefore became government policy to shift the risk on to peasant producers rather than to encourage plantations involving European capital and manpower. In designated cotton zones each local inhabitant was required to use his own land, his own time and his own family labour-force to grow cotton. In good years he received payment for the crop. In bad years he received nothing. But he had no choice in whether to gamble on a cash crop or not. He was forbidden from giving first consideration to food crops for himself. The consequences of this policy were endemic famine. As early as 1945 responsible district officers recognised the dangers of compelling Kimbundu-speaking farmers to grow cotton, which might fail one year in three, yet the imperial government denounced the Angolan famine as a figment of the black imagination. The 'Bantu', said doctors Salazar and Caetano in a considered statement, were psychologically resistant to regular work and must be

---

1 Luis Bernardo Honwana, *We Killed Mangy Dog*, English ed., London, 1969.
2 Eduardo Mondlane, *The Struggle for Mozambique*, Harmondsworth, 1969.

compelled to it. Once they had adopted 'civilised' standards of compliance there would be no imaginary famines.[3]

For fifteen years compulsory cotton-growing continued without local officials daring further to question its desirability. In January 1961 despair among black planters was heightened by low prices, and delayed payment. Violence broke out in 'Maria's war', cotton seed was burnt, European stores were attacked, river barges were sunk, cattle were killed, roads were barricaded.[4] The cotton war was short-lived, and the insurgent villages were indiscriminately strafed by the embryonic Portuguese air force; resistance was crushed and people fled. The fuse on the Central African powder keg had been lit, however, and war continued in one or another of the border states of Central Africa for the next nineteen years.

While low cotton prices were fuelling rural resentment, a different kind of nationalist movement had slowly emerged in Luanda, the colonial capital. The Movement for the Popular Liberation of Angola (MPLA) began as a nationalist discussion forum for educated city dwellers. It was related to the Portuguese communist party, which had survived thirty years of Salazar's fascist-style dictatorship as virtually the only opposition in either Portugal or the colonies. The movement came to prominence in February 1961. In the wake of the cotton war an attempt was made to free nationalist leaders held in Luanda gaol. Two unsuccessful attacks on prisons unleashed a wave of white panic. Vigilante groups were mobilised, armed, and sent ranging through the black slums, where hundreds were killed in fear and revenge. The Luanda pogrom of February 1961 was unexpectedly well publicised by foreign journalists. They had been following a stunt by Portugal's dissident democrats who, thirteen days before the gaol attack, had hijacked an ocean liner in the Atlantic and were thought to be heading for Luanda to raise the flag of white rebellion against Salazar. The liner never arrived, but its manoeuvres gave wide publicity to the simultaneous, but equally abortive, *coup* by the MPLA.[5]

The reasons for the February week of urban warfare are deeply embedded in the colonial changes of the 1950s. In the ten years before 1961 many white immigrants, poor, unlettered, insecure, had reached Angola. They competed with black Angolans for jobs as carpenters, drivers, mechanics, hotel porters, chambermaids, hawkers, shop assistants, prostitutes, clerks, cleaners and sellers of lottery tickets. Elsewhere in Africa the 1950s was a time of growing black opportunity; new jobs and skills were drawing men, and some women, up the economic ladder as the

---

3 The reaction of the president, prime minister and colonial minister of Portugal to the Angolan famine of 1945 was published at the time. The best account of colonial Angola is René Pélissier, *La Colonie du Minotaure* (Orgeval, 1978).
4 John Marcum, *The Angolan Revolution volume I: the Anatomy of an Explosion 1950–1962*, Cambridge, Mass., 1969, I, 124–6.
5 Marcum, *The Angolan Revolution*, I, pp. 126–30.

colour bar weakened. In Angola the opposite was happening. The floating colour bar was moving downward, and immigrants from the black countryside were losing their jobs, as foreign whites, with less skill and experience, were preferred.[6] Black élites lost their place in both government and business and bitterly resented the illiterate and semi-literate migrants from Portugal's most backward provinces. However, the relatively privileged white immigrants were not happy either. This 'land of convicts' was not an obvious escape route from European poverty like Brazil or California. The jobs it offered were lowly and dull.[7] Many whites lived in the twilight areas of the city, in dusty wooden houses squeezed between the end of the ashphalt and the twisting lanes of the black shanties. Luanda's murderous white mob bore little resemblance to the British settlers under the jacarandas of Rhodesia. The magnet which had brought them to Africa was a boom in Angolan coffee-planting.

The coffee zones of Angola lie north and south of the cotton belt. The south was primarily managed by large colonial companies with multinational capital and expertise. The north, however, had more opportunity for individual planters. And it was in the north that the Angolan revolution exploded, forty days after the Luanda uprising.

Coffee is the oldest colonial export crop of Angola. It dates back to the early nineteenth century. Much of it was grown by Kikongo-speaking small farmers who sold their beans to white store-keepers. When prices were high, store-keepers were tempted to go into direct production and buy, or even seize, good coffee land from traditional land-users.[8] In the 1950s prices were particularly high, and the shopkeeper–planters were joined by several thousand new coffee speculators from Portugal. The consequences were stressful as more land was alienated to whites, and dispossessed black land-owners were turned into wage-dependent labourers. Despite this proletarianisation, labour was insufficient and a system of forced contract workers revived and expanded. Central Angola sent Ovimbundu migrants to tend the trees and harvest the beans. Both local and contract workers became dependent on European wages, in cash, tokens or kind, which made them vulnerable to economic fluctuations in the coffee industry. The contrasting white population became a privileged colonial élite living off a colonised society suffering deprivations in education, in health, in job mobility and in economic prospects. The tinder was touched on 15 March 1961 when the workers on the Primavera plantation asked the bailiff for wages by then six months overdue. This

6 David Birmingham, 'Colonialism in Angola', *Tarikh*, 1980, gives a dramatised account of the conflicting aspirations of rural blacks and immigrant whites in Angola's cities.
7 Gerald J. Bender, *Angola under the Portuguese; the myth and the reality*, London, 1978, has the most comprehensive history of Portuguese emigration to Angola.
8 David Birmingham, 'The coffee barons of Cazengo', *Journal of African History*, xix, 1978, 523–38.

reasonable request met with such violent planter denunciations that fighting broke out. In its wake several hundred white settlers and black migrant workers were killed. In retaliation several thousand black northerners, some indiscriminate victims, others singled out as mission-educated 'subversive elements', were massacred. The violence spread throughout northern Angola. A hundred thousand Angolan refugees streamed across the border into Zaire. Portugal launched a full-scale war of reconquest.[9]

The first question that needs to be asked about the Angolan war of 1961 is, why did Portugal mobilise such a large army to dragoon its rebellious colony back to submission? Even a rich world power such as Britain had found considerable difficulty in containing the smaller nationalist uprising in colonial Kenya. Yet a poor, small, weak Portugal launched a full-scale military counter-offensive. Portugal did not have the economic muscle to switch from formal colonial domination to neo-colonial partnership. Portugal in 1961 could not supply industrial produce in return for colonial coffee, diamonds, sisal and cotton. West Germany[10] and the United States,[11] the main industrial powers without African colonies, would have economically adopted ex-Portuguese colonies had the metropolitan government in Lisbon not decided to stem the tide of African independence.

In 1961 it was commonly predicted that the war would be over within the year and that Angola would join Zaire in the search for a viable form of independence and prosperity. In fact that war lasted thirteen years and ran through three phases. The two-year dragoon phase, from 1961 to 1963, sowed the seeds of military stalemate and political fragmentation. The next five years saw a widescale internationalisation of the conflict as Portugal gave up its narrow economic nationalism and allowed foreign investors to increase their activities in the colony. Finally, the last five colonial years saw yet a different policy. The Africanisation of the colonial structures was attempted, and Angolans were given new educational and economic opportunities in return for cooperation against armed nationalism.

The greatest problem facing Angolan nationalists in 1961 was how to follow up in quick unity the initiative which had been explosively and unexpectedly thrust into their hands. Angola was a divided society. Instead of having a single pole of attraction around which education, opportunity

9 Marcum, *The Angolan Revolution*, I, pp. 130–5. There is an extensive contemporary literature on the outbreak of the Angolan war.
10 For indications of German economic interest, see Manfred Kuder, *Angola: eine geographische und wirtschaftliche Landeskunde*, Darmstadt, 1971; Günter Borchert, *Die Wirtschafträume Angolas*, Hamburg, 1967; Hermann Pössinger, *Angola als Wirtschaftspartner*, Cologne, 1966.
11 Early indications of American interest may be found in D. M. Abshire and M. A. Samuels, *Portuguese Africa: a Handbook*, London, 1969; A. B. Herrick *et al.*, *Area Handbook for Angola*, Washington, D.C., 1967.

and politics revolved, it had two. One was Kinshasa, outside the country, and it was to Kinshasa that northern Angolans had looked for advancement ever since the early twentieth century. The city attracted aspiring young mission-leavers from both the Belgian and the Portuguese halves of the old Kongo empire. When war broke out in Angola, refugees increased the numbers who looked north. As the Baptist Missionary Society mounted relief work among the exiles, the well-established network of Baptist old-school links was strengthened. A political party emerged which eventually became the FNLA, the Front for the National Liberation of Angola. Its leaders were at home in the political climate of Kinshasa and made Zaire the base for their military institutionalisation of the anti-colonial conflict.[12]

The second urban focus of Angola's colonial bipolarity was, of course, Luanda, the Portuguese capital. It was to Luanda that Portuguese-speaking black Catholics looked. Luanda was also the city of Angola's Methodists, many of whom, including Agostinho Neto, played an important role in building up the MPLA. Luanda, however, proved too dangerous a base for active nationalist agitation. In 1961 some MPLA leaders retreated to the Ndembu forest, 50 miles outside the city, to create a small guerrilla presence; this survived through thirteen years of warfare. Other leaders went into exile and eventually created a new military front in the remote eastern savanna 'at the ends of the world'.[13]

In 1962 Portugal succeeded in clawing its way back to achieve a military stalemate with both the Kinshasa–Kikongo–Baptists nationalists and the Luanda–Kimbundu–Methodist nationalists. This colonial success, this partial reversal of the African tide, was due in large measure to a carefully manipulated reversal of the colonial policy of the United States of America. António Salazar, the dictatorial prime minister of Portugal, effectively blackmailed the administration of John Kennedy into abandoning his Africa-for-the-Africans stance of 1961. Continued sympathy for the Angolan cause, Portugal said, would lead to the withdrawal of United States military rights to refuel planes in the Azores Islands – a then necessary staging post between America and the Middle East.[14] This strategic pressure came at a time of American doubts about the viability of post-colonial republics in Africa. Maintaining an anti-communist unitary government in Zaire (then still called Congo) was proving expensive to America. Continued Portuguese colonial rule seemed a safer, and cheaper, way of keeping the Soviet Union out of Central Africa. In 1961, therefore, Portugal was quietly permitted to divert NATO military equipment, including napalm, from the North Atlantic to the South Atlantic to further colonial aggression. Twenty thousand people probably died in the initial

12 John Marcum, *The Angolan Revolution volume II: Exile Politics and Guerrilla Warfare*, Cambridge, Mass., 1978, describes the environment of the exile community.
13 Basil Davidson, *In the Eye of the Storm: Angola's People*, London, 1972.
14 Marcum, *The Angolan Revolution*, I, pp. 181–8.

two-year phase of the war, almost as many as in the whole of the subsequent Zimbabwe war of liberation.[15]

In the middle years of the 1960s the Angolan war of liberation was internationalised and formalised on both sides. On the nationalist side both movements found regional bases in neighbouring countries and a limited level of international support. Holden Roberto's FNLA maintained generally good relations with the emerging military government of Zaire and received covert assistance from the United States and from China as well as from African countries. The MPLA began operating from Zambia once independence was achieved there in 1964. Its overseas support came from the Soviet Union by way of the long, over-land route through Tanzania. The problem which both movements faced in mobilising political support and guerrilla armies was the remoteness of their friendly frontiers from the main centres of Angolan population and economic strength. The cities, the highlands, the plantations were all several hundred miles inside Angola. The only strategic targets near a border were Cabinda and the Benguela railway. However, Cabinda was a difficult target because it was small, easy to defend, and had a local separatist movement which inhibited recruitment by the two big parties.[16] The railway was also a difficult target: the transport of Belgian and British copper to the Atlantic was so important to Zaire and Zambia that neither could allow nationalists to attack the railway, on pain of expulsion. Each guerrilla army, and its host population of northern and eastern peasants, could hold down a large Portuguese expeditionary force but not win the war.

The Portuguese inability to rid the colony of armed nationalists proved an unacceptable burden on the weak metropolitan economy. New policies were therefore drawn up in 1963 which allowed foreign investors to enter colonial sectors previously reserved for Portuguese domestic capital. The aim was two-fold. Countries such as Britain, Germany, France, Brazil and the United States would be expected to support the capital risked by their nationals and refrain from advocating Angolan independence. Secondly, new investment would create wealth with which to modernise the country's economy, infrastructure and transport system and so facilitate and finance counter-insurgency campaigns.

The policy worked well. International support for Angolan freedom was minimised. The political parties remained so frustrated and divided that severe schisms and enmities arose within them and between them. One such division led to the creation of yet a third nationalist movement. From about 1965 the UNITA (Union for Total Independence in Angola), led by Jonas Savimbi, succeeded in finding a new base among the Ovimbundu, a new political target in the central highlands, and a new administrative network of catechists and school-leavers from the Presbyterian missions

15 *Ibid.*, p. 144.
16 Phyllis Martin, 'The Cabinda Connection', *African Affairs*, lxxvi, 1977, 47–59.

along the Benguela railway. Although UNITA seceded from the northern FNLA, its main competitor was the MPLA, which it rivalled in the search for a corridor from the Zambian border to the Angolan heartlands. Such rivalry, discreetly encouraged by the intelligence forces of Portugal, prolonged the colonial hold on Angola. It still did not win the war for Portugal, however, and a third policy option evolved in the late 1960s to win over black hearts and minds.

The policy of minimising dissent arose from the army's growing conviction, most clearly expressed in 1973 by General António Spínola, that Portugal could not win outright a war in Africa.[17] In the late 1960s, therefore, the colonial military command began to advocate economic development plans in which Angolans featured as beneficiaries, not merely as docile cheap labour. The first project, using the international profits of coffee, and expertise in rural development from Germany, aimed to create rising prosperity among black peasants on the north-eastern plateau. The Andulu region was closer to Zaire and Zambia than any other part of the highlands, and likely to be the focus of a fourth MPLA military front. To prevent such a nationalist breakthrough a peasant-oriented, government-financed, highland development scheme was introduced. Although aspects of the plan were hopelessly uneconomic, it did symbolise an entirely new direction in colonial counter-insurgency, and sowed the seeds of a black capitalist peasantry which would resist the communal models of agricultural production favoured by MPLA nationalists.

A more important extension of economic counter-insurgency occurred in the north. From the late 1960s the Portuguese army insisted, despite vehement protests from white truckers, planters, merchants and middlemen, that prosperity should be restored to a section of the northern black peasantry. Producer cooperatives were set up with right of access to shippers in Luanda. Agricultural extension services were created to advise small and medium-sized coffee farms. The new black rural capitalists were even allowed to recruit paid migrant labour from the south. At a social level the influence of state Catholicism was soft-pedalled, and Baptist churches were informally allowed to revive without the need for subversive secrecy.[18] This small-scale reversal of policy did little to prolong the Portuguese colonial tenure in Angola. It did, however, create an élite which after independence became vocally opposed to socialist ideals for national reconstruction in the rural economy.

Education was another sector where improvement, rather than oppression, became the new policy of the late 1960s. Hitherto the expansion of education had been primarily designed for the children of

17 António Spínola, *Portugal e o Futuro*, Lisbon, 1973.
18 The rural development projects were funded by the Coffee Institute; see Jeremy Grest, 'Agriculture in Angola: the State and Coffee Production 1945–1975', M.A. thesis, SOAS, 1979.

Angola's quarter of a million settlers, immigrants and expatriates. In order to create opportunities for black advancement, African education was expanded so that by 1974 significant numbers of Angolans had entered the secondary and trade schools, though barely a handful passed on to the university. As in other late colonial educational systems, however, African children suffered severe, and in Angola deliberate, handicaps, so that a frustrated cohort of drop-outs created an angry young generation whose unfulfilled ambitions were a painful legacy to the post-colonial government.

The Africanisation of the colonial army in Angola was modelled on the United States experience in recruiting Vietnamese troops to fight against their own forces of liberation in south-east Asia. The Angolan policy of using black privates was subsequently adopted in turn by the Rhodesian army in Zimbabwe. The advantage to Lisbon of hiring the underemployed and of conscripting the better-educated to serve as black soldiers was both political and financial. By this policy sensitive and expensive European casualty rates were lowered, as black soldiers were driven to undertake the high-risk tasks of mine-detecting and anti-guerrilla patrolling. It was, however, yet another example of sowing the wind to reap the whirlwind. At independence Angola inherited some tens of thousands of frightened citizens who had served in the colonial army. Their search for a secure future played a significant role in the decolonisation conflict of 1974 to 1976, which followed the collapse of the Portuguese empire in Africa.

A more severe cause of long-term internal stress in the last colonial years was labour policy. The Ovimbundu highlands had been a source of slaves, of indentured estate workers, and of forced migrants since the earliest Portuguese attempts at colonial development in the late nineteenth century. The war of the 1960s led to revisions in the labour codes, but the crux of the Angolan economy remained the interlocking of northern land and southern labour. In the south, village store-keepers became the recruiters of the now 'voluntary' migrant labour. Any southern farmer requiring credit to buy roofing thatch, to tide his family over the hunger gap in the crop season, to pay his son's school fees, to get his wife to hospital, to buy a new cow or seed corn, had to approach his local Portuguese store. In return for credit he not only had to agree to sell his maize crop at disadvantageous prices, but also to contract himself, or his relations, for periods of labour service on the northern estates. The official ending of compulsory government recruitment did little to brighten the prospects for southern peasants, because the manipulation of rural credit kept them in uncertainty, and in subservience to the fattening class of small white merchants. In some areas this uncertainty was compounded by the growth of white cattle ranching which took land away from communities already reaching the limits of their productive territory. The south, therefore, was as tense as the north on the eve of independence.

East Angola's main colonial significance was as a corridor for Britain's Benguela railway. From 1965 onwards, however, it became a major war zone where for eight years the MPLA held down a large colonial army. In order to prevent the sparse local population from offering hospitality to passing guerrilla bands, Portuguese strategists adopted a policy of 'villagization' made familiar by Britain in Kenya during the 1950s. Neither the herding of people into concentrated hamlets, nor the destructive spraying of crops, could uproot the liberation army, small though it was. By the early 1970s security villages were being imposed on an ever-widening swath. Even some of the hard-pressed peasant communities in the highlands, 400 miles inside Angola, were relocated along the strategic roads. This long war of attrition, with a severe disruption of civilian life and peasant economies, came to a sudden end in 1974. This end of the first war of Angolan liberation came not through any military breakthrough by the MPLA or from any renewed colonial offensive; it came as a direct consequence of another Portuguese colonial war, in Mozambique, which took a dramatic turn in the early months of 1974. This transformation, which led to the overthrow of the dictatorship in Portugal, amounted to a military defeat of the colonial army on the Zambezi by nationalist forces.

THE LIBERATION OF MOZAMBIQUE

The ten-year war of liberation in Mozambique was, in many respects, very different from the first war of liberation in Angola. Mozambique had a different economy, a different strategic geography, a different history of national awakening. The Mozambique war took place in two phases – a northern phase, in the middle 1960s, and a Zambezian phase in the early 1970s.

There were two anti-colonial strands from which Mozambican nationalism was woven in the early 1960s. The first was rural and predominantly northern. The peoples of Cabo Delgado and Niassa had suffered as much from colonial exploitation as any in South-Central Africa. Before 1929 chartered company government had brought violent forms of surplus extraction and severe outbursts of physical brutality. Direct rule did not greatly improve the peasant lot. Makonde peoples were administered, like most Africans, under the Native Charter (*régime do indigenato*), which allowed few civic rights. Forced labour could be compelled to work at uneconomic rates on government projects as far away as Maputo (then known as Lourenço Marques), 1 000 miles south. It was in the farming sector, however, that the most severe strains were felt. Rural taxation was increased when the farmer's price for cotton remained low. An attempt to organise a peaceful demonstration of cotton-growers at Mueda, in June 1960, led to the unpublicised shooting of many protesters. Peasants fled into exile in Tanzania (called Tanganyika until its 1964 union with Zanzibar).

Like their fellows from Angola, they began to plan a future of national independence.

The second strand of Mozambique nationalism was spun among the small communities of blacks who had succeeded in escaping the native obligation to perform unskilled labour. They had joined the colonial cadres of schoolmen assimilated into the so-called 'civilised' colonial class. Before 1961 they aimed primarily at liberalising the Portuguese colonial state in collaboration with their democratic and Marxist class-mates, both black and white, from Bissau, Luanda and Lisbon. After 1961 the reformist movement split into predominantly white collaborators, who tried to change the system from within, and predominantly black nationalists, who sought to create a broad-fronted coalition dedicated to the overthrow of foreign rule. Internal reform was led by Adriano Moreira, who joined the Salazar government and carried through a legal revision of the native statutes and labour obligations. His legislative efforts had only limited practical effect, however, and he was swept away by a new generation of hard-line colonial planners from the army. They rightly saw Africa as a sphere in which to increase the power of the military wing of Salazar's corporative New State. Meanwhile the nationalist reformers turned to exile and revolution. They found their leader in Eduardo Mondlane.

The leaders of the Mozambique revolution found in Tanzania a much more stable environment in which to plan their strategy than the Angolans had found in Zaire. In the two years leading to 1964 Mondlane successfully blended the broad national vision of the urban exiles with the local territorial knowledge of the northern refugees. These twin strengths, backed with unofficial material support from the liberal West and official military support from the Soviet and Chinese East, enabled a considered guerrilla war to be planned. A unified front for the liberation of Mozambique, Frelimo, sent its members throughout the north, at great personal risk, to recruit supporters, sell membership cards, establish party cells, organise the election of local chairmen, and find publicity agents and couriers. On 25 September 1964 coordinated Frelimo attacks were launched on widely scattered targets throughout the north.[19]

Mozambique's northern war progressed towards liberation for five years. The large colonial army which was drafted in could hold only a few strong points that were inadequately linked by much-mined dirt roads. It could not restore the white extractive economy nor protect the old network of colonial bush traders. The introduction of a 'secret' political police, far from preventing local young men from joining Frelimo, frightened them into doing so all the sooner by their insensitive brutality which shocked even the civil administration. The regular flow of new

---

19 John Paul, *Mozambique: Memoirs of a Revolution*, Harmondsworth, 1975. This eye-witness account of the war in the north is one of the best documents available for the early history of Frelimo.

recruits, often the ablest of Protestant-educated sons, and the guerrilla successes against the cumbersome army convoys, gave Frelimo a momentum, a unity and a strength which Angolan nationalists always lacked. It nevertheless began to incur similar problems of stagnation and disillusion when five years of achievement had not led to victory.

It had been easy for guerrillas to destroy the network of Portuguese rural stores, but it was difficult to create a new market for peasant surpluses. In the tiny West African colony of Guinea-Bissau anti-Portuguese nationalists, led by Amilcar Cabral, achieved some success in setting up people's shops. In Mozambique the distances were far greater, communications more difficult, the river frontier more dangerous, and the Tanzanian havens far removed from coasts, ports and good roads. Equally difficult was the organisation of essential supplies of kerosene, candles, sugar, pencils, medicine and schoolbooks to the liberated areas. Freed populations were caught between the long-term visions of liberty-with-austerity or of collaboration and minimal material comforts. Both involved danger, insecurity and reprisals for not conforming. The further south people were, the more difficult they found it to trust to the nationalist vision of an alternative society in their own time. The northern war thus ran into the sand. Leaders began to question the correctness of their ideology, the effectiveness of their method, the loyalty of their allies. In February 1969, five years after war broke out, Mondlane was assassinated and the movement lost its unifying leader.[20]

The second phase of the Mozambique war of liberation got under way in 1971, through the leadership of Samora Machel. The new initiative was preceded by an intense Portuguese counter-offensive designed in 1968 by Marcello Caetano, a former colonial minister who succeeded Salazar as Prime Minister of Portugal. His reshaping of colonial strategy had both an internal military facet and an international economic facet.[21]

The military strategy involved an intensification of 'anti-terrorist' colonial action modelled on American experience in Vietnam. A new Portuguese commander, General Kaulza de Arriaga, was given an increased budget to 'mop up' Frelimo. He greatly increased the number of African soldiers in the colonial army, and by 1974 there were about 30 000 black troops in operation compared to some 20 000 white soldiers.[22] Some were ethnically recruited infantry units, with their own officers, who were encouraged to think tribally and divisively rather than nationally. They were better paid than government labour and were given five months of

20 Eduardo Mondlane, *The Struggle for Mozambique*, was written shortly before his death and published posthumously.
21 Keith Middlemas, *Cabora Bassa: Engineering and Politics in Southern Africa*, London, 1975, is one of the most important works of scholarship published on Mozambique and has a wider political, economic and even military focus than its title implies. It has been heavily relied on in the following pages.
22 Middlemas, *Cabora Bassa*, p. 144.

military training. The recruitment of an élite of black paratroops was also accelerated. Arriaga's second military innovation was 'psychological warfare'. In Cabo Delado 300 000 people were moved into security hamlets in two years. The objective was a mixed, almost contradictory one. Development policy required villagisation in order that services might be improved, water supplies laid on, schools and clinics centrally provided, a colonial version of *ujamaa* attempted. Strategic policy required that people be concentrated quickly, that villages be sited near military roads rather than near fertile fields, that barbed wire and curfews insulate villagers from nationalists. Hostility to forced relocation meant that the Portuguese gained little credit for the positive side of the policy. After independence it was difficult for Frelimo to turn communities which had been so arbitrarily concentrated into genuine centres of rural self-improvement.

The third branch of Arriaga's offensive was a conventional escalation of the military attacks on the north. The cost in lives, in money, in political effort, was enormous. The assault, known as Gordian Knot, had short-term military successes but finally exhausted the last vestiges of Portuguese enthusiasm for their 'Coca-Cola' war. It was profoundly counter-productive in that it finally drove Frelimo to open its long-planned second front. It was on this new, western front that Portugal was eventually defeated.[23]

The international facet of Caetano's revived colonial dynamism led the war into the western province of Tete in its final, decisive phase. The story revolves round the Zambezi gorge at Cabora Bassa. Plans to build a hydro-electric dam in the gorge were debated throughout the twentieth century. In April 1969 engineering, and financial proposals were finalised and Caetano decided to dam the Zambezi, create nearly two thousand megawatts of electricity, and pave the way for agricultural, extractive and manufacturing industries in the lower Zambezi valley. The decision was a major policy choice by the new Portuguese leader. On succeeding Salazar he had to decide whether Portugal's future lay in Europe, as a junior supplier of cheap labour and Mediterranean produce, or in Africa as a senior supplier of colonial technology and management. He chose Africa. This choice could be turned into reality only with strong international backing, and the Cabora Bassa dam provided succulent, if tainted, bait. It was used to entice advanced industrial countries to commit support for a long-term colonial future in Mozambique. Britain, France, Germany, Sweden, the United States and Italy competed fiercely for the right to participate in the £300 million project. They were discreetly encouraged by South Africa, which saw every advantage in encouraging more Western governments to develop a vested interest in white domination. For political reasons South Africa was also willing to buy most of the

---

23 Middlemas, *Cabora Bassa*, ch. 6.

electricity. In the final contractors' bargaining the United States was underbid by Europe, Britain was excluded because the guarantees of its enthusiastic Labour government were considered suspect, and Swedish industry withdrew lest its profitable relationship with anti-colonial trading partners and its liberal government policies be impaired. The poisoned bait was otherwise swallowed whole, and France, Germany and Italy built the dam, and the thousand-kilometre power-line to Pretoria.[24] Mozambique seemed more inexorably shackled by colonialism than ever before. Ironically, however, the real consequence of building the dam was the exact opposite. Cabora Bassa became the dowry for Mozambique's independence.

Frelimo, after running into both logistical and military problems in the north, was able to use the consolidation of white power around Cabora Bassa to embark on a highly successful publicity campaign. The involvement of South Africa, and the unrealistically ambitious scheme to settle a million peasants, some of them new white immigrants, in the newly regulated flood basin below the dam, were unacceptable to liberal world opinion. They were also unacceptable to President Kaunda of Zambia who, in 1970, gave Frelimo a new western sanctuary from which to open its second front. By early 1971 Frelimo was operating within striking range of Cabora Bassa. The new colonial dream was threatened, and defence costs escalated. The colonial government was stampeded into herding the Tete provincial population into security hamlets with even greater haste, more agony, and fewer planned services than in the north. Frelimo speeded up military penetration of Mozambique even where political mobilisation of host populations lagged behind. The columns needed rest havens, food supplies and carriers for their increasingly heavy and sophisticated weapons. Villages which supplied such amenities became the subject of draconian Portuguese reprisals. One search-and-destroy operation, at Wiriyamu, took place on 16 December 1972. The names are known of eighty-five men, women and children who were shot or killed by hand. Altogether the patrol probably killed 300 people that afternoon, many herded into thatched huts and set alight. When news of this type of counter-insurgency finally leaked out of Mozambique[25] the now demoralised colonial régime had less than twelve months left to live.

The final year of colonial rule in Mozambique saw the nationalist offensive penetrate areas of real economic importance. The site of Cabora Bassa was by-passed, and the hydro-electric project proceeded ready to be plucked ripe at independence. The new target was the Rhodesian railway to the port of Beira which it began to sabotage regularly in January

24 Middlemas, *Cabora Bassa*, chs. 2 and 3.
25 Adrian Hastings, *Wiriyamu*, London, 1974.

1974. The effect was to bring panic to the white highlands of Portuguese Manica, to damage the credibility of Portuguese security measures in the eyes of the Rhodesians, now also at war with their black subjects, and to bring home the reality of impending defeat to the dismayed expatriate middle classes on the city boulevards of Beira. The acute last phase of the war was gruesomely illustrated in the diary of a Dutch priest living in the small railway town of Inhaminga, in the early months of 1974.

The white population of Inhaminga felt constantly threatened by the large surrounding black population. Frelimo regularly attacked their railway, and even their water-tower, their saw-mill, their army barracks. It recruited local young men and threatened government-appointed chiefs. In their panic the Portuguese community petitioned the local security police, the DGS (Direcção Geral de Segurança), to arrest young men who were liable to be 'subverted' by 'terrorists'. The police agreed, and soon the local gaol was full of suspected nationalist sympathisers. People fled to the *maquis* more quickly than ever for fear of arrest. In order to house more suspects in the prison, the police agreed to remove a lorry-load of men whom informers considered especially subversive. A bulldozer was taken up to the woods behind the town to cover their bodies with earth. By April many more people had been killed, not in battle, but in cold-blooded civilian purges.[26]

The rising power of the Mozambique security police was a central phenomenon of the last phase of the war. The police had for some time been permitted to recruit their own black arrow commandos, the *flechas*. These dehumanised and heavily armed units had particular responsibility for spreading terror as a government weapon. They were responsible for indiscriminate police raids on infiltrated rural areas. Their white colleagues specialised in identifying, arresting and cruelly interrogating specific suspects. The DGS security police also ran the prison camps, such as Ibo fortress, where maltreatment led to intentionally high mortality rates. The police policy of restoring power through intimidation undermined the short-lived army policy of winning over moderate-minded Mozambicans, yet government came to have more faith in the police than in the failing army. After ten war-weary years army morale could not withstand the barrage of condemnation brought forth by the sudden spate of Frelimo victories in the heartlands of middle Mozambique.

The army *coup d'état* which overturned the Caetano government on the morning of 25 April 1974 was not triggered off solely by the success of Frelimo in winning the political and military initiative in Mozambique. The colonial war in Guinea-Bissau had also gone badly for Portugal, and the former commander there, General Spinola, had become publicly

26 *The Inhaminga Diary.* Reprinted in the Portuguese edition of Hastings, *Wiriyamu*, Porto, 1974.

convinced that a military victory was impossible and political accommodation with the liberation movement in Guiné and Cabo Verde would have to be negotiated. Even Angola, where neither side had succeeded in gaining the upper hand, was a burden which Portugal could no longer carry. Although Angola, unlike Mozambique, was rich enough to bear half the cost of its own military budget, it still absorbed large numbers of European conscripts and drove many into exile in France. The war also created tension within the army. The increased power of the police threatened the position of senior officers and lack of promotions and preferment of conscripts threatened the junior professionals. It was the junior officers who planned the *coup*, but senior officers, including Spinola himself, initially took over the government. Within six months, peace had been formalised, the integration of the nationalist and colonial armies followed soon after, and on 25 June 1975 Mozambique became an independent republic ready to turn from ten years of war to the real problems of creating a viable, stable economy on the south-east coast of Central Africa.

THE COLONIAL LEGACY IN MOZAMBIQUE AND ANGOLA

The colonial economy of Mozambique was founded on three pillars, none of which was attractive to a free country. They were tropical plantations, rail and harbour services, and the export of labour. The tropical plantations had been little affected by the war, which did not penetrate the lower Zambezia districts. Sugar, copra and tea continued initially to be grown by the great tropical companies, and a transfer to government ownership occurred slowly over the first years of independence. Cotton, a compulsory tax crop rather than a cash crop, proved harder to maintain than sugar, and the sisal estates of the north had been almost wholly disrupted by war. More difficult policy decisions than those relating to agribusiness concerned the role of Mozambique in providing harbour facilities and rail transport to both Rhodesia and South Africa. The Machel government closed the Rhodesian railway in support of Zimbabwean nationalists and of United Nations resolutions to ban trade with the illegal white régime which had been in power since 1965. The world community provided some international aid to offset the loss of government revenue, but commercial decline and rising unemployment were severe consequences of the decision to comply with international law.

The second Mozambique railway, to South Africa, was even more important. The government decided to keep that one open, and brought in South African technicians to manage the harbour and replace the Portuguese expatriate personnel who left the colony in the years immediately before and after independence. Mozambique remained inextricably linked to the southern economic complex. From 1975 electricity revenue from South Africa began to supplement railway revenue and pay off the construction debts on the Cabora Bassa dam.

Even more difficult to unravel than transport and energy was the question of labour migration. South Mozambicans began travelling to South Africa in search of jobs in the mid-nineteenth century. Some went privately, even illegally. Since early in the twentieth century many went under the auspices of the gold-mine recruiting agency WENELA (Witwatersrand Native Labour Association). The advantage of this, for Portugal, was that a whole range of fees, taxes, dues and premiums could be levied on recruiters, on recruits, on remittances to families, and on goods brought back from the mines. The 100 000 and more miners thus put money into government coffers, in gold, as well as into the village economies of south Mozambique. To cut migration at a stroke would create budgetary stress at a time of rising expectations for improved services in health and education. It would also create a loss of cash revenue in the villages, an unemployed manpower surplus which the new régime was not yet ready to absorb productively, and likelihood of increased clandestine emigration to South Africa. The government therefore adopted a prudent policy of pragmatism in its relations with its large industrial neighbour, and labour, like energy and railway goods, continued to flow, albeit in reduced volume.

The forward-looking economic policies concerned industrialisation. Here the colonial legacy proved to be an unbalanced one. The Caetano reforms had more to do with economic controls and financial institutions than with genuine development. Processing of local crops and raw materials and the manufacture of agricultural equipment remained limited. Coal was mined in Tete for export rather than for local industry. Processing was concerned with such typically colonial enterprises as brewing, furniture-making and plastic goods. Even the cement industry had been inadequate to meet the demands of Cabora Bassa, and supplies had been discreetly, and illegally, bought in Rhodesia. The great weakness of the economy, however, was that production and consumption were heavily oriented to the white 2 per cent of the population. Mozambique industry, like Mozambique administration, depended on white planning, white administration, white craftsmanship, white clerical skills and white purchasing power. The real legacy of underdevelopment that Portugal bequeathed to Mozambique was an almost complete failure of education, whether academic, commercial or practical.

Frelimo, throughout the war and the transition to independence, tenaciously maintained its policy of non-racial even-handedness. Party membership and even high office were open to Mozambicans of European and Asian as well as African ancestry. The new government could not, however, reconcile its socialist vision of equality of opportunity with the economic privileges enjoyed by the 180 000 settler, immigrant and expatriate members of the colonial élite. Half of these began to question their future and left to seek new openings in Brazil, South Africa or Rhodesia. Their departure created gaps in the fabric of both government and private institutions which could only partially be filled by second-generation settlers and Mozambican Asians. The system of rural trade was temporarily restored to Asian commercial expertise after a generation of white domination. After independence a second round of emigration further reduced both European and Asian expertise and acumen. Commerce was taken up by state institutions comparable to the peoples' shops of the liberation movement. Administrative and professional gaps had to be filled by recruiting a new generation of expatriates from a kaleidoscopic variety of friendly countries such as Scandinavia, North Korea, Poland, Portugal, the Soviet Union, China, Britain and Bulgaria. The pattern of Mozambique's foreign relations became more varied than any in Africa. The drive towards national restructuring was interrupted, however, by a new war. This war was fought between South Africa and its three Central African neighbours. It culminated in extensive joint South African and Rhodesian air raids and commando attacks on Zambia and Mozambique in 1979. South Africa's military drive to the north had begun, however, five years earlier, in Angola.

On 25 April 1974 it was easy for a reasonably detached Portuguese observer to see that power in Mozambique would be transferred to the successful Frelimo leadership. The future of Angola was less clear. For the rest of the year it was commonly assumed in Lisbon and Luanda that a colonial, or neo-colonial, partnership would be woven which would ensure the Portuguese future of the newly-struck oil-wells, the continued annual production of quarter of a million tons of coffee and the survival of the 300 000-strong white bourgeoisie. The colonial war, which had been stagnant for several years, petered out without victors convincingly emerging to claim the nationalist heritage. In January 1975 the Portuguese, with help from President Kenyatta of Kenya, cobbled together a tripartite power-sharing executive of the three main political parties, MPLA, FNLA and UNITA. Its coherence and authority were almost immediately subverted, however, first by Zaire, secondly by the Soviet Union, thirdly by South Africa, and finally by a rabble of American, French and British mercenaries. Before the year was out a foreign-fuelled civil war had become a full-scale war of foreign intervention. It was known as the 'asphalt war' because foreign armoured columns ebbed and flowed along the strategic highways which the Portuguese had built.[27]

The descent into war was triggered by Zaire. President Mobutu rightly

27 The literature on the second war of liberation in Angola is extensive. A guide to it may be found in F. W. Heimer, *The Decolonization Conflict in Angola 1974–76: an Essay in Political Sociology*, Geneva, 1979, and in the same author's more extensive treatment of the subject in German.

357

feared that a socialist government in Angola would re-inspire the severely repressed opposition to his own privileged urban military élite. In an effort to forestall renewed peasant rebellion in the decaying agrarian economic sector, Mobutu lent Zairian troops to Holden Roberto with which to mount a putsch and install the FNLA as a friendly government unrestricted by its coalition partners. In the short term, Mobutu was successful in destroying the transitional coalition in Angola. In the long run, he nearly destroyed his own régime as well. Zairian troops proved much less well trained and equipped than he had anticipated, and their defeats in Angola underlay several attempts to overthrow Mobutu in the following years. His survival was eventually ensured only by a large injection of United States aid, by two military interventions by France against armed rebellions, and by a state visit to Luanda to bury the hatchet with Agostinho Neto's MPLA which he had so ardently tried to exclude from office.

When Zaire, with discreet but growing support from the North Atlantic powers, tried to ensure that the FNLA inherited Angola's independence, the MPLA turned to the Warsaw Pact nations for military equipment to re-arm, modernise and expand the guerrilla force which emerged from the eastern war zone. In April 1975 crates of military hardware were being unloaded from Yugoslav freighters at small ports unobserved by the now nominal Portuguese authorities. Soon after, street fighting began in Luanda between the rival parties. In July the MPLA won the last of a series of urban battles. The consequences were the expulsion of the coalition partners from government and the beginnings of a white exodus which swelled to a flood of ninety per cent of the European population by November. The Zairian endeavour to mould the independence policies of Angola failed spectacularly. That was not, however, the end of foreign intervention. The second attempt to exclude the MPLA from office came not across the northern border, but across the southern one, from South Africa.

In 1975 South Africa's policy of emerging from its *laager* to create a security zone, and an economic market, far to the north of its borders was progressing smoothly. Relations with Malawi were cordial, the French connection gave South Africa access to Gabon, Zaire shared strong mutual interests, Zambia was sourly dependent on southern technology and expertise to maintain its copper industry, and Mozambique had been skilfully manoeuvred into a shot-gun marriage at Cabora Bassa. Angola was the only threat to Prime Minister Vorster's strategic web of dialogue partners stretching to the Equator. South Africa therefore felt compelled to forestall accession to power by a hostile MPLA which could endanger its whole Central African edifice and provide a sanctuary for nationalist guerrillas seeking the independence of Namibia. Laws restricting the use of South African troops beyond the Cunene–Limpopo frontiers were amended to allow military strikes as far as the Equator. A secret agreement was concluded with the most southerly of the Angolan political parties, UNITA. Covert encouragement by at least some parts of the United States government system was ensured. In October 1975 an invasion was launched after several months of reconnoitring.[28]

The South African invasion of Angola had a dramatic effect on the politics of Africa. Suddenly it became legitimate to seek the support of foreign troops to defend black independence. In particular, the old African fear of Soviet imperialism waned in the face of a virulent new threat of Afrikaner imperialism. The *de facto* government of the MPLA in Angola sought urgent reinforcements from the Soviet Union, with which it had maintained a discontinuous and volatile relationship over twenty years. The response was as shrewd a diplomatic *coup* as any yet seen in independent Africa. An expeditionary force of ten or more thousand men was raised in Cuba and lifted to Africa in a geriatric fleet of old planes which dodged from country to country in search of refuelling rights. The Spanish-speaking Cubans could learn Angolan Portuguese speedily, could meld into the multi-racial environment invisibly, and could adapt to the low level of material comforts painlessly. They could also turn back the South African column and expose its venture to the world. The last vestige of Portuguese authority melted away, on 11 November 1975, leaving power to 'the people of Angola' rather than to any party or leader. The MPLA, beleaguered in the capital, set out to reconquer the country with Cuban help. The South Africans withdrew in an unwelcome glare of publicity, the resurgent Zairians were again driven back to their border, the American-financed mercenaries were defeated, and their leaders convicted of murder and shot. The price of freedom, however, proved enormous. The cooperation between north Angola and south Angola, which underpinned the agrarian export economy, had been torn apart, the communications systems of road and rail had been mined and counter-mined, the transport fleets of lorries and planes had been destroyed in scorched-earth vendettas by fleeing refugees. Sorely needed men and women of skill and education had been massacred when caught on the wrong side. Postwar reconstruction in Angola was a far harder task than in Mozambique.

Agostinho Neto presided over the difficult first three years of reconstruction until his death in September 1979. Throughout his presidency the central issues of national integration and economic recovery were regularly obscured by border conflicts with threatening neighbours. Two domestic problems, of far greater importance were the rural highlands, and the urban city centres. The rural problem concerned the highland supporters of UNITA. In 1974 the leadership of the party, dominated by Jonas Savimbi, had gained a head-start in politicising and

28 Robin Hallett, 'The South African Intervention in Angola', *African Affairs*, LVII, 1978, 347–86; R. W. Johnson, *How Long Can South Africa Survive?* London, 1977; F. W. Heimer, *The Decolonization Conflict in Angola*.

mobilising its natural constituency of Ovimbundu-speaking Presbyterians. The church network lent itself readily to the organisation of a party, and the church hymns gave zest to its political rallies. Solidarity was enhanced by the horrors of the civil war, and remained surprisingly unscarred by the military collaboration with South Africa. The highland peoples shared a common fear of city politicians in general and of the colonial and post-colonial Luanda bourgeoisie in particular. The sudden departure of settlers who in the 1950s and 1960s had encroached on the Ovimbundu's limited and crowded lands gave a new impetus to mixed subsistence farming which city planning could only threaten. The highlanders therefore resisted government policies of national reintegration. Long after the civil war was over they continued to keep the Benguela railway closed and to ambush agents of government and Cuban security forces. Their recalcitrance was regularly encouraged by contacts with South Africa, which welcomed the deviation of MPLA energies and initially hoped for a long-delayed triumph by Savimbi. By the time of his death, however, Neto had begun to recover the initiative and had reintegrated the central high-lands into the national economic network. There was still some way to go, however, in restoring maize production and supplying migrant coffee labour.

The urban challenge to the independent government of Angola was more serious than the rural once since it stemmed from the MPLA's own city base. After twenty years of deferred hope, however, the city expected freedom to be sweet and golden. Party supporters were not conditioned to expecting blood, sweat and tears as the fruits of independence. Within a year of its victory the MPLA faced a serious uprising in the capital organised by a young man in a hurry called Nito Alves. He challenged the party leadership for resting on its laurels when the slums went hungry; he challenged the pragmatism of policies which deviated from Maoist visions of a new society; he challenged the subversion of trade unions from being the champion of workers' rights to guarantors of government productivity schedules; he challenged the mobilisation of unemployed city youth for 'degrading' work in the sugar and coffee harvest, and he challenged the non-racial preferment of *mestiços* and whites in management and administration. In short, he created a coalition of slum grievances which he publicised through political education cells and among members of a popular football club. By 27 May 1977 he was ready to overthrow the old guard of MPLA leaders and install a young radical alternative. His plan-ning, however, was deficient, his army contacts unreliable, his faith in Soviet support unproven and his calculation of Cuban neutrality wrong. The *coup* was crushed within a day, but it left the new country shaken and paranoid. The political leaders once again went back to the drawing board.[29]

29 David Birmingham 'The twenty-seventh of May: the abortive *coup* in Angola', *African Affairs*, LVII, 1978, 554–64.

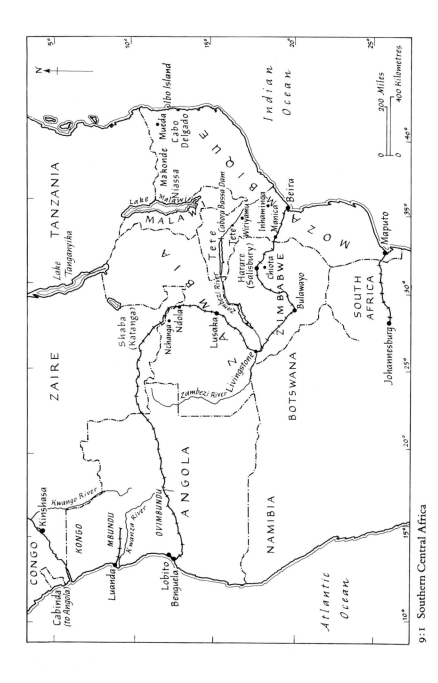

9:1 Southern Central Africa

Angola did still retain one asset which promised security and well-being for the future. In the northern enclave of Cabinda, protected by 4 000 Cuban troops, ten million tons of increasingly valuable oil continued to be pumped out of the sea-bed each year. The royalty constituted eighty per cent of government revenue – not a fortune, but enough with which to plan a genuinely free strategy of development for an otherwise poor country of peasant farmers. After a lifetime of pain and disillusion, President Neto could, by the time of his death, at last look forward with quiet optimism. He had not only achieved the decolonisation of Angola but had, as an increasingly mature statesman, paved the way for the front-line nations of South-Central Africa to help bring Zimbabwe to independence too.

BRITISH CENTRAL AFRICA: THE FEDERATION OF RHODESIA AND
NYASALAND

Historians are increasingly coming to see the 1930s as the key decade in colonial Africa. In the 1930s, so the argument runs, colonial economies ran out of steam and never convincingly recovered; the early optimism and commitment to the transformation of the African environment, and African society, gave way to pessimism and an emphasis upon 'tradition' and stability. Moral initiative passed from whites to blacks. This change of climate was certainly noticeable in British Central Africa in general and in Southern Rhodesia in particular. The 1930s in Southern Rhodesia were a time of retreat from ambition. It was realised that the great areas of land which the whites had claimed exceeded their capacity for developing them. A defensive, narrow, local white nationalism replaced the old arrogant imperialism. The difference between the history of Southern Rhodesia and that of, say, Tanganyika was that in Rhodesia the colonial economy did eventually recover. During the Second World War there was a rapid development of secondary industry and a growth of prosperity for white farmers. When the war was over, some of the new industries proved to be too inefficient to survive. There was no general post-war slump, however, and both industrial and agricultural growth continued. A turning point came in 1948 with two remarkable events. The first was the Southern Rhodesia general strike of African workers in Bulawayo, Salisbury and other towns. The second was a parliamentary election which roundly defeated the isolationists and the not-so-well-off white farmers and artisans. This election virtually destroyed the white Labour Party and marked a signal victory for the prosperous business and industrial element in colonial society.[30]

30 L. H. Gann and M. Gelfand, *Huggins of Rhodesia: the Man and His Country*, London, 1964, p. 206.

The 1948 election gave the Southern Rhodesia prime minister, Godfrey Huggins, the opportunity to press ahead with a strategy of renewed optimism. The expansionists were not content with merely occupying the land of Southern Rhodesia, but revived Rhodes's early dream of a northern El Dorado.[31] The economic logic which led to the establishment of the Central African Federation in 1953 was straightforward. Demand for Northern Rhodesian copper remained strong after the war, and its price was consequently high. The industrialists of Southern Rhodesia realised that the foreign-exchange earnings from copper could be used to finance improvements in communications and the development of hydro-electric power. Moreover, the creation of a single Central African tariff area would give Southern Rhodesian products advantageous access to the markets of the north. At the same time the creation of political links might ensure the continued flow to Southern Rhodesia's mines and farms of unskilled migrant labour from the north. This optimism about the prospect of rapid and large-scale economic development was shared by British governments during the negotiations over Federation. They also believed that Federation would bar South African influence from Central Africa.

So far as Southern Rhodesia was concerned the first years of the Federation of Rhodesia and Nyasaland were a success story. The claim, however, that economic development would equally benefit Northern Rhodesia and Nyasaland soon looked hollow. A careful examination of the economics of the Federation in 1960 found that the rate of growth in the economies of Northern Rhodesia and Nyasaland in the years before they joined the Federation was much greater than the rate of growth after they had joined it. Only in Southern Rhodesia did the data indicate an acceleration in the rate of growth since the establishment of the Federal connection. Investments by the federal government, though underwritten by Northern Rhodesian copper sales, almost entirely benefited industrial growth in Southern Rhodesia. Southern Rhodesian textiles and utensils began to drive out imports from India and Hong Kong on the Nyasaland African market; this meant that 'the poorest sections of the people' had to pay more for necessities than they had done before Federation. The striking 42-per-cent increase in manufacturing output in British Central Africa in the two years after 1955 took place almost entirely in Southern Rhodesia, where observers hailed it as an 'industrial revolution'.[32]

In the political field the consequences of federation were, not surprisingly, as disparate in the three territories as were the economic consequences. In Southern Rhodesia the federal boom between 1953 and 1957 enabled government effectively to buy off most elements of both

31 *Ibid.*, p. 243.
32 A. Hazlewood and P. D. Henderson, *Nyasaland: the Economics of Federation*, Oxford, 1960; P. Deane, 'The Industrial Revolution in British Central Africa', *Civilisations*, Brussels, Vol. XII, no. 3, 1962, pp. 331–47.

white and black opposition. On the white side, poor whites were absorbed into industry, immigrants created new employment, skilled technicians got jobs in the factories and all worried less about competition from Africans than had done the white 'painters and bricklayers of the old school'.[33]

In a different, but equally effective, way government was able to undercut African labour discontent. The 1948 general strike had aroused a great expectation that black proletarian power would henceforth be regularly exercised. 'The old Africa of tribalism and selfishness has died away,' proclaimed Jasper Savanhu. 'Africans realise as never before that united they stand and divided they fall.'[34] Change, however, was not as imminent as it seemed. The Bulawayo and Salisbury African work-force was not a mass of united proletarians. Rapid industrial growth had not created a general 'stabilisation' of workers. Some industries had certainly come to need more semi-skilled and skilled workers, but even they continued to depend for their profits upon low-paid and unskilled migrants.

The chief organisers of the Bulawayo strike of 1948 were semi-skilled workers, who aspired to live permanently in town and thus especially resented poor conditions of work, of accommodation and of pay. In individual firms these employees began to create proto-unions which gained and retained effective freedom of action. They did not wish to be hampered by the coordinating associations led by recognised union leaders such as Savanhu, Mzingeli or Burumbo. The 'leaders' advised against a strike in 1948, but were defied by the 'agitators' from the semi-skilled work-force, who were then able to bring out on strike the mass of unskilled workers. Once the strike was over, employers and government rapidly realised that they had to concentrate on buying off the semi-skilled minority. In order better to control labour some African unions therefore came to be recognised. Labour Boards were set up in several industries and made awards of higher rates of pay to semi-skilled workers. For many years trade unionists worked within the official conciliation machinery. There was some spin-off for unskilled workers, and living conditions slowly improved. Through the 1950s the wages of unskilled African workers, although so low, rose relatively faster than those of white workers. The prosperity of Southern Rhodesian industry in the early years of Federation thus enabled urban discontent to be at least partly bought off. The only significant strikes took place in the mining industry, which still depended largely on unskilled northern migrants and established no Labour Boards.

The early federal years in the south also brought an improvement in the relations of government with African entrepreneurs and with the educated élite. African master-farmers in the Native Purchase Areas began to get

33 Gann and Gelfand, *Huggins*, p. 206.
34 Quoted in Richard Gray, *The Two Nations*, London, 1960, p. 319.

official recognition, and received support at a time when white agricultural success was sufficient to quieten white fears of black competition. There was a noticeable increase in the numbers of black store-keepers and traders in the rural areas. Because the proclamation of 'partnership', as the ideology of Federation, persuaded the African élite to seek achievement within the framework of establishment politics, the great challenge of 1948 was followed by years of quiet almost everywhere.

The quiet politics of Southern Rhodesia after 1948 contrast sharply with what happened in Northern Rhodesia and Nyasaland. On the Copperbelt the African Mineworkers' Union, which had achieved recognition in 1949, demanded that its members should be given some share of federal prosperity. There were strikes of African workers in October and November 1954 and in January and February 1955. A series of 'rolling strikes' began in June 1956 and culminated in the declaration of a state of emergency on the Copperbelt in September. Meanwhile the Northern Rhodesian African National Congress organised boycotts of Copperbelt stores, and popular violence broke out in Ndola and Nchanga. In Nyasaland there had been 'blank, bitter, obstinate refusal' to cooperate since the very beginning of Federation. Educated Africans felt frustrated in their ambitions. 'The Nyasaland Government,' complained Kanyama Chiume, 'is making very slow progress in the promotion of Africans in the field of the civil service.... Federation is opposed by the people and by parents of the children; the discontent in the schools is a symptom of the unsatisfactory constitutional set-up in the country, reflected through an equally unsatisfactory educational system.' Peasant farmers resented and resisted compulsory agricultural rules. 'Nyasaland,' Chiume continued, 'is becoming one of the few countries in which agriculture is taught to the people by imprisonment of the people.'[35]

Even in Southern Rhodesia, however, the apparent peace of the mid-1950s was deceptive. In particular the government failed signally to buy off discontent in the African reserves. During the Second World War the implementation of the Land Apportionment Act had been delayed so as not to cause unrest, but after the war there were large-scale clearances of families off 'European' land and into the reserves. People were moved with their cattle, and herds in the reserves grew so excessive that compulsory destocking was enforced. There was, moreover, increasing government intervention in African peasant farming. The Native Trade and Production Commission of 1944 had painted an alarming picture of 'traditional' sloth and destructiveness, disregarding the earlier history of vigorous peasant response to market opportunity. The Commission recommended that conservation measures be enforced and that compulsory labour be employed. It also recommended that the whole basis of land tenure be

35 M. W. Kanyama Chiume, *Kwacha: an Autobiography*, Nairobi, 1975, pp. 106–12.

changed, so that only those with registered individual titles be permitted to hold land. Residential settlements were also to be regrouped. All these provisions were embodied in the Native Land Husbandry Act of 1951.

Government statements about Land Husbandry spoke of their intention to create a contented and prosperous peasantry. An official publication in 1955, when the act began to be implemented more thoroughly, predicted a doubling of rural cash incomes within five years and a 140-per-cent increase within eight years. It also predicted the emergence of a stable urban work-force which had surrendered its rights to land.[36] The act did not work out as intended, and almost everyone in the reserves opposed it. In many reserves, entrepreneurial peasants farmed quite large areas of land. Under Land Husbandry they would have been allocated the standard 6 or 7 acres, so they naturally opposed its implementation. Many chiefs resented the loss of their power to allocate land. Even peasants who were allocated more or less the same amount of land that they had previously farmed resented new and unpopular patterns of residence and the coercive commands of agricultural demonstrators and land development officers. Above all, those young men who were away in the towns and who lost land rights at the time of registration opposed implementation very strongly. On the side of the employers and the municipalities there was little interest in keeping the implicit Land Husbandry bargain. Employers did not want all their work-force to be 'stabilised' and thereby to have to pay them a full living wage without a rural subsidy. Failure was compounded when the agricultural methods imposed by the new policy were unsuccessful. The predicted increase in output did not occur. The reports of Native Commissioners – and more especially oral records of the period – make it clear that there was very widespread discontent in the reserves between 1948 and 1958.

The dissatisfaction of the unpropitiated peasantry was only one part of Southern Rhodesia's problem. The rest of the government's policy of co-option depended upon the continuance of a federal economic boom. Even before Federation came to an end things began to look bleaker. There was a fall in copper, and by 1958 prices were down to 60 per cent of their 1956 level. The rapid growth of the federal economy until 1956 was geared to the price of copper, and with the fall in that price the growth of the domestic product came to an end.[37] From 1957 the rate of industrial growth in Southern Rhodesia slowed; in mid-1958 the Foreign Migratory Labour Act was introduced to keep Mozambicans and other alien workers out of Southern Rhodesian towns. Even with this measure indigenous unemployment grew, and the 1958–1959 federal recession brought an economic crisis in which unemployment manifested itself significantly.[38]

36 *What the Native Land Husbandry Act Means to the Rural Africans*, Salisbury, 1955.
37 Hazlewood and Henderson, *Nyasaland*, p. 13.
38 Duncan Clarke, *The Unemployment Crisis*, London, 1978, p. 6.

This economic recession formed the background to the political crisis of the Federation in 1958 and 1959.

A series of events in all three territories led to the crisis of the Central African Federation. In September 1957 the African National Congress of Southern Rhodesia was established under the leadership of Joshua Nkomo at a meeting in Salisbury. Congress rapidly established itself as the dominant African political movement in the territory. It at once began to make contact with unskilled migrants in the towns whose wage increases were slowing down, and who feared that they would lose their land rights. Congress also recruited peasants in the reserves whose opposition to Land Husbandry had intensified as more vigorous implementation was pursued. In January 1958 the Southern Rhodesian cabinet revolted against the leadership of Garfield Todd, whose policies were held to be too 'liberal'. Southern Rhodesian whites had failed to take advantage of the time bought for them by economic prosperity, and had not made sufficient reforms to hold the loyalty of the African middle class. Todd's overthrow, and the sense of curtailed opportunity which came with the recession, initiated a movement of the African educated élite towards Congress. In July 1958 Dr Hastings Banda returned to Nyasaland from his long absence overseas to take command of the Nyasaland National Congress. 'Human nature is such,' wrote Henry Chipembere to Banda, 'that it needs a hero to be hero-worshipped if the political struggle is to succeed.'[39] Flamboyant, peppery, profoundly conservative in everything save his detestation of the 'stupid Federation', Banda proclaimed himself an 'extremist' and soon had 'the whole of Nyasaland on fire'.[40] At the end of 1958 Kenneth Kaunda and others broke away from the African National Congress of Northern Rhodesia to form their own Zambia African National Congress dedicated to destroying the new Northern Rhodesian constitution and supplanting the ANC as the major national party. Zambia African National Congress gained support in a majority of the rural areas and there was a marked increase in rural unrest and even arson.[41]

Unrest throughout the Federation came to a head early in 1959. On 26 February a state of emergency was declared in Southern Rhodesia. The ANC was banned, and hundreds of its officers were arrested. Congress was accused of having made the implementation of Land Husbandry impossible. Godfrey Huggins, now Lord Malvern, frankly admitted, however, that 'the Southern Rhodesian African Congress must be put behind wire so that they could not create a diversion and prevent the sending of necessary police to Nyasaland'.[42] White Southern Rhodesian troops were flown to Nyasaland, where on 3 March a state of emergency

39 Clyde Sanger, *Central African Emergency*, London, 1960, p. 198.
40 *Ibid.*, p. 200.
41 D. C. Mulford, *The Northern Rhodesian General Election, 1962*, Oxford, 1964, p. 15.
42 Philip Mason, *Year of Decision: Rhodesia and Nyasaland, 1960*, London, 1960, p. 216.

was declared and the Nyasaland Congress was banned. Thereafter hundreds of people were arrested, crowds were dispersed, villages were searched, collective fines were imposed. Hastings Banda and other Congress leaders were taken to prisons in Southern Rhodesia. On 11 March the Zambia Congress was also declared illegal and its leaders were similarly arrested.

The 1959 emergencies were the turning point for the Federation. They made nakedly clear the dominance of Southern Rhodesia over the reluctant north. As Philip Mason wrote the following year: 'The effect on the people of Nyasaland can hardly be overestimated. What they had feared most about Federation was that they would be ruled by Southern Rhodesia. They had been told that under Federation they would keep their own government. . . . Yet they had seen Southern Rhodesian white troops come into Nyasaland and search their villages; aircraft had been used, as if against an enemy, to frighten them. . . . From Southern Rhodesia many Nyasalanders who were not active politicians . . . had been suddenly arrested, detained for weeks without trial, and at last released and returned to Nyasaland without jobs.'[43]

In 1959 the southern prime minister, Edgar Whitehead, and the two northern governors, claimed that they had secured at least two years of freedom from 'extremist' African oppostion. It was soon plain, however, that support for Congress in Nyasaland and for the Zambia Congress in Northern Rhodesia had in no way been broken. More important developments, however, occurred in Southern Rhodesia. The emergency there was followed by draconian security legislation and long months of stunned African inactivity. Change came in January 1960 when the National Democratic Party was founded and inaugurated four years of confrontation between government and mass nationalism. When Whitehead banned the National Democratic Party it was immediately succeeded by the Zimbabwe African People's Union (ZAPU). In the north Southern Rhodesian troops could not again be made available to hold the disintegrating Federation together. The British government realised this, and set up conferences which unavailingly devised several new constitutions with complex racial franchises. By March 1959, however, the break-up of the Federation had already become inevitable. It occurred in 1964.

The break-up of the British Central African Federation led to the emergence of two independent nations under African majority rule – Malawi and Zambia. Forced interaction between the three component territories was replaced by an almost complete lack of interaction between them. Relations between Zambia and Southern Rhodesia grew increasingly hostile until a complete closure of the frontier between them was

43 *Ibid.*, p. 217.

imposed in 1973. Much coolness developed between Zambia and Malawi. One major beneficiary of the break-up of the Federation was South Africa, which traded with Zambia, opened diplomatic relations with Malawi and supplied aid, export goods, petrol and finance capital to Southern Rhodesia. The main loser was Zambia. The long-delayed resolution of the struggle between black and white in Southern Rhodesia put severe constraints on the exercise of Zambian independence.

NATIONALIST POLITICS IN SOUTHERN RHODESIA, 1962–1972

Many people in Zambia, and elsewhere, blamed the costly delay in resolving the federal legacy of conflict on the inadequacies of the African political movements in Southern Rhodesia. Such critics argued that the leaders of the successive parties made an erroneous analysis of their situation. They had been misled by the successes of nationalism in Zambia and Malawi, and thought they could win independence by appealing to Britain or to the United Nations. They demonstrated the mass support they enjoyed by means of large public rallies, but never realised that force might be necessary to overthrow a settler régime. They launched no effective training programme for guerrilla struggle. They also failed to prepare a network of underground cells which might have perpetuated political organisation in the countryside. The critics applied a class analysis to the successive nationalist parties: their leadership was stigmatised as 'petty bourgeois reformist', with distinctions between the 'petty bourgeois populist' atmosphere of Congress and ZAPU, and the 'petty bourgeois élitist' atmosphere of the National Democratic Party and ZANU (Zimbabwe African National Union). Some of these criticisms plainly were justified, and were indeed voiced within the liberation movement. Others, however, revealed too little appreciation of circumstances and too scholastic a desire to make distinctions within a short sequence of parties.

In Southern Rhodesia the period of open mass nationalism produced a single sequence of parties which shared the same social character. All were led by the same sort of people in class terms, and all enjoyed a following among urban workers and rural cultivators. The major difference between Congress, in 1957, and ZAPU, in 1963, was that ZAPU had grown larger and had penetrated more areas. ZAPU had also become more militant, though still without conceiving of a protracted guerrilla struggle. By means of public meetings, of impassioned oratory and of symbolic action, a massive political education campaign was carried out. Ndabaningi Sithole described the atmosphere of nationalist meetings in colourful language: 'The crowds cheered wildly. It was clear that the natural eloquence of the Son of the Soil . . . moved them to the very core of their being. His words had broken loose the chains around their souls . . . lifted a downtrodden, third-rate people out of the valley of depression . . . to the very top of the

369

Mount of Transfiguration.'[44] In 1957 most Africans had been reluctant to be seen in open opposition to their employers or to the state. They did not even believe that majority rule was a possible target. They lacked the confidence to escape the contempt with which white Rhodesians regarded African society. The lack of inner conviction made it impossible to plan a guerrilla war or even to imagine one. By 1962 change had brought immeasurable gains in self-confidence and increased expectations.

The rapid growth of self-confidence and expectation brought another criticism of the Southern Rhodesian nationalist leadership. This was its unrealistic lack of concrete political and military planning. ZAPU was banned in 1962, both ZAPU and ZANU were banned in 1964, Ian Smith declared unilateral independence from Britain in 1965, and yet none of these disasters was countered by effective nationalist action. The contrast between the 1962 prediction that majority rule would be achieved within six months, and the humiliating reversals of the next three years, caused deep popular disillusion. In Chiota Reserve people turned inward with a new fatalism: 'After the events of 1964 and 1965 hope turned almost to despair as it became clear that majority rule would not easily be achieved. ... Africans began a hunt for "sell-outs". The confrontation between white and black had been diverted into a search for the enemy within.'[45]

Mass disillusion was paralleled and intensified by divisions within the political leadership. ZAPU had agreed that if the party were banned no further party should be founded. It was held essential to break the cycle of banning, confiscation of assets, re-formation, and banning again. After ZAPU was banned in 1962, months passed and the absence of any formal nationalist voice seemed increasingly dangerous. In March 1963 Nkomo began to fear that Britain might concede independence to white Southern Rhodesia when the Federation broke up. A new nationalist initiative had somehow to be taken. Nkomo concluded that the best course was to prepare for a Rhodesian independence – whether conceded by Britain or unilaterally declared by Smith – by establishing an alternative nationalist government, which could appeal for support to Africa and the world. In April 1963 members of ZAPU's executive were ordered to make their way to Dar-es-Salaam to set up a government-in-exile. Such a government-in-exile could have focused world opposition to Smith. The plan, however, did not enjoy the backing of the presidents of Tanganyika or Zambia. They told Nkomo to return and fight alongside his people. Inside Rhodesia rumours seethed about the mysterious flight of the ZAPU executive. The situation in the African nationalist ranks was confused, and an African moderate wrote wryly that 'Everybody who is anybody is running away and only stooges and political fools like ourselves remain. ... I do not think

44 Ndabaningi Sithole, *Roots of a Revolution*, Oxford, 1977, p. 103.
45 Peter Fry, *Spirits of Protest*, Cambridge, 1976, p. 120.

anybody here knows what to do next.'[46] The fiery Maurice Nyagumbo was equally confused, and wrote from Tanganyika, 'I don't know what's going on. I am being pushed from one place to another. That's why I feel I must say No to staying here in Tanganyika even if it means expulsion from the party. . . . Some of us must remain at home to be with the people, even if it means to be in gaol with them.'[47]

Confusion in exile and anxiety to be home 'with the people' gave rise to fierce criticism of Nkomo's leadership. Leaflets attacking him were circulated in the townships inside Rhodesia. In Dar-es-Salaam members of the executive felt foolish and humiliated. They decided to wait until Nkomo was fund-raising in Europe and depose him. They planned to elect Ndabaningi Sithole as their new leader and then to return to Rhodesia to announce a new phase of the struggle. Nkomo learned of the plan, flew to Rhodesia and put his absent critics at a serious disadvantage: 'A voice from Dar-es-Salaam could not contend with a voice from Highfields.'[48] Nkomo rallied support and retained control of most of the old party. From those who opposed him came ZANU, launched in August 1963. ZANU gained the support of men such as Herbert Chitepo, Leopold Takawira, Maurice Nyagumbo and Robert Mugabe. They declared a policy of confrontation with the Smith régime.

Confrontation between black nationalists and white settlers was delayed, however, by confrontation between Nkomo's ZAPU and the new ZANU. The Smith government was able to sit back for several months while the rivals assailed each other. ZAPU probably retained majority support, not only in Matabeleland, where Nkomo's long trade-union and political career brought him widespread loyalty, but also in Salisbury and many rural areas of Mashonaland. ZANU's support was drawn partly from individuals and groups who had become frustrated with the old reformist strategies and partly from local loyalty to individual leaders. The region around Umtali knew Chitepo well; the region around Chilimanzi heard the appeal of Takawira; and the region around Mount Silinda responded to Ndabaningi Sithole. It was clear, however, that neither party spoke in tribal or regional terms and both argued their case on the basis of national emancipation.

In 1964 the Smith régime shut the leaders of both ZAPU and ZANU away for ten years, and a difficult period ensued for the nationalist movement. A new leadership had to emerge in exile and faced many difficulties in planning for guerrilla war. Neither party could recruit men for military training from inside the country since the well-policed Zambezi border prevented travel from Southern Rhodesia. Most of those sent to train were therefore immigrants from Southern Rhodesia living in

46 Stanlake Samkange to Terence Ranger, 22 April 1963.
47 Maurice Nyagumbo to Shelagh Ranger, 14 May 1963.
48 Sarah Chavunduka to Terence Ranger, 28 Aug. 1963.

Zambia. None of the new men in charge of ZAPU and ZANU had any experience of warfare, and supplies of arms and money were slow to arrive. Worst of all, the Zambezi was a formidable barrier to guerrilla incursions. Once across, you faced 'a terrible situation: there are not people there ... you see animals only.'[49]

Guerrilla groups which did get through to Shona-speaking or Ndebele-speaking rural areas did not find universal support. The young guerrillas were largely strangers inside Southern Rhodesia, and there had been little preparation for their arrival. Rural communities had not recovered from their in-turned pessimism of 1964, and the edge had been taken off their rural grievances. Even in these years, however, guerrilla activity possessed an important symbolic quality. In 1966 a ZANU guerrilla group from Zambia fought a pitched battle with white security forces in Sinoia. Survivors correctly perceived the battle as a lesson in how not to attempt guerrilla penetration. 'We failed our battle because we could not mobilise the masses, we had no contacts inside the country, we did not hide weapons inside the country.'[50] But the news of this readiness to confront the white army did much to counter fatalism. 'We heard of the first shot in Sinoia,' remembered Samuel Mamutsi Mrimbo. 'We had no idea that there were some people inside. ... A big number of people [joined] the party because of what happened at Sinoia.'[51]

The external difficulties of the years between 1964 and 1970 were compounded by an unpropitious internal environment. The great strike of 1948 had been succeeded by years of apparent acquiescence to colonial rule, and the nationalist agitation of 1963 and 1964 was similarly followed by a long lull. The new Rhodesian régime was able to undercut African opposition in ways very different from those used in the 1950s. The Rhodesia Front made clear that it would abandon the Land Husbandry Act, which had created a landless class harbouring a great deal of ill-feeling towards the agents of government. The act had seriously disturbed social stability.[52] The régime disavowed any intention to interfere with African 'tradition' or with communal agriculture. Instead, it proposed a policy of 'community development' allegedly to restore decision-making to Africans.

The new policy meant that primary schools controlled by mission churches were handed over to local community control. The influence of the chiefs was recognised and buttressed. All over the country Native Commissioners began to delineate and define the boundaries of chiefdoms and their constituent communities. All these moves were aspects of the

49 Interview between John Conradie and Samuel Mrimbo, Maputo, Aug. 1979.
50 *Ibid.*
51 *Ibid.*
52 Rhodesia Government report of 1964, cited in A. J. B. Hughes, *Development in Rhodesian Tribal Areas*, Salisbury, 1974, p. 148.

Rhodesia Front's belief in segregation, in a half-hearted apartheid, which matched its refusal to recognise African rights in the towns. The policy was intended to leave the poor to pay for their own needs. 'Make the African aware,' proclaimed a Rhodesia Front document in 1974, 'that he must look primarily to the African area to provide him with his living and occupation, skilled and unskilled ... [and] remove pressure on the European tax payer to supply unlimited finance to provide ever increasing services.'[53] In the long run such a policy was bound to intensify the social and economic problems of the African rural areas, but in the short run it gave both rural Africans and the Smith government a breathing space.

The Unilateral Declaration of Independence (UDI) and the international economic sanctions which followed it gave the Rhodesian industrial economy an unexpected boost. After the boom of the early Federal years, employment stagnated until the late 1960s when the post-UDI boom occurred under enforced protection.[54] New import substitution industries were promoted. Industrial output grew steadily between 1966 and 1974. Zambia suffered much more from sanctions in this period than did Southern Rhodesia. For some years the growth in jobs satisfied the ever-increasing numbers of youthful job seekers, though a segregationist philosophy prevented the adequate development of town accommodation and facilities. When the economic prosperity tailed off and unemployment began to mount, the Rhodesia Front faced serious internal discontent. In the years between 1964 and 1970, however, an illusory calm prevailed.

The turning point in the nationalist struggle came in the years 1970 to 1972. In 1970 Frelimo opened its second front, south of the Zambezi, in the Tete region of Mozambique. In the same year ZANU commanders came to the conclusion that their guerrilla action across the Zambezi from Zambia was leading nowhere. The Zimbabwe struggle also needed a second front, preferably one across a land frontier where guerrillas could gain immediate access to large populations of Shona-speakers familiar with the nationalist movement. ZANU approached Frelimo for transit facilities through the Tete operational area to the eastern war zone of Rhodesia. 'We support ZAPU,' replied Samora Machel, 'but we are not married to ZAPU. We are married to the people of Zimbabwe. So Frelimo will not support ZANU, no, Frelimo will support the people of Zimbabwe.'[55] Facilities were given, and very quietly small-scale preparations were made for war in the north-east. A handful of ZANU militants infiltrated the villages and discovered a welcoming response. Weapons and ammunition

---

53 Rhodesia Front document of 1974, cited in Michael Bratton, 'Settler State, Guerrilla War, and Rural Underdevelopment in Rhodesia', *Rural Africana*, 4–5, spring/fall 1979, p. 123.
54 Colin Stoneman, *Skilled Labour and Future Needs*, London, 1978, p. 8.
55 Interview between John Conradie and Josiah Tongogara, Maputo, Aug. 1979. I am very grateful to Dr Conradie for allowing me to make use of this material.

373

were concealed in local caches, and recruits were trained on the spot. For two years a steady build-up of support and resources took place, quite unknown to the Rhodesian régime. Then 'on 21 December 1972, at 3.00 a.m., a few miles from Centenary village, the Altena tobacco farm, owned by de Borchgrave, was riddled with machine gun fire and torn apart by hand grenades. ... For the white farmers of the north-east a new era had begun.'[56]

Meanwhile change went on inside Rhodesia also. On 24 November 1971 the British prime minister, Sir Alec Douglas-Home, announced that he and Ian Smith had agreed on a constitutional settlement. If this settlement proved to be acceptable to African opinion it would be implemented. It was immediately denounced by Nkomo and Sithole from prison. 'Let every bush ... be alive with our clear, unmistakable "NO",' wrote Sithole to his supporters.[57] The Smith government was confident that Nkomo and Sithole were forgotten men and that it could win adequate expressions of African support. It was deluded by its own political success in creating acquiescence to its authority in the rural areas. This confidence was misplaced and on 16 December 1971 a new African organisation came into being. The African National Council (ANC), under Bishop Abel Muzorewa, vigorously revived mass nationalism. The Rhodesian government was obliged to allow it some freedom to campaign against the settlement proposals, and within weeks the ANC had branches all over the territory. In May 1972 the Pearce Commission reported that African opinion was overwhelmingly against the proposed constitution. This effective African veto revived Zimbabwean self-confidence and brought a whole new generation into nationalist politics. The revival of internal mass nationalism and the simultaneous opening of guerrilla action marked a decisive new phase in the country's history.

In 1972 the support which ZANU received in the north-east, and which the ANC enjoyed throughout the territory, indicated that rural grievance was once again sharp. Community development had brought none of the promised benefits. African cultivators had, moreover, been indirectly but sharply affected by economic sanctions. The first sufferers from sanctions had been European producers of export cash crops. Prior to UDI white farmers had been happy to concentrate on tobacco and to leave a considerable share of the home food market to African producers. After UDI the Rhodesian régime assisted white farmers to diversify their production and to move out of tobacco and into maize and beef. Capital investment from South Africa assisted in the process, and white farmers began to drive African producers out of the local market. A massive impoverishment of the peasantry was beginning.[58]

56 Michael Raeburn, *Black Fire*, London, 1978, pp. 217–18.
57 Ndabaningi Sithole, *Letters from Salisbury Prison*, Nairobi, 1976, p. 68.
58 Clarke, *The Unemployment Crisis*, p. 13.

THE ZIMBABWE WAR 1972–1980

African economic grievance and the escalation of the war were closely interlinked. The north-eastern war flared brightly between December 1972 and the end of 1974. In April 1974 the whole eastern border was opened to ZANU infiltration as a consequence of the revolution in Portugal, and the Rhodesian régime had to pour men and money into the war. Economic decline followed the 1972 intensification of the war. Growth rates slipped downwards although they remained positive until 1975. The real GDP fell in 1976 by 3·2 per cent and in 1977 by a further 7 per cent. Falling GDP was quickly translated into sizeable reductions in the volume of African employment.[59] In 1960 18·6 per cent of all Africans in Rhodesia were in wage employment. This number fell to 15·6 per cent by 1975 and only 13 per cent by 1978. African boys and girls at school no longer believed that their qualifications would find them employment. Many therefore joined the stream of guerrilla volunteers leaving Rhodesia. The sharp fall in the African share of the agricultural market also persuaded peasant cultivators to shelter these young guerrillas and sustain their attack on the régime.

The development of the war alarmed Rhodesia's friends. South Africa foresaw that a long, wasting war would produce a revolutionary African régime on its border, and supplied the Smith régime with oil and the fighting men, and the capital long kept out by federal tariffs. The United States and Britain also disliked the prospect of radical change and sought to avert it.

From 1974 to 1978 the Smith régime adopted several broad tactics to meet the nationalist challenge. They undercut the war effort by promising to negotiate peace and sought out the most 'moderate' sections of the nationalist leadership with offers of partnership. They put pressure on Zambia and Mozambique by closing supply routes, supporting armed opposition groups, and launching land and air raids into their territory. Pressure on these front-line states was designed to force ZAPU and ZANU to the conference table. Internally the war in the African rural areas was fought with ever-increasing ferocity and thought of winning hearts and minds or of protecting the rural economy was abandoned. More African soldiers, police and 'auxiliaries' were recruited and armed. Ultimately conscripts bore the brunt of the fighting in rural areas. African unemployment, which generated recruits for the guerrillas, also drove young men to military employment by the régime.

The complex consequences of the government's tactics enabled Smith to play on the divisions within the nationalist ranks. Not only were there divisions between ZAPU and ZANU and Muzorewa's ANC, but also between the 'generations' of leaders within each movement. At times the

59 *Ibid.*, p. 10.

nationalist thrust seemed fatally fragmented, and some commentators went so far as to predict civil war. Despite delay and confusion the remorseless growth of the war brought forth solidarity and commitment by the great majority of African people.

In 1974 an attempt was made at *détente*. It successfully disrupted the nationalist war effort. South Africa, Britain and the United States put pressure on Smith to negotiate while Zambia, Tanzania and Mozambique put even greater pressure on the nationalists. Nkomo, Sithole, Mugabe and others were released from gaol by Smith and compelled by the front-line states to unite in an umbrella organisation led by Muzorewa. The negotiations produced nothing, and were much resented by ZANU. It was the ZANU offensive in the north-east which had put the Smith régime under pressure, and ZANU guerrilla commanders were the ones most reluctant to call a ceasefire or to join a unitary force. Leaders who had been in prison for ten years were deeply suspicious of the motives both of the front-line states and of Britain. They tried to depose Ndabaningi Sithole lest he cooperate too willingly in *détente*. They agreed in form only to the front-line presidents' demand for a ceasefire, and secretly continued to train guerrillas for an intensified offensive. ZANU was seen by the protagonists of *détente* as the major obstacle.

Events inside ZANU gave its enemies an opportunity. Tension between guerrillas in the field and their commanders in Zambia had taken on both ideological and ethnic overtones and led to faction fighting in Lusaka. On 18 March 1975, Herbert Chitepo, the national chairman of ZANU, was killed by a bomb outside his house in Lusaka. The murder remains one of the mysteries of Zimbabwean history, but ZANU members argued that he was killed by Rhodesian or South African agents. The Zambian government, however, thought he had been killed by Tongogara and the ZANU military commanders. The accused were held in prison until late 1976, and ZANU camps were occupied by the Zambian army. In March 1976 an international commission of inquiry supported the Zambian action.[60] For over a year the war of liberation was stalled.

The 1974 *détente* had other effects. While the military commanders of ZANU were placed in gaol, the political founders of the party were released from their Rhodesian prisons. Men like Robert Mugabe, Edgar Tekere and Maurice Nyagumbo kept the war going by setting up training camps in Mozambique. During the 'ceasefire' a communications network was established inside Zimbabwe and thousands of young recruits travelled to Mozambique and Botswana. The men trying to hold ZANU together were overwhelmed by the response: 'They are taking up arms in their thousands,' said Tekere. 'People of seven to sixteen years of age, thousands

---

60 The report of the Commission of Inquiry into Chitepo's death was published in Lusaka in March 1976; ZANU radicals in England produced a very effective critique, *The Price of Détente*, soon thereafter.

of them ... coming to fight. Seven year olds. To fight. It is a battle with them, with these little kids, to persuade them to go back to school.'[61] But there were enough 'big kids' to make good the loss of the fighting men held in Zambia. When the war resumed in 1976 it was on a wider basis than before.

The release of the original political leaders reduced the fragmentation of Zimbabwe politics. Nkomo once again became the unchallenged leader of ZAPU and built a formidable force of equipped and trained men. After complex and obscure struggles Robert Mugabe emerged at the end of 1976 as the leader of the ZANU forces. Once again, as in 1964, opposition to the régime was simply divided between ZAPU and ZANU. From the end of 1976 they worked together in the Patriotic Front alliance. The underlying simplicity and strength of this alliance was revealed in the 1980 election in which the popular vote went overwhelmingly to Nkomo and Mugabe. All other parties were swept aside.

Renewed war, and success in the field by the Patriotic Front, caused the Smith régime to play its cards with desperation and ferocity. It forced hundred of thousands of rural Africans into consolidated villages where they were unable to support the guerrillas. Curfews were imposed. Standing crops were destroyed. Food stores and grain mills were closed down to deny the guerrillas access to food. Villages and schools were attacked from the air when guerrilla sightings were reported. Tight censorship was imposed, but the widespread brutalities were none the less publicised, particularly by the Catholic Commission for Justice and Peace.[62]

As the war grew, the régime gave up the struggle to control African rural areas. They had become economically marginal to the government and were more or less abandoned by the administration. White troops and regular African soldiers were withdrawn. Instead, the régime came to rely on 'auxiliaries' and African irregulars who instituted a campaign of counter-terror in the Tribal Trust Lands. By 1978 the Tribal Trust Lands had in effect passed from government control to nationalist control. Guerrilla offensives could now be aimed at the white farming region. Official military strategy concentrated on protecting the core of the white economy, the towns and the line-of-rail, as well as the limited number of heavily capitalised, highly productive farms and plantations run by white entrepreneurs. The rest of the white farming area was tacitly abandoned, and an informal 'squatter' resettlement by Africans took place. In the towns intense police action prevented African workers from expressing open opposition to government. In the rural areas, however, peasant support for the guerrillas persisted in spite of great suffering.

61 Speech by Edgar Tekere, 28 Aug. 1976, *Revolutionary Zimbabwe*, 4, p. 11.
62 For the publications of the commission see in the bibliography below the section on the war and its impact.

A costly and bloody stalemate was eventually reached in 1979. Holding even to the core area had become a long-term burden too great for the Smith régime. A new effort had to be made to end the war, and an 'Internal Settlement' exercise was launched in 1978 and 1979. Smith sought to bargain a deal with those African leaders who no longer commanded guerrilla forces. Muzorewa and Sithole, in particular, had nothing to expect from continued war; both, on the other hand, retained some support which could be consolidated if they could bring about peace. Their mistake, and that of Smith, was not to realise that the African peasantry was not ready to seek peace at any price.

The internal attempt to buy off African opposition was much less successful than the previous *détente*. The domestic economic crisis meant that the régime could offer little prospect of prosperity to workers or to farmers. Externally the settlement gained no international recognition, and no front-line states pressurised guerrillas to accept a ceasefire. Rhodesian whites still did not realise the scale of the concessions that they would have to make to African demands. The elections for African majority rule produced an impressive turn-out of voters in April 1979. Muzorewa gained 67 per cent of the votes cast and Sithole 14 per cent, but neither man could deliver the promised peace. Sithole had relied upon his reputation as the founding president of ZANU. In his name, he said, the boys had gone out into the bush, and in his name they would come back. They did not, and Sithole failed to attract support. Instead, the war was intensified and martial law further extended. Muzorewa, who won the election and became the country's first black prime minister, could not deliver peace either. He presided over the bloodiest period of military repression. The war escalated with a series of devastating raids into Zambia and Mozambique. Participation in the white military offensive undermined Muzorewa. Equally seriously, he was unable to redistribute land, to increase urban wages or to reduce unemployment. The white structures continued to function under his formal authority while dearth and death were experienced on the Tribal Trust Lands. Vast, plastic-tented shanties grew up around each major town. Rural refugees, men and women, ceased to be part of rural society without being able to enter the urban economy.

The total failure of the internal settlement led to another attempt at *détente* in mid-1979. This time the front-line states, Britain and South Africa were all involved. Heavy military and economic pressure was again put on the front-line states, who again pressurised ZAPU and ZANU to negotiate under threat of discontinuing support. Once again the guerrillas and their leaders entered the negotiations with profound suspicion. The ZANU leaders particularly wanted to achieve an outright military victory. They believed that the Lancaster House negotiations were designed to eliminate the armed nationalists and to present Muzorewa with a rigged electoral victory.

The Lancaster House settlement did not work out in the way in which ZANU had feared and others had hoped. The African population of Zimbabwe, particularly in the rural areas but also significantly in the towns, had broken out of the cycle of protest and quiescence and were determined to achieve a proper reward for their suffering. The ideologies of self-help taught by the guerrillas, together with other forms of radicalism, had influenced many. A rigged election had become impossible. Furthermore, the internal settlement, despite all its inadequacy, had decisively weakened Ian Smith and given deceptive prominence to Muzorewa. South Africa believed that Muzorewa could win a new election, and gain increased power under the Lancaster House constitution. Without this South African belief it is unlikely that the elections would have been permitted to take place. ZANU and ZAPU, however, made other calculations and also decided to work within the terms of the Lancaster House agreement. 'I would be the last to praise the constitution and say it is perfect,' wrote Mugabe in an address to the people in January 1980, 'but it is a viable political instrument. ... We have to seize that instrument which after all is a logical product of our revolutionary efforts and place it firmly in the hands of our people.... We have decided to declare 1980 the Year of People's Power, the year in which we shall, as the great people of Zimbabwe, take control of ... all the institutions of government.'[63]

Mugabe's confidence in accepting the Zimbabwe independence constitution was justified. In February 1980 the voters gave fifty-seven of the eighty African seats to Mugabe's ZANU and twenty of them to Nkomo's ZAPU. It was a return to the two-party politics of 1964, except that a decisive shift in the balance of support between the two parties had taken place. In 1964 ZAPU enjoyed three supporters to every one of ZANU's. In 1980 ZANU won 63 per cent of the vote and ZAPU 24 per cent. This shift had been brought about by the war. ZANU had committed more guerrillas to the field and its armies had spread more widely. With few exceptions the areas they reached voted for ZANU and Mugabe.

ZIMBABWE AND INDEPENDENCE

The belated achievement of African majority rule in Zimbabwe opened up all sorts of possibilities which had been in abeyance since the break-up of the Central African Federation in 1964. In 1964 an African successor government in Zimbabwe might have been able to construct a more equitable association among the three former British territories. It might also have met the grievances of African peasants and workers and so avoided their immersion in the violence of the 1970s. Such aspirations

63 Robert Mugabe, *1980 – the Year of the People's Power*, Jan. 1980.

constituted much of the political agenda in Zimbabwe after the election of 1980. Meetings between representatives of Zimbabwe, Zambia, Malawi, Mozambique and other states of the region attempted to construct mechanisms of collaboration which could break the regional dependence on the South African economy. Zimbabwe's role in such an association was to supply industrial goods and food to the rest of the region. In return, the associates offered Zimbabwe routes to the coast to reduce or eliminate the use of South African roads and railways. Such a plan optimistically anticipated international investment on a generous scale. The huge maize harvest of 1981 helped arrangements for regional cooperation off to a good start; much of the maize was set aside to supply Zambia's needs, and more was purchased by international agencies for famine relief elsewhere in Africa.

To satisfy the aspirations of peasants and workers, the government of Zimbabwe announced far-reaching schemes of land distribution and wage increases. In 1980 rural peasant families were given free food, free seed and free fertiliser to reconstruct the agrarian economy ravaged by war. Their large maize surplus was bought by government at a high guaranteed price. The authority of chiefs and district commissioners was replaced by that of village committees, village courts and elected rural councils. Workers received large wage increases and were promised participation in, and even control of, industries taken over by government. The Mugabe government planned both for a permanently settled urban work-force and for a group of full-time peasant cultivators. In the 1980s, however, unlike the 1950s, government aimed to help ensure that urban dwellers got a living wage and adequate accommodation. Similarly, they aspired to guarantee peasants enough land to subsist and a fair price for any cash crop they grew.

In 1980 it did not prove easy for Zimbabwe to escape from the legacy of its own recent history or from that of South-Central Africa in general. Relations with Zambia were complicated by the fact that Kaunda had supported Nkomo and his guerrillas during the war and had imprisoned many ZANU activists. When fighting broke out between Nkomo's men and Mugabe's men in Bulawayo in 1980, or when buried arms were found on Nkomo's farms in February 1982, this intensified the stress between the ZANU–Mugabe regions in the centre and east of the country and the ZAPU–Patriotic Front regions in the west. The tension also made more delicate relations between Zambia and Zimbabwe. The export of maize was also held up by Zambia's crippling shortage of foreign exchange. Relations with Malawi were affected by President Banda's past links with South Africa and with the enemies of Frelimo in Mozambique. On the other hand, Zimbabwe itself was still very dependent on South Africa. South Africa emphasised this dependence by withdrawing railway engines lent to the Smith régime when they were most needed for moving the maize harvest. South Africa also restricted the flow of petrol or diesel fuel, though much South African capital was still invested in Zimbabwe industry. The extensive penetration of South African economic influence could not be rapidly eliminated. In the field of politics, moreover, South Africa made it clear to Zimbabwe that a 'destabilisation' campaign would be launched should open support be offered to the African National Congress of South Africa and its guerrillas. Both black and white soldiers of the Smith and Muzorewa régimes fled into South Africa in 1980 and were established in camps just south of the Limpopo frontier. No convincing international guarantees against South African intervention across the Limpopo were offered to Zimbabwe.

When independence finally came to Zimbabwe, popular expectations were so high that great difficulties arose in carrying through programmes of reform. The government did not receive compensation aid for the acquisition of white land, as had been promised under the Lancaster House agreement, from any nation except Britain. Even the British contribution was inadequate to fund any ambitious programme of land resettlement. The government's approach to resettlement was deliberate and slow and involved surveys, farm plans, grazing and cultivating licences, and the advice of the demonstrators. The cumbersome procedures were expensive and unpopular with peasants who had been resisting directed agriculture for decades. Moreover, the government anxiously protected efficient commercial farms upon which agricultural productivity largely depended. White farmers with highly capitalised and mechanised operations made handsome profits from the sale of maize in 1981. Their land did not become available for peasant resettlement, and land-hungry Africans were therefore offered marginal zones previously used for cattle-ranching rather than for agriculture. In the arid Gutu district, for example, peasant cultivation was attempted on ranching land which had never been intensively cultivated before. At the other extreme, the government allowed the old Rural District Councils to continue to operate in commercial farming areas in order to maintain production. These councils enjoyed a good rate of local taxation and possessed elaborate equipment. The African peasant areas felt the contrast acutely. Their councils had to operate on funds raised by peasants themselves. Many peasants therefore complained that they did not receive due reward for their contribution to the war.

Similarly, protests began to arise in the towns. Strikes were called by workers in industry, on the railways, down the mines, at the hospitals. In manufacturing industry white control remained almost unimpaired. Increased wages did not always compensate for increased food prices and general inflation. Inevitably, workers made claims for remuneration on the old white scales of pay. Although rented town cottages were given in freehold to their occupants, grave shortages of accommodation persisted.

381

The difficulties of national reconstruction should not appear to overshadow the remarkable recovery after the war. According to the London *Times* the war had cost 27 500 African dead, 275 000 wounded, 750 000 displaced from their homes, 225 000 refugees in neighbouring territories and 225 000 removed to consolidated villages.[64] The return of all survivors to their homes was largely achieved within two years. A more difficult task for the government was the harnessing of guerrillas to productive and structural change in Zimbabwe. Some had been trained as medical orderlies and were dispatched to clinics in rural areas; others were employed by the new rural councils. Most, however, were integrated into a very large national army. This army was employed to good national effect, but the mobilisation of people achieved in the war was not enough in itself to solve all Zimbabwe's post-colonial problems. Twenty years after majority rule had been achieved in Zambia and Malawi the difficulties of post-colonial nationhood in South-Central Africa still looked familiar and often formidable.

64 *The Times*, 31 March 1980.

Sources and Further Reading

THE VIOLENCE OF EMPIRE

There is an array of books and articles on the subject of European imperialism. They contain 'answers' to the questions raised in the chapter on the timing, speed and patterns of expansion. They range over diverse topics, from ideology to diplomacy and from economics to individual idiosyncracies. The literature has become so diverse that only specialists on imperialism can begin to take a close look at even the main titles. Fortunately for the Africanist, there are several good anthologies. Among these are Raymond F. Betts (ed.), *The Scramble for Africa: Causes and Dimensions of Empire,* Lexington, Mass., 1972; W. Roger Louis (ed.), *Imperialism: the Robinson and Gallagher Controversy,* New York, 1976; William B. Cohen (ed.), *European Empire-Building: Nineteenth-Century Imperialism,* St Louis, Mo., 1980. Collections of essays include Roger Owen and Bob Sutcliffe (eds), *Studies in the Theory of Imperialism,* London, 1972; John E. Flint and Glyndwr Williams (eds), *Perspectives of Empire,* London, 1973; and H. L. Wesseling, *Expansion and Reaction,* Leiden, 1978. There are also some essays relevant to European expansion in Central Africa in P. Gifford and W. R. Louis (eds), *Britain and Germany in Africa,* New Haven, Conn., 1967, and *Britain and France in Africa,* New Haven, Conn., 1971.

Some influential works deal with the interest and impact of certain European countries in the partition of Africa. On Britain there is the now classic account by R. E. Robinson and J. Gallagher, *Africa and the Victorians,* London, 1961, and the work of G. N. Uzoigwe, *Britain and the Conquest of Africa,* Ann Arbor, Mich., 1974. The economic impetus to British imperialism is the focus of P. J. Cain, *Economic Foundations of British Expansion Overseas, 1815–1914,* London 1980. On France, there are Henri Brunschwig's influential studies, *Mythes et réalités de l'impérialisme colonial français,* Paris, 1960, and *Le Partage de l'Afrique Noire,* Paris, 1971; also C. W. Newbury and A. S. Kanya-Forstner, 'French policy and the origins of the scramble for Africa', *Journal of African History,* x, 3, 253–73. On

Leopold II of Belgium, the many works by Jean Stengers include 'King Leopold's imperialism' in *Studies in the Theory of Imperialism*, Roger Owen and Bob Sutcliffe (eds), London, 1972, pp. 248–76, and 'King Leopold and Anglo-French Rivalry, 1882–1884', in *France and Britain in Africa*, P. Gifford and W. R. Louis (eds), New Haven, Conn., 1971; a different interpretation of the Belgian king's motives can be found in P. A. Roeykens, *Leopold II et l'Afrique, 1880–1885*, Brussels, 1958. On Portuguese interests, the standard work is by R. J. Hammond, *Portugal and Africa 1815–1910*, Stanford, Ca., 1966, but his interpretation has come under heavy criticism, for example by W. G. Clarence-Smith. 'The myth of uneconomic imperialism: the Portuguese in Angola, 1836–1926', *Journal of Southern African Studies*, v, 2, 1979, 165–80. On Germany, a good introduction is in Woodruff D. Smith, *The German Colonial Empire*, Chapel Hill, N.C., 1978.

Several other works should be mentioned for their usefulness to the general reader. D. K. Fieldhouse, *Economics and Empire, 1830–1914*, London, 1973, is important because it deals with events on the African periphery which helped to draw Europe into Africa, as well as with developments in the metropoles; G. N. Sanderson's 'The European partition of Africa: coincidence or conjuncture?', *Journal of Imperial and Commonwealth History*, iii, Oct. 1974, 1–54, is an excellent broad overview of the subject; and J. Forbes Munro's *Africa and the International Economy, 1800–1960*, London, 1976, is indispensable for its clear discussion of the international economy as it affected developments in Africa. Also, on broad economic trends see Samir Amin, 'Underdevelopment and dependence in Black Africa: origins and contemporary forms', *Journal of Modern African Studies*, x, 4, 1972, 50–5; and Robin Palmer and Neil Parsons (eds), *The Roots of Rural Poverty in Central and Southern Africa*, London, 1977.

The hundredth anniversary of the 1876 Brussels Geographical Conference was the occasion for the publication of a collection of papers, *La Conférence de Géographie de 1876*, Brussels, 1976, which sum up the state of European knowledge of Central Africa in the 1870s. Robin Hallett, 'Changing European attitudes to Africa', in *The Cambridge History of Africa*, John E. Flint (ed.), Cambridge, 1976, vol. v, pp. 468–96, is a good survey of intellectual perspectives on Africa; and the state of European technology as it related to empire-building is the subject of Daniel R. Headrick, *The Tools of Empire*, New York, 1981.

Accounts of European rivalries in specific regions of Central Africa are only briefly mentioned here since several relevant works are included in the bibliographical essays of individual chapters in both volumes of this *History*. The controversy over control of the lower Zaire is dealt with in Roger Anstey, *Britain and the Congo in the Nineteenth Century*, Oxford, 1962, and Françoise L. da Veiga Pinto, *Le Portugal et le Congo au dix-neuvième siècle*, Paris, 1972. The partition in the region which became

French Equatorial Africa is considered in Henri Brunschwig, *L'Avènement de l'Afrique Noire*, Paris, 1963, and in *Brazza explorateur: les traités Makoko, 1880–1882*, Paris, 1972. The major French expedition which occupied the Congo is the subject of C. Coquery-Vidrovitch, *Brazza et la prise de possession du Congo, 1883–1885*, Paris, 1969. The expansion of Leopold II and his Congo State into the Zaire basin has been extensively studied, for example in Ruth Slade, *King Leopold's Congo*, London, 1962; Robert O. Collins, *King Leopold, England and the Upper Nile, 1899–1909*, New Haven, Conn., 1968; and the classic account by P. Ceulemans, *La Question arabe et le Congo, 1883–1892*, Brussels, 1958. The horrors of marching huge expeditions through the forest zone are graphically portrayed from both African and European perspectives in Iain R. Smith, *The Emin Pasha Relief Expedition, 1886–1890*, Oxford, 1972. The German thrust into Cameroun is discussed in Harry R. Rudin, *Germans in the Cameroons, 1884–1914*, New Haven, Conn., 1938, and essays in *Kamerun Unter Deutscher Kolonial-herrschaft*, Helmuth Stoecker (ed.), Berlin, 1960, two volumes. Portuguese actions in Angola and Mozambique are dealt with in Douglas Wheeler and René Pélissier, *Angola*, New York, 1971; Eric Axelson, *Portugal and the Scramble for Africa*, Johannesburg, 1967; and Philip R. Warhurst, *Anglo-Portuguese Relations in South-Central Africa, 1890–1900*, London, 1962. Finally, for British Central Africa, on which there are many studies, three notable contributions are John Galbraith, *Crown and Charter: the Early Years of the British South Africa Company*, London, 1974; I. R. Phimister, 'Rhodes, Rhodesia and the Rand', *Journal of Southern African Studies*, i, 1, 1974, 74–90; and the account by Roland Oliver, *Sir Harry Johnston and the Scramble for Africa*, London, 1957.

The literature on African response to the expansion of Europe is much less extensive than the accounts of European imperialism, but the topic has stimulated an increasing number of thoughtful studies. A good starting point for the reactions of the African élite are the mini-biographies published in C. Julien *et al.*, *Les Africains*, Paris, 1977. For a single country, nothing matches the information contained in René Pélissier's two volumes, *Les Guerres grises: résistance et révoltes en Angola, 1845–1941* and *La Colonie du Minotaure: nationalisme et révoltes en Angola, 1926–1961*, Orgeval, 1977 and 1978. The grass-roots of African response, both individual and collective, are now receiving more attention, for example in Allen F. Isaacman, *The Tradition of Resistance in Mozambique*, Los Angeles and Berkeley, 1976, and in Allen Isaacman and Barbara Isaacman, 'Resistance and collaboration in southern and Central Africa c. 1850–1920', *International Journal of African Historical Studies*, x, 1, 1977, 31–62. Also important are the many studies of Charles van Onselen, for example, 'The role of collaborators in the Rhodesian mining industry, 1900–1935', *African Affairs*, lxxii, 1973, 401–18. Finally, the influential work of T. O. Ranger on this subject must be mentioned. Starting with his work on specific examples of African response in Zimbabwe, he has stimulated discussion of possible links between early resistance and post-1945 nationalism and liberation movements. His writings on the subject include *Revolt in Southern Rhodesia, 1896–1897*, London, 1967; 'Connexions between "primary resistance" movements and modern mass nationalism in East and Central Africa', *Journal of African History*, ix, 3, 1968, 437–53, and, in the same volume, no. 4, 631–41; and 'The people in African resistance: a review', *Journal of Southern African Studies*, iv, 1, 1977, 125–47.

EQUATORIAL AFRICA UNDER COLONIAL RULE

In the uneven literature on the colonial history of equatorial Africa, three books stand out as monumental pieces of scholarship: Catherine Coquery-Vidrovitch, *Le Congo au temps des grands compagnies concessionnaires, 1898–1930*, Paris, 1972, which blends wide-ranging economic history with a sensitivity to social developments; Harry Rudin, *Germans in the Cameroons, 1884–1914: a Case Study in Modern Imperialism*, New Haven, Conn., 1938, a thorough, well-documented and balanced account; and Gilles Sautter, *De l'Atlantique au fleuve Congo: une géographie du sous-peuplement*, Paris, 1966, 2 volumes, a series of regional studies accompanied by detailed maps, indispensable for understanding the demography of Gabon or Moyen-Congo.

Other works which provide valuable surveys of the major topics of this chapter are John A. Ballard, 'Four equatorial states' in *National Unity and Regionalism in Eight African States*, Gwendolen M. Carter (ed.), Ithaca, N.Y., 1966, pp. 231–324, especially good on political issues in the decolonisation and early independence period for AEF; Raymond Leslie Buell, *The Native Problem in Africa*, New York, 1928, important for documentation, first-hand observations and comparisons between colonies; Richard Joseph, *Radical Nationalism in Cameroon: Social Origins of the U.P.C. Rebellion*, Oxford 1977, important for a far wider range of topics than the title implies; Victor T. Le Vine, *The Cameroons: From Mandate to Independence*, Berkeley, Ca., 1964; Elikia M'Bokolo, 'French colonial policy in Equatorial Africa in the 1940s and 1950s', in Prosser Gifford and William Roger Louis (eds), *The Transfer of Power*, New York, 1982; Jean Suret-Canale, *French Colonialism in Tropical Africa 1900–1945* (translated by Till Gottheimer), New York, 1971, and *Afrique Noire, Occidentale et Centrale de la colonisation aux independences 1945–1960*, vol. I, *Crise du système colonial et capitalisme monopoliste d'état*, Paris, 1972; and Virginia Thompson and Richard Adloff, *The Emerging States of French Equatorial Africa*, Stanford, Ca., 1960, particularly strong on economic and administrative issues.

For Cameroun, there are three relatively recent German works containing monographic studies on a variety of political, economic and social topics: Karin Hausen, *Deutsche Kolonialherrschaft in Afrika: Wirtschaftsinterressen und Kolonialverwaltung in Kamerun vor 1914*, Zurich, 1970; the two volumes edited by Helmuth Stoecker, *Kamerun unter deutscher Kolonialherrschaft*, East Berlin, 1960, 1968; and Albert Wirz, *Vom Sklavenhandel zum kolonialen Handel: Wirtschaftsräume und Wirtschaftsformen in Kamerun vor 1914*, Zurich, 1972. On specific territories and regions of AEF see Georges Balandier, *The Sociology of Black Africa* (translated by Douglas Garman), New York, 1970, basically a study of the reactions to colonialism of the Fang in Gabon and Bakongo in Moyen-Congo; Robert Buijtenhuijs, *Le Frolinat et les révoltes populaires du Tchad, 1965–1976*, The Hague, 1978; Samuel Decalo, *Historical Dictionary of Chad*, Metuchen, N.J., 1977, far richer than other volumes in this series; Pierre Kalck, *The Central African Republic* (translated by Barbara Thomson), New York, 1971, a greatly condensed version of his thesis, *Histoire centrafricaine des origines à nos jours*, 4 volumes, University of Lille, Service de reproduction des thèses, 1973; Guy Lasserre, *Libreville, la ville et sa région*, Paris, 1958; Georges Mazenot, *La Likouala-Mossaka: histoire de la pénétration du Haut-Congo, 1878–1920*, Paris, 1971; Pierre-Philippe Rey, *Colonialisme, néo-colonialisme et transition au capitalisme: exemple de la 'Comilog' au Congo-Brazzaville*, Paris, 1971; Brian Weinstein, *Gabon: Nation-Building on the Ogooué*, Cambridge, Mass., 1966.

The following works deal with topics which have been somewhat neglected in the text of this chapter. On pre-colonial trade in AEF: Phyllis M. Martin, *The External Trade of the Loango Coast 1576–1870: the Effects of Changing Commercial Relations on the Vili of Loango*, Oxford, 1972; K. David Patterson, *The Northern Gabon Coast to 1875*, Oxford, 1975. On exploration and annexation of AEF: Henri Brunschwig, *Brazza explorateur: les traités Makoko, 1880–1882*, Paris, 1972; Catherine Coquery-Vidrovitch, *Brazza et la prise de possession du Congo*, Paris, 1969. On the second partition and reunification of Cameroun see C. M. Andrews and S. Kanya-Forstner, 'The French colonial party and French colonial war aims, 1914–1918', *Historical Journal*, xvii, 1974, 79–106; William Roger Louis, *Great Britain and Germany's Lost Colonies, 1914–1919*, Oxford, 1967; Claude Welch, *Dream of Unity: Pan-Africanism and Political Unification in West Africa*, Ithaca, N.Y., 1966. On missionary politics, Rudolph Stumpf, *La Politique linguistique au Cameroun de 1884 à 1960*, Berne, 1979; Jehan Gaspar Marie Witte, *Un explorateur et un apôtre du Congo français: Mgr. Augouard*, Paris, 1924, a hagiographical account of a controversial and powerful churchman active in AEF for forty years.

Annual government reports on Cameroun are available as: Germany, Auswärtiges Amt, *Jahresberichte über die Entwicklung der Deutschen Schutzgebiete* (1895–1907); Germany, Reichskolonialamt, *Denkschrifte über die Entwicklung der Schutzgebiete in Afrika und Südsee* (1907–1909); *Die deutschen Schutzgebiete in Afrika und Südsee* (1910–1912); France, *Rapport* annuel au Conseil de la Société des Nations sur l'administration sous mandat du territoire du Cameroun (1921–1938); France, Rapport annuel à l'Assemblée Générale des Nations Unies sur l'administration du Cameroun placé sous la tutelle de la France (1947–1960). There are no such published reports for AEF; the closest equivalent is Afrique Equatoriale Française, Haut Commissariat, Annuaires statistiques, vol. I, giving selected and summary information to 1936 and greater detail from 1937 to 1950. Earlier statistics are incorporated in France, Ministère des Colonies, Office Colonial, Statistiques coloniales (1890–1914), and France, Agence Générale des Colonies, Renseignements généraux sur le commerce des colonies françaises (1914–1928). These sources can be supplemented by the official Deutsches Kolonialblatt and the semi-official L'Afrique Française, containing less systematic but more discursive articles often presenting criticisms of the French régime for purposes of refuting them.

More intimate impressions of the colonial experience are conveyed through less formal literature. André Gide, Voyage au Congo, Paris, 1927, is the most widely available example of travel accounts describing abuses in AEF and is one of the few of these works published in English (Travels in the Congo, New York, 1937) although the translation is not entirely reliable. For guidance to the other scandal literature on AEF, mostly by obscure authors and in French, see Coquery-Vidrovitch, Le Congo, pp. 558–62, and Thompson and Adloff, Emerging States, pp. 14–20. Albert Schweitzer, On the Edge of the Primeval Forest and More from the Primeval Forest, New York, 1948, reveals a good deal both about health and medicine in Gabon and about the racial attitudes of even the most famous medical missionary. The twelve volumes of Charles-André Julien et al. (eds), Les Africains, Paris, 1977, contain brief but well-researched biographies of Charles Atangana, Barthélémy Boganda, Karnou (leader of the 1929 Baya revolt), André Matsoua, and Sultan Njoya of Bamoun. Brian Weinstein, Eboué, London, 1972, is highly readable and based on detailed written and oral documentation of Eboué's career in AEF. The best writings by equatorial Africans themselves about this period come from Cameroun; for example, the autobiographical work of Jacques Kuoh-Moukouri, Doigts noirs: je fus écrivain–interprète au Cameroun, Montréal, 1963. A number of Cameroun novelists have written wonderful satires on the colonial period, including Mongo Beti, The Poor Christ of Bomba (translated by Gerald Moore), London, 1971; King Lazarus (no translator given), London 1966; Mission to Kala (translated by Peter Green), London, 1966; and Ferdinand Oyono, House Boy (translated by John Reed), London, 1966, and The Old Man and the Medal (translated by John Reed), London, 1967.

RURAL SOCIETY AND THE BELGIAN COLONIAL ECONOMY

There is no general survey offering adequate coverage of the period and problems analysed in this chapter. The best history of Zaire to date is by M. Merlier, *Le Congo, de la colonisation belge à l'indépendance*, Paris, 1962. This stimulating book of Marxist persuasion does not constitute a work of ready reference for the uninitiated, and contains documentary evidence which is sometimes faulty. R. Lemarchand, *Political Awakening in the Belgian Congo*, Berkeley and Los Angeles, 1964, is still important, as are R. Anstey, *King Leopold's Legacy: the Congo under Belgian Rule*, London, 1966, and C. Young, *Politics in the Congo*, Princeton, 1965. As these works were written at the time of independence and during the following crisis, their chief aim was to explain the political failure of decolonisation. The chapters by J. Stengers with J. Vansina, B. Jewsiewicki and C. Young in volumes VI, VII and VIII of *The Cambridge History of Africa* (forthcoming) are attempts at an up-dated composite study.

The best survey of colonial history from the Belgian point of view is by J. Stengers, 'La Belgique et le Congo, politique coloniale et décolonisation', in *Histoire de la Belgique contemporaine, 1914–70*, Brussels, 1974. The only survey written by a Zairois, Thimanga wa Thibangu, *Histoire du Zaire*, Bukavu, 1976, follows the tradition of R. Cornevin. The chapters devoted to the Belgian Congo in P. Duignan and L. H. Gann (eds), *Colonialism in Africa*, Cambridge, 1970–5, 5 volumes, are very useful. Finally, Duignan and Gann have recently published an account of European involvement in the Congo during the reign of Leopold, *The Rulers of Belgian Africa 1884–1914*, Princeton, 1979.

The best economic survey of the Belgian Congo is by J. P. Peemans, *Diffusion du progrès et convergence des prix: Congo-Belgique, 1900–1960*, Louvain, 1970, although this book does not entirely supplant G. Vandewalle's *De conjoncturele evolutie in Kongo en Ruanda-Urundi van 1920 tot 1939, en van 1949 tot 1958*, Ghent, 1966; see also Peemans, 'Capital accumulation in the Congo under colonialism: the role of the state' in P. Duignan and L. H. Gann (eds), *The Economics of Colonialism*, Vol. IV, *Colonialism in Africa 1870–1960*, Cambridge, 1973, and a general survey by B. Jewsiewicki, 'Zaire enters the world system: its colonial incorporation in the Belgian Congo, 1885–1960' in *Zaire: the Political Economy of Underdevelopment*, G. Gran (ed.), New York, pp. 29–53.

The closing years of the 1950s and the 1960s saw the publication of several vindicatory works on the topic of agriculture. They emphasised the technical side of the Belgian operation, confident of 'progress' introduced by the coloniser. In 1962 the Académie Royale des Sciences d'Outre-Mer published a *Livre blanc*, Brussels, 3 volumes, in the tradition of Inforcongo, *Le Congo Belge*, Brussels, 1958, 2 volumes, and G. Hostelet's *L'Oeuvre colonisatrice de la Belgique au Congo de 1885 à 1953*, Brussels, 1954, 2 volumes. Two agricultural histories are available: *Bulletin agricole du Congo Belge et du Ruanda-Urundi, 1910–1960: volume jubilaire*, Brussels, 1960, a valuable survey and source, and R. J. Cornet's *Les Phares verts*, Brussels, 1965, which expand the information found in E. Van der Straeten, *L'Agriculture et les industries agricoles au Congo Belge*, Brussels, 1945.

A basic survey of traditional African agriculture appeared in the form of P. De Schlippe's *Shifting Cultivation in Africa: the Zande System of Agriculture*, London, 1956. Two works which have become authorities on the economic and technical aspects of African agriculture are M. Miracle, *Agriculture in the Congo Basin*, Madison, 1967, and F. Jurion and J. Henry, *De l'agriculture itinérante à l'agriculture intensive*, Brussels, 1967. Two years earlier V. Drachoussoff, formerly an agronomist with the colonial government, as were F. Jurion and J. Henry, published *Agricultural Change in the Belgian Congo, 1945–1960*, Stanford, Ca., 1965. Geographers have produced some excellent critical studies of rural development, for example, H. Beguin, *La Mise en valeur du Sud-Est du Kasai*, Brussels, 1960; J. Wilmet, *Systèmes agraires et techniques agricoles au Katanga*, Brussels, 1963; and, best of all, O. Tulippe and J. Wilmet, 'Géographie de l'agriculture en Afrique centrale: essai de synthèse', *Bulletin de la société belge d'études géographiques*, 1964, no. 2, 303–73.

It is only recently that studies of the social history of the African farmer have appeared, for instance, Mulambu-Mvuluya, *Cultures obligatoires et colonisation dans l'ex-Congo Belge* in *Cahiers du CEDAF*, 1974, nos. 6–7, and B. Jewsiewicki, *Agriculture nomade et économie capitaliste: histoire des essais de modernisation de l'agriculture africaine au Zaire à l'époque coloniale*, Lubumbashi, 1975, 2 volumes, mimeographed. In English, see the chapters by B. Jewsiewicki in *Roots of Rural Poverty in Central and Southern Africa*, R. Palmer and N. Parsons (eds), London, 1977, as well as the important chapter by J.-L. Vellut, 'Rural poverty in Western Shaba, c. 1890–1930', M. Klein (ed.), *Peasants in Africa: Historical and Contemporary Perspectives*, Beverly Hills, 1980; and D. Crummey and C. Stewart, *Modes of Production in Africa, the Precolonial Era*, Beverly Hills, 1981.

A forewarning of the importance of the ecological issue was provided at the end of the 1940s by P. Harroy, *L'Afrique, terre qui meurt*, but this was confined to the technical aspect of soil erosion. The issue is considered in greater depth by B. Jewsiewicki (ed.), *Contributions to a History of Agriculture and Fishing in Central Africa* in *African Economic History*, 7 (special issue), 1979.

Our knowledge of the social history of Zaire, particularly that pertaining to the rural population, is very scant; see J.-L. Vellut, 'Pour une histoire sociale de l'Afrique centrale', *Cultures et développement*, viii, 1976, 61–86. Anthropological contributions are also important; see the excellent W. MacGaffey, *Custom and Government in the Lower Congo*, Berkeley, California, 1970. There are numerous surveys of the political history of Kimbanguism and some accounts of the Kitawala from this standpoint. The Kwango Revolt of 1931 is the subject of a systematic survey by Sikitele Gize in his doctoral thesis in progress, 'Les Racines de la révolte pende de

1931'; *Etudes d'histoire africaine*, v, 1973, 99–154, provides a rough summary. A description of the Masisi (Bushiri) Revolt has been published by M. Lovens, *La Révolte de Maesisi-Lubutu (Congo belge: janvier-mai 1944)* in *Cahiers du CEDAF*, 1974, nos. 3–4. The best analyses of the non-Christian religious movements have been published by J. Vansina; a summary is W. de Craemer, J. Vansina and R. C. Fox, 'Religious movements in Central Africa: a theoretical study', *Comparative Studies in Society and History*, xviii, 1976, 458–75. For a composite historical study of the social movements, plus a bibliography, see B. Jewsiewicki, 'La Contestation sociale et la naissance du prolétariat au Zaire au cours de la première moitié du XXᵉ siècle', *Canadian Journal of African Studies*, x, 1976, 47–71, and 'Political consciousness among African peasants in colonial Zaire', *Review of African Political Economy*, xix, 1980, 23–32.

A history of European agricultural activity has yet to be undertaken. A general account has recently been published by B. Jewsiewicki, 'Le Colonat agricole européen au Congo Belge, 1910–1960, problèmes politiques et économiques', *Journal of African History*, xx, 1979, 559–72. D. K. Fieldhouse has published a study of Unilever, which had an important oil-producing subsidiary in the Belgian Congo, *Unilever Overseas: the Anatomy of a Multinational, 1895–1965*, London, 1978. Works produced during the colonial period, like that of A. Brixie, *Le Coton au Congo Belge*, assume an apologetic nature.

For a demographic history of the rural areas, P. Gourou, *La Densité de la population rurale au Congo Belge*, Brussels, 1955, remains an essential source, now complemented by A. Romaniuk, *La Fécondité des populations congolaises*, Paris, 1967.

A socio-economic history of pre-colonial agriculture is in progress. J. Vansina makes an extremely valuable contribution to the field in *The Children of Woot: a History of the Kuba Peoples*, Madison, Wisconsin, 1978, and in *The Tio Kingdom of the Middle Congo 1880–1892*, London, 1973. D. Lloyd, 'The Precolonial Economic History of the Avongara-Zande c. 1750–1916', Ph.D. thesis, Berkeley, 1977, lends a historical dimension to Schlippe's book.

Some highly important works were completed in the 1970s in the History Department at the National University of Zaire in Lubumbashi. Unfortunately, these masters' and doctoral theses remain virtually inaccessible. Mumbanza mwa Bawele's thesis, 'Histoire des peuples riverains de l'entre Zaire-Ubangi', Lubumbashi, 1981, mimeographed, and that of Tshundolela Epanya, 'Politique coloniale, économie capitaliste et sous-développement au Congo Belge; le cas du Kasai (1920–1959)', Lubumbashi, 1980, mimeographed, are essential for an understanding of the issues involved. See also Bishikwabo Chubaka, 'Histoire d'un Etat shi en Afrique des Grands Lacs: Kaziba au Zaïre (ca. 1850–1940)', Ph.D. thesis, Université Catholique de Louvain, 1982.

Among several bibliographical aids which might serve as a guide for the student of the history of Zaire, the best is the work of J.-L. Vellut, *Guide de l'étudiant en Histoire du Zaire*, Kinshasa, 1974. Specialist bibliographies have recently been published by CEDAF and by the Musée Royal de l'Afrique Centrale at Tervuren, see B. de Halleux *et al.*, *Bibliographie Analytique pour L'Agronomie Tropicale: Zaïre, Rwanda, Burundi*, 2 vols.

MINING IN THE BELGIAN CONGO

In terms of published books and articles, the social and economic history of colonial Congo has lagged behind that of southern Africa. Substantial research, often based on unpublished archive material, has, however, been conducted by staff and students of the National University of Zaire. This material is unfortunately not readily available for consultation.

There exists a vast colonial literature which covers various aspects of mining in the Congo, from a technical, economic or social point of view, but this lacks a truly historical perspective as we understand it today. Generally speaking, this literature approaches industrial history as a process of modernisation imposed upon a passive African mass by benevolent employers.

Recent general surveys which provide a reliable background include:
Peemans, J. P. *Diffusion du progrès et convergence des prix. Congo-Belgique, 1900–1960*, Louvain–Paris, 1970.
————, 'Capital Accumulation in the Congo under Colonialism: the Role of the State', in P. Duignan and L. H. Gann, *Colonialism in Africa 1870–1960*, Vol. IV, *The Economics of Colonialism*, Cambridge, 1975, pp. 165–212. The author gives a broad macro-economic interpretation of colonial history with a wide-ranging bibliography.
Stengers, J. 'La Belgique et le Congo, politique coloniale et décolonisation', in *Histoire de la Belgique contemporaine, 1914–1970*, Brussels, 1974, pp. 391–440.
———— 'Une décolonisation précipitée: le cas du Congo Belge', *Cultures et Développement*, 1978, x, 4, Louvain, 521–56. These two essays are strong on the political dimension.

Modern surveys of mining
Bezy, F. 'Changements de structure et conjoncture de l'industrie minière du Congo, 1938–1960', *Notes et Documents*, Institut de Recherches Economiques et Sociales, Léopoldville, 1961. The only attempt at a general view on the economics of mining in the country, valuable for post-second World War.
Recent historical work has concentrated on the copper basin of Upper Katanga (Shaba).

Gouverneur, J. *Productivity and Factor Proportions in Less-Developed Countries: the Case of Industrial Firms in the Congo*, Oxford, 1971, includes a discussion of Union Minière. See also Georges, F., and Gouverneur, J., 'Les Transformations techniques et l'évolution des facteurs de production à l'UMHK de 1910 à 1965', *Cultures et Développement*, 1969–70, ii, 1, Louvain, 53–100. Both important for long-term trends in the labour/capital ratio in industrial Congo.

Katzenellenbogen, S. E. *Railways and the Copper Mines of Katanga*, Oxford, 1973. Basic for the history of financial control over transportation to and from the Copperbelt.

Perrings, C. *Black Mineworkers in Central Africa*, London, 1979. A path-breaking social history of the Copperbelt region, very densely covering both the Congo and Rhodesia. Avowedly adverse to the humanist school in social history.

Surveys on mining dating from the colonial period

Leonard, H. 'Les Mines du Congo et les problèmes que l'exploitation pose aujourd'hui', *Bulletin de l'Institut Royal Colonial Belge*, 1938, 78–99. The mining industry is recommended to turn to more capital-intensive forms of production.

Marthoz, A. *L'Industrie minière et métallurgique au Congo Belge*, Brussels, 1955. Surveys technology in the mining industry.

U.S. Department of the Interior, *Mineral Resources of the Belgian Congo and Ruanda-Urundi*, Washington, D.C., 1947, Foreign Mineral Surveys, vol. 2, no. 6. The first systematic approach to mining in the country.

Vaes, A. J. 'Production minière et main-d'oeuvre indigène en ...', yearly report, 1948–58, published by *Annales des Mines de Belgique* since 1949. Basic for the 1950s.

Monographs

Specific mineral zones are unevenly covered. Popular topics as reflected by an extensive literature include company histories, social medicine and, generally, the material dimension of history.

Company histories, published under company auspices:

Symetain, *Maniema. Le pays de l'étain*, Brussels, 1953.

Union Minière du Haut Katanga, 1906–56, *Evolution des techniques et des activités sociales*, Brussels, 1957.

These two volumes are the most informative in an otherwise uneven collection.

Social medicine is extensively covered by the colonial literature:

Mouchet R., and van Nitsen, R. *La Main-d'oeuvre indigène au Congo Belge*, Brussels, 1940.

Daco, Dr. 'Situation sanitaire et organisation du service médical aux mines de Kilo–Moto', *Bruxelles-Médical*, ix, 1926, 273–90.

Two examples of informative works on the physical conditioning of a working class in the Congo.

Fields which are poorly covered. The hinterlands developed by mining zones have hardly been studied as such. See, however:

Jewsiewicki, B. 'Unequal Development: Capitalism and the Katanga Economy', in R. Palmer and N. Parsons (eds), *The Roots of Rural Poverty in Central and Southern Africa*, Berkeley and London, 1977, pp. 317–44.

Vellut, J.-L. 'Rural Poverty in Western Shaba c. 1900–1930', *ibid.*, pp. 294–321.

Much information on the hinterland of Kilo–Moto may be found in the writings of an articulate exponent of mining interests in the Congo, G. Moulaert, *Vingt années à Kilo–Moto, 1920–1940*, Brussels, 1950.

Social history for the colonial period is in its infancy:

Fetter, B. *The Creation of Elisabethville, 1910–1940*, Stanford, Ca., 1976. Contains much information on the beginnings of Lubumbashi.

———. 'L'Union Minière du Haut-Katanga, 1920–1940: la naissance d'une sous-culture totalitaire', *Cahiers du CEDAF*, 6, Brussels, 1973.

Jewsiewicki, B. 'La Contestation sociale et la naissance du prolétariat au Zaïre au cours de la première moitié du XXème siècle', *Canadian Journal of African Studies*, x, 1, 1976, 47–71. Original piece of research, important bibliography.

Vellut, J.-L. 'Le Katanga industriel en 1944: malaises et anxiétés dans la société coloniale', *Le Congo Belge dans la Deuxième Guerre Mondiale*, Brussels, in press.

For the history of class formation as seen by the employers, the works of L. Mottoulle are essential. See, for example, his *Contribution à l'étude du déterminisme fonctionnel de l'industrie dans l'éducation de l'indigène congolais*, Brussels, 1934. Mottoulle was director of the Labour Division at Union Minière, and a firm believer in its 'stabilisation' policy.

CAPITAL ACCUMULATION AND CLASS FORMATION IN ANGOLA

The best general survey of the Portuguese empire in this period is M. Newitt, *Portugal in Africa: the Last Hundred Years*, London, 1981. It replaces the older surveys, J. Duffy, *Portuguese Africa*, Cambridge, Mass., 1959, and his shorter *Portugal in Africa*, Harmondsworth, 1962.

Portuguese imperial expansion in the nineteenth century is the subject of the highly influential R. J. Hammond, *Portugal and Africa, 1815–1910: a Study in Uneconomic Imperialism*, Stanford, Ca., 1966. For a critique, see

W. G. Clarence-Smith, 'The myth of uneconomic imperialism, the Portuguese in Angola, 1836–1926', *Journal of Southern African Studies*, v, 2, 1979, 165–80. There is also an excellent rebuttal of Hammond in Portuguese, V. Alexandre, *Origens do colonialismo português moderno, 1822–1891*, Lisbon, 1979.

For the twentieth century, E. A. Ross, *Report on the Employment of Native Labour in Portuguese Africa*, New York, 1925, is a good primary source for the 1920s. A. Castro, *O sistema colonial português em África (meados do século XX)*, Lisbon, 2nd ed., 1978, originally published under a pseudonym in Russian in 1962, provides an excellent survey, based on first-hand experience, of the 1950s.

The standard general history of Angola proper is D. Wheeler and R. Pélissier, *Angola*, London, 1971. The part by Wheeler, is useful on the creoles and early politics. L. Henderson, *Angola, Five Centuries of Conflict*, Ithaca, N.Y., 1979, written by a Protestant missionary with long experience of Angola, is a modest summary of secondary sources in English, particularly good for missions. In French, R. Pélissier's two massive tomes, *Les Guerres grises, résistance et révoltes en Angola, 1845–1941*, and *La Colonie du Minotaure, nationalisme et révoltes en Angola, 1926–1961*, Orgeval, 1977 and 1978, are centred on military history, but provide an enormous quarry of information on a wide variety of topics. G. J. Bender, *Angola under the Portuguese, the myth and the reality*, London, 1978, has a rather misleading title, and is in fact a series of essays on white settlement and racism in Angola. F. W. Heimer edited a set of essays, *Social Change in Angola*, Munich, 1973, which, although uneven and concentrated on the more recent period, fill a great gap in the literature. F. W. Heimer is editing another set of essays, *The Formation of Angolan Society*, forthcoming, which should become a standard history of Angola.

Of the many monographs and articles on particular aspects of Angolan history, the following are all of importance. M. Martins Contreiras, *A província de Angola*, Lisbon, 1894, and H. de Paiva Couceiro, *Angola, dous annos de governo*, Lisbon, 1910, are general surveys for the period up to 1910. M. A. Samuels, *Education in Angola, 1878–1914*, New York, 1970, covers the missions as well as education. W. G. Clarence-Smith, *Slaves, Peasants and Capitalists in Southern Angola, 1840–1926*, Cambridge, 1979, is a regional monograph. J. R. Dias, 'Black chiefs, white traders and colonial policy near the Kwanza: Kabuku Kambilo and the Portuguese, 1873–1896', *Journal of African History*, xvii, 2, 1976, 245–65, is an important first result of major continuing work on the Mbundu. Two other useful regional articles are D. Birmingham, 'The coffee barons of Cazengo', *Journal of African History*, xix, 4, 1978, 523–38, and J. C. Miller, 'Cokwe trade and conquest in the nineteenth century' in *Pre-colonial African Trade*, R. Gray and D. Birmingham (eds), London, 1970, pp. 175–201. Two economic surveys of the 1940s and 1950s are G. Lefebvre, *L'Angola, son histoire, son économie*,

Liège, 1947, and J. Cerqueira de Azevedo, *Angola, exemplo de trabalho*, Luanda, 1958.

THE POLITICAL ECONOMY OF EAST–CENTRAL AFRICA

The historical literature available on East-Central Africa is uneven, with Zambia fairly well-covered but Malawi and Mozambique less so. For useful discussions of the social and ecological changes that occurred during the last six decades of the nineteenth century, see John Iliffe, *A Modern History of Tanganyika*, Cambridge, 1979, which although specifically concerned with Tanganyika, is suggestive for East-Central Africa. Helge Kjekshus, *Ecology Control and Economic Development in East Africa: the Case of Tanganyika, 1850–1950*, London, 1977, stresses the importance of ecological changes in shaping human history. Two articles specifically on ecological change in Central Africa are Charles van Onselen, 'Reactions to rinderpest in Southern Africa, 1896–7', *Journal of African History*, xiii, 3, 1972; 473–88, and Leroy Vail, 'Ecology and history: the example of eastern Zambia', *Journal of Southern African Studies*, iii, 2, 1977. For a general assessment of the impact of Nguni migrations on East-Central Africa, see John Omer-Cooper, *The Zulu Aftermath*, London, 1966. Edward A. Alpers, *Ivory and Slaves in East Central Africa*, London, 1975, is primarily concerned with the period before 1800 but has some useful information on the slave-trade of the nineteenth century. On the gradual suppression of the slave-trade in the Indian Ocean basin, see S. Miers, *Britain and the Ending of the Slave Trade*, London, 1975, pp. 40–166. The trade's internal impact on societies in this region has been assessed in various local studies, of which the best is Andrew Roberts, *A History of the Bemba*, London, 1973.

The impact of the development of the South African mines has been widely discussed. The *Journal of Southern African Studies* is an essential source for information on the mines, as well as for articles of relevance to all of South-Central Africa. A detailed discussion of gold-mining finance is found in Robert V. Kubicek, *Economic Imperialism in Theory and Practice: the Case of South African Gold Mining Finance, 1886–1914*, Durham, N.C., 1979; the later history of the mines is found in Sheila T. van der Horst, *Native Labour in South Africa*, London, 1942, and Francis Wilson, *Labour in the South African Gold Mines, 1911–1969*, Cambridge, 1972. Shula Marks and Stanley Trapido have written an important article on 'Lord Milner and the South African State', *History Workshop*, No. 8, 1979. For a theoretical article on the relationship between the mines and the rural areas of South-Central Africa see Harold Wolpe, 'Capitalism and Cheap Labour-Power in South Africa: from Segregation to Apartheid', *Economy and Society*, i, 1972. Fundamental to an understanding of the whole phenomenon of labour migrancy in the area is Charles van Onselen's excellent *Chibaro: African*

Mine Labour in Southern Rhodesia, 1900–1933, London, 1976, with particularly valuable sections on labour control.

Portuguese reluctance to permit historical research in Mozambique means that the literature on colonial Mozambique is poor. A general overview of the country's history is found in Thomas H. Henrickson, *Mozambique: a History*, London, 1978. From a specifically European point of view, four books are useful for an appreciation of Portuguese efforts to secure control of the area: R. J. Hammond, *Portugal and Africa, 1815–1910*, Stanford, California, 1966; Eric Axelson, *Portugal and the Scramble for Africa*, Johannesburg, 1967; and two books by James Duffy, *Portuguese Africa*, Cambridge, Mass., 1961, and *A Question of Slavery*, Oxford, 1967. The one area of the country which has received specialised concern is the Zambezi valley and its *prazos*, analysed in M. D. D. Newitt, *Portuguese Settlement on the Zambesi*, London, 1973, and Allen Isaacman, *Mozambique: the Africanization of a European Institution: the Zambesi Prazos, 1750–1902*, Madison, Wis., 1972. More specifically concerned with African responses to colonialism in this area is Allen Isaacman, *The Tradition of Resistance in Mozambique: Anti-Colonial Activity in the Zambesi Valley, 1850–1921*, London, 1976. Again concerned with the Zambezi valley, but encompassing a broader time span and concerned with a wide range of topics, including the policies of the government of António Salazar, is Leroy Vail and Landeg White, *Capitalism and Colonialism in Mozambique: a Study of Quelimane District*, London, 1980. The area governed by the Mozambique Company before 1942 has not yet been adequately researched by historians. One useful article is Barry Neil-Tomlinson, 'The growth of a colonial economy and the development of African labour: Manica and Sofala and the Mozambique Chartered Company, 1892–1942', in University of Edinburgh, Centre for African Studies, *Mozambique*, Edinburgh, 1979. Another article dealing with the area of the Mozambique Company, as well as touching upon the less well-known area governed by the Niassa Company, is Leroy Vail, 'Mozambique's chartered companies: the rule of the feeble', *Journal of African History*, xvii, 3, 1976. Useful as a background to the rise of Mozambican nationalism are Eduardo Mondlane, *The Struggle for Mozambique*, Harmondsworth, 1969, and Keith Middlemas, *Cabora Bassa: Engineering and Politics in Southern Africa*, London, 1975.

The historical literature concerning Malawi has, like that of Mozambique, been seriously affected by official restraints upon research. There is no adequate history of the country. Perhaps the best introduction is T. David Williams, *Malawi: the Politics of Despair*, Ithaca, N.Y., 1978. B. Pachai, *Malawi: the History of the Nation*, London, 1973, is long on detail but short on interpretation. Nineteenth-century Malawi history is touched on in B. Pachai (ed.), *The Early History of Malawi*, London, 1972; and R. J. MacDonald, (ed.), *From Nyasaland to Malawi: Studies in Colonial History*,

Nairobi, 1975, discusses aspects of twentieth-century history. Robin Palmer and Neil Parsons (eds), *The Roots of Rural Poverty in Central and Southern Africa*, London, 1977, contains essays on Malawi history as well as essays on Zambian and Mozambique history. Specialised studies on Malawi include George Shepperson and Thomas Price, *Independent African*, Edinburgh, 1958, a careful study of the Chilembwe rising of 1915 and a useful overview of early colonial history in Nyasaland; Ian Linden, *Catholics, Peasants and Chewa Resistance in Nyasaland, 1889–1939*, London, 1974, discusses the establishment of the Catholic church in Nyasaland and its impact upon the Ngoni and Chewa peoples; John McCracken, *Politics and Christianity in Malawi, 1875–1940*, Cambridge, 1977, analyses the important Scottish Presbyterian mission of Livingstonia in northern Malawi. The history of Zambian and Malawian nationalism is treated in Robert I. Rotberg, *The Rise of Nationalism in Central Africa: the Making of Malawi and Zambia, 1873–1964*, Cambridge, Mass., 1966.

Because of government encouragement to research in the colonial period, and a laudably liberal government attitude towards historical research since independence, there is a rich historical literature on Zambia. Two important journals published in the country are essential for an understanding of its history; they are *Human Problems in Central Africa*, which appeared until independence, and its successor, *African Social Research*. The best general history of the country is Andrew Roberts, *A History of Zambia*, London, 1976, a book valuable both for itself and for its splendid bibliographical guide; all students of Zambian history should begin their work with this volume and refer to it for the many studies available on Zambia. A useful survey of the colonial period is L. H. Gann, *A History of Northern Rhodesia: Early Days to 1953*, London, 1964. Richard Gray, *The Two Nations: Aspects of the Development of Race Relations in the Rhodesias and Nyasaland*, London, 1960, although primarily concerned with Southern Rhodesia, contains material on Northern Rhodesia's economic and social history to 1953. Specialised studies on the copper industry include E. L. Berger, *Labour, Race and Colonial Rule: the Copperbelt from 1924 to Independence*, Oxford, 1974, and Charles Perrings, *Black Mineworkers in Central Africa: Industrial Strategies and the Evolution of an African Proletariat in the Copperbelt, 1911–1941*, London, 1979.

ZIMBABWE: THE PATH OF CAPITALIST DEVELOPMENT

For a discussion of Zimbabwe historiography, including many of the books, articles and theses on which this chapter draws, see Terence Ranger, 'The historiography of Southern Rhodesia', *Trans-African Journal of History*, i, 1971; and Ian Phimister, 'Zimbabwean economic and social historiography since 1970', *African Affairs*, lxxvii, 1979. The following is a select list of useful works.

Arrighi, G. *The Political Economy of Rhodesia*, The Hague, 1967.
———. 'Labour supplies in historical perspective: a study of the proletarianisation of the African peasantry in Rhodesia', *Journal of Development Studies*, vi, 1970.
Barber, W. J. *The Economy of British Central Africa*, London, 1961.
Beach, D. N. '"Chimurenga": the Shona Rising of 1896–97', *Journal of African History*, xx, 1979.
Clarke, D. G. 'The political economy of discrimination and underdevelopment in Rhodesia with special reference to African workers, 1940–1973', Ph.D. thesis, University of St Andrews, 1975.
Clements, F., and Harben, E. *Leaf of Gold*, London, 1962.
Cobbing, J., 'The Ndebele under the Khumalos, 1820–96', Ph.D. thesis, University of Lancaster, 1976.
Galbraith, J. S. *Crown and Charter*, Berkeley, Ca., 1974.
Gann, L. H. *A History of Southern Rhodesia*, London, 1965.
———, and Gelfand, M. *Huggins of Rhodesia*, London, 1964.
Gray, R. *The Two Nations*, London, 1960.
Keyter, C. *Maize Control in Southern Rhodesia 1931–1941: the African Contribution to White Survival*, Salisbury, 1978.
Lee, E. 'Politics and Pressure Groups in S. Rhodesia, 1898–1923', Ph.D. thesis, University of London, 1974.
Mackenzie, J. M. 'Colonial labour policy and Rhodesia', *Rhodesian Journal of Economics*, viii, 1974.
Murray, D. J. *The Governmental System in Southern Rhodesia*, Oxford, 1970.
Palmer, R. H. *Land and Racial Domination in Rhodesia*, London, 1977.
Phimister, I. R. 'History of Mining in Southern Rhodesia to 1953', Ph.D. thesis, University of Rhodesia, 1975.
———. 'The reconstruction of the Southern Rhodesian gold mining industry, 1903–10', *Economic History Review*, xxix, 1976.
———. 'Peasant production and underdevelopment in Southern Rhodesia, 1890–1914, with particular reference to the Victoria district', in *The Roots of Rural Poverty in Central and Southern Africa*, R. H. Palmer and N. Parsons (eds), London, 1977.
———, and Van Onselen, C. *Studies in the History of African Mine Labour in Colonial Zimbabwe*, Gwelo, 1978.
Ranger, T. O. *Revolt in Southern Rhodesia*, London, 1967.
———. *The African Voice in Southern Rhodesia*, London, 1970.
———. 'Growing from the roots: reflections on peasant research in Central and Southern Africa', *Journal of Southern African Studies*, v, 1978.
Thompson, C. H., and Woodruff, H. H. *Economic Development in Rhodesia and Nyasaland*, London, 1953.
Van Onselen, C. 'Worker consciousness in black miners: Southern Rhodesia, 1900–1920', *Journal of African History*, xiv, 1973.
———. 'Black workers in Central African industry: a critical essay on the

historiography and sociology of Rhodesia', *Journal of Southern African Studies*, i, 1975.

————. *Chibaro: African Mine Labour in Southern Rhodesia 1900–1933*, London, 1976.

Yudelman, M. *Africans on the Land*, Cambridge, Mass., 1964.

Zachrisson, P. *An African Area in Change. Belingwe 1894–1946*, Bulletin of Department of History No. 17, University of Gothenburg, 1978.

THE NORTHERN REPUBLICS, 1960–1980

Materials available for the study of the contemporary history of the seven countries covered in this chapter vary widely in quantity and quality. Although there are major gaps for all seven states, Zaire is by far the most thoroughly covered. At the other extreme, virtually no post-independence research has been done in Equatorial Guinea or São Tomé e Príncipe, and very little in Central African Republic.

Given the lag between actual research and publication, scholarly treatment of the later 1970s is scarce. For events after 1975, the student is obliged to rely heavily upon such current sources as *Africa Contemporary Record, Africa Research Bulletin*, and *Keesing's Contemporary Archives*. For the francophone states, such reviews as *Marchés Tropicaux et Méditerranéen* and *Revue Française d'Etudes Politiques Africaines* are useful. On Zaire, the publications of the Centre d'Études et de Documentation Africaines, and the journal *Zaire-Afrique* offer reliable analyses of current issues.

For Zaire the First Republic's years of crisis gave rise to an immense literature. The most important single source is the series of yearbooks published by the Centre de Recherches et d'Informations Socio-Politiques (*Congo 1959* to *Congo 1967*). An invaluable bibliography covering the period until 1970 was compiled by Edouard Bustin, 'Congo-Kinshasa, Guide Bibliographique I and II', *Cahiers du CEDAF*, 3 and 4, 1971. The most useful over-all treatments of the 1960s crisis and the first phase of independence are Herbert Weiss, *Political Protest in the Congo*, Princeton, N.J., 1967; Crawford Young, *Politics in the Congo*, Princeton, N.J., 1965; René Lemarchand, *Political Awakening in the Congo*, Berkeley, Ca., 1964, and Paule Bouvier, *L'Accession du Congo Belge à l'indépendance*. The later phases of the First Republic and beginning of the Second are covered in Jean-Claude Willame, *Patrimonialism and Political Change in the Congo*, Stanford, Ca., 1972.

On more specific aspects of the First Republic and on the 1964–5 uprisings, see the monumental study by Benoît Verhaegen, *Rébellions au Congo*, Brussels, two volumes, 1966, 1969, and a brief treatment by Crawford Young, 'Rebellion and the Congo', in Robert Rotberg and Ali Mazrui (eds), *Protest and Power in Black Africa*, New York, 1970. For the Katanga secession, see Jules Gérard-Libois, *Katanga Secession*, Madison,

Wis., 1966. On the UN role, see Arthur House, *The UN in the Congo*, Washington, D.C., 1978; Conor Cruise O'Brien, *To Katanga and Back*, New York, 1962; Rajeshwar Dayal, *Mission for Hammarskjold*, Princeton, N.J., 1976. Concerning American involvement, Stephen Weissman, *American Foreign Policy in the Congo 1960–1964*, Ithaca, N.Y., 1974, is detailed and forthright; see also his contribution to René Lemarchand (ed.), *American Policy in Southern Africa*, Washington, D.C., 1978. For an overview of the economic impact of the early crisis, consult Institut de Recherches Economiques et Sociales, *Indépendence, inflation, développement*, Paris, 1968.

For the Mobutu era, there is still no integrated, over-all treatment. For a useful collection of critical pieces, see Guy Gran (ed.), *Zaire: the Political Economy of Underdevelopment*, New York, 1980. The best single book, a case study of the small administrative centre of Lisala, is Michael G. Schatzberg, *Politics and Class in Zaire*, New York, 1980. For brief recent treatments, see Jean Rymenam, 'Comment le régime Mobutu a sapé ses propres fondements', *Le Monde Diplomatique*, cclxxviii, May 1977; and Crawford Young, 'Zaire: the unending crisis', *Foreign Affairs*, lvii, 1, Fall, 1978, 169–85. Several critical works have been published by régime opponents; special mention should be made of Comité du Zaire, *Zaire – le dossier de la recolonisation*, Paris, 1978; Kamitatu Massamba (Cléophas), *Le Pouvoir au portée du peuple*, Paris, 1977; and *La Grande Mystification du Congo–Kinshasa*, Paris, 1971.

On the economic side, see International Bank for Reconstruction and Development, *Zaire: Current Economic Situation and Constraints*, Washington, D.C., 1980; the annual reports of the Bank of Zaire, issued since 1967, are important documents, and generally reliable. The contributions of J. P. Peemans are especially valuable; see in particular 'The social and economic development of Zaire since independence: an historical outline', in *African Affairs*, ccvc, 1975, 148–79. On the role of external capital, see Jean-Claude Willame, 'Le Secteur multinational au Zaire,' *Cahiers du CEDAF*, 1, 1981. On the 1977 and 1978 Shaba crises, see especially 'Contribution à l'étude des mouvements d'opposition au Zaire: le F.L.N.C.', *Cahiers du CEDAF*, 6, 1981.

For Cameroun, more recent studies include Marcel Prouzet, *Le Cameroun*, Paris, 1974; Victor T. LeVine, *The Cameroon Federal Republic*, Ithaca, N.Y., 1971, and François Bayart, 'L'Union Nationale Camerounaise', *Revue Française de Science Politique*, xx, 4, Aug. 1970. The first years of independence are well covered by Willard Johnson, *The Cameroon Federation*, Princeton, N.J., 1970. On the UPC phenomenon, see Johnson's contribution to Rotberg and Mazrui (eds), *Protest and Power in Black Africa*, and especially Richard Joseph, *Radical Nationalism in Cameroon*, Oxford, 1977.

On Congo, the most cogent comprehensive study is Hugues Bertrand,

Le Congo, Paris, 1975. Also useful are Samuel Decalo, *Coups and Army Rule in Africa*, New Haven, Conn., 1976, and his chapter in Carl G. Rosberg and Thomas M. Callaghy, *Socialism in Sub-Saharan Africa: a New Assessment*, Berkeley, Ca., 1979, pp. 231–64.

For the first post-independence years, René Gauze, *The Politics of Congo-Brazzaville*, Stanford, Ca., 1973, is well informed; the author is a former agent of the French security police who served in Brazzaville in the years just before independence. See also John Ballard's contribution in Gwendolen M. Carter (ed.), *National Unity and Regionalism in Eight African States*, Ithaca, N.Y., 1966. Some useful reference material is found in Virginia Thompson and Richard Adloff, *Historical Dictionary of the People's Republic of the Congo*, Metuchen, N.J., 1974.

No good comprehensive political study of Gabon has emerged since that by Brian Weinstein, *Nation-Building on the Ogooué*, Cambridge, Mass., 1966. Since that time, the political economy has been transformed by the mineral boom, whose impact on society is inadequately documented. The Central African Republic has only one major monograph, Pierre Kalck, *Central African Republic: a Failure in Decolonization*, New York, 1971; for the period covered, until 1970, it is an informed and judicious account.

The micro-states of Equatorial Guinea and São Tomé e Príncipe are virtually undocumented. René Pélissier covers the colonial period for both; see *Etudes hispano-guinéenes*, Paris, 1969, and *São Tomé e Príncipe: do colonialismo à independência*, Lisbon, 1975. The post-independence period offers extremely slender pickings; note only Suzanne Cronjé, *Equatorial Guinea: the Forgotten Dictatorship*, London, 1976; Laurie S. Wisenberg and Gary F. Nelson, 'São Tomé and Príncipe: mini-state with maxi-problems', *Africa Report*, xxi, 2, March–April 1976, 15–17.

SETTLERS AND LIBERATORS IN THE SOUTH

The first half of Chapter nine is primarily concerned with lusophone Africa during the period of decolonisation. The latest work on the over-all history of Portuguese-speaking Africa is Malyn Newitt, *Portugal in Africa: the Last Hundred Years*, London, 1981, which supplants previous syntheses. For an imaginative description of the metropolitan society of Portugal and its attitudes to Africa, see John Sykes, *Portugal and Africa: the People and the War*, London, 1971. The nature of Portuguese colonialism is vividly illustrated in relation to Angola in René Pélissier, *La Colonie du Minotaure*, Orgeval, 1978. This sequel to his detailed work on nineteenth-century resistance in Angola also contains an extensive collection of published data on the outbreak of the Angolan revolution in 1961. The only other work of comparable scale and importance is the two-volume analysis of the politics of Angolan exile by John Marcum, *The Angolan Revolution*, Cambridge, Mass., 1969 and 1978, which is essential reading.

The war of liberation in Angola generated a plethora of publications about a country previously ignored. Some were official or semi-official works mainly published in Portugal, Germany and the United States. One of the most comprehensive is Irving Kaplan (ed.), *Angola: a Country Study*, 2nd ed., Washington, D.C., 1979. Its bibliography is a valuable guide to both official and unofficial works but is limited to material in the English language. For works in German and Portuguese it is necessary to consult the 40-page bibliography in Franz-Wilhelm Heimer, *Der Entkolonisierungs-konflict in Angola*, Munich, 1979. A shortened version of Heimer's scholarly analysis on the last stage of the war is available in *The Decolonisation Conflict in Angola 1974–76*, Geneva, 1979. Even more extensive than the official materials and the scholarly analyses are the works by committed observers of the war. Many of them, on both sides, were crudely polemical, but some, such as Thomas Okuma, *Angola in Ferment: Background and Prospects of Angolan Nationalism*, Boston, Mass., 1962, and Basil Davidson, *In the Eye of the Storm: Angola's People*, London, 1972, offered profound contemporary insights. Journalists also provided a rich vein of contemporary comment. In the 1970s both *Facts and Reports* (Amsterdam, fortnightly) and the *Africa Contemporary Record* (London, annual) gave prominent treatment to Portuguese-speaking Africa.

The complex politics and numerous personalities of the Angolan revolution have been unravelled in Phyllis M. Martin, *Historical Dictionary of Angola*, Metuchen, N.J., 1980, which also contains an invaluable thematic bibliography. Some further analysis beyond the account presented here may be found in two slight essays by David Birmingham, 'War in Africa' in *Contemporary Review*, March 1981, and 'A question of coffee: black enterprise in Angola', in Catherine Coquery-Vidrovitch (ed.), *Entreprises et entrepreneurs en Afrique*, Paris, 1983.

Mozambique did not attract the same international attention as Angola in the 1960s, but the more limited bibliography falls into the same categories of semi-official, scholarly and partisan writings. A. B. Herrick (ed.), *Area Handbook for Mozambique*, Washington, D.C., 1969, provides an American overview; and Manfred Kuder, *Moçambique*, Darmstadt, 1975, gives the perspective of a German economic geographer. The most perspicacious scholarly analysis of terminal Portuguese rule in Mozambique is Keith Middlemas, *Cabora Bassa: Engineering and Politics in Southern Africa*, London, 1975. A remarkable eye-witness account of Portuguese colonialism and the origins of the northern war of liberation is given by John Paul, *Mozambique: Memoirs of a Revolution*, Harmondsworth, 1975. The partisan works of participants vary in quality from the fundamental nationalist analysis by Eduardo Mondlane, *The Struggle for Mozambique*, Harmondsworth, 1969, to the self-important Portuguese account by Jorge Jardim, *Moçambique: terra queimada*, Lisbon, 1976. A useful pamphlet by Allen Isaacman, *A luta continua: creating a new society in*

Mozambique, Binghamton, N.Y., 1978, gives an insight into post-independence aspirations. The first major research book to be published on Mozambique after independence was Leroy Vail and Landeg White, *Capitalism and Colonialism in Mozambique*, London, 1980, which analyses the Mozambique inheritance.

The second half of Chapter nine examines the modern history of Zimbabwe and its anglophone neighbours in South–Central Africa. Of these neighbours Zambia is historically well served by Andrew Roberts, *A History of Zambia*, London, 1976, which not only gives a treatment of the independence period but also provides an annotated bibliography of more detailed works. The early politics of independent Malawi are clearly analysed in Caroline McMaster, *Malawi: Foreign Policy and Development*, London, 1974. A rather more episodic overview of Malawi's history can be acquired from Bridglal Pachai, *Malawi: the History of the Nation*, London, 1973. Further reading on both Zambia and Malawi is included in the bibliographical essay for Chapter six by Leroy Vail. No overview exists for Zimbabwe, and the account given here has been built up from the following extended range of books, pamphlets and articles.

Over-all narrative:
David Martin and Phyllis Johnson, *The Struggle for Zimbabwe*, London, 1981.
Martin Meredith, *The Past Is Another Country: Rhodesia 1890–1979*, London, 1979.

Post-war strikes:
Richard Gray, *The Two Nations*, London, 1960.

White politics and policies before UDI:
Robert Blake, *A History of Rhodesia*, London, 1977.
Larry Bowman, *Politics in Rhodesia: White Power in an African State*, Cambridge, Mass., 1973.
D.J. Murray, *The Governmental System in Southern Rhodesia*, Oxford, 1970.

Land husbandry:
Ken Brown, *Land in Southern Rhodesia*, Africa Bureau, London, 1959.
Hans Holleman, *Chief, Council and Commissioner*, Assen, Netherlands, 1969.
Nathan Shamuyarira, *Crisis in Rhodesia*, London, 1965.
M. Yudelman, *Africans on the Land*, Cambridge, Mass., 1964.

African nationalism:
Robert Cary and Diana Mitchell, *African Nationalist Leaders in Rhodesia: Who's Who*, Johannesburg, 1977, 2nd and rev. ed., 1980.

Enoch Dumbutshena, *Zimbabwe Tragedy*, Nairobi, 1975.

Eshamael Mlambo, *Rhodesia: the Struggle for a Birthright*, London, 1972.

W. Nyagoni, *African Nationalism in Zimbabwe*, Washington, D.C., 1978.

M. Nyagumbo, *With the People*, London, 1980.

Terence Ranger, 'Reviewing the Old Guard: Robert Mugabe and the Revival of ZANU', *Journal of Southern African Studies*, vii, 1, Oct. 1980.

John Saul, 'Transforming the Struggle in Zimbabwe', in *The State and Revolution in Eastern Africa*, London, 1979.

Masipula Sithole, *Zimbabwe – Struggle Within the Struggle*, Salisbury, 1979.

Ndabaningi Sithole, *African Nationalism*, Cape Town, 1959; 2nd ed., London, 1968.

———. *Obed Mutezo. The Mudzimu-Christian Nationalist*, Nairobi, 1970.

———. *Letters from Salisbury Prison*, Nairobi, 1976.

———. *Roots of a Revolution*, Oxford, 1977.

Henry Slater, 'The Politics of Frustration. The ZAPU/ZANU Split in Historical Perspective', *Kenya Historical Review Journal*, iii, 2, 1975.

Lawrence Vambe, *From Rhodesia to Zimbabwe*, London, 1976.

Rural introversion after 1964:

Peter Fry, *Spirits of Protest*, Cambridge, 1976.

The Policy of the Rhodesia Front in the rural areas:

Michael Bratton, *Beyond Community Development: (From Rhodesia to Zimbabwe 6)* London, 1978.

A. J. B. Hughes, *Development in Rhodesian Tribal Areas: an Overview*, Salisbury, 1974.

Didymus Mutasa, *Rhodesian Black Behind Bars*, London, 1974.

Gloria Passmore, *The National Policy of Community Development in Rhodesia*, Salisbury, 1972.

A. K. H. Weinrich, *Chiefs and Councils in Rhodesia*, London, 1971.

The successive constitutional negotiations after UDI:

R. C. Good, *U.D.I.: the International Politics of the Rhodesian Rebellion*, London, 1973.

Anthony Lake, *The 'Tar Baby' Option: American Policy Towards Southern Rhodesia*, New York, 1976.

Elaine Windrich, *Britain and the Politics of Rhodesian Independence*, London, 1978.

The 1971 constitutional proposals and the Pearce Commission:

E. Mlambo, *No Future Without Us: the Story of the African National Council in Zimbabwe*, London.

Abel Muzorewa, *Rise Up and Walk: an Auto-biography*, London, 1978.

Report of the Commission on Rhodesian Opinion, Cmnd. 4964, London, May 1972.

Judith Todd, *The Right to Say No*, London, 1972.
S. E. Wilmer, *Zimbabwe Now*, London, 1973.

The 'front-line' states:
Wilfred Burchett, *Southern Africa Stands Up*, New York, 1978.
Richard Hall, *The High Price of Principles: Kaunda and the White South*, London, 1969.
International Defence and Aid, *The Rhodesia–Zambia Border Closure*, May 1973.
Colin Legum, *Southern Africa: the Secret Diplomacy of Détente*, London, 1975.

Recent socio-economic change:

From Rhodesia to Zimbabwe, Catholic Institute for International Relations, London:

1 Roger Riddell, *Alternatives to Poverty*, 1977.
2 Roger Riddell, *The Land Question*, 1978.
3 Duncan Clarke, *The Unemployment Crisis*, 1978.
4 Colin Stoneman, *Skilled Labour and Future Needs*, 1978.
5 Rob Davies, *The Informal Sector*, 1978.
6 Michael Bratton, *Beyond Community Development*, 1978.
7 John Gilmurray, Roger Riddell and David Sanders, *The Struggle for Health*, 1979.
8 Vincent Tickner, *The Food Problem*, 1979.
9 Roger Riddell, *Education for Employment*, 1980.

The Mambo Occasional Papers – Socio-economic series, Gwelo:

1 Duncan Clarke, *Domestic Workers in Rhodesia*, 1974.
2 Peter Harris, *Black Industrial Workers in Rhodesia*, 1974.
3 Duncan Clarke, *Contract Workers and Underdevelopment in Rhodesia*, 1974.
4 Roger Riddell and Duncan Clarke, *The Poverty Datum Line*, 1975.
5 Eric Garbett, *The Administration of Transition. African Urban Settlement*, 1977.
6 Duncan Clarke, *Agricultural and Plantation Workers in Rhodesia*, 1977.
7 Duncan Clarke, *The Distribution of Income and Wealth in Rhodesia*, 1977.
8 A. K. H. Weinrich, *The Tonga People of the Southern Shore of Lake Kariba*, 1977.
9 Duncan Clarke, *Unemployment and Economic Structure in Rhodesia*, 1978.
10 Duncan Clarke, *The Economics of African Old Age Subsistence*, 1978.
11 Roger Riddell, *The Land Problem in Rhodesia*, 1978.
12 Joan May, *African Women in Urban Employment*, 1979.

The Rhodesian Journal of Economics:

ix, 4, December 1975:

Duncan Clarke, 'African Mine Labourers and Conditions of Labour in the Rhodesian Mining Industry, 1940/74'.

x, 1, March 1976:

Ian Phimister, 'Gold Mining in Southern Rhodesia, 1919 to 1953'.

Centre of African Studies, Maputo, *Zimbabwe: Notes and Reflections*, 1977.

Duncan Clarke, *Foreign Companies and International Investment in Zimbabwe*, London, 1980.

Peter Harris, 'Industrial Workers in Rhodesia, 1946–1972', *Journal of Southern African Studies*, i, 2, April 1975.

Oliver Pollak, 'Black Farmers and White Politics in Rhodesia', *African Affairs*, lxxiv, 296, July 1975.

————. *African Farmers in Rhodesia*, London, 1975.

The war and its impact:

Anon., 'Southern Africa. A Smuggled Account from a Guerrilla Fighter', *Ramparts*, viii, 4, 1969.

M. Bratton, 'Settler State, Guerrilla War and Rural Development in Rhodesia', *Rural Africana*, 4–5, spring/fall 1979.

Catholic Commission for Justice and Peace, *The Man in the Middle*, London, 1975.

————. *Civil War in Rhodesia*, London, 1976.

————. *Rhodesia: the Propaganda War*, 1977.

————. *Rhodesia at War*, London, 1979.

B. Cohen, 'The War in Rhodesia: a Dissenter's View', *African Affairs*, lxxvi, 305, Oct. 1977.

Ole Gjerstad (ed.), *The Organiser: Story of Temba Moyo, Life Histories from the Revolution, Zimbabwe, ZAPU*, 1, Richmond, 1974.

Ian Linden, *The Catholic Church and the Struggle for Zimbabwe*, London, 1980.

Kees Maxey, *The Fight for Zimbabwe*, London, 1975.

————. 'The Continuing Fight for Zimbabwe', *African Perspectives*, Leiden, 1976.

————. *The War of Liberation: Zimbabwe Briefings*, 6, London, 1978.

Michael Raeburn, *Black Fire: Accounts of the Guerrilla War in Rhodesia*, London, 1978.

A. K. H. Weinrich, 'Strategic Resettlement in Rhodesia', *Journal of Southern African Studies*, iii, 2, April 1977.

A. R. Wilkinson, *Insurgency in Rhodesia, 1957–1973*, London, 1973.

————. 'From Rhodesia to Zimbabwe', in *Southern Africa: the New Politics of Revolution*, Basil Davidson, Jo Slovo and A. R. Wilkinson (eds), London, 1976.

————. 'The Impact of the War', in *From Rhodesia to Zimbabwe: Behind and*

Beyond Lancaster House, by W. H. Morris-Jones (ed.), London, 1980.

The Internal Settlement and the 1979 elections:
Lord Chitnis, *Free and Fair? The 1979 Rhodesian Election*, London, May 1979.
Mick Delap, 'The 1979 Elections in Zimbabwe-Rhodesia', *African Affairs*, lxxviii, 313, Oct. 1979.
International Defence and Aid, *Smith's Settlement*, London, 1978.
K. N. Mufuka, 'Rhodesia's Internal Settlement: a Tragedy', *African Affairs*, lxxviii, 313, Oct. 1979.
Claire Palley, *The Rhodesian Election*, London, April 1979.
————. *Zimbabwe Rhodesia: Should the Present Government be Recognised?*, London, 1979.
Ndabaningi Sithole, *In Defence of the Rhodesian Constitutional Agreement: a Power Promise*, Salisbury, 1978.

Lancaster House and thereafter:
Catholic Institute of International Relations, *The 1980 Rhodesian Elections*, Salisbury, March 1980.
International Defence and Aid, *Focus. Zimbabwe: Independence at Last*, April, 1980.
W. H. Morris Jones (ed.), *From Rhodesia to Zimbabwe: Behind and Beyond Lancaster House*, London, 1980.

Acknowledgements

The editors wish to thank the British Social Science Research Council for a grant to enable the authors to discuss their work at a conference in Canterbury in July 1980. They also wish to thank all those from Central African universities and elsewhere who attended the conference or sent advice. Eliot College in the University of Kent at Canterbury, the African Studies Program and History Department of Indiana University and the publisher all contributed generously to the administrative work of preparing and distributing the typescripts of successive drafts. Several Indiana graduate students helped translate the contributions submitted in French. The editors also wish to thank Bettina Wilkes for her careful copy-editing, N. S. Hyslop for his skilled rendering of the numerous maps, and Roger G. Thomas for his meticulous page-proof corrections.

Phyllis Martin wishes to thank David Easterbrook, Scotch Ndlovu, George Brooks and William Cohen for their advice and assistance. She received financial support from the Overseas Conference Fund of the Office of International Programs at Indiana University.

Ralph Austen received a travel grant from the American Council of Learned Societies. He and *Rita Headrick* wish to thank Joseph Hanc for his cartographic work.

Rita Headrick received a travel grant from the Fulbright-Hays Doctorate Dissertation Abroad Fellowship programme and was supported during part of the writing of her chapter by the American Association of University Women.

Bogumil Jewsiewicki wishes to thank the Social Science and Humanities Research Council of Canada and the Université Laval for grants. He is grateful to Jan Vansina for commenting on his chapter.

Jean-Luc Vellut thanks Charles Perrings for valuable comment on the first version of his chapter.

Gervase Clarence-Smith wishes to thank the British Academy and the University of York for travel and conference grants.

Leroy Vail thanks Landeg White for valuable comment on the draft and for permission to use material freely from their joint *Capitalism and Colonialism in Mozambique* (London, 1980). Gervase Clarence-Smith and Shula Marks helpfully criticised an earlier version. Chipasha Luchembe helped with discussions on Zambian history, and the essay is gratefully dedicated to Julius Bambala Mulenga. The American Council of Learned Societies provided a grant which is gratefully acknowledged.

Ian Phimister gratefully acknowledges financial assistance from the University of Cape Town, the University of the Witwatersrand, the Human Sciences Research Council and the Social Sciences Research Council for research and conference expenses.

Crawford Young drafted his chapter while gratefully enjoying the remarkable hospitality which the Institute for Advanced Study in Princeton extends to its visiting members.

Index

ABAKO (Alliance des Bakongo), 307
Abeche, 80
Abir, 53, 97
Adamawa plateau, 30, 37, 46, 76, 77, 84–5
administration, Africans employed in the,
    15–16, 21, 41, 63, 70, 71, 73–5, 79, 87,
    89, 93, 122, 170–2, 180, 183, 192, 197,
    298, 302–5, 315, 322, 324, 343, 350, 357,
    365
administrative councils, 87, 88
Adoula, Cyrille, 292, 326–7, 329
AEF *see* French Equatorial Africa
African:
    auxiliaries, 68–9, 75, 79, 80, 98, 107, 123,
        138, 142, 375, 377, 382
    clergy, 183, 301
    militiamen, 40, 41–2
    rulers *see* chiefs
    soldiers, 122, 161, 208, 348, 351–2, 377
African National Congress, 365, 367–8,
    369, 381
African National Council (ANC), 374, 375
African Workers Voice Association, 280,
    287, 289
Africanisation, 119, 183, 294, 344, 348
Afrikaners, 147, 148, 192, 336, 359
Afrique Equatoriale Française (AEF) *see*
    French Equatorial Africa
age ratios, 17, 214, 300
agriculture:
    chitemene systems, 229
    cooperatives, 59, 100, 101, 114, 116, 269,
        347
    demonstrators, 271–2, 366, 381
    development, 86, 96, 111–14, 134, 152,
        153, 347

extensive, 204
intensive, 58, 112, 134, 204
mechanisation, 100, 110–11, 116, 264,
    356
processing, 58, 101, 111, 113, 114, 116,
    151, 268, 269, 356
productivity, 41, 85, 92, 105, 114, 116,
    148–52, 204–5, 224, 237, 243, 262, 269,
    278–9, 282, 285, 306, 366
research, 112
subsidies, 275–6
subsistence, 104, 195
surpluses, 3, 16, 35, 112, 151, 185–6, 195,
    269, 274, 283, 380
women in, 17, 36, 124, 210, 215, 236,
    237
see also animal husbandry; crops *and*
    plantations
agoardente, 167, 169, 170, 177, 179
Ahidjo, Ahmadou, 92, 292, 297, 315–17,
    333
aid *see* development aid
aides de santé, 69
air transport, 190, 195
akapolo (domestic slaves), 222
alcohol, 215–16
    addiction, 167, 174, 191, 192, 216
    see also agoardente; beer *and* wines and
        spirits trade
Algeria, 39, 327, 329, 340
Alima river, 64
Altena tobacco farm, 374
aluminium, 85, 86
Alves, Nito, 360
Amboim, 168, 173, 182, 185
American missionaries, 71–2, 74